ANN

THE COLLECTION

VOLUME THREE:
SEVEN BOOKS ON MAN:
PRINCIPLES, PEDIGREE,
PROBLEMS, LAWS, ETC.

THE SEVEN PRINCIPLES OF MAN

THE PEDIGREE OF MAN

MAN AND HIS BODIES

EVOLUTION OF LIFE AND FORM

THE LAWS OF HIGHER LIFE

THE SPIRITUAL LIFE

SOME PROBLEMS OF LIFE

CONTENTS

THE TIMELESS WISDOM COLLECTION

Emerson once said: *"Consider what you have in the smallest chosen library. A company of the wisest and wittiest men that could be picked out of all civil countries in a thousand years, have set in best order the results of their learning and wisdom. The men themselves were hid and inaccessible, solitary, impatient of interruptions, fenced by etiquette; but the thought which they did not uncover to their bosom friend is here written out in transparent words to us, the strangers of another age."*

TWC is YOUR small library. Thousands of individual books and anthologies, the best of the best in fiction and non-fiction from the 19th and 20th Centuries, written by men and women whose lives were committed to enlighten the world with the wisdom of the ages.

Our fiction features names as Hemingway, Faulkner, Wells, Orwell, Huxley, Doyle, Twain, Burroughs, Chesterton, Alcott, C. S. Lewis, J. M. Barrie, Edgar Wallace, and hundreds more... Authors who have enriched our lives and forever enlarged our capacity to dream, to get enamoured by the characters, to suffer their pain, tragedies, and triumphs as if they were ours; as if they were true...

In self-development and positive-thinking, our authors include Napoleon Hill, Dale Carnegie, Charles Haanel, William Atkinson, Orison Swett Marden, Wallace Wattles, James Allen, Christian D. Larson, Florence Scovell-Shinn, Robert Collier and many more.

In Psychology, we have the works of Freud, Jung, Coué, Coriat, Adler and many others; and in philosophy, the works of Kant, Russell, Whitehead and Eucken, among others. In theosophy and mysticism, our authors include Blavatsky, Bulwer, Besant, Leadbeater, and Sinnet. We feature the works of scientists as Eddington, Darwin, and J.W.Dunne; successful industrialists as Henry Ford, Andrew Carnegie and Charles Schwab; and Economists as John Maynard Keynes...

Thousands of carefully selected masterpieces that have brilliantly captured the essence of life, are now being placed in your hands. *The results of the learning and wisdom of the greatest minds, set in best order,* as Emerson would say. Books for enlightenment, learning, illumination... that will provide the seeker —the one who is ready and is paying attention—, some of the deepest answers to life.

Mauricio Chaves-Mesén, Author of

12 Laws of Successful Entrepreneurs;

Think Success, and The Knights of Nostradamus

BOOK ONE
THE SEVEN PRINCIPLES
OF MAN

PREFACE

Few words are needed in sending this little book out into the world. It is the first of a series of Manuals designed to meet the public demand a simple exposition of Theosophical teachings. Some have complained that our literature is at once too abstruse, too technical, and too expensive for the ordinary reader, and it is our hope that the present series may succeed in supplying what is a very real want. Theosophy is not only for the learned; it is for all. It may be that among those who in these little books catch their first glimpse of its teachings, there may be a few who will be led by them to penetrate more deeply into its philosophy, its science, and its religion, facing its abstruser problems with the student's zeal and the neophyte's ardour. But these Manuals are not written for the eager student whom no initial difficulties can daunt; they are written for the busy men and women of the work-a-day world and seek to make plain some of the great truths that render life easier to bear and death easier to face. Written by servants of the Masters who are the Elder Brothers of our race, they can have no other object than to serve our fellowmen.

ANNIE BESANT

Inquirers attracted to Theosophy by its central doctrine of the brotherhood of man, and by the hopes which it holds out of wider knowledge and of spiritual growth, are apt to be repelled when they make their first attempt to come into closer acquaintance with it, by the, to them, strange and puzzling names which flow glibly from the lips of Theosophists in conference assembled. They hear a tangle of Âtma-Buddhi, Kâma-Manas, Triad, Devachan, and what not, and feel at once that for them Theosophy is far too abstruse a study. Yet they might have become very good Theosophists, had not their initial enthusiasm been quenched with the *douche* of Sanskrit terms. In the present manual the smoking flax shall be more tenderly treated, and but few Sanskrit names shall be flung in the face of the enquirer. As a matter of fact, the use of these terms has become general among Theosophists because the English language has no equivalents for them, and a long and clumsy sentence has to be used in their stead if the idea is to be conveyed at all. The initial trouble of learning the names has been preferred to the continued trouble of using roundabout descriptive phrases – "Kâma", for instance, being shorter and more precise than "the passional and emotional part of our nature".

Man according to the Theosophical teaching is a sevenfold being, or, in the usual phrase, has a septenary constitution. Putting it in another way, man's nature has seven aspects, may be studied from seven different points of view, is composed of seven principles. The clearest and best way of all in which to think of man is to regard him as one, the Spirit or True Self; this belongs to the highest region of the universe, and is universal, the same for all; it is a ray of God, a spark from the divine fire. This is to become an individual, reflecting the divine perfection, a son that grows into the likeness of his father. For this purpose the Spirit, or true Self, is clothed in garment after garment, each garment belonging to a definite region of the universe, and enabling the Self to come into contact with that region, gain knowledge of it, and work in it. It thus gains experience, and all its latent potentialities are gradually drawn out into active powers. These garments, or sheaths, are distinguishable from each other both theoretically and practically. If a man be looked at clairvoyantly each is distinguishable by the eye, and they are separable each from each either during physical life or at death, according to the nature of any particular sheath. Whatever words may be used, the fact remains the same – that he is essentially sevenfold, an evolving being, part of whose nature has already been manifested, part remaining latent at present, so far as the vast majority of humankind is concerned. Man's consciousness is able to function through as many of these aspects as have been already evolved in him into activity.

This evolution, during the present cycle of human development, takes place on five out of seven planes of nature. The two higher planes – the sixth and seventh – will not be reached, save in the most exceptional cases, by men of this humanity in the present cycle, and they may therefore be left out of sight for our present purpose. As, however, some confusion has arisen as to the seven planes through differences of nomenclature, two diagrams are given at the end of this treatise showing the seven planes as they exist in our division of the universe, in correspondence with the vaster planes of the universe as a whole, and also the subdivision of the five into seven, as they are represented in some of our literature. A"plane" is merely a condition, a stage, a state; so that we might describe man as fitted by his nature, when that nature is fully developed, to exist consciously in seven different conditions, or seven different stages, in seven different states; or technically, on seven different planes of being. To take an easily verified illustration: a man may be conscious on the physical plane, that is, in his physical body, feeling hunger and thirst, and pain of a blow or cut. But let the man be a soldier in the heat of battle, and his consciousness will be centred in his passions and emotions, and he may suffer a wound without knowing it, his consciousness being away from the physical plane and acting on the plane of passions and emotions: when the excitement is over, consciousness will pass back to the physical, and he will "feel" the pain of his wound. Let the man be a philosopher, and as he ponders over some knotty problem he will lose all consciousness of bodily wants, of emotions, of love and hatred; his consciousness will have passed to the plane of intellect, he will be "abstracted", i. e.., drawn away from considerations pertaining to his bodily life, and fixed on the plane of thought. Thus may a man live on these several planes, in these several conditions, one part or another of his nature being thrown into activity at any given time; and an understanding of what man is, of his nature, his powers, his possibilities, will be reached more easily and assimilated more usefully if he is studied along these clearly defined lines, that if he be left without analysis, a mere confused bundle of qualities and states.

It has also been found convenient, having regard to man's mortal and immortal life, to put these seven principles into two groups – one containing the three higher principles and therefore called the Triad, the other containing the four lower, and therefore called the Quaternary. The Triad is the deathless part of man's nature, the "spirit" and soul of Christian terminology; the Quaternary is the mortal part, the "body", of Christianity. This division into body, soul and spirit is used by St. Paul, and is recognised in all careful Christian philosophy, although generally ignored by the mass of Christian people. In ordinary parlance soul and body make up the man, and the words soul and spirit are used interchangeably, with much confusion of thought as the result. This looseness is fatal to any clear view of the constitution of man, and the Theosophist may well appeal to the Christian philosopher as against the causal Christian non-thinker if it be urged that he is making distinctions difficult to be grasped. No philosophy worthy of the name can be stated even in the most elementary fashion without making some demand on the intelligence and the attention of the would be learner, and carefulness in the use of terms is a condition of all knowledge.

PRINCIPLE 1. THE DENSE PHYSICAL BODY

The dense physical body of man is called the first of his seven principles, as it is certainly the most obvious. Built of material molecules, in the generally accepted sense of the term – with its five organs of sensation - the five senses - its organs of locomotion, its brain and nervous system, its apparatus for carrying on the various functions necessary for its continued existence, there is little to be said about this physical body in so slight a sketch as this of the constitution of man. Western science is almost ready to accept the Theosophical view that the human organism consists of innumerable "lives", which build up the cells. H. P. Blavatsky says on this: "Science has never yet gone so far as to assert with the Occult doctrine that our bodies, as well as those of animals, plants, and stones, are themselves altogether built up of such beings [bacteria, etc.]: which, with the exception of the larger species, no microscope can detect .... The physical and chemical constituents of all being found to be identical, chemical science may well say that there is no difference between the matter which composes the ox and that which forms the man. But the Occult doctrine is far more explicit. It says: Not only the chemical compounds are the same, but the same infinitesimal *invisible* lives compose the atoms of the bodies of the mountain and the daisy, of man and the ant, of the elephant and of the tree which shelters him from the sun. Each particle – whether you call it organic or inorganic – *is* a life. Every atom and molecule in the universe is both *life-giving and death-giving* to such forms (*Secret Doctrine*, vol. I, p. 281, new edition). The microbes thus "build up the material body and its cells", under the constructive energy of vitality – a phrase that will be explained when we come to deal with "life", as the Third Principle, and with these microbes as part of it. When the "life" is no longer supplied the microbes "are left to run riot as destructive agents", and they break up and disintegrate the cells which they built, and so the body goes to pieces.

The purely physical consciousness is the consciousness of the cells and the molecules. The selective action of the cells, taking from the blood what they need, rejecting what they do not need, is an instance of this self consciousness. The process goes on without the help of our consciousness or volition. Again that which is called by physiologists unconscious memory is the memory of the physical consciousness, unconscious to us indeed, until we have learned to transfer our brain consciousness there. What we feel is not what the cells feel. The *pain* of a wound is felt by the brain-consciousness, acting, as before said, on the physical plane; but the consciousness of the molecule, as of the aggregation of molecules we call cells, leads it to hurry to the repair of the damaged tissues – actions of which the brain is *un*conscious – and its memory makes it repeat the same act again and again, even when it has become unnecessary. Hence cicatrices on wounds, scars, callosities, etc. The student may find many details on this subject in physiological treatises.

The death of the dense physical body occurs when the withdrawal of the controlling life-energy leaves the microbes to go their own way, and the many lives, no longer co-ordinated, separate from each other and scatter the particles of the cells of "the man of dust", and what we call decay sets in. The body becomes a whirlpool of unrestrained, unregulated lives, and its form, which resulted from their correlation, is destroyed by their exuberant individual energy. Death is but an aspect of life, and the destruction of one material form is but a prelude to building up of another.

PRINCIPLE 2. THE ETHERIC DOUBLE

The Linga Sharira, the astral body, the ethereal body, the fluidic body, the double, the wraith, the döppelganger, the astral man – such are a few of the many names which have been given to the second principle in man's constitution. The best name is the Etheric Double, because this term designates the second principle only, suggesting its constitution and appearance: whereas the other names have been used somewhat generally to describe bodies formed of some more subtle matter than that which affects our physical senses, without regard to the question whether other principles were or were not involved in their construction. I shall therefore use this name throughout.

The etheric double is formed of matter rarer or more subtle than that which is perceptible to our five senses, but still matter belonging to the physical plane, to which its functioning is confined. It is the state of physical matter which is just beyond our "solid, liquid and gas", which form the dense portions of the physical plane.

This etheric double is the exact double or counterpart of the dense physical body to which it belongs, and is separable from it, although unable to go very far away therefrom. In normal healthy human beings the separation is a matter of difficulty, but in persons known as physical or materialising mediums, the ethereal double slips out without any great effort. When separated from the dense body it is visible to the clairvoyant as an exact replica thereof, united to it by a slender thread. So close is the physical union between the two that an injury inflicted on the etheric double appears as a lesion on the dense body, a fact known under the name of repercussion. A. d'Assier, in his well-known work – translated by Colonel Olcott, the President-Founder of the Theosophical Society, under the title of *Posthumous Humanity* – gives a number of cases (see p. 51-57) in which this repercussion took place.

Separation of the etheric double from the dense body is generally accompanied by a considerable decrease in vitality in the latter, the double becoming more vitalised as the energy in the dense body diminishes. Colonel Olcott says (page 63):

"When the double is projected by a trained expert, even the body seems torpid, and the mind in a 'brown study' or dazed state; the eyes are lifeless in expression, the heart and lung actions feeble, and often the temperature much lowered. It is very dangerous to make any sudden noise or burst into the room, under such circumstances; for the double, being by instantaneous reaction drawn back into the body, the heart convulsively contracts, and death may even be caused. "

In the case of Emilie Sagée (quoted on page 62-65) the girl was noticed to look pale and exhausted when the double was visible: "the more distinct the double and more material in appearance, the really material person was effectively wearied, suffering and languid; when on the contrary, the appearance of the double weakened, the patient was seen to recover strength. "This phenomenon is perfectly intelligible to the Theosophical student, who knows that the etheric double is the vehicle of the life-principle, or vitality, in the physical body, and that its partial withdrawal must therefore diminish the energy, with which this principle plays on the denser molecules. Clairvoyants, such as the Seeress of Prevorst, state that they can see the ethereal arm or leg attached to a body from which the dense limb has been amputated, and D'Assier remarks on this: -

"Whilst I was absorbed in physiological studies, I was often arrested by a singular fact. It sometimes happens that a person who has lost an arm or leg experiences certain sensations at the extremities of the fingers and toes. Physiologists explain this anomaly by postulating in the patient an inversion of sensitiveness or of recollection, which makes him locate in the hand or the foot the sensation with which the nerve of the stump is alone affected ...I confess that these explanations seemed to me laboured and have never satisfied me. When I studied the problem of the duplication of man, the question of amputations recurred to my mind, and I asked myself if it was not more simple and logical to attribute the anomaly of which I have spoken to the doubling of the human body, which by its fluid nature can escape amputation" (*loc. Cit., p. 103-104*).

7

The etheric double plays a great part in spiritualistic phenomena. Here again the clairvoyant can help us. A clairvoyant can see the etheric double oozing out of the left side of the medium, and it is this which often appears as the "materialised spirit," easily moulded into various shapes by the thought-currents of the sitters, and gaining strength and vitality as the medium sinks into a deep trance. The Countess Wachtmeister, who is clairvoyant, says she has seen the same "spirit" recognised as that of a near relative or friend by different sitters, each of whom saw it according to his expectations, while to her own eyes it was the mere double of the medium. So again, H. P. Blavatsky told me that when she was at the Eddy homestead, watching the remarkable series of phenomena there produced, she deliberately moulded the "spirit" that appeared into the likenesses of persons known to herself and to no one else present, and the other sitters saw the types which she produced by her own will-power, moulding the plastic matter of the medium's etheric double.

Many of the movements of objects that occur at such séances, and at other times, without visible contact, are due to the action of the etheric double, and the student can learn how to produce such phenomena at will. They are trivial enough: the mere putting out of the etheric hand is no more important than the putting out of the dense counterpart, and neither more or less miraculous. Some persons produce such phenomena unconsciously, mere aimless overturnings of objects, making of noises, and so on: they have no control over their etheric double, and it just blunders about in their near neighbourhood, like a baby trying to walk. For the etheric double, like the dense body, has only a diffused consciousness belonging to its parts, and has no mentality. Nor does it readily serve as a medium of mentality, when disjoined from the dense counterpart.

This leads to and interesting point. The centres of sensation are located in the fourth principle, which may be said to form a bridge between the physical organs and the mental perceptions; impressions from the physical universe impinge on the material molecules of the dense physical body, setting in vibration the constituent cells of the organs of sensations, or our "senses". These vibrations, in their turn, set in motion the finer material molecules of the etheric double, in the corresponding sense organs of its finer matter. From these vibrations pass to the astral body, or fourth principle, presently to be considered, wherein are the corresponding centres of sensation. From these vibrations are again propagated into the yet rarer matter of the lower mental plane, whence they are reflected back until, reaching the material molecules of the cerebral hemispheres, they become our "brain consciousness". This correlated and unconscious succession is necessary for the normal action of consciousness as we know it. In sleep and in trance, natural or induced, the first two and the last stages are generally omitted, and the impressions start from and return to the astral plane, and thus make no trace on the brain memory; but the natural or trained psychic, the clairvoyant who does not need trance for the exercise of his powers, is able to transfer his consciousness from the physical to the astral plane without losing grip thereof, and can impress the brain-memory with knowledge gained on the astral plane, so retaining it for use.

Death means for the etheric double just what it means for the dense physical body, the breaking up of its constituent parts, the dissipation of its molecules. The vehicle of the vitality that animates the bodily organism as a whole, it oozes forth from the body when the death hour comes, and is seen by the clairvoyant as a violet light, or violet form, hovering over the dying person, still attached to the physical body by the slender thread before spoken of. When the thread snaps, the last breath has quivered outwards, and the bystanders whisper "He is dead".

The etheric double, being of physical matter, remains in the neighbourhood of the corpse, and is the "wraith", or "apparition", or "phantom", sometimes seen at the moment of death and afterwards by persons near the place where the death has occurred. It disintegrates slowly *pari passu* with its dense counterpart, and its remnants are seen by sensitives in cemeteries and church yards as violet lights hovering over graves. Here is one of the reasons which render cremation preferable to burial as a mode of disposing of the physical enveloped of man; the fire dissipates in a few hours the molecules which would otherwise be set free only in the slow course of gradual putrefaction, and thus quickly restores to their own plane the dense and etheric materials, ready for use once more in the building up of new forms.

PRINCIPLE 3. PRÂNA, THE LIFE

All universes, all worlds, all men, all brutes, all vegetables, all minerals, all molecules and atoms, all that *is*, are plunged in a great ocean of life, life eternal, life infinite, life incapable of increase or diminution. The universe is only life in manifestation, life made objective, life differentiated. Now each organism, whether minute as a molecule or vast as a universe, may be thought of as appropriating to itself somewhat of life, of embodying, in itself as its own life some of this universal life. Figure a living sponge, stretching itself out in the water which bathes it, envelops it, permeates it; there is water, still the ocean, circulating in every passage, filling every pore; but we may think of the ocean outside the sponge, or of part of the ocean, appropriated by the sponge, distinguishing them in thought if we want to make statements about each severally. So each organism is a sponge bathed in the ocean of life universal, and containing within itself some of that ocean as its own breath of life. In Theosophy we distinguish this appropriated life under the name Prâna, breath, and call it the third principle in man's constitution.

To speak quite accurately, the "breath of life" – that which the Hebrews termed *Nephesh*, or the breath of life breathed into the nostrils of Adam – is not Prâna only, but Prâna and the fourth principle conjoined. It is these two together that make the "vital spark" (*Secret Doctrine*, vol. 1., page 262), and that are the "breath of life in man, as in beast or insect, or physical, material life" (*Secret Doctrine*, vol. 1., note to page 263). It is "the breath of animal life in man – the breath of life instinctual in the animal" (*Secret Doctrine*, vol. 1., diagram page 262). But just now we are concerned with Prâna only, with vitality as the animating principle in all animal and human bodies. Of this life the etheric double is the vehicle, acting, so to say, as means of communication, as bridge, between Prâna and the dense body.

Prâna is explained in the *Secret Doctrine* as having for its lowest subdivision the microbes of science; these are the "invisible lives" that build up the physical cells (se *ante*, page 8-9); these are the "countless myriads of lives" that build the "tabernacle of clay", the physical bodies (*Secret Doctrine* vol. 1, page 245). "Science, dimly perceiving the truth, may find bacteria and other infinitesimals in the human body, and see in them only, occasional and abnormal visitors to which diseases are attributed. Occultism – which discerns a life in every atom and molecule, whether in a mineral or human body, in air, fire, or water – affirms that our whole body is built of such lives; the smallest bacterium under the microscope being to them a comparative size like an elephant to the tiniest infusoria" (*ibid.*, p. 245). The "fiery lives" are the controllers and directors of these microbes, these invisible lives, and "indirectly" build, *i. e.*, build by controlling and directing the microbes, the immediate builders, supplying the latter with what is necessary, acting as the life of these lives; the "fiery lives" the synthesis, the essence, of Prâna, are the "vital constructive energy" that enables the microbes to build the physical cells. One of the archaic commentaries sums up the matter in stately and luminous phrases: "The worlds, to the profane, are built up of the known elements. To the conception of an Arhat, these elements are themselves collectively a divine life; distributively, on the plane of manifestations, the numberless and countless crores – (a crore is ten millions) – of lives. Fire alone is ONE, on the plane of the One Reality; on that of manifested, hence illusive, being, its particles are fiery lives which live and have their being at the expense of every other life that they consume. Therefore they are named the Devourers.... Every visible thing in this universe was built by such lives, from conscious and divine primordial man, down to the unconscious agents that construct matter..... From the One Life, formless and uncreate, proceeds the universe of lives (*Secret Doctrine*, Vol. I, page 269). As in the universe, so in man, and all these countless lives, all this constructive vitality, all this is summed up by the Theosophist as Prâna.

PRINCIPLE 4. THE DESIRE BODY

In building up our man we have now reached the principle sometimes described as the animal soul, in Theosophical parlance Kâma Rûpa, or the desire-body. It belongs to in constitution, and functions on, the second or astral plane. It includes the whole body of appetites, passions, emotions, and desires which come under the head of instincts, sensations, feelings and emotions, in our Western psychological classification, and are dealt with as a subdivision of mind. In Western psychology mind is divided – by the modern school – into three main groups, feelings, will, intellect. Feelings are again divided into sensations and emotions, and these are divided and subdivided under numerous heads. Kâma, or desire, includes the whole group of "feelings", and might be described as our passional and emotional nature. All animal needs, such as hunger, thirst, sexual desire, come under it; all passions, such as love (in its lower sense), hatred, envy, jealousy. It is the desire for sentient experience, for experience of material joys – "the lust of the flesh, the lust of the eyes, the pride of life". This principle is the most material in our nature, it is the one that binds us fast to earthly life. "It is not molecularly constituted matter, least of all the human body, Sthula Sharîra, that is the grossest of all our 'principles' but verily the *middle* principle, the real animal centre; whereas our body is but its shell, the irresponsible factor and medium through which the beast in us acts all its life" (*Secret Doctrine,* vol. I, p. 280-81).

United to the lower part of Manas, the mind, as Kâma-Manas, it becomes the normal human brain-intelligence, and that aspect of it will be dealt with presently. Considered by itself, it remains the brute in us, the "ape and tiger" of Tennyson, the force which most avails to keep us bound to earth and to stifle in us all higher longings by the illusions of sense.

Kâma joined to Prâna is, as we have seen, the "breath of life," the vital sentient principle spread over every particle of the body. It is, therefore, the seat of sensation, that which enables the organs of sensation to function. We have already noted that the physical organs of sense, the bodily instruments that come into immediate contact with the external world, are related to the organs of sensation in the etheric double (*ante* p. 14). But these organs would be incapable of functioning did not Prâna make them vibrant with activity, and their vibrations would remain vibrations only, motion on the material plane of the physical body, did not Kâma, the principle of sensation translate the vibration into feeling. Feeling indeed, is consciousness on the kâmic plane, and when a man is under the dominion of a sensation or a passion, the Theosophist speaks of him as on the kâmic plane, meaning thereby that his consciousness is functioning on that plane. For instance, a tree may reflect rays of light, that is, ethereal vibrations, and these vibrations striking on the outer eye will set up vibrations in the physical nerve-cells; these will be propagated as vibrations to the physical and on to the astral centres, but there is no *sight* of the tree until the seat of the sensation is reached, and Kâma enables us to *perceive*.

Matter of the astral plane – including that called elemental essence – is the material of which the desire-body is composed, and it is the peculiar properties of this matter which enable it to serve as the sheath in which the Self can gain experience of sensation. (The constitution of the elemental essence would lead us too far from an elementary treatise). The desire–body, or astral body, as it is often called, has the form of a mere cloudy mass during the earlier stages of evolution, and is incapable of serving as an independent vehicle of consciousness. During deep sleep it escapes from the physical body, but remains near it, and the mind within it is almost as much asleep as the body. It is, however, liable to be affected by forces of the astral plane akin to its own constitution, and gives rise to dreams of a sensuous kind. In a man of average intellectual development the desire-body has become more highly organised, and when separated from the physical body is seen to resemble it is outline and features; even then, however, it is not conscious of its surroundings on the astral plane, but encloses the mind as a shell, within which the mind may actively function, while not yet able to use it as an independent vehicle of consciousness. Only in the highly evolved man does the desire-body become thoroughly organised and vitalised, as much the vehicle of consciousness on the astral plane as the physical body is on the physical plane.

After death, the higher part of man dwells for awhile in the desire-body, the length of its stay depending on the comparative grossness or delicacy of its constituents. When the man escapes from it, it persists for a time as a "shell" and when the departed entity is of a low type, and during earth life infused such mentality as it possessed into the passional nature, some of this remains entangled with the shell. It then possesses consciousness of a very low order, has brute cunning, is without conscience – an altogether objectionable entity, often spoken of as a "spook. " It strays about, attracted to all places in which animal desires are encouraged and satisfied, and is drawn into the currents of those whose animal passions are strong and unbridled. Mediums of low type inevitably attract these eminently undesirable visitors, whose fading vitality is reinforced in their séance rooms, who catch astral reflections, and play the part of "disembodied spirits" of a low order. Nor is this all; if at such a séance there be present some man or woman of correspondingly low development, the spook will be attracted to that person, and may attach itself to him or to her, and thus may be set up currents between the desire-body of the living person and the dying desire-body of the dead person, generating results of the most deplorable kind.

The longer or shorter persistence of the desire-body as a shell or a spook depends on the greater or less development of the animal and passional nature in the dying personality. If during earth-life the animal nature was indulged and allowed to run riot, if the intellectual and spiritual parts of man were neglected or stifled, then, as the life-currents were set strongly in the direction of passion, the desire-body will persist for a long period after the body of the person is dead. Or again, if earth-life has been suddenly cut short by accident or by suicide, the link between Kâma and Prâna will not be easily broken, and the desire-body will be strongly vivified. If, on the other hand, desire has been conquered and bridled during earth-life, if it has been purified and trained into subservience to man's higher nature, then there is but little to energise the desire-body and it will quickly disintegrate and dissolve away.

There remains one other fate, terrible in its possibilities, which may befall the fourth principle, but it cannot be clearly understood until the fifth principle has been dealt with.

THE QUATERNARY, OR FOUR LOWER PRINCIPLES

Diagram of the Quaternary; transitory and mortal; see Secret Doctrine, Volume I, page 262 [The etheric double is here named the Linga Sharira, a name now discarded in consequence of the confusion caused by employing a

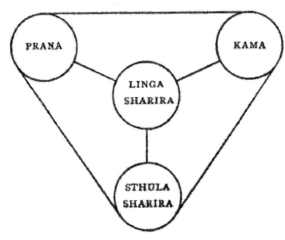

well-known term in Hindu philosophy in an entirely new sense. Before her departure H. P. B. urged her pupils to reform the terminology, which had been too carelessly put together, and we are trying to carry out her wish.]

We have thus studied man, as to his lower nature, and have reached the point in his path of evolution to which he is accompanied by the brute. The quaternary, regarded alone, ere it is affected by contact with the mind, is merely a lower animal; it awaits the coming of the mind to make it man. Theosophy teaches that through past ages man was thus slowly built up, stage by stage, principle by principle, until he stood as a quaternary, brooded over but not in contact with the Spirit, waiting for that mind which could alone enable him to progress farther, and to come into conscious union with the Spirit, so fulfilling the very object of his being. This aeonian evolution, in its slow progression, is hurried through in the personal evolution of each human being, each principle which was in the course of ages successively evolved in man on earth, appearing as part of the constitution of each man at the point of evolution reached at any given time, the remaining principles being latent, awaiting their gradual manifestation. The evolution of the quaternary until it reached the point at which further progress was impossible without mind, is told in eloquent sentences in the archaic stanzas on which the *Secret Doctrine* of H. P. Blavatsky is based (*breath* is, the Spirit, for which the human tabernacle is to be built; the *gross body* is the dense physical body; the *spirit of life* is Prâna; the *mirror of its body* is the etheric double; the *vehicle of desires is* Kâma):
-

"The Breath needed a form; the Fathers gave it. The Breath needed a gross body; the Earth moulded it; The Breath needed the Spirit of Life; the Solar Lhas breathed into it its form. The Breath needed a Mirror of its Body; 'We gave it our own', said the Dhyânis. The Breath needed a Vehicle of Desires; 'It has it', said the Drainer of Waters. But Breath needs a Mind to embrace the Universe; 'We cannot give that, 'said the fathers, 'I never had it,' said the Spirit of the Earth. 'The form would be consumed were I

14

to give it mine,' said the Great Fire .... Man remained an empty senseless Bhûta" (phantom).

And so is the personal man without mind. The quaternary alone is not man, the Thinker, and it is as Thinker that man is really man.

Yet at this point let the student pause, and reflect over the human constitution, so far as he has gone. For this quaternary is the mortal part of man, and is distinguished by Theosophy as the *personality*. It needs to be very clearly and definitely realised, if the constitution of man is to be understood, and if the student is to read more advanced treatises with intelligence. True, to make the personality *human* it has yet to come under the rays of mind, and to be illuminated by it as the world by the rays of the sun. But even without these rays it is a clearly defined entity, with its dense body, its etheric double, its life, and its desire body or animal soul. It has passions, but no reason; it has emotions, but no intellect; it has desires, but no rationalised will; it awaits the coming of its monarch, the mind, the touch which shall transform it into man.

PRINCIPLE 5.
MANAS, THE THINKER, OR MIND

We have reached the most complicated part of our study, and some thought and attention are necessary from the reader to gain even an elementary idea of the relation held by the fifth principle to the other principles in man.

The word Manas comes from the Sanskrit word *man,* the root of the verb to think; it is the Thinker in us, spoken of vaguely in the West as mind. I will ask the reader to regard Manas as Thinker rather than as mind, because the word Thinker suggests some one who thinks, *i.e.,* an individual, an entity. And this is exactly the Theosophical idea of Manas, for Manas is the immortal individual, the real " I", that clothes itself over and over again in transient personalities, and itself endures for ever. It is described in the *Voice of the Silence* in the exhortation addressed to the candidate for initiation: "Have perseverance as one who doth for evermore endure. Thy shadows [personalities] live and vanish; that which in thee shall live for ever, that which in thee *knows*, for it is knowledge, is not of fleeting life; it is the man that was, that is, and will be, for whom the hour shall never strike" (p. 31). H. P. Blavatsky has described it very clearly in the *Key to Theosophy*: "Try to imagine a 'Spirit', a celestial being, whether we call it by one name or another, divine in its essential nature, yet not pure enough to be one with the ALL, and having, in order to achieve this, to so purify its nature as finally to gain that goal. It can do so only be passing *individually* and *personally*, i. e., spiritually and physically, through every experience and feeling that exists in the manifold or differentiated universe. It has, therefore, after having gained such experience in the lower kingdoms, and having ascended higher and still higher with every rung on the ladder of being, to pass through every experience on the human planes. In its very essence it is Thought, and is, therefore, called in its plurality *Manasaputra*, 'the Sons of (universal) Mind. ' This *individualised* 'Thought' is what we Theosophists call the *real* human Ego, the thinking entity imprisoned in a case of flesh and bones. This is surely a spiritual entity, not *matter* [that is, not matter as we know it, on the plane of the objective universe] – and such entities are the incarnating Egos that inform the bundle of animal matter called mankind, and whose names are *Manasa* or minds" (*Key to Theosophy*, p. 183-184).

This idea may be rendered yet clearer perhaps by a hurried glance cast backward over man's evolution in the past. When the quaternary had been slowly built up, it was a fair house without a tenant, and stood empty awaiting the coming of the one who was to dwell therein. The name Mânasaputra (the sons of mind) covers many grades of intelligence, ranging from the mighty "Sons of the Flame" whose human evolution lies far behind them, down to those entities who gained individualisation in the cycle preceding our own, and were ready to incarnate on this earth in order to accomplish their human stage of evolution. Some superhuman intelligences incarnated as guides and teachers of our infant humanity, and became founders and divine rulers of the ancient civilisations. Large numbers of the entities spoken of above, who had already evolved some mental faculties, took up their abode in the human quaternary, in the mindless men. These are the reincarnating Mânasaputra, who became the tenants of the human frames as then evolved on earth, and these same Mânasaputra, reincarnating age after age, are the Reincarnating Egos, the Manas in us, the persistent individual, the fifth principle in man. The remainder of mankind through successive ages received from the loftier Mânasaputra their first spark of mind, a ray which stimulated into growth the germ of mind latent within them, the human soul thus having its birth in time there. It is these differences of age, as we may call them, in the beginning of the individual life, of the specialisation of the eternal Divine Spirit into a human soul, which explain the enormous differences in mental capacity found in our present humanity.

The multiplicity of names given to this fifth principle has probably tended to increase the confusion surrounding it in the minds of many who are beginning to study Theosophy. *Mânasaputra* is what we call the historical name, the name that suggests the entrance into humanity of a class of already individualised souls at a certain point of evolution; *Manas* is the ordinary name, descriptive of the intellectual nature of the principle; the *Individual* or the "!", or *Ego*, recalls the fact that this principle is permanent, does not die, is the individualising principle, separating itself in thought from all that is not itself, the *Subject* in Western terminology as opposed to the *Object*; the *Higher Ego* puts it into contrast with the *Personal Ego*, of which something is to be presently said. The *Reincarnating Ego* lays stress on the fact that it is the principle that reincarnates continually, and so unites in its own experience all the lives passed through on earth. There are various other names, but they will not be met with in elementary treatises. The above are those most often encountered, and there is no real difficulty about them, but when they are used interchangeably, without explanation, the unhappy student is apt to tear his hair in anguish, wondering how many principles he has got hold of, and what relation they bear to each other.

We must now consider Manas during a single incarnation, which will serve as the type of all, and we will start when the Ego has been drawn – by causes set a-going in previous earth-lives – to the family in which is to be born the human being who is to serve as its next tabernacle. (I do not deal here with reincarnation, since that great and most essential doctrine of Theosophy must be expounded separately). The Thinker, then, awaits the building of the "house of life" which he is to occupy; and now arises a difficulty; himself a spiritual entity living on the mental or third plane upwards, a plane far higher than that of the physical universe, he cannot influence the molecules of gross matter of which his dwelling is built by the direct play upon them of his own most subtle particles. So, he projects part of his own substance, which clothes itself with astral matter, and then with the help of etheric matter permeates the whole nervous system of the yet unborn child, to form, as the physical apparatus matures, the thinking principle in man. This projection from Manas, spoken of as its reflection, its shadow, its ray, and by many another descriptive and allegorical name, is the lower Manas, in contradistinction to the higher Manas – Manas, during every period of incarnation, being dual. On this, H. P. Blavatsky says: "Once imprisoned, or incarnate, their (the Manas) essence becomes dual; that is to say the *rays* of the eternal divine Mind, considered as individual entities, assume a twofold attribute which is (a) their essential, inherent, characteristic, heaven-aspiring mind (higher Manas), and (b) the human quality of thinking, or animal cogitation, rationalised owing to the superiority of the human brain, the Kâma-tending or lower Manas" (*Key to Theosophy*, p. 184).

We must now turn our attention to this lower Manas alone, and see the part which it plays in the human constitution.

It is engulfed in the quaternary, and we may regard it as clasping Kâma with one hand, while with the other it retains its hold on its father, the higher Manas. Whether it will be dragged down by Kâma altogether and be torn away from the triad to which by its nature it belongs, or whether it will triumphantly carry back to its source the purified experiences of its earth-life – that is the life-problem set and solved in each successive incarnation. During earth-life, Kâma and the lower Manas are joined together, and are often spoken of conveniently as Kâma-Manas. Kâma supplies, as we have seen, the animal and passional elements; the lower Manas rationalises these, and adds the intellectual faculties; and so we have the brain-mind, the brain-intelligence, *i. e.,* Kâma-Manas functioning in the brain and nervous system, using the physical apparatus as its organ on the material plane. In man these two principles are interwoven during life, and rarely act separately, but the student must realise that "Kâma-Manas" is not a new principle, but the interweaving of the fourth with the lower part of the fifth.

As with a flame we may light a wick, and the colour of the flame of the burning wick will depend on the nature of the wick and of the liquid in which it is soaked, so in each human being the flame of Manas set alight the brain and Kâmic wick, and the colour of the light from that wick will depend on the Kâmic nature and the development of the brain-apparatus. If the Kâmic nature be strong and undisciplined it will soil the pure manasic light, lending it a lurid tinge and fouling it with noisome smoke. If the brain-apparatus be imperfect or undeveloped, it will dull the light and prevent it from shining forth to the outer world. As was clearly stated by H. P. Blavatsky in her article on "Genius"; "What we call 'the manifestations of genius' in a person are only the more or less successful efforts of that Ego to assert itself on the outward plane of its objective form – the man of clay – in the matter-of-fact daily life of the latter. The Egos of a Newton, an Aeschylus, or a Shakespeare are of the same essence and substance as the Egos of a yokel, an ignoramus, a fool, or even an idiot; and the self-assertion of their informing *genii* depends on the physiological and material construction of the physical man. No Ego differs from another Ego in its primordial or original essence and nature. That which makes of one mortal a great man and of another a vulgar silly person is, as said, the quality and make-up of the physical shell or casing, and the adequacy or inadequacy of brain and body to transmit and give expression to the light of the real *inner* man; and this aptness or inaptness is, in its turn, the result of Karma. Or, to use another simile, physical man is the musical instrument, and the Ego the performing artist. The potentiality of perfect melody of sound is in the former – the instrument – and no skill of the latter can awaken a faultless harmony out of a broken or badly made instrument. This harmony depends on the fidelity of transmission, by word and act, to the objective plane, of the unspoken divine thought in the very depths of man's subjective or inner nature. Physical man may – to follow our simile – be a priceless Stradivarius, or a cheap and cracked fiddle, or again a mediocrity between the two, in the hands of the Paganini who ensouls him" (*Lucifer* November, 1889, p. 228).

Bearing in mind these limitations and idiosyncrasies [Limitations and idiosyncrasies due to the action of the Ego in previous earth-lives, be it remembered] imposed on the manifestations of the thinking principle by the organ through which it has to function, we shall have little difficulty in following the workings of the lower Manas in man; mental ability, intellectual strength, acuteness, subtlety – all these are its manifestations; these may reach as far as what is often called genius, what H. P. Blavatsky speaks of as "artificial genius, the outcome of culture and of purely intellectual acuteness". Its nature is often demonstrated by the presence of Kâmic elements in it, of passion, vanity and arrogance.

The higher Manas can but rarely manifest itself at the present stage of human evolution. Occasionally a flash from those loftier regions lightens the twilight in which we dwell, and such flashes alone are what the Theosophist calls true genius; "Behold in every manifestation of genius, *when combined with virtue*, the undeniable presence of the celestial exile, the divine Ego whose jailer thou art, O man of matter. "For theosophy teaches "that the presence in man of various creative powers" – called genius in their collectivity – is due to no blind chance, to no innate qualities through hereditary tendencies – though that which is known as atavism may often intensify these faculties – but to an accumulation of individual antecedent experiences of the Ego in its preceding life and lives. For, omniscient in its essence and nature, it still requires experience, through its *personalities*, of the things of earth, earthly on the objective plane, in order to apply the fruition of that abstract experience to them. And, adds our philosophy, the cultivation of certain aptitudes through out a long series of past incarnations must finally culminate, in some one life, in a blooming forth as *genius,* in one or another direction" – (*Lucifer* November, 1889, p. 229-30). For the manifestation of true genius, purity of life is an essential condition.

Kâma-Manas is the personal self of man; we have already seen that the quaternary, as a whole, is the personality, "the shadow". and the lower Manas gives the individualising touch that makes the personality recognise itself as "!". It becomes intellectual, it recognises itself as separate from all other selves; deluded by the separateness it *feels*, it does not realise a unity beyond all that it is able to sense. And the lower Manas, attracted by the vividness of the material-life impressions, swayed by the rush of the Kâmic emotions, passions and desires, attracted to all material things blinded and deafened by the storm voices among which it is plunged – the lower Manas is apt to forget the pure and serene glory of its birthplace, and to throw itself into the turbulence which gives rapture in lieu of peace. And, be it remembered, it is this very lower Manas that yields the last touch of delight to the senses and to the animal nature; for what is passion that can neither anticipate nor remember, where is ecstasy without the subtle force of imagination, the delicate colours of fancy and of dream?

But there may be chains yet more strong and constraining, binding the lower Manas fast to the earth. They are forged of ambition, of desire for fame, be it for that of the statesman's power, or of supreme intellectual achievement. So long as any work is wrought for sake of love, or praise, or even recognition that the work is "mine" and not another's; so long as in the heart's remotest chambers one subtlest yearning remains to be recognised as separate from all; so long, however grand the ambition, however far reaching the charity, however lofty the achievement, Manas is tainted with Kâma, and is not pure as its source.

MANAS IN ACTIVITY

We have already seen that the fifth principle is dual in its aspect during each period of earth-life, and that the lower Manas united to Kâma, spoken of conveniently as Kâma-Manas, functions in the brain and nervous system of man. We need to carry our investigation a little further in order to distinguish clearly between the activity of the higher and of the lower Manas, so that the working in the mind of man may become less obscure to us that it is at present to many.

Now the cells of the brain and nervous system (like all other cells) are composed of minute particles of matter, called molecules (literally, little heaps). These molecules do not touch each other, but are held grouped together by that manifestation of the Eternal Life which we call attraction. Not being in contact with each other they are able to vibrate to and fro if set in motion, and, as a matter of fact, they are in a state of continual vibration. H. P. Blavatsky points out (*Lucifer*, October, 1890, p. 92-93) that molecular motion is the lowest and most material form of the One Eternal Life. Itself motion as the "Great Breath", and the source of all motion on every plane of the universe. In the Sanskrit, the roots of the terms for spirit, breath, being and motion are essentially the same, and Râma Prâsad says that "all these roots have for their origin the sound produced by the breath of animals" – the sound of expiration and inspiration.

Now, the lower mind, or Kâma-Manas, acts on the molecules of the nervous cells by motion, and set them vibrating, so starting mind-consciousness on the physical plane. Manas itself could not affect these molecules; but its ray, the lower Manas, having clothed itself in astral matter and united itself to the kâmic elements, is able to set the physical molecules in motion, and so give rise to "brain consciousness," including the brain memory and all other functions of the human mind, as we know it in its ordinary activity. These manifestations, "like all other phenomena on the material plane. .. *must* be related in their final analysis to the world of vibration," says H. P. Blavatsky. But, she goes on to point out, "in their origin they belong to a different and higher world of harmony". Their origin is in the manasic essence, in the ray; but on the material plane, acting on the molecules of the brain, they are translated into vibrations.

This action of the Kâma-Manas is spoken of by Theosophists as *psychic*. All mental and passional activities are due to this psychic energy, and its manifestations are necessarily conditioned by the physical apparatus through which it acts. We have already seen this broadly stated, and the *rationale* of the statement will now be apparent. If the molecular constitution of the brain be fine, and if the working of the specifically kâmic organs (liver, spleen, etc.) be healthy and pure – so as not to injure the molecular constitution of the nerves which put them into communication with the brain – then the psychic breath, as it sweeps through the instrument, awakens in this true Aeolian harp harmonious and exquisite melodies; whereas if the molecular constitution be gross or poor, if it be disordered by the emanations of alcohol, if the blood be poisoned by gross living or sexual excesses, the strings of the Aeolian harp become too loose or too tense, clogged with dirt or frayed with harsh usage, and when the psychic breath passes over them they remain dumb or give out harsh discordant notes, not because the breath is absent, but because the strings are in evil case.

It will now, I think, be clearly understood that what we call mind, or intellect, is in H. P. Blavatsky's words, "a pale and too often distorted reflection" of Manas itself, or our fifth principle; Kâma-Manas is "the rational, but earthly or physical intellect of man, incased in, and bound by, matter, therefore subject to the influence of the latter"; it is the "lower self, or that which manifesting through our *organic* system, acting on this plane of illusion, imagines itself the *Ego sum*, and thus falls into what Buddhist philosophy brands as the 'heresy of separateness.' It is the human personality, from which proceeds "the psychic, *i. e.*, 'terrestrial wisdom' at best, as it is influenced by all the chaotic stimuli of the human or rather animal passions of the living body" (*Lucifer*, October, 1890, p. 179).

A clear understanding of the fact that Kâma-Manas belongs to the human personality, that it functions in and through the physical brain, that it acts on the molecules of the brain, setting them into vibration, will very much facilitate the comprehension by the student of the doctrine of reincarnation. That great subject will be dealt with in another volume of this series, and I do not propose to dwell upon it here, more than to remind the student to take careful note of the fact that the lower Manas is a ray from the immortal Thinker, *illuminating a personality*, and that all the functions which are brought into activity in the brain-consciousness are functions correlated to the particular brain, to the particular personality, in which they occur. The brain-molecules that are set vibrating are material organs in the man of flesh; they did not exist as brain molecules before his conception, nor do they persist as brain molecules after his disintegration. Their functional activity is limited by the limits of his personal life, the life of the body, the life of the transient personality.

Now the faulty of which we speak as memory on the physical plane depends on the response of these very brain-molecules to the impulse of the lower Manas, and there is no link between the brains of successive personalities except through the higher Manas, that sends out its ray to inform and enlighten them successively. It follows, then, inevitably, that unless the consciousness of man can rise from the physical and Kâma-manasic planes to the plane of the higher Manas, no memory of one personality can reach over to another. The memory of the personality belongs to the transitory part of man's complex nature, and those only can recover the memory of their past lives who can raise their consciousness to the plane of the immortal Thinker, and can, so to speak, travel in consciousness up and down the ray which is the bridge between the personal man that perishes and the immortal man that endures. If, while we are cased in the human flesh, we can raise our consciousness along the ray that connects our lower with our true Self, and so reach the higher Manas, we find there stored in the memory of that eternal Ego the whole of our past lives on earth, and we can bring back those records to our brain-memory by way of that same ray, through which we can climb upwards to our "Father". But this is an achievement that belongs to a late stage of human evolution, and until this is reached the successive personalities informed by the manasic rays are separated from each other, and no memory bridges over the gulf between. The fact is obvious enough to any one who thinks the matter out, but as the difference between the personality and the immortal individuality is somewhat unfamiliar in the West, it may be well to remove a possible stumbling-block from the student's path.

Now the lower Manas may do one of three things; It may rise towards its source, and by unremitting and strenuous efforts become one with its "Father in heaven," or the higher Manas – Manas uncontaminated with earthly elements, unsoiled and pure. Or it may partially aspire and partially tend downwards, as indeed is mostly the case with the average man. Or saddest fate of all, it may become so clogged with the kâmic elements as to become one with them, and be finally wrenched away from its parent and perish.

Before considering these three fates, there are a few more words to be said touching the activity of the lower Manas.

As the lower Manas frees itself from Kâma, it becomes the sovereign of the lower part of man, and manifests more and more of its true and essential nature. In Kâma is desire, moved by bodily needs, and Will, which is the outgoing energy of the Self in Manas, is often led captive by the turbulent physical impulses. But the lower Manas, "whenever it disconnects itself, for the time being, from Kâma, becomes the guide of the highest mental faculties, and is the organ of the free will in physical man" (*Lucifer*, October 1890, page 94). But the condition of this freedom is that Kâma shall be subdued, shall lie prostrate beneath the feet of the conqueror; if the maiden Will is to be set free, the manasic St. George must slay the kâmic dragon that holds her captive; for while Kâma is unconquered, Desire will be master of the Will.

Again, as the lower Manas frees itself from Kâma, it becomes more and more capable of transmitting to the human personality with which it is connected the impulses that reach it from its source. It is then, as we have seen, that genius flashes forth, the light from the higher Ego streaming through the lower Manas to the brain, and manifesting itself to the world. So also, as H. P. Blavatsky points out, such action may raise a man above the normal level of human power. "The higher Ego", she says, "cannot act directly on the body, as its consciousness belongs to quite another plane and planes of ideation; the lower self does; and its action and behaviour depend on its freewill and choice as to whether it will gravitate more towards its parent ('the Father in heaven') or the 'animal' which it informs, the man of flesh. The higher Ego, as part of the essence of the Universal Mind, is unconditionally omniscient on its own plane, and only potentially so in our terrestrial sphere, as it has to act solely through its *alter ego* the personal self. Now ...the former is the vehicle of all knowledge of the past, the present and the future, and ...it is from this fountain head that its 'double' catches occasional glimpses of that which is beyond the senses of man, and transmits them to certain brain-cells (unknown to science in their functions), thus making of man a *seer*, a soothsayer and a prophet" (*Lucifer, November, 1890, p. 179*). This is the real seership, and on it a few words must be said presently. It is, naturally, extremely rare, and precious as it is rare. A "faint and distorted reflection" of it is found in what is called mediumship, and of this H. P. Blavatsky says: "Now what is a medium? The term medium, when not applied to things and objects, is supposed to be a person through whom the action of another person or being is either manifested or transmitted. Spiritualists believing in communications with disembodied spirits, and that these can manifest through, or impress sensitives to transmit messages from them, regard mediumship as a blessing and a great privilege. We Theosophists, on the other hand, who do not believe in the 'communion of spirits', as Spiritualists do, regard the gift as one of the most dangerous of abnormal nervous diseases. A medium is simply one in whose personal Ego, or terrestrial mind, the percentage of the astral light so preponderates as to impregnate with it his whole physical constitution. Every organ and cell thereby is attuned, so to speak, and subject to an enormous and abnormal tension" (*Lucifer, November 1890, page 183*).

To return to the three fates spoken of above, any one of which may befall the lower Manas.

It may rise towards its source and become one with the Father in heaven. This triumph can only be gained by many successive incarnations, all consciously directed towards this end. As life succeeds life, the physical frame becomes more and more delicately attuned to vibrations responsive to the manasic impulses, so that gradually the manasic ray needs less and less of the coarser astral matter as its vehicle. "It is part of the mission of the manasic ray to get gradually rid of the blind deceptive element which, though it makes of it an actual spiritual entity on this plane, still brings it into so close contact with matter as to entirely becloud its divine nature and stultify its intuitions" (*Lucifer, November, 1890, p. 182*). Life after life it rids itself of this "blind deceptive element", until at least, master of Kâma, and with body responsive to mind, the ray becomes one with its radiant source, the lower nature is wholly attuned to the higher, and the Adept stands forth complete, the "Father and the Son", having become one on all planes, as they have been always "one in heaven". For him the wheel of incarnation is over, the cycle of necessity is trodden. Henceforth he can incarnate at will, to do any special service to mankind; or he can dwell in the planes round the earth without the physical body, helping in the further evolution of the globe and of the race.

It may partially aspire and partially tend downwards. This is the normal experience of the average man. All life is a battlefield, and the battle rages in the lower manasic region, where Manas wrestles with Kâma for empire over man. Anon aspiration conquers, the chains of sense are broken, and the lower Manas, with the radiance of its birthplace on it, soars upwards on strong wings, spurning the soil of earth. But alas! too soon the pinions tire, they flag, they flutter, they cease to beat the air; and downwards falls the royal bird whose true realm is that of the higher air, and he flutters heavily to the bog of earth once more, and Kâma chains him down.

When the period of incarnation is over, and the gateway of death closes the road of earthly life, what becomes of the lower Manas in the case we are considering?

Soon after the death of the physical body, Kâma-Manas is set free, and dwells for a while on the astral plane clothed with a body of astral matter. From this all of the manasic ray that is pure and unsoiled gradually disentangles itself, and, after a lengthy period spent on the lower levels of Devachan, it returns to its source, carrying with it such of its life-experiences as are of a nature fit for assimilation with the Higher Ego. Manas thus again becomes one during the latter part of the period which intervenes between two incarnations. The manasic Ego, brooded over by Âtma-Buddhi – the two highest principles in the human constitution, not yet considered by us – passes into the devachanic state of consciousness, resting from the weariness of the life-struggle through which it has passed. The experiences of the earth-life just closed are carried into the manasic consciousness by the lower ray withdrawn into its source. They make the devachanic state a continuation of earth-life, shorn of its sorrows, a completion of the wishes and desires of earth-life, so far as those were pure and noble. The poetic phrase that "the mind creates its own heaven" is truer than many may have imagined, for everywhere man *is* what he *thinks*, and in the devachanic state the mind is unfettered by the gross physical matter through which it works on the objective plane. The devachanic period is the time for the assimilation of life experiences, the regaining of equilibrium, ere a new journey is commenced. It is the day that succeeds the night of earth-life, the alternative of the objective manifestation. Periodicity is here, as everywhere else in nature, ebb and flow, throb and rest, the rhythm of the Universal Life. This devachanic state of consciousness lasts for a period of varying length, proportioned to the stage reached in evolution, the Devachan of the average man being said to extend over some fifteen-hundred years.

Meanwhile, that portion of the impure garment of the lower Manas which remains entangled with Kâma gives to the desire-body a somewhat confused consciousness, a broken memory of the events of the life just closed. If the emotions and passions were strong and the manasic element weak during the period of incarnation, the desire-body will be strongly energised, and will persist in its activity for a considerable length of time after the death of the physical body. It will also show a considerable amount of consciousness, as much of the manasic ray will have been overpowered by the vigorous kâmic elements, and will have remained entangled in them. If, on the other hand, the earth-life just closed was characterised my mentality and purity rather than by passion, the desire-body, being but poorly energised, will be a pale simulacrum of the person to whom it belonged, and will fade away, disintegrate and perish before any long period has elapsed. The "spook" already mentioned will now be understood. It may show very considerable intelligence, if the manasic element be still largely present, and this will be the case with the desire-body of persons of strong animal nature and forcible though coarse intellect. For intelligence working in a very powerful kâmic personality will be exceedingly strong and energetic, though not subtle or delicate, and the spook of such a person, still further vitalised by the magnetic currents of persons yet living in the body, may show much intellectual ability of a low type. But such a spook is conscienceless, devoid of good impulses, tending towards disintegration, and communications with it can work for evil only, whether we regard them as prolonging its vitality by the currents which it sucks up from the bodies and kâmic elements of the living, or as exhausting the vitality of these living persons and polluting them with astral connections of an altogether undesirable kind.

Nor should it be forgotten that, without attending séance-rooms at all, living persons may come into objectionable contact with these kâmic spooks. As already mentioned, they are attracted to places in which the animal part of man is chiefly catered for; drinking houses, gambling saloons, brothels – all these places are full of the vilest magnetism, are very whirlpools of magnetic currents of the foulest type. These attract the spooks magnetically, and they drift to such psychic maelstroms of all that is earthly and sensual. Vivified by currents so congenial to their own, the desire-bodies become more active and potent; impregnated with the emanations of passions and desires which they can no longer physically satisfy, their magnetic current reinforce the similar currents in the live persons, action and reaction continually going on, and the animal natures of the living become more potent and less controlled by the will as they are played on by these forces of the kâmic world. Kâma-loka (from *loka,* a place, and so the place for Kâma) is a name often used to designate that plane of the astral world to which these spooks belong, and from this ray forth magnetic currents of poisonous character, as from a pest-house float out germs of disease which may take root and grow in the congenial soil of some poorly vitalised physical body.

It is very possible that many will say, on reading these statements, that Theosophy is a revival of mediaeval superstitions and will lead to imaginary terrors. Theosophy explains mediaeval superstitions, and shows the natural facts on which they were founded and from which they drew their vitality. If there are planes in nature other than the physical, no amount of reasoning will get rid of them and belief in their existence will constantly reappear; but knowledge will give them their intelligible place in the universal order, and will prevent superstition by an accurate understanding of their nature, and of the laws under which they function. And let it be remembered that persons whose consciousness is normally on the physical plane can protect themselves from undesirable influences by keeping their minds clean and their wills strong. We protect ourselves best against disease by maintaining our bodies in vigorous health; we cannot guard ourselves against invisible germs, but we can prevent our bodies from becoming suitable soil for the growth and development of the germs. Nor need we deliberately throw ourselves in the way infection. So also as regards these malign germs from the astral plane. We can prevent the formation of Kâma-manasic soil in which they can germinate and develop, and we need not go into evil places, nor deliberately encourage receptivity and mediumistic tendencies. A strong active will and a pure heart are our best protection.

There remains the third possibility for Kâma-Manas, to which we must now turn our attention, the fate spoken of earlier as "terrible in its consequences, which may befall the kâmic principle".

It may break away from its source made one with Kâma instead of with the higher Manas. This is fortunately, a rare event, as rare at one pole of human life as the complete re-union with the higher Manas is rare at the other. But still the possibility remains and must be stated.

The personality may be so strongly controlled by Kâma that, in the struggle between the kâmic and manasic elements, the victory may remain wholly with the former. The lower Manas may become so enslaved that its essence may be frayed and thinner and thinner by the constant rub and strain, until at last persistent yielding to the promptings of desire bears its inevitable fruit, and the slender link which unites the higher to the lower Manas, the "silver thread that binds it to the Master", snaps in two. Then, during earth-life, the lower quaternary is wrenched away from the Triad to which it was linked, and the higher nature is severed wholly from the lower. The human being is rent in twain, the brute has broken itself free, and it goes forth unbridled, carrying with it the reflections of that manasic light which should have been its guide through the desert of life. A more dangerous brute it is than its fellows of the unevolved animal world, just because of these fragments in it of the higher mentality of man. Such a being, human in form but brute in nature, human in appearance but without human truth, or love or justice – such a one may now and then be met with in the haunts of men, putrescent while still living, a thing to shudder at with deepest, if hopeless compassion. What is its fate after the funeral knell has tolled?

Ultimately, there is the perishing of the personality that has thus broken away from the principles that can alone give it immortality. But a period of persistence lies before it.

The desire-body of such a one is an entity of terrible potency, and it has this unique peculiarity, that it is able under certain rare circumstances to reincarnate in the world of men. It is not a mere "spook" on the way to disintegration; it has retained, entangled in its coils, too much of the manasic element to permit of such natural dissipation in space. It is sufficiently an independent entity, lurid instead of radiant, with manasic flame rendered foul instead of purifying, as to be able to take to itself a garment of flesh once more and dwell as man with men. Such a man – if the word may indeed be applied to the mere human shell with brute interior – passes through a period of earth-life the natural foe of all who are still normal in their humanity. With no instincts save those of the animal, driven only by passion, never even by emotion, with a cunning that no brute can rival, a deliberate wickedness that plans evil in fashion unknown to the mere frankly natural impulses of the animal world, the reincarnated entity touches ideal vileness. Such soil the page of human history as the monsters of iniquity that startle us now and again into a wondering cry, "Is this a human being?" Sinking lower with each successive incarnation, the evil force gradually wears itself out, and such a personality perishes separated from the source of life. It finally disintegrates, to be worked up into other forms of living things, but as a separate existence, it is lost. It is a bead broken off the thread of life, and the immortal Ego that incarnated in that personality has lost the experience of that incarnation, has reaped no harvest from that life-sowing. Its ray has brought nothing back, its lifework for that birth has been a total and complete failure, whereof nothing remains to weave into the fabric of its own eternal Self.

SUBTLE FORMS OF THE FOURTH AND FIFTH PRINCIPLE

The student will already have fully realised that "an astral body" is a loose term that may cover a variety of different forms. It may be well at this stage to sum up the subtle types sometimes inaccurately called the astral that belong to the fourth and fifth principles.

During life a true astral body may be projected – formed, as its name implies, of astral matter – but, unlike the etheric double, dowered with intelligence, and able to travel to a considerable distance from the physical body to which it belongs. This is the desire-body, and it is, as we have seen, a vehicle of consciousness. It is projected by mediums and sensitives unconsciously, and by trained students consciously. It can travel with the speed of thought to a distant place, can there gather impressions from surrounding objects, can bring back those impressions to the physical body. In the case of a medium it can convey them to others by means of the physical body still entranced, but as a rule when the sensitive comes out of trance, the brain does not retain the impressions thus made upon it, and no trace is left in the memory of the experiences thus acquired. Sometimes, but this is rare, the desire-body is able sufficiently to affect the brain by the vibrations it set up, to leave a lasting impression thereon, and then the sensitive is able to recall the knowledge acquired during trance. The student learns to impress on his brain the knowledge gained in the desire-body, his will being active while that of the medium is passive.

This desire-body is the agent unconsciously used by clairvoyants when their vision is not merely the seeing in the astral light. This astral form does then really travel to distant places, and may appear there to persons who are sensitive or who chance for the time to be in an abnormal nervous condition. Sometimes it appears to them – when very faintly informed by consciousness – as a vaguely outlined form, not noticing its surroundings. Such a body has appeared near the time of death at places distant from the dying person, to those who were closely united to the dying by ties of the blood, of affection, or of hatred. More highly energised, it will show intelligence and emotion, as in some cases on record, in which dying mothers have visited their children residing at a distance, and have spoken in their last moments of what they had seen and done. The desire-body is also set free in many cases of disease – as is the etheric double – as well as in sleep and in trance. Inactivity of the physical body is a condition of such astral voyagings.

The desire-body seems also occasionally to appear in séance-rooms, giving rise to some of the more intellectual phenomena that takes place. It must not be confounded with the "spook" already sufficiently familiar to the reader, the latter being always the kâmic or Kâma-Manasic remains of some dead person, whereas the body we are now dealing with is the projection of an astral double from a living person.

A higher form of subtle body, belonging to Manas, is that known as the Mâyâvi Rûpa, or "body of illusion". The Mâyâvi Rûpa is a subtle body formed by the consciously directed will of the Adept or disciple; it may, or may not, resemble the physical body, the form given to it being suitable to the purpose for which it is projected. In this body the full consciousness dwells, for it is merely the mental body rearranged. The Adept or disciple can thus travel at will, without the burden of the physical body, in the full exercise of every faculty, in perfect self-consciousness. He makes the Mâyâvi Rûpa visible of invisible at will – on the physical plane – and the phrase often used by chelâs and others as to seeing an Adept "in his astral", means that he was visited by them in his Mâyâvi Rûpa. If he so chose, he can make it, indistinguishable from a physical body, warm and firm to the touch as well as visible, able to carry on a conversation, at all points like a physical human being. But the power thus to form the true Mâyâvi Rûpa is confined to Adepts and chelâs; it cannot be done by the untrained student, however psychic he may naturally be, for it is a manasic and not a psychic creation, and it is only under the instruction of his Guru that the chelâ learns to form and use the "body of illusion".

THE HIGHER MANAS

The immortal Thinker itself, as will by this time have become clear to the reader, can manifest itself but little on the physical plane at the present stage of human evolution. Yet we are able to catch some glimpses of the powers resident in it, the more as in the lower Manas we find those powers "cribbed, cabined and confined" indeed, but yet existing. Thus we have seen (p. 37) that the lower Manas "is the organ of the freewill in physical man". Freewill resides in Manas itself, in Manas the representative of Mahat, the Universal Mind. From Manas comes the feeling of liberty, the knowledge that we can rule ourselves – really the knowledge that the higher nature in us can rule the lower, let that lower nature rebel and struggle as it may. Once let our consciousness identify itself with Manas instead of with Kâma, and the lower nature becomes the animal we bestride, it is no longer the "I". All its plungings, its struggles, its fights for mastery, are then outside us, not within us, and we rein it in and hold it as we rein in a plunging steed and subdue it to our will.

On this question of freewill I venture to quote from an article of my own that appeared in the *Path* – "Unconditioned will, alone can be absolutely free: the unconditioned and the absolute are one: all that is conditioned must, by virtue of that conditioning, be relative and therefore partially bound. As that will evolves the universe, it becomes conditioned by the laws of its own manifestation. The manasic entities are differentiations of that will, each conditioned by the nature of its manifesting potency, but, while conditioned without, it is free within its own sphere of activity, so being the image in its own world of the universal will in the universe. Now as this will, acting on each successive plane, crystalises itself more and more densely as matter, the manifestation is conditioned by the material in which it works, while, relatively to the material, it is itself free. So at each stage the inner freedom appears in consciousness, while yet investigation shows that, that freedom works within the limits of the plane of manifestation on which it is acting, free to work upon the lower, yet hindered as to manifestation by the unresponsiveness of the lower to its impulse. Thus the higher Manas, in whom resides free will, so far as the lower quaternary is concerned – being the offspring of Mahat, the third Logos, the Word, *i. e.,* the Will in manifestation – is limited in its manifestation in our lower nature by the sluggishness of the response of the personality to its impulses. In the lower Manas itself – as immersed in that personality - resides the will with which we are familiar, swayed by passions, by appetites, by desires, by impressions coming from without, yet able to assert itself among them all, by virtue of its essential nature, one with that higher Ego of which it is the ray. It is free, as regards all below it, able to act on Kâma and on the physical body, however much its full expression may be thwarted and hindered by the crudeness of the material in which it is working. Were the will the mere outcome of the physical body, of the desires and passions, whence could arise the sense of the "!" that can judge, can desire, can overcome? It acts from a higher plane, is royal as touching the lower whenever it claims the royalty of birthright, and the very struggle of its self-assertion is the best testimony to the fact that in its nature it is free. And so, passing to lower planes, we find in each grade this freedom of the higher as ruling the lower, yet, on the plane of the lower, hindered in manifestation. Reversing the process and starting from the lower, the same truth becomes manifest. Let a man's limbs be loaded with fetters, and crude material iron will prevent the manifestation of the muscular and nervous force with which they are instinct: none the less is that force present, though hindered for the moment in its activity. Its strength may be shown in its very efforts to break the chains that bind it there, is no power in the iron to prevent the free giving out of the muscular energy, though the phenomena of motion may be hindered. But while this energy cannot be ruled by the physical nature below, its expenditure is determined by the kâmic principle; passions and desires can set it going, can direct and control it. The muscular and nervous energy cannot rule the passions and desires, they are free as regards it, it is determined by their interposition. Yet again Kâma may be ruled, controlled, determined by the will; as touching the manasic principle it is bound, not free, and hence the sense of freedom in choosing which desire shall be gratified, which act performed. As the lower Manas rules Kâma, the lower quaternary takes its rightful position of subserviency to the higher triad, and is determined by a will it recognises as above itself, and, as it regards itself, a will that is free. Here in many a mind will spring the question, 'And what of the will of the higher Manas; is that in turn determined by what is above it, while it is free to all below? But we have reached a point where the intellect fails us, and where language may not easily utter that which the Spirit senses in those higher realms. Dimly only can we feel that there, as everywhere else, "the truest freedom must be in harmony with law, and that voluntary acceptance of the function of acting as channel of the Universal Will must unite into one perfect liberty and perfect obedience".

This is truly an obscure and difficult problem, but the student will find much light fall on it by following the lines of thought thus traced.

Another power resident in the higher Manas and manifested on the lower planes by those in whom the higher Manas is consciously master, is that of creation of forms by the will. The *Secret Doctrine* says: "Kriyashakti". The mysterious power of thought which enables it to produce external, perceptible, phenomenal results by its own inherent energy. The ancient held that *any idea will manifest itself externally if one's attention is deeply concentrated upon it. Similarly an intense volition will be followed by the desired results"* (vol. I, p. 312). Here is the secret of true "magic", and as the subject is an important one, and as Western science is beginning to touch its fringe, a separate section is devoted to its consideration farther on, in order not to break the connected outline here given on principles.

Again we have learned from H. P. Blavatsky that Manas, or the higher Ego, as "part of the essence of the Universal Mind, is unconditionally omniscient on its own plane", when it has fully developed self-consciousness by its evolutionary experiences, and "is the vehicle of all knowledge of the past and present, and the future". When this immortal entity is able through its ray, the lower Manas, to impress the brain of a man, that man is one who manifests abnormal qualities, is a genius or seer. The conditions of seership are thus laid down: "The former [the visions of the true seer] can be obtained by one of two means: (a) on the condition of paralysing at will the *memory* and the instinctual independent action of all the material organs and even cells in the body of flesh, an act which, when once the light of the higher Ego has consumed and subjected for ever the passional nature of the personal lower Ego, is easy, but requires an adept; (b) of being a reincarnation of one who, in a previous birth, had attained through extreme purity of life and efforts in the right direction almost to a Yogi-state of holiness and saintship. There is also a third possibility of reaching in mystic visions the plane of the higher Manas; but it is only occasional, and does not depend on the will of the seer, but on the extreme weakness and exhaustion of the material body through illness and suffering. The Seeress of Prevorst was an instance of the latter case; and Jacob Boehme of our second category" (*Lucifer, November, 1890, p. 183*).

The reader will now be in a position to grasp the difference between the workings of the higher Ego and of its ray. Genius, which *sees* instead of arguing, is of the higher Ego; true intuition is one of its faculties. Reason, the weighing and balancing quality which arranges the facts gathered by observation, balances them one against the other, argues from them, draws conclusions from them – this is the exercise of the lower Manas through the brain apparatus; its instrument is ratiocination; by induction it ascends from the known to the unknown, building up a hypothesis; by deduction it descends again to the known, verifying its hypothesis by fresh experiment.

Intuition, as we see by its derivation, is simply insight – a process as direct and swift as bodily vision. It is the exercise of the eyes of the intelligence, the unerring recognition of a truth presented on the mental plane. It sees with certainty, its vision is unclouded, its report unfaltering. No proof can add to the certitude of its recognition, for it is beyond and above the reason. Often our instincts, blinded and confused by passions and desires, are miscalled intuitions, and a mere kâmic impulse is accepted as the sublime voice of the higher Manas. Careful and prolonged self-training is necessary, ere the voice can be recognised with certainty, but of one thing we may feel very sure: so long as we are in the vortex of the personality, so long as the storms of desires and appetites howl around us, so long as the waves of emotion toss us to and fro, so long the voice of the higher Manas cannot reach our ears. Not in the fire or the whirlwind, not in the thunderclap of the storm, comes the mandate of the higher Ego: only when there has fallen the stillness of a silence that can be felt, only when the very air is motionless and the calm is profound, only when the man wraps his face in a mantle which closes his ears even to the silence that is of earth, then only sounds the voice that is stiller than the silence, the voice of his true Self.

On this H. P. Blavatsky has written in *Isis Unveiled*: "Allied to the physical half of man's nature is reason, which enables him to maintain his supremacy over the lower animals, and to subjugate nature to his uses. Allied to his spiritual part is his conscience, which will serve as his unerring guide through the besetment of the senses; for conscience is that instantaneous perception between right and wrong which can only be exercised by the spirit, which, being a portion of the divine wisdom and purity, is absolutely pure and wise. Its promptings are independent of reason, and it can only manifest itself clearly when unhampered by the baser attractions of our dual nature. Reason being a faculty of our physical brain, one which is justly defined as that of deducing inferences from premises, and being wholly dependent on the evidence of other senses, cannot be a quality pertaining directly to our divine spirit. The latter *knows* – hence all reasoning, which implies discussion and argument, would be useless. So an entity which, if it must be considered as a direct emanation from the eternal Spirit of wisdom, has to be vied as possessed of the same attributes as the essence of the whole of which it is part. Therefore it is with a certain degree of logic that the ancient Theurgists maintained that the rational part of a man's soul (spirit) never entered wholly into the man's body, but only overshadowed him more or less through the irrational or astral soul, which serves as an intermediary agent, or a medium between spirit and body. The man who has conquered matter sufficiently to receive the direct light from his shining *Augoeides,* feels truth intuitionally; he could not err in his judgement, notwithstanding all the sophisms suggested by cold reason, for he is *illuminated.* Hence prophesy, vaticination, and the so-called divine inspiration, are simply the effects of this illumination from above by our own immortal spirit" (Volume I, page 305-306).

This Augoeides, according to the belief of the Neo-Platonists, as according to the Theosophical teachings, "sheds more or less its radiance on the inner man, the astral soul" (Volume, page 315) *i. e..,* in the now accepted terminology, on the Kâma-Manasic personality or lower Ego. (In reading *Isis Unveiled*, the student has to bear in mind the fact that when the book was written, the terminology was by no means even as fixed as it is now; in *Isis Unveiled* is the first modern attempt to translate into Western language the complicated Eastern ideas, and further experience has shown that many of the terms used to cover two or three conceptions may with advantage be restricted to one and thus rendered precise. Thus the "astral soul" must be understood in the sense given above.) Only as this lower Ego becomes pure from all breath of passion, as the lower Manas frees itself from Kâma, can the "shining one" impress it; H. P. Blavatsky tells how initiates meet this higher Ego face to face. Having spoken of the trinity in man, Âtma-Buddhi-Manas, she goes on: "It is when this trinity, in anticipation of the final triumphant reunion beyond the gates of corporeal death, became for a few seconds a unity, that the candidate is allowed, at the moment of the initiation, to behold his future self. Thus we read in the Persian *Desatir* of the 'resplendent one'; in the Greek philosopher-initiates of the Augoeides – the self-shining 'blessed vision resident in the pure light'; in Porphyry, that Plotinus was united to his 'god' six times during his lifetime, and so on" *(Isis Unveiled, Vol. II, pp. 114-115)*.

This trinity made into unity, again, is the "Christ" of all mystics. When in the final initiation, the candidate has been outstretched on the floor or altar stone and has thus typified the crucifixion of the flesh, or lower nature, and when from this "death" he has "risen again" as the triumphant conqueror over sin and death, he then, in the supreme moment, sees before him the glorious presence and becomes "one with Christ," is himself the Christ. Thenceforth he may live in the body, but it has become his obedient instrument; he is united with his true Self, Manas made one with Âtma-Buddhi, and through the personality which he inhabits he wields his full powers as an immortal spiritual intelligence. While he was still struggling in the toils of the lower nature, Christ, the spiritual Ego, was daily crucified in him; but in the full Adept Christ has arisen triumphant, lord of himself and of nature. The long pilgrimage of Manas is over, the cycle of necessity is trodden, the wheel of rebirth ceases to turn, the Son of man has been made perfect by suffering.

So long as this point has not been reached, "the Christ" is the object of aspiration. The ray is ever struggling to return to its source, the lower Manas ever aspiring to re-become one with the higher. While this duality persists the continual yearning towards reunion felt by the noblest and purest natures is one of the most salient facts of the inner life, and it is this which clothes itself as prayer, as inspiration, as "seeking after God," as the longing for union with the divine. "My soul is athirst for God, for the living God", cries the eager Christian, and to tell him that this intense longing is a fancy and is futile to make him turn aside from you as one who cannot understand, but whose insensibility does not alter the fact. The Occultist recognises in this cry the inextinguishable impulse upwards of the lower Self to the higher from which it is separated, but the attraction of which it vividly feels. Whether the person pray to the Buddha, to Vishnu, to Christ, to the Virgin, to the Father, it matters not at all; these are questions of mere dialect, not of essential fact. In all the Manas united to Âtma-Buddhi is the real object, veiled under what name the changing time or race may give; at once the ideal humanity and the "personal God", the "God Man" found in all religions, "God incarnate", the "Word made flesh", "the Christ who must be born in each", with whom the believer must be made one.

And this leads us on to the last planes with which we are concerned, the planes of Spirit, using that much abused word merely as the opposite pole to matter; here only very general ideas can be grasped by us, but it is necessary none the less to try to grasp these ideas if we are to complete, however poorly our conception of man.

PRINCIPLES 6 and 7.
ÂTMA – BUDDHI, THE SPIRIT

As the completion of the thought of the last section, we will look at Âtma-Buddhi first in its connection with Manas, and will then proceed to a somewhat more general view of it as the "Monad. " The clearest and best description of the human trinity, Âtma-Buddhi-Manas, will be found in the *Key to Theosophy*, in which H. P. Blavatsky gives the following definitions:-

THE HIGHER SELF is	*Atma,* the inseparable ray of the Universal and ONE SELF. It is the God *above,* more than within us. Happy the man who succeeds in saturating his *inner Ego* with it
THE SPIRITUAL divine EGO is	the spiritual soul, or *Buddhi,* in close union with *Manas,* the mind-principle, without which it is no EGO at all, but only the Atmic Vehicle.
THE INNER or HIGHER EGO is	*Manas,* the fifth principle, so called, independently of Buddhi. The mind-principle is only the Spiritual Ego when merged into one with Buddhi. . It is the permanent individuality or the reincarnating Ego.

Âtmâ must then be regarded as the most abstract part of man's nature, the "breath" which needs a body for its manifestation. It is the one reality, that which manifests on all planes, the essence of which all our principles are but aspects. The one Eternal Existence, wherefrom are all things, which embodies one of its aspects in the universe, that which we speak of as the One Life – this Eternal Existence rays forth as Âtmâ, the very Self alike of the universe and of man; their innermost core, their very heart, that in which all things inhere. In itself incapable of direct manifestation on lower planes, yet That without which no lower planes could come into existence, It clothes Itself in Buddhi, as Its vehicle, or medium of further manifestation. "Buddhi is the faculty of cognising, the channel through which divine knowledge reaches the Ego, the discernment of good and evil, also divine conscience, and the spiritual Soul, which is the vehicle of Âtmâ" (*Secret Doctrine*, Volume I, page 2). It is often spoken of as the principle of spiritual discernment. But Âtma-Buddhi, a universal principle, needs individualising ere experience can be gathered and self-consciousness attained. So the mind-principle is united to Âtma-Buddhi, and the human trinity is complete. Manas becomes the *spiritual*Ego only when merged in Buddhi; Buddhi becomes the spiritual *Ego* only when united to Manas; in the union of the two lies the evolution of the Spirit, self-conscious on all planes. Hence Manas strives upward to Âtma-Buddhi, as the lower Manas strives upward to the higher, and hence, in relation to the higher Manas, Âtma-Buddhi, or Âtma, is often spoken of as "the Father in Heaven", as the higher Manas is itself thus described in relation to the lower. (See ante page 40) The lower Manas gathers experience to carry it back to its source; the higher Manas accumulates the store throughout the cycle of reincarnation; Buddhi becomes assimilated with the higher Manas; and these, permeated with the Âtmic light, one with that True Self, the trinity becomes a unity, the Spirit is self-conscious on all planes, and the object of the manifested universe is attained.

But no words of mine can avail to explain or to describe that which is beyond explanation and beyond description. Words can but blunder along on such a theme, dwarfing and distorting it. Only by long and patient meditation can the student hope vaguely to sense something greater than himself, yet something which stirs at the innermost core of his being. As to the steady gaze directed at the pale evening sky, there appears after while, faintly and far away, the soft glimmer of a star, so to the patient gaze of the inner vision there may come the tender beam of the spiritual star, if but as a mere suggestion of a far off world. Only to a patient and persevering purity will that light arise, and blessed beyond all earthly blessedness is he who sees but the palest shimmer of that transcendent radiance.

With such ideas as to "Spirit", the horror with which Theosophists shrink from ascribing the trivial phenomena of the séance-room to "spirits" will be readily understood. Playing on musical boxes, talking through trumpets, tapping people on the head, carrying accordions round the room – these things may be all very well for astrals, spooks and elementals, but who can assign them to "spirits", who has any conception of Spirit worthy of the name? Such vulgarisation and degradation of the most sublime conceptions as yet evolved by man are surely subjects for the keenest regret, and it may well be hoped that ere long these phenomena will be put in their true place, as evidence that the materialistic views of the universe are inadequate, instead of being exalted to a place they cannot fill as proofs of Spirit. No physical, no intellectual phenomena are proofs of the existence of Spirit. Only to the spirit can Spirit be demonstrated. You cannot prove a proposition in Euclid to a dog; you cannot prove Âtma-Buddhi to Kâma and the lower Manas. As we climb, our view will widen, and when we stand on the summit of the Holy Mount the planes of Spirit shall lie before our opened vision.

THE MONAD IN EVOLUTION

Perhaps a slightly more definite conception of Atmâ-Buddhi may be obtained by the student, if he considers its work in evolution as the Monad. Now Atmâ-Buddhi is identical with the universal Over-soul, "itself an aspect of the Unknown Root", the One Existence. When manifestation begins the Monad is "thrown downwards into matter", to propel forward and force evolution (See *Secret Doctrine,* Volume 2, page 115); it is the mainspring, so to speak, of all evolution, the impelling force at the root of all things. All the principles we have been studying are mere "variously differentiated aspects" of Atmâ, the One Reality manifesting in our universe; it is in every atom, "the root of every atom individually and of every form collectively", and all the principles are fundamentally Atmâ on different planes. The stages of its evolution are very clearly laid down in *Five Years of Theosophy,* pages 273 *et seq.* There we are shown how it passes through the stages termed elemental, "nascent centres of forces", and reaches the mineral stage; from this it passes up through vegetable, animal, to man, vivifying every form. As we are taught in the *Secret Doctrine*: "The well-known Kabbalistic aphorism runs:

"A stone becomes a plant; the plant a beast; the beast, a man; the man, a spirit; and the spirit, a god."

The 'spark' animates all the kingdoms in turn before it enters into and informs divine man, between whom and his predecessor, animal man, there is all the difference in the world.... The Monad...is first of all, shot down by the law of evolution into the lowest form of matter – the mineral. After a sevenfold gyration incased in the stone, or that which will become mineral and stone in the Fourth Round, it creeps out of it, say as a lichen. Passing thence, through all the forms of vegetable matter, into what is termed animal matter, it has now reached the point in which it has become the germ, so to speak, of the animal, that will become the physical man" (Vol. I, pages 266-267).

It is the Monad, Âtma-Buddhi, that thus vivifies every part and kingdom of nature, making all instinct with life and consciousness, one throbbing whole. "Occultism does not accept anything inorganic in the Kosmos. The expression employed by science, ' inorganic substance,' means simply that the latent life, slumbering in the molecules of so-called 'inert matter,' is incognisable. All is life and every atom of even mineral dust is a life, though beyond our comprehension and perception, because it is outside the range of the laws known to those who reject Occultism "(*Secret Doctrine*, Vol. I, pages 268-69). And again: "Everything in the universe, throughout all its kingdoms, is conscious, *i. e..*, endowed with a consciousness of its own kind and on its own plane of perception. We men must remember that simply because *we* do not perceive any signs of consciousness which we can recognise, say in stones, we have no right to say that no consciousness exists there. There is no such thing as either 'dead' or 'blind' matter, as there is no 'blind' or 'unconscious' law" (page 295).

How many of the great poets, with the sublime intuition of genius, have sensed this great truth! To them all nature pulses with life; they see life and love everywhere, in suns and planets as in the grains of dust, in rustling leaves and opening blossoms, in dancing gnats and gliding snakes. Each form manifests as much of the One Life as it is capable of expressing, and what is man that he should despise the more limited manifestations, when he compares himself as a life-expression, not with the forms below him, but with the possibilities of expression that soar above him in infinite heights of being, which he can estimate still less than the stone can estimate him?

The student will readily see that we must regard this force at the centre of evolution as essentially *one*. There is but one Âtma-Buddhi in our universe, the universal Soul, everywhere present, immanent in all, the One Supreme Energy whereof all varying energies or forces are only differing forms. As the sunbeam is light or heat or electricity according to its conditioning environment, so is Âtma all-energy, differentiating on different planes. "As an abstraction, we will call it the One Life; as an objective and evident reality, we speak of a septenary scale of manifestation, which begins at the upper rung with the one unknowable causality, and ends as Omnipresent Mind and Life immanent in every atom of matter" (*Secret Doctrine*, Volume I, p.163).

Its evolutionary course is very plainly outlined in a quotation given in the *Secret Doctrine*, and as students are very often puzzled over this unity of the Monad, I subjoin the statement. The subject is difficult, but it could not, I think, be more clearly put than it is in these sentences:-

"Now the monadic or cosmic essence (if such a term be permitted) in the mineral, vegetable, and animal, though the same throughout the series of cycles from the lowest elemental up to the Deva kingdom, yet differs in the scale of progression. It would be very misleading to imagine a Monad as a separate entity trailing its slow way in a distinct path through the lower kingdoms, and after incalculable series of transformations flowering into a human being; in short, that the Monad of a Humboldt dates back to the Monad of an atom of hornblende. Instead of saying a 'Mineral Monad,' the more correct phraseology in physical science, which differentiates every atom, would of course have been to call it 'the Monad manifesting in that form of Prakriti called the mineral kingdom. ' The atom, as represented in the ordinary scientific hypothesis, is not a particle of something, animated by a psychic something, destined after aeons to blossom as a man. But it is a concrete manifestation of the universal energy which itself has not yet become individualised; a sequential manifestation of the one universal Monad The ocean of matter does not divide into its potential and constituent drops until the sweep of the life-impulse reaches the stage of man-birth. The tendency towards segregation into individual Monads is gradual, and in the higher animals comes almost to the point. The Peripatetics applied the word Monad to the whole Kosmos in the pantheistic sense; and the Occultists, while accepting this thought for convenience sake, distinguish the progressive stages of the evolution of the concrete from the abstract by terms of which the 'mineral, vegetable, animal, Monad,' etc., are examples. The term merely means that the tidal wave of spiritual evolution is passing through that arc of its circuit. The 'Monadic Essence' begins imperfectly to differentiate towards individual consciousness in the vegetable kingdom. As the Monads are un-compounded things, as correctly defined by Leibnitz, it is the spiritual essence which vivifies them in their degrees of differentiation, which properly constitutes the Monad – not the atomic aggregation, which is only the vehicle and the substance through which thrill the lower and the higher degrees of intelligence" (vol. I, p. 201).

The student who reads and weighs this passage will, at the cost of a little present trouble, save himself from much confusion in days to come. Let him first realise clearly that the Monad – "the spiritual essence" to which alone in strict accuracy the term Monad should be applied – is *one* all the universe over, that Âtma-Buddhi is not his, nor mine, nor the property of anybody in particular, but the spiritual essence energising in all. So is electricity *one* all the world over; though it may be active in his machine or in mine, neither he nor I can call it distinctly our electricity. But – and here arise confusion – when Âtma-Buddhi energises in man, in whom Manas is active as an individualising force, it is often spoken of as though the "atomic aggregation" were a separate Monad, and then we have "Monads," as in the above passage. This loose way of using the word will not lead to error if the student will remember that the individualising process *is not on the spiritual plane*, but Âtma-Buddhi *as seen through Manas* seems to share in the individuality of the latter. So if you hold pieces of variously coloured glass in your hand you may see through them a red sun, a blue sun, a yellow sun, and so on. None the less there is only the one sun shining down upon you, altered by the media through which you look at it. So we often meet the phrase "human Monads"; it should be "the Monad manifesting in the human kingdom"; but this somewhat pedantic accuracy would be likely only to puzzle a large number of people, and the looser popular phrase will not mislead when the principle of the unity on the spiritual plane is grasped, any more than we mislead by speaking of the rising of the sun. "The Spiritual Monad is one, universal, boundless, and impartite, whose rays, nevertheless, form what we, in our ignorance, call the 'individual Monads' of men" (*Secret Doct.*, Vol.I, p.200)

Very beautifully and poetically is this unity in diversity put in one of the Occult Catechisms in which the Guru questions the Chela:-

"Lift thy head, O Lanoo; dost thou see one or countless lights above thee, burning in the dark midnight sky?"

"I sense one Flame, O Gurudeva; I see countless undetached sparks burning in it."

"Thou sayest well. And now look around and into thyself. That light which burns inside thee, dost thou feel it different in any wise from the light that shines in thy brother-men?"

"It is in no way different, though the prisoner is held in bondage by Karma, and though its outer garments delude the ignorant into saying, 'thy soul' and 'my soul'" (*Secret Doctrine*, Vol., I, p. 145).

There ought not to be any serious difficulty now in grasping the stages of human evolution; the Monad, which has been working its way as we have seen, reaches the point at which the human form can be built up on earth; an etheric body and its physical counterpart are then developed, Prâna specialised from the great ocean of life, and Kâma evolved, all these principles, the lower quaternary, being brooded over by the Monad, energised by it, impelled by it, forced onward by it towards continually increasing perfection of form and capacity for manifesting the higher energies in Nature. This was animal, or physical man, evolved through two and a half Races. But the Monad and the lower quaternary could not come into sufficiently close relation with each other; a link was yet wanting. "The Double Dragon [the Monad] has no hold upon the mere form. It is like the breeze where there is no tree or branch to receive and harbour it. It cannot affect the form where there is no agent of transmission, and the form knows it not" – (Secret Doctrine, vol. II, p. 60). Then, at the middle point just reached, in the middle, that is, of the Third race, the lower Mânasaputra stepped in to inhabit the dwellings thus prepared for them, and to form the bridge between animal man and the Spirit, between the evolved quaternary and the brooding Âtma-Buddhi, to begin the long cycle of reincarnation which is to issue in the perfect man.

The "monadic inflow," or the evolution of the Monad, from the animal into the human kingdom, continued through the Third Race on to the middle of the Fourth, the human population thus continually receiving fresh recruits, the birth of souls thus continuing through the second half of the Third race and the first half of the Fourth. After this, the "central turning point" of the cycle of evolution, "no more Monads can enter the human kingdom. The door is closed for this cycle" (Secret Doctrine, vol. I, p. 205). Since then reincarnation has been the method of evolution, this individual reincarnation of the immortal Thinker in conjunction with Âtma-Buddhi replacing the collective indwelling of Âtma-Buddhi in lower forms of matter.

According to Theosophical teachings, humanity has now reached the Fifth Race, and we are in the fifth sub-race thereof, mankind on this globe in the present stage having before it the completion of the Fifth race, and the rise, maturity and decay of the Sixth and Seventh Races. But during all the ages necessary for this evolution, there is no increase in the total number of reincarnating Egos; only a small proportion of these are reincarnated at any special time on our globe, so that the population may ebb and flow within very wide limits, and it will have been noticed that there is a rush of birth after a local depopulation has been caused by exceptional mortality. There is room and to spare for all such fluctuations, having in view the difference between the total number of reincarnating Egos and the number actually incarnated at a given period.

LINES OF PROOF FOR AN UNTRAINED ENQUIRER

It is natural and right that any thoughtful person brought face to face with assertions such as those put forth in the preceding pages, should demand what proof is forthcoming to substantiate the propositions laid down. A reasonable person will not demand full and complete proof available to all comers, without study and without painstaking. He will admit that the advanced theories of a science cannot be demonstrated to one ignorant of its first principles, and he will be prepared to find that very much will have been alleged which can only be proved to those who have made some progress in their study. An essay on the higher mathematics, on the correlation of forces, on the atomic theory, on the molecular constitution of chemical compounds, would contain many statements the proofs of which would only be available for those who had devoted time and thought to the study of the elements of the science concerned; and so an unprejudiced person, confronted with the Theosophical view of the constitution of man, would readily admit that he could not expect complete demonstration until he had mastered the elements of the Theosophical science.

None the less are there general proofs available in every science which suffice to justify its existence and to encourage study of its more recondite truths; and in Theosophy it is possible to indicate lines of proof which can be followed by the untrained enquirer, and which justify him in devoting time and pains to a study which gives promise of a wider and deeper knowledge of himself and of external nature than is otherwise attainable.

It is well to say at the outset that there is no proof available to the average enquirer of the existence of the three higher planes of which we have spoken. The realms of Spirit, and of the higher mind are closed to all save those who have evolved the faculties necessary for their investigation. Those who have evolved these faculties need no proof of the existence of those realms; to those who have not, no proof of their existence can be given. That there is *something* above the astral and the lower levels of the mental plane may indeed be proved by the flashes of genius, the lofty intuitions, that from time to time lighten the darkness of our lower world; but what that something is, only those can say whose inner eyes have been opened, who see where the race as a whole is still blind. But the lower planes are susceptible to proof, and fresh proofs are accumulating day be day. The Masters of Wisdom are using the investigators and thinkers of the Western world to make "discoveries" which tend to substantiate the outposts of the Theosophical position, and the lines which they are following are exactly those which are needed for the finding of natural laws which will justify the assertions of Theosophists with regard to the elementary "powers" and "phenomena" to which such exaggerated importance has been given. If it is found that we have undeniable facts which establish the existence of planes other than the physical on which consciousness can work; which establish the existence of senses and powers of perception other than those with which we are familiar in daily life; which establish the existence of powers of communication between intelligences without the use of mechanical apparatus, surely, under these circumstances, the Theosophist may claim that he has made out a *prima facie* case for further investigation of his doctrines.

Let us then, confine ourselves to the lower planes of which we have spoken in the preceding pages, and the four lower principles in man which are correlated with these planes. Of these four, we may dismiss one, that of Prâna, as none will challenge the fact of the existence of the energy we call "life"; the need of isolating it for purposes of study may be challenged, and in very truth the plane of Prâna, or the principle of Prâna, runs through all other planes, all other principles, interpenetrating all and binding all in one. There remain for our study the physical plane, the astral plane, the lower levels of the manasic plane. Can we substantiate these by proofs which will be accepted by those who are not yet Theosophists? I think we can.

First, as regards the physical plane. We need here to notice how the senses of man are correlated with the physical universe outside him, and how his knowledge of that universe is bounded by the power of his organs of sense to vibrate in response to vibrations set up outside him. He can hear when the air is thrown into vibrations into which the drum of his ear can also be thrown; if the vibration be so slow that the drum cannot vibrate in answer, the person does not hear any sound; if the vibration be so rapid that the drum cannot vibrate in answer, the person does not hear any sound. So true is this, that the limit of hearing in different persons varies with this power of vibration of the drums of their respective ears; one person is plunged in silence, while another is deafened by the keen shrilling that is throwing into tumult the air around both. The same principle holds good for sight; we see so long as the light waves are of a length to which our organs of sight can respond; below and beyond this length we are in darkness, let the ether vibrate as it may. The ant can see where we are blind, because its eye can receive and respond to etheric vibrations more rapid than we can sense.

All this suggests to any thoughtful person the idea that if our senses could be evolved to more responsiveness, new avenues of knowledge would be opened up even on the physical plane; this realised, it is not difficult to go a step farther, and to conceive that keener and subtler senses might exist which would open up, as it were, a new universe on a plane other than the physical.

Now this conception is true, and with the evolution of the astral senses the astral plane unfolds itself, and may be studied as really, as scientifically, as the physical universe can be. These astral senses exist in all men, but are latent in most, and generally need to be artificially forced, if they are to be used in the present stage of evolution. In a few persons they are normally present and become active without any artificial impulse. In very many persons they can be artificially awakened and developed. The condition, in all cases, of the activity of the astral senses is the passivity of the physical, and the more complete passivity on the physical plane the greater the possibility of activity on the astral.

It is noteworthy that Western psychologists have found it necessary to investigate what is termed the "dream consciousness", in order to understand the workings of consciousness as a whole. It is impossible to ignore the strange phenomena which characterise the workings of consciousness when it is removed from the limitations of the physical plane, and some of the most able and advanced of our psychologists do not think these workings to be in any way unworthy of the most careful and scientific investigation. All such workings are, in Theosophical language, on the astral plane, and the student who seeks for proof there is an astral plane may here find enough and to spare. He will speedily discover that the laws under which consciousness works on the physical plane have no existence on the astral. E. g., the laws of space and time, which are here the very conditions of thought, do not exist for consciousness when its activity is transferred to the astral world. Mozart hears a whole symphony as a single impression, "as in a fine and strong dream" (*Philosophy of Mysticism*, Du Prel, vol. I, p. 106), but has to work it out in successive details when he brings it back with him to the physical plane. The dream of the moment contains a mass of events that would take years to pass in succession in our world of space and time. The drowning man sees his life history in a few seconds. But it is needless to multiply instances.

The astral plane may be reached in sleep or in trance, natural or induced, *i. e..*, in any case in which the body is reduced to a condition of lethargy. It is in trance that it can best be studied, and here our enquirer will soon find proof that consciousness can work apart from the physical organism, unfettered by the laws that bind it while it works on the physical plane. Clairvoyance and clairaudience are among the most interesting of the phenomena that here lie for investigation.

It is not necessary here to give a large number of cases of clairvoyance, for I am supposing that the enquirer intends to study for himself. But I may mention the case of Jane Rider, observed by Dr. Belden, her medical attendant, a girl who could read and write with her eyes carefully covered with wads of cotton wool, coming down from to the middle of the cheek (*Isis Revelata,* vol. 1, page 37); of a clairvoyant observed by Schelling who announced the death of a relative at a distance of 150 leagues, and stated that the letter containing the news of the death was on its way (*ibid.,* vol. 2, pages 89-92); of Madame Lagrandré, who diagnosed the internal state of her mother, giving a description that was proved to be correct by the post-mortem examination (*Somnolism and Psychism,* Dr. Haddock, pages 54-56); of Emma, Dr. Haddock's somnambule, who constantly diagnosed diseases for him (*ibid.,* chap. 7). Speaking generally, the clairvoyant can see and describe events which are taking place at a distance, or under circumstances that render physical sight impossible. *How is this done?* The facts are beyond dispute. They require explanation. We say that consciousness can work through senses other than the physical, senses unfettered by the limitations of space which exist for our bodily senses, and cannot by them be transcended. Those who deny the possibility of such working on what we call the astral plane should at least endeavour to present a hypothesis more reasonable than ours. Facts are stubborn things, and we have here a mass of facts proving the existence of conscious activity on a superphysical plane, of sight without eyes, hearing without ears, obtaining knowledge without physical apparatus. In default of any other explanation, the Theosophical hypothesis holds the field.

There is another class of facts: that of etheric and astral appearances, whether of living or dead persons, wraiths, apparitions, doubles, ghosts, etc., etc. Of course the omniscient person of the end of the nineteenth century will sniff with lofty disdain at the mention of such silly superstitions. But sniffs do not abolish facts, and it is a question of evidence. The weight of evidence is enormously on the side of such appearances, and in all ages of the world human testimony has borne witness to their reality. The enquirer whose demand for proof I have in view may well set to work to gather first hand evidence on this head. Of course if he is afraid of being laughed at he had better leave the matter alone, but if he is robust enough to face the ridicule of the superior person he will be amazed at the evidence which he will collect from persons who have themselves come into contact with astral forms. "Illusions!

hallucinations!" the superior person will say. But calling names settles nothing. Illusions to which the vast majority of the human race bears witness are at least worthy of study, if human testimony is to be taken as of any worth. There must be something which gives rise to this unanimity of testimony in all ages of the world, testimony which is found today among civilised people, amid railways and electric lights, as well as among barbarous races.

The testimony of millions of Spiritualists to the reality of etheric and astral forms cannot be left out of consideration. When all cases of fraud and imposture are discounted there remain phenomena that cannot be dismissed as fraudulent, and that can be examined by any persons who care to give time and trouble to the investigation. There is no necessity to employ a professional medium; a few friends well know to each other, can carry on their search together; and it is not too much to say that any half-dozen persons, with a little patience and perseverance, may convince themselves of the existence of forces and of intelligences other than those of the physical plane. There is danger in this research to any emotional, nervous, and easily influenced natures, and it is well not to carry the investigations too far, for the reasons given on the previous pages. But there is no readier way of breaking down the unbelief in the existence of anything outside the physical plane than trying a few experiments, and it is worth while to run some risk in order to effect this breaking down.

These are but hints as to lines that the enquirer may follow, so as to convince himself that there is a state of consciousness such as we label "astral". When he has collected evidence enough to make such a state probable to him, it will be time for him to be put in the way of serious study. For real investigation of the astral plane, the student must develop in himself the necessary senses, and to make his knowledge available while he is in the body, he must learn to transfer his consciousness to the astral plane without losing grip of the physical organism, so that he may impress on the physical brain the knowledge acquired during his astral voyagings. But for this he will need to be not a mere enquirer but a student, and he will require the aid and guidance of a teacher. As to finding that teacher, "when the pupil is ready the teacher is always there".

Further proofs of the existence of the astral plane are, at the present time, most easily found in the study of mesmeric and hypnotic phenomena. And here, ere passing to these, I am bound to put in a word of warning. The use of mesmerism and hypnotism is surrounded by danger. The publicity which attends on all scientific discoveries in the West has scattered broadcast knowledge which places within the reach of the criminally disposed powers of the most terrible character, which may be used for the most damnable purposes. No good man or woman will use these powers, if he finds that he possesses them, save when he utilises them purely for human service, without personal end in view, and when he is very sure that he is not by their means usurping control over the will and the actions of another human being. Unhappily the use of these forces is as open to the bad as to the good, and they may be, and are being, used to most nefarious ends. In view of these new dangers menacing individuals and society, each will do well to strengthen the habits of self-control and of concentration of thought and will, so as to encourage the positive mental attitude as opposed to the negative, and thus to oppose a sustained resistance to all influences coming from without. Our loose habits of thought, our lack of distinct and conscious purpose, lay us open to the attacks of the evil-minded hypnotiser, and that this is a real, not a fancied, danger has been already proved by cases that have brought the victims within grasp of the criminal law. It may be hoped that ere long such hypnotic malpractices may be brought within the criminal code.

While thus in the attitude of caution and of self-defence, we may yet wisely study the experiments made public to the world, in our search for preliminary proofs of the existence of the astral plane. For here Western science is on the very verge of discovering some of those "powers" of which Theosophists have said so much, and we have the right to use in justification of our teachings all the facts with which that science may supply us.

Now, one of the most important classes of these facts is that of thoughts rendered visible as forms. A hypnotised person, after being awakened from trance and being apparently in normal possession of his senses, can be made to see any form conceived by the hypnotiser. No word need be spoken, no touch given; it suffices that the hypnotiser should clearly image to himself some idea, and that idea becomes a visible and tangible object to the person under his control. This experiment may be tried in various ways; while the patient is in trance, "suggestion" may be used; that is, the operator may tell him that a bird is on his knee, and on awaking from the trance he will see the bird and will stroke it (*Etudes Cliniques sur la Grande Hystérie*, Richet, p. 645); or that he has a lampshade between his hands, and on awaking he will press his hands against it, feeling resistance in the empty air (*Animal Magnetism*, translated from Binet and Féré, page 213); scores of these experiments may be read in Richet or in Binet and Féré. Similar results may be effected without "suggestion", by pure concentration of the thought; I have seen a patient thus made to remove a ring from a person's finger, without word spoken or touch passing between hypnotiser and hypnotised.

The literature of mesmerism and hypnotism in English, French, and German is now very extensive, and it is open to every one. There may be sought the evidence of this creation of forms by thought and will, forms which, *on the astral plane*, are real and objective. Mesmerism and hypnotism set the intelligence free on this plane, and it works thereon without the hindrance normally imposed by the physical apparatus; it can see and hear on that plane, and sees thoughts as things. Here, again, for real study, it is necessary to learn how thus to transfer the consciousness while retaining hold of the physical organism; but for preliminary inquiry it suffices to study others whose consciousness is artificially liberated without their own volition. This reality of thought images on a superphysical plane is a fact of the very highest importance, especially in its bearing on reincarnation; but it is enough here to point to it as one of the facts which go to show the *prima facie* probability of the existence of such a plane.

Another class of facts deserving study is that which includes the phenomena of thought-transference, and here we reach the lower levels of the mental, or manasic, plane. The *Transactions of the Psychical Research Society* contain a large number of interesting experiments on this subject, and the possibility of the transference of thought from brain to brain without the use of words, or of any means of ordinary physical communication, is on the verge of general acceptance. And two persons, gifted with patience, may convince themselves of this possibility, if they care to devote to the effort sufficient time and perseverance. Let them agree to give, say, ten minutes daily to their experiment, and fixing on the time, let each shut himself up alone, secure from interruption of any kind. Let one be the thought projector, the other the thought-receiver, and it is safer to alternate these positions, in order to avoid risk of one becoming permanently abnormally passive. Let the thought projector concentrate himself on a definite thought and the will to impress it on his friend; no other idea than the one must enter his mind; his thought must be concentrated on the one thing, "one–pointed" in the graphic language of Patanjali. The thought-receiver, on the other hand, must render his mind a blank, and must merely note the thoughts that drift into it. These he should put down as they appear, his only care being to remain passive, to reject nothing, to encourage nothing. The thought-projector, on his side, should keep a record of the ideas he tries to send, and at the end of six months the two records should be compared. Unless the persons are abnormally deficient in thought and will, some power of communication will by that time have been established between them: and if they are at all psychic they will probably also have developed the power of see in each other in the astral light.

It may be objected that such an experiment would be wearisome and monotonous. Granted. All first hand investigations into natural laws and forces are wearisome and monotonous. That is why nearly every one prefers second-hand to first-hand knowledge; the "sublime patience of the investigator" is one of the rarest gifts. Darwin would perform an apparently trivial experiment hundreds of times to substantiate one small fact. The supersensuous domains certainly do not need for their conquest less patience and less effort than the sensuous. Impatience never yet accomplished anything in the questioning of nature, and the would-be student must, at the very outset, show the tireless perseverance which can perish but cannot relinquish its hold. Finally, let me advise the inquirer to keep his eyes open for new discoveries, especially in the sciences of electricity, physics, and chemistry. Let him read Professor Lodge's address to the British Association at Cardiff in the autumn of 1891 and Professor Crookes' address to the Society of Electrical Engineers in London the following November. He will there find pregnant hints of the lines along which Western science is preparing to advance, and he will perchance begin to feel that there may be something in H. P. Blavatsky's statement that the Masters of Wisdom are preparing to give proofs that will substantiate the Secret Doctrine.

The Seven Planes and the principles functioning thereon	
7 x	
6 x	
5 Atmâ. Spirit	Spiritual
4 Buddhi. Spiritual Soul	Spiritual
3 Manas. Human Soul.	Mental
2 Kâma. Astral or Desire-Body	Astral
1 Prâna. Etheric Double. Dense Physical Body	Physical

Another Division according to the Principles			
	7	Atmâ	Spiritual
	6	Buddhi	Spiritual
	5	Higher Manas	
Principles closely interwoven during earth life. Sometimes called high Psychic Plane	4	Lower Manas	Mental
	3	Kâma	Astral
	2	Prâna. Etheric Double	Physical
	1	Dense Physical Body	Physical

Another Division also according the Principles		
7	Atmâ	Spiritual
6	Buddhi	Spiritual
5	Manas	Mental
4	Kâma	Astral
3	Prâna	
2	Etheric Double	Physical
1	Dense Physical Body	Physical

These two latter divisions are matters of convenience in classification. The first diagram gives the planes themselves as they exist in nature.

THE END.

BOOK TWO
THE PEDIGREE OF MAN

A series of four Lectures delivered during the Annual Convention of the Theosophical Society, at Adyar, December 1903.

I. THE SPIRITUAL PEDIGREE

IN WESTERN LANDS, science during the last fifty years has been trying to trace what is called the pedigree of man. In Germany, in France, in England, scientific men have tried to arrange the vast number of facts collected, so as to draw a genealogical tree and represent the way in which man has evolved from the fire-mist to the civilized human being. The great difficulty with regard to these pedigrees of man has been the fact that they only apply to his physical nature; in the tracing of his body, scientists trace from step to step the way in which that wonderful and complicated organism has been built up cell by cell in all the kingdoms of nature; and this they have done with wonderful patience and with a large degree of success, although their ignorance of successive cycles of growth has caused much confusion, much linking together of types separated by incalculable aeons of time, and much turning upside down of sequences, and translation of descendants into the seats of ancestors.

But when you have traced even accurately the pedigree of man's body, you have not traced the pedigree of man. Man is not his body; the body is but the garment that he wears; and man can never be understood, when you leave out of his pedigree the Spirit that makes him eternal, and the intelligence, which is an aspect of that Spirit differentiating itself in the world of matter, and manifesting as intellect and as mind. Thus the scientific pedigrees of man are all thrown out of court by the partial nature of the pedigree, and by the fact that you find the least human part of man exclusively dealt with.

In theosophical teachings - those which have been given to us by the great Sages of the past, reinforced, verified, and repeated in scripture after scripture of all the great religions of the world - in these you will find a truer pedigree, that deals with every part of the nature of man. It is not alone in the Hindu Scriptures, though they are the fullest in this respect, that you can find traces of that primeval revelation, that you can understand something of the long road that man has travelled in his journey from the mineral to the God; nay, rather should I say, from the mineral to the God, for as is truly said, not only in Hindu writings, but by our brothers of Islam: "From God we came, and unto God do we return. "

In order, then, that we may trace man's pedigree aright, we shall do well to follow the broad outlines laid down by that great disciple of the Sages, H. P. B. whom here I salute, with my heart's gratitude for the light and the knowledge that she has brought to the modern world. At the very outset of these lectures, I would acknowledge my debt to her great work, The Secret Doctrine, from which the whole plan and innumerable details are taken; I have added some facts, filled up some lacunae, bridged some gulfs, perhaps, but most of the materials are here, and are drawn from that record of her vast occult knowledge, her giant grasp of facts.

She taught us that, in trying to understand man and his pedigree, we must mark three great lines of evolution: first, the spiritual, which is by far the most important, for Spirit is the master of matter, guides it, shapes it, builds it into form; and unless the spiritual pedigree be known, man remains an insoluble problem. Then, at the other pole of human nature, the physical, the pedigree of man's body. The spiritual pedigree is the coming down by slow degrees of Spirit into Matter. The physical pedigree is the result of the upward climbing of the Spirit through the Matter, which it shapes for the expression of its own inherent powers, Then, looking at these two great lines, one from above downwards, the other from below upwards, we come to a point at which a third line of the evolution of man's pedigree joins these others and links them both to form the human being. That is the intellectual evolution; that is the coming of the Ego to take possession of his physical tabernacle, and to link to that tabernacle the Spirit which has brooded over it, which has by its subtle influence Shaped and fashioned it. When we have traced the spiritual evolution, the physical evolution, the intellectual evolution, then there unfolds before us a vast picture, in which we can see the whole pedigree of man traced in broad illuminative outlines, and we can begin to understand something of the wonder of that Human Nature which is God, God in manifested form, divine in essence and in powers.

H. P. B. says: "There exists in Nature a triple evolutionary scheme, for the formation of the three periodical Bases; or rather three separate schemes of evolution, which in our system are inextricably interwoven and interblended at every point. 1. The Monadic, as the name implies, is concerned with the growth and development into still higher phases of activity of the Monad, in conjunction with: 2. The Intellectual, represented by the "Mind-intelligence's" (the Solar Gods, or the Fathers devoid of the creative fire), the 'givers of intelligence and consciousness' to man; and: 3. The Physical, represented by the shadows of the Lunar Fathers, round which Nature has consecrated the present physical body. ... . It is the union of these three streams in him, which makes him the complex being he now is. "

Now that is the great task that lies before us in these lectures. To my hands, too feeble for the task, to my lips, not sufficiently articulate to speak it, has fallen this work, really far too great for one like myself, so limited alike in knowledge and in power to gain it; and all that I can hope to do is to place before you the results of some study, guided by knowledge far greater than my own, hoping that, not to dictate to you a scheme that you are bound to accept, but to throw out such hints as a student may throw out to students, which may help you in your own study and in your own research; to serve, if I may be so fortunate, as a clue through the labyrinth of Nature, which may aid you in your struggle to traverse it.

We take the first of these three lines of human pedigree, the spiritual pedigree of man, In order to understand that, we must begin with two vast outlines. The first, the outline of those great Hierarchies of intelligences, of spiritual Intelligences, who, in past aeons, past universes, having completed their own human evolution, have climbed up to be co-workers with God in the shaping of a new Mundane Egg; these are the Hierarchies that guide and mould, the Architects, the Builders, of Solar systems. We need to get some idea, however vague, however imperfect, however paltry, of these vast Hierarchies that fill our solar system, and to whom we owe our spiritual evolution; some idea, traced with reverence, however imperfect it may be, for They are the life of the universe. They are the guides of spiritual, intellectual and physical evolution. The second outline is that of the Field of Evolution, the place wherein the evolution goes on.

Now according to the old occult records, identical on this point with the most ancient Hindu teachings, we find that our solar system has a life stretching behind it into what to us, is an illimitable past, counting, it is said, some 1,955,884,703 years up to the present time (as in the year 1903), a period so vast that it is but words that I utter; the words convey no idea to the human mind save that of illimitable antiquity.

Going back into that far off past, we see, to use the splendid simile of Manu, God as a Mountain of Light appearing to illuminate the darkness. No words can better convey the idea of that dawn of a new universe; words are almost hindrances in the way of the vague idea of the upspringing Light in the midst of darkness unfathomable. That is the simile chosen by the

Father of Mankind, when he desired to describe to men the dawn of the solar system.

Then we are told-and we can only reverently repeat what we are told-that God unfolds Himself into a triple manifestation, into three Forms, and from that marvellous light we see issuing in wondrous magnificent outlines three mighty and divine Forms. They are the Powers, the Aspects of God to be manifested In the coming universe-He who creates, He who preserves, He who destroys when the end of the system approaches. The One In three Forms, the Three whose essence is One-we may phrase it as we will. Dimly we feel that we gaze at three Bases that appear for purposes of functioning, but that divide not the all-embracing Consciousness that ensouls Them. Those wondrous Forms we call the Logo), using that Greek term which means the Word, because the idea of sound beat expresses the incalculable potencies of manifested Deity- sound which creates, supports, destroys. Now this triplicity appears in every religion, save here and there, where for passing and temporary causes it has not been clearly and definitely stated. Go back to far Chaldea, study the remains plucked from the opened tombs of dead Egypt, the secrets which its mummies unfold, and everywhere, as well as in Hindu Scriptures, do you find shining out the Three from the One, One in the divinity of Their nature, Three in their manifested powers.

Then, around that wondrous Trinity, we see standing in the light coming forth from Them, Those, the fruits of past universes, who have won to that marvellous spiritual height; and the next Forms that we dimly glimpse, in the middle of the light, are of those who are called the Seven. The descriptive words, the names, applied to that number, the Seven differ in different religions. The Hindu speaks of the seven sons of Aditi- the eighth was the Sun, each son, having his own "house. " They have been called the Seven Spirits in the Sun; the seven Mystery Gods was Their name in ancient Egypt. They were called in the religion of Zoroaster the seven Amshaspends. Among the Jews, They are the seven Sephiroth, among the Christians and Muhammadans, They are the seven Archangels. The names do not matter. Suffice it that every religion points to Them as standing round the manifested trinity, forming the Viceroys, as it were, of God in the vast Empire of the solar system, each one with His own kingdom, each one administering His own department. We call Them in Theosophy the Planetary Logoi, because these seven Spirits in the Sun have ever been identified with the seven sacred planets, which are Their physical bodies; those planets in their outer form here are globes, some of the globes that make up our solar system; but in their spiritual nature they are these mighty Sons of Aditi, who has each His own house, that is, His own planet, ruling over His own kingdom, a definite department of the solar universe.

Round these again, in wider circles, there come the mighty Ones, the Hierarchies that are the creative Hierarchies, or the Twelve Creative Orders, of the universe.

These are headed by the Twelve Great Gods, that appear in very ancient stories, looming vast and magnificent from the great distances in which They dwell. These are symbolized in. the familiar Signs of the Zodiac; for the Zodiac is no modern fancy, but was given to the Fourth race of men by the mighty Teachers, and you may read in your own records the names of some of these teachers, one of whom, Asuramaya, is known as the first of the great astronomers; it was he who gave the Zodiacs to Egypt and to India.

Those astronomical wheels are the symbols, the pictures in which the plan of the solar system is written, and in the traditions of the past we find the clue to the labyrinth, and we realize why we are told that a planet "rules" or is the Lord of, one of the signs of the Zodiac. For the planet is the Planetary Spirit, and His sign of the Zodiac is one of the chief Creative Hierarchies, containing within itself the remaining Hierarchies as sub-hierarchies, and these, under His control and direction, build up His kingdom, and help the Monads in it to evolve. If you bear this in mind, the picture, though wonderful, will not be confused. First comes the great Trinity; round that Trinity the seven Spirits who are the Viceroys in his universe.

Around them the twelve Creative Hierarchies, busy with the work of the construction of the universe. Now at the present stage of evolution, out of these twelve Creative Hierarchies, five have passed away from the ken of even the greatest and most developed Teachers of our world; four of them have passed onward into liberation, and one is touching the threshold of liberation; so that in our own evolution we have now only to deal with seven.

These all touch us, as it were, our fragment of Deity, the portion of God, the Living Self, the living being, that presently we find composes one of these very Hierarchies in his highest, most spiritual nature. Let us try to glimpse the main characteristics of These, for we need, however vaguely, to characterize each of them, so that They may not be wholly blurred in our eyes, dazzled by the radiance in which They dwell.

First comes the Order that is only describable by words connected with fire; Formless Fiery Breaths,

They are called, Lords of Fire, Divine Flames, Divine Fires, Fiery Lions, Lions of Life: name after name, epithet after epithet, all circling round the attribute of fire, for they, it is written, are the Life and the Heart of the universe, the Self, the kosmic Will, and through Them comes the divine ray of Supreme Self, that awakens self in the Monad of Man.

Below them comes the second great Hierarchy, two-fold in its nature, the "two-fold units," Fire and Ether, manifested Reason, the wisdom of the system, that we speak of as Kosmic Soul, that arouses Soul in the Monad of man.

Below Them again, the third, the Great, or Kosmic Mind, "the triads," Fire, Ether, Water, the Kosmic Activity, that will also bestow part of its essence on the Monad of man as he descends.

These are the Formless Creative Orders, dwelling in matter too subtle to assume a limiting form, matter in which all forms intermingle and interpenetrate.

Below these come the Creative Orders having Forms and first of these, fourth among the Hierarchies, is that which is ours, the Hierarchy of human Monads, not yet having left the bosom of our Highest Father, wherein in truth we ever remain, inseparable from him, although to us, in the mazes of matter, we seem to be utterly separated and distinct. We can dimly glimpse them as they stand there in the glory of their birth, with a "certain spiritual individuality," it is written, which has become more separate on the lower planes, these we shall come back to in a moment, after this rough and hasty outlining of the seven great Hierarchies, meant to give us a bird's eye view of the whole; these, called the Imperishable Lives, are the fourth of the seven Creative Orders - out of the twelve - with which we are concerned.

Then we come to the later three, that contain within them many who have already entered evolution in our own planetary scheme in past aeons, and of whom we may learn a little more, because they touch our own evolution.

The fifth hierarchy is named that of the Crocodile, and has for its symbol the pentagon; in this the dual spiritual and the dual physical aspects of Nature appear, the positive and the negative, at war with each other; these are the turbulent, the "rebels" of many a mythos.

Much shall we hear of some of these presently, of those who are called the Asuras born of the first body of Brahma which, cast off, became Darkness. A great host of Beings in this hierarchy have come from a past universe, and spring forth, full grown as it were, from the Planetary Logos.

These also seem to be called Asuras but we are specially concerned with those born from the Body of Darkness, and belonging to this universe by their evolution. These are beings of great spiritual power and spiritual knowledge, but hide deep within themselves the germ, the essence, of Ahamkara, of that l-making faculty which is necessary for human evolution. They are the fruitage of the first planetary chain, a word that will become more familiar as we proceed.

The sixth of these great Hierarchies contains some that we can also recognize, who are born of the Body of Brahma which is known as the Body of Light, or of Day; a group of Devas is seen, shining out amid this host of Devas with especial glory, the Pitrs of the Devas, who are known by the name of Agnishvattas, Those who are called the "six-fold Dhyanis," They give to man all but the Atma and the physical body, and so are called the givers of the "five middle human principles," They guide the Monad in obtaining the permanent atoms connected with these principles, or the "five-fold plasm. " They are the fruitage if the second planetary Chain. The Hierarchy includes also great hosts of Devas, the highest Nature Spirits, or Elementals of the Middle Kingdom.

The seventh Hierarchy contains those whom we know best under the name of the Lunar Pitris, or the Barhishad Pitris, born of the Body of Brahma which is called that of the Twilight, the Sandhya. They have to do with physical evolution, as the Agnishvatta Pitris have to deal with the intellectual evolution of man, so that we shall meet with both of these as we go on with our study. Then, those we see crowding round them, belonging to their Hierarchy, are their agents in the work that lies before them, vast hosts of Devas, the lower Nature Spirits, or Elementals of the Lowest Kingdom, who will have to do with the actual building of the body of man. And here too are the "spirits of atoms," the seeds of evolution in future kalpas, with which we have here nothing to do.

Thus the seven great Hierarchies, or Creative Orders, stretch before us in their splendour, ready for the work of directing the unfolding of spiritual powers in a universe of matter.

Now glance with me at the second great outline, that of the Field of Evolution. Over this I pass rapidly, because its outlines will come to be very distinct as we deal with physical evolution; but we cannot catch the points of the spiritual evolution, unless we have before us the broad outlines of the Field in which that evolution is taking place. I call it the Field borrowing that term from The Bhagavad-Gita, because it is the very type of Matter. That word expresses, better than any term I can fashion for myself, all that is included under the name of Matter, in which evolution is to go on. We confine ourselves now to the kingdom of one Planetary Logos, that to which we belong, for each Planetary Logos presides over one Field of Evolution, and this we must study. I only deal with the fundamental principles. First, grasp clearly and strongly the phases of the Field. They are repeated over and over again, and, if once grasped, will be the Ariadne's clue to the labyrinth.

There are seven great stages of spiritual evolution. During three the Spirit descends. As it descends, it broods over Matter certain powers, certain qualities, certain attributes, and those qualities, powers, and attributes are the outcome of the first three stages of the descent of the Spirit. Then comes a stage, the fourth, that stands alone, where Matter, having been thus gifted with various powers and various attributes, comes into manifold relations with the reforming Spirit, which now enters it. This is the great battle of the universe, the conflict between Spirit and Matter, the Battle Field, of the vast hosts of the two opposing armies. Here, in this part of the field, is the point of balance; the Spirit, coming into innumerable relations with Matter, is at first overpowered; then comes the point of balance, when neither has the advantage over the other; then slowly the Spirit begins to triumph over Matter, so that, when this fourth stage is over, Spirit is the master of Matter, and is ready for his ascent through the three stages that complete the seven. The Spirit, in these, organises the Matter which he has mastered, and ensouled, and turns it to his own purposes, shapes it for his own expression, so that Matter may become the means whereby all the powers of the Spirit shall be made manifest and active; the last three stages are taken up by that spiritual ascent. Three, then, of descent, giving qualities; one of struggle, forming manifold relations; three of ascent, wherein Matter is fashioned by Spirit into the perfect vehicle he needs for his own manifestation.

Now cling to that main idea, for it is repeated at every stage, and governs each stage, no matter how many additional complexities may mark the stage; over and over again it gives you the clue, when you are losing yourselves in that confusion of Chains, Rounds, Globes and Races, that is so fertile a source of trouble to the theosophical student.

What is the next thing to grasp? That which is called the planetary Chain. Considered as a whole, it forms the Vehicle of the planetary Logos, in which His life incarnates. Seven stages must be passed through, so seven the Chains will be; three Chains in which Spirit will be descending; one Chain, the fourth, in which Spirit and Matter will be inter-linking and inter-weaving and forming innumerable relations; then three chains of upward climbing, at the end of which all shall return into the bosom of the

Planetary logos, to merge into God with the fruitage of evolution. The planetary Chain may thus be thought of as the bodies in which the life of the Planetary logos reincarnates itself seven times, each Chain beginning with the fruitage of its predecessor, each handing on to its successor that which itself has made.

The period during which a planetary Chain lasts is called a planetary evolution, and each evolution is followed by a planetary Dissolution; the beings whose highest principles have been evolved during the evolution pass at its close, into a blissful state of super-consciousness, the planetary Nirvana, while those who have not evolved so far sink into peaceful sleep. These 'nirvanees' do not come back to birth until the succeeding chain has evolved vehicles suitable to their further growth.

Let us examine a single planetary Chain, and see how it is composed, what are the links that make up the Chain. Each link of the chain is a round, or circle, of life; a wave of life makes a complete circle, on the principle already enunciated, passing through seven stages; during three stages the life descends into matter, and gives birth to more and more material forms; in the fourth the life-wave evolves forms in which conflict is carried on; in the remaining three the life-wave" ascends, and the forms to which it has given birth become more and more spiritual; moreover, each Round of the life-wave evolves one kingdom of nature - the three elemental, the mineral, vegetable, animal, human - to the highest perfection of its own type, the future types, not belonging to the round, being indeed present, but more or less embryonic, compared with their future development. Thus seven rounds, seven successive circles of the life-wave, are the links which compose the planetary Chain.

Let us take a single Round, a single life-circle, and we find this again has its own seven stages, but this time each stage is a Globe, a world. In the first three forms are evolved; in the middle, the gulf is spanned between the forms and the overbrooding spirits, and the forms become ensouled; in the later three, the Spirits shape the forms to their will. To distinguish these Globes from each other, the letters of the alphabet from A to G have been used, and the Globes in the arc of descent and the globes in the arc of ascent correspond with each other: those in the upward are showing out in completion that which those in the downward arc embryonically adumbrate, while the middle Globe is the point of balance of conflict, of turning. Globe A is of subtle mental matter, and is archetypal i. e. contains the archetypes of the forms to be produced in the Round; H>P>B. explains: 'The word "archetypal" must not be taken here in the sense that the Platonists gave to it, i. e. the world as it existed in the mind of the Deity; but in that of a world made as a first model, to be followed and improved upon by the worlds which succeed it physically. 'Globe G corresponding with A as to matter, on the upward arc, contains the archetypes of Globe A, worked out in detail and perfected. Globe B is of denser mental matter, and is creative, or intellectual, i. e. contains the concrete types derived from the archetypes, the qualities marked, the forms crude and rough; Globe F, corresponding with B on the upward arc, contains these forms elaborated and refined. Globe C is of astral matter and is substantial or formative, i. e. builds the crude forms in denser matter; and its corresponding Globe E shows them in similar matter, but exquisitely adapted for their functions. Globe D is of physical matter, and is the turning point, the field of conflict between Spirit and Matter. In each Globe successively is evolved one stage in the kingdom which is being developed in the Round, so that when the life-wave has completed its circuit round the seven Globes, i. e. has completed a Reund, the kingdom is completely evolved. And all the kingdoms, behind the one characteristic of the Round, are advanced a stage in their embryonic career. Thus in the first Round, the Highest Elemental Kingdom is completed, the remaining two elemental and the mineral shew all their types, and the vegetable, animal and human are sketched out, but inchoate, and so on. This will be more fully dealt with under physical evolution. These Globes of our own Chain are often spoken of in the Puranas as Dvipas, Jambudvipa being our own earth.

Our own Field of Evolution, so that we may realise where we are standing now, must be clearly seen. Out Planetary Logos, spoken of as Brahma, in His creative function to us, has already carried His kingdom into the fourth stage of its evolution; we are in the fourth planetary Chain. Of the first planetary Chain, the archetypal, we know nothing, save that it is spoken as His Body of Darkness, or of Night, and that its fruitage was the Asuras. Of the second planetary Chain, the creative, we know nothing, save that it was His Body of Light, or of Day, and produced the Agnishvatta Pitrs. Of the third planetary Chain, the formative, we know a little for its Globe D was the Moon, and it was His body of Twilight, and the evolved the Barhishad Pitris and seven classBS of Monads for its successor; we call it the lunar Chain. The fourth planetary chain, the physical, is the terrene, its globe D being our Earth, and it is His Body of Dawn, and is evolving men. Having thus laid down the broad outlines of the Hierarchies and the Field, we may return to the study of the fourth Hierarchy, that of the Human Monads, those who are to become "Men" in the terrene planetary Chain. And this Chain is the fourth, the Chain of struggle, of balance, the Chain in which Spirit and Matter are to be interlinked and interwoven, so that the highest and the lowest, the two poles of nature, shall join in one complex being, Man — Man who is the starting point for the higher evolution. Moreover, the Monads are now on the fourth Globe, Globe D, which is our earth, the Globe of this Chain, being placed with regard to the other Chains. The Monads are thus at the very centre of the struggle, at the point of keenest combat and of greatest difficulty, truly on the planetary Kurukshetra; here, in the fourth Globe of the fourth Chain must be waged the greatest conflict of Spirit and Matter, to end in the triumph of Spirit.

I have used the word 'Human Monad. ' Let me define what is meant in Occultism by the word "man. " " Man" is that being in the universe, in whatever part of the universe he may be, in whom highest Spirit and lowest Matter are joined together by intelligence, thus ultimately making a manifested God, who will then go forth, conquering and to conquer, through the illimitable future that stretches before him. "Man is not necessarily of just the form that you now see. He may have a million forms: "Man" means that being in whom Spirit and Matter have joined hands, in whom they have become, or are becoming, balanced, in whom ultimately Spirit has conquered or will conquer, Matter.

In whatever being those conditions are found, "Man" is the word which is used in the occult writings to describe him. It is not limited simply to ourselves, one puny race of the vast human Hierarchy. To show his position in evolution, and that is the medium position I have described, H. P. B. has said that every being in this universe has passed through the human kingdom, or must pass, if he has not already passed it; if he has passed beyond it; he must have passed through it; if he has not reached it, he will have to pass through it in the future. It does not depend on third globe, nor on this race. "Man" is the battle ground of Matter and Spirit, and every being must, like Yudhishtira, fight his Kurukshetra, and conquer, before he enters on his divine kingdom. Such then is "Man. "

The Monad is the divine Spirit which is man's upper pole, bom from Ishvara Himself, or rather born within Him, as a centre in His life, "a portion of Myself. " "'Lift thy head, O Lanoo; dost thou see one, or, countless, lights above thee, burning in the dark midnight sky?' ' I sense one Flame, O Gurudeva; I see countless undetached sparks shining in it. "

The Flame is Ishvara, in His manifestation as the First Logos; the undetached sparks are the human and other Monads. The will of Ishvara to manifest works in these portions of Himself, undetached from Him, and this will turns them towards the world of matter, and they pass into the Second Logos, and dwell in Him, the Sons of the Father; from the Third Logos they receive the touch that gives to each a "spiritual individuality," the faint adumbration of separateness. They. enter the streams which from the Three divide into the Seven, and each group takes on the colour belonging to the Planetary Logos into whom it has flowed, and then the seven colours interweave in wondrous maze of flashing lights - the first great choral heavenly dance, the solar Rasalila - until within each Planetary Logos the seven rays of colour are seen, a sevenfold splendor, dominated in each by His own colour, which lends its hue to all the rays within it. Hence is it said that "every man is born under a planet,' since on each Globe in every planetary Chain appear the seven groups of Monads, each coloured by his "Father-Star. "

Still is the Monad not ready to issue on his long pilgrimage, for it's attention is not turned outwards, and the three aspects of his nature, reproductions of the three aspects of Ishvara, play upon each other within him and are not turned to the Universe. But now they begin to descend through the Creative Orders. From the first Creative Hierarchy comes the life-thrill that awakens to outward turning life the Will, the atmic aspect; from the second Creative Hierarchy proceeds the impulse that similarly awakens the Wisdom, the buddhic, aspect; from the third that which awakens the Activity, the manasic, aspect. Thus amused to turn his attention outwards, the Monad is ready for his descent. These preparatory stages accomplished, the vast host of the Monads that are to become human have reached their abiding place, where they will dwell for innumerable ages. They are the fourth Creative Hierarchy, ready for their pilgrimage. Each of them is 'an individual Dhyan Chohan, distinct from others,' but they are too subtle, too lofty, in their nature to be able to enter into the five-fold universe, the universe of grosser-matter.

Yet they must find a vehicle, since their divine powers are to become effective in the worlds before them, and as the mighty vibrations of the Sun throw matter into the vibrations we call his rays, so does the Monad cause the atomic matter of the atmic, buddhic and manasic planes - surrounding him as the ether of space surrounds the Sun - to vibrate, and thus makes for himself a Ray, triple like his own three-fold nature. In this he is aided by the fifth and sixth Creative hierarchies, who have passed through a similar experience before; the fifth Hierarchy guides the vibratory wave from the Will-aspect to the atmic atom, and the atmic atom, vibrating to the Will-aspect, is called Atma; the sixth Hierarchy guides the vibratory wave from the wisdom-aspect to the buddhic atom, and the buddhic atom, vibrating to the Wisdom-aspect is called Buddhi; also it guides the vibratory wave from the activity-aspect to the manasic atom, and the manasic atom, vibrating to the Activity-aspect, is called Manah. Thus

Atma-Buddhi-Manah, the Monad in the world of manifestation, is formed, the Ray of the true Monad beyond the five-fold universe.

Here is the mystery of the Watcher, the spectator, the actionless Atma, who abides ever in his triple nature on his own plane, and lives in the world of men by his Ray, which animates his shadows, the fleeting lives on earth. It is written in the stanzas of Dzyan: 'Said the Flame to the Spark: "Thou art myself, my Image and my Shadow. I have clothed myself in thee, and thou art my vahan(vehicleO to the day be with us, when thou shalt rebecome myself and others, thy self and me. '" The Flame, the Monad, sends out the thread of Life, the triple thread, woven out of his own nature, and on this, the Sutratma, 'the Thread-soul' are all the incarnations, the shadows, strung. "The Watcher and his shadows - the latter numbering as many as there are reincarnations for the Monad - are one. The Watcher, or the Divine Prototype, is at the upper end of the ladder of being; the shadow at the lower. " He, the Watcher, is our Father in Heaven, and " I and my Father are one. " We are the shadows in our personalities, the Image - the Son of the Father - in our individualities; the innumerable shadows are cast by the Ray, and are the pearls strung on the thread of Life. The shadows do the work on the lower planes, and are moved by the Monad through his image, or Ray, at first so feebly that his influence is well-nigh imperceptible later with ever-increasing power: The thread between the Silent Watcher and his Shadow becomes more strong and radiant with every change. "

We must now give to the Son the name of the Father, to the Image the name of the Watcher, and call him the Monad; for there is no other name by which fitly to describe him, and truly is he one and the same. But the Image is now clothed in matter, veiled in Avidya, and blinded by the envelope he has not yet essayed, he is weak and limited in the world he has entered. He comes to be his master, but has first to learn obedience: "though he were a son, yet learned he obedience by the things that he suffered, and being made perfect. " He becomes Master of Life and Death. He forgets his birth place, as he falls asleep in matter, and only gradually will the impacts from without stir his dreamy divinity into answer in manifestation.

The Monads are now, as we have seen, ready, and they pass into the first planctary Chain, the Archetypal. All that we know of them there is that the most progressed of them became Asuras, and passed into the fifth Creative Hierarchy. Others, less progressed, took up their evolution in the second planetary Chain, the Creative, and the most progressed of them became Agnishvattas, and entered the sixth Creative Hierarchy. Once more, the less progressed took up their evolution in the third planetary Chain, the lunar, and here we see them, on their emergence from it, classed in three great groups.

1. First, come the true Pitrs, sometimes called the Lunar, but better the Barhishad, Pitrs, who are the most progressed entities from the lunar Chain, who entered, at its close, the seventh Creative Hierarchy. These are the 'Lunar Gods. ' the 'Lords of the Moon of the airy bodies,' who are to be charged with the duty of guiding physical evolution in the fourth planetary Chain, the terrene. With these, but less developed, are two classes of Monads, variously named Lower Dhyanis, Solar Pitrs - the ranks in the lunar Chain immediately below the Barhishad Pitrs - the first class of whom had developed the causal body, and the second class of whom were just ready for its formation, too far advanced to enter the fourth Chain in its earlier Round, in the third and fourth Root Races. Thus this first great group contains three classes of Monads.

2. Four classes, sufficiently evolved to reach the human stage during the first three and a half Rounds of the terrene Chain. These are also often spoken of as 'Inner Pitrs,' and the name is not wholly inapplicable, since they come from the lunar Chain; still they are not 'ancestors' of men, but are evolving into men, and should not therefore be called Pitrs. This name was, however, given to them by H. P. B., and has become incorporated into theosophical terminology. It does not much matter, if they are not confused with the true Lunar Pitrs of Group 1, the Lords of the Moon.

3. Three classes, who dropped out of the lunar evolution by falling too far behind the general advance. These will only touch humanity at the close of the seventh Round of the terrene Chain, and will form the humanity of the fifth planetary Chain, the one that will succeed our own. They are at present climbing their slow way upwards in the mineral, vegetable and animal kingdoms.

These seven classes, forming Groups 2 and 3, are the seven classes of 'lunar Pitrs' often mentioned by H. P. B. In order to avoid confusion, I shall speak of them merely as 'monads of the lunar Chain' - a term also used by her - or ex-lunar monads, and shall restrict the use of the term 'Lunar Pitrs' to the 'Lords of the Moon of the airy bodies. ' These Monads of the lunar Chain are said to be classed according to 'evolution consciousness and merit,' and this fixed their entry in succession in time.

These seven classes, due to these evolutionary differences, must not be confused with the seven types of Monads, due to the colorings received from the seven Planetary Logoi, previously mentioned. In each of the seven classes will be found Monads of all the seven types, so that each class has representations of each of the seven colours. These seven types, therefore, appear simultaneously and side by side, when a class enters the planetary Chain, and each successive class shews not within itself the seven types.

For our tracing of the monadic pedigree of man, we omit Group 1 altogether for the present, the Lunar Pitrs, because they are, concerned with physical evolution, and the two classes of Lower Dhyanis, because they are in the lower Nirvana, assimilating the spiritual and mental results of past experiences, and will not enter the earth Chain until the fourth Round. We have to do here only with Groups 2 and 3, the seven classes of which arrive successively on the earth.

The Monad, Atma-Buddhi-Manah, broods over the evolving forms, not descending below the atomic level of the manasic plane, and represented by the three atoms, acquired for this Chain, as previously said, by the aid of the fifth and sixth Creative Orders. A thread of life, clothed in buddhic matter, is sent forth, and becomes attached to the atoms available for appropriation at each successive stage as 'permanent atoms' and these make part of the forms prepared for him by the activities of the Lords of the Moon, in the order we shall study under 'Physical evolution. ' It will suffice to say here that on each Globe the seven kingdoms - three elemental, one mineral, one vegetable, one animal, one human - are represented, those belonging to the Round, or to previous Rounds, fully, those beyond the evolution of the round, embryonically. And though it may seem strange to speak of our present humanity as embryonic, yet truly is it so in comparison with the beings of at present unimaginable splendor who shall be the humanity of the seventh, the human, Chain. Each kingdom is divided into seven stages - departments or provinces - as we see plainly when we come to man, with his seven Root Races, through these stages are not so marked to our eyes in the lower kingdoms. And in fact we only recognise their existence by the fact that the Monads, who travel more slowly in proportion as they are less progressed, gradually trail off in ever-lengthening procession, failing more and more behind as the younger travel along the Globes of the terrene Chain.

When the ex-lunar Monads of the first class in Group 2 - the most developed - arrive on Globe A of the terrene Circle, they pass very rapidly through the forms - prepared by the Barhishad Pitrs - of the six lower kingdoms and reach the lowest stage of the human kingdom. They repeat the process on Globe B, C, D, E, F and G, adding one human stage on each Globe, until on Globe G they complete the seven human stages, and have passed through the whole forty-nine stages- sever in each of the seven kingdoms - that occur in each Round. I may again remind you that 'human' here does not mean anything like the 'human' that we know; even on Globe D of the Round these Monads do not find any physical human forms.

The ex-lunar monads of class 2 follow 1, but travel less rapidly than their predecessors, so that at the end of the round only completed the animal and touched the border of the human; only in the next Round will they complete the seven stages of the human kingdom.

The ex-lunar Monads of class 3 follow class 2, but fall a little further behind, and see only ready to escape from a little further behind, and are only ready to escape from the vegetable into the animal kingdom at the close of the first Round; while those of class 4 are only ready to escape from the mineral.

The remaining three classes, forming Group 3 of the ex-lunar Monads, are respectively on the borders of the mineral, the higher and the middle elemental kingdoms, at the close of the first Round.

Thus class 1 has accomplished forty-nine stages; class 2, forty-two; class 3, thirty-five; class 4, twenty-eight; class 5, twenty-one; class 6, fourteen; class 7, seven. Or, taking the last class as the unit, class 1 travels seven times as fast; class 2, six times; class 3, five times class 4, tour times; class 5, three times; class 6, twice.

It must be remembered that only the archetypes of the mineral kingdom are on globe A in the first Round, and that the densest type of matter available in this round is only touched in the mineral kingdom on Globe D, the higher types, vegetable, animal, and human, existing only as, mental germs.

In the second round the ex-lunar Monads of the first class entered only the human kingdom, strengthening the germs in which they dwelt; those of the second class reached the human and acquired one stage of progress on each Globe completing the seven stages on Globe G; the third class touched the human in the second Round, while the fourth completed the vegetable and were ready for the animal.

In the third round the ex-lunar Monads of the first and second classes still worked at the developing germs of humanity, while the third conquered the seven stages of the human kingdom in this round, and the fourth just received its borders, thus passing into the human kingdom with the beginning of the fourth Round.

Meanwhile the three laggard classes climbed slowly upwards, so that in the fourth round all had escaped from the elemental kingdom, and they are now the Monads of animals, vegetables and minerals, not to reach the human kingdom in this chain, since human forms of a type sufficiently low for their humanising are no longer produced by nature.

The fourth round is often called the human round, since the archetypes of each Root Race appeared on Globe A at the beginning of the round; but it is really the Round in which the mineral reaches its perfection, i. e. the point of greatest hardness and density.

When the foremost of the circling Monads reached, Globe D on the fourth Round, they were ready for the development of man on a far higher model, and the Chhaya of the Barhishad Pitrs now became the form to which the permanent physical atom attached itself, the chhaya being of etheric matter. The Aiteraya Brahmana sketches in a few phrases this long evolution, this passing of the Monads through the mineral, vegetable and animal kingdoms, and the reaching of human; ' In herbs and trees life is seen: intelligence in breathing creatures, and in these breathing creatures the Self is more manifest; he is most supplied with knowledge. He speaks that which he knows; he sees that which he knows; he knows what occurred yesterday; he knows the visible and the invisible; by the mortal he desires the immortal. Thus supplied is he. 'On this runs the commentary of Sayana:' In the unconscious, earth, stones, etc. only Sat is manifest, and the Atma has not yet attained to the form of Jiva. The unmoving Jivas, namely the herbs and trees, and also the moving Jivas, which have Prana as breath, both these are stages of manifestation in a higher degree. '

The foremost Monads are now brooding over the embryonic forms of the first Root Race, and shaping the growth of the human foetus in the womb of time. Their Rays warm into activity the envelopes of matter that enshroud them, and shape them into organs of communication with the outer world. The sense of hearing is the first to be developed, that which will respond to the rate of vibrations hereafter to be known as sound. Awake on its own plane, the monadic consciousness responds dimly, very dimly, through the enveloping matter, so that the forms are well-nigh senseless; they feel on the physical plane the presence of fire, the first impact to which consciousness there responds through the new forms.

As the monad passes into the second Root Race, he adds to his physical plane consciousness the sense of touch, and begins to respond to the impact of air as well as of fire; as we listen, we hear faint chant-like sounds issuing from the varied nondescript forms that represent humanity, open vowel like sounds, inarticulate, faintly indicating the stirrings of emotions moved from hidden springs. Such consciousness as there is belongs to above rather than to below; there is dreamy quiet enjoyment, arising from within, but little sense of pleasure or pain, stimulated from without. It is the monadic consciousness, awake on the higher planes but not on the lower, and the forms are but slightly responsive, almost senseless, though more responsive than those of the first race.

With the entry of the Monad into the third root race, progress quickens; sight is slowly added to the senses of hearing and touch, and with this the recognition of the outer world becomes clearer and more definite. Language, consisting of mere cries through the first and second sub-races, cries of pleasure and pain, of love and wrath, becomes monosyllabic in the third sub-race. Consciousness of the impacts of water is added to that of the impacts of fire and air, and the human form, crude and clumsy, but now distinctly human, brooded over by the Monad, is ready for the incoming of the intelligence which shall make it man. It is now fairly responsive to the thrills of life that reach it from above, but on the physical plane is stupid, ignorant, moved by rushes of pain and pleasure stimulated from without, and blindly yielding to their currents, drifted hither and thither. The Monad cannot check its physical vehicle, answering to the strong impacts of its own plane, and answering the more strongly as more life is poured into it from above; the life is transmuted into sense-responses, and flows along the channels of animal instincts. For the Monad to increase the life-flow will be to increase the danger; it is like increasing stream-pressure in an engine without a driver.

Then come in the sons of Mind, to add the element needed for safety and for progress, The intellectual evolution must now begin, and for a time obscure the spiritual. The spiritual must give way before the rush of intelligence, and retire into the background for awhile, leaving intelligence to grasp the reins and guide the next stage of evolution. The Monad will silently and subtly begin to inform the intelligence, working through it indirectly, stimulating it by its energies, evolving it by a ceaseless flow of potent influence from within, while intelligence grapples with the lower vehicles, to be at first conquered and enslaved but slowly to master and to rule. And here we leave monadic evolution, now to go on silently beneath the surface, till the time shall come when the triumphant intellect shall merge in the Spirit. Such, briefly stated, is our pedigree on the side of Spirit; we see our birth in God; we see the groups of Mighty Ones that nurtured our infancy; we see the stages of our growth, as we descend from Chain to Chain, from Round to Round, from Globe to Globe, until we reach our own familiar earth, and touch the ground we know. Then we sense dimly the coming of the 'Sons of Night,' the 'Sons of the Dark Wisdom,' those who bring ahamkara for the building of man, and we know that here is another line of our pedigree, that they too are ourselves. We see the

Spirit obscured, and know that the Spirit must mature in silence, while the warrior Intellect carries on the combat; until the time shall come when Intellect shall lay his spoils at the feet of Spirit, and man, become divine, shall reign on earth.

II. THE PHYSICAL PEDIGREE

IN DEALING WITH the physical side of man's evolution, we shall have the difficulty that is always found when we come to deal with the Physical; and that is, that we have a mass of details, details most complicated in their character; as all of you know, even Modern Science, dealing with a fraction of the whole, is fairly difficult to study, when you desire to understand thoroughly the story that it tells. How much more difficult, then, is it when you have to deal with things as they are, in all their various planes, in all their various states; and when, instead of confining yourself to the differentiation of the physical tattva, you have also to take into consideration the differentiations of those tattvas that belong to the higher planes as well. I say this because I am aware that I shall have a little to tax your attention, if you desire really to follow the stages of man's physical evolution, and if you desire to grasp the part he plays in the world in which he is the highest example of life, the one from whom are drawn all seeds of life, so far as the present evolution is concerned, the one who stands at the head of the evolution of the globe, and on whom depend for their life and guidance the various kingdoms below him in nature. We shall want to discover how it comes to be that in the very body of man there exist the germs of life which populate all the great kingdoms of the globe. The only theory which seems to afford a glimpse of the truth, though the only of a fragment, is that theory of Weissman which, in its wonderful complication, is fairly difficult to fully grasp, but which shows us how, even from the standpoint of modern science, you may have complications so varied, so numerous, so inter-lacing, within the limits of a germ, that you can find there the limits of a germ, that you can find there the traces of thousands of generations, and the possibility of any one of those traces evolving and appearing in the man of today. Now with regard to the physical evolution, there is one great class of beings who guide it, who control it, who, in fact, give the patterns on which the whole of that evolution is moulded.

This is the class known to you in Hindu literature under the general name of Pitrs, or ancestors.

Now there is much confusion about these Pitrs, and that for a very simple reason. First of all, the original Pitrs - those to whom I would like, if possible, to confine the name, for the sake of clearness - reappear over and over and over again, in different characters. They appear in every Round, and when we come down to the evolution of our own Globe, they appear in the different cycles of growth upon that Globe. Then we find them almost, as it were, merging in man; then we find them again reborn in fresh characters; so that they are somewhat like the players on the stage of a theatre, who, clothing themselves in different garments, appear in different characters though the same men are under the changed clothes. This change of characters were assumed, and part of our work to-day will be trace these beings, and see how the Pitrs reappear cycle after cycle, but always with the characteristic that they are the Lords of the physical kingdom, that they are the guides, the moulders, and the architects of mortal man.

That same name of Pitrs is also used for those who are spoken of as Agnishvattas, who have nothing to do with the physical body of man. Those we shall for a moment put aside entirely. They are the three higher classes of the seven classes of Pitrs, more or less familiar to you in the Hindu Shastras, but they are distinguished as being Arupa, without form, and they belong to a different evolution. They have to do with the Devas, and are sometimes called Pitrs of the Devas. Again, they have to do with the intellectual evolution of man, and we shall have to meet them under another title, the title of Manasaputras, which includes these and many other.

The Pitrs who have to do with the pnysical ancestry of man, who are literally his physical ancestors, the ancestors of his body, are grouped into the remaining four great classes, and in the occult teachings these four classes are given a single name, Barhishad. Now that name appears again as the name of one class out of the four, which makes part of our confusion. The general name is the name of Barhishad Pitrs, or those possessing the creative fire. Although you find that name specially given to the sons of one of the mind-born Sons of Brahma, it is none the less true that it is also used for the whole of the four classes of the Rupa Pitrs who have to do with physical evolution, So that when I speak of the Barhishad Pitrs, if I use the term without further explanation, I shall mean all the four classes of Rupa Pitrs.

Now these four classes, the Barhishad Pitrs, come from the Moon. You know how you read of the Moon as the gate way of Svarga, as being one of the Lokas, as being the home of the Pitrs. This is indeed true as regards human beings, for they pass out of Pretaloka into Pitrloka, and thence into Svarga. In a cosmic sense the Moon serves as a gateway, through which its inhabitants pour into the earth. These Pitrs come to the Earth Chain from the Moon Chain, and therefore we speak of them as Lunar Pits, as Pits who have come from the Moon.

Now if we want to understand their nature, the first question that we naturally ask is: What did they do on the Moon, and what was the result of their living there? We already know that the lunar Chain is the Chain that preceded our own, and that we are bound by the closest ties with the evolution that was carried on the Moon, or on the lunar Chain. You will best estimate the achievements of the Lunar Pits on the lunar Chain, if, for a moment, you think of Those whom we generally speak of as the Masters on our earth. They are Masters, who, having come through human evolution here, have transcended humanity. They are the flower of humanity, as They have been called -Those who have triumphed over all the difficulties of matter and have become here the Lords of matter, the Guardians, the Protectors of humanity. Just such a function was played by the Lunar Pitrs in the evolution on the lunar Chair. They passed through all that through the equivalent human stage; they were the successes of that evolution; they rose higher and higher until they had utterly conquered all the matter of the lunar Chain, and could use it for their own purposes. Therefore, they are sometimes called the Cubes, because on the lunar Chain they conquered matter in its quaternary, or four-fold, form, and they brought that matter with them for its further evolution in the Earth Chain. Think of them then as the Lords of the Moon, a title which is very often given to them in the occult writings. They, are also called the 'Sons of Twilight,' for a reason we shall see in a moment, again connecting them with the Moon; or. Again, celestial Men, Sons of the Moon, Progenitors. Do not confuse them - for here one of the difficulties of the student comes in - with those classes of Pitrs, the ex-Monads of the lunar Chain, who come from the Moon to pass into human evolution on our Globe. These have nothing to do with those great Lunar Pitrs, save that they evolved under their protecting care on the Moon, as we evolve here under the care of the Masters of Wisdom and Compassion. These ordinary Pitrs, so often confused with these others, are the ex-Monads from the Moon, who make the bulk of our humanity at the present time, and who also are imprisoned in the animal, the vegetable and the mineral kingdoms of our Globe, the whole, indeed, of the forms of our Chain being occupied by these Monads from the Moon. These are indeed called Pitrs, but they are not the great Lunar Pitrs.

You may notice that this identity of name appears also in Hindu literature, in the Shraddhas and in ordinary talk, in speaking of the Pitrs; for every deceased man at a certain stage, after the Preta stage, passes into Pitrloka, and is numbered among the Pitrs; and yet you know very well that those human beings, who are numbered or classed with the Pitrs are rather "under their roof, under their protection, are kept, guarded and shielded by them, than share their nature; and do not really confuse those of our humanity who pass on into Pitrloka at a certain time after death with the great and mighty Pitrs who are constantly invoked in the shraddha, and who are children of the mind-born Sons of Brahma. The confusion is thus very general, and it has persisted in our own nomenclature. Let us then, for the purpose of these lectures, keep the name of Pitrs only for the Lords of the Moon, and not confuse them with our ordinary humanity, which they are going to guide as regards the physical evolution.

Now these Pitrs, at the end of their evolution on the Moon Chain, merged into the planetary Logos, the Ruler of the Chain, As we might say now, they reached Nirvana; they entered the consciousness of the great Lord under whose rule they had been evolving; they passed into His being; they became, as it were, the germs of life within His body.

When the Earth Chain is to begin, the new body of the Planetary Logos - now called because of his functions, Brahma, the Creator, the reflection of the great Brahrha of the system - these Pitrs are born from His 'Body of Twilight. ' These four bodies of Brahma are the four planetary Chains; the first is His body of Darkness; the second His Body of Day; the third, the lunar, his body of Twilight, the fourth, the terrene, the turning-point, His Bodyy of Dawn. Born thus from Him, they are called the Sons of the twilight, the Will born, and the Lords of Yoga; they are ever spoken of sometimes as Swayambhuva, since they have no birth, save the coming forth from the Body of the Lord. They were born, it is written in the Vishnu Purana, from His body of Twilight, when He was meditating on Himself as the father of the world, and the coming forth of the world of men; and the Varaha Purana speaks similarly, saying that they came forth, the color of smoke, as He meditated on the bringing forth of all classes of beings. When He thus thought of Himself as the Father, then it was that these issued forth from His body of Twilight, these will-born Pitrs, the Lords of the lunar Chain.

Possessing the four-fold matter, and also the creative fire, they were able to give to man his etheric double, prana, animal kama, and animal germ of mind. Beyond this they could not go, but this sufficed for the shaping of physical evolution, for the building of animal man and all lower forms.

These Pitrs are spoken of as under the rule of Yama, the Lord of Death; he is called "Pitrpati," the Lord of the Pitrs; hence the bodies they give to man are mortal, born under the domination of the Lord of Change and of Death. They cannot give the Immortal, under the dominance of the Lord of death. Men are their progeny, and must therefore form part of Death's kingdom; and thus the children of earth differ from the children of Buddha, the planet Mercury, for his men are immortal, whereas the children of Earth are mortal. Moreover, these Pitrs themselves by their work on the terrene chain, and they will escape from the dominion of the Lord of death by this evolution, and in the next planetary Chain, the fifth, they will play the part of Sons of Mind and Lords of death.

Such then is our first glance of the Lunar Pitrs. We shall find them, as I said, re-emerging over and over and over again; first they appear before us in their character as Rulers of matter, when the Globes are formed, but are still devoid of living inhabitants, only the matter of the Globe being moulded into globular form. We meet them at the beginning of the first Round. How shall I give to you some picture of what might be seen by the 'Divine Eye,' if it were turned by some Yogi to that first Round? I would fain give you a picture which, however imperfect, would convey some kind of definite thought to the mind. Behold a vast mass of heaving, tossing, whirling, fiery matter, flashing, rolling, changing, in billowing masses, slowly aggregating itself according to three varying densities, into seven flimsy forms. Scarce forms indeed we can call them, for even when we descend to the fourth, the most material of the globes, we can only catch a dim glimpse of Earth's first form, a mere film of Ether, tenuous, radiant, luminous, fiery.

There is nothing visible save embodied fire in this Round. Seven of these globes we dimly see, of which this fourth, that is to be our Earth, is the most perceptible. Above it, on the descending arc, vague and vaguer shadows loom through the fiery mists. Above it, on the ascending arc, three other shadows, fiery, scarce perceptible. A vast panorama of flames, that take and lose again the form of globes, huge, wondrous, awe-inspiring, in restless force and overwhelming energy. The four classes of Barhishad, or Lunar Pitrs, the Rupa Pitrs, preside respectively over the four successive Rounds of our terrene Chain, those with the most subtle bodies guiding the first Round, the next second, the denser bodies of all the fourth, the Round in which the denser matter is formed. Each of these four classes presents its own seven grades, or sub-classes, so that in any given Round, or Globe, we meet with what are called ' seven classes of Pitrs,' and many a student, noting this, has been puzzled, since he remembers another statement about seven classes of Pitrs, among whom the Agnishvatta Pitrs were named, whereas these are all Barhishad Pitrs. The puzzle is solved when he understands that in each of the first seven classes, divided into Arupa and Rupa, there are seven subclasses, marked out from each other by differences in evolution: in the four great classes of Rupa Pitrs we have thus twenty eight subclasses, seven in each class, and it is these sub-classes alone with which we have to do in each successive Round. Only one of the great classes is concerned with each Round, and it is the sub-classes of these which we meet in 'the seven classes of Lunar Pitrs. '

The four great classes are distinguished by the differences in their Upadhis; the first has no lower Upadhi than the Karana Sarira; the second has for its acting vehicle the mental body; the third uses the astral body; and the fourth is clothed in the etheric double. Thus, as the Globes grow denser in successive Rounds, the Pitrs who successively guide physical evolution bring to their work these successively denser vehicles of activity, suitable for the task entrusted to them. The more we study the plan of evolution, the more are we struck with the exquisite adaptations of part to part.

These Barhishad Pitrs belong - as stated in the first lecture - to the last of the Creative Hierarchies, or Orders, called by us the seventh, though in reality the twelfth. They have under them vast hosts of nature spirits, who are the actual builders of the forms, the masons, while the Pitrs themselves may be compared to the architects, a name which is indeed very often given to then. They give the forms, the models, the plans, which are followed, actually worked out, by their subordinates, the innumerable beings who select the material particles and put each in its proper place. I may remark, in passing, that since, in Hindu literature, the word 'Deva' is applied to the whole of these, the need of the familiar thirty-three crores of Devas to carry on the workings of nature becomes very obvious, and should cause no surprise.

The Puranas, when they speak of the earth and its six Globes, draw you that strange picture at which I am afraid many an Indian graduate has often laughed - the seven zones, or even the seven dvipas, as they are called, and the curious oceans of milk and curds, etc.; dividing one from the other. "What foolish tales these old men write," our modern critics say. Yet they wrote much more wisely than the scientists of the 19th century, for they give you, through a graphic picture, an idea of the appearance of the planetary Chain, and every dvipa, or world, is a Globe of the planetary

Chain, and that which is called the ocean is the matter between each globe and the next, dividing them by a sea that none can cross, save those who have built their higher upadhis and are therein able to navigate those wondrous seas of matter. And if you could stand on some higher plane and look down on the Chain from above, you would see exactly what is figured in the Puranas - the seven dvipas and the seven oceans that surround them, billowy masses of matter of varying densities, heaving between the Globes, and named according to the earthly liquids they most resemble in their general appearance. The mistake has been that men have tried to identify these with things on the physical globe, whereas they are seven worlds of the Chain, differing utterly from each other, and the Jambudvipa of that Chain is our earth, our own world. These descriptions may not be according to modern ideas of precise and accurate scientific nomenclature, but they convey vivid and graphic ideas to the ordinary mind, for which they were intended; and the modern seer easily recognises the objects described when, from the standpoint at which the pauranic writer surveyed the scene, he also lets his gaze wander over the wondrous panorama, and sees the seven Globes amid their encircling oceans of unorganised matter. Let us return to our picture of fire, with the filmy globes rolling amid the billowing flames.

On to the first of these, vaguest, must fiery of all, the first class of Lunar Pitrs descend. Theirs to give the first models of form which all who follow after them will use as tabernacle; these are based upon Ideas in the mind of the Planetary Logos, but theirs to shape the forms, theirs to give the first moulding to the fiery matter which is to serve as the dwelling of the incoming Monads from the lunar Chain. They must assimilate the matter of the Chain, else how shall they be able to build therewith the forms? They cannot work with the matter which is not theirs. Hence the first thing to do is themselves to pass through every kind of matter, and, gathering it round their airy bodies, shape it by their creative fire into germinal forms, which will slowly develop and mature, and become in the course of ages, the forms that we know in the fourth Round on our fourth Globe. Seven typical forms must each sub-class mould in each kingdom on each Globe, for in every kingdom of nature there are seven types existing side by side, and there are the seven types in each of the seven sub-classes of the Pitrs of each Round. These are mere films of fiery matter in this first Round.

Now the characteristic of the first Globe, Globe A, is that nothing there is form as we know it; so unlike is all to the forms we know that it is even called Arupa, formless; and yet there is form though not form as known to mortal man. Archetypal forms they are called, i. e., ideal forms made out of the stuff of abstract thinking, vague, changing, and indefinite, inconceivable and ungraspable by the concrete mind, only to be known in this way, that when such a form passes to a lower plane, it bursts into innumerable concrete forms all of which bear a likeness to itself, in that they present its essential characteristics, have in them something after its image. Perhaps this will be more readily intelligible if I remind you of a curious device, resorted to in the early days of biological science, to show the type of an order. Professor Owen, dealing with the great complexity of the mammalian order, sought to find out and combine what was common to all. He found certain things existing in every mammal - back bone, four limbs, and so on. He connected together, from his study of many mammalian forms, all the things that were common to every one of them, and he put these together into a form that was like nothing in heaven or earth or in the waters of the sea, and he called it the archetypal mammal. That was the exercise of scientific fancy, in order to guide and aid scientific investigation. He 'builded truer than he knew. 'Such archetypal forms exist in the mind of the Logos as the ideas of every kingdom - the archetypal minerals, the archetypal vegetables, the archetypal animals, and the archetypal men. They existed as ideas - Platonic ideas they are sometimes called, because Plato laid so much stress upon them in his philosophy. These ideas are in the mind of the Logos, and the architects, who are the Barhishad Pitrs, reproduce these ideas from the mind of the Logos in the highest Globe of the planetary Chain; this is Globe A. Hence it is spoken as the archetypal Globe, for it contains in every Round the archetypes that underlie the evolution of forms in that Round.

These forms are sometimes described, or hinted at, in the Puranas, and the descriptions seem to you strange, grotesque and unintelligible. Many of our learned men, who know a little of modern science, laugh at the ancient Rshis who tried to describe these extraordinary forms, unlike anything that the human mind can conceive. But the Rshis knew something more than modern science knows; they knew archetypal forms, the basis of all forms, and those strange creatures that you read of in the early pauranic histories are archetypes, and not forms as they exist on the lower planes. I know of no language, of no description, which conveys an idea of this wondrous building, better than you can find in the pauranic accounts, dim, strange and grotesque as they may seem. They are at least the best description that human language is able to give.

Let us come to the next point. Every Round, as I told you yesterday, produces an evolution of a particular kind, elemental, mineral, vegetable, animal, human. The other forms, that are not yet born on to a Globe of the Chain, none the less exist in the mind of the creative Logos. They surround these globes as embryos, so that in the atmosphere of the Globe you might read its history. That is one of the things meant by the phrase 'reading in the astral light.' Thus in the first Globe, in the first Round of our Chain, the Pitrs form the archetypes of the three elemental kingdoms and of the mineral; only the types of the highest elemental kingdom are mature and complete; those of the middle and lower elemental kingdom are embryonic types, and those of the mineral kingdom are mere germs, though representing all that will be contained in the perfected mineral kingdom of the fourth Round. The first class of Barhishad Pitrs produce these archetypes in filmy matter, populating with them the fiery Globe. In the atmosphere of the Globe, surrounding it, the other three classes of Barhishads Pitrs are busy with the embryos of the future vegetable kingdom for the second Round, with the embryos of the animal kingdom for the third Round, and with the embryos of the human kingdom for the fourth Round; these have no resemblance to the future vegetable, animal, and human forms, but are mere crystallisations - if the word may be used of matter so tenuous - aggregations of material; these embryos are in the womb of nature as embryos in the womb of the mother, and truly has it been written that when we come to understand the mystery of human growth, the whole chart of creative activity will lie open before our eyes.

On that first Globe A our Pitris are busy; they form the archetypes as aforesaid, they clothe themselves in the forms they have made, and then pass rapidly through the embryonic forms in the atmosphere around, touching them with the first thrill of nascent foetal life; they pass to the second Globe, Globe B, where they shape the multiplied concrete forms which spring out from the archetypal origin. Little change is perceptible in the form in the atmosphere; the whole stress is on the elemental and mineral, in which much progress is made. Then to the third Globe of the Chain, Globe C, where they shape far denser forms; but still it is but the densification of the fire, as you might see in a fire the layers of the whiter and the yellower flame, and then a redder glow; only such differences are there in the fire of the successive Globes. At last they came to the Earth, whereon the mineral touches the physical, the other forms remaining still in the atmosphere around. The germinal forms of minerals dimly appear in our growing fiery earth as tenuous films, and so on until the seventh Globe is reached and the whole germinal mineral kingdom is formed, although formed only in filmy shapes, not minerals as you know them - solid, crystalline, or in many other forms - but always as glowing gaseous masses; everything that now exists in the mineral kingdom is found on the last Globe of that first Round, in filmy, tenuous germs, to be enriched, densified, strengthened, and made complicated, in the succeeding Rounds. We may sum up their task by saying that on Globe A they give seven archetypal forms for each kingdom; on Globe B they multiply forms containing the essentials of each archetype; on Globe C they densify these forms; on Globe D they shape them in yet denser matter; on Globe E they make them more complex and slightly refine them; on Globe F they build them on finer matter; on Globe G they finally perfect them. This is the method on every Round, and thus the Pitrs work, though on the first Round only do they gather the matter round themselves, and dwell within it for awhile to assimilate it. They only use in their building the four upper sub-planes of the matter of each plane.

Now as the first class of Barhishad Pitrs do this work in each Globe, the ex-lunar Monads arriving on the terrene Chain, slip into the forms they shape and leave. The Monads flowing from the Moon pass first into the elemental kingdoms, and through them into the mineral and other forms left by the Pitrs. The seven classes of them, as we saw yesterday, are at different stages of evolution, and hence show ever decreasing powers from the highest to the lowest. Some, the youngest, had scarcely touched sentient life on the lunar Chain; others had passed through the lunar kingdoms and had reached the types of lunar animal forms. Now this difference of growth, of evolution of consciousness, has one remarkable effect. The more the Monad is evolved, the more rapid his progress through the kingdoms of forms. Hence an ever-increasing gulf divides class from class as they evolve. The lower ones fall further and further behind, because of the swiftness of the progress of the more developed. I can perhaps best symbolise that - only symbolise it for the difference is by 1/7 of retardation in every class - if I remind you of the arithmetical way of increasing by addition or by powers. Suppose I start with 3 and go on adding 3; then we get 3, 6, 9, 12. That might be taken as symbolical of one rate of progress. Now suppose I proceed by geometrical proportion - 3, 9, 27, 81. My first only gave me 12 at the fourth remove; and my second gives me 81 at the fourth remove; and the difference of amount is caused by the difference of the rate of progression. Something of that sort occurs with these ex-lunar Monads; so that, on Globe A, when the first class of them has reached the lowest of the seven stages of the sub-organic human form, having passed through forty-three types of form, the last class has only passed through one stage, that of the lowest in the seven stages of the lowest elemental kingdom. The first proceeds seven times as fast as the last. At the end of the first Round, the first class of ex-lunar Monads have passed through forty-nine evolutionary stages of form, seven stages in each of the seven kingdoms. The lowest, the seventh class, have during the same time passed through only seven evolutionary changes of form, the seven which make up the lowest elemental kingdom. During the remaining

Rounds those of the first class do not pass through the lower kingdoms, but enter the human directly. When the first Round is over, pralaya supervenes, and there are ages of rest, ere yet again the work of the building of forms proceeds.

Then the second Round begins; and the second great class of Barhishad Pitrs take up the work. They bring down the archetypes of the vegetable forms to Globe A, work them into concrete forms on Globe B, densify them on Globe C, and these touch the physical on Globe D, the animal and human remaining in the atmosphere, and all progressing; and the human embryos which in the first Round, only took on the strange crystalline kind of form analogous to the mineral kingdom, now spread out like a plant or a tree in a gigantic filamentous shape, nothing recognisable as human, though still to be found in human embryonic growth with the impress of the vegetable kingdom on it. Gaseous particles are built into all bodies throughout this Round, particles of the third sub-planes.

We pass on to the third Round; the worlds are becoming far denser than they were, though still luminous and ethereal. Now animals are developing. The third great class of the Barhishad Pitrs are in charge of this Round, and as the work of densification goes on, they bring down the archetypes of the embryonic animals, and work them into concrete forms, which, on Globe D, take more definite and exact shapes. Looking at the human embryos, which have received a large addition in numbers from the second Round, we see them, still in the atmosphere around the Globe, taking on strange animal shapes, monstrous, to our eyes repellent, and they appear as huge apelike creatures, with the stamp of the animal kingdom branded deeply into the embryonic form. The human embryo still shews this stage in his growth. Watery particles are built into all bodies during this Round, particles from the second subplanes.

The fourth Round opens. The fourth class of Barhishad Pitrs, the densest in form, possessing the ethereal body, comes to its work, and the archetypes of men are brought down to the first Globe; wondrous archetypes and beautiful are they, showing what man will be as well as what man is, for the archetypes of the seven Races are there. The sixth and seventh stand out radiant in the splendor of their beauty, and hint at what the developed types will be in the Races and the Rounds that lie in front. Now, coming down slowly, multiplying, densifying as they come, we see the forms which are to be produced on the fourth Globe - our earth. At last we touch the solid ground. We seem now in breathe again after our flight through space. We have come to the earth, not quite as we know it indeed, but still our own earth and therefore more familiar.

Having arrived here and taken breath, let us look at our world for a moment. Strange world, a world of such terrible turmoil, of such gigantic convulsions of nature, that you can hear nothing but the crash of falling mountain summits, the roar of volcanoes as they throw up the burning lava, the dash of giant waves loaded with rocks, with avalanches of lava, which they picked up as they rushed in mighty billows, and toss up as though in play, masses that are almost mountains; fire breaking out everywhere, storm, whirlwind and tornado - one vast turmoil and turbulence where you would think that life could not exist. It recalls the first Round in miniature, save that the greater density of matter makes the crash and tumult far greater than in those subtle worlds. But here, too, fire seems the dominant agent, fire furious, tumultuous. For 20 crores [200,000,000] of years these convulsions go on 'uninterruptedly, after which they become periodical and at long intervals.' The Pitrs are here, master of all this tumultuous turmoil of matter.

Three hundred million years have passed away in this fourth Round, on Globe D, and the nature-spirits have been busy at work, forming minerals, vegetables, and animals of the lower kinds. In the midst of the great turmoil they labor, and out of the remnants of the preceding Round they have taken the empty shells of forms, left when the life-wave left Globe D, and have tried to shape them into new living organisms - they are strange hybrid monsters of all mixed kinds of generations, half human and half animal; reptilian forms of all sorts and kinds appear, amid the fires and the whirling spray and clouds; they were produced by the 'prentice hand of nature' as science might say, but we see them as works of the lower Devas, the nature-spirits, unassisted by the guidjng power of the Lords of form. The Lords come to look if the earth is ready for the making of man, when the incessant turmoil is nearing its ending; all these lower forms are swept away, and there the earth lies, a vast ocean of heaving tepid water, emptied of inhabitants, solid hard ground beneath the watery desert. At one point, gradually, the first land appears. It is the peak of Mount Mem; it is the cap of the North Pole; it is the beginning of the imperishable Sacred land, the Holy land, the Land of the devas, called also Svetadvipa, the White Island, the Central land, and sometimes Jambudvipa, the name given to the earth as a whole. The Parsis call it Airyana Vaejo, and say truly that their great prophet Zarathushtra was born there. Mount Meru, the axis of the globe, though emerging at the Pole, has its roots struck deep in the Himalayan chain, the 'belt of the earth. ' Slowly that land emerges from the swelling waves of the tepid watery globe, and like the lotus of seven leaves, their centre Mount Mem, at the Pole, seven great promontories of land appear, to the edges of which the name Pushkara is sometimes given, though this name belongs more accurately to the seventh continent, and those promontories and their centre form the Imperishable Land. On that Land every human Race in turn is to be born, no matter whither it be led after its birth. It is the birth place of every Race under the rule of Dhruva, who is Lord of the Pole-Star. The Pole-Star has in its watchful eye upon it, from the dawn to the close of the twilight of a Day of the Great Breath. ' That land appears, and is ready to receive its inhabitants, and the climate is an exquisite spring; and the cry goes out, the ringing cry of the Lords who are the Governors of all. List to the stately rhythm of the Stanzas of the Book of the Wisdom:

" The great Chohans called the Lords of the Moon, of the airy bodies: ' Bring forth men, men of your nature. Give them their forms within. She will build coverings without. Males-Females will they be. Lords of the Flame also' — They went each on his allotted land; seven of them, each on his lot. The Lords of the Flame remain behind. They would not go, they would not create. The Seven Hosts, the Will-born Lords, propelled by the spirit of Life-giving, separate men from themselves, each on his own zone. Seven times seven shadows of future men were born, each of his own color and kind, each inferior to his Father. The fathers, the boneless, could give no life to beings with bones. Their progeny were Bhuta, with neither form nor mind. Therefore they are called the chhaya. "

There are four classes of lunar Monads ready for human incarnation, and the Barhishad Pitrs, descending on our earth on the Imperishable Land, separate off from their own ethereal bodies, a chhaya, a 'shadow,' a seed of life, which contains within it the potentialities of developing into the human form. It is huge, filamentous, sexless, an empty Bhuta, floatong about in the dense atmosphere, and in the seething seas. They sway and drift about, huge, indefinite, protista-like forms in ethereal matter, with changing outline, containing the seeds of all forms, gathered up by the Pitrs during preceding evolution, of a moon-like color, yellow-white of varying shades. Within the fourth classes of Barhishad Pitrs, who thus gave the seed of life for the shaping of the form of their progeny, physical man, there were, as we have seen, seven distinct sub-classes, and each subclass populates one of the seven promontories: "Seven of them each on his lot... separate men from themselves, each on his own zone. " But the phrase occurs: "Seven times seven shadows of future men were born," and the question naturally arises: whence this seven-fold increase? Each class of Barhishad Pitrs not only showed its seven sub-classes, as previously mentioned, at different stages of growth; but each of these seven sub-classes, successive grades of evolution, also contained members of each of the seven types, also spoke of earlier, and thence the "seven times seven. "

The ex-lunar Monads, being themselves at such different grades of evolution, could not have found fitting tabernacles in chhayas of one evolutionary grade. According to the respective stages reached by the four classes in their upward climbing through the preceding three and a half Rounds, were the respective chhayas into which they passed. Many forms, many kinds, many shades, were needed, so that each Monad might find his appropriate tabernacle, and the forty-nine orders provided yielded the necessary conditions.

These protista-like forms, oozed out from the ethereal bodies of their progenitors - as the etheric double may be seen oozing out from the side of a medium - were the first human Race. "Human?" you say. "But what is this, that calls itself human, this strange spreading indefinite form, more like a piece of slimy ooze, like the supposed Bathybius, than a human being. Why do you call it human?" Why do you call human, in the womb of the mother, the first foetal conglomeration of cells, unlike the human form? Because in that form, which is not human, the future man is evolving and the development must be human, can be nothing else. And therefore, though the form has nothing of human appearance in it, though it be but the mere embryo of the coming man, none the less we stamp it "human," for the Monad brooding over it has reached the human stage, and we name the form by the life within it and not by the mere outward similitude. And therefore we also say that the first human Race is here.

These huge forms are drifted about hither and thither, senseless and passive. As we have seen, the consciousness, being on the atmic level, can very slightly affect these clumsy bodies, which only show vaguely the sense of hearing and a dim consciousness of fire. Because such consciousness as touched them was of so lofty a character, they are sometimes spoken of as the Race of the Gods; also as sons of Yoga - the Pitrs sending out their chhayas when immersed in yogic meditation -and even the self-born, as not being produced of human parents. They are the second Adam of the Jewish Scriptures. The Pitrs have given out their etheric chhayas, have animated them with their own electric fire, galvanised them, as it were, into activity; the Sun aided in the task by sending upon them his vivifying beams, the solar fire, in answer to the cry of the Ruler of the nature-spirits for his help: "These three produced by their joint efforts a good rupa. It could stand, walk, run, recline or fly. Yet it was still but a chhaya, a shadow with no sense. "The presiding planet of the first Race is the Sun, or rather the mystic planet Uranus, that he represents.

Multiplication of these beings was by fission or by budding, the only forms of reproduction possible for them, as even today for the protista, their nearest physical likeness. They grew, expanding in size, and then divided, at first into two equal halves, and in their later stages into unequal portions budding off progeny smaller than themselves, that grew in their turn and again budded off their young. A study of the amoeba and the hydra will make the reproduction methods clear. No definite sub-races can be spoken of in this first Race, though you may mark seven stages of growth, or evolutionary changes. Nor does any die; "neither fire nor water could destroy them," fire was their element, of water they were unconscious. When the time is ripe for the second Root Race to appear, the nature-spirits build round the chhayas denser particles of matter forming a kind of stiffer shell on the outside, and "the outer of the first became the Inner of the second. "Thus imperceptibly the first Race vanished into, merged in, became, the second, and the chhaya, which was all the body of the first, became the etheric double of the second.

During the ages of unknown length through which the first Race lived, the earth was settling down into quieter conditions, and cataclysms were local, no longer general. More land slowly appeared above the surface of the watery desert, stretching out from the promontories of the first continent, and forming a vast horseshoe, the second continent, called the Hyperborean, or Plaksha. It occupied the area now called northern Asia, joining Greenland and Kamschatka, and was bounded on the south by the great sea which rolled where the Gobi desert now stretches its wastes of sand; Spitzbergen formed part of it, together with Sweden and Norway, and it extended south-westwards over the British Isles; Baffin's Bay was then land, which included the islands now existing there. The climate was tropical, and richly luxuriant vegetation clothed the sunny plains. We must not connect with the name Hyperborean the associations now carried with it, for it was a glowing gladsome land, full of exuberant vitality. The name Hyperborean took on its gloomy associations in later days, when the land had been swept of its inhabitants by a change of climate, and many cataclysms had broken it up.

The second Race appears, as we have seen, and it shows during its existence two marked types, responding slightly to the buddhic consciousness; it shows the duality which is characteristic of that consciousness, coming out in its physical changes, as in its two senses of hearing and touch, and its consciousness of fire and water, already noted in following the Monadic evolution. They are called Kimpurushas, the children of the Sun and the Moon, "the yellow Fattier and the White mother," hence of fire and water, and they were born under the planet Brihaspati, Jupiter. Their color was a golden-yellow, sometimes glowing almost into orange, sometimes of palest lemon shades, and these gorgeously-hued forms, filamentous, tree-like often in shape, some approaching animal types, others semi-human in outline, very heterogeneous in appearance, drifting, floating, gliding, climbing, crying to each other in flute-like notes, through the splendid tropical forests, brilliantly green in the sunlight, with flowering creepers starred with dazzling blossoms - all these make up a picture of gorgeous hues, the splendour of nature in her exuberant youth, running over with life, movement, color, outlines sketched in with a giant's hand, colors flung from an overflowing palette.

Two main types appear as just said, in this second Race, the earlier and the later. In the first type there is no trace of sex, they are a-sexual, and it multiplies by expansion and budding like the first Race; as the forms become harder, coated with a thicker shell of earthy particles, this form of reproduction becomes impossible, and small bodies are extruded from them, figuratively termed "drops of sweat," since they ooze out like sweat from the human skin, viscid, opalescent, and these gradually harden, grow, and take on various shapes. You may remember how it is said in the Puranas that all races were born from the pores of the skin of their ancestors. You may remember how Virabhadra, sent by Mahadeva to break up Daksha's sacrifice, produced myriads of strange forms from the pores of his skin. Many traces of this mode of reproduction are to be found in the pauranic stories, and these facts in the evolution of the physical side of man will enable you to understand the meaning of those stories better than you did before. In process of time slight indications of sexuality begin to appear in these "sweat-born" of the second Race, and they shew within themselves adumbrations of the two sexes, and hence are spoken of as latent androgynes. As we study the development of the lower kingdoms to-day, we see all these stages still persisting, and realise how steadily the nature-spirits have been guided along a single plan, endlessly modified in details but ever the same in principles. From germs thrown off by these second Race "men," the mammalian kingdom was gradually developed in all its immense variety of forms; the animals below the mammalian being shaped by the nature- spirits from the types elaborated in the third Round, sometimes aided by human emanations.

Meanwhile the earth is slowly changing; "The great Mother travailed under the waves.... she travailed harder for the third (Race), and her waist and navel appeared above the water. It was the Belt, the sacred Himavat, which stretches round the world. " The huge sea to the south of Plaksha covered the desert of Gobi, Tibet and Mongolia, and from the southern waters of this the vast Himalayan chain emerged. Southwards the land slowly appeared, stretching from the foot of the Himalayan range, southward to Ceylon, Sumatra, to far off Australia and Tasmania and Easter Island; westwards, till Madagascar and part of Africa emerge, and claiming Norway, Sweden, east and west Siberia and Kamschatka from its predecessor - a vast continent, the huge Lemuria, cradle of the Race in which human intelligence appeared. Shalmali, it is called in ancient story. In the course of ages, the vast continent undergoes many disruptions, and is broken up into great islands. Volcanic outbreaks, mighty earthquakes, from time to time shiver huge fragments from its giant bulk. A slow sinking begins at Norway, and that ancient land disappears for a while from sight, 700,000 years before the Tertiary, the Eocene of the Tertiary, began, there was a great outburst of volcanic fire, chasms opened up in the ocean floor, and Lemuria, as Lemuria, disappeared, leaving only such fragments as Australia and Madagascar behind, as traces of its story, which Easter Island, submerged and re-uplifted. During the life of Lemuria, at about the middle of its racial development, took place the great change of climate, which slew the remnants of the second Race, together with their progeny, the early third. The axle of the wheel tilted. The Sun and Moon shone no longer over the heads of that portion of the sweat-born; people knew snow, ice, frost, and men, plants and animals were dwarfed in their growth. " The gorgeous hues of the tropics faded away before the breath of the ice-kind; the polar days and nights of six months began, and for a while the remnants of Plaksha showed but a scanty population. Beyond it, in the polar region, smiled ever the Imperishable Sacred Land. The third Race showed out, as we might expect from analogy, three strongly marked types, which we will call the early, middle, and later third. As the first Race, in touch with Atma, showed a unity; as the second, in touch with Atma-Buddhi, a duality; so did the third, in touch with Atma-Buddhi-Manas, show a triplicity.

In type I, the early third, the mode of reproduction is similar to that of the later second- the extrusion of soft, viscid bodies, the "sweat," these bodies harden during the second sub-race:" the drops become hard and round. The Sun warmed it; the Moon cooled and shaped it; the wrnd fed it until its ripeness". The soft bodies gradually became encrusted, and took the form of eggs, the ovum, which thenceforth, even to the present day, is the natal home of the germ. Within the egg, now the form passed its earlier stages of growth, more human in outline, latently androgyne. The early third includes two sub-races; the first sub-race was sweat-born, and the sexes scarcely showed within the body; the second sub-race was still sweat-born, and evolved into definitely androgynous creatures, distinctly human in type, the outer covering of the envelope hardening. Sons ef passive Yoga these are called, so abstracted they seem from outer things. In type II, the middle third, in the third sub-race, the young creature developed within the envelope, which was now a shell, evolved double sexual organs, and when born, by the breaking of the envelope, was fully developed -like the chick of the present day-able to walk and run; they were the hermaphrodites, of whom we shall hear. again presently, for they became the vehicles of the Lords of Wisdom, and this phase is taken as the name of the middle third; in the fourth sub-race, reproduction was still by eggs, but in the developing creature one sex began to predominate over the other, until, from the egg, males and females were born; as this process went on, the babes became more helpless, and by the end of the fourth sub-race, the young creature could no longer walk, on emerging from the protective envelope. The human embryo still reproduces these stages in its developments; it shows the amaeba-like form of the first Race; the filamentoid form of the second; the sexlessness of the early stages is replaced by a androgynous state, and slowly male or female predominates, determining the sex, as in the third; it may be noted that the traces of sex-duality never disappear, even in maturity, the male retaining the rudimentary organs of the female, the female of the male.

It is interesting to notice the many traces in Hindu literature, in the "myths" that are truer than history, of the varied modes of reproduction current in early days; in the account of Daksha's sacrifice various modes are given: "from the egg, from the vapour, vegetation, pores of the skin, and, finally, only, from the womb. "

In type III, the later third, the fifth sub-race at first still reproduces itself by extruded eggs, within which the human babe matures, but gradually the egg is retained within the mother, and the child is born, as at present, feeble and helpless; in the sixth and seventh sub-race, sexual reproduction is universal. This later third is ready for the reception of the Manasaputras.

The separation of the sexes, in the fourth sub-race, in the middle third, took place in the later part of the Secondary Period, 18,000,000 years ago, the race having then existed for at least 18,000,000 years and perhaps for much longer; for it began in the Jurassic period of the Secondary, or Mesozoic, age, the Reptilian period, as it is sometimes called. After this the earlier sub-races perished off quickly, chiefly in the catastrophe already spoken of. The Divine Kings, as we shall see, came to earth before the separation of the sexes, taking from the middle third their best forms; the Divine Androgynes, the Divine Hermaphrodites, they were called, and they moulded these forms into divinest beauty, towering giants, splendid in figure and feature. With their coming, and the subsequent separation of the sexes, ended the Satya Yuga of the earth.

The early third was born under Shukra, Venus, and under this influence the hermaphrodites were evolved; the races separated under Lohitanga, Mars, who is the embodiment of Kama, the passion-nature. Like all the forms then on earth, man was gigantic in bulk, compared with his present size; he was the contemporary of the pterodactyl, the megolosaurus, and other gigantic animals, and had to hold his own among them. Organs of vision were evolved in this third Race, at first the single eye in the midst of the forehead-later called "the third eye"-and then the two eyes; but these were little used by third Race men till the seventh sub-race, and only in the fourth Race-the third eye having retreated inwards, to become the pineal gland-did they become the normal organs of vision. The color of the third Race is red, varying much in its shades. The Divine Androgynes are of a glorious red-gold hue, indescribably glowing and splendid, and adding largely to the glory of their general aspect, the single eye flashing like a jewel from its dazzling setting. It is a shock to turn from them to the earthen reds of the crude and clumsy forms of the first men and women after the separation. Gigantic in height and correspondingly broad, they give the impression of tremendous power, as far beyond the men of our own generation as the Anoplatheridae and Paleotheridae, which surround them in their later days, are beyond the oxen, deer and pigs, and the horses, tapirs and rhinoceroses that have descended from them. The head with retreating forehead, the dully lurid eye, glowing redly over the flattened nose, the projecting heavy jaws, offer a repulsive ensemble according to the modern taste. The memory of the third eye persisted in Grecian story, where we read of the one-eyed "Cyclops," as the one-eyed were called in later days, and of Ulysses, a man of the fourth Race, slaying a Cyclops of the third-he who had a central eye. That third eye, developed under the influence of the Monad, of the Spirit in man, possessed far greater powers of vision than the two later eyes, or, to speak more accurately, offered less obstruction to the perceptive power of the Monad; but as the Monad drew back before the intellect, the physical triumphed, and the two feeble organs of vision, that are called our eyes, were gradually developed, greater obstacles to the wide power of perception of the Monad, but yet giving a sharper definition of objects, and on the way to a keener vision than before. The third eye gave impressions of the physical in the mass rather than in detail, and the temporary closing in was the way to clearer sight. These apparent savages, savages in form, were none the less intuitional, responding quickly to the impulses sent out by the Divine Kings who ruled them, under whose tutelage they build mighty cities, huge cyclopean temples, mighty and massive, builded so that fragments yet remain, and Shamballah itself, the Holy City, the Sacred Dwelling-place, stands still unshaken, to tell of the strength that built, of the skill that planned. Of this civilisation a little must be said in dealing with intellectual Evolution.

Let us, ere leaving Physical Evolution, in which the Barhishad Pitrs play so great a part, glance at their subsequent share in racial evolution. After giving out their chhayas for the first Race, they leave the earth, ascending to Mahaloka for a while. "Having projected their shadows and made men of one element, the Progenitors re-ascend to Mahaloka: whence they descend periodically, when the world is renewed, to give birth to new men. " To a new Race, that is, and for the birth of a new Race they ever descend, guiding it for a while, and taking birth in it, to aid the Manu of the Race. They are reborn as the children of some of the Mind-born Sons of Brahma, the Planetary Logos, the Sons called the Sapta Rshis, the seven Rshis, and take up their function in the shaping of forms, elaborating the forms of the third Race for the coming changes, and preparing the A Androgynes to become the vehicles of the Sons of Wisdom. After the separation into sexes, the sons of Atri, to whom the specific name of Barhishads is given-called in some Puranas also the sons of Marichi- preside over the further evolution of the third Race, to whom the name of Danavas is given in Hindu literature. You may remember the story of the moral deterioration of the Danavas, told in the Mahabharata, as ahamkara-the intellectual principle-takes possession of them; how the Devi Shri dwelt with them in their early days, when they were pure and pious, and left them as they grew selfish and grasping. The Pitrs became the Divine Kings of these later. Lemurians, ruling under the sway of the Divine Androgynes, and teaching arts and sciences to the infant humanity in their charge. They are therefore called "the Pitrs of the Danavas," and these same beings are also "the Pitrs of the Daityas," the Atlanteans, appearing among them also as the early Divine Kings.

In the firth Race, members of the four great classes appear, to aid Vaivasvan Manu in His building of the polity of the first family of that Race. The sons of Bhrigu, they in whom the causal body is the active vehicle, are the Somapas, the Kavyas, and the Saumyas; and these are they who give their chhayas for the typical Sukshma Sharira of the most advanced Egos then ready for incarnation, who formed the caste of Brahmanas in those early days. The sons of Angiras, the Havishmats, in whom the mental body is the active vehicle, give their chhayas for the type of the Sukshma Shrira of the warrior caste, the Kshattriyas. The sons of Pulastya, the Ajapas, in whom the astral body is the active vehicle, give their chhayas for the type of the Sukshma Sharira of the Vaishyas. The sons of Vashishta-sometime called the sons of Daksha-the Sukalins, in whom the etheric double is the active vehicle, give their chhayas as the type of the Sukshma Sharira of the Shudras. Each of these types having a different color predominating in it, the four castes were called the four Varnas, or the four colors, and to the clairvoyant eye the Sukshma Sharira of each caste was at once recognisable by its dominant color, due to the relative density of its materials.

This is the secret of the difficulty of the change of caste, apart from all moral qualifications, The Sukshma Sharira, shaped by karma for the new incarnation, has to be rebuilt if the caste is to be changed. It is not a thing that can be done by a legislative enactment, nor by the decision of any body of men. None the less it can be done-it has been done in the past, it is done in the present-but only by the help of the Pitrs. That was the help that Vishvamitra sought by tapas and by yoga, until he won their assistance, and they gave a new chhaya, the chhaya of the Brahmana. It is not then true that change from one caste to another is impossible, nor could you regard it as impossible, if you really believed your sacred books. But it is difficult, very difficult, and can only be done by the aid of the Pitrs, not by the word of man. There is the truth which lies between the two extremes, between the man who says that caste is nothing but birth, and the man who says that caste is nothing but merit. Neither of them speaks the full truth. Birth has a great deal to do with it, because the physical body and the Sukshma Sharira are modelled upon a similar plan and because the Ego, coming with the Sukshma Sharira of one type, has the body moulded as far as possible on the same type.

So far we have traced the spiritual, we have traced the physical. To-morrow we will bring in the bridge that unites the two-the intellectual ancestry of man.

III. THE INTELLECTUAL PEDIGREE

WE HAVE STUDIED the spiritual and physical evolution. The two lines of evolution, approaching each other, find themselves separated by a gulf. There is no bridge whereby they reach each other. " They who fashion the physical man descend from the material Worlds. They are inferior Spirits possessed of a dual body. They are the fashioners and creators of our body of illusion. Into the forms, projected by the Pitrs the Two Letters (the Monad, called also the Double Dragon) descend from the spheres of expectation. But they are like a roof with no walls nor pillars to rest upon.

Man needs four Flames and three Fires to become one on earth, and he requires the essence of forty-nine fires to be perfect. It is those who have deserted the superior spheres, the Gods of Will, who complete the Manu of Illusion. For the Double Dragon has no hold upon the mere form. It is like the breeze, where there is no tree or branch to receive and harbour it. It cannot affect the form where there is no agent of transmission, and the form knows it not. -- They are like the two lines of a triangle that has lost its bottom line. " That, then is the description in the Occult Commentary of the position at which human evolution is now standing - above, the Monad, or Double Dragon; below, the physical form that knows not the over-brooding Spirit. Nothing more can be done by either of these. The Monad can come no further downwards; the Double Dragon cannot breathe the coarse atmosphere of earth. That helpless, senseless empty form can mount no further; that is the bhuta, the shadow, that cannot climb any higher up the ladder of evolution. It is the senseless, the weak, the powerless, that demands some help from outside.

But the divine plan for the building of man cannot be frustrated here any more than anywhere else. And they from the heavenly spheres, they who are able to bridge the gulf between the spiritual and the material. It is the bridge of intellect they will build, the bridge of mind. Now the mind cannot be given by the Lords of the Twilight; for although they themselves possess it, it is not in them so thoroughly transcended that they are able to throw it off from them for the helping of others. Those who are able to spare of their own mind must of themselves have transcended mind, for only when we transcend can we two lines of the ancestry of man.. We traced his spiritual ancestry, and tried to catch some glimpses of the mighty Hierarchies of Spiritual Intelligences who co-operated in the sending forth of the Spirit, of the Monad, on his long pilgrimage through the worlds. We also traced the up-climbing of Matter, ever organised into better and better forms; and we saw how this building of Matter was guided by other spiritual Intelligences, who, having conquered Matter in their own previous evolution, were fitted to control and shape it for the practically helpless incoming human Monads. Now our two lines of evolution, approaching each other, find themselves separated by a gulf. The one has been descending from the celestial sphere, and the other has been up-climbing from the mud and slime of earth. But they now face each other across a gulf, and there is no bridge whereby they may reach each other, whereby they come into touch, the one with the other. That is the position in which we find ourselves; and this is graphically described in an ancient Occult Commentary. It is written there:" It is from the material worlds that descend they who fashion physical man at the new

Manvantaras. They are give. While we still identify ourselves with anything it remains our own possession; we cannot part with it for another.

Thus the mind cannot be given by the Lords of the Twilight; they have, indeed achieved intelligence for themselves, but they have not yet reached the stage in which they can give that intelligence to others. The stately poetry of the Book of Dzyan sketches for us the difficulty which confronted those who had done so much to shape man, but who had now reached the limit of their powers. Listen: "The Breath needed a form; The Fathers gave it. The Breath needed a gross body; the earth moulded it. The breath needed the Spirit of life; the solar Lhas breathed it into its form. The Breath needed a mirror of its body; 'We gave it our own,' said the Dhyanis. The Breath needed a vehicle of desires; 'It has it,' said the Drainer of Waters. " So far had they gone. "But Breath needs a mind, to embrace the universe; 'We cannot give that,' said the Fathers. 'I never had it,' said the Spirit of the earth. The form would be consumed were I to give it mine,' said the great Fire... Man remained an empty senseless Bhuta. "

Hence arose the need for some who had conquered the mind, who were the Lords of Mind, to come forward and help to awaken the powers of Manah, latent in the forms; at the same time, many of them were to incarnate within the forms, to become the Kings, the Teachers, the Guides of human evolution. There will be the intellectual Ancestors, as the Lunar Pitrs were the Physical Ancestors.

We have come to a time since when eighteen million years have rolled over our earth; eighteen million years ago the Lords of the Flame descended. Now we notice, coming to the earth, three distinct classes of great Beings. These we dwell upon for a moment, for, hidden in their varied nature, lies the secret of the intellectual growth of man, and by their play upon the forms, and the different stages that these forms have reached, we shall be able, when once we understand it, to solve the problem of the differences that we find in the intellectual development of the human races. Remember, on the one side, that you find among those who are called "men" such beings as are rapidly dying out; such men as the Veddas of Ceylon, arboreal beings with scarcely a language, making only inarticulate and animal cries; such beings as the wild men of Bornea, hardly distinguishable from giant apes; such men as the aborigines of Australia, that are so little developed in intelligence that they do not remember from one day to another, that they cannot count more than two - one, two, more to signify all beyond two. Compare with those who are still reckoned, and rightly reckoned, within the human pale, such men as a Newton, such men as a Descartes, such men as the past great Teachers in India or like the mighty Rshi Vyasa, who still wore the human form; or take the great teachers, the great Mystics, and range them on the one side and these backward, disappearing, races on the other. It seems as though the name 'human' could scarce be stretched to cover the two, as though the difference in intelligence were too wide to be explained simply by evolution. We shall only solve the problem by an understanding of the mystery of the intellect, of the mystery of the Sons of Mind.

Now those who come to the earth are summed up under that last name; Manasputras, they are called, literally the Sons of Mind. But the name, in itself, does not convey much information, beyond the fact that they were endowed with mind; and a good deal of difficulty has arisen in the thought of our students, because to some of the Manasaputras the loftiest terms are applied, and they were spoken of by names that imply the highest spiritual intelligence, while on the other hand, the same name is applied to beings who are obviously interior, who are obviously inferior, who are obviously of very limited intelligence. You have to recognise the fact that the name of Manasaputra means nothing more than it says, a son of mind, i. e. a being possessed of mind, possessed of intelligence; and just as 'man' is a wide term, covering many grades of humanity, and indicating nothing as to the grade in evolution of the man, so is the term Manasaputra employed by HPB following the usages of the ancient Hindu Shastras, and it is a term of the widest signification, covering many, many grades on the ladder of intelligence.

Let us, then, separate off the first three great classes, who are all far above our humanity, when They come to our globe; the fourth class are the Solar Pitrs from the Moon. The first class are spoken of as the Sons of Night, as the Sons of the Dark Wisdom, and this word "dark" or "night" comes over and over again in regard to them. If we speak quite accurately, this adjective should be used to distinguish them from the Agnishvatta Pitrs, who form the second class of the Manasaputras, and are called the Lords of the Flame, or the Sons of Wisdom. And I shall use the adjective when the first class is in question, so as to avoid confusion. These are Asuras, born of the Body of Brahma, which, thrown aside, became the Body of Night. If you look over the Hindu scriptures, you will find beings named Asuras playing a very active part in the early stories of the world, and the name covers a larger class than these with whom we are now concerned. It is worth while to delay upon it for a moment, for the influence of modern religious thought has cast a lurid light upon the name, and has made it almost equivalent to the Christian "Devil," a being who has no representative in Hinduism. The word Asura is derived from Asu, breath or life, asumat meaning simply a living being; in the Rigveda.

Varuria, Indra Agni, are called Asuras, the living ones, and it designates spiritual beings, and by no means those who were evil. It is true that later on, Asuras and Suras are put in opposition to each other, for their functions in evolution were different; moreover the Suras were on the whole far more passive than the Asuras, more moved by the sense of unity and of a common purpose, and hence yielding more ready obedience to the loss of the system, and promoting their smooth working, and keeping things in status quo, while the asuras were turbulent and aggressive, independent and separative, prone to discontent and eager for change. The Suras embody Order, the Asuras Progress, and hence they are constantly in opposition, though in reality both are equally necessary. You may remember that, in the churnjng of the ocean, the Asuras were at one end of Shesha and the Suras at the other, both employed in the churning, and there was a struggle for Amruta, the nectar of immortality, which was denied to the Asuras, eagerly as they desired to quaff it. Let us see why it was denied. The principle that is embodied in the Asuras, their very essence, their dominating characteristic, is Ahamkara, the 1-making faculty, the will to be separate. This is the over-mastering force to them, their characteristic mark, and by this you may know them. They are ever the rebels, and where they are there is war. Ahamkara develops in struggle, in isolation, in rebellion, and calls all tumultuous forces into exercise, and thus establishes the I. The time comes when that I learns that its truest self-expression is in the divine will, is the I of the universe, and then the Asura breaks the bonds of matter and knows himself to be one with the Supreme with whom he battled. Then he may drink the nectar of immortality, which is poured ever into the cup of unity alone, and may be drunk by those in whom it is transcended, but not by those in whom it is triumphant, who embody its very essence. Such beings, then, formed the first class of the Manasaputras who came to our earth; they had developed extraordinary intelligence; reaching the human stage in the first planetary Chain, they had during incalculable aeons of time been developing and growing in the subtler spheres, playing the part of Barhishad Pitrs in the second Chain, of Agnishvatta Pitrs in the third, and into ours they came as the Sons of Dark Wisdom for the tremendous struggle of the fourth Chain, and the fourth Round, and the fourth Globe, the ne plus ultra of the separateness of matter and the truimph of Ahamkara. When the order goes forth from the Planetary Logos to the "Sons" to "create their images," they begin their last struggle for separate independence, the struggle which, in its ending, will teach them the true nature of the "I. " They will not create; " One third refuses. Two obey. The curse is pronounced. They will be born in the Fourth, suffer and cause suffering. " These will be the "Lords of the dark Faces" in Atlantis, striving against the "Lords of the Dazzling Face" and in, their terrible overthrow, learning the final lesson, and turning to seek unity through the foremost races of humanity. These asuras form the fifth of the great Creative Orders, that of Makara, fitly named the most mysterious of all.

The second class of Manasaputras are those so familiar to theosophists under the name of the Agnishvatta Pitrs; they are the fruitage of the second Planetary Chain, born of Brahma's Body of Light, or of the Day, radiant, splendid Beings, Pitrs of the Devas, the Suras, in the subtler spheres, and Deva-like in their nature, with the sense of unity stronger than the sense of separateness. They occupy various grades in evolution, some more advanced than others. They form a part of the sixth Creative Order. Their names are many in ancient story; the occultist calls them the Sons of Wisdom - not of the Dark Wisdom, observe - the Lords of the Flame, the Sons of the Fire, the Fire Dhyanis, the "Heart of the Body:" also he speaks of them as the Triangles - since the three aspects, Atma-Buddhi- Manas are all active in them - who on earth become the Pentagons; for Manah becoming dual, and Buddhi reflecting itself in Karma, they become five-fold; Atma they cannot give to man, that is too high a task, but they send its force into etheric matter and so make the truly human Prana, thus giving the "spiritual plasm," the life-side of the permanent atoms, that flows from "the six-fold Heavenly Man. " Yet again he calls then the Pranidhananath, the Lords of profound meditation, the Lords of Yoga. They are the Virgins, the Kumaras, who cannot create the man of flesh, when Brahma desires to populate the earth, being too pure and subtle for the task. On the third Chain, they had brought forth the men of that Chain, but now matter was denser and they more subtle. After accomplishing their task on earth - the task we have to deal with now - they were reborn as the sons of Marichi, or some say of Pulastya, and become the Pitrs of the Devas; their heavenly abode is Viraja Loka, named after another of their many cognomens, the Vairajas. Many are the forms they have taken, and many their names in the Puranas; they are Ajitas, Satyas, Haris, Vaikunthas, Sandhyas, Adtyas, Rajasas, etc.

The third class of Manasaputras consists of Beings who come to our earth from another planetary Chain. They are not, like the other two classes, the results of the evolution of our own Chains in the earlier phases, but come from outside, from the Chain wherein the planet Venus, Shukra, is Globe D. You may have noticed certain phrases in old stories which give a relation between our earth and Shukra, the planet Venus. It is said that the earth is the adopted child of Shukra. You may have read that Shukra was the preceptor of the Asuras, Danavas and Daityas, or you may have read again that Shukra was incarnated as Ushanas on our earth. What is the meaning of these puzzling phrases? They refer to this third class of Manasaputras; Venus is earlier in evolution than our globe; she is older. She is in her seventh Round while we are only in or fourth, so that she is capable of acting as a parent to the earth by virtue of the far higher evolution of her humanity; hence it is said that she adopted the earth as her child, the earth which was her younger brother. That, translated into more intelligible language, means that she sent to the earth some of her own sons, Men marvellous in Knowledge and in power, Men of her seventh Round. She sent them to the younger earth, in order that they might act there as the Instructors of mankind. They duty was not to throw out the sparks of mind, but to take bodies on earth, and become the teachers and the Guides of the young humanity. They came to the earth when the third Race, was under the presiding power of Shukra, the planet whence they came, a radiant splendid band, and made to Themselves outer coatings, drawing round themselves translucent material, through which shine Their starry subtle bodies. The First of Them, Their Chief, is known by many mystic names in the old writings. HPB speaks of Him as the Root-Base of the occult Hierarchy; she speaks of Him as the spreading Banyan-tree, because from Him, by His creation of the Sons of will and of yoga, the occult Hierarchy was formed which over-shadows the earth, the Tree of Life under which we take shelter. She calls Him also the Great Initiator, because alone from Him the power of true Initiation descends. By these and other descriptive names He is indicated in H's mysterious Being; and sometimes He is called the Virgin, the Kumara, the One above all others. Round Him is a small, a very small, band of Beings from His own sphere. His own planet, who come to earth to labor with Him for the evolution of mankind. The humanity of this fourth Round had not evolved far enough to yield any sons for the great emprise; all needed teaching; none could teach. Hence the need for help from outside. They form what has been called the nursery of adepts. It is the nucleus of the first great White Lodge upon earth, which - from that day, more than eighteen million years ago, until now, in this modern 20th century - has never ceased to function, has never changed its character; it is the one supreme Lodge of the Guides and the Teachers of humanity, without which spiritual evolution were practically impossible, without which the earth would wander in the darkness, and for long ages could not find her way home to the Supreme. These, then, the Sons of Venus, are the third class of the Manasaputras, the root of the great White Lodge. There remains still one more class of Manasaputras: they are the Solar Pitrs from the Moon, grouped into two large divisions according to their stage of evolution; they have been abiding in the lunar Nirvana between the lunar and terrene Chains, and have dwelt there still through the vast period occupied by the three and a half Rounds of the terrene Chain, which have passed. On this a teacher remarks: "These 'failures' are too far progressed and spiritualised to be thrown back forcibly from Dhyan-chohanship into the vortex of a new primordial evolution through the lower kingdoms. " The "successes" of the Moon were the Lunar Pitrs, the Lords of the twilight, the rest being, comparatively, "failures". Of these, the second division entered the humanity of earth after the separation of the sexes in the third Race, the first division entered during the fourth Race, the Atlantean. They did, however, hover round the earth from the early stages of its activity in this fourth Round, as though watching for the time when their tabernacles would be ready for their incoming.

We must now take up the coming of the Sons of Mind in definite order, seeing the condition of the third Race at their coming, and the various events that surrounded and followed immediately on that coming. A preparatory touch was given to the second Root race, to quicken its evolution, and it was "endowed with the first primitive and weak spark" of intelligence; but we need not dwell on this, but may pass to the definite coming of the Manasaputras.

We must return for a moment to the stanza already quoted: "At the fourth the Sons are told to create Their Images. One-third refuse. Two obey. The curse is pronounced. They will be born in the fourth, suffer and cause suffering. " Now these sentences are good examples of the difficulty of unravelling the old writings. The word "fourth" occurs twice, and it is used in two entirely different senses. In the first phrase you must supply Round: at the fourth Round the Sons of Mind, the Manasaputras, were told to create their Images; one-third-the Asuras, the rebels-refused, and two-thirds-the Agnishvatta Pitrs, and the children of Venus-obeyed; the curse was pronounced; they, the Asuras, will be born in the fourth Race, suffer and cause suffering. That is a good example as I said, of the difficulty of translating old books. Rounds, Kalpas, Globes, Races-they are mixed up anyhow. The significant number is given, and the reader has to discover to what particular cycle of evolution the number applies. Once you have the key, the key of the cycles, then you can turn it in the lock, but until you have the key the sentence is more puzzling than illuminating; and that is what is called by the name of "blind. " it does not mean that any thing untrue is stated, but it means that the truth is stated in a way which needs explanation to be understood by the uninitiated. The key is given when the man is ready. But as it was important to keep the knowledge in a convenient form, which could not be readily under-stood until men were ready-because of the harm that had come in the old days of Atlantis by giving knowledge to those who were morally unprepared-the distinctive words that enable one to identify the time and place were removed from the commentaries that became public property. Thus, by the removal of these specific words, the whole thing became confused. You will find exactly the same thing in the Puranas. They are practically largely unintelligible until some of the keys are given; and, as you know, it is the function of Theosophy to give those keys to men.

One-third have refused; they are to be born in the fourth Race. They will come, and come in the Atlantean Race, and play there a mighty part. For the present they remain behind; the doom of rebirth under worse conditions is upon them; they would not descend at the right moment, they would not help in the human evolution. It is said that they came down and looked on the forms, "the vile forms of the first third" Race. Notice the Ahamkara coming out, the sense of separation, the pride, the contempt. They looked on these forms, the early third, and they despised them. "They rejected," "They spurned," are the phrases used, Ahamkara reigned supreme; they would not descend; hence the curse, and- the curse which came in a terrible form, making their work more difficult when they came, making their struggle keener, harsher and more turbulent, teaching the needed lesson. So we can leave our Asuras for the present, awaiting their time. Two-thirds obeyed. They are the Agnishvatta Pitrs, and the children of Venus. They are willing to take up their work, to perform their duty. The third Race is evolving. Recall what I said to you yesterday about the three stages of the third Race. First, the sexual form; the second, hermaphrodite; the hermaphrodite is divided into two sexes, separation'occurs. The divine men from Venus descend when the time is ripe for the second stage of the third Race, and by their influence the latent androgynity is quickened into definite hermaphroditism, and some very beautiful forms are produced. "It is through Shukra that the 'double ones' of the third descended from the first Sweat-born. While the majority of the third and fourth sub-races slowly evolved the human form through, to us, repulsive forms, animal-like, ape-like in type, a few, specially shaped for the indwelling of the sons of Venus were "towering giants of godly strength and beauty. "

Glance over the earth for a moment and see the differences of form. There is the wonderful Hermaphrodite, beautiful, strong and mighty, evolved under the immediate direction of the Lords of Venus for their own use, they being a perfected humanity, male-female having passed beyond the separation of sexes; these contained no ex-lunar Monads, but were evolved as forms, the incoming tenants from Venus acting as the Monads of the forms. There are the slowly evolving third and fourth sub-races, passing through the hermaphrodite stage, and slowly separating off into male and female, as explained in the last lecture. They are tenanted by the four classes of ex-lunar Monads that have touched the human stage; the three of them that became human in the first, second and third Rounds show out different stages of development, and the forms over which they brood develop human characteristics at a rate proportioned to the stage reached by the brooding Monads. Far behind them come in the less evolved, occupying lower and lower forms, until you come to those who have only begun their human evolution in the fourth Round itself; the forms of these are naturally very crude, very animal-like, and they are called the "narrow-headed. " These, neglected and despised by their more advanced brethren, became, as we shall see later, the source of a terrible degradation, and may serve as a lesson to the more developed classes - a lesson, alas! Only too sadly needed still-of the Nemesis entailed on the whole, by the law of collective karma, when the higher neglects and despises the lower, and they in turn re-act upon the higher by the degradation into which they drag it.

To the earth, showing these varied conditions, come the Lords of Venus, and, immediately following them, the Lords of the Flame, the Agnishvatta Pitrs. A few of the Lords of Venus make for themselves bodies by will and yoga, as before mentioned, and a few enter the hermaphrodite forms. They have evolved from the egg-born. As the Agnishvatta Pitrs come, some of them take the embryonic forms within the eggs, evolve them and enter into them; "Those who entered became Arhats." Thus was established upon earth the first great occult Hierarchy, which has ever since continued its gracious work, with the various grades appearing in it.

Then begins the labor of the gradual lifting of humanity, by imparting to "animal man" the spark of intellect, and thus evolving the 6th and 7th sub-races. This is the special work of the Agnishvatta Pitrs. The Lords of Venus do not take part in this. They are the highest grade of the Hierarchy of Sages, who train great Teachers for men, and from among whom in the rarest cases, One appears among me. We read of Them as settling at Shamballah, that mystic Holy City in the Central Gobi desert. They come down there from the far North, where Their earlier home had been, from the Land of the Gods, and They build Shamballah and settle therein, where ever since They dwell unchanged. It is said that Shamballah is over the heart of the Earth, a mystic phrase, meaning that within it dwell. They who are the heart of humanity's life, for from Them and back to Them flow all the streams of spiritual life. As from the heart in man the life-blood goes forth to nourish every part of the body, and returns thither charged with impurities, to be cleansed and again sent forth, so from this spiritual Heart go forth the currents of spiritual life; to that Heart the currents return loaded with impurity, when they have become polluted by their contact with the lower world; there are re-purified, and thence are again sent out. Thus is carried on the perpetual Sacrifice by which human evolution is sustained and quickened.

When the Lords of Venus - the Dragons of Wisdom as They are often called - came to our earth, they brought with them the seeds of various types of living things evolved on Venus, to improve and quicken the terrene evolution. You may remember that when the coming of Manu with other Rshis is mentioned, it is said that he brought with Him in His ship - the Ark - many seeds of life. And these seeds were not only the seeds of life spiritual and life intellectual, but also of physical life as it existed in Venus. Wheat, for instance, does not belong to our earth, and much are the botanists puzzled as to its origin; by crossing the wheat produced from the Venus seeds with earth-born grasses, the early Instructors evolved the various food-grains. Bees and ants, with their extraordinary social systems and well-regulated activities, are natives of Ve'nus, coming from a sphere where all evolution had progressed much further than our own, so that even in the realms of vegetable and animal life all stands on a higher level than we have yet reached.

These Dragons of Wisdom are the "the primitive Adepts of the third Race, and later of the fourth and fifty Races," says H. P. B. and were the "Sons of the Fire," the immediate disciples of the "Fathers," the "Primordial Flame. " They gave the Buddhas, i. e. the supreme Buddha and the Bodhisattva for the Third Race, as well as many Arhats, a few of the Agnishvatta Pitrs also entering into this glorious company; from Them also the Beings who occupied similar stations in the fourth Race, and in the fifth Race twenty-four are found, these mostly being Agnishvatta Pitrs, and recognised among the Jains as the twenty-four Tirthankaras.

The divine Hermaphrodites of the middle third Race, the "holy Fathers," as They are called, created Sons by will and yoga for the incarnation of the highest Agnishattas, the "Ancestors- the spiritual forefathers- of all the subsequent and present Arhats or Mahatmas," that is their Gurus; and we are told that, in the seventh Race, these Sons of will and yoga, with others like them, will produce mind-born sons.

These again are They who, watching over the evolution of the later third and the fourth Races, became wroth with the children of Atlantis, as we shall see later, when they became steeped in degradation, and brought about the great catastrophes which whelmed Atlantis beneath the waves of ocean They are ever spoken of as the divine instructors, They who superintended the spiritual evolution of humanity, and guided the cosmic forces so as to subserve that evolution. The divine Kings - of the earliest dynasties - who guided humanity intellectually, teaching them sciences and arts and superintending their social evolution, were some of the highest Agnishvatta Pitrs. These were the Titan-Kaborim, to whom allusions are made in the records of very ancient peoples. Says H. P. B.: "They are truly the great beneficent and powerful Gods, as Cassius Hermone calls them. At Thebes Core and Demeter, the Kabirim, had a sanctuary, and at Memphis, the Kabiri had a temple so sacred, that none excepting the priests, were suffered to enter its holy precincts.. . They were also, in the beginning of times, the Rulers of mankind, when incarnated as Kings of the 'divine dynasties. ' They gave the first impulse to civilisation, and directed the mind, with which they had endued men, to the invention and perfection of all the arts and science. Thus the Kabiri are said to have appeared as the benefactors of men, and as such they lived for ages in the memory of nations. To these Kabiri or Titans is ascribed the invention of letters ... of laws and legislature, of architecture, as also of the various modes of magic, so-called and of the medical use of plants'. Occultists speak of these divine Beings also as the Manushis, who taught and sacred language the Senzar, to the third and fourth Races.

Let us turn from the Rulers to the humanity They ruled. The highest grades of this humanity, the immediate pupils and ministers of the divine Kings, were Agnishvattas of lower classes, some of whom gradually evolved into Arhats in the better types of body in the fourth and fifth sub-races. The second class of the Solar Pitrs from the Moon came into incarnation in the sixth and seventh sub-races, leading the advance under these of humanity-untii superseded by the first class, who came into the fourth Race. Below these came the four classes of ex-lunar. Monads previously mentioned, thus presenting to our gaze an immense variety of human grades, from the semi-divine men, surrounding the divine Kings, down to the narrow-headed semi-animal types. In all the higher classes the third eye functioned actively, so that the astrai worlds were as open to them as the physical; its powers decreased in the lower classes, until in the narrow-headed vision was very dim. In the sixth and seventh sub-races, as we have seen, it gradually retreated inwards, to-disappear altogether among the Atlanteans.

We see in Lemuria, during the earlier part of the later third Race, the dawn of an exquisite civilisation, in which the Elders guide the youngers, who are still obedient, tractable, intuitive -the youngest of all following blindly and submissively in the wake of their seniors. The organisation is due only to the Elders; hence its beauty. But it obviously cannot be permanent, for it is the beauty of infancy, carefully guarded and shielded, not the beauty of manhood, self-sustaining and self-directed. Guided by the divine Kings, the sixth sub-race built the first rock and lava cities in the region of Madagascar, and many such cities followed, whereof, here and there, vast fragments remain, rocks that no modern engineer could handle, ruins of huge temples-cyclopean ruins, they are called. To the early Greeks and the early Egyptians they handed on the types of such building, and in the temples of Egypt, such as that of Karnac, we see traces of Lemurian building as practised by their later descendants of the fourth Race. So, again, in southern India traces of this massive style of building appear in some of the old temples. Judging by the ruins of Karnac, you may imagine the building of those who were mightier yet than they who raised those ponderous stones; or see the mighty pyramid of Egypt, and measure the knowledge and the skill that reared its stupendous strength. But those stones were not raised by mere bulk of muscles, nor by skilful apparatus, strong beyond modern making; they were raised by those who understood and could control the forces of terrestrial magnetism, so that the stone lost its weight, and floated, guided by the touch of a finger, to rest on its appointed bed. Some of the extra-ordinary rocking-stones still remain, that were poised by Lemurian fingers-or to use a name more familiar to you, by the fingers of Danavas. For the Danavas were the sixth and seventh sub-races of the Third Race. Those stones are one of the puzzles modern science has failed to solve, trying explanations of erosion by ice and water, that are manifestly inadequate. And what are they, the rocking-stones? Means by which messages might come from. Those above to those below, in which the swayings of the Morse telegraph needle spell out messages to-day.

I have just named the Danavas, and you remember that in the ancient stories the Danavas were pure and pious in their early days, and dually deteriorated in their later. Let us follow this downward process, and see how it came about.

We are still on the downward arc, though nearing its close. Matter is rapidly becoming denser, and the bodies grow more and more material; they are gigantic, strong, vigorous, and with the separation of the sexes, the creative instinct that is inherent in all life takes on the surging vehement form of sexual passion, hitherto unknown. That creative instinct in the sexless had worked smoothly, calmly, in the production of new forms. But now, violent physical excitement and pleasure mingled with it, and sexual passion arose, first in the animals and then in man. The Agnishvatta Pitrs who had incarnated, and the Solar Pitrs -clad in bodies growing denser and more robust with every birth conscious of their intellectual power and feeling themselves as Gods upon earth, sending down into their bodies strong currents of vitality that became transmuted in the densifying bodies into currents of sexual passion, hitherto unknown - were oft-times attracted by women of the less evolved classes, and, mating with them, produced a progeny of lower type than themselves. The bright Sons of Light wedded the more earthly women - "the Sons of God saw the daughters of men that they were fair, and took them wives of ail that they chose," says the old Hebrew tradition truly enough and humanity descended deeper into matter. It was necessary to go down into the depths of matter in order to conquer it, and in that first Kurukshetra many were conquered. A separation arose between those who, in the fierce struggle, still clung to the laws of the divine Hierarchy, and those who, succumbing to the intoxicating delights of sense encased in gross matter, turned their backs on the Lords of Light. As they drew apart quarrels arose, wars broke out, between them. The purer gravitated slowly northwards; the coarser wandered far and wise, southwards, eastwards, westwards, made alliance with the grosser Elementals, and became worshippers of matter rather than of Spirit. They became the fathers of the Atlantean Race, the Race in which matter was to reach its densest state, and win its greatest triumphs. It is the first division between the followers of the light and the dark, the division which become more marked and with more terrible results in Atlantis. The deified images of these Lemurian giants were worshipped as those of Gods and heroes in the fourth and fifth Races, and many an ancient mythos records their great achievements, their colossal combats, their superb strength.

As the separation went on gigantic and far-reaching convulsions began to rend Lemuria apart; earthquakes shook the land, and volcanoes burst out, sending far and wide raging floods of fiery lava. The huge continent split up into great islands, each itself as large as a continent, and these in turn were rent by new convulsions, until at last, some 700,000 years before the beginning of the Tertiary age, Lemuria as such disappeared, devastated by fire, channelled by lava, in great explosions of steam generated as fire warred with water, and amid roaring flames and surging billows, it sank, island after island, into the whirlpools of fire and sea.

On many districts which were not destroyed, some remaining as part of Atlantis, others isolated-such as Australia-some of the third Race people long survived. The aboriginal Australians and Tasmanians, how well-nigh extinct, belong to the seventh Lemurian sub-race; the Malays and Papuans have descended from a cross between this sub-race and the Atlanteans; and the Hottentots form another remnant. The Dravidiana of southern Indian are a mixture of the seventh sub-race with the second Atlantean sub-race. Where a really black race is found, such as the negro, Lemurian descent is strongly marked.

One other fact remains to place on record, ere we close to-day's study, for it resulted from the refusal of the Asuras to take their due place in evolution, and brought about a sore degradation, a descent instead of an ascent, of those who should have become truly men.

In this the occult record comes sharply into conflict with modern scientific teaching. Modern science posits a common animal ancestor for the anthropoid apes and man. Occultism asserts that the anthropoid apes are the late descendants of a mixture of the human and animal kingdoms that took place in the later third Race. You will remember that the lowest human class of the ex-lunar Monads-those who had touched the threshold of humanity at the close of the third Round, the "narrow-headed"-were not ready to receive the spark of mind; they had separated into sexes, but were ruled wholly by animal instincts. Some of these, in the seventh sub-race, mated with ape-like animals, not very far from themselves in form, but with Monads far less evolved than their own, still belonging to the animal kingdom, and from this union sprang a race half-human and half-animal; some of its descendants again inter-bred with some of the most degraded of the later Atlanteans, and the beings known as Satyrs in old Greek story, denizens of forests and lonely places, the terror of all more highly evolved men, bestial exceedingly-these were the progeny of that degrading alliance. From these according to occultism, descent the anthropoid apes, and these alone, of all now in the animal kingdom, will reach humanity on our Chain. In the sixth and seventh Races of this Round on our globe, they will attain to the astral human form, and in the fifth Round will enter definitely into the human kingdom. Such was the "sin of the mindless" and its results.

"Seeing which, the Lhas (Asuras) who had not built men, wept, saying: "The Amanasa (mindless) have defiled our future abodes. This is Karma. Let us dwell in the others. Let us teach them better, lest worse should happen. They did. .. .. Then all men became endowed with Manah." The earth was ready for the Atlantean evolution. The fourth Race was born.

IV. THE HUMAN RACES

WE HAVE SEEN that the sexes became separate in man in the middle third Race, some 18,000,000 years ago; nevertheless, while the third eye was not entirely obstructed by dense matter, the Monad exercised some slight influence directly upon his vehicles; this influence lessened as the density of matter increased, and the developing lower mind more and more took possession, thrusting the Monad into the background, and compelling all influence to pass through itself. When the time arrived for the birth of the fourth Race, the most advanced section of humanity had reached this point, and hence it is said that the Atlantean was the "first truly human and terrestrial race. "

The Atlantean continent was slowly rising as the Lemurian was broken up by earthquakes and volcanic outbursts, the one emerging as the other sank. The most suitable types for the fourth Race - the most intellectually developed and the most robust and dense in body - were chosen out of the third Race by the Manu of the fourth, and were led away northwards to the Imperishable Sacred Land, to be isolated and evolved, and to settle, on leaving that cradle of the races, on the northern parts of Asia, unaffected by the great Lemurian catastrophes. The first two sub-races of the Atlanteans overlap the sixth and seventh sub-races of the Lemurian during the later part of the Secondary Age, ante-dating the great Lemurian catastrophe, which took place 700,000 years before the close of that age. The most glorious period as regards spirituality of the fourth Race - that under its divine dynasty - was in the Eocene Age, and the first great cataclysm which destroyed it, took place about the middle of the Miocene Age, some four million years ago. Another splendid civilisation - the Toltec - grew up after this first cataclysm, and was destroyed in the catastrophe of 850,000 years ago. Others, but none so splendid, followed. These we shall glance at presently. The last remnant of Atlantis, the island called Poseidonis by Plato, was submerged eleven thousand years ago, 9564 B. C.

The huge continent we call Atlantis, the continent of the fourth Race, named Kusha in the occult records, embraced northern Asia - untouched, as said, from Lemurian times - stretching far to the north of the great sea, now the Gobi Desert; it extended eastwards, in a solid block of land, including China and Japan, and passed beyond them across the present northern Pacific Ocean, till it almost touched the western coast of North America; southwards it covered India and Ceylon, Burmah, and the Malay peninsula, and westwards included Persia, Arabia and Syria, the Red Sea and Abyssinia, occupying the basin of the mediterranean, covering southern Italy and Spain, and, projecting from Scotland and Ireland, then above the waters, into what is now sea, it stretched westwards, covering the present Atlantic Ocean and a large part of North and South America. The catastrophe which rent it, in the mid-Miocene, about four million years ago, into seven islands, of varying size, brought to the surface Norway and Sweden, much of southern Europe, Egypt, nearly all Africa, and much of North America, while sinking northern Asia, and breaking Atlantis off from the Imperishable Sacred Land. The lands later called Ruta and Daitya, the present bed of the Atlantic, were rent away from America, but a great belt of land still connected them, a belt submerged in the catastrophe of 850,000 years ago, in the later Pliocene, leaving the two lands as separate islands. These, again, perished, some 200,000 years ago, leaving Poseidonis in the midst of the Atlantic.

It must be remembered with regard to the dates of catastrophes, and the relative distribution of sea and land, that these vary according to the catastrophes selected for chronicling, and the point between widely separated periods at which a map is made. The available information is fragmentary, and is not always easily pieced together; hence the above outlines as existing at given dates must be taken provisionally. The Lemurians selected as the parents of the Atlantean stock, and led by their Manu to the Imperishable Sacred Land, separated off into groups, occupying the seven zones, or promontories, of the land. "Thus, two by two, on the seven zones," says the Book by Dzyan, "the third Race gave birth to the fourth," about eight million years ago, towards the later part of the Secondary Age. They were born under the Moon and Saturn - Soma and Shani - and much of the black magic developed among them, especially in the Toltec sub-race, was wrought by a skilled use of the "dark rays" of the moon, the emanations from the dark part of the moon. To Saturn was partly due the immense development of the concrete mind which marked the same sub-race, and much of Egyptian lore was gained under his influence. They were called also the "children of Padmapani," the flower of the lotus being a symbol of generation, an allusion to the fact that the fourth Race was produced by a union of the sexes. The marked density reached now by the human body brought about the clear recognition of impacts from solids, to which the subtler forms of earlier times had offered little resistance.

Into the first sub-race of the fourth Race, the Rmoahal, fair in color, came the Asuras; and the first class of Solar Pitrs, ex-lunar Monads, also came crowding in. They moved southward after long ages, when the Atlantean type of their divine Kings, the Agnishvatta Pitrs, gradually established a powerful civilisation. They drove before them the Lemurians, still dwelling in Africa and in the adjoining lands which had risen from the Atlantic, building strong cities, and becoming a settled people. The third eye was still used, but the two ordinary physical eyes had developed and were replacing it; the astral world was not yet shut out from the general vision, and much susceptibility to astral impressions remained, and much tractability as regarded the divine Rulers, looked up to, practically worshipped by those They guided and trained. The Asuras were not yet masters enough of their bodies to be able to turn their attention to the mastery of others, and the young civilisation went quietly on. The second sub-race, the Tlavatli, yellow in color, grew up on the land now beneath the Atlantic, still ruled and guided from above, by the divine Kings. The Asuras steadily came to the front of human evolution, as the ages went on, but were still obedient to the Lords of Light, ruling large districts and laboring for the improvement of agriculture and architecture, both of which made great progress under their brilliant leadership. There is nothing else in Atlantean civilisation so peacefully great as this early period, under the divine Kings. Meanwhile, under the western sky, were beginning to grow the seeds of a more intellectual but more densely physical sub-race, that called the Toltec, destined to carry the fourth Race civilisation to its highest material point, and also to experience is most tremendous fall. The most powerful of the Asuras and the best of the Solar Pitrs took birth in this, and settled on lands which did not come within the sweep of the mighty convulsion that rent Atlantis into the seven great islands. This convulsion destroyed the greater part of the first and second sub-races, leaving only remnants; the first drifted northwards, dwindled in stature, and declined into barbarism. The second gravitated southwards and eastwards, intermarried with the Lemurians still left in the district into which they wandered, and gave rise to the Dravidian peoples.

Thus was cleared the theatre for the great Toltec sub-race, a race handsome and well cut in feature, gigantic still, some twenty-seven feet in height, but well-modelled in figure, red to re-brown in color. Their bodies and those of the fourth and fifth sub-races were denser in material than any before or since, of a hardness sufficient to bend a bar of the iron of the present day, were it launched against them, or to break a bar of our steel, were they heavily struck by it; one of our knives would not cut their flesh, any more than it would cut a piece of present-day rock. Needless to add that the minerals of their day were so much harder than our own, that their relative hardness to these human bodies was much as that our minerals to our bodies now. Another peculiarity was the extraordinary recuperative power they possessed; they recovered from the most ghastly and extensive wounds, received in battle or accident, the flesh joining and healing with the most astonishing rapidity; nor did they at all suffer from nervous shock, consequent on serious laceration, nor suffer very keenly from physical torture, even that inflicted by deliberate human cruelty. The nervous organisation was strong but not fine, nor was it delicately balanced in its internal co-ordinations; hence it could stand, without injury, shocks which would prostrate a man of the fifth Race, and could endure strains and convulsions that would leave him a nervous wreck. Flesh like rock, nerves like wires of steel, would best describe the bodies of these sub-races. The developing sense of taste answered only to very powerful stimulants, and could not distinguish any delicate flavours; putrid meat, strongly smelling fish, garlic and all herbs of very pungent flavor, the sharpest and most fiery solids and liquids, were, to them, the only delicious foods. All else was tasteless and vapid. As they possessed no sense of smell, they could dwell undisturbed amid the most appalling stenches, and although the higher classes were most scrupulously clean in their persons and dwellings, the neighbourhood of malodorous filth - provided it did not offend the eye - troubled them not at all. Traces of these physical peculiarities still remain in many of their descendants. The North American Indians recover from wound which would kill the fifth Race man, whether from injury to tissue or from nervous shock; he can bear, unblenching, tortures under which the fifth Race man would incontinently faint away. The Burmans will bury fish and meat, and find them, in their putrid condition, a toothsome delicacy. And all can live amid smells that would turn the fifth Race man sick. The third eye, which, as we have seen, had retreated inwards and had been becoming more and more obscured with the increasing density of matter, disappeared altogether as physical organ during the Toltec sub-race, but remained functionally active for long ages in the succeeding sub-races. Even after it complete disappearance as a physical organ, much susceptibility to astral impulses remained, and superphysical impressionability was general. In the days of Toltec degradation, processes of black magic were resorted to by the upper classes, in order to deprive of this faculty those whom they oppressed and enslaved. They not only ceased to train it, as was done in the earlier days, but sought actively to stunt and even to destroy it. Despite all, I however, it still survives, to some extent, in many fourth Race nations and tribes.

Language was at this time. agglutinative, both among the Toitecs and among the fourth and fifth sub-races - the Turanian and Semitic - and this was the most ancient from of the Rakshasa language, so called as typical of the Turanian giants, to whom the name of Rakshasas was specially given. As time went on, language became inflectional, and this passed on to the fifth Race.

Stature, as said above, was gigantic - giants, Titans, are names often met with - but it gradually diminished, sub-race after sub-race. The Easter Island statues run to about twenty-seven feet in height, and represent fourth Race men in the middle period: the Bamian statues, five in number, are said, by H. P. B. to be the handiwork of fourth Race Initiates, and to represent the gradually diminishing height of the five Races; the first is 173 feet in height, representing the first Race; the second, that of the Sweat-born, is 120 feet high; the third, that of the third Race, 60 feet; the fourth and fifth are smaller, the last being a little over the height of a tall man of the fifth Race. The statues have been modelled over in plaster, and made to represent the Lord Buddha, but the rock-cut figures antedate His coming by ages.

Into this third sub-race, the Toltec, came some of the greatest Asuras, Intelligences of highly developed power and knowledge, and they found, in the splendid highest type of Toltec bodies, fit vehicles for their further evolution, and vehicles, moreover, that took on swiftly a still higher development, under the stimulating pressure from within. Behind them gathered the Asuras, who had already previously incarnated in the first and second sub-races, and also the Solar Pitrs, who had therein experienced their first terrene incarnations. Such were the higher classes of the early Toitecs, and below them a vast mass of less developed, but pliable and receptive peoples, ready to be led and guided. To these came the divine Kings, to aid them in the building of a great civilisation, and the Dragons of Wisdom watched this new development of the human race, so promising in the vigor of its splendid and eager youth. Hence this sub-race, named the Daityas in the Puranas, is said to have taught by Shukra, the divine Agnishattva Kings ruling it under the instruction and protection of the Dragons of Wisdom from Venus. Hence, too, is Shukra spoken of as the preceptor of the Asuras.

Under these favoring conditions of divine Instructors and Rulers and apt pupils, the Toltec civilisation grew and developed. In it appeared Asuramaya, greatest of astronomers, who began the astronomical records ever since guarded by the White Lodge, he who constructed the Zodiac, handing it down to the Atlanteans of Ruta, from whom it passed to the Egyptians after the lapse of ages. Among them, from time to time, appeared the mysterious Narada, Son of will and yoga, he who had learned the secret of appearing upon earth during incalculable ages, b stepping from one body to another, arbiter of the destiny of nations, guider of the whirling wheels of change, the sparks whereof are wars and natural convulsions. Study of the energies of nature was carried further by these quick pupils of the Stages than man has since been able to carry it. They yoked to their service the subtle energies that have the ether for their medium; they learned to plough the air in airships as steamers plough the waves of oceans, and these air-ships were used in the great wards which marked the later ages of Toltec supremacy. Many a reference to these may be found in the ancient stories, telling of combats waged in air between contending hosts. In those later days also they used their knowledge of chemistry to construct weapons dealing out a wide-spreading destruction; a war-ship, high in air over the heads of the combatants, would suddenly pour down a rain of heavy poisonous vapor, that would stupefy or slay thousands of hapless warriors; or they would hurl down huge bombs that, on striking the ground, exploded, scattering in all directions hundreds of thousands of fiery arrows, spreading the ground with the mutilated corpses of the slain.

In earlier days, their scientific studies were turned in more beneficent directions: to the improvement of agriculture, the breeding of improved types of animals, the production of grain-stuffs, the cultivation of fruit-tress, the enriching of the soil, the use of light of various colors for the stimulation of the growth of animals and plants, and for the eradication of germinal diseases.

Nor must be forgotten the wide use of alchemy, the parent of chemistry, in the production of the metals now called 'precious,' but then esteemed merely for their beauty as decorative agents. Gold was freely used on houses and temples, and gilded pillars were seen in the houses of the wealthy, the palaces of rulers, the temples of religion. Many beautiful alloys were also made for decorative purposes, contributing their metallic glint to the splendor of the cities.

Architecture was the art that rose highest under the Toltecs, and some of their great cities were models of strength and beauty. Supreme among them all was the famous "City of the Golden Gates," built on a hill which was crowned by the gorgeous Golden Temple, at once a temple and a palace, for its pillared galleries and richly adorned courts wee the home of the divine Kings, who raised the Toltec Empire to its splendid height. Painting and gilding were largely used on the outside of the houses, and statuary, bas-reliefs and mouldings of all kinds were freely employed as decorations.

The social polity established by the divine Kings was based on the general idea that knowledge and power must bear burden and responsibility, and that weakness gave a claim for protection not a reason for oppression. Education was universal, but of many kinds, suited to the life which lay about the student. In the days of the zenith of the Toltec civilisation, every capital of a province had its central college, with a department for each art, science, and branch of literature, and with affiliated colleges through the whole province, by means of which was spread the knowledge of al discoveries that tended to improvement in the application of science to production. Progress in science was promoted by the rule that removed men from the active duties of executive work when they had passed the zenith of their physical powers and relegated them to the study and the laboratory, if not needed for the direction of great industrial enterprises, the discharge of judicial functions, the guiding of the State. The less developed classes were trained in agricultural, manufacturing, and all. kinds of manual labor, and their welfare and comfort, with the provision of abundant food and clothing, were regarded as among the first duties of government. A Governor whose people were discontented, unruly, ill-provided, was removed from his post, as being either incapable or neglectful, and for any serious troubles he was punished by fine or imprisonment.

Many traces of these methods and views are still to be found in the fragments of very ancient literature, embedded in the books of nations with an antique past. They appear in some of the Chinese books, and some of the fragments unearthed from comparatively modern, though now dead, civilisations, shew the paternal and minute care exercised by Rulers over their people. The beautiful, though effete, civilisation of Peru, destroyed by Pizarro and his Spaniards, shews some faint traces of the elder world, whence it was derived.

The Toltec sway spread its centre in Atlantis proper - the land now beneath the Atlantic - westwards over the land now embraced in North and South America; eastwards also it extended itself over northern Africa and Egypt, bringing under its rule many nations springing from the mixture of the second sub-race with the Lemurians, and of the younger fourth and fifth sub-races, growing up in their respective centres.

When the Toltec Empire had been raised to its highest point, the divine dynasty came to an end, for the wisdom of the great Hierarchy saw that the time had come when humanity should try to walk for a while aione, gaining knowledge by its experiments and strength from its falls. A long line of Adept Kings followed, disciples of the great Lords, but now the ahamkara of the incarnated Asuras, nourished by power and rule, began to assume dangerous dimensions as their strength and dominance increased, and as the strong hand of the divine Kings was removed, and the reins of empire fell into a weaker grasp. The Stanzas tell the story in brief bold outline: Then the third and fourth became tall with pride". 'We are the Kings; we are the Gods. ' They took wives fair to look upon, wives from the mindless, the narrow-headed. They bred monsters, male and female, also khado, with little minds. They built temples for the human body. Male and female they worshipped. Then the third eye acted no longer. They built huge cities, of rare earths and metals they built. Out of the fires vomited, out of the white stone of the mountains and of the black stone, they cut their own images, in their size and likeness, and worshipped them. They built great images, nine yatis high, the size of their bodies. Inner fires had destroyed the land of their fathers. The water threatened the fourth.

Let us fill in the outline. First I would suggest, with all deference, that "the third and fourth" does not mean, the third and fourth Races, but the third and fourth sub-races of the fourth Race. It is distinctly said in the first shloka of Stanza X: "the third Race gave birth to the fourth," and then mention is made of the first four sub-races, thus produced. To bring in at this stage the third race, of which the degraded remnants were scattered through the fourth Race Kingdoms, seems incongruous, and the story is thrown out of gear. Whereas, if we read "third and fourth" as applying to the sub-races, the whole story is then congruous and sequential. At this stage of the third sub-race, the Toltec the fourth sub-race, the Turanian, had risen into power in the eastern lands, though still tributary to the white Emperor of the City of the Golden Gates, and, in the later struggle, it allied itself with the southern rebels; these were the "third and fourth" that grew "tall and pride. " The fifth sub-race was also differentiated, and was fighting its turbulent way to power in the north; we need not, however, concern ourselves with it at the moment.

Against the rule of the White emperor, the incarnated asuras gradually rebelled; at first secretly, disregarding the orders from the capital, spreading the idea that the far-off Sovereign was less useful to the people than the nearer Viceroys, themselves, assuming greater and greater state, and encroaching in every direction on the imperial authority. To increase their own greatness in the eyes of the people, they dazzled them with exhibitions of magical power, using their great resources of superphysical knowledge to aggrandise themselves, and to surround themselves with mystery, breeding awe in the minds of the ignorant. In order more fully to detach the hearts of the people from the White Emperor, they gradually introduced changes in religious worship, and substitutes luxurious feasts, dazzling spectacles, and sensuous pageantry for the stately and somewhat severe ritual instituted by the divine Kings. The early temples were of massive grandeur, splendid with gold and rich with jewels, but all was chaste, simple and grandiose. A dazzling Sun of gold was the central object, image and symbol of the celestial Sun, and that, in turn, but the symbol, the radiant garment, of the Lord of Light and Love, the Ruler of the solar system, in which He veiled His Presence of light ineffable. The worship was in sonorous chants and stately mazes of rhythmic dance, with flower-garlands and rolling clouds of fragrant incense, splendid and gorgeous indeed, but yet to chaste simplicity and stateliness. In connection with the

Golden Temple in the capital city was the White Hall, or cave, of Initiation, wherein the disciples of the Dragons of Wisdom received the holy chrism, wherein shone the Star of Initiation over the head of the Hierophant wherein from time to time appeared the radiant forms of the Sons of the Fire. This it was which gave to the Temple its supreme sanctity, and made it the focus of spiritual power. To it turned the hearts of the people; round it ever shone the halo of their devotion; it was the visible symbol of the protecting care of the Dragons of Wisdom.

Well did the ambitious Asuras know that so long as the Golden Temple and the White Hall remained the cynosure of all eyes, the acknowledged heart of the Toltec Empire, the hearts of the people would still turn thither. Hence they determined to create a new capital, and to set up a rival Emperor - his name is recorded as Thevatat - building within his palace a new temple and a new hall of Initiation. To give to this new centre the sanction of the super-physical, they called to their aid the powerful Elementals of the lower astral world, to appear in their midst at high festivals, and receive, clad in dazzling guise, the offerings and adoration of the people; after a while, to bind these dread beings more closely to their service, they began to offer to them sacrifices of slain animals, and, on great festivals, even of slain men; then, in connection with these, began licentious practices, cruelty and lust having natural affinities, until orgies of the vilest kinds filled the nights, which followed days spent in spectacular combats and bloody sacrifices.

The next downward step was taken when the chiefs of the Asuras proclaimed themselves as objects of divine worship; "We are the Kings; we are the Gods" and, carving huge figures of themselves, they set these up in these temples as objects of worship, and the creative power of man, reflection of the divine, was substituted for that spiritual energy of which it was the physical correspondence; thus phallicism arose surrounded by all its attendant abominations.

The great super-physical powers of the Asuras, now become Magicians of the darkest and most terrible type, imposed a reign of terror over the portion of the earth they swayed. The blackest practices of magic were resorted to, to terrorise and to crush. Aided by the half-animal women of the narrow-headed of the third Race, and by magical processes of unspeakable loathsome-ness, they produced powerful monsters, with the strength of the brute and the cunning of the savage; and ensouled these gruesome forms with the worst type of elementals. These became their guards and their messengers, the terrible symbols of their power, and the

Lord of the dark Face rose to the height of power, embodied ahamkara, veritable kings of Darkness.

Thus were all the forces of matter rallied round a single centre, while on the other side the White Emperor strengthened his forces to resist. In the higher spheres, preparations for the future were going on. Among the Sons of Light, several reached the supreme illumination, becoming Buddhas, a vast reserve of spiritual strength, ready for the uplifting of the world, after its plunge into matter. Two hundred thousand years had still to run their course before the great struggle, when the Dragons of Wisdom bade one of their number, Vaivasvata, choose out of the turbulent fifth sub-race, and lead them to the Imperishable Sacred Land, the cradle, as before said, of every Root Race. One million years have rolled away since the seeds of the fifth Race were thus separated out from the fourth. To that impregnable fortress were led successive emigrations of the Elect Race, to be guarded in safety though the coming tumults, far away from the scenes of strife. In that peaceful sunny land we may see Vaivasvata, presiding over His disciples and the infant, nay, embryonic Race. There is the future Zarathustra, the future Hermes, the future Orpheus, the future Gautama, the future Maitreya, with many another, watching over the growing seed. But we must turn away from that peaceful scene to the turmoil of the struggling fourth.

The armies of the Lords of the dark Face now began to advance northwards, and a long series of combats opened between these and the armies of the White Emperor. Now the dark, and now the white forces conquered, but the tide of victory set, none the less, northwards; for the cycle was against the triumph of Spirit, it was the time for the triumph of Matter. From every side flocked hosts to the banners of the Dark Lords, for they appealed to the passions of the animal side of man; fierce hatred arose against the clean living followers of the Good Law, the hatred ever felt by the luxurious for the "pale ascetic," the hatred of the unclean for those whose purity is a silent rebuke to themselves. Slowly, with ebb and flow, the tide rolled onwards; fierce combats, vast slaughters took place, but surely the dark forces won their way. At last the White emperor was driven from his capital, and the City of the Golden Gates, where divine Kings had ruled, sweetened by the feet of the Holy Ones, became the prey of the Lords of the Dark Face, and the Dark Emperor, the famous Hiranyaksha, was enthroned on the seat whence the Good Law had been proclaimed. The Cave of Initiation was found to be a heap of ruins, the great entrance pillars rent in twain, and the roof shivered into fragments; but in the Golden Temple, where a divine Priesthood had ministered, the blood of guiltless animals flowered in polluting streams, and the great statues of the dark magicians frowned where the Disk of the Sun had shone.

At last the cup of evil was full. Some 50,000 years had passed since the pollution of the Golden Temple; sorcery had spread in all directions, and the lowest stage of materiality had been reached. It was time that the earth should be relieved from the weight of cruelty, lust and oppression under which she was sinking.

The Dragons of Wisdom saw that the time was come, and that the forces of nature must be turned against "the dark brood of sorcerers. "From Shambhallah the word went forth, the signal for the overwhelming of the land, polluted beyond cleansing, and for the saving of any who would obey the summons to leave the doomed land. The Commentary tells the story: "And the 'great Kind of the Dazzling Face,' the Chief of all the yellow-faced, was sad, seeing the sins of the black-faced. He sent his air-vehicles to all his brother-chiefs, with pious men within, saying: 'Prepare. Arise, ye men of the Good Law, and cross the land while dry. The Lords of the Storm are approaching. Their chariots are nearing the land. One night and two days only shall the Lords of the Dark Face live on this patient land. She is doomed, and they have to descend with her. The nether Lords of the Fires are preparing their magic fire-weapons. But the Lords of the Dark Eye are stronger than they, and they are the slaves of the mighty ones. They are versed in weapons. Come and use yours. Let every Lord of the Dazzling Face cause the air-vehicle of every Lord of the Dark Face to come into his hands, lest any should, by its means, escape from the waters, avoid the rod of the Four, and save his wicked one. May every Yellow Face send sleep from himself to every Black Face. May even they avoid pain and suffering. May every man true to the Solar Gods bind every man under the Lunar Gods, lest he should suffer, on escape his destiny. And may every Yellow Face offer of his life-water to the speaking animal of the Black Face, lest he awaken his master. The hour has struck, the black night is ready.. . Let their destiny be accomplished. We are the servants of the great Four. May the Kings of Light return'... Stars showered on the lands of the Black Faces, but they slept. The speaking beasts kept quite. The nether Lords waited for orders, but they came not, for their masters slept. The waters arose, and covered the valleys from one end of the earth to the other. High lands remained, the bottom of the earth remained dry. There dwelt those who escaped; the men of the Yellow Faces and of the straight eye. When the Lords of the Dark Faces awoke and bethought themselves of their air-vehicles in order to escape from the rising waters, they found them gone. "

Such is a fragment of the story as told in the Commentary. The "speaking animals" are the monsters before mentioned, and the "life-water" is blood; the "men of the Good Law" escaped from the impending disaster, and then the storm broke. Furious blasts of air lifted the ocean billows into mountain-heights: underground convulsions hurled vast tidal waves on the rocking lands; deluges of rain swamped the valleys, and turned the rivers into cataracts; hills, riven by earth-quakes, were flung high in air, and fell in avalanches of fragments on the vales beneath; the earth itself seemed to shiver under the impacts of whirling waters and rushing rivers; the deafening roar of waters mingled with the cries of drowning men, the howls of drowning animals, and the glory of Atlantis sunk beneath the waters, leaving memories of a deluge that crept into the literature of nations, giving rise to many a legend and song in later years.

Thus was the earth relieved of her burden, and the Black Art received a blow from which it has never recovered. And the Asuras themselves received a lesson which wrought their redemption, and sent them onwards in evolution on a sure ascent.

The fourth sub-race, the Turanian, need not delay us; they were pre-eminently the Rakshasas, giants of a brutal and ferocious type, and their conflicts with the young fifth Race find much place in Indian Story. From the fifth sub-race, the Semitic, as we have seen, came the seeds of the fifth Race; they were a turbulent, fighting, people, and a branch of one of their families, selected by Vaivasvata Manu as the seed of the fifth Race, and rejected again because of its lack of plasticity, is the far-off ancestor of the Hebrew people.

The sixth sub-race, the Akkadian, was born after the catastrophe that destroyed two-thirds of the Toltec race - one third going north and later blending with the evolving fifth Race. The Pelasgians came from these, with some admixture of seventh sub-race blood. The Etruscans and Carthaginians derived from the same root, whence also the Scythians.

The seventh sub-race, the Mongolian, developed from the Turanian, the fourth sub-race, stock, and from this have descended the inland Chinese - not those of the coasts - the Malays, Tibetans, Hungarians, Finns and Esquimaux; some of their offshoots mixed with the Toltecs in North America, and thus the Red Indians have in them some Mongolian blood. The Japanese are one of their latest off-shoots. Many of this sub-race travelled westwards, settling down in Asia Minor, Greece, and adjoining countries; there, improved by intermixture of fifth Race blood, from the second sub-race of the fifth, they gave rise to the old Greeks and the Phoenicians.

After the disappearance of Poseidonis, the deterioration of the scattered Atlantean tribes was rapid, though the Atlanteans in the east of Asia held their own. The Polynesians, Samoans and Tongas are surviving relics. Some of the tribes even sank so low as to intermarry with the hybrid creatures that sprang from the sin of the mindless. Others intermarried with the degraded remnants of the seventh Lemurian sub-race, and the Veddahs of Ceylon are the descendants from such unions, as are the hairy men of Borneo, the Andaman Islanders, Bushmen, and some Australian aborigines. The majority of the inhabitants of the earth are still fourth Race people, but the only ones that seem to have future are the Japenese, and perhaps the Chinese.

Let us go northward now, northward to the Sacred Land, and see our Manu, the holy Vaivasvata, evolving, with infinite patience, His chosen Race. For ages upon ages He labors thee, He and His band of co-workers, shaping the nucleus of the future humanity, repressing the undesirable, stimulating the desirable, encouraging, warning, persuading, rebuking. There the fifth sense is added to the other four, and man is shaped as we know him now. Thither He guides for re-birth the great Asuras, to turn their powers to nobler ends. Thither He calls the brightest intelligences, the purest characters, to take re-birth in the forms He is evolving. And there they dwell under the Pole-Star far away from the tumults of earth, slowly shaping into a new and finer type.

Meanwhile the surface of the globe is under going-manifold changes of land sea. The new continent Krauncha, the Europe, Asia, Africa, America, Australia, of our own age, is not yet born: with many throes one portion after another is up-heaved and others are submerged, until the great convulsion of 200,000 years ago left Poseidonis alone in Mid-Atlantic, and the outlines of the great continents much as they are to-day. This fifth "continent" -meaning by this word all the land surface prepared for a Root Race - will, in the course of ages, perish by earthquakes and by volcanic fires, much as Lemuria perished in the elder days. For fire and water destroy the world in turns, and our world will perish by fire, as did Lemuria.

Under Budha - Mercury - was the fifth Race evolved, for the development of the mind was its chief work, and the planet of knowledge shed its beneficent rays upon its birth-hour. Hence, in pauranic story, is Budha said to be the son of Indu-Indu, the Moon, being the Lord of the fourth Race, the progenitor, and Budha of the fifth Race, the progeny.

When the Manu had established the type of His Race, He led them southward to Central Asia, and there another age-long halt was made, and the home of the Race, whence its several streams should issue, was established.

Then came the first great emigration, perhaps some 850,000 years ago; the first sub-race - often specifically called the Aryan, though the name applies to the whole fifth Race - was led southwards, across the mighty belt of the Himalayas, and settled in the northern India, in Aryavarta. At its head were the "seven Rshis," Marichi, Atri, Pulastya, Pulaha (?Kavi) Angiras (?Kratu,) Kardama, and Daksha - the names vary in different lists - who had long been guiding their evolution. In Manusmrti we find them given as above, save that Daksha is called Prachetas. With these were three, others, making up "ten Rshis," Vashishtha, Bhrgu and Narada. These led the sub-race into India, already built into the fourfold order by the Manu, the Barshishad Pitrs - as we saw, in studying physical evolution -having lent their aid in the shaping of the type of subtle body for each caste. We have not time to trace the long history of this great sub-race; moreover it is, more or less, known to all of you. Under its divine Kings, it warred against the peoples occupying the lands into which it came, Titans left from the third Race, Daityas and Rakshasas of the fourth. Who does not know the story of Ramachandra, warring against the Rakshasas under their mighty King, Ravana, and establishing His kingdom from the Himalayas to the southern sea? It must suffice us to recall that these Aryans received the Zodiac directly from the Sons of will and yoga, who came among them as Teachers - we are told of The Serpents who re-descended, who made peace with the fifth, who taught and instructed it, " that they had brought with them from Central Asia the Senzar language, the "secret sacerdotal tongue," the true "language of the Gods," from which Samskrt was derived, still the "mystery tongue" of Initiates; that among them arose the twenty-four Buddhas, still reverenced among the Jains as the twenty-four Tirthamkaras.

The second sub-race of the fifth Race, the Aryo-Semitic, migrated westwards from Central Asia, peopling Afghanistan, passing along the Oxus, and crossing the Euphrates into Arabia and Syria; these aryanised many of the Turanian and Akkadian tribes, dwelling along this route, and the great Empires of Assyria and Babylonia arose as the result of their impulse. The Phoenicians and the later Egyptians, and the old Greeks, arose from their intermixture with the seventh Atlantean sub-race, as has been already mentioned. "The last seven dynasties referred to in the Egyptian and Chaldean records," says H. P. B. belonged to the fifth Race. Some off-shoots of this Race travelled eastwards, and mingling with the Mongolian sub-race along the coasts of China, gave rise to the Chinese of the coasts, and also to the family which now sits on the Dragon Throne of China.

The third sub-race, the Iranian, led by Zarathushtra, went forth northwards and eastwards, following in the track of the second, but settling down for the most part in Afghanistan and Persia, the great Prophet dwelling in this latter country. Some wandered as far as Arabia and thence into Egypt, intermarrying there with the Egyptian Atlanteans.

Both these sub-races found the fourth Race people they settled among worshippers of Surya, the Sun, the priests bearing the name of Magas. These Magas claimed to have come from Shakudvipa, or Shvetadvipa, the White Island, and the claim was true enough, as regards their remote origin, for all true teaching was derived from the Dwellers in that Holy Land, whether the name be used for the Imperishable Sacred land, or, by substitution, for the Holy City, Shamballah, in the Gobi Desert. Taught by the Instructors of the second sub-race, these Empires followed Saboeanism, the worship of the Beings who rule the celestial bodies, the "Star-Angels," and the Chaldean worship rose to a splendid being of wisdom and purity, the Magi of Chaldea being astronomers and astrologers, versed profoundly in the science of the celestial bodies, and guiding the State by advice, based on a study of the stars.

The third sub-race, under its Instructors, headed by the first Zarathushtra - whose name descended to Teacher after Teacher, to the number of fourteen - was forbidden the worship of the Star-Angels, in consequence of the abuses which had arisen in connexion with it, and was given Fire as the sole permissible symbol of Deity. The wise men of Persia, often also called Magi, were followers more of chemistry than of astronomy, partly in consequence of its value in agriculture to which the Iranian sub-race was specially devoted. This led to a great development among them of alchemy, and many traces may be found in Egypt of their influence in this direction. The fourth sub-race, the Keltic, led by Orpheus, migrated westwards, beyond the track of its fore-runners, first peopling Greece with the later Greeks, and then spreading over Italy, northwards over France, still more northwards into the old Atlantean lands of Ireland and Scotland, and peopling also the younger land of England. It is interesting to notice how the familiar symbology of the Dragon and the Serpent, as names for high Initiates, appears among all these closely related peoples. The Hierophants of Babylon and of Egypt, the Druids, the Phoenicians, are all sons of the Dragon, or Serpents. The symbol came down from Atlantis, even from Lemura, and has ever been preserved, down to the fifth Race; and in Mexico, and scattered over America, it recurs, one of the universal symbols, belonging to the early Teachers of humanity.

The fifth sub-race, the Teutonic, also migrating westwards, occupied all Central Europe, and is now spreading over the world; it has occupied the greater part of North America, driving before it the old Atlantean stock; it has seized Australia and New Zealand, the remnants of still more ancient Lemuria and the poor relics of that dying Race are vanishing before it. High is it rearing its proud head over the countries of the globe, destined to build a world-wide Empire, and to sway the destinies of civilisation.

Yet it too shall pass away, as the ages roll on their course, and Krauncha shall follow Plaksha, Shalmali and Kusha. Then shall Shaka rise to be continent of the sixth Root Race, emerging where North America now is, most of that land having been previously broken up by earthquakes and subterranean fires. Shaka shall also pass away, whelmed under floods, as was Kusha, and Pushkara, the seventh continent, shall emerge and flourish, its centre about where South America is now to be found. And then will come the end of our globe, the close of its long and eventful history, and it will sink peacefully to sleep, after its long day of waking. For worlds pass away, and Round succeeds Round, and Chain follows Chain, but the eternal Spirit, who now clothes himself in human bodies, he, he alone, remains, and he endureth for ever.

PEACE TO ALL BEINGS

BOOK THREE
MAN AND HIS BODIES

(Theosophical Manual No. VII, 1912)

PREFACE

FEW words are needed in sending this little book out into the world. It is the seventh of a series of Manuals designed to meet the public demand for a simple exposition of theosophical teaching. Some have complained that our literature is at once too abstruse, too technical, and too expensive for the ordinary reader, and it is our hope that the present series may succeed in supplying what is a very real want. Theosophy is not only for the learned; it is for all. It may be that among those who in these little books catch their first glimpse of its teachings, there may be a few who will be led by them to penetrate more deeply into its philosophy, its science, and its religion, facing its abstruser problems with the student's zeal and the neophyte's ardour. But these manuals are not written for the eager student, whom no initial difficulties can daunt; they are written for the busy men and women of the work-a-day world, and seek to make plain some of the great truths that render life easier to bear and death easier to face. Written by servants of the Masters who are the Elder Brothers of our race, they can have no other object than to serve our fellow-men.

INTRODUCTION

So much confusion exists as to consciousness and its vehicles, the man and the garments that he wears, that it seems expedient to place before Theosophical students a plain statement of the facts so far as they are known to us. We have reached a point in our studies at which much that was at first obscure has become clear, much that was vague has become definite, much that was accepted as theory has become matter of first-hand knowledge. It is therefore possible to arrange ascertained facts in a definite sequence, facts which can be observed again and again as successive students develop the power of observation, and to speak on them with the same certainty as is felt by the physicist who deals with other observed and tabulated phenomena. But just as the physicist may err so may the metaphysicist, and as knowledge widens new lights are thrown on old facts, their relations are more clearly seen, and their appearance changes - often because the further light shows that the fact which seemed a whole was only a fragment. No authority is claimed for the views here presented; they are offered only as from a student to students, as an effort to reproduce what has been taught but has doubtless been very imperfectly apprehended, together with such results of the observations of pupils as their limited powers enable them to make.

At the outset of our study it is necessary that the Western reader should change the attitude in which he has been accustomed to regard himself, and that he should clearly distinguish between the man and the bodies in which the man dwells. We are too much in the habit of identifying ourselves with the outer garments that we wear, too apt to think of ourselves as though we were our bodies; and it is necessary, if we are to grasp a true conception of our subject, that we shall leave this point of view and shall cease to identify ourselves with casings that we put on for a time and again cast off, to put on fresh ones when we are again in need of such vestures. To identify ourselves with these bodies that have only a passing existence is really as foolish and as unreasonable as it would be to identify ourselves with our clothes; we are not dependent on them - their value is in proportion to their utility. The blunder so constantly made of identifying the consciousness, which is our Self, with the vehicles in which that consciousness is for the moment functioning, can only be excused by the fact that the waking consciousness, and to some extent the dream consciousness also, do live and work in the body and are not known apart from it to the ordinary man; yet an intellectual understanding of the real conditions may be gained, and we may train ourselves to regard our Self as the owner of his vehicle and after a time this will by experience become for a definite fact, when we learn to separate our Self from his bodies, to step out of the vehicle, and to know that we exist in a far fuller consciousness outside it then within it, and that we are in no sense dependent upon it; when that is once achieved, any further identification of our Self with our bodies is of course impossible, and we can never again make the blunder of supposing we are what we wear. The clear intellectual understanding at least is within the grasp of all of us, and we may train ourselves in the habitual distinguishment between the Self - the man - and his bodies; even to do this is to step out of the illusion in which the majority are wrapped, and changes our whole attitude towards life and towards the world, lifting us into a serener region above "the changes and chances of this mortal life," placing us above the daily petty troubles which loom so largely to embodied consciousness, showing us the true proportion between the ever-changing and the relatively permanent, and making us feel the difference between the drowning man tossed and buffeted by the waves that smother him, and the man whose feet are on a rock while the surges break harmlessly at its base.

By man I mean the living, conscious, thinking Self, the individual; by bodies, the various casings in which this Self is enclosed, each casing enabling the Self to function in some definite region of the universe. As a man might use a carriage on the land, a ship on the water, an aeroplane in the air, to travel from one place to another, and yet in all places remain himself, so does the Self, the real man, remain himself no matter in what body he is functioning; and as carriage, ship and aeroplane vary in materials and arrangement according to the element in which each is destined to move, so does each body vary according to the environment in which it is to act. One is grosser than another, one shorter-lived than another, one has fewer capacities than another; but all have this in common - that relatively to the man they are transient, his instruments, his servants, wearing out and renewed according to their nature, and adapted to his varying needs, his growing powers. We will study them one by one, beginning with the lowest, and then take the man himself, the actor in all the bodies.

I. THE PHYSICAL BODY

Under the term physical body must be included the two lower principles of man - called in our old terminology the Sthūla Sharīra and Linga Sharīra - since they both function on the physical plane, are composed of physical matter, are formed for the period of one physical life, are cast off by the man at death, and disintegrate together in the physical world when he passes on into the astral.

Another reason for classing these two principles as our physical body or physical vehicle is that so long as we cannot pass out of the physical world - or plane, we are accustomed to call it - we are using one or other or both of these physical vestures; they both belong to the physical plane by their materials, and cannot pass outside it; consciousness working in them is bound within their physical limitations, and is subject to the ordinary laws of space and time. Although partially separable, they are rarely separated during earthly life and such separation is inadvisable and is always a sign of disease or of ill-balanced constitution.

They are distinguishable by the materials of which they are composed into the gross body and the etheric double, the latter being the exact duplicate of the visible body, particle for particle, and the medium through which play all the electrical and vital currents on which the activity of the body depends. This etheric double has hitherto been called the Linga Sharīra, but it seems advisable, for several reasons, to put an end to the use of the name in this relation. "Linga Sharīra" has from time immemorial been used in Hindu books in another sense, and much confusion arises among students of Eastern literature, whether Easterns or Westerns, in consequence of its arbitrary wresting from its recognized meaning; for this reason, if for no other, it would be well to surrender its improper use. Further, it is better to have English names for the subdivisions of the human constitution, and thus remove from our elementary literature the stumbling block to beginners of a Sanskrit terminology. Also, the name etheric double exactly expresses the nature and constitution of the subtler portion of the physical body, and is thus significant and therefore easy to remember, as every name should be; it is "etheric" because made of ether, "double" because an exact duplicate of the gross body - its shadow, as it were.

Now physical matter has seven subdivisions, distinguishable from each other, and each showing a vast variety of combinations within its own limits. The subdivisions are: solid, liquid, gas, ether, the latter having four conditions as distinct from each other as liquids are distinct from solids and gases. These are the seven states of physical matter, and any portion of such matter is capable of passing into any one of these states, although under what we call normal temperature and pressure it will assume one or other of these as its relatively permanent condition, as gold is ordinarily solid, water is ordinarily liquid, chlorine is ordinarily gaseous. The physical body of man is composed of matter in these seven states - the gross body consisting of solids, liquids and gases; and the etheric double of the four subdivisions of ether, known respectively as Ether I, Ether II, Ether III, and Ether IV.

When the higher Theosophical truths are put before people, we find them constantly complaining that they are too much in the clouds, and asking: "Where ought we to begin? If we want to learn for ourselves and prove the truth of the assertions made, how are we to start? What are the first steps that we should take? What, in fact, is the alphabet of this language in which Theosophists discourse so glibly? What ought we to do, we men and women living in the world, in order to understand and verify these matters, instead of merely taking them on trust from others who say they know?" I am going to try to answer that question in the following pages, so that those who are really in earnest may see the earlier practical steps they ought to take - it being always understood that these steps must belong to a life, the moral, intellectual and spiritual parts of which are also under training. Nothing that a man can do to the physical body alone will turn him into a seer or a saint; but it is also true that inasmuch as the body is an instrument that we have to use, certain treatment of the body is necessary in order that we may turn our footsteps in the direction of the Path; while dealing with the body only will never take us to the heights to which we aspire, still to let the body alone will make it impossible for us to scale those heights at all. The bodies in which he has to live and work are the instruments of the man, and the very first thing we have to realize is this: that the body exists for us, not we for the body; the body is ours to use - we do not belong to it to be used by it. The body is an instrument which is to be refined, to be improved, to be trained, to be moulded into such a form and made of such constituents as may best fit it to be the instrument on the physical plane for the highest purposes of the man. Everything which tends in that direction is to be encouraged and cultivated; everything which goes contrary to it is to be avoided. It does not matter what wishes the body may have, what habits it may have contracted in the past, the body is ours, our servant, to be employed as we desire, and the moment it takes the reins into its own hands and claims to guide the man instead of being guided by the man, at that moment the whole purpose of life is subverted, and any kind of progress is rendered utterly impossible.

Here is the point from which any person who is in earnest must start. The very nature of the physical body makes it a thing which can be turned fairly easily into a servant or an instrument. It has certain peculiarities which help us in training it and make it comparatively easy to guide and mould, and one of these peculiarities is that when once it has been accustomed to work along particular lines it will very readily continue to follow those lines of its own accord, and will be quite as happy in doing so as it was previously in going along others. If a bad habit has been acquired, the body will make considerable resistance to any change in that habit; but if it be compelled to alter, if the obstacle it places in the way be overcome, and if it be forced to act as the man desires, then after a short time the body will of its own accord repeat the new habit that the man has imposed on it, and will as contentedly pursue the new method as it pursued the old one to which the man found reason to object.

Let us now turn to the consideration of the dense body that we may roughly call the visible part of the physical body, though the gaseous constituents are not visible to the untrained physical eye. This is the most outward garment of the man, his lowest manifestation, his most limited and imperfect expression of himself.

The Dense Body. — We must delay sufficiently long on the constitution of the body to enable us to understand how it is that we can take this body, purify it, and train it; we must glance at a set of activities which are for the most part outside the control of the will, and then at those which are under that control. Both of these work by means of nervous systems, but by nervous systems of different kinds. One carries on all the activities of the body which maintain its ordinary life, by which the lungs contract, by which the heart pulsates, by which the movements of the digestive system are directed. This is composed of the involuntary nerves, commonly called the "sympathetic system. " At one time during the long past of physical evolution during which our bodies were built, this system was under the control of the animal possessing it, but gradually it began to work automatically - it passed away from the control of the will, took on its own quasi-independence and carried on all the normal vital activities of the body. While a person is in health, he does not notice these activities; he knows that he breathes when the breathing is oppressed or checked, he knows that his heart beats when the beating is violent or irregular, but when all is in order these processes go on unnoticed. It is, however, possible to bring the sympathetic nervous system under the control of the will by long and painful practice, and a class of Yogi in India - Hatha Yogis they are called - develop this power to an extraordinary degree, with the object of stimulating the lower psychic faculties. It is possible to evolve these (without any regard to spiritual, moral or intellectual growth) by direct action on the physical body. The Hatha Yogi learns to control his breathing even to the point of suspension for a considerable period to control the beating of his heart, quickening or retarding the circulation at will, and by these means to throw the physical body into a trance and set free the astral body. The method is not one to be emulated; but still it is instructive for Western nations (who are apt to regard the body as of such imperative nature) to know how thoroughly a man can bring under his control these normally automatic physical processes, and to realize that thousands of men impose on themselves a long and exquisitely painful discipline in order to see themselves free from the prison-house of the physical body, and to know that they live when the animation of the body is suspended. They are at least in earnest, and are no longer the mere slaves of the senses.

Passing from this we have the voluntary nervous system, one far more important for our mental purposes. This is the great system which is our instrument of thought, by which we feel and move on the physical plane. It consists of the cerebro-spinal axis - the brain and spinal cord - whence go to every part of the body filaments of nervous matter, the sensory and motor nerves - the nerves by which we feel running from the periphery to the axis, and the nerves by which we move running from the axis to the periphery. From every part of the body the nerve-threads run, associating with each other to make bundles, these proceeding to join the spinal cord, forming its external fibrous substance, and passing upwards to spread out and ramify in the brain, the centre of all feeling and all purposive motion controllable by the will. This is the system through which the man expresses his will and his consciousness, and these may be said to be seated in the brain. The man can do nothing on the physical plane except through the brain and nervous system; if these be out of order, he can no longer express himself in orderly fashion. Here is the fact on which materialism has based its contention that thought and brain-action vary together; dealing with the physical plane only, as the materialist is dealing, they do vary together, and it is necessary to bring in forces from another plane, the astral, in order to show that thought is not the result of nervous actions. If the brain be affected by drugs, or by disease, or by injury, the thought of the man to whom the brain belongs can no longer find its due expression on the physical plane. The materialist will also point out that if you have certain diseases, thought will be peculiarly affected There is a rare disease, aphasia, which destroys a particular part of the tissue of the brain, near the ear, and is accompanied by a total loss of memory so far as words are concerned; if you ask a person who is suffering from this disease a question, he cannot answer you; if you ask him his name, he will give you no reply; but if you speak his name he will show recognition of it, if you read him some statement he will signify assent or dissent; he is able to think, but unable to speak. I seems as though the part of the brain that has been eaten away were connected with the physical memory of words, so that with the loss of that the man loses on the physical plane the memory of words and is rendered dumb, while he retains the power of thought and can agree or disagree with any proposition made. The materialistic argument at once breaks down, of course, when the man is set free from his imperfect instrument; he is then able to manifest his powers, though he is again crippled when reduced once more to physical expression. The importance of this as regards our present inquiry lies not in the validity or invalidity of the materialistic position, but in the fact that the man is limited in his expression on the physical plane by the capabilities of his physical instrument, and that this instrument is susceptible to physical agents; if these can injure it they can also improve it - a consideration which we shall find to be of vital importance to us.

These nervous systems, like every part of the body, are built up of cell, small definite bodies, with enclosing wall and contents, visible under the microscope, and modified according to their various functions; these cells in their turn are made up of small molecules, and these again of atoms - the atoms of the chemist, each atom being his ultimate indivisible particle of a chemical element. These chemical atoms combine together in innumerable ways to form the gases, the liquids, and the solids of the dense body. Each chemical atom is to the Theosophist a living thing capable of leading its independent life, and each combination of such atoms into a more complex being is again a living thing; also each cell has a life of its own, and all these chemical atoms and molecules and cells are combined together into an organic whole, a body, to serve as vehicle of a loftier form of consciousness than any which they know in their separated lives. Now, the particles of which these bodies are composed are constantly coming and going, these particles being aggregations of chemical atoms too minute to be visible to the naked eye, though many of them are visible under the microscope. If a little blood be put under the microscope, we see moving in it a number of living bodies, the white and red corpuscles, the white being closely similar in structure and activity to ordinary amoebas; in connection with many diseases microbes are found, bacilli of various kinds, and scientists tell us that we have in our bodies friendly and unfriendly microbes, some that injure and others that pounce upon and devour deleterious intruders and effete matter. Some microbes come to us from without that ravage our bodies with disease, others that promote their health, and so these garments of ours are continually changing their materials, which come and stay for a while, and go away to form parts of other bodies - a continual change and interplay.

Now, the vast majority of mankind know little and care less for these facts, and yet on them hinges the possibility of the purification of the dense body, thus rendering it a fitter vehicle for the indwelling man The ordinary person lets his body build itself up anyhow out of the materials supplied to it, without regard to their nature, caring only that they shall be palatable and agreeable to his desires, and not whether they be suitable or unsuitable to the making of a pure and noble dwelling for the Self, the true man that liveth for ever more. He exercises no supervision over these particle as they come and go, selecting none, rejecting none, but letting everything build itself in as it lists, like a careless mason who should catch up any rubbish as materials for his house, floating wool and hairs, mud, chips, sand, nails, offal, filth of any kind - the veriest jerry-builde is the ordinary man with his body. The purifying of the dense body will then consist in a process of deliberate selection of the particles permitted to compose it; the man will take into it in the way of food the purest constituents he can obtain, rejecting the impure and the gross; he knows that by natural change the particles built into it in the days of his careless living will gradually pass away, at least within seven years - though the process may be considerably hastened - and he resolves to build in no more that are unclean; as he increases the pure constituents he makes in his body an army of defenders, that destroy any foul particles that may fall upon it from without or enter it without his consent; and he guards it further by an active will that it shall be pure, which, acting magnetically, continually drives away from his vicinity all unclean creatures that would fain enter his body, and thus shields it from the inroads to which it is liable, while living in an atmosphere impregnated with uncleannesses of every kind.

When a man thus resolves to purify the body and to make it into an instrument fit for the Self to work with, he takes the first step towards the practice of Yoga - a step which must be taken in this or in some other life before he can seriously ask the question, "How can I learn to verify for myself the truths of Theosophy?" All personal verification of superphysical facts depends on the complete subjection of the physical body to its owner, the man; he has to do the verification, and he cannot do it while he is fast bound within the prison of the body, or while that body is impure. Even should he have brought over from better-disciplined lives partially developed psychic faculties, which show themselves despite present unfavourable circumstances, the use of these will be hampered when he is in the physical body, if that body be impure; it will dull or distort the exercise of the faculties when they play through it, and render their reports untrustworthy.

Let us suppose that a man deliberately chooses that he will have a pure body, and that he either takes advantage of the fact that his body completely changes in seven years, or prefers the shorter and more difficult path of changing it more rapidly - in either case he will begin at once to select the materials from which the new clean body is to be built, and the question of diet will present itself. He will immediately begin to exclude from his food all kinds which will build into his body particles which are impure and polluting. He will strike off all alcohol, and every liquor which contains it, because that brings into his physical body microbes of the most impure kinds, products of decomposition; these are not only offensive in themselves, but they attract towards themselves - and therefore towards any body of which they form part - some of the most objectionable of the physically invisible inhabitants of the next plane. Drunkards who have lost their physical bodies, and can therefore no longer satisfy their longing for intoxicants, hang round places where drink is taken, and round those who take it, endeavouring to push themselves into the bodies of people who are drinking, and thus to share the low pleasure to which they surrender themselves. Women of refinement would shrink from their wines if they could see the loathly creatures who seek to partake in their enjoyment, and the close connection which they thus set up with beings of the most repellent type. Evil elementals also cluster round the thoughts of drunkards clad in elemental essence, while the physical body attracts to itself from the surrounding atmosphere other gross particles given off from drunken and profligate bodies, and these also are built into it, coarsening and degrading it. If we look at people who are constantly engaged with alcohol, in manufacturing or distributing spirits, wines, beers, and other kinds of unclean liquors, we can see physically how their bodies have become gross and coarse. A brewer's man, a publican - to say nothing of persons in all ranks of society who drink to excess - these show fully what everyone who builds into his body any of these particles is doing in part and slowly; the more of these he builds in, the coarser will his body become. And so with other articles of diet, flesh of mammals, birds, reptiles and fish, with that of crustaceous creatures and mollusks which feed on carrion - how should bodies made of such materials be refined, sensitive, delicately balanced and yet perfectly healthy, with the strength and fineness of tempered steel, such as the man needs for all the higher kinds of work? Is it necessary again to add the practical lesson that may be learned by looking at the bodies of those living in such surroundings? See the slaughterman and the butcher, and judge if their bodies look like the fittest instruments for employment on high thoughts and lofty spiritual themes. Yet they are only the highly finished products of the forces that work proportionately in all bodies that feed on the impure viands they supply. True, no amount of attention paid to the physical body by the man will of itself give him spiritual life, but why should he hamper himself with an impure body? Why should he allow his powers, whether great or small, to be limited, thwarted, dwarfed in their attempts to manifest by this needlessly imperfect instrument?

There is, however, one difficulty in our way that we cannot overlook; we may take a good deal of pains with the body and may resolutely refuse to befoul it, but we are living among people who are careless and who for the most part know nothing of these facts in nature. In a town like London, or indeed in any Western town, we cannot walk through streets without being offended at every turn, and the more we refine the body the more delicately acute do the physical senses become, and the more we must suffer in a civilization so coarse and animal as is the present. Walking through the poorer and the business streets, where there are beerhouses at every corner, we can scarcely ever escape the smell of drink, the effluvium from one drinking-place overlapping that from the next - even reputedly respectable streets being thus poisoned; so, too, we have to pass slaughter-houses and butchers' shops. Of course one knows that when civilization is a little more advanced better arrangements will be made, and something will be gained when all these unclean things are gathered in special quarters where those can seek them who want them. But meanwhile particles from these places fall on our bodies, and we breathe them in with the air. But as the normally healthy body gives no soil in which disease-microbes can germinate, so the clean body offers no soil in which these impure particles can grow. Besides, as we have seen, there are armies of living creatures that are always at work keeping our blood pure, and these regiments of true lifeguards will charge down upon any poisonous particle that comes into the city of a pure body and will destroy it and cut it to pieces. For us it is to choose whether we will have in our blood these defenders of life, or whether we will people it with the pirates that plunder and slay the good. The more resolutely we refuse to put into the body anything that is unclean, the more shall we be fortified against attacks from without.

Reference has already been made to the automatism of the body, to the fact that it is a creature of habit, and I said that use could be made of this peculiarity. If the Theosophist says to some aspirant who would fain practise Yoga and win entrance to higher planes being: "You must then begin at once to purify the body, and this must precede the attempt to practise a Yoga worthy of the name; for real Yoga is as dangerous to an impure and undisciplined body as a match to a cask of gunpowder"; if the Theosophist should thus speak, he would very probably be met with the answer that health would suffer if such a course were to be adopted. As a dry matter of fact the body does very much care in the long run what you give it, provided that you give it something that will keep it in health; and it will accommodate itself in a short time to a form of pure and nutritious food that you choose to adopt. Just because it is an automatic creature, it will soon stop asking for things that are steadily withheld from it, and if you disregard its demands for the coarse and ranker kinds of food it will soon get into the habit of disliking them. Just as even a moderately natural palate will shrink with a sickening feeling of disgust from the decaying game and venison if yclept[1] "high", so a pure taste will revolt against all coarse foods. Suppose that a man has been feeding his body with various kinds of unclean things, his body will demand them imperiously, and he will be inclined to yield to it; but if he pays no attention to it, and goes his own way and not the way of the body, he will find, perhaps to his surprise, that his body will soon recognize its master and will accommodate itself to his orders; presently it will begin to prefer the things that he gives it, and will set up a liking for clean foods and a distaste for unclean. Habit can be used for help as well as for hindrance, and the body yields when it understands that you are the master and that you do not intend the purpose of your life to be interfered with by the mere instrument that is yours for use. The truth is that it is not the body which is chiefly in fault, but Kama, the desire-nature. The adult body has got into the habit of demanding particular things, but if you notice a child, you will find that the child's body does not spontaneously make demands for the things on which adult bodies feast with coarse pleasure; the child's body, unless it has a very bad physical heredity, shrinks from meat and wine, but its elders force meat on it, and the father and mother give it sips of wine from their glasses at dessert, and bid it "be a little man," till the child by its own imitative faculty and by the compulsion of others is turned into evil ways. Then, of course, impure tastes are made, and perhaps old kamic cravings are awakened which might have been starved out, and the body will gradually form the habit of demanding the things upon which it has been fed. Despite all this in the past, make the change, and as you get rid of the particles that crave these impurities you will feel your body altering its

---

[1] Archaic English, meaning 'called' or 'named'

habits and revolting against the very smell of the things that it used to enjoy. The real difficulty in the way of the reformation lies in Kāma, not in the body. You do not want to do it; if you did, you would do it. You say to yourself: "After all, perhaps it does not matter so much; I have no psychic faculties, I am not advanced enough for this to make any difference. " You will never become advanced if you do not endeavour to live up to the highest that is within your reach - if you allow the desire-nature to interfere with your progress. You say, "How much I should like to possess astral vision, to travel in the astral body!" but when it comes to the point you prefer a "good" dinner. If the prize for giving up unclean food were a million pounds at the end of a year, how rapidly would difficulties disappear and ways be found for keeping the body alive without meat and wine! But when only the priceless treasures of the higher life are offered, the difficulties are insuperable. If men really desired what they pretend to desire, we should have much more rapid changes around us than we now see. But they make believe, and make believe so effectually that they deceive themselves into the idea that they are in earnest, and they come back life after life to live in the same unprogressive manner for thousands of years; and then in some particular life they wonder why they do not advance, and why somebody else has male such rapid progress in this one life while they make none. The man who is in earnest - not spasmodically but with steady persistence - can make what progress he chooses; while the man who is making believe will run round and round the mill-path for many a life to come.

Here, at any rate, in this purification of the body lies the preparation for all Yoga practice - not the whole preparation most certainly, but an essential part of it. This much must suffice as to the dense body, the lowest vehicle of consciousness.

The Etheric Double. — Modern physical science holds that all bodily changes, whether in the muscles, cells, or nerves, are accompanied by electric action, and the same is probably true even of the chemical changes which are continually going on. Ample evidence of this has been accumulated by careful observations with the most delicate galvanometers. Whenever electric action occurs ether must be present, so that the presence of the current is proof of the presence of the ether, which interpenetrates all, surrounds all; no particle of physical matter is in contact with any other particle, but each swings in a field of ether. The Western scientist asserts as a necessary hypothesis that which the trained pupil in East science asserts as a verifiable observation, for as matter of fact ether is as visible as a chair or a table, only a sight different from the normal physical is need to see it. As has already been said, it exists in four modifications, the finest of these consisting of the ultimate physical atoms - not the so-called chemical atom which is really a complex body - ultimate, because they yield astral matter on disintegration. [2]

The etheric double is composed of these four ethers which interpenetrate the solid, liquid and gaseous constituents of the dense body, surrounding every particle with an etheric envelope, and thus presenting a perfect duplicate of the denser form. This etheric double is perfectly visible to the trained sight, and is violet-grey in colour, coarse or fine in its texture as dense body is coarse or fine. The four ethers enter into it, as solids, liquids and gases enter into the composition of the dense body, but they can be in coarser or finer combinations just as can the denser constituents; it is important to notice that the dense body and its etheric double vary together as to their quality, so that as the aspirant deliberately and consciously refines his dense body, the etheric double follows suit without his consciousness and without any additional effort. [3]

It is by means of the etheric double that the life-force, Prâna, runs along the nerves of the body and thus enables them to act as the carriers of motor force and of sensitiveness to external impacts. The powers of thought, of movement and of feeling are not resident in physical or ether nerve-substance; they are activities of the Ego working in his inner bodies, and the expression of them on the physical plane is rendered possible by the life-breath as it runs along the nerve-threads and round the nerve-cells; for Prâna, the life-breath, is the active energy of the Self, as Shri Shankaracharya has taught us. The function of the etheric double is to serve as the physical medium for this energy, and hence it is often spoken of in our literature as the "vehicle of Prâna".

It may be useful to note that the etheric double is peculiarly susceptible to the volatile constituents of alcohols.

---

[2] See *Occult Chemistry* by Annie Besant and C. W. Leadbeater
[3] On looking at a man's lower bodies with astral vision, the etheric double (Linga Sharīra) and the astral body (kâmic body) are seen interpenetrating each other, as both interpenetrate the dense physical, and hence some confusion has arisen in the past and the names Linga Sharīra and astral body have been used interchangeably, while the latter name has also been used for the kâmic or desire-body. This loose terminology has caused much trouble, as the functions of the kâmic body, termed the astral body, have often been understood as the functions of the etheric double, also termed the astral body, and the student, unable to see for himself, has been hopelessly entangled in apparent contradictions. Careful observations on the formation of these two bodies now enable us to say definitely that the etheric double is composed of the physical ethers only, and cannot, if extruded leave the physical plane or go far away from its denser counterpart; further, that it is built after the mould given by the Lords of Karma, and is not brought with him by the Ego, but awaits him with the physical body formed upon it. The astral or kâmic body, the desire-body, on the other hand, is composed of astral matter only, is able to range the astral plane when freed from the physical body, and is the proper vehicle of the Ego on that plane; it is brought with him by the Ego when he comes to re-incarnate. Under these circumstances it is better to call the first the etheric double, and the second the astral body, and so avoid confusion.

Phenomena connected with the Physical Body. — When a person "goes to sleep" the Ego slips out of the physical body, and leaves it to slumber and so to recuperate itself for the next day's work. The dense body and its etheric double are thus left to their own devices, and to the play of the influences which they attract to themselves by their constitution and habits. Streams of thought-forms from the astral world of a nature congruous with the thought-forms created or harboured by the Ego in his daily life, pass into and out of the dense and etheric brains, and, mingling with the automatic repetitions of vibrations set up in waking consciousness by the Ego, cause the broken and chaotic dreams with which most people are familiar. These broken images are instructive as showing the working of the physical body when it is left to itself; it can only reproduce fragments of past vibrations without rational order or coherence, fitting them together as they are thrown up, however grotesquely incongruous they may be; it is insensible to absurdity or irrationality, content with a phantasmagoria of kaleidoscopic shapes and colours, without even the regularity given by the kaleidoscope mirrors. Looked at in this way, the dense and etheric brains are readily recognized as instruments of thought, not as creators thereof, for we see how very erratic are their creations, when they are left to themselves.

In sleep the thinking Ego slips out of these two bodies, or rather this one body with its visible and invisible parts, leaving them together; in death it slips out for the last time, but with this difference, that it draws out the etheric double with it, separating it from its dense counterpart and thus rendering impossible any further play of the life-breath in the latter as an organic whole. The Ego quickly shakes off the etheric double, which, as we have seen, cannot pass on to the astral plane, and leaves it to disintegrate with its lifelong partner. It will sometimes appear immediately after death to friends at no great distance from the corpse, but naturally shows very little consciousness, and will not speak or do anything beyond "manifesting" itself. It is comparatively easily seen, being physical, and a slight tension of the nervous system will render vision sufficiently acute to discern it. It is also responsible for many "churchyard ghosts," as it hovers over the grave in which its physical counterpart is lying, and is more readily visible than astral bodies for the reason just given. Thus even "in death they are not divided" by more than a few feet of space.

For the normal man it is only at death that this separation takes place, but some abnormal people of the type called mediumistic are subject to a partial division of the physical body during earth-life, a dangerous and fortunately a comparatively rare abnormality which gives rise to much nervous strain and disturbance. When the etheric double is extruded the double itself is rent in twain; the whole of it could not be separated from the dense body without causing the death of the latter, since the currents of the life-breath need its presence for their circulation. Even its partial withdrawal reduces the dense body to a state of lethargy, and the vital activities are almost suspended; extreme exhaustion follows the re-uniting of the severed parts, and the condition of the medium until the normal union is reestablished is one of considerable physical danger. The greater number of the phenomena that occur in the presence of mediums are not connected with this extrusion of the etheric double, but some who have been distinguished for the remarkable character of the materializations which they have assisted in producing offer this peculiarity to observation. I am informed that Mr. Eglinton exhibited this curious physical dissociation to a rare extent, and that his etheric double might be seen oozing from his left side, while his dense body shrivelled perceptibly; and that the same phenomenon has been observed with Mr. Husk, whose dense body became too reduced to fill out his clothes. Mr. Eglinton's body once was so diminished in size that a materialized form carried it out and presented it for the inspection of the sitters - one of the few cases in which both medium and materialized form have been visible together in light sufficient to allow of examination. This shrinkage of the medium seems to imply the removal of some of the denser "ponderable" matter from the body - very possibly part of the liquid constituents - but, so far as I am aware, no observations have been made on this point, and it is therefore impossible to speak with any certainty. What is certain is that this partial extrusion of the etheric double results in much nervous trouble, and that it should not be practised by any sensible person if he finds that he is unfortunate enough to be liable to it.

We have now studied the physical body both in its dense and etheric parts, the vesture which the Ego must wear for his work on the physical plane, the dwelling which may be either his convenient office for physical work, or his prison-house of which death alone holds the key. We can see what we ought to have and what we can gradually make - a body perfectly healthy and strong, and at the same time delicately organized refined and sensitive. Healthy it should be - and in the East health is insisted on as a condition of discipleship - for everything that is unhealthy in the body mars it as an instrument of the Ego, and is apt to distort both the impressions sent inwards and the impulses sent outwards. The activities of the Ego are hindered if his instrument be strained or twisted by ill-health. Healthy then, delicately organized, refined, sensitive, repelling automatically all evil influences, automatically receptive of all good - such a body we should deliberately build choosing among all the things that surround us those that conduce to that end, knowing that the task can be accomplished only gradually, but working on patiently and steadily with that object in view. We shall know when we are beginning to succeed even to a very limited extent, for we shall find opening up in us all kinds of powers of perception that we did not before possess We shall find ourselves becoming more sensitive to sounds and sights, to fuller, softer, richer harmonies, to tenderer, fairer, lovelier hues. Just as the painter trains his eye to see the delicacies of colour to which common eyes are blind; just as the musician trains his ear to hear overtones of notes to which common ears are deaf so may we train our bodies to be receptive to the finer vibrations of life missed by ordinary men. True, many unpleasant sensations will come, for the world we are living in is rendered rough and coarse by the humanity that dwells in it: but, on the other hand, beauties will reveal themselves that will repay us a hundred-fold for the difficulties we face and overcome. And this, not that we may possess such bodies for selfish purposes either of vanity or of enjoyment, but in order that we, the men who own them, may own them for wider usefulness, for added strength to serve. They will be more efficient instruments with which to help the progress of humanity, and so more fit to aid in that task of forwarding human evolution which is the work of our great Masters, and in which it may be our privilege to co-operate.

Although we have been only on the physical plane throughout this part of our subject, we may yet see that the study is not without importance, and that the lowest of the vehicles of consciousness needs our attention and will repay our care. These cities of ours, this land of ours, will be cleaner, fairer, better, when this knowledge has become common knowledge, and when it is accepted not only as intellectually probable, but as a law of daily life.

II. THE ASTRAL OR DESIRE BODY

We have studied the physical body of man both as to its visible and invisible parts, and we understand that man - the living, conscious entity - in his "waking" consciousness, living in the physical world, can only show so much of his knowledge and manifest so much of his powers as he is able to express through his physical body. According to the perfection or imperfection of its development will be the perfection or imperfection of his expression on the physical plane; it limits him while he functions in the lower world, forming a veritable "ring pass-not" around him. That which cannot pass through it cannot manifest on earth, and hence its importance to the developing man. In the same way when the man is functioning without the physical body in another region of the universe, the astral plane or astral world, he is able to express on that plane just so much of his knowledge and his powers, of himself in short, as his astral body enables him to put forth. It is at once his vehicle and his limitation. The man is more than his bodies; he has in him much that he is unable to manifest either on the physical or on the astral plane; but so much as he is able to express may be taken as the man himself in that particular region of the universe. What he can show of himself down here is limited by the physical body; what he can show of himself in the astral world is limited by the astral body; so we shall find as we rise to higher worlds in our study, that more and more of the man is able to express itself as he himself develops in his evolution, and also gradually brings towards perfection higher and higher vehicles of consciousness.

It may be well to remind the reader, as we are entering on fields comparatively untrodden and to the majority unknown, that no claim is here put forward to infallible knowledge or to perfect power of observation. Errors of observation and of inference may be made on planes above the physical as well as on the physical, and this possibility should always be kept in mind. As knowledge increases and training is prolonged, more and more accuracy will be reached, and such errors will thus gradually be eliminated. But as the writer is only a student, mistakes are likely to be made and to need correction in the future. They may creep in on matters of detail, but will not touch the general principles nor vitiate the main conclusions.

First, let the meaning of the words astral plane or astral world be clearly grasped. The astral world is a definite region of the universe, surrounding and interpenetrating the physical, but imperceptible to our ordinary observation because it is composed of a different order of matter. If the ultimate physical atom be taken and broken up, it vanishes so far as the physical world is concerned; but it is found to be composed of numerous particles of the grossest kind of astral matter – the solid matter of the astral world. [4] We have found seven sub-states of physical matter - solid, liquid, gaseous, and four etheric - under which are classified the innumerable combinations which make up the physical world. In the same

---

[4] The word "astral", starry, is not a very happy one, but it has been used during so many centuries to denote super-physical matter that it would now be difficult to dislodge it. It was probably at first chosen by observers in consequence of the luminous appearance of astral as compared with physical matter. The student is advised to read, on this whole subject, Manual No. V., *The Astral Plane*, by C. W. Leadbeater.

way we have seven sub-states of astral matter corresponding to the physical, and under these may be classified the innumerable combinations which similarly make up the astral world. All physical atoms have their astral envelopes, the astral matter thus forming what may be called the matrix of the physical, the physical being embedded in the astral. The astral matter serves as a vehicle for Jīva, the One Life animating all, and by means of the astral matter currents of Jīva surround, sustain, nourish every particle of physical matter, the currents of Jīva giving rise not only to what a popularly called vital forces, but also to all electric, magnetic, chemical, and other energies, attraction, cohesion, repulsion and the like, all of which are differentiations of the One Life in which universes swim as fishes in the sea. From the astral world, thus intimately interpenetrating the physical, Jīva passes to the ether of the latter, which then becomes the vehicle of all these forces to the lower sub-states of physical matter, wherein we observe their play. If we imagine the physical world to be struck out of existence without any other change being made, we should still have a perfect replica of it in astral matter; and if we further imagine everyone to be dowered with working astral faculties, men and women would at first be unconscious of any difference in their surroundings; "dead" people who wake up in the lower regions of the astral world often find themselves in such a state and believe themselves to be yet living in the physical world. As most of us have not yet developed astral vision, it is necessary to enforce this relative reality of the astral world as a part of the phenomenal universe, and to see it with the mental eye, if not with the astral. It is as real as - in fact, not being quite so far removed from the One Reality, it is more real than - the physical; its phenomena are open to competent observation like those of the physical plane. Just as down here a blind man cannot see physical objects, and as many things can only be observed with the help of apparatus - the microscope, spectroscope, etc. - so is it with the astral plane. Astrally blind people cannot see astral objects at all, and many things escape ordinary astral vision, or clairvoyance. But at the present stage of evolution many people could develop the astral senses and are developing them to some extent, thus enabling themselves to receive the subtler vibrations of the astral plane. Such persons are indeed liable to make many mistakes, as a child makes mistakes when he begins to use physical senses, but these mistakes are corrected by wider experience, and after a time they can see and hear as accurately on the astral as on the physical plane. It is not desirable to force this development by artificial means, for until some amount of physical strength has been evolved the physical world is about as much as can conveniently be managed, and the intrusion of astral sights, sounds and general phenomena is apt to be disturbing and even alarming. But the time comes when this stage is reached and when the relative reality of the astral part of the invisible world is borne in upon the waking consciousness.

For this it is necessary not only to have an astral body, as we all of us have, but to have it fully organized and in working order, the consciousness being accustomed to act in it, not only to act through it on the physical body. Everyone is constantly working through the astral body, but comparatively few work in it separated from the physical. Without the general action through the astral body there would be no connection between the external world and the mind of man, no connection between impacts made on the physical senses and the perception of them by the mind. The impact becomes a sensation in the astral body, and is then perceived by the mind. The astral body, in which are the centres of sensation, is often spoken of as the astral man, just as we might call the physical body the physical man; but it is of course only a vehicle - a sheath, as the Vedāntin would call it - in which the man himself is functioning, and through which he reaches, and is reached by, the grosser vehicle, the physical body.

As to the constitution of the astral body, it is made up of the seven sub-states of astral matter, and may have coarser or finer materials drawn from each of these. It is easy to picture a man in a well-formed astral body; you can think of him as dropping the physical body and standing up in a subtler, more luminous copy of it, visible in his own likeness to clairvoyant vision, though invisible to ordinary sight. I have said "a well-formed astral body," for an undeveloped person in his astral body presents a very inchoate appearance. Its outline is undefined, its materials are dull and ill-arranged, and if withdrawn from the body it is a mere shapeless, shifting cloud, obviously unfit to act as an independent vehicle; it is, in truth, rather a fragment of astral matter than an organized astral body - a mass of astral protoplasm of an amoeboid type. A well-formed astral body means that a man has reached a fairly high level of intellectual culture or of spiritual growth, so that the appearance of the astral body is significant of the progress made by its owner; by the definiteness of it outline, the luminosity of its materials, and the perfection of its organization, one may judge of the stage of evolution reached by the Ego using it.

As regards the question of its improvement - a question important to us all - it must be remembered that the improvement of the astral body hinges on the one side on the purification of the physical body, and on the other on the purification and development of the mind. The astral body is peculiarly susceptible to impressions from thought, for astral matter responds more rapidly than physical to every impulse from the world of mind. For instance, if we look at the astral world we find it full of continually changing shapes; we find there "thought-forms" - forms composed of elemental essence and animated by a thought - and we also notice vast masses of this elemental essence, from which continually shapes emerge and into which they again disappear; watching carefully, we may see that currents of thought thrill this astral matter, that strong thoughts take a covering of it and persist as entities for a long time, while weak thoughts clothe themselves feebly and waver out again, so that all through the astral world changes are ever going on under thought-impulses. The astral body of man, being made of astral matter, shares this readiness to respond to the impact of thought, and thrills in answer to every thought that strikes it, whether the thoughts come from without, from the minds of other men, or come from within, from the mind of its owner.

Let us study this astral body under these impacts from within and without. We see it permeating the physical body and extending around it in every direction like a coloured cloud. The colours vary with the nature of the man, with his lower, animal passional nature, and the part outside the physical body is called the kâmic aura, as belonging to the Kâma or desire-body, commonly called the astral body of man. 5 For the astral body is the vehicle of man's kâmic consciousness, the seat of all animal passions and desires, the centre of the senses, as already said, where all sensations arise. It changes its colours continually as it vibrates under thought-impacts; if a man loses his temper, flashes of scarlet appear; if he feels love, rose-red thrills through it. If the man's thoughts are high and noble they demand finer astral matter to answer to them, and we trace this action on the astral body in its loss of the grosser and denser particles from each sub-plane, and its gain of the finer and rarer kinds. The astral body of a man whose thoughts are low and animal, is gross, thick, dense and dark in colour - often so dense that the outline of the physical body is almost lost in it; whereas that of an advanced man is fine, clear, luminous and bright in colour - a really beautiful object. In such a case the lower passions have been dominated, and the selective action of the mind has refined the astral matter. By thinking nobly, then, we purify the astral body, even without

---

5 This separation of the "aura" from the man, as though it were something different from himself, is misleading, although very natural from the point of view of observation. The "aura" is the cloud round the body, in ordinary parlance; really, the man lives on the various planes in such garments as befit each, and all these garments or bodies interpenetrate each other; the lowest and smallest of these is called "the body", and the mixed substances of the other garments are called the aura when they extend beyond that body. The kâmic aura, then, is merely such part of the kâmic body as extends beyond the physical.

having consciously worked towards that end. And be it remembered that this inner working exercises a potent influence on the thoughts that are attracted from without to the astral body; a body which is made by its owner to respond habitually to evil thoughts acts as a magnet to similar thought-forms in its vicinity, whereas a pure astral body acts on such thoughts with a repulsive energy, and attracts to itself thought-forms composed of matter congruous with its own.

As said above, the astral body hinges on one side to the physical, and it is affected by the purity or impurity of the physical body. We have seen that the solids, liquids, gases and ethers of which the physical body is composed may be coarse or refined, gross or delicate Their nature will in turn affect the nature of their corresponding astral envelopes. If, unwisely careless about the physical, we build into our dense bodies solid particles of an impure kind, we attract to ourselves the corresponding impure kind of what we will call the solid astral. As we, on the other hand, build into our dense bodies solid particles of purer type, we attract the correspondingly purer type of solid astral matter. As we carry on the purification of the physical body by feeding it on clean food and drink, by excluding from our diet the polluting kinds of aliment - the blood of animals, alcohol and other things that are foul and degrading - we not only improve our physical vehicle of consciousness, but we also begin to purify the astral vehicle and take from the astral world more delicate and finer materials for its construction. The effect of this is not only important as regards the present earth-life, but it has a distinct bearing also - as we shall see later - on the next post-mortem state, on the stay in the astral world, and also on the kind of body we shall have in the next life upon earth.

Nor is this all: the worse kinds of food attract to the astral body entities of a mischievous kind belonging to the astral world, for we have to do not only with astral matter, but also with what are called the elementals of that region. These are entities of higher and lower types existing on that plane, given birth to by the thoughts of men; and there are also in the astral world depraved men, imprisoned in their astral bodies, known as elementaries. The elementals are attracted towards people whose astral bodies contain matter congenial to their nature, while the elementaries naturally seek those who indulge in vices such as they themselves encouraged while in physical bodies. Any person endowed with astral vision sees, as he walks along our London streets, hordes of loathsome elementals crowding round our butchers' shops; and in beer-houses and gin-palaces elementaries specially gather, feasting on the foul emanations of the liquors, and thrusting themselves, when possible, into the very bodies of the drinkers. These beings are attracted by those who build their bodies out of these materials, and such people have these surroundings as part of their astral life. So it goes on through each stage of the astral plane; as we purify the physical we draw to ourselves correspondingly pure stages of the astral matter.

Now, of course, the possibilities of the astral body largely depend on the nature of the materials we build into it; as by the process of purification we make these bodies finer and finer, they cease to vibrate in answer to the lower impulses, and begin to answer to the higher influences of the astral world. We are thus making an instrument which, though by its very nature sensitive to influences coming to it from without, is gradually losing the power of responding to the lower vibrations, and is taking on the power of answering to the higher - an instrument which is tuned to vibrate only to the higher notes. As we can take a wire to produce a sympathetic vibration, choosing to that end its diameter, its length and its tension, so we can attune our astral bodies to give out sympathetic vibrations when noble harmonies are sounded in the world around us. This is not a mere matter of speculation or of theory; it is a matter of scientific fact. As here we tune the wire on the string, so there we can tune the strings of the astral body; the law of cause and effect holds good there as well as here; we appeal to the law, we take refuge in the law, and on that we rely. All we need is knowledge, and the will to put the knowledge into practice. This knowledge you may take and experiment on first, if you will, as a mere hypothesis, congruous with facts known to you in the lower world; later on, as you purify the astral body, the hypothesis will change into knowledge; it will be a matter of your own first-hand observation, so that you will be able to verify the theories you originally accepted only as working hypothesis.

Our possibilities, then, of mastering the astral world, and of becoming of real service there, depend first of all on this process of purification. There are definite methods of Yoga by which development of the astral senses may be helped forward in a rational and healthy way, but it is not of the least use to try to teach these to anyone who has not been using these simple preparatory means of purification. It is a common experience that people are very anxious to try some new and unusual method of progress, but it is idle to instruct people in Yoga when they will not even practice these preparatory stages in their ordinary life. Suppose one began to teach some very simple form of Yoga to an ordinary unprepared person; he would take it up eagerly and enthusiastically because it was new, because it was strange, because he hoped for very quick results, and before he had been working at it for even a year he would get tired of the regular strain of it in his daily life and disheartened by the absence of immediate effect;

unused to persistent effort, steadily maintained day after day, he would break down and give up his practice; the novelty outworn, weariness would soon assert itself. If a person cannot or will not accomplish the simple and comparatively easy duty of purifying the physical and astral bodies by using a temporary self-denial to break the bonds of evil habits in eating and drinking, it is idle for him to hanker after more difficult processes which attract by reason of their novelty and would soon be dropped as an intolerable burden. All talk even of special methods is idle until these ordinary humble means have been practiced for some time; but with the purification new possibilities will begin to show themselves. The pupil will find knowledge gradually flow into him, keener vision will awaken, vibrations will reach him from every side, arousing in him response which could not have been made by him in the days of blindness and obtuseness. Sooner or later, according to the Karma of his past, this experience becomes his, and just as a child mastering the difficulties of the alphabet has the pleasure of the book it can read, so the student will find coming to his knowledge and under his control possibilities of which he had not dreamed in his careless days, new vistas of knowledge opening out before him, a wider universe unfolding on every side.

If, now, for a few moments, we study the astral body as regards its functions in the sleeping and waking states, we shall be able easily and rapidly to appreciate its functions when it becomes a vehicle of consciousness apart from the body. If we study a person when he is awake and when he is asleep, we shall become aware of one very marked change as regards the astral body; when he is awake, the astral activities - the changing colours and so on - all manifest themselves in and immediately around the physical body; but when he is asleep a separation has occurred, and we see the physical body - the dense body and the etheric double - lying by themselves on the bed, while the astral body is floating in the air above them. * [* See for a fuller description the articles on "Dreams" before referred to.] If the person we are studying is one of mediocre

development, the astral body when separated from the physical is the somewhat shapeless mass before described; it cannot go far away from its physical body, it is useless as a vehicle of consciousness and the man within it is in a very vague and dream condition, unaccustomed to act away from his physical vehicle; in fact, he may be said to be almost asleep, failing the medium through which he has been accustomed to work, and he is not able to receive definite impressions from the astral world or express himself clearly through the poorly-organized astral body. The centres of sensation in it may be affected by passing thought-forms, and he may answer in it to stimuli that rouse the lower nature; but the whole effect given to the observer is one of sleepiness and vagueness, the astral body lacking all definite activity and floating idly, inchoate, above the sleeping physical form. If anything should occur tending to lead or drive it away from its physical partner, the latter will awaken and the astral will quickly reenter it. But if a person be observed who is much more developed, say one who is accustomed to function in the astral world and to use the astral body for that purpose, it will be seen that when the physical body goes to sleep and the astral body slips out of it, we have the man himself before us in full consciousness; the astral body is clearly outlined and definitely organized, bearing the likeness of the man, and the man is able to use it as a vehicle - a vehicle far more convenient than the physical. He is wide awake, and is working far more actively, more accurately, with greater power of comprehension, than when he was confined in the denser physical vehicle, and he can move about freely and with immense rapidity at any distance, without causing the least disturbance to the sleeping body on the bed.

If such a person has not yet learned to link together his astral and physical vehicles, if there be a break in consciousness when the astral body slips out as he falls asleep, then, while he himself will be wide awake and fully conscious on the astral plane, he will not be able to impress on the physical brain on his return to his denser vehicle the knowledge of what he has been doing during his absence; under these circumstances his "waking" consciousness - as it is the habit to term the most limited form of our consciousness - will not share the man's experiences in the astral world, not because he does not know them, but because the physical organism is too dense to receive these impressions from him. Sometimes, when the physical body awakes, there is a feeling that something has been experienced of which no memory remains; yet this very feeling shows that there has been some functioning of consciousness in the astral world away from the physical body, though the brain is not sufficiently receptive to have even an evanescent memory of what has occurred. At other times, when the astral body returns to the physical, the man succeeds in making a momentary impression on the etheric double and dense body, and when the latter is awake there is a vivid memory of an experience gained in the astral world; but the memory quickly vanishes and refuses to be recalled, every effort rendering success more impossible, as each effort sets up strong vibrations in the physical brain, and still further overpowers the subtler vibrations of the astral. Or yet again, the man may succeed in impressing new knowledge on the physical brain without being able to convey the memory of where or how that knowledge was gained; in such cases ideas will arise in the waking consciousness as though spontaneously generated, solutions will come of problems before uncomprehended, light will be thrown on questions before obscure. When this occurs, it is an encouraging sign of progress, showing that the astral body is well organized and is functioning actively in the astral world, although the physical body is still but very partially receptive. Sometimes, however, the man succeeds in making the physical brain respond, and then we have what is regarded as a very vivid, reasonable and coherent dream, the kind of dream which most thoughtful people have occasionally enjoyed, in which they feel more alive, not less, than when "awake," and in which they may even receive knowledge which is helpful to them in their physical life. All these are stages of progress marking the evolution and improving organization of the astral body.

But, on the other hand, it is well to understand that persons who are making real and even rapid progress in spirituality may be functioning most actively and usefully in the astral world without impressing on the brain when they return the slightest memory of the work in which they have been engaged, although they may be aware in their lower consciousness of an ever-increasing illumination and widening knowledge of spiritual truth. There is one fact which all students may take as a matter of encouragement, and on which they may rely with confidence, however blank their physical memory may be as regards super-physical experiences: as we learn to work more and more for others, as we endeavour to become more and more useful to the world, as we grow stronger and steadier in our devotion to the Elder Brothers of humanity, and seek ever more earnestly to perform perfectly our little share in Their great work, we are inevitably developing that astral body and that power of functioning in it which render us more efficient servants; whether with or without physical memory, we leave our physical prisons in deep sleep and work along useful lines of activity in the astral world, helping people we should otherwise be unable to reach, aiding and comforting in ways we could not otherwise employ. This evolution is going on with those who are pure in mind, elevated in thought, with their hearts set on the desire to serve. They may be working for many a year in the astral world without bringing back the memory to their lower consciousness, and exercising powers for good to the world far beyond anything of which they suppose themselves to be capable: to them, when Karma permits, shall come the full unbroken consciousness which passes at will between the physical and astral worlds; the bridge shall be made which lets the memory cross from the one to the other without effort, so that the man returning from his activities in the astral world will don again his physical vesture without a moment's loss of consciousness. This is the certainty that lies before all those who choose the life of service. They will one day acquire this unbroken consciousness; and then to them life shall no longer be composed of days of memoried work and nights of oblivion, but it will be a continuous whole, the body put aside to take the rest necessary for it, while the man himself uses the astral body for his work in the astral world; then they will keep the links of thought unbroken, knowing when they leave the physical body, knowing while they are passing out of it, knowing their life away from it, knowing when they return and again put it on: thus they will carry on week after week, year after year, the unbroken, unwearied consciousness which gives the absolute certainty of the existence of the individual Self, of the fact that the body is only a garment that they wear, put on and off at pleasure, and not a necessary instrument of thought and life. They will know that so far from its being necessary to either, life is far more active, thought far more untrammelled without it.

When this stage is reached a man begins to understand the world and his own life in it far better than he did before, begins to realize more of what lies in front of him, more of the possibilities of the higher humanity. Slowly he sees that just as man acquires first physical and then astral consciousness, so there stretch above him other and far higher ranges of consciousness that he may acquire one after the other, becoming active on loftier planes, ranging through wider worlds, exercising vaster powers, and all as the servant of the Holy Ones for the assistance and benefit of humanity. Then physical life begins to assume its true proportion, and nothing that happens in the physical world can affect him as it did ere he knew the fuller, richer life, and nothing that death can do can touch him either in himself or in those he desires to assist. The earth-life takes its true place as the smallest part of human activity, and it can never again be as dark as it used to be, for the light of the higher regions shines down into its obscurest recesses.

Turning from the study of the functions and possibilities of the astral body, let us consider now certain phenomena connected with it. It may show itself to other people apart from the physical body, either during or after earth-life. A person who has complete mastery over the astral body can, of course, leave the physical at any time and go to a friend at a distance. If the person thus visited be clairvoyant, *i. e.,* has developed astral sight, he will see his friend's astral body; if not, such visitor might slightly densify his vehicle by drawing into it from the surrounding atmosphere particles of physical matter, and thus "materialize" sufficiently to make himself visible to physical sight. This is the explanation of many of the appearances of friends at a distance, phenomena which are far more common than most people imagine, owing to the reticence of timid folk who are afraid of being laughed at as superstitious. Fortunately that fear is lessening, and if people would only have the courage and common sense to say what they know to be true, we should soon have a large mass of evidence on the appearances of people whose physical bodies are far away from the places where their astral bodies show themselves. These bodies may, under certain circumstances, be seen by those who do not normally exercise astral vision, without materialization being resorted to. If a person's nervous system be overstrained and the physical body be in weak health, so that the pulses of vitality throb less strongly than usual, the nervous activity so largely dependent on the etheric double may be unduly stimulated, and under these conditions the man may become temporarily clairvoyant. A mother, for instance, who knows her son to be dangerously ill in a foreign land, and who is racked by anxiety about him, may thus become susceptible to astral vibrations, especially in the hours of the night at which vitality is at its lowest; under these conditions, if her son be thinking of her, and his physical body be unconscious, so as to permit him to visit her astrally, she will be likely to see him. More often such a visit is made when the person has just shaken off the physical body at death. These appearances are by no means uncommon, especially where the dying person has a strong wish to reach someone to whom he is closely bound by affection, or where he desires to communicate some particular piece of information, and has passed away without fulfilling his wish.

If we follow the astral body after death, when the etheric double has been shaken off as well as the dense body, we shall observe a change in its appearance. During its connection with the physical body the sub-states of astral matter are intermixed with each other, the denser and the rarer kinds inter-penetrating and intermingling. But after death a rearrangement takes place, and the particles of the different sub-states separate from each other, and, as it were, sort themselves out in the order of their respective densities, the astral body thus assuming a stratified condition, or becoming a series of concentric shells of which the densest is outside. And here we are again met with the importance of purifying the astral body during our life on earth, for we find that it cannot, after death, range the astral world at will; that world has its seven sub-planes, and the man is confined to the sub-plane to which the matter of his external shell belongs; as this outermost covering disintegrates he rises to the next sub-plane, and so on from one to another. A man of very low and animal tendencies would have in his astral body much of the grossest and densest kind of astral matter, and this would hold him down on the lowest level of Kâmaloka; until this shell is disintegrated to a great extent the man must remain imprisoned in that section of the astral world, and suffer the annoyances of that most undesirable locality. When this outermost shell is sufficiently disintegrated to allow escape, the man passes to the next level of the astral world, or perhaps it is more accurate to say that he is able to come into contact with the vibrations of the next sub-plane of astral matter, thus seeming to himself to be in a different region: there he remains till the shell of the sixth sub-plane is worn away and permits his passage to the fifth, his stay on each sub-plane corresponding to the strength of those parts of his nature represented in the astral body by the amount of the matter belonging to that sub-plane. The greater the quantity, then, of the grosser sub-states of matter, the longer the stay on the lower kâmalokic levels, and the more we can get rid of those elements here the briefer will be the delay on the other side of death. Even where the grosser materials are not eliminated completely - a process long and difficult being necessary for their entire eradication - the consciousness may during earth-life be so persistently withdrawn from the lower passions that the matter by which they can find expression will cease to function actively as a vehicle of consciousness - will become atrophied, to borrow a physical analogy. In such case, though the man will be held for a short time on the lower levels, he will sleep peacefully through them, feeling none of the disagreeables accompanying them; his consciousness, having ceased to seek expression through such kinds of matter, will not pass outwards through them to contact objects composed of them in the astral world.

The passage through Kâmaloka of one who has so purified the astral body that he has only retained in it the purest and finest elements of each sub-plane - such as would at once pass into the matter of the sub-plane next above if raised another degree - is swift indeed. There is a point known as the critical point between every pair of sub-states of matter; ice may be raised a point at which the least increment of heat will change it into liquid; water may be raised to a point at which the next increment will change it into vapour. So each sub-state of astral matter may be carried to a point of fineness at which any additional refinement would transform it into the next sub-state. If this has be done for every sub-state of matter in the astral body, it has been purified to the last possible degree of delicacy, then its passage through Kâmaloka will be of inconceivable rapidity, and the man will flash through it untrammeled in his flight to loftier regions.

One other matter remains in connection with the purification of the astral body, both by physical and mental processes, and that is the effect of such purification on the new astral body that will in due course of time be formed for use in the next succeeding incarnation. When the man passes out of Kâmaloka into Devachan, he cannot carry thither with him thought-forms of an evil type; astral matter cannot exist on the devachanic level, and devachanic matter cannot answer to the coarse vibrations of evil passions and desires. Consequently all that the man can carry with him when he finally shakes off the remnants of his astral body will be the latent germs or tendencies which, when they can find nutriment or outlet, manifest as evil desires and passions in the astral world. But these he does take with him, and they lie latent throughout his devachanic life. When he returns for rebirth he brings these back with him and throws them outwards; they draw to themselves from the astral world by a kind of magnetic affinity the appropriate materials for their manifestation, and clothe themselves in astral matter congruous with their own nature, so forming part of the man's astral body for the impending incarnation. Thus we are not only living in an astral body now, but are fashioning the type of the astral body which will be ours in another birth - one reason the more for purifying the present astral body to the utmost, using our present knowledge to ensure our future progress.

For all our lives are linked together, and none of them can be broken away from those that lie behind it or from those that stretch in front. In truth, we have but one life in which what we call lives are really only days. We never begin a new life with a clean sheet on which to write an entirely new story; we do but begin a new chapter which must develop the old plot. We can no more get rid of the karmic liabilities of a preceding life by passing through death, than we can get rid of the pecuniary liabilities incurred on one day by sleeping through a night; if we incur a debt today we are not free of it tomorrow, but the claim is presented until it is discharged. The life of man is continuous, unbroken; the earth lives are linked together, and not isolated. The processes of purification and development are also continuous, and must be carried on through many successive earth-lives. Some time or other each of us must begin the work; some time or other each will grow weary of the sensations of the lower nature, weary of being in subjection to the animals, weary of the tyranny of the senses. Then the man will no longer consent to submit, he will decide that the bonds of his captivity shall be broken. Why, indeed, should we prolong our bondage, when it is in our own power to break it at any moment? No hand can bind us save our own, and no hand save our own can set us free. We have our right of choice, our freedom of will, and inasmuch as one day we shall all stand together in the higher world, why should we not begin at once to break our bondage, and to claim our divine birthright? The beginning of the shattering of the fetters, of the winning of liberty, is when a man determines that he will make the lower nature the servant of the higher, that here on the plane of physical consciousness he will begin the building of the higher bodies, and will seek to realize those loftier possibilities which are his by right divine, and are only obscured by the animal in which he lives.

III. THE MIND BODIES

We have already studied at some length the physical and astral bodies of man. We have studied the physical both in its visible and invisible parts, working on the physical plane; we have followed the various lines of its activities, have analysed the nature of its growth, and have dwelt upon its gradual purification. Then we have considered the astral body in a similar fashion, tracing its growth and functions, dealing with the phenomena connected with its manifestation on the astral plane, and also with its purification. Thus we have gained some idea of human activity on two out of seven great planes of our universe. Having done so, we can now pass on to the third great plane, the mind world; when we have learned something of this we shall have under our eyes the physical, the astral, and the mental worlds - our globe and the two spheres surrounding it - as a triple region, wherein man is active during his earthly incarnations and wherein he dwells also during the periods which intervene between the death that closes one earth-life and the birth which opens another. These three concentric spheres are man's school-house and kingdom: in them he works out his development, in them his evolutionary pilgrimage; beyond them he may not consciously pass until the gateway of Initiation has opened before him, for out of these three worlds there is no other way.

This third region, that I have called the mind world, includes, though it is not identical with, that which is familiar to Theosophists under the name of Devachan or Devaloka, the land of the Gods, the happy or blessed land, as some translate it. Devachan bears that name because of its nature and condition, nothing interfering with that world which may cause pain or sorrow; it is a specially guarded state, into which positive evil is not allowed to intrude, the blissful resting-place of man in which he peacefully assimilates the fruits of his physical life.

A preliminary word of explanation regarding the mind world as a whole is necessary in order to avoid confusion. While, like the other regions, it is sub-divided into seven sub-planes, it has the peculiarity that these seven are grouped into two sets - a three and a four. The three upper sub-planes are technically called arûpa, or without body, owing to their extreme subtlety, while the four lower are called rûpa, or with body. Man has two vehicles of consciousness, consequently, in which he functions on this plane, to both of which the term mind body is applicable. The lower of these, the one with which we shall first deal, may, however, be allowed to usurp the exclusive use of the name until a better one be found for it; for the higher one is known as the causal body, for reasons which will become clear further on. Students will be familiar with the distinction between the Higher and Lower Manas; the causal body is that of the Higher Manas, the permanent body of the Ego, or man, lasting from life to life; the mind body is that of the Lower Manas, lasting after death and passing into Devachan, but disintegrating when the life on the rûpa levels of Devachan is over.

(a) The Mind Body. — This vehicle of consciousness belongs to, and is formed of, the matter of the four lower levels of Devachan. While it is especially the vehicle of consciousness for that part of the mental plane, it works upon and through the astral and physical bodies in all the manifestations that we call those of the mind in our ordinary waking consciousness. In the undeveloped man, indeed, it cannot function separately on its own plane as an independent vehicle of consciousness during his earthly life, and when such a man exercises his mental faculties, they must clothe themselves in astral and physical matter ere he can become conscious of their activity. The mind body is the vehicle of the Ego, the Thinker, for all his reasoning work, but during his early life it is feebly organized and somewhat inchoate and helpless, like the astral body of the undeveloped man.

The matter of which the mind body is composed is of an exceedingly rare and subtle kind. We have already seen that astral matter is much less dense than even the ether of the physical plane, and we have now to enlarge our conception of matter still further, and to extend it to include the idea of a substance invisible to astral sight as well as to physical, far too subtle to be perceived even by the "inner" senses of man. This matter belongs to the fifth plane counting downwards, or the third plane counting upwards, of our universe, and in this matter the Self manifests as mind, as in the next below it (the astral) it manifests as sensation. There is one marked peculiarity about the mind body, as its outer part shows itself in the human aura; it grows, increases in size and in activity, incarnation after incarnation, with the growth and development of the man himself. This peculiarity is one to which so far we are now accustomed. A physical body is built incarnation after incarnation, varying according to nationality and sex, but we think of it as very much the same in size since Atlantean days. In the astral body we found growth in organization as the man progressed. But the mind body literally grows in size with the advancing evolution of the man. If we look at a very undeveloped person, we shall find that the mind body is even difficult to distinguish - that it is so little evolved that some care is necessary to see it at all. Looking then at a more advanced man, one who is not spiritual, but who has developed the faculties of the mind, who has trained and developed the intellect, we shall find that the mind body is acquiring a very definite development, and that it has an organization that can be recognized as a vehicle of activity; it is a clear and definitely outlined object, fine in material and beautiful in colour, continually vibrating with enormous activity, full of life, full of vigour, the expression of the mind in the world of the mind.

As regards its nature, then, made of this subtle matter; as regards its functions, the immediate vehicle in which the Self manifests as intellect; as regards its growth, growing life after life in proportion to the intellectual development, becoming also more and more definitely organized as the attributes and the qualities of the mind become more and more clearly marked. It does not, like the astral body, become a distinct representation of the man in form and feature when it is working in connection with the astral and physical bodies; it is oval - egg-like - in outline, interpenetrating of course the physical and astral bodies, and surrounding them with a radiant atmosphere as it develops - becoming, as I said, larger and larger as the intellectual growth increases. Needless to say, this egg-like form becomes a very beautiful and glorious object as the man develops the higher capacities of the mind: it is not visible to astral sight, but is clearly seen by the higher vision which belongs to the world of mind. Just as an ordinary man living in the physical world sees nothing of astral world - though surrounded by it - until the astral senses are opened, so a man in whom only the physical and astral senses are active will see nothing of the mind world, or of forms composed of its matter, unless mental senses be opened, albeit it surrounds us on every side.

These keener senses, the senses which belong to mind world, differ very much from the senses with which we are familiar here. The very word "senses" in fact, is a misnomer, for we ought rather to say mental "sense. " The mind comes into contact with the things of its own world as it were directly oven its whole surface. There are no distinct organs for sight, hearing, touch, taste and smell; all the vibrations which we should here receive through separate sense-organs, in that region give rise to all these characteristics once when they come into touch with the mind. The mind body receives them all at one and the same time and is, as it were, conscious all over of everything which is able to impress it at all.

It is not easy to convey in words any clear idea of the way this sense receives an aggregate of impressions without confusion, but it may perhaps be best described by saying that if a trained student passes into that region, and there communicates with another student, the mind in speaking speaks at once by colour, sound and form, so that the complete thought is conveyed as a coloured and musical picture instead of only a fragment of it being shown, as is done here by the symbols we call words. Some readers may have heard of ancient books written by great Initiates in colour-language, the language of the Gods; that language is known to many chelâs, and is taken, so far as form and colour are concerned, from the mind-world "speech," in which the vibrations from a single thought give rise to form, to colour, and to sound. It is not that the mind thinks a colour, or thinks a sound, or thinks a form; it thinks a thought, a complex vibration in subtle matter, and that thought expresses itself in all these ways by the vibrations set up. The matter of the mind world is constantly being thrown into vibrations which give birth to these colours, to these sounds, to these forms; and if a man be functioning in the mind body apart from the astral and the physical, he finds himself entirely freed from the limitations of their sense-organs, receptive at every point to every vibration that in the lower world would present itself as separate and different from its fellows.

When, however, a man is thinking in his waking consciousness and is working through his astral and physical bodies, then the thought has its producer in the mind body and passes out, first to the astral and then to the physical; when we think, we are thinking by our mind body - that is, the agent of thought, the consciousness which expresses itself as "I". The "I" is illusory, but it is the only "I" known to the majority of us. When we were dealing with the consciousness the physical body, we found that the man himself was not conscious of all that was going on in the physical body itself, that its activities were partially independent of him, that he was not able to think as the tiny separate cells were thinking, that he did not really share the consciousness of the body as a whole. But when we come to the mind body we come to a region so closely identified with the man that it seems to be himself. "I think," "I know" - can we go behind that? The mind is the Self in the mind body, and it is that which for most of us seems the goal of our search after the Self. But this is only true if we are confined to the waking consciousness. Anyone who has learned that the waking consciousness, like the sensations of the astral body, is only a stage of our journey as we seek the Self, and who has further learned to go beyond it, will be aware that this in its turn is but an instrument of the real man. Most of us, however, as I say, do not separate, cannot separate in thought the man from his mind body, which seems to them to be his highest expression, his highest vehicle, the highest self they can in any way touch or realize. This is the more natural and inevitable in that the individual, the man, at this stage of evolution, is beginning to vivify this body and to bring it into preeminent activity. He has vivified the physical body as a vehicle of consciousness in the past, and is using it in the present as a matter of course. He is vivifying the astral body in the backward members of the race, but in very large numbers this work is at least partially accomplished; in this Fifth Race he is working at the mind body, and the special work on which humanity should now be engaged is the building, the evolution of this body.

We are, then, much concerned to understand how the mind body is built and how it grows. It grows by thought. Our thoughts are the materials we build into this mind body; by the exercise of our mental faculties, by the development of our artistic powers, our higher emotions, we are literally building the mind body day by day, each month and year of our lives. If you are not exercising your mental abilities; if, so far as your thoughts are concerned, you are a receptacle and not a creator; if you are constantly accepting from outside instead of forming from within; if, as you go through life, the thoughts of other people are crowding into your mind; if this be all you know of thought and of thinking, then, life after life, your mind body cannot grow; life after life you come back very much as you went out; life after life you remain as an undeveloped individual. For it is only by the exercise of the mind itself, using its faculties creatively, exercising them, working with them, constantly exerting them - it is only by these means that the mind body can develop, and that the truly human evolution can proceed.

The very moment you begin to realize this you will probably try to change the general attitude of your consciousness in daily life; you will begin to watch its working; and as soon as you do this you will notice that, as just said, a great deal of your thinking is not your thinking at all, but the mere reception of the thoughts of other people; thoughts that come you not know how; thoughts that arrive you do not know whence; thoughts that take themselves off again you not know whither; and you will begin to feel, probably with some distress and disappointments that instead of the mind being highly evolved it is little more than a place through which thoughts are passing. Try yourself, and see how much of the content of your consciousness is your own, and how much of it consists merely of contributions from outside. Stop yourself suddenly now and then during the day, and see what you are thinking about, and on such a sudden checking you will probably either find that you are thinking about nothing

- a very common experience - or that you are thinking so vague that a very slight impression is made upon anything you can venture to call your mind. When you have tried this a good many times, and by the very trying have become more self-conscious than you were, then begin to notice the thoughts you find in your mind, and see what difference there is between their condition when they came into the mind and their condition when they go out of it - what you have added to them during their stay with you. In this way your mind will become really active, and will be exercising its creative powers, and if you be wise you will follow some such process as this: first, you will choose the thoughts that you will allow to remain in the mind at all; whenever you find in the mind a thought that is good you will dwell upon it, nourish it, strengthen it, try to put into it more than it had at first; and send it out as a beneficent agent into the astral world; when you find in the mind a thought that is evil you will turn it out with all imaginable promptitude. Presently you will find that as you welcome into your mind all thoughts that are good and useful, and refuse to entertain thoughts which are evil, this result will appear: that more and more good thoughts will flow into your mind from without, and fewer and fewer evil thoughts will flow into it. The effect of making your mind full of good and useful thoughts will be that it will act as a magnet for all the similar thoughts that are around you; as you refuse to give any sort of habourage to evil thoughts, those that approach you will be thrown back by an automatic action of the mind itself. The mind body will take on the characteristic of attracting all thoughts that are good from the surrounding atmosphere, and repelling all thoughts that are evil, and it will work upon the good and make them more active, and so constantly gather a mass of mental material which will form its content, and will grow richer every year. When the time comes when the man shall shake off the astral and physical bodies finally, passing into the mind world, he will carry with him the whole of this gathered-up material; he will take with him the content of consciousness into the region to which it properly belongs, and he will use his devachanic life in working up into faculties and powers the whole of the materials which it has stored.

At the end of the devachanic period the mind body will hand on to the permanent causal body the characteristics thus fashioned, that they may be carried on into the next incarnation. These faculties, as the man returns, will clothe themselves in the matter of the rûpa planes of the mind world, forming the more highly organized and developed mind body for the coming earth-life, and they will show themselves through the astral and physical bodies as the "innate faculties," those with which the child comes into the world. During the present life we are gathering together materials in the way which I have sketched; during the devachan life we work up these materials, changing them from separate efforts of thought into faculty of thought, into mental powers and activities. That is the immense change made during the devachanic life, and inasmuch as it is limited by the use we are making of the earth-life, we shall do well to spare no efforts now. The mind body of the next incarnation depends on the work we are doing in the mind body of the present; here is, then, the immense importance to the evolution of the man of the use which he is now making of his mind bodes; it limits his activities in Devachan, and by limiting those activities it limits the mental qualities with which he will return for his next life upon earth. We cannot isolate one life from another, nor miraculously create something out of nothing. Karma brings the harvest according to our sowing: scanty or plentiful is the crop as the labourer gives seed and tillage.

The automatic action of the mind body, spoken of above, may perhaps be better understood if we consider the nature of the materials on which it draws for its building. The Universal Mind, to which it is allied in its inmost nature, is the storehouse in its material aspect from which it draws these materials. They give rise to every kind of vibration, varying in quality and in power according to the combinations made. The mind body automatically draws to itself from the general storehouse matter that can maintain the combinations already existing in it, for there is a constant changing of particles in the mind body as in the physical, and the place of those which leave is taken by similar particles that come. If the man finds that he has evil tendencies and sets to work to change them, he sets up a new set of vibrations, and the mind body, moulded to respond to the old one resists the new, and there is conflict and suffering. But gradually, as the older particles are thrown out and are replaced by others that answer to the new vibrations - being attracted from outside by their very power to respond to them - the mind body changes its character, changes, in fact, its materials, and its vibrations become antagonistic to the evil and attractive to the good. Hence the extreme difficulty of the first efforts, met and combated by the old form-aspect of the mind; hence the increasing ease of right thinking as the old form changes, and finally, the spontaneity and the pleasure that accompany the new exercise.

Another way of helping the growth of the mind body is the practice of concentration; that is, the fixing of the mind on a point and holding it there firmly, not allowing it to drift or wander. We should train ourselves in thinking steadily and consecutively, not allowing our minds to run suddenly from one thing to another, not to fritter their energies away over a large number or insignificant thoughts. It is a good practice to follow a consecutive line of reasoning, in which one thought grows naturally out of the thought that went before it, thus gradually developing in ourselves the intellectual qualities which make our thoughts sequential and therefore essentially rational; for when the mind thus works, thought following thought in definite and orderly succession, it is strengthening itself as an instrument of the Self for activity in the mind world. This development of the power of thinking with concentration and sequence will show itself in a more clearly outlined and definite mind body, in a rapidly increasing growth, in steadiness and balance, the efforts being well repaid by the progress which results from them.

(b) the Causal Body. — Let us now pass on to the second mind body, known by its own distinctive name of causal body. The name is due to the fact that all the causes reside in this body which manifest themselves as effects on the lower planes. This body is the "body of Manas," the form-aspect of the individual, of the true man. It is the receptacle, the storehouse, in which all the man's treasures are stored for eternity, and it grows as the lower nature hands up more and more that is worthy to be built into its structure. The causal body is that into which everything is woven which can endure, and in which are stored the germs of every quality, to be carried over to the next incarnation; thus the lower manifestations depend wholly on the growth and development of this man for "whom the hour never strikes."

The causal body, it is said above, is the form-aspect of the individual. Dealing, as we do here, only with the present human cycle, we may say that until that comes into existence there is no man; there may be the physical and etheric tabernacles prepared for his habitation; passions, emotions and appetites may gradually be gathered to form the kâmic nature in the astral body; but there is not man until the growth through the physical and astral planes has been accomplished, and until the matter of the mind world is beginning to show itself within the evolved lower bodies. When, by the power of the Self preparing its own habitation, the matter of the mind plane begins slowly to evolve, then there is a downpouring from the great ocean of Âtmâ-Buddhi which is ever brooding over the evolution of man - and this, as it were, meets the upward-growing, unfolding mind-stuff, comes into union with it, fertilizes it, and at that point of union the causal body, the individual, is formed. Those who are able to see in those lofty regions say that this form-aspect of the true man is like a delicate film of subtlest matter, just visible, marking where the individual begins his separate life; that delicate, colourless film of subtle matter is the body that lasts through the whole of the human evolution, the thread on which all the lives are strung, the reincarnating Sûtrâtmâ, the "thread-self". It is the receptacle of all which is in accordance with the Law, of every attribute which is noble and harmonious, and therefore enduring. It is that which marks the growth of man, the stage of evolution to which he has attained. Every great and noble thought, every pure and lofty emotion, is carried up and worked into his substance.

Let us take the life of an ordinary man and try to see how much of that life will pass upwards for the building of the causal body, and let us imagine it pictorially as a delicate film; it is to be strengthened, to be made beautiful with colour, made active with life, made radiant and glorious, increasing in size as the man grows and develops. At a low stage of evolution he is not showing much mental quality, but rather he is manifesting much passion, much appetite. He feels sensations and seeks them; they are the things to which he turns. It is as though this inner life of the man puts forth a little of the delicate matter of which it is composed, and round that the mind body gathers; and the mind body puts forth into the astral world, and there comes into contact with the astral body, and becomes connected with it, so that a bridge is formed along which anything capable of passing can pass. The man sends his thoughts downwards by this bridge into the world of sensations, of passions, of animal life, and the thoughts intermingle with all these animal passions and emotions; thus the mind body becomes entangled with the astral body and they adhere to each other and are difficult to separate when the time of death comes. But if the man, during the life which he is spending in these lower regions, has an unselfish thought, a thought of service to someone he loves, and makes some sacrifice in order to do service to his friend, he has then set up something that is able to endure, something that is able to live, something that has in it the nature of the higher world; that can pass upwards to the causal body and be worked into its substance, making it more beautiful, giving it perhaps its first touch of intensity of colour; perhaps all through the man's life there will only be a few of these things that are able to endure, to serve as food for the growth of the real man. So the growth is very slow, for all the rest of his life does not aid it; all his evil tendencies born of ignorance and fed by exercise, have their germs drawn inward and thrown into latency, as the astral body which gave them home and form is dissipated in the astral world; they are drawn inward into the mind body and lie latent there, lacking material for expression in the devachanic world; when the mind body in its turn perishes, they are drawn into the causal body, and there still lie latent, as in suspended animation. They are thrown outwards as the Ego, returning to earth-life reaches the astral world, reappearing there as evil tendencies brought over from the past. Thus the causal body may be spoken of as the storehouse of evil as well as good, being all that remains of the man after the lower vehicles are dissipated, but the good is worked into its texture and aids its growth, while the evil, with the exception noted below, remains as germ.

But the evil which a man works in life, when he puts into its execution his thought, does more injury to the causal body than merely to lie latent in it, as the germ of future sin and sorrow. It is not only that the evil does not help the growth of the true man, but where it is subtle and persistent it drags away, if the expression may be permitted, something of the individual himself. If vice be persistent, if evil be continually followed, the mind body becomes so entangled with the astral that after death it cannot free itself entirely, and some of its very substance is torn away from it, and when the astral dissipates this goes back to the mind stuff of the mind world and is lost to the individual; in this way, if we think again of our image of a film, or bubble, it may be to some extent thinned by vicious living - not only delayed in its progress, but something wrought upon it which makes it more difficult to build into. It is as though the film were in some way affected as to capacity of growth, sterilized or atrophied to some extent. Beyond this, in ordinary cases, the harm wrought to the causal body does not go.

But where the Ego has become strong both in intellect and will without at the same time increasing in unselfishness and love, where it contracts itself round its own separated centre instead of expanding as it grows, building a wall of selfishness around it and using its developing powers for the "I" instead of for the all; in such cases arises the possibility alluded to in so many of the world-scriptures, of more dangerous and ingrained evil, of the Ego setting itself consciously against the Law, of fighting deliberately against evolution. Then the causal body itself, wrought on by vibrations on the mental plane of intellect and will, but both turned to selfish ends, shows the dark hues which result from contraction and loses the dazzling radiance which is its characteristic property. Such harm cannot be worked by a poorly developed Ego nor by ordinary passional or mental faults; to effect injury so far-reaching the Ego must be highly evolved, and must have its energies potent on the mânasic plane. Therefore is it that ambition, pride and the powers of the intellect used for selfish aims are so far more dangerous, so far more deadly in their effects, than the more palpable faults of the lower nature, and the "Pharisee" is often further from the "kingdom of God" than "the publican and the sinner. " Along this line is developed the "black magician," the man who conquers passion and desire, develops will and the higher powers of the mind, not to offer them gladly as forces to help forward the evolution of the whole, but in order to grasp all he can for himself as unit, to hold and not to share. These set themselves to maintain separation as against unity, they strive to retard instead of to quicken evolution: therefore they vibrate in discord with the whole instead of in harmony, and are in danger of that rending of the Ego which means the loss of all the fruits of evolution.

All of us who are beginning to understand something of this causal body can make its evolution a definite object in our life; we can strive to think unselfishly and so contribute to its growth and activity. Life after life, century after century, millennium after millennium, this evolution of the individual proceeds, and in aiding its growth by conscious effort we are working in harmony with the divine will, and carrying out the purpose for which we are here. Nothing good that is once woven into the texture of this causal body is ever lost, nothing is dissipated: for this is the man that lives for ever.

Thus we see that by the law of evolution everything that is evil, however strong for the time it may seem, has within itself the germ of its own destruction, while everything that is good has in it the seed of immortality; the secret of this lies in the fact that everything evil is inharmonious, that it sets itself against the cosmic law; it is therefore sooner or later broken up by that law, dashed into pieces against it, crushed into dust. Everything that is good, on the other hand, being in harmony with the law, is taken on by it, carried forward; it becomes part of the stream of evolution, of that "not ourselves which makes for righteousness," and therefore it can never perish, can never be destroyed. Here lie not only the hope of man but the certainty of his final triumph; however slow the growth, it is there; however long the way, it has its ending. The individual which is our Self is evolving, and cannot now be utterly destroyed; even though by our folly we may make the growth slower than it need be, none the less everything we contribute to it, however little, lasts in it for ever and is our possession for all the ages that lie in front.

IV. OTHER VEHICLES

We may rise one step further, but in doing so we enter a region so lofty that it is well-nigh beyond our treading, even in imagination. For the causal body itself is not the highest, and the "Spiritual Ego" is not Manas, but Manas united to, merged in, Buddhi. This is the culmination of the human evolution, the end of the revolution on the wheel of births and deaths. Above the plane with which we have been dealing lies a yet higher, sometimes called that of Turīya, the plane of Buddhi *(this plane has also been called that of Sushupti).* Here the vehicle of consciousness is the spiritual body, the Ânandamayakosha, or body of bliss and into this Yogïs can pass, and in it taste the eternal bliss of that glorious world, and realize in their own consciousness the underlying unity, which then becomes to them a fact of experience and no longer only an intellectual belief. We may read of a time that comes to the man when he has grown in love, wisdom and power, and when he passes through a great gateway, marking a distinct stage in his evolution. It is the gateway of Initiation, and the man led through it by his Master rises for the first time into the spiritual body, and experiences in it the unity which underlies all the diversity of the physical world and all its separateness, which underlies the separateness of the astral plane and even of the mental region. When these are left behind and the man, clothed in the spiritual body, rises beyond them, he then finds for the first time in his experience that separateness belongs only to the three lower worlds; that he is one with all others, and that, without losing self-consciousness, his consciousness can expand to embrace the consciousness of others, can become verily and indeed one with them. There is the unity after which man is always yearning, the unity he has felt as true and has vainly tried to realize on low planes; there it is realized beyond his loftiest dreaming and all humanity is found to be one with his innermost Self.

Temporary Bodies. — We cannot leave out of our review of man's bodies certain other vehicles that are temporary, and may be called artificial, in their character. When a man begins to pass out of the physical body he may use the astral, but so long as he is functioning in that he is limited to the astral world. It is possible, however, for him to use the mind body - that of the Lower Manas - in order to pass into the mental region, and in this he can also range the astral and physical planes without let or hindrance. The body thus used is often called the Mâyâvi Rûpa, or body of illusion, and it is the mind body re-arranged, so to speak, for separate activity. The man fashions his mind body into the likeness of himself, shapes it into his own image and likeness, and is then in this temporary and artificial body free to traverse the three planes at will and rise superior to the ordinary limitations of man. It is this artificial body that is often spoken of in Theosophical books, in which a person can travel from land to land, passing also into the world of mind, learning there new truths, gathering new experience, and bringing back to the waking consciousness the treasures thus collected. The advantage of using this higher body is that it is not subject to deception and glamour on the astral plane as is the astral body. The untrained astral senses often mislead, and much experience is needed ere their reports can be trusted, but this temporarily formed mind body is not subject to such deceptions; it sees with a true vision, it hears with a true hearing; no astral glamour can overpower, no astral illusion can deceive; therefore this body is preferably used by those trained for such journeyings, made when it is wanted, let go again when the purpose for which it was made is served. Thus it is that the student often learns lessons that otherwise could not reach him, and receives instructions from which he would otherwise be entirely shut off.

Other temporary bodies have been called by the name of Mâyâvi Rûpa, but it seems better to restrict the term to the one just described. A man may appear a distance in a body which is really a thought-form more than a vehicle of consciousness, thought clothed in elemental essence of the astral plane. These bodies are, as a rule, merely vehicles of some particular thought, some special volition, and outside this show no consciousness. They need only be mentioned in passing.

The Human Aura. — We are now in a position to understand what the human aura, in its fullest sense, really is. It is the man himself, manifest at once on the four planes of consciousness, and according to its development is his power of functioning on each; it is the aggregate of his bodies, of his vehicles of consciousness; in a phrase, it is the form-aspect of the man. It is thus that we should regard it, and not as a mere ring or cloud surrounding him. Most glorious of all is the spiritual body, visible in Initiates, through which plays the living âtmic fire; this is the manifestation of man on the buddhic plane. Then comes the causal body, his manifestation in the highest mental world, on the arûpa levels of the plane of mind, where the individual has his home. Next the mind body, belonging to the lower mental planes, and the astral, etheric and dense bodies in succession, each formed of the matter of its own region, and expressing the man as he is in each. When the student looks at the human being he sees all these bodies making up the man, showing themselves separately by virtue of their different grades of matter, and thus marking the stage of development at which the man has arrived. As the higher vision is developed the student sees each of these bodies in its full activity. The physical body is visible as a kind of dense crystallization in the centre of the other bodies, the others permeating it and extending beyond its periphery, the physical being the smallest. The astral comes next, showing the state of the kâmic nature that forms so great a part of the ordinary man, full of his passions, lower appetites and emotions, differing in fineness, in colour, as the man is more or less pure - very dense in the grosser types, finer in the more refined, finest of all if the man be far advanced in his evolution. Then the mind body, poorly developed in the majority but beautiful in many, very various in colouring according to the mental and moral type. Then the causal, scarcely visible in most, visible only if careful scrutiny be brought to bear on the man, so slightly is it developed, so comparatively thin is its colouring, so feeble is its activity. But when we come to look at an advanced soul, it is this and the one above it that at once strike the eye as being emphatically the presentation of the man; radiant in light, most glorious and delicate in colouring, showing hues that no language can describe, because they have no place in earth's spectrum - hues not only most pure and beautiful, but entirely different from the colour known on the lower planes, additional ones which show the growth of the man in those higher regions in the loftier qualities and powers that there exist. If the eye be fortunate enough to be blessed with the sight of one of the Great Ones, He appears as this mighty living form of life and colour, radiant and glorious, showing forth His nature by His very appearance to the view: beautiful beyond description, resplendent beyond imagination. Yet what He is, all shall one day become: that which He is in accomplishment dwells in every son of man a possibility.

There is one point about the aura that I may mention as it is one of practical utility. We can to a great extent protect ourselves against the incursions of thoughts from outside by making a spherical wall round us from the auric substance. The aura responds very readily to the impulse of thought, and if by an effort of the imagination we picture its outer edge as densified into a shell we really make such a protective wall around us. This shell will prevent the incoming of the drifting thoughts that fill the astral atmosphere, and thus will prevent the disturbing influence they exercise over the untrained mind. The drain on our vitality that we sometimes feel, especially when we come into contact with people who unconsciously vampirize their neighbours, may also be guarded against by the formation of a shell, and anyone who is sensitive and who finds himself very exhausted by such a drain will do wisely thus to protect himself. Such is the power of human thought on subtle matter that to think of yourself as within such a shell is to have it formed around you.

Looking at human beings around us on every side we may see them in every stage of development, showing themselves forth by their bodies according to the point in evolution which they have reached, living on plane after plane of the universe, functioning in region after region, as they develop the corresponding vehicles of consciousness. Our aura shows just what we are; we add to it as we grow in the true life; we purify it as we live noble and cleanly lives; we weave into it higher and higher qualities.

Is it possible that any philosophy of life should be more full of hope, more full of strength, more full of joy than this? Looking over the world of men with the physical eye only, we see it degraded, miserable, apparently hopeless, as in truth it is to the eye of flesh. But that same world of men appears to us in quite another aspect when seen by the higher vision. We see indeed the sorrow and the misery, we see indeed the degradation and the shape; but we know that they are transient, that they are temporary, that they belong to the childhood of the race, and that the race will outgrow them. Looking at the lowest and vilest, at the most degraded and most brutal, we can yet see their divine possibilities, we can yet realize what they shall be in the years to come. That is the message of hope brought by Theosophy to the Western world, the message of universal redemption from ignorance, and therefore of universal emancipation from misery - not in dream but in reality, not in hope but in certainty. Everyone who in his own life is showing the growth is, as it were, a fresh realization and enforcement of the message; everywhere the first-fruits are appearing, and the whole world shall one day be ripe for harvest, and shall accomplish the purpose for which the Logos gave it birth.

V. THE MAN

We have now to turn to the consideration of the man himself, no longer studying the vehicles of consciousness but the action of the consciousness on them, no longer looking at the bodies but at the entity who functions in them. By "the man" I mean that continuing individual who passes from life to life, who comes into bodies and again leaves them, over and over again, who develops slowly in the course of ages, who grows by the gathering and by the assimilation of experience, and who exists on that higher mânasic or mental plane referred to in the last chapter. This man is to be the subject of our study, functioning on the three planes with which we are now familiar - the physical, the astral and the mental.

Man begins his experiences by developing self-consciousness on the physical plane; it is here that appears what we call the "waking consciousness," the consciousness with which we are all familiar, which works through the brain and nervous system, by which we reason in the ordinary way, carrying on all logical processes, by which we remember past events of the current incarnation, and exercise judgment in the affairs of life. All that we recognize as our mental faculties is the outcome of the man's work through the preceding stages of his pilgrimage, and his self-consciousness here becomes more and more vivid, more and more active, more and more alive, we may say, as the individual develops, as the man progresses life after life.

If we study a very undeveloped man, we find his self-conscious mental activity to be poor in quality and limited in quantity. He is working in the physical body through the gross and etheric brains; action is continually going on, so far as the whole nervous system is concerned, visible and invisible, but the action is of a very clumsy kind. There is in it very little discrimination, very little delicacy of mental touch. There is some mental activity, but it is of a very infantile or childish kind. It is occupied with very small things; it is amused by very trivial occurrences; the things that attract its attention are things of a petty character; it is interested in passing objects; it likes to sit at a window and look out at a busy street, watching people and vehicles go by, making remarks on them, overwhelmed with amusement if a well-dressed person tumbles into a puddle or is badly splashed by a passing cab. It has not much in itself to occupy its attention, and therefore it is always rushing outwards in order to feel that it is alive; it is one of the chief characteristics of this low stage of mental evolution that the man working at the physical and etheric bodies, and bringing them into order as vehicles of consciousness, is always seeking violent sensations; he needs to make sure that he is feeling and to learn to distinguish things by receiving from them strong and vivid sensations; it is a quite necessary stage of progress, though an elementary one, and without this he would continually be becoming confused, confused between the processes within his vehicle and without it; he must learn the alphabet of the self and the not-self by distinguishing between the objects causing impacts and the sensations caused by impacts, between the stimulus and the feeling. The lowest types of this stage may be seen gathered at street-corners, lounging idly against a wall and indulging occasionally in a few ejaculatory remarks and in cackling outbursts of empty laughter. Anyone able to look into their brains finds that they are receiving somewhat blurred impressions from passing objects, and that the links between these impressions and others like them are very slight. The impressions are more like a heap of pebbles than a well-arranged mosaic.

In studying the way in which the physical and etheric brains become vehicles of consciousness, we have to run back to the early development of the Ahamkâra, or "I-ness", a stage that may be seen in the lower animals around us. Vibrations caused by the impact of external objects are set up in the brain, transmitted by it to the astral body, and felt by the consciousness as sensations before there is any linking of these sensations to the objects that caused them, this linking being a definite mental action - a perception. When perception begins, the consciousness is using the physical and etheric brains as a vehicle for itself, by means of which it

166

gathers knowledge of the external world. This stage is long past in our humanity, of course, but its fleeting repetition may be seen, when the consciousness takes up a new brain in coming to rebirth; the child begins to "take notice," as the nurses say, that is, to relate a sensation arising in itself to an impression made upon its new sheath, or vehicle, by an external object, and thus to "notice" the object, to perceive it.

After a time the perception of an object is not necessary in order that the picture of the object may be present to the consciousness, and it finds itself able to recall the appearance of an object, when it is not contacted by any sense; such a memoried perception is a idea, a concept, a mental image, and these make up the store which the consciousness gathers from the outside world. On these it begins to work, and the first stage of this activity is the arrangement of the ideas, the preliminary to "reasoning" upon them. Reasoning begins by comparing the ideas with each other, and then by inferring relations between them from the simultaneous or sequential happening of two or more of them, time after time. In this process the consciousness has withdrawn within itself, carrying with it the ideas it has made out of perceptions, and it goes (on) to and [projects on] to them something of its own, as when it infers a sequence, relates one thing to another as cause and effect. It begins to draw conclusions, even to forecast future happenings, when it has established a sequence, so that when the perception regarded as "cause" appears, the perception regarded as "effect" is expected to follow. Again, it notices in comparing its ideas that many of them have one or more elements in common, while their remaining constituents are different, and it proceeds to draw these common characteristics away from the rest and to put them together as the characteristics of a class, and then it groups together the objects that possess these, and when it sees a new object which possesses them, it throws it into that class; in this way it gradually arranges into a cosmos the chaos of perceptions with which it began its mental career, and infers law from the orderly succession of phenomena, and the types it finds in nature. All this is the work of the consciousness in and through the physical brain, but even in this working we trace the presence of that which the brain does not supply. The brain merely receives vibrations; the consciousness working in the astral body changes the vibrations into sensations, and in the mental body changes the sensations into perceptions, and then carries on all the processes which, as just said, transform the chaos into cosmos. And the consciousness thus working is, further, illuminated from above with ides that are not fabricated from materials supplied by the physical world, but are reflected into it directly from the Universal Mind. The great "laws of thought" regulate all thinking, and the very act of thinking reveals their pre-existence, as it is done by them and under them, and is impossible without them.

It is unnecessary almost to remark that all the earlier efforts of consciousness to work in the physical vehicle are subject to much error, both from imperfect perception and from mistaken inferences. Hasty inferences, generalizations from limited experience, vitiate many of the conclusions arrived at, and the rules of logic are formulated in order to discipline the thinking faculty and to enable it to avoid the fallacies into which it constantly falls while untrained. But none the less the attempt to reason, however imperfectly, from one thing to another is a distinct mark of growth in the man himself, for it shows that he is adding something of his own to the information contributed from outside. This working on the collected materials has an effect on the physical vehicle itself. When the mind links two perceptions together, it also sets up - as it is causing corresponding vibrations in the brain - a link between the sets of vibrations from which the perceptions arose. For as the mind body is thrown into activity, it acts on the astral body, and this again on the etheric and dense bodies, and the nervous matter of the latter vibrates under the impulses sent through; this action shows itself as electrical discharges, and magnetic currents play between molecules and groups of molecules causing intricate inter-relations. These leave what we may call a nervous track, a track along which another current will run more easily than it can run, say, athwart it, and if a group of molecules that were concerned in a vibration should be again made active by the consciousness repeating the idea that was impressed upon them, the disturbance there set up readily runs along the track formed between it and another group by a previous linking, and calls that other group into activity, and it sends up to the mind a vibration which, after the regular transformations, presents itself as an associated idea. Hence the great importance of association, this action of the brain being sometimes exceedingly troublesome, as when some foolish or ludicrous idea has been linked with a serious or a sacred one. The consciousness calls up the sacred idea in order to dwell upon it, and suddenly, quite without its consent, the grinning face of the intruding idea, sent up by the mechanical action of the brain, thrusts itself through the doorway of the sanctuary and defiles it. Wise men pay attention to association, and are careful how they speak of the most sacred things, lest some foolish and ignorant person should make a connecting link between the holy and the silly or the coarse, a link which afterwards would be likely to repel itself in the consciousness. Useful is the precept of the great Jewish Teacher: "Give not that which is holy to the dogs, neither cast ye your pearls before swine."

Another mark of progress appears when a man begins to regulate his conduct by conclusions arrived at within instead of by impulses received from without. He is then acting from his own store of accumulated experiences, remembering past happenings, comparing results obtained by different lines of action in the past, and deciding by these as to the line of action he will adopt in the present. He is beginning to forecast, to foresee, to judge of the future by the past, to reason ahead by remembering what has already occurred, and as a man does this there is a distinct growth of him as man. He may still be confined to functioning in his physical brains, he may still be inactive outside them, but he is becoming a developing consciousness which is beginning to behave as an individual, to choose its own road instead of drifting with circumstances, or being forced along a particular line of action by some pressure from without. The growth of the man shows itself in this definite way, and he develops more and more of what is called character, more and more of will-power.

Strong-willed and weak-willed persons are distinguished by their difference in this respect. The weak-willed man is moved from outside, by outer attractions and repulsions, while the strong-willed man is moved from inside, and continually masters circumstances by bringing to bear upon them appropriate forces, guided by his store of accumulated experiences. This store, which the man has in many lives gathered and accumulated, becomes more and more available as the physical brains become more trained and refined, and therefore more receptive: the store is in the man, but he can only use so much of it as he can impress on the physical consciousness. The man himself has the memory and does the reasoning; the man himself judges, chooses, decides: but he has to do all this through his physical and etheric brains; he must work and act by way of the physical body, of the nervous mechanism, and of the etheric organism therewith connected. As the brain becomes more impressible, as he improves its material and brings it more under his control, he is able to use it for better expression of himself.

How, then, shall we, the living men, try to train our vehicles of consciousness in order that they may serve as better instruments? We are not now studying the physical development of the vehicle, but its training by the consciousness that uses it as an instrument of thought. The man decides that in order to make more useful this vehicle of his, to the improvement of which physically he has already directed his attention, he must train it to answer promptly and consecutively to the impulses he transmits to it; in order that the brain may respond consecutively, he will himself think consecutively, and so sending to the brain sequential impulses he will accustom it to work sequentially by linked groups of molecules, instead of by haphazard and unrelated vibrations. The man initiates, the brain only imitates, and unconnected, careless thinking sets up the habit in the brain of forming unconnected vibratory groups. The training has two stages; the man, determining that he will think consecutively, trains his mental body to link though to thought and not to alight anywhere in a casual way; and then, by thinking thus, he trains the brain which vibrates in answer to his thought. In this way the physical organisms - the nervous and the etheric systems - get into the habit of working in a systematic way, and when their owner wants them, they respond promptly and in an orderly fashion; when he require them they are ready to his hand. Between such a trained vehicle of consciousness and one that is untrained, there is the kind of difference that there is between the tools of a careless workman, who leave them dirty and blunt, unfit for use, and those of the man who makes his tools ready, sharpens them and cleans them, so that when they are wanted they are ready to his hand and he can at once use them for the work demanding his attention. Thus should the physical vehicle be ready always to answer to the call of the mind.

The result of such continued working on the physical body will be by no means exhausted in the improved capacity of the brain. For every impulse sent to the physical body has had to pass through the astral vehicle, and has produced an effect upon it also. For, as we have seen, astral matter is far more responsive to thought-vibrations than is physical, and the effect on the astral body of the course of action we have been considering is proportionally great. Under it the astral body assumes a definite outline, a well-organized condition, such as has already been described. When a man has learned to dominate the brain, when he has learned concentration, when he is able to think as he likes and when he likes, a corresponding development takes place in what - if he be physically conscious of it - he will regard as his dream-life. His dreams will become vivid, well-sustained, rational, even instructive. The man is beginning to function in the second of his vehicles of consciousness, the astral body, is entering the second great region or plane of consciousness, and is acting there in the astral vehicle apart from the physical. Let us for a moment consider the difference between two men both "wide-awake," *i. e.*, functioning in the physical vehicle, one of whom is only using his astral body unconsciously as a bridge between the mind and the brain, and the other of whom is using it consciously as a vehicle. The first sees in the ordinary and very limited way, his astral body not yet being an effective vehicle of consciousness; the second uses the astral vision, and is no longer limited by physical matter; he sees through all physical bodies, he sees behind well as in front, walls and other "opaque" substances are to him transparent as glass; he sees astral forms and colours also, auras, elementals, and so on. If he goes to a concert he sees glorious symphonies of colours as the music swells; to a lecture, he sees the speaker's thoughts in colour and form, and so gains a much more complete representation of his thoughts than is possible to one who hears only the spoken words. For the thoughts that issue in symbols as words go out also as coloured and musical forms, and clothed in astral matter impress themselves on the astral body. Where the consciousness is fully awake in that body, it receives and registers the whole of these additional impressions, and many persons will find, if they closely examine themselves, that they do catch from a speaker a good deal more than the mere words convey, even though they may not have been aware of it at the time when they were listening. Many will find in their memory more than the speaker uttered; sometimes a kind suggestion continuing the thought, as though something rose up round the words and made them mean more than they meant to the ear. This experience shows that the astral vehicle is developing, and as the man pays attention to his thinking and unconsciously uses the astral body, it grows and becomes more and more organized.

The "unconsciousness" of people during sleep is due either to the undevelopment of the astral body, or to the absence of connecting conscious links between it and the physical brain. A man uses his astral body during his waking consciousness, sending mind-currents through the astral to the physical brain; but when the physical brain is not in active use, the brain through which the man is in the habit of receiving impressions from without, he is like David in the armor which he had not proved: he is not so receptive to impressions coming to him only through the astral body, to the independent use of which he is not yet accustomed. Further, he may learn to use it independently on the astral plane, and yet not know that he has been using it when he returns to the physical - another stage in the slow progress of the man - and he thus begins to employ it in its own world, before he can make connection between that world and the world below. Lastly, he makes those connections and then he passes in full consciousness from the use of one vehicle to-the use of the other, and is free of the astral world. He has definitely enlarged the area of his waking consciousness to include the astral plane, and while in the physical body his astral senses are entirely at his service, he may be said to be living at one and the same time in the two worlds, there being no break, no gulf between them, and he walks the physical world as a man born blind, whose eyes have been opened.

In the next stage of his evolution, the man begins to work consciously on the third, or mental plane; he has long been working on this plane, sending down from it all the thoughts that take such active form in the astral world and find expression in the physical world through the brain. As he becomes conscious in the mind body, in his mental vehicle, he finds that when he is thinking he is creating forms; he becomes conscious of the creative act, though he has long been exercising the power unconsciously. The reader may remember that in one of the letters quoted in the Occult World, a Master speaks of everyone as making thought-forms but draws the distinction between the ordinary man and the Adept, that the ordinary man produces them unconsciously, while the Adept produces them consciously. (The word Adept is here used in a very wide sense to include Initiates of various grades far below that of a "Master") At this stage of a man's development his powers of usefulness very largely increase, for when he can consciously create and direct a thought-form - an artificial elemental, as it is often called - he can use it to do work in places to which, at the moment, it may not be convenient for him to travel in his mind body. Thus he can work at a distance as well as at hand, and increase his usefulness; he controls these thought-forms from a distance, watching and guiding them as they work, and making them the agents of his will. As the mind body develops, and the man lives and works in it consciously, he knows all the wider and greater life he lives on the mental plane; while he remains in the physical body and is conscious through that of his physical surroundings, he is yet wide-awake and active in the higher world, and he does not need to put the physical body to sleep in order to enjoy the use of the higher faculties. He habitually employs the mental sense, receiving by it impressions of every kind from the mental plane, so that all the mental workings of others are sensed by him as he senses their bodily movements.

When the man has reached this stage of development - a relatively high one, compared with the average, though low when compared with that to which he aspires - he functions then consciously in his third vehicle, or mind body, traces out all he does in it, and experiences its powers and its limitations. Of necessity, also, he learns to distinguish between this vehicle he uses and himself; then he feels the illusory character of the personal "I", the "I" of the mind body and not of the man, and he consciously identifies himself with the individuality that resides in that higher body, the causal, which dwells on the loftier mental planes, those of the arûpa world. He finds that he, the man, can withdraw himself from the mind body, can leave it behind, and, rising higher, yet remain himself; then he knows the many lives are in verity but one life, and that he, the living man, remains himself through all.

And now as to the links - the links between these different bodies. They exist at first without coming into the consciousness of the man. They are there, otherwise he could not pass from the plane of the mind to that of the body, but he is not conscious of their existence, and they are not actively vivified, they are almost like what are called in the physical body rudimentary organs. Every student of biology knows that rudimentary organs are of two kinds: one kind affords the traces of the stages through which the body has passed in evolution, while the other gives hints of the lines of future growth. These organs exist but they do not function; their activity in the physical body is either of the past or of the future, dead or unborn. The links which I venture by analogy to call rudimentary organs of the second kind, connect the dense and etheric bodies with the astral, the astral with the mind body, the mind body with the causal. They exist, but they have to be brought into activity; that is, they have to be developed, and, like their physical types, they can only be developed by use. The life-current flows through them, the mind-current flows through them, and thus they are kept alive and nourished; but they are only gradually brought into functioning activity as the man fixes his attention on them and brings his will to bear on their development. The action of the will begins to vivify these rudimentary links, and, step by step, very slowly perhaps, they begin to function; the man begins to use them for the passage of his consciousness from vehicle to vehicle.

In the physical body there are nervous centres, little groups of nervous cells, and both impacts from without and impulses from the brain pass through these centres. If one of these is out of order, then at once disturbances arise and physical consciousness is disturbed. There are analogous centres in the astral body, but in the undeveloped man they are rudimentary and do not function. These are links between the physical and the astral bodies, between the astral and the mind bodies, and as evolution proceeds they are vivified by the will, setting free and guiding the "serpent-fire", called Kundalini in Indian books. The preparatory stage for the direct action that liberates Kundalini is the training and purifying of the vehicles, for if this be not thoroughly accomplished, the fire is a destructive instead of a vivifying energy. That is why we have laid so much stress on purification and urge it as a necessary preliminary for all true Yoga.

When a man has rendered himself fit to safely receive assistance in the vivifying of these links, such assistance comes to him as a matter of course from those who are ever seeking opportunity to aid the earnest and the unselfish aspirant. Then, one day, the man finds himself slipping out of the physical body while he is wide-awake, and without any break in consciousness he discovers himself to be free. When this has occurred a few times the passage from vehicle to vehicle becomes familiar and easy. When the astral body leaves the physical in sleep, there is a brief period of unconsciousness, and even when the man is functioning actively on the astral plane he fails to bridge over that unconsciousness on his return. Unconscious as he leaves the body, he will probably be unconscious as he re-enters it; there may be full and vivid consciousness on the astral plane, and yet a complete blank may be all that represents it in the physical brain. But when the man leaves the body in waking consciousness, having developed the links between the vehicles into functional activity, he has bridged the gulf; for him it is a gulf no longer, and his consciousness passes swiftly from one plane to the other, and he knows himself as the same man on both.

The more the physical brain is trained to answer to the vibrations from the mind body, the more is the bridging of the gulf between day and night facilitated. The brain becomes more and more the obedient instrument of the man, carrying on its activities under the impulses from his will, and like a well-broken horse answering to the lightest touch of hand or knee. The astral world lies open to the man who has thus unified the two lower vehicles of consciousness, and it belongs to him with all its possibilities, with all its wider powers, its greater opportunities of doing service and of rendering help. Then comes the joy of carrying aid to sufferers who are unconscious of the agent though they feel the relief, of pouring balm into wounds that then seem to heal of themselves, of lifting burdens that become miraculously light to the aching shoulders on which they pressed so heavily.

More than this is needed to bridge over the gulf between life and life; to carry memory through day and night unbrokenly merely means that the astral body is functioning perfectly, and that the links between it and the physical are in full working order. If a man is to bridge over the gulf between life and life he must do very much more than act in full consciousness in the astral body, and more than act consciously in the mind body; for the mind body is composed of the materials of the lower planes of the mânasic world, and reincarnation does not take place from them. The mind body disintegrates in due course, like the astral and physical vehicles, and cannot carry anything across. The whole question on which memory of past lives turns is this: Can the man, or can he not, function on the higher planes of the mânasic world in his causal body? It is the causal body that passes from life to life: it is in the causal body that everything is stored; it is in the causal body that all experience remains, for into it the consciousness is drawn up, and from its plane is the descent made into rebirth. Let us follow the stages of the life out of the physical world, and see how far the sway of King Death extends. The man draws himself away from the dense part of the physical body; it drops off him, goes to pieces, and is restored to the physical world; nothing remains in which the magnetic link of memory can inhere. He is then in the etheric part of the physical body, but in the course of a few hours he shakes that off, and it is resolved into its elements. No memory, then, connected with the etheric brain will help him to bridge the gulf. He passes on into the astral world, remaining there till he similarly shakes off his astral body, and leaves it behind as he had left the physical; the "astral corpse," in its turn, disintegrates, restores its materials to the astral world, and breaks up all that might serve as basis for the magnetic links necessary for memory. He goes onward in his mind body and dwells in the rûpa levels of Devachan, living there for hundreds of years, working up faculties, enjoying fruit. But from this mind body also he withdraws when the time is ripe, taking from it to carry on into the body that endures the essence of all that he has gathered and assimilated. He leaves the mind body behind him, to disintegrate after the fashion of his denser vehicles, for the matter of it - subtle as it is from our standpoint - is not subtle enough to pass onward to the higher planes of the mânasic world. It has to be shaken off, to be left to go back into the materials of its own region, once more a resolution of the combination into its elements. All the way up the man is shaking off body after body, and only on reaching the arûpa planes of the mânasic world can he be said to have passed beyond the regions over which the disintegrating sceptre of Death has sway. He passes finally out of his dominions, dwelling in the causal body over which Death has no power, and in which he stores up all that he has gathered. Hence its very name of causal body, since all causes that affect future incarnations reside in it. He must then begin to act in full consciousness on the arûpa levels of the mânasic world in his causal body ere he can bring memory across the gulf of death. An undeveloped soul, entering that lofty region, cannot keep consciousness there; he enters it, carrying up all the germs of his qualities; there is a touch, a flash of consciousness embracing past and future, and the dazzled Ego sinks downwards towards rebirth. He carries the germs in this causal body and throws outward on each plane those that belong to it; they gather to themselves matters severally befitting them. Thus on the rûpa levels of the lower mânasic world the mental germs draw round them the matter of those levels to form the new mind body, and the matter thus gathered shows the mental characteristics given to it by the germ within it, as the acorn develops into an oak by gathering into it suitable materials from soil and atmosphere. The acorn cannot develop into a birch or a cedar, but only into an oak, and so the mental germ must develop after its own nature and none other. Thus does Karma work in the building of the vehicles, and the man has the harvest of which he sowed the seed. The germ thrown out from the causal body can only grow after its kind, attracting to itself the grade of matter that belongs to it, arranging that matter in its characteristic form, so that it produces the replica of the quality the man made in the past. As he comes into the astral world, the germs are thrown out that belong to that world, and they draw round themselves suitable astral materials and elemental essences. Thus reappear the appetites, emotions and passions belonging to the desire body, or astral body, of the man, reformed in this fashion on his arrival on the astral plane. If, then, consciousness of past lives is to remain, carried through all these processes and all these worlds it must exist in full activity on that high plane of causes, the plane of the causal body. People do not remember their past lives because they are not yet conscious in the causal body as a vehicle; it has not developed functional activity of its own. It is there, the essence of their lives, their real "I", that from which all proceeds, but it does not yet actively function: it is not yet self-conscious, though unconsciously active, and until it is self-conscious, fully self-conscious, the memory cannot pass from plane to plane and therefore from life to life. As the man advances, flashes of consciousness break forth that illumine fragments of the past, but these flashes need to change to a steady light ere any consecutive memory can arise.

It may be asked: Is it possible to encourage the recurrence of such flashes? Is it possible for people to hasten this gradually growing activity of consciousness on the higher planes? The lower man may labour to this end, if he has patience and courage; he may try to live more and more in the permanent self, to withdraw thought and energy more and more, so far as interest is concerned, from the trivialities and impermanences of ordinary life. I do not mean that a man should become dreamy, abstracted and wandering, a most inefficient member of the home and of society; on the contrary, every claim that the world has on him will be discharged, and discharged the more perfectly because of the greatness of the man who is doing it; he cannot do things as clumsily and imperfectly as the less developed man may do them, for to him duty is duty, and as long as anyone or anything has a claim upon him, the debt must be paid to the uttermost farthing; every duty will be fulfilled as perfectly as he can fulfill it, with his best faculties, his best attention. But his interest will not be in these things, his thoughts will not be bound to their results; the instant that the duty is performed and he is released his thought will fly back to the permanent life, will rise to the higher level with upward-striving energy, and he will begin to live there and to rate at their true worthlessness the trivialities of the worldly life. As he steadily does this, and seeks to train himself to high and abstract thinking, he will begin to vivify the higher links in consciousness and bring into this lower life the consciousness that is himself.

A man is one and the same man on whatever plane he may be functioning, and his triumph is when he functions on all the five planes in unbroken consciousness. Those whom we call the Masters, the "Men made perfect," function in Their waking consciousness, not only on the three lower planes, but on the fourth plane - that plane of unity spoken of in the *Mândûkyopanishad* as the Turîya, and on that yet above it, the plane of Nirvana. In them evolution is completed, this cycle has been trodden to its close, and what they are, all in time shall be who are climbing slowly upwards. This is the unification of consciousness; the vehicles remain for use, but no longer are able to imprison, and the man uses any one of his bodies according to the work that he has to do.

In this way matter, time and space are conquered, and their barriers cease to exist for the unified man. He has found in climbing upwards that there are less and less barriers in each stage: even on the astral plane, matter is much less of a division than it is down here, separating him from his brothers far less effectually. Traveling in the astral body is so swift that space and time may be said to be practically conquered, for although the man knows he is passing through space it is passed through so rapidly that its power to divide friend from friend is lost. Even that first conquest sets at nought physical distance. When he rose to the mental world he found another power his; he thought of a place: he was there; he thought of a friend: the friend was before him. Even on the third plane consciousness transcends the barriers of matter, space and time, and is present anywhere at will. All things that are seen are seen at once, the moment attention is turned to them; all that is heard is heard at a single impression; space, matter and time, as known in the lower worlds, have disappeared, sequence no longer exists in the "eternal now. " As he rises yet higher, barriers within consciousness also fall away, and knows himself to be one with other consciousness other living things; he can think as they think, feel as they feel, know as they know. He can make their limitations his for the moment, in order that he can understand exactly how they are thinking, and yet have his own consciousness. He can use his own great knowledge for the helping of the narrower and more restricted thought, identifying himself with it in order gently to enlarge its bounds. He takes on altogether new functions in nature when he is no longer divided from others, but realizes the Self that is one in all and sends down his energies from the plane of unity. With regard even to the lower animals he is able to feel how the world exists to them, so that he can give exactly the help they need, and can supply the aid after which they are blindly groping.

Hence his conquest is not for himself but for all, and he wins wider powers only to place them at the service of all lower in the scale evolution than himself; in this way he becomes self-conscious in all the world; for this he learns to be responsive to every cry of pain, to every throb of joy or sorrow. All is reached, all is gained, and the Master is the man "who has nothing more to learn. " By this we mean not that all possible knowledge is at any given moment within His consciousness, but that so far as this stage of evolution is concerned there is nothing that to Him is veiled, nothing of which He does not become fully conscious when He turns His attention to it; within this circle of evolution of everything that lives - and all things live - there is nothing He cannot understand, and therefore nothing that He cannot help.

That is the ultimate triumph of man. All that I have spoken of would be worthless, trivial, were it gained for the narrow self we recognize as self down here; all the steps, my reader, to which I have been trying to win you would not be worth the taking did they set you at last on an isolated pinnacle, apart from all the sinning, suffering selves, instead of leading you to the heart of things, where they and you are one. The consciousness of the Master stretches itself out in any direction in which He sends it, assimilates itself with any point to which He directs it, knows anything which He wills to know; and all this in order that He may help perfectly, that there may be nothing that He cannot feel, nothing that He cannot foster, nothing that He cannot strengthen, nothing that He cannot aid in its evolution; to Him the whole world is one vast evolving whole, and His place in it is that of a helper of evolution; He is able to identify Himself with any step, and at that step to give the aid that is needed. He helps the elementary kingdoms to evolve downwards, and, each in its own way, the evolutions of the minerals, plants, animals and men, and He helps them all as Himself. For the glory of His life is that all is Himself and yet He can aid all, in the very helping realizing as Himself that which He aids.

The mystery how this can be gradually unfolds itself as man develops, and consciousness widens to embrace more and more while yet becoming more vivid, more vital, and without losing knowledge of itself. When the point has become the sphere, the sphere finds itself to be the point; each point contains everything and knows itself one with every other point; the outer is found be only the reflection of the inner; the Reality is the One Life, and the difference an illusion that is overcome.

THE END.

BOOK FOUR
EVOLUTION OF LIFE AND FORM

Four Lectures delivered at the Twenty-third Anniversary Meeting of the Theosophical Society at Adyar, Madras, 1898.

I. ANCIENT AND MODERN SCIENCE.

MY BROTHERS:—The subject on which I am to address you this morning, and the three mornings that follow, is one of considerable complexity and difficulty. I do not apologise to you for the difficulty of my theme. When we meet here in our Anniversary Meeting, we meet as students and not simply as superficial men and women of the world. We try to prepare ourselves, by study, for the exchange of thought which in these gatherings takes place, and although the subject is a difficult one, although it is not possible to make it clear and intelligible without the use of certain technical terms, yet, to the student technical terms—being precise—are really the easiest to understand, and inasmuch as, in a great majority at least, we are students, I who speak, and you who listen, we may be content to treat the subject in a somewhat formal and technical way. Roughly, my outline is this. I want to lay before you an intelligible conception of evolution, taking it on its two sides, that of the evolving life and that of the developing forms. I begin by laying before you a sketch of the methods of "Ancient and Modern Science," the direction in which each has worked, and is working, the ultimate union that, we hope, may take place between them. For what could more fully presage the good of the whole world, what could promise more happily for the relationship between the different races of humanity, than to draw together on the plane of mind the science of antiquity and of modern days, the science of the East and of the West, and, by wedding them to each other, draw together the nations that are now divided, and make objective that brotherhood of humanity of which we dream.

Dealing first with ancient and modern science in this broad and general way, and taking that as my subject for this morning, I shall pass on to-morrow to speak on the "Functions of the Gods," meaning by that phrase the activities of that invisible side of nature on which the whole of the visible depends. Whether we use here the name "Devas" to represent those developed spiritual intelligences, or whether with the child of Islâm, with the Hebrew or the Christian, we speak of the "Angels" and "Archangels," the name matters nothing; the conception is common to every faith of man. We shall study their functions in the universe, and try to understand how they act as the ministers of the Divine Will. Then we shall pass on to treat of that "Evolution of Life" which lies underneath the evolution of forms. Finally, we shall treat the "Evolution of Forms," and see how, in that evolution, is the promise of final perfection, how all is working to a perfect ending, how the best that we can dream of is less than the performance of God.

That is the outline of our work. Let us at once begin the first section of the subject—Ancient and Modern Science.

Now, in the olden times, in those times to which in this land our thought turns back most fondly with reverence and with pride, in those times, here, as in every other ancient land, Religion and Science were wedded together, and there was no discord between the intelligence and the spirit. It matters not whither you wander amid the ancient nations of the world: you may travel through the whole of Chaldea; you may study the remains of ancient Egypt; you may go through Persia and search amid her monuments; you may cross the Atlantic to America, and unbury the cities that were lost ere yet the Aztecs had made the mighty State which fell under the blows of the Spaniards; you may go into China and, in the vast recesses of that well-nigh unknown land, you may search for what has been left there from ancient days; or without going outside the limits of your own land, you may take the literature that is our pride, the mighty books written by the Ṛishis of the past; and everywhere antiquity speaks with a single tongue. Religion reveals the spirit, the spiritual truth which is one. Intelligence studies that truth in its manifold manifestations, and its work; science, studying the phenomena which are images of aspects of the Divine, is the handmaid, is the sister, of religion, and between them discord is unnatural and fatal to progress. That is the ancient view; but when we come to our own century a new phenomenon presents itself to our gaze—religion on the one side suspicious of science in its progress, science on the other hand apt to be proudly contemptuous of religious claims. How has the divorce arisen? Why this discord between two of the great helpers of human evolution? The reason is not far to seek. In the western world the science of the elder time, the science of antiquity, disappeared in the great flood of barbaric invasions, underneath the whirlpool caused by the ruins of the Roman Empire, and later on, underneath the wreckage of that same Empire with its new centre in Constantinople. The invasions of barbarians, both from the East and the North, sweeping over the European continent, brought ignorance in the wake of barbaric conquest. The result was that night came down upon knowledge and thick darkness enveloped the lands which were to be the nursery of a new civilisation. When the Sun of science again began to rise upon the Western world, it presented itself in a form which was alien, nay, which was more than alien, which was hostile to the dominant religion of the time. It came from the children of Islâm. It came from those who recognised Muhammed as their Prophet. From the Muslim schools of Arabia came the first teachers of modern science to Europe. True, they were really by their intellectual ancestry descended from the thought of Greece. They drew their inspiration from the school of Plato through the Neo-Platonists; they reproduced the ideas of Porphyry and Ptolemy, and of other Grecian and Egyptian thinkers, Neo-Platonic and even Gnostic. But they threw over it the garb of Islâm, they presented it in the form of Arabic thought. The result of this was that, as it made its way into Spain in the wake of the conquering Moors, as it came with those who drove out of the Southern Peninsula the rule of the Spanish Christian monarchy, so the first aspect of science to Christians was an aspect of hostility. It came as an invading enemy and not as an illuminant to all. Hence conflict arose; some who were within the limits of the mighty Church of Rome, touched by a longing for the new learning, stretched out their hands to take the gifts that science was bringing. These men were regarded with suspicion, nay, with more than suspicion, with hatred that broke out in bitter persecution. Who can read the history of Roger Bacon, the wondrous monk; who can picture Copernicus on his death-bed as his immortal work is brought to him ere yet his eyes are closed, he having shrunk from earlier publication, lest the stake should be his portion; who can stand in the Field of Flowers in Rome, and see there the statue erected where he was burned to death, who dying in one century, lives for all centuries to come—Giordano Bruno; who can listen to Galileo, as with faltering lips he denies the truth he knows and utters the falsehood that he knows not; who can follow these martyr-steps, led on by bitter memories of blood and fire, without understanding the reason for the hostility of science to religion, without confessing with shame and sorrow that that hostility was caused and was justified by the cruelties wreaked by religion on science, when science was young and feeble? Every one of us who stands upon the side of religion should recognise that we are reaping the bitter harvest of our own past errors, and that the law is just which brings upon us the difficulties and opposition we encounter in our modern days. For as science grew strong, she grew strong with the sword in her hands. She fought for every inch of the ground on which she stood, and only so far as she could guard herself was she safe from the flame or from the prison. Hence she searched for everything in nature that could serve as a weapon against the foe that attacked her. Hence she welcomed eagerly everything which seemed to show that materialism was the true philosophy of life. If we go back twenty-five years, to the time when I and some of you were young, we shall find that over western science there hung the shadow of materialism, and that stronger and stronger grew the scientific tendency to "see in matter the promise and the potency of every form of life." You remember those famous words of Professor Tyndall, no materialist in his thought and a religious man in his aspirations, but wellnigh driven by despair to claim fair field for science, and to fling back the claims of religion, because among them was included the right to gag, the refusal to allow thought to be honestly uttered by the thinker. But things are changing more and more; as religion has been growing more liberal and more rational, science is becoming less materialistic and less aggressive; and we shall see presently that the most modern of modern science—not quite the science that you get in your textbooks, for that is practically out-of-date in the rush of thought which comes from the West, but the science of the leaders of thought, the science of the first men in the scientific camp—is more and more approaching the domain where scientists will recognise religion as helper and not as enemy. In fact, speaking from the same chair from which Tyndall had uttered his famous phrase that "in matter he saw the promise and potency of every form of life," his successor, Sir William Crookes, a member of our own Theosophical Society, declared, reversing those words of his predecessor, that "In life I see the promise and potency of all forms of matter. "

Such is the great change. Let us now examine in detail. The fundamental difference between ancient and modern science is that ancient science studies the world from the standpoint of life which is evolving, while modern science studies the world by observing the forms through which that life is manifesting. The first studies life, and sees in forms the expressions of life. The second studies forms, and tries, by the process of induction, to find out if there be an underlying principle by which the multiplicity of forms may be explained. The first works from above downwards, the second from below upwards, and in that very fact is the promise of a meeting place where the two will join hand in hand. But this fundamental difference carries with it very important results. If we are to study the world from the standpoint of forms, our study will be almost endless in its multiplicity. Think of a tree; the one trunk through which the life is pouring, innumerable leaves in which that life is ultimately expressed; it is an image of the tree of life, that great Ashvattha, the tree of which we have heard, whose roots are in the heavens and whose branches spread out over the earth. If we are to study it where its trunk is, the trunk of life, we have the unity of purpose and can trace why we have multiplicity of forms; but if we are to start at the parts where the leaves are growing, leaf by leaf we must examine, every difference of outline we must record, each little variety in shape we must carefully note and study. Science studies the leaves in modern days—the old science studied the life. There is the fundamental difference. There is also the reason of the difference of methods by which the study must be carried on. What is the method of modern science? The use of clear observation, keen judgment, power of placing like things together, and seeing the differences that divide the classes of the like from the classes of the unlike. But in order that this may be done, inasmuch as nature is infinite both in the vast and in the minute, man demands, to supplement his limited senses, instruments and apparatus of the most exquisite and delicate character; so that it has been even said that the progress of science is the progress of the exquisite nature of the apparatus which science uses, and scientific men will devise a more delicate balance, a more dainty way of adjustment, instrument after instrument, until perfection seems well-nigh to be reached; the modern man of science, to carry on his researches, demands a vast array of apparatus that he must use for his work, for according to the delicacy of his apparatus is the extent of his observation of the forms to which his attention is directed. But the man of science of the ancient type does not ask for instruments; he is not studying the evolution of forms; he has to study life, not form; and for such study he must evolve himself, the life that is within him, for only life can measure life, only life can respond to the vibrations of the living; his work is to unfold himself, to bring out of the depths of his own nature the divine powers that lie hidden therein, not in the senses but in the Self. His investigations can only be carried on by means of these powers, and only as he develops the divine within him will he be able to understand and measure the divine without him. Now this is only possible because, in essence, the natures of God and man are identical. This sounds a bold statement, but it is the fundamental truth of all religions. Need I quote to you the famous saying, "Thou art That"? Shall I take an equivalent phrase from the Hebrew Scripture, accepted by the whole Christian world: "God created man in His own image, in the image of God created He him"? The teaching is identical as all great truths are identical in the various religions; but what does it mean? God is manifest in His universe. Would you understand His work, you must develop the

God within yourself, else will He for ever be veiled from your eyes. Not by the eyes of sense may you behold Him, not by the vision of intellect may you see that Form, invisible even to the intelligence. Only as the Self that is God is unfolded within you, will the Self that is the God without you manifest to you the full glory of His life. That is the ancient starting point. Thus what the man of old had to do, if indeed he were to be a man of science, was to become divine; he was to be a saint before he could be a sage. No man could be wise until he was pure, for how should impure eyes behold the Pure? There is the hall-mark of the man of science of the ancient days: he is developed within before he can be learned without. But from the modern man of science is not demanded this condition. He must indeed lead a life that is self-restrained, orderly, and fairly clean; were he to yield to the riot of the senses, his intelligence would become clouded. He must have keen power of observation, balanced strength of judgment, strong patience, unwearied industry, clear insight for differences and similarities. All these are demanded from him, if he is to be great, and these are among the noblest powers of intelligence. But all he asks of religion is to leave him alone. Of old, religion opened the gateway to science; now-a-days science asks nothing from religion save to stand aside. That is the difficulty in our way. We have to show that life cannot be understood until the student lives that which he seeks. That even the understanding of forms is very imperfect until the life expressed through them is recognised and partially understood. That fundamental difference of method then, will cover the whole field, and will enable us to comprehend the difference of the results.

Now let us try to understand more clearly why it was that the ancient man of science was taught that the first step to true knowledge, or wisdom, was the unfolding of the Self. What is life or consciousness—for the two terms are synonymous? It is the power to answer to vibrations, the power to respond—that is consciousness. Evolution is the unfolding of a continually increasing power to respond. The whole universe is full of the vibrations of Íshvara, of God. He sustains and moves the whole. Consciousness is the power in us to answer to those vibrations. All powers lie hidden within us as the oak tree lies hidden in the acorn. But it is in the process of evolution that the sapling slowly grows out of the seed. In Eternity, in the Now, all is existent, perfect; in Time only is there succession, the unfolding of one thing after another. In the changeless Point everything is present: Space is but the field for diverse sequences. Hence Time and Space are the basic illusions, and are yet the fundamental conditions of thinking. Keep, I pray you, that definition of consciousness in mind, for it will govern the remainder of our study.

The Self in man, being in the image of God, is triple as the Self, the Divine, is triple. I need not stop to argue this. You know it from that great literature which lies at the foundation of all Hindu Philosophy. Whether you speak in abstract terms and say with the Upanishad that Brahman is threefold, whether you speak of Him as Sat-chit-ânanda, or whether, instead of using philosophical, abstract terms, you say He is manifest as Íshvara in the Trimûrti as Mahâdeva, Vishnu and Brahmâ, it matters not. You may take the concrete form or the abstract, the fundamental idea is the same: that the Divine Self in manifestation is triple, and therefore in every great religion God is spoken of as a Trinity. If this were not so, the relationship between God and man would remain for ever unintelligible, for man shows a triplicity as he evolves. The human reflection of that triple Divine Self is the triple Self in man.

One by one are the Divine aspects unfolded as manifestation proceeds. The lowest, if I may dare to use such a term, is the aspect which is first brought into activity for the building of the universe. So also in man the intelligence awakens and becomes active, the lowest aspect of the human Self. That is the reflection of Brahmâ, of the Universal Mind, the creative energy from which all comes forth; and you may find in yourselves, as you evolve, that creative faculty of imagination which, working at present in subtle matter, will, when man is perfect, work in grosser matter as well; for the imaginative power in man is the reflection of the power that in God created the universe. Brahmâ meditated, and all forms came forth; and in the creative power of mind lies every possibility of form. So in man is later evolved the next aspect, that of A'nanda, where unity is recognised instead of diversity. Chit, in man, is the intelligence that *knows*, that separates and divides and analyses, and it has to do with the multiplicity of forms and with their inter-relations; A'nanda is the wisdom that realises the unity of all things, and that accomplishes union, thus finding the joy that lies at the very heart of life; last of all in human evolution, is developed the third and highest aspect of Deity, Self-Existence, the Unity that lies beyond union, and this can be developed in man only because man is one with the Eternal in his nature. By this evolution, in ages to come, through the countless kalpas that lie in front, Íshvara after Íshvara arises, each as the fruitage of a universe, to carry on still more mightily the will of the "One without a second," and to manifest something of that perfection to the whole of the then manifested nature. Such, very roughly, is the course of human evolution into divinity, and this is carried on by races succeeding one another; as we come to the higher Root-races of man, to those that we speak of as the Fifth, in which we are, the Sixth, that shall succeed us, and the Seventh that finishes this cycle of human evolution, we learn that the characteristic of each of these three Root-races is that each gradually develops that aspect of God which belongs to it in the due sequence of evolution. The Fifth is developing the aspect of Chit, Intelligence, the mind is being evolved, and all the progress of modern science, so marked in our own days, is but part of the fruitage of that evolution, of that growth of intelligence which looks on the outer world as not itself—as the Not-Self— and seeks to study and understand it. The characteristic attributes belonging to the evolution of the two following races are even now to be reached by special methods, by individuals who are willing to take the pains to make the required sacrifices. That which we know as Yoga is the method by which evolution is quickened in the individual, and all the powers of the Self, up to the threshold of divinity, may by it be brought into manifestation in the man of the present. That is why Yoga training was necessary for the ancient scientist; he must develop in himself the three aspects of God, if he were to understand them as manifested in the universe around him.

Now, at our own stage of evolution, it is specially the life of Brahmâ— or the Brahmâ aspect of God—with which the human mind is coming into touch, because the mind in man is the reflection of the universal mind in Kosmos. That life is the life that is the force in the atom, that vivifies every atom, nay, that brings the atom into existence, as we shall see, and remains during the whole of the growth of the universe as the fundamental life that keeps those atoms as active particles building up innumerable forms. Only as the life of Brahmâ, the aspect of Brahmâ, is developed in the human Self will man be able to study the workings of that life in the atomic forms that are filled by it; and it is very significant that some of the greatest problems of modern science are now turning on the nature of the atom, and that scientists are asking, what is it? Is it matter or force? Is it a particle or a vortex? Never will that question be answered with certainty until man has developed in himself the power to respond to the life that thrills in the atom, until, developing intelligence within himself to the fullest point, he is able to answer by that intelligence to the vibrations of the atomic life outside him. We have defined consciousness as the power to answer to vibrations, and if man is to measure life, if he is to know the underlying causes of phenomena, he must develop in himself the power to respond to that life outside him; and in the perfection of human intelligence—the reflection of the Brahmâ aspect of God—lies the only possibility of solution for this much debated problem in science. I said it was significant, for this problem belongs to the Fifth race, and the Western world is at present peopled largely by the fifth sub-race of the great Fifth. Thus it takes to the very highest point the concrete mind of man, that marvellous activity of the intellect, that swift and yet patient study, bringing about the achievements that modern science is performing. All these are a testimony of the truth of the ancient teaching that sub-race after sub-race arises, each one with its own work to do, and we should look on the work of each sub-division of humanity as good in itself: each should not be regarded as an isolated and hostile expression, but as part of the Divine manifestation, expressing that portion which it is destined to express.

Looking thus, then, on the problem of the life that exists in the atom, we find that in order to understand it, we must develop the pure intellect in man; but to understand the life that clothes itself in organic forms, to unravel the secrets which will explain to us why one is formed thus and another thus, the next great aspect of the Self must be developed within us—that of the all-pervading life of Vishnu, that sustains the world as the mighty supporter of everything, the basis, the foundation of the whole. There alone is unifying energy and there the root from which all divisions have arisen; only as we realise this aspect of unifying energy in the Self will the secrets of organised forms in nature unravel themselves before our eyes. This work is that of the Sixth Root-race, and those who would ante-date their evolution must develop Sixth-race powers in themselves by Yoga. Remains one mightier problem, subtlest and most difficult of all, that of the life of the human spirit, of man evolving into God. The mysteries of that life may only be understood when the human Self, which comes forth from the Father of all—from the mighty One who is sometimes the Destroyer, sometimes the Creator, but always the Regenerator, the name that includes them both, Mahâdeva, the mighty God who is Sat, Existence—has developed the aspect of Sat, of pure Existence, thus becoming the triple Unity, a Logos, an Íshvara. That is the work of the Seventh Root-race, and when that is accomplished, then only will the final problems of the human spirit lie open before our gaze.

The scientific man of antiquity, then, began by that self-attention, unfolding in himself one by one all those potentialities under a suitable Guru, passing from step to step till he reached the highest, and ever worshipping the Mahâguru, the Guru of the universe. Having unfolded his highest powers, he began to study life, life in its outpouring, not life in its manifold and veiled manifestations in the lower worlds. Hence the lofty point at which he started, no less than the arising of Íshvara enveloped in Mâyâ.

What is Íshvara? What is Mâyâ? There is the first great problem. Let us reverently address ourselves to it. The philosophers of India have answered these questions in different ways, each one containing part of the eternal truth. Íshvara is that mighty centre of consciousness that exists unchanged in the bosom of the One Existence. There are innumerable such Centres of Consciousness, of which you may remember your own Svâmi Subba Rao wrote as existing in the bosom of the One Existence. Íshvara in manifestation is like a lamp, a light enclosed in a shade. Íshvara, enveloped in Mâyâ, brings forth a universe and is enclosed, as it were, in the universe of which He is the Light. Breaking the shade, the light shines forth in every direction. Dissolving the universe, He still remains. The centre remains, but the circumference that circumscribed it is gone. So is that mighty centre when the universe vanishes; He alone remains, holding His centre unshaken in the very act of merging in, expanding into, the Infinite, the Absolute, the Super-Consciousness, the One. Let us think of Him as an eternal centre of self-consciousness, able to merge in super-consciousness and to again limit Himself to self-consciousness.

What, then, is Mâyâ? Mâyâ is prepared in every case by the merging in Íshvara of the whole of the universe which is come to its ending. As one loka rolls up and merges in the one above it, all forms in the loka thus merged disappear, but the consciousness that ensouled those forms does not vanish; a modification of consciousness remains, a modification expressing itself by a vibratory power—not a vibration, but a power to vibrate in a particular way; and though the form vanishes as the loka is merged in the one above it—because the matter disappears, being disintegrated into finer matter—in consciousness there remains the power to vibrate in the way in which it had vibrated in the grosser matter, and power persists although the forms caused by such vibrations disappear, for lack of material sufficiently coarse to respond to such vibrations. As one region passes into the next, this process is repeated over and over and over again, and loka after loka vanishes. The forms are gone, the vibrations are gone, only the modifications in consciousness capable of giving rise to similar vibrations remain until finally, when Íshvara—whose consciousness was the one consciousness in the universe, whose life was the one life, who supported every form, who made the possibility of every separated existence—gathers up His universe into Himself ere He merges Himself in the ONE, everything has vanished that we know as form, nothing remains save the centre of consciousness. There remains in Íshvara the power of vibrating in particular fashions, resulting from the evolution of His universe, in endless multiplicity of vibrations; when He merges Himself in the One Existence all has vanished as form, but powers remain in these subtle modifications, preserved in that unchangeable centre in the mightiness of the One Life. Is that only a dream?

There was a great teacher, Vâsishtha. He taught Râmâ, as you will remember, and in the record of his teaching there are hints on some of the mysteries of life. If you keep what I have now said in mind, if I have succeeded by the clumsy words which are all that the human tongue can utter on these great problems, in clarifying at all your thoughts, then just listen to that same thought as expressed by Sûryadeva, when he was speaking of the same thing—the ending and the new beginning of a universe. We have only to add to what I have already said, that when Íshvara arises in order that a new universe may be formed, He throws His life into these modifications that had apparently disappeared, and the Mâyâ in which He arises, enveloped and circumscribed, is His own re-vivified memory, which can never be separated from Himself; He draws in His consciousness, under the impulse of the Great Breath, limiting it to self-consciousness, and turning His attention to the contents of that self-consciousness, its powers start into activity, and that is Mâyâ. So it is written: "Thereafter, Thou, O Lord, intent on [maintaining] the reign of night, fixed within the Self, having indrawn that order of things, [or universe] ... To-day, Thou hast awakened, and art most joyfully desirous of again throwing out [manifesting] the universe in mighty gradations [hierarchies of beings]. " [*Yoga Vâsishtha*, lxxxvii, 7, 8.] These nights and days are the "Nights and Days of Brahmâ," the inbreathing and outbreathing of the One Existence, and Mâyâ is this indrawn "order of things" that remains fixed through the Night, and starts forth as Íshvara awakens at the coming of Day. That is Mâyâ and if you take up the definitions given in the different schools, you will find that this includes and illumines every one of them, that it shows you what is meant by illusion, and explains to you what is implied in dreaming. The joyful throwing out into manifestation of all the powers that are remembered by Íshvara the moment His attention is turned to His own Self, that memory-prompted "desire" which arises in the bosom of the Eternal, is the root of the coming universe. Now this thought will prove to you the key of much ancient teaching. You have, in the Universal Mind full of ideas which are not yet concreted into phenomena, the world of ideas of Plato, the invisible world of the Hebrew Kabbalah; in every great teaching you find the same thought expressed. If, instead of being fettered by words, as for the most part we are, and if, instead of repeating phrases that carry with them no idea in the mind of the repeater, we would try to read the thought that underlies the words, we should find the Hindu philosophy in every modern philosophy that is worthy of the name, and see the traces of ancient India in Greece and in Rome, in Germany and in the England of to-day.

What is the next stage? The Life-Breath goes forth. Íshvara, the Centre of all, enveloped in Mâyâ sends forth His breath; as that vibrating breath falls on the enveloping Mâyâ, Mâyâ becomes Prakriti, or Matter—rather, perhaps, Mûlaprakriti, the root of matter. As that breath, with its triple vibratory force falls on this matter, it throws it into three modifications, or "attributes"—Tamas, inertia, or better, stability; Rajas, activity, vigour; Sattva, a difficult word to translate: I am inclined to translate it as Harmony; for this reason, that wherever there is pleasure, Sattva is present. Without harmony no pleasure can anywhere exist. All pleasure is due to harmonious vibration, and that quality of harmonious inter-related vibrations is the quality that Sattva gives to matter. These three fundamental qualities of matter—answering to three fundamental modifications in the consciousness of Íshvara—inertia, activity, and harmony, these are the famous three Gunas without which Prakriti cannot manifest. Fundamental, essential, and unchangeable, they are present in every particle in the manifested universe, and according to their combinations is the nature of each particle.

Then comes the seven-fold division. In a moment I will tell you why we speak of it as seven-fold instead of five-fold, which is the more familiar division to you. The seven-fold division, what is this? Here is matter with its three Gunas, now ready to receive another impulse from the Life-Breath; that breath comes forth from Brahmâ, for Íshvara has unfolded His triple nature into its three aspects, and it comes forth in seven great waves. Each one modifies matter, and evolves and ensouls those that follow it. The first two are absolutely beyond our knowing, and belong not to our present stages of evolution at all; therefore they are ordinarily left out, and only the five that make up the evolution of our universe are spoken of in the sacred books. Here and there the seven are mentioned, but only rarely. You may remember the seven tongues of fire, for instance, and one or two other similar phrases. But generally five-fold is Prâna, the five-fold evolving life. First, in every case, is a modification of consciousness sent forth as a power by Íshvara. Turn to the *Vishnu Purâna* and you will see exactly the stage that I am pointing out to you in more modern phrases. Íshvara Himself, as Brahmâ, sends forth a power, due to a modification of His consciousness, called in the *Vishnu Purâna* a Tanmâtra. In the English translation the word rudiment is used. You remember the rudiments of sound, of touch, of colour, and so on. All these rudiments are the tanmâtras. These tanmâtras are the powers due to modifications in consciousness or life, without which no modification in matter can be. The consciousness first, then the form. The first great vibration that goes forth is the vibration that gives rise to what we speak of here as sound—all our terms being drawn from the lowest, or physical, manifestations; the form that it brings into manifestation is A'kâsha, the mighty element of Ether; not the ether of modern science, of course, although that is its physical representative. Then into that the next tanmâtra, the next power due to a modification of consciousness, is sent forth; the A'kâsha, with the primary vibration within it, receives the second vibration sent out by Îshvara, and this, pervading the matter around it, brings about the next modification of matter, the element Vâyu, or Air. Vâyu, permeated, ensouled and enveloped in A'kâsha, receives a fresh impulse from Îshvara, the third tanmâtra, or power resulting from a modification of consciousness; this tanmâtra, working on Vâyu, produces the modification of matter called the element Agni, or Fire, and this fire-matter is permeated, ensouled, and enveloped in Vâyu, as Vâyu in A'kâsha. A similar process brings into manifestation the elements Apas and Prithivî. The "magnetic field" of an atom is composed of all the tanmâtras and elements above it. Try to realise this process if you can, though I know the conception is difficult. What has occurred? A modification of life or consciousness in Îshvara, manifested as a power, a vibration; everything depends on vibration; ancient and modern science speak alike on this. The universe is made up of vibrations, the vibrations which are the modifications of the Divine outpouring of life. These clothe themselves in fundamental forms of matter, out of which all multiplicity is developed. These modifications in matter, these great, or primary, elements are also called tattvas. Tanmâtras, then, are the powers sent out by modifications of consciousness, and these are awkwardly translated by the word rudiments; we have next the modifications in matter, the great elements, the primary elements, or tattvas. The first of the tattvas is called A'kâsha; then Vâyu, then Agni, then Apas, then Prithivî, the five following one after the other; the keynote of this evolution is that the modification of the previous higher tattva is reproduced within the lower, pervades it and expands outside it. If you will take the *Vishnu Purâna*, the second chapter, and read over again the evolution of the five tattvas, you will find that the Sanskrit word which is used comes from a root which means to pervade as well as to enclose, giving the idea of permeation as well as of expanding around to form an envelope. And you must understand that the central life of each tattva is the preceding tattva with its tanmâtra; that, with the new tanmâtra, makes up the life; and the outer form is the new tattva that by that productive action comes into existence.

Now leaving that, for I cannot go into further details, let me just say to you one word about the seven and the five, because that has been a source of great dispute between some of our Hindu Pandits and some of our

Theosophists. In the universe, taken as a whole, seven-fold is the life of Íshvara. Beyond the tattva that we know as A'kâsha, there is that tattva which has been called Anupâdaka, and beyond that A'ditattva, the first. Those are far beyond our knowing; we cannot think so far. For our life-evolution, the five mark the limit; and only the five, therefore, as a rule, are given in the books which are to be studied to show you how to evolve.

Rapidly we must pass onward, then, to these tattvas as, modifying themselves by aggregations, and by disintegrations and re-combinations of these, they make innumerable forms. The fundamental conception is that there are as many basic forms of atoms in the universe as there are tattvas. The tattva of ancient science is the atom of modern science, but modern science makes the mistake of supposing that there is only one fundamental atom. The truth is that modern science is only seeking to get hold of the Prithivî Tattva, the lowest, or physical, atom, and it has not yet recognized even the existence of the four (or six) higher atoms that stretch beyond. These atoms form the regions of the universe. All that is physical is made up from the Prithivî Tattva. Not only is this so, but within the limits of this physical region, correspondences of all the higher six atomic forms are reproduced. The sub-divisions of the physical region, due to combinations of the Prithivî Tattva, show forth the characteristics of the great regions which make up the universe; so that we have here in our solid, liquid, gas, three ethers and atoms, correspondences of the six higher tattvas, but we have them all in their Prithivî form; they are the modifications of Prithivî, reproducing on a lower plane the great primary elements. We might call them Prithivî A'ditattva, Prithivî Anupâdhakatattva, Prithivî A'kâshatattva, Prithivî Vâyutattva, Prithivî Agnitattva, Prithivî Apastattva, Prithivî Prithivîtattva. Above the region of Prithivî comes the great realm of Apas, with similar sub-divisions, all of the Apastattva, and so again another seven above that in the higher realm of Agni, and above that the same in the still higher realm of Vâyu, and above that again in the A'kâsha, and then the highest two unknown realms. When you remember that all these regions interpenetrate the one the other, you will gain some glimpse of a complexity dizzying to think of, the vast complexity of the universe in which the One Life is working. Yet that complexity is simplified by thus working downwards, and there is the line of the study of the ancient science. Working out from this originally simple life into the endless multiplicity of forms, we may trace the One among the many, and see the Self in all things, and all things in Him.

At the ending of a universe, the tattvas merge in each other by disintegration; Prithivî Tattva, having disintegrated into atoms, these atoms are themselves broken up, and the tanmâtra that formed them, being no longer able to express itself for lack of suitable material, ceases to be a power, and remains only represented by a modification in consciousness—a permanent possibility. Thus Apas Tattva becomes the lowest manifestation, and, by a repetition of the above process, ceases to exist. In like fashion each successively vanishes. Hence, Mahâdeva is represented as saying in the *Shivâgama*: "The universe proceeded from the tattvas; it goes on through the tattvas; it vanishes into the tattvas. "

Such is the grandiose conception of the kosmos given by the science of antiquity; one life, pulsing into innumerable vibrations, and these throwing matter into forms. On this was based the Pythagorean system of numbers; on this mathematics and music were founded; on this the "Great Science," or Magic, of long-perished nations was built up. That science only survives in its purity in the Great White Brotherhood, but its traces may yet be seen in the scriptures and the religions of the world.

We take up modern science, and pass into a different atmosphere. Now phenomena are to be studied, forms are to occupy our attention. But as we look at modern science we find that it is beginning to transcend the study of forms; we find the efforts of its greatest men are turned to seek unity amid diversity. Do not think that, in speaking of modern science as studying forms, I am indifferent to the mighty achievements that it has made, or that I would say one word in derogation of the ability of the leading men of science, and the priceless value of the work that they are doing for humanity. Their achievements during the present century are achievements that are worthy of the very deepest respect, not only for the "sublime patience of the investigator," of which William Kingdon Clifford so rightly spoke, but also for the self-abnegation with which many of them have given their lives to follow truth, to study in the innermost recesses of the phenomena of nature what secrets she has hidden, what may be underneath the "Veil of Isis. " I do not, then, speak a word against modern science, but I point out to you this fact, that the greatest work of science has been the generalisations that have been suggested in the attempt to reach simplicity, to reduce multiplicity to unity. How far has science gone from that generally accepted view of the materialistic school of thirty years ago, that the universe is made up of an indefinite number of atoms, the atoms being our chemical elements! A phrase from one of the most famous of the then leading men of science, Dr. Ludwig Büchner, will mark the greatness of the change: he declared that the carbon atom will always remain a carbon atom, and has been a carbon atom from all eternity; that the hydrogen atom from all eternity has been a hydrogen atom, and to all eternity a hydrogen atom it will remain; for atoms with their properties are indestructible, and are therefore eternal. What man of science would dare to allege that to-day, knowing that he would be laughed to scorn by all his scientific brethren; who would say that these atoms are eternally of the same nature as they have till now been made out to be? What is science in fact, doing as to the atom? It is finding in what is called the atom a composite body, a compound, not an element. This discovery is chiefly due to the researches of Sir William Crookes, who is guided in his investigations by a deeper philosophy of the universe than is common among scientists. It is gradually finding out that these atoms are things that are built up gradually, and that the qualities of atoms are not fixed, but are properties that change with every difference of conditions. Late investigations have shown that when chemical bodies are submitted to extraordinary conditions of cold—such cold as makes the air into a liquid and solidifies hydrogen and oxygen—they suffer the destruction of their supposedly permanent properties. It is proved that, as these conditions are changed, and as lower and lower ranges of temperature are brought to bear upon these chemical elements, one by one their eternal properties disappear, and they lie there changed in their activities, and lose the characteristic traits which enabled them to be discovered as parts of the moving world. Downward and downward falls the temperature, property after property disappears, until science asks, bewildered, what will happen when we reach the absolute zero, what will then become of the properties of matter, what will remain of the characteristics of the elements? Is there not but one Matter, and are not all chemical elements but modifications, aggregations, of this one ultimate matter? Similarly with Force, modern science has made the magnificent generalisation that all the forces that we know are modifications of one Force, and are identical in their essential nature; that heat, and light, and all the various forces around us, electricity, magnetism and the rest, that all these are but vibrations of varying lengths and activities in a subtle medium, and that they may be transmuted the one into the other. They are not fundamentally different, but are one and the same in their root. But if this be so, if there be but one Matter, if there be but one Force, then science is now tending towards unity; and as that unity is traced or aimed at, science will have to pass out of the grosser realm of dense matter into the realm of forces working in subtle media; and we find this wondrous change that, whereas in old days the existence of force was argued for inductively, by studying the changes in matter, now science is beginning to posit the existence of force and to question whether matter is anything more than the action of force. Instead of regarding an atom as a solid indivisible particle, the tendency is to regard it as a vortex of energy, a centre of force. One writer even goes so far as to suggest that an atom is a source "through which an invisible fluid is pouring into three-dimensional space. " Other atoms, "anti-atoms," may be "sinks" through which the fluid pours out. If these unite, may not inertia be neutralised as well as gravity? May there not be potential matter, and may there not be such in space, without any of the attributes which characterise matter, but ready to be vivified and form a system of worlds? Here we have H. P. B. 's atoms and laya centres, put forward tentatively as a scientific problem. Science is mounting into the invisible world and is trying to measure and to weigh that which therein it finds. Now this tendency to unity is the testimony to the One that underlies all manifestation; only one Force, only one Matter; endless diversity of forces, transmutable into each other; endless diversity of forms, which break up again to recombine; only one Force under all forces, one Matter under all forms. It is seen that the very fact of harmony and of evolution points to a root unity, and that eternally independent self-moving particles would only perpetuate a chaos.

As science travels along this most hopeful line, we find great changes are arising in the nature of the studies that are being carried on, and we have that wonderful theory of Sir William Crookes of the genesis of the elements. He takes protyle as a starting-point, which is really Vâyu in its form on this physical plane—Prithivî Vâyu—and out of that builds one atom after another, making all the chemical elements to be bodies aggregated together by the action of a positive and a negative force. Let me just remind you of this, because some amongst you go so eagerly after modern science and despise your own literature. If you had read your *Vishnu Purâna*, with your brain, and not merely with your eyes through modern spectacles, you might have learnt that theory of Sir William Crookes long, long before he gave it. He has drawn a picture, and the picture shows an immovable axis, and around it a spiral coil, and at points in that coil are atoms of the chemical elements, generated by that coil which represents a swinging and cooling force. That spiral is in the great ocean of protyle, or primeval matter, and, as that spiral goes round and round the immovable axis, it generates chemical elements one after another, and so brings into existence the materials out of which the world is to be formed. That is the dry scientific statement summarised from his own address. But I have read in an ancient book of a mountain—which is the emblem of stability, of an axis round which everything is to revolve— thrown into a mighty ocean; and I have read of a great serpent turned round that mountain in spiral coils; on the one side the Suras are pulling and on the other side the Asuras are equally busy. Between the two—the positive and negative of modern science—evolution is started and the serpent spiral begins to turn and turn round that axis. They call the axis

Mount Mandara, and they call the spiral coil the serpent Vâsuki while the axis rests on Hari as a pivot; they call the positive and the negative forces the Gods and Demons, and their churning of the ocean gives rise to the materials of the universe. Aye! That is from the seer, who, looking at the ocean of matter, described pictorially what the eyes of the spirit beheld there; while the other is the dry scientific statement of the modern thinker, who works out his magnificent generalisation as the result of his study of the forms. The seer and the scientist have met.

I shall show you, when I come to deal with life, that modern science is coming towards our view of life. I shall give you, from the latest declarations of our modern scientific teachers, points which will show you how they are climbing towards the ancient view which is found in our sacred books; and I will now finish this first part of our subject this morning by one plea addressed to all of you, which I would pray you to think over at your leisure.

There is but One Life, the Life of God, within everything in His universe. No life save His life, no consciousness save His consciousness, no thought save His thought. This is our glory; for inasmuch as we are in His image, we can answer to the vibrations of His thinking, and can reproduce in our minds that which He has initiated in order that we may be evolved. In all the different parts of this universe, different lines of evolution are going on; the sun is doing part of it, the vegetable world another part, the animal world another, the world of man another; but in the world of man there is more diversity, because there Self-consciousness is arising. The final image of the Supreme on earth is man; in man alone is the highest life; the others are climbing towards it, but in them it has not yet evolved. Therefore in man there is more difference; therefore in man, for the time, more separation; therefore in man the great danger of antagonism that the lower kingdoms know not, because they are not sufficiently evolved. Then comes the conflict: I take my own poor reflection of one tiny bit of thought of Íshvara, and I say: "This is Íshvara Himself," and not my poor thought of Him; "Worship this as I see it," that is, "Worship me instead of Íshvara, and my thought of Him instead of Him. " So man after man puts up his idea of God as God, and we see all the world divided into many forms of thought and of worship. Then a man imagines that his brother men are worshipping other Gods, and he becomes anxious and troubled, not realising that Gods are many because we are worshipping our own thoughts of God instead of God, our own limited representations instead of the Universal Self. Nay more—I, perhaps, not only say to you that you must worship my conception of God instead of your own, that my knowledge is the limit of manifestation, that my small fancies make up the universe instead of the infinite diversity that alone can represent His might; but perhaps I go further and say: "If you do not worship my idea of God, you are outcaste, you are alien, you belong to a different faith, you belong to a different creed; stand outside; for I am orthodox, you are heretic and blasphemous your faith. " So speaks religion after religion, fanatic after fanatic; so one man after another makes his own reflection the God of the universe, and hence antagonises his brethren, whose representations of the divine image are as necessary to its completeness as his own.

That is what I ask you to realise. God cannot be expressed wholly in you or in me, in our miserable limitations, in our poverty of thought, in our wretchedness of impudent assumption. He can only be even partially expressed by all the worlds together; His whole universe is His mirror, and every fragment in the universe gives back to Him, in part His own perfections. Is it not nobler, greater, more glorious, to be a fragment of a perfect whole, making a part of the whole unity itself, subserving it in mirroring Íshvara, than to be shut in with our own fragment of a looking glass, trying vainly to make it perfectly reflect the whole, and refusing any partial reflection of the perfect in our brethren on every side? That is the thought which these lectures will embody, and they will fail in their purpose if they do not carry it home to your minds. For Íshvara, who is Existence and Intelligence, is also A'nanda, Joy, Bliss inexpressible, and that Bliss is only realized when union is consciously accomplished, when the whole is known as one. May I but help you to see the Self in all things: what better service may man do for man?

II. THE FUNCTIONS OF THE GODS.

My Brothers:—Those of you who are familiar with your own sacred literature will know how great a part is played therein by those spiritual Intelligences who are spoken of as the Devas, or Gods. As I said yesterday, the existence, the presence, and the working of these Intelligences in the administration of nature, in the carrying out of the will of Íshvara, are recognised in every great faith that the world has known. The Hindu speaks of them sometimes as Suras, sometimes as Devas; the Hebrew, the Christian, the Mussulman, speak of them as Angels and Archangels, making the distinction between the higher and the lower; the Zoroastrian also recognises their work, speaking of them as Feristhas; and so, in each of the great religions, we find the presence of these workers in the Kosmos recognised, and we see their functions defined. Now it is exceedingly important, especially perhaps for the Hindu, to understand how wide is the area of their working, how general their functions, for no subject perhaps is more often made a subject for attack by those who desire to injure the ancient religion of India, than the actions of the Gods as detailed in the sacred books. You will continually find that those actions are being misunderstood or mis-represented. The mis-representation, one may always hope, is not deliberate and conscious. It is due to the general materialism of the age. It is due to the fact that men who believe in a religion nominally do not realise the effect of that religion in their consciousness. So that while a man may say that he believes in Angels and Archangels and so on, he leads his life as though they did not exist. Among our Christian brothers there is considerable difference of opinion with regard to these Angels. In the different sections of the great Christian community, the vast majority of those that profess Christianity—making up the old Greek Church, sometimes called the Eastern Christian Church, and those who are numbered in the Roman Communion, the Roman Catholic Church, the two ancient Churches which have preserved an unbroken antiquity and an unbroken tradition from the time of Christ and His Apostles—have maintained and maintain, uninjured and complete, the ancient belief in the ministry of angels. They really lead their lives as recognising the part that is played in the world by the angelic hosts, and not only do they regard the Archangels as the great rulers of animated nature—the seven chief Archangels taking the place of the seven Gods in other faiths—but they also recognise the lower host of angels as concerned continually in administering natural laws, in guiding human evolution; and indeed they go so far as to say that every individual man is in special charge of a guardian angel, who ministers to him from the cradle to the grave, who tries to help him in danger, to advise him in temptation, to protect him in peril, to ward off all the evils levelled against him, and who, helping him through the gateway of death, accompanies him on the other side through the invisible world, until he surrenders up his charge into the hands of Christ Himself. The Protestant communities, however, breaking off as they did, roughly and abruptly, from the ancient tradition, full of occult truth, have lost, among many other valuable things, this real belief in the work of the angels. Most members of the Protestant communities, while they acknowledge the existence of the angels and vaguely regard them as "ministers of God," have no very definite idea of the part that they play in the world. They do not address them, as do the Roman Catholics and the Greeks. They do not pay them reverence and homage day by day, or look on them as helpers, as intelligences superior to themselves, always willing to render assistance. Practically the angels have passed out of their lives, so far as any conscious realisation of their presence is concerned; and I cannot help thinking that the loss is a very serious loss when you are dealing with spiritual evolution; the whole idea of the Supreme tends to become degraded and anthropomorphised when the intermediate agents are forgotten, and when every petty concern of human life is, as it were, thrown directly under the immediate superintendence of the Supreme. We must not, of course, in recognising the working of the Gods, or the Devas, as I shall call them for the rest of the lecture, lose sight of the unity of the Supreme Deity. We do not, in Hinduism, deny or ignore the existence of Íshvara because we recognise the hosts of the Devas; we do not cloud our belief in the One because we recognise the innumerable hosts of the ministers of His will; there is nothing more against the unity of God in the recognition of the hosts of the Devas, than there is in recognising the diversity of men, yet it is not pretended that we are clouding the unity of the Divine Existence when we recognise the hosts of individuals who make up the whole of humanity. It is mere prejudice or ignorance that makes any one think that because the Hindu recognises the action of the Devas, therefore he has lost his belief in the One Existence beyond even Íshvara Himself, in the fundamental unity that underlies diversity. What he does is, that instead of regarding the world as superintended by an extra-kosmic God, separated as it were from His universe, with a mighty gulf existing between Him and it, he sees in Íshvara the manifestation of the one Life that pervades and sustains all, he sees in Íshvara the one Root out of which all separated existences spring; and he sees, stretching between himself and that Supreme, innumerable hosts of Intelligences, step after step, rank after rank, and he looks to climbing up that celestial ladder until he also stands at its very top; for he knows that he also is divine, although as yet in an early stage of evolution, and he recognises the more highly evolved divinity above him, as he recognises the divinity in the stone beneath his feet, in everything that exists in this universe of God.

With that beginning, so that our study may not lead to a misconception, let us pass on to ask what are the functions of these Devas, of these Intelligences, who work in the world. You will at once realise that the functions must be very different, according to the grade of the Devas that we may happen to be studying. Through the whole of the Kosmos they are working. Some are very lofty, some are very little evolved above the level of humanity. One great difference there is between us and them, that whatever may be the grade of their mental, emotional, and spiritual life, they do not, normally, use a physical body. That is a clear mark or line of separation. The being functioning as man, while spiritual, intellectual and emotional, uses a physical body, in order to carry on the activities connected with the physical world. All the hosts of Devas are without that physical covering or vehicle; they normally use as their vehicle a body which belongs to the particular region in the universe in which their normal activities lie. Suppose, for instance, that a Deva belongs essentially to the spiritual world, he will normally use a spiritual body; if he wants to function on the mânasic plane, he will create for himself a temporary mânasic body, drawing together for this purpose the matter of that plane and holding it as his vehicle during the period of his functioning thereupon; if he wants to function in the kâmic region, he will draw together the material of that region and make of it for himself a temporary body; if he wants to function visibly in the world of man, he will draw round himself the matter of the physical plane, and make for himself a body suitable to the immediate purpose that he has in view. So with every other grade. The Devas of the mânasic world use normally the mânasic body, and create the kâmic or physical body as they may want a temporary vehicle. Those of the kârmic region use the kârmic body normally, and create a physical vehicle when they require it. Thus, in every case, the Deva's ordinary body is composed of the matter of the region of the universe to which he belongs; but he has always the power to create any vehicle that he needs for carrying out any purpose with which he is charged. This will perhaps suggest to you one reason for the great variety of forms which a single God may assume. Those whose inner sight is developed, who can see in the regions which to ordinary men are invisible, say that the Gods use many forms. And some of their forms have come down traditionally, described originally perhaps by a great Ṛishi, preserved by his disciples, then thrown into some form of earth, or stone, or metal, painted or sculptured as the case may be; then such an image of the God is handed down generation after generation, and represents that Deva under that particular form to his worshippers. We find many forms for one Deva, just because of the fact that the God makes the form he wants for the particular work he has upon hand, and that none of those forms bind him. They are merely transitory vehicles created for a definite purpose. Some of these forms are indeed relatively permanent, partly because of the worship which is addressed to them. For the Deva will often graciously use a particular form in order to meet the thought of his worshippers. Suppose for instance, taking a lofty example, that Shrî Krishna willed to reveal Himself to some Bhakta of His, in order that that devotee might have the joy of consciously realising the presence of his Lord, He then most certainly would clothe Himself in the form which that Bhakta was in the habit of worshipping and which drew up the deepest emotions of his heart. For these forms are taken for the very purpose of

200

stimulating devotion, for the very object of attracting the heart by presenting the illimitable Deity in some conditioned form which the concrete mind of man is able more or less to grasp, to understand, to admire and to worship. You cannot love the void of space. You cannot fix your heart on the depths of infinity; you deceive yourself if, with your limited intelligence, untrained even in the lowest forms of Yoga, you think that you can realise Brahman, the Supreme. Too often when we speak of THAT, no real thought responds to our speaking; the lips speak, not the intelligence or the heart. Step by step we have to climb from the manifested to the unmanifested, and, in His compassionate love, God veils Himself in forms of beauty to attract the human heart, in order that the human heart may rise adoringly to His Feet, and that some portion of His life, pouring down thereinto, may enable the Self of the worshipper to realise even partially its unity with Him.

The Devas, then, in their many ranks and divisions, perform functions according to their grade. Speaking generally, their work in the world is to guide evolution according to the design of Íshvara. That really sums up their functions, although we are going to study them in detail. I say nothing of the vast functions of the higher Devas that lie beyond our knowing, beyond the teaching that Ṛishis have given. I deal only with those lower functions that are concerned with our world, and with the solar system of which our world is part. Taking that limitation, suitable to our ignorance, we can study some of the functions of the Gods within the limits of our solar system.

Speaking generally, as I said, that function is to guide evolution, to adapt, to correlate, to carry out the living will of the Supreme, and to carry out that will by bringing together in time and space all the agents and conditions necessary for carrying it out. There is only one supreme Will that guides the universe, and that Will points steadily to progress, to the goal set forth for the universe, the goal towards which it is evolving. Unchangeable, stable, perpetual, that Will knows no swerving; to use a Christian phrase, "there is no shadow of turning" in that immutable Will. The universe rolls along the road traced out by the Divine Will. It cannot be diverted from that road; it cannot change its path; that is the law of the universe, the law on which we rest with faith unshakable. But in the working out of the law in this universe where men are evolving—men in whom is the germ of that same sovereign and imperial Will of God, man being made in the Divine image and containing within himself the germ of the Divine powers—in this universe, as man evolves, wills also evolve which are separate, personal, individual. All the confusion in the world of man is due to this evolution of the separated wills that do not recognise their root in God, but try to follow their own diverse ways, and want to move after their own separated fashions; so that in the world of man, as nowhere else in nature, you have discord instead of harmony, clash instead of peace, struggle and war instead of tranquillity. The world of minerals obeys the compulsion of the law; the world of vegetables obeys the compulsion of the law; the world of animals obeys the compulsion of the law; but when man arises, man in whom the Supreme is to be developed after he has climbed through the lower stages, in man there awakens the germ of the will, and the separated wills bring about the discord which will yet end in something greater and richer than the harmony of the stones, of the vegetables, of the animals. For when human evolution is over, millions of separated wills will join in one mighty chord of harmonious union, and that union of the wills that voluntarily give themselves is mightier in its powers, more beautiful in its expression, than compelled obedience can ever be. The music that humanity sends up to God, in all its varied melody, is a far more perfect expression of Divinity than can be drawn from the monochord that we find in the lower kingdoms of nature; but you will readily understand that when these warring wills arise, something, some one, is wanted in order to adapt, to correlate, to bring about equilibrium among the contending forces, so that the one purpose may be steadily subserved. Let me take a concrete illustration. Suppose I had here a ball which I want to move. That ball can be moved along a straight line in innumerable ways. I might give it a single impulse in the direction in which I want it to move; and it would move straight on in that direction following my primary impulse. So would the universe move if it contained only minerals, vegetables and animals, if there were no clashing wills within it, if it were within the iron grip of compulsion, which never in any fashion could be resisted. But I can equally well drive my ball along that straight line, if I know enough of physics, by correlating different and opposed forces. I may send two forces against it at a particular angle, and if my angle be properly measured according to the strength of the forces, then the ball will travel along the same line by the interaction of the two forces as well as by the impact of the one; and I may bring three, or four, or five, or a million forces, to bear upon that ball, and still it will move along that one definite line, if only the forces are calculated and balanced so that their resultant shall always be a force along that straight line. That balancing is one of the functions of the Gods. They take these warring wills, these different directions that are being impressed, as it were, on the rolling world that is going along the road of evolution; they balance, adapt, and correlate them, and thus always keep the world travelling along the straight line, always bringing about the same resultant, the accomplishment of the Will of the Supreme; without them, these wills of ours would work infinite confusion, and the world would never complete its evolution, would never roll upwards to its place at the Feet of God.

We find the Gods discharging other functions which subserve the same purpose. They mould the forms in which the growing life is to express itself. Evolution depends upon the growing power of the unfolding life, but it needs forms whereby that growth shall be carried on. These forms are moulded by the Devas, so that the life, which breaks by expansion its containing form that is out-worn, may have another form into which to go fitted for the capacity that was evolved in the form it has out-grown. We shall find also that they break up forms as well as build them; being always fixed on the one object of serving the evolution of the life. Then again they act as teachers, as guides, as councillors, to those that have gone beyond the normal evolution, that are the first fruits of the human race. Not acting as teachers directly to the masses, they take the more advanced human beings in charge, directly instruct them, test them and try them, as presently we shall see. So that while the general purpose is the helping forward of evolution, this help is rendered in a million ways, according to the needs of the time.

Now, in the past, this working of the Gods was recognised, and the sacred books are full of it. They showed themselves continually among men, they carried on their work, as it were, in the full blaze of day. But now no longer do they show themselves to men at large, and many have forgotten even their existence, and very many people, even in India, materialised by the thought in which they have been trained, are half ashamed to say that they believe in the existence and the working of the Devas. The unbelief makes no difference, save to those who disbelieve. The working of the Gods remains ever the same. They are ever busy in carrying out the Supreme Will. Only they do not show themselves, and to those alone who recognise their existence and their work will they manifest themselves. If in the old days they showed themselves as they do not now, it was because men then had reverence and love and were willing to bow down to those who were wiser and greater than themselves; because then democracy was not reigning; because then the ignorant did not think themselves equal to the learned, nor did man deem himself equal to the Gods. In those days, because they could help they came to the helping; but they will never come visibly again to earth until men have learnt to reverence once more what is above them, and to understand their place in the Kosmos, to worship as well as to command. The Gods work all the same. They are not deprived of their functions by our folly, by our conceit, by our ignorance. Only they work unseen, and we forfeit the sweet comfort of their visible presence, the strength and joy of the old heroic days, the dignity of conscious companionship with the Immortals, the ever-renewed assurance of super-physical life. Not one death that happens on our earth, but a God has struck away that body whose work is over; not one "natural catastrophe," but a God has guided it to the happening; not one help given to a man in need, but a God is the agent behind the visible helper; not one answer to the cry of man in his distress, that is not the response of a God to human sorrow. Everywhere they are working. Everywhere they are bringing about what we see as dead mechanical nature. Every phenomenon is the veil of a God, and there is nothing done in which an Intelligence does not take part.

Seven are the great Gods below the Trinity, below the Trimûrti. Every religion, again, acknowledges these Seven. The Christian speaks of the "Seven Spirits that are before the throne of God. " The Zoroastrian tells us of the seven Ameshaspendas who rule the world. The Chaldean spoke of the seven great Gods. Five only are working and two are concealed, for the universe is in process of evolution and only five stages of it have been reached. Therefore only with regard to five can we definitely speak as to working. The two concealed are beyond our knowing; they are related to future stages of the evolution of the Kosmos. But the five we will now consider. Their names in connection with their functions you know well enough. They are connected with the tattvas of which we were speaking yesterday—the Lord of A'kâsha, Indra; the Lord of Air, Vâyu; the Lord of Fire, Agni; the Lord of Water, Varuna; the Lord of Earth, sometimes called Kshiti (various names are used for him); each of these great Gods has what we may call one region marked out for his working. The matter of that region is the matter in which he works; but in addition to that, each one is represented in the realms of the others by a sub-division on which his impression is especially made. These are the great kosmic planes that I have spoken of marked off from each other by the tattvas. But if we come down to the physical plane, dealing only with Prithivî Tattva, we shall then find that that is also seven-fold in division and that we have physical solid, physical earth or Prithivî, physical water or Apas, physical fire or Agni, physical air or Vâyu, physical ether or A'kâsha. Each of these great Gods works on each plane through the medium that corresponds to the region which belongs to him in the Kosmos as a whole. How often we see those correspondences as it were printed in physical nature. We have light with its seven sub-divisions as seen in the solar spectrums showing the seven colours, and the scale with its seven notes. Colours and notes alike result from vibrations, and are determined by the number of vibrations occurring in a unit of time. As the universe is built by vibrations, colour and sound are factors of the universe at large, and every region is said to have its own colour; the God of that region has his colour—dependent on his vibratory force—which he imprints on the region over which he rules; so that if a Ṛishi looks at the solar system from a higher plane, he not only hears the seven fundamental notes of music, making "the harmony of the spheres," but he sees a gorgeous display of colours, as the sphere of every great Deva with his own colour interpenetrates the others, yielding an iridescent splendour of interfering radiances, the marvellous "rainbow that is round the throne of God. " Such mystic expressions have lost their meaning for the majority, because the sight of those who wrote them is but little developed in these days, and few are they who can see as the seer saw of old.

Each of these great Gods has under him a host of subordinate Gods who carry out his decrees. The constitution of an ordinary state will give you a very good picture of the government of the solar system. We have at the head an Emperor or an Empress; then the officers who represent that supreme authority in separate divisions of the realm; there is the one central authority over the whole, and the officers who wield it in different areas of the Empire. Then these officers are graded in rank, and we have higher and subordinate Ministers, Judges, Magistrates, in descending order, each with a smaller and smaller district to administer, the functions of each becoming more limited as you descend the official ladder; and each responsible to his official superior. That is really a very good picture of the government of the solar system; the head of all is Íshvara Himself; His Viceroys are the great Gods, each with his own vast area over which he rules, and each with his official hierarchy under him, until you come down to the lowest Devas, who carry on the work in the limited area of a village of the solar system.

Such is the outline, then, of the functions. The next thing to grasp is, that, when we see on this plane in which our consciousness is working— the physical plane—any one of these fundamental forms of manifestation, we should try to realise the presence of the God behind the material phenomenon. Not a fire that burns upon the earth, whether the fire of the volcanic mountain, whether the fire ranging through the vast forest, whether the fire burning on the household hearth, or on the sacrificial altar, that is not Agni in manifestation, with the possibility of his powers coming into visibility. They were not dreamers, they who bade you of old keep safe the fire, the household fire which husband and wife at the bridal kindled, and which, when the life of the married was over in the home, they still carried out into the forest; they carried with them the fire, and it took with them the presence of the God, who through the household life had blessed, had guided, had given prosperity and made the final withdrawal from the household life possible and desirable. That is one of the many truths which modern India is losing.

But when these things were believed in, and the ceremonies connected with them were carried on, then nature worked in a definite order, and there were not the same continual irregularities that we have in our modern days. By that harmonious working between man and the Gods, nature answered to man as man answered to nature; while man did his duty, nature in her turn did her duty also; the failure of rain, the failure of crops, the failure of sunshine, the presence of plague, or of any other form of human misery, was seen as having its root in the failure of humanity; and man turned dutifully to that which he had neglected, and thus readjusted the balance which his irregularity had displaced. Let us try and see, as an example, one concrete working in what we call natural evolution. We will turn to the great God Varuna. He works through water; every manifestation of water is his, whether on the physical or on any other plane, in any of the forms that it may take, for what we call "water" is naturally the lowest, coarsest manifestation, his physical body, as it were. He works with it in nature in endless ways—to dissolve, to combine, to dissociate. When we take the greater workings, how very grand is the conception we may gain of the might of the God. Come back with me, far back, into the past, ere humanity had taken form; there see the world as it then was; see how, as fire and water, Agni and Varuna are working on every material to fit the world to be the birthplace of the yet unborn humanity. See how Varuna is working in order to prepare what is wanted of mountain and of valley, of river and of plain; see the might of his work as well as that of his brother Agni, in apparent clash but really in harmony; fire and water meet, explode, and toss up a mountain-chain where before there was none; see how he gathers snow on the mountain peaks, and gradually fills with masses of this snow, frozen into ice, the mountain ravines made by the combined volcanic action; see how the slow ploughing begins; ploughing, ploughing and ploughing again, as the mighty God works onward in the form of glaciers, grinding his furrow through the earth, and preparing for the future; see, ages later, how the channel cut out by the glacier is filled by the tumbling cataracts from melted snow, and a turbulent torrent rolls downwards, and against its resistless waves nothing is able to stand; the valley dug out by the plough of the ice is filled with water, and from it the soil is gradually deposited, which in the future will make fertile land for crops in order that man may live. Then Varuna binds his waters into a narrower and narrower channel, until there is mountain range and valley and a river flowing through it: and he carries his river downwards and pours it into the sea and his brother Agni draws it up again to form the clouds. There has come by that mighty action, destructive as it seems in appearance, the building of the plain and the valley where men shall live and love, where children shall be playing, where horses shall graze, where corn shall grow and ripen in the sunshine, and where, on the peaceful banks of the river, men shall worship the God who made possible their happy life.

We talk about the "cruelty of nature. " Let us try and understand what this cruelty means. The world now is inhabited. Crowds of men are here, and lo! the river, that made the habitation of the valley possible and keeps it fruitful, now overflows its banks and the mighty flood sweeps away village and town, men, women, children, and cattle, and only desolation is left behind. What is this? Is this horror a divine working? What is this that Varuna has done? Varuna is working for evolution. His thought is not fixed on the forms in which the life is cabined, but on the life that is evolving within them, which can make for itself new forms. When those men are swept away, it is only the breaking of the forms that happens; the life up-springs uninjured and set free; for the body is the prison-house of the evolving life, and if the prison doors were never thrown open, we should be in jail all our lives and make no progress for the future. The God to whom form is nothing and life everything, to whom form is but a changing, convenient vehicle, and the life that moulds the form is the one thing that is worthy of thought, he strikes away the form when its purpose is completed; to him such destruction is the act of mightiest charity; it is the deed most helpful to evolution. We err, my brothers, when we look on death with eyes that are full of tears, with hearts that are breaking. Death is he who brings us to a higher birth, and who sets free the imprisoned soul; it is the liberation of the bird confined within the limits of a cage, enabling it to soar upwards into the heavens, singing, as it goes, with joy at the freedom it has recovered. Does that seem strange? Let us take an illustration from the *Mahâbhârata:*—

There was a council among the Gods in Svarga, how some of them would take incarnation upon earth for the sake of helping men at a great crisis in the world's history. Great men were needed, and the question arose whether some of the Gods were willing to bind themselves within the limits of human form, in order to give special help to human progress; among those who were needed for the work that was coming was the son of Soma Deva, Varchas, as he was called, and the Gods desired that this Deva should be born on earth. Soma Deva hesitated. He was not willing that his son should leave him and the heavenly life, and although he finally consented that he should be born as Abhimanyu, the son of Arjuna, it was only on the condition that he should live but for sixteen years, and be killed in the great battle of Kurukshetra. You say, what a strange view of life! What an extraordinary condition for love to make, that this youth should die at the age of sixteen, in the very flower of his dawning manhood, should die a death of violence. Yet that was the will of the one who loved him best, for heaven sees with different eyes from earth. Soma saw the life, and cared not for the form; to a God the form is a prison, death is the gaoler that liberates; hence the condition was made that only for sixteen years might the divine youth live a human life, and then "my son of mighty arms shall come back to me," and that from a battle field, dying gloriously in the midst of the fight.

Do you know that sometimes the swamping of a civilisation by a natural convulsion—such as the going down of Atlantis below the waves of the ocean that we now call the Atlantic, the wiping out of the whole nation or race—is the best proof of love that the Supreme Íshvara through His intermediate agents can show to the lives therein embodied. For there are stages in the world's story where man is so passionately set on a line of action that is against his real progress, when he so determinately sets his desires on objects that hold him back and delay his evolution, that the only mercy that the Gods can show him is to break his form in pieces, and give him as it were a new start for the evolving of himself—the life. Sometimes I have felt, as I have gone through some of the miseries of our great cities in the West, when, in the pursuance of my duty, I have gone with breaking heart through the slums of eastern and southern London, or through those of Glasgow, or Edinburgh, or Sheffield, as I have noted the types of men and women around me, as I have seen the human almost veiled by the brute, and humanity degraded well-nigh beyond possibility of recognition, that no appeal for help was fitting save one that would set free that imprisoned life. I have felt that nothing save the destruction of the forms could give any hope for those imprisoned within them; that for those men and women, as they were, degraded, brutal, drunken, profligate, their very forms with the impress of the animal, the best mercy that God could show them would be an earthquake that would swallow the whole great city and set free the lives pent hopeless within it. For not one life would be lost, not one life would pass away, but they would be set free to go into somewhat less unplastic forms and give scope for that divine working towards evolution, which is in extreme cases only possible when the forms, forms of evil, are gone. We speak sometimes of the training of children being easier than that of grown-up people, because they are more plastic. So also the Gods want oftentimes the child-ego in the plastic form instead of in the prison-house grown rigid by age; and they therefore break that environment in order that the young life may grow.

Another great function of the Gods is the dealing with the karma of nations, "collective karma," as it is sometimes called. Suppose a nation is acting in its collective capacity—I am not now thinking of the individuals brought into it by their individual karma but of the nation acting as a unit— and suppose it commits a crime against another nation. There has been one working of karma so tremendous during the last year, that I will take it as an illustration—Spain. Some centuries ago Spain was at the summit of her power; mighty was she among the western nations. There was sent to her, in order to help her forward, the gift of new knowledge. It came truly in a somewhat unacceptable guise, for it came from Arabia, with the stamp of Muhammed upon it; it was brought by the children of Islâm; they brought the light of science with them, and, as they established themselves in southern Spain, they gave that light to Spain. Universities were established. Large classes were formed. From every part of Europe men come crowding to the Schools of Cordova, and there they learnt the beginnings of the Science that has since grown into so mighty a tree in western lands. What did Spain do? Spain called up against these Moors, and against the Hebrews—who also were learned in the learning of the East—the frightful weapons of the Inquisition, the stake, the rack, the dungeon, the torture of exile. Who can count the hundreds of thousands driven out from home, the broken families, the miseries, the poverty and starvation intolerable, which marked the expulsion of the Jews and of the Moors from Spain? Still her karma of success was not complete. Across the Atlantic Ocean she sped, Italy lending one of her sons for the glory of the Spanish Empire. In the wake of the ships of Columbus there followed the ships of the conquerors of America, full of Spanish soldiers. I cannot dwell on the story of the conquest of Mexico, and the still more terrible conquest of Peru; I have no time to wring your hearts, as I might, with the tale of the destruction of a great civilisation, of the killing out of the last exquisite traces in Peru of one of the most perfect civilisations that our world has ever known, of the crushing of the gentle Indian race there by chains, by imprisonment, shut out from the glorious Sun whose children their Incas were. Too gentle to struggle, accustomed only to a life of flowers, of music, and of sunshine, they were crammed into caves that they were made to dig in ancient cliffs, dying by thousands upon thousands in the digging out of the gold and silver which their Spanish conquerors demanded, until the very name of the ancient nation perished, and only a few scattered Peruvian Indians remained to represent what was one of the fairest civilisations of the world. Such was the karma made by Spain in the days of her glory, and the horror of her conquests sank into the oblivion of the past. But do the Gods forget? Nay, their memory is perfect. They are the administrators of the divine law, and give the harvest to the sowers. From the very country which they outraged, from the very land that they conquered, a new nation springs up as the centuries go on to take up the old struggle between the two hemispheres, and to-day we have seen America and Spain closing again in the death-grip, but the scale of balance is now weighed down on the other side, and America becomes the karmic agent for working out the woes of the Aztecs and the Peruvians, and for driving from the western hemisphere the nation that there outraged humanity in the centuries gone by. Thus the Gods are needed to bring nations together to balance up these accounts between the races, and so to restore equilibrium once again. Thus they work, using men as their agents, and they bring about these national results. Partly they do it by bringing to birth, at a particular time, men whose individual karma fits them to be the agents of the collective karma of the nation. What was more striking in the Spanish war which has just closed, than the absolute incapacity shown by the men who were the rulers of Spain? Whence came they? They were men who in the past by their individual karma had fitted themselves for the sorry fate of incapable rulers, and they were guided by the Gods to take birth in the families which give rulers to Spain, in order that, by their weakness and ineptitude, by their cowardice and their want of foresight, they might serve as men to lead their nation to destruction, the fitting instruments for the working out of Spain's evil karma. See also how at the fit time great men arise to lead a nation to victory. These men are also chosen by the Gods beforehand because of their individual karma, and they are brought to birth in the place and at the time when they are wanted for the working out of the collective karma of a nation. Not by chance is a man brought into the world, not by the compulsion of a dead law, or of a blind necessity; the Gods are working here with an intelligence that foresees and guides, and they choose for the accomplishment of their ends the men whose own karma fits them to be their agents for the work in hand, and then guide them to take birth at the place where that karma can subserve the collective karma of their people.

This also is true in a much more limited way with regard to the working of individual karma. Sometimes you must have wondered how, with all the interfering activities of men, the karmic law could work out with undeviating justice; it is because the Gods are guiding the working. You see somewhere a man who is starving and if you misunderstand karma— as too many of you do, to the shame of India, in a land where this teaching is of immemorial antiquity—you turn aside from that starving man and say that it is his karma to starve and perish; in those hardened hearts of yours you use the will of God as a cover for your own selfishness, for your indifference and your lack of love. That man's karma to starve? Aye, and therefore he is starving! But if a Deva guides you to the place where your brother is starving, it is because he would make you the agent of his beneficence to that man whose evil karma of the present moment has been exhausted by his suffering; the Deva thus says to you: "Man, your brother man is starving, give him the relief it is his karma to receive, and be my agent in carrying out the law." But if you refuse the God, if, blinded by ignorance or indifference, you turn aside and will not carry his message to your brother, he will not for that be thwarted, he will find some other agent, or, as a last resource, he will do it himself by some act that may seem miraculous in the eyes of the blind, for the purpose of the God may not be blocked; but for those who have refused to act as his agents, who have refused to act as his messengers, they have made for themselves the karma of being left unassisted when the hour of their own need shall strike in the future. For the administrators of the good law forget not; every debt is collected, every creditor is paid in full. But you may say that it does not follow that a man's karma is exhausted when you meet him; true, but that is not your business, it is the business of the guiding God, and he will frustrate the physical aid if the karma be still evil. If you have that opportunity given you of making good karma, you have all the merit of your willingness to act, you have all the virtue of your readiness to sacrifice; but if it is not yet his time to be relieved, you will not find the object of your charity; by circumstances, as you will say, he will have been taken outside your reach. Leave you the Gods to do the work of the Gods, the administration of the law; do you that charity, that love and compassion, which it is ever their will that man should show to man. We cannot break the law; we cannot change their purpose; but we have the choice of co-working or refusing, and on that our individual karma depends.

Then we find further that Devas bring people together and carry them apart, always for the working out of their individual karmas; that men are guided to places and positions at definite times, according to those circumstances which, by their karma, they must meet.

Now men are related especially to one or other of the great Gods, by the constitution of their bodies visible and invisible. That gives them a special affinity for one Deva rather than for another. For instance, the lower hosts of Devas who, we will say, belong to Agni, build into a man's invisible and visible bodies, the kind of matter in which that God normally works. That gives the man a relationship to that particular God. Every man is connected with a special manifestation of God, to whom by his constitution and evolution he should turn. Unhappily ignorance has so widely taken the place of knowledge, that it is difficult for a man to discover to which Deva he is thus related. I have not time to work that out but you will see how thoroughly it supports the ancient idea that men rightly worshipped different manifestations of the Divine, and profited by such worship.

But we must hurry on with this outline, for we have yet to deal with the more highly evolved souls, and on your understanding this last part of our subject will depend your power to defend our sacred literature when it is attacked by those who do not understand it. Therefore I will ask you to follow it carefully, and you can apply the principles that I will illustrate by special stories in a hundred other cases.

The Devas, in their relationship to the more advanced human lives, have that function of teaching that I have alluded to, and also the function of testing and trying them, to see how far they are worthy and reliable, testing all their weak points in order that those weak points may be gotten rid of, trying them, where there is a germ of vice still remaining, in order that that germ of vice may be eradicated. Let us try to realise the nature of that working. Suppose we see a man who has made great progress. He is approaching the end of his births. In that man there is some germ of evil still remaining that has not been brought out yet into manifestation by the working of karma. He is going to be liberated, but he cannot be liberated while that germ remains. What shall be done with him? That germ of evil must be hastened to its ripening. It must be made to grow more quickly than otherwise it would grow. It must be gotten rid of, at any cost of pain, of anguish, and of temporary degradation, and the God will take such action as will ripen that germ and bring it to fruitage; so that, the man acting as he would act when that germ had been ripened by evolution, may suffer the results which would follow from the error, and by such suffering may get rid of that evil in his nature, which would otherwise have prevented him from attaining liberation.

Let me give you a story for each of these to make the action clear. You see that a man is strong; well and good; but that strength must be tested to see if there be a flaw anywhere; if there is a rope on which the life of a man is going to depend, he holding it and descending a precipice, that rope must be pulled and tested to see if there be any weak point in it which might break when the man's body is hanging upon it, so that he would fall. There may be a flaw in the rope, and not till it has been tested will the man risk his life upon it. How much less then will the Deva risk the progress of an advanced man on a virtue not strong enough to bear every strain? He will test it with every possibility of strain, until it has proved itself strong enough to bear the weight which it may be called upon to hold up. We will take our stories from the *Mahâbhârata*, which you all know, or ought to know. Arjuna was seeking to get divine weapons; he was to be a great leader in a battle still in the future. We are at the time of the thirteen years' exile, and you may remember that he spent many of these years in the search for these weapons. During his search, he sought Maheshvara, who had promised to give him His own weapon, and he performed many austerities in order that he might come pure into the presence of God. One day as he was performing worship, a wild boar came along; at the same time a hunter appeared, a hunter of a very low caste, a hunter of the hills. Now you remember that Arjuna was a Kshattriya, and he accordingly caught up his bow to shoot at the wild boar; the hunter also raised his bow to shoot at the wild boar. Two arrows went from the two sides and the boar was struck dead. Arjuna was very angry at the interference of this low-caste hunter, and cried: "How dare you shoot at the wild boar which was mine?" and he began to quarrel and to threaten to slay him. Said the hunter: "If you wish to fight, fight"; at that, Arjuna showered his arrows on the hunter but they all fell off from him. The hunter, laughing, said: "Excellent! Excellent! go on! go on!"; and Arjuna hurled at him weapon after weapon, but everything failed. Arrows fell off him, everything broke against him— trees, rocks, everything; he remained untouched and uninjured, until at last He showed Himself as Mahâdeva, and praised the man who had held his own against the God. Thus He tried Arjuna's strength; could he be sent to Kurukshetra with celestial weapons if his strength were too little for the fight? Try him against the Divine potency, limited in order to be faced and fought; when his courage is found to be dauntless and his strength sufficient, then send him to Kurukshetra tried and proved, able to lead his men to victory.

Take another case, more difficult. Yudhishthira is sad at heart; he is struggling, has failed, and is in danger. Drona is there, leading the hosts of his enemies, and he has been driven by him from the battle-field. No one is able to stand against Drona; every one flies before the face of that mighty warrior; he turns back every attack. What can be done? Yudhishthira is in despair. Is he to be conquered? A stainless king was this son of Pându, one of the noblest and most blameless figures that ancient literature paints; but with a strain of weakness in him which in critical times would sometimes show a too great readiness to yield, too little of the Kshattriya's power of standing alone against any force that might be brought to bear against him; a little germ of weakness was there, that had in it the possibility of a fatal fall. Shrî Krishna is there, the great Avatâra, and Bhîma comes rushing up from the battle-field saying that he has slain an elephant, whose name is the same as the name of the son of Drona.

If Drona hear that his son Ashvatthâmâ is dead, he will drop his weapons, he will let go his enemy; no further will he fight when his beloved is gone. "I told him that Ashvatthâmâ was dead, but he would not believe me; he sent me to you saying that Yudhishthira is a devotee of truth, he will not tell a lie for the sovereignty of the three worlds. If he says Ashvatthâmâ is dead, I will believe." Terrible is the strain; mighty the force brought to bear against the man who has a weakness in him; and Shrî Krishna, standing by him, watching him steadfastly, advises him to utter that which is not true. God advises this almost blameless man to tell a lie? How strange the scene! Yudhishthira, yielding to Shrî Krishna, tells the falsehood, and Drona lets fall his weapons and is killed. If the story stopped there, we might well be puzzled. If Yudhishthira's life was no further told, we might well ask: what is this that we have studied?

But when we remember that one of the great functions of the Teacher, the Gurudeva, is to bring out any weakness inherent in His pupil, because otherwise that weakness will keep the man tied, and he will not be fit to be liberated, we pause and read on. When that lie was spoken, the chariot of Yudhishthira sank downwards to the ground, no longer able to support itself, truth having been violated. And as years went on, the bitterness of that memory of a falsehood remained; the sorrow of the slaying of the preceptor by a lie ate deep into the heart of the king; he never recovered from it, he never got rid of its effect; over and over again, he breaks from his repose in anguish; "I have slain my Guru." The sorrow worked and the shame, till the anguish purified that noble soul from the last stain of weakness; and when the Great Journey is over, when wife and brothers lie dead behind him and he utters not a word of protest against the death of his beloved, when he stands ready to ascend to heaven, when only one living creature remains with him, the dog who had followed after him faithfully through all his wanderings since he left his capital, when that dog remained his sole companion, trusting his master's love faithfully unto death, then comes down a mighty God and stands beside him. "Your time has come; mount on my celestial chariot, and ascend in your body unto the heaven where you have won the right to sit and reign."

Will he now yield to the invitation of the God? He said: "This dog is here; he has trusted to my protection and I cannot leave him alone; I must take him with me." The God answered: "Dogs have no place in heaven;

dogs are unclean, no place for them is there; you have left your dead brothers behind, and your wife when she perished; why should you remain still with this dog?" "They are all dead," he answered "for the dead, the living can do nothing. This creature is still living and has sought my protection; I will not abandon him. " "Nay," the God said, "be not so foolish; leave the dog there. " But Yudhishthira stood firm; he was strong enough to stand against the God, and to show righteousness and fidelity to the poor brute that had placed his love in him; unless he might take the dog with him, he would stay on the earth and do his duty. Such lesson had he learnt from his fall; such is the result of the working of Shrî Krishna on his evolution. We can see this same working throughout the whole of that struggle. Trace Shrî Krishna through the pages of the *Mahâbhârata*, and you will find that He never deviates from one steady purpose—to bring the great struggle to a foreseen ending, where justice shall triumph and the Kshattriyas of India shall disappear; He was at once destroying injustice and preparing for the future of India, breaking down the iron wall of her warring caste that ringed her around with safety. There is a particular aim in everything that He does, and you will see that His purpose is immovable, if you study carefully. He is working towards its accomplishment the whole way through. Look at the way in which He steps in when His strength or protection is needed; see how He tries to stimulate the Pândavas to do their duty, and only takes their place when they fail. See the case where Shrî Krishna having promised that he would do no battle, Arjuna falters before the face of Bhîshma and has no heart to strike; you remember how sad was the struggle.

Arjuna was not able to strike harshly at Bhîshma, the greatest of all men and all warriors, perfect in Dharma, the grandsire and the teacher of all. "How can I slay him?" insisted Arjuna; "I remember when as a child soiled with dust, I climbed on to his knees and throwing my arms around him called him 'Father,' and he said to me, 'I am thy father's father. ' How can I bring myself to slay him?" And you will remember how Shrî Krishna Himself told him not to shrink, 'bade him slay him. ' Hard was the task; Arjuna's memory was too strong for him; he only fought in appearance with restrained might, not with vigour, until at last Shrî Krishna saw that He must stimulate this man to do his duty, and to fight, though it were against his old teacher himself; He throws down the reins of His horses, takes the whip, and leaps down from the chariot, and with the whip He rushes through the brunt of the battle to attack Bhîshma Himself. Ah! that sight is hard for Arjuna; it appeals to him as Kshattriya, and duty is remembered instead of emotion; throwing his arms round Shrî Krishna to stop him he says, "Go back! Go back! and drive me yet again, and I will do my duty even to the slaying of Bhîshma. " Now what does that mean? It means that the purpose of the God will be accomplished, whether or not a man is found to do it; that evolution will proceed, no matter who may falter or who may hinder; that while evolution will go on under the Will of God, individual progress depends on individual co-operation with that Will; that God evolves His agents by setting them to His work, and that their progress depends on the extent to which they are able to receive the impulse that He imparts. Only one other case I will take to show you how Shrî Kṛishṇa worked when the force was too great for Arjuna to meet, when He saw Arjuna could do nothing with all the valour at his command, that no force of appeal, no stimulus, could enable him to defend himself. One weapon was thrown that might not err in its aim, one weapon a celestial weapon that He had given as a boon, when He waked from His thousand years of sleep. That weapon was cast against Arjuna. Arjuna could not avert it. Alone of all the weapons in earth and heaven, that weapon must go to its ending, and Arjuna would have been slain in the midst of the battle. What can be done? He could not cut it with the arrows from Gândîva, he could not use against it any of the mighty weapons that the Gods had given him. This was the weapon of the Supreme, which nothing was able to oppose. Shrî Kṛishṇa then, at that last moment, as the weapon flies straight at the breast of the warrior throws Himself in front, and, as it strikes His bosom, it knows its Master and is changed into a garland of flowers. So also with the chariot on which He drove. He bade Arjuna first get down. He bade him take his weapons, and until Arjuna had left it, Shrî Kṛishṇa stood there immovable, He would not stir; and the moment He left it the whole chariot burst into flames, for only His presence had kept it together, He who was the Lord of fire, as well as the Lord of all else. You see, my brothers, how fruitful is the study of this subject, when you are dealing with the sacred literature; how you may be able to explain it to men of your own faith, and defend it against the attacks of men of other creeds. Do not defend it with bitter words, do not defend it with harsh language, do not defend it with wrath in your mind, and indignation making your tongue poisonous; but remember that where ignorance attacks, it is the duty of knowledge to defend; and that when that which ignorance attacks is the spiritual food of millions, every man of knowledge should spring forward to defend it, lest the ignorant of that faith should swerve, when they see the truths in their books assailed by those who do not understand.

That then is the outcome of this lecture. I ask you to remember that in every stage of your life, Gods are around you. No karma that you make, that they will not remember; no appeal that you utter, that they will not answer. If for a moment no answer seems to come, or if sorrow that you shrink from falls upon you, remember that the hand of love allows it thus to fall, and that in bearing that sorrow bravely, you are swiftly working out your own deliverance. You are to be men, not children, in the future; men-sons of the living Íshvara whose image you are, and not babies that He must for ever carry in His arms. He asks from you the strength of men to help the Gods. He is evolving you as the agents for His future universe. You may delay, if you will. You may lose time, if you will. Kalpa after Kalpa, you may remain at a low stage. If so you choose, He will not force your will; but your wisdom lies in letting His Will work in you to your swift and perfect evolution, that you may have the joy of carrying out that Will in other worlds, of consciously being His agents under other conditions; for men are Gods in the making, and we are preparing to discharge the functions of the Gods.

III. EVOLUTION OF LIFE.

MY BROTHERS,—We have reached a point in our study from which we may begin to trace the Evolution of Life in our own system that evolution takes place on the various planets, but it is similar in its general outline, though modified in its details on the different globes. We shall chiefly confine ourselves to our own world and our own humanity at the outset we shall be obliged to go somewhat further afield, but for the greater part of our study we may confine ourselves to the evolution of life on our earth. Now we are seeking in our study to find a common ground of agreement on which co-operation may arise between peoples of different faiths and of different schools of thought. If we are trying to find a meeting-place for western and for eastern Science, if we are seeking in the light of Religion to understand some of the mysteries of life, it is right and fitting that we should remember that no one religion has a monopoly of truth, and that any one who is seeking to expound the truth should be able to fortify his position from the different religions of the world, and to show that on all great, essential, and fundamental truths they speak with a single voice, they teach an identical lesson. Therefore in dealing with my subject this morning, I shall, as before, draw your attention on the main points where challenge might arise to the consensus of religious opinion, to the definite statements of the world's Teachers; so that the tendency towards unity, on which the future evolution of life depends, may be helped to develop amongst us. And there is a special reason for that just now. We shall see, as we trace out the evolution of life, that we are in the very crisis of the intellectual evolution, and we shall find that the characteristic of that stage of evolution is division and separation, and the placing of the individual apart from, and somewhat in conflict with, other individuals. And we shall find that the next stage in the evolution of life is the seeking for union amid the individualised units; that the next divine aspect that man has to develop in the Self within him is the aspect of union and not the aspect of diversity; and it is of importance that those who are seeking the light, those who are striving to co-operate with nature by understanding her hidden ways, should realise the next step of evolution as well as the present, in order that they may co-operate with nature by themselves taking that step, thus quickening the possibility of similar taking for all mankind.

Now with regard to life in its relation to forms, change at the present time is coming over the thought of western Science. I pause on this for a moment in order to substantiate that assertion, for it is important in the search for the means of drawing together the two kinds of science, ancient and modern, to notice how much the position of the leading scientists of the West has been modified with regard to life and form during the last ten years. I take as a declaration on this subject of life, issued some years ago, the article on Biology in the last edition of the *Encyclopædia Britannica*, written, as all the articles in that *Cyclopædia* are written, by a prominent man in the scientific world. In dealing then with life, the writer of the article in question distinctly states that "a mass of living protoplasm is simply a molecular machine of great complexity, the total results of the working of which, or its vital phenomena, depend, on the one hand, upon its construction, and on the other, upon the energy supplied to it and to speak of 'vitality' as anything but the name of a series of operations is as if any one should talk of the 'horology' of a clock. " That is to say, that to regard life as being in any sense a common existing principle, as anything more than a mere succession of phenomena in connection with a particular apparatus of matter, is as foolish and unreasonable as if, looking at a clock, you should separate its going property from the mechanism of the clock itself. A purely mechanical view of nature is thus taken, and life-processes are regarded as being due to the unstable equilibrium of protoplasm; the series of these life-processes is brought about merely by mechanical and chemical changes, the actions called vital being thus mechanical in their character. But at the last meeting of the British Association, the President of the Chemical Section—chemistry having been the very science to lead the scientific world towards materialism in this respect—has taken up an entirely different standpoint, a point that brings the question into a line with ancient thinking, and that starts the investigations of western Science along a road whereon the most fruitful results are likely to be encountered. Dr. Japp, the President of that Section, compares the action of life to the action of an operator who is deliberately working with a purpose, using knowledge and will in order to bring about a definite result. "The operator," he says, "exercises a guiding power which is akin, in its results, to that of the living organism," and, going on to explain in very technical language the ground on which this view is based, he concludes by saying: "Every purely mechanical explanation of the phenomenon must necessarily fail. I see no escape from the conclusion that at the moment when life first arose a directive force came into play— a force precisely of the same character as that which enables the intelligent operator, by the exercise of his will, to select one crystallised enantiomorph and reject its asymmetric opposite. " That is the declaration: that with the arising of life there is an arising of consciousness which exercises a directive force in nature, as we see it exercising a directive force in the choice exercised by men. Put those two statements side by side, see the entire reversal of the attitude, and then you will be able to measure to some extent the change that has come over western thinking—the recognition of life as identical with consciousness, a position which has ever been taken in the hoary Science of the East.

Now let me, before going into details, suggest to you the path that we are to follow. From the One Existence, that One without a second, arises, as we saw in our first study—Íshvara, God in His creative and manifested aspect, Íshvara clothed in Mâyâ, out of which a new universe is to be builded. Threefold we found Him to be in His manifestation, threefold in the aspect that He showed forth; so that a Trimûrti, or Trinity, is the aspect towards this universe of the manifested God; His working will show this triple character, and the evolution of life is threefold, whether we study it in nature or in man. I know the thought that arises in many of you, accustomed to the broad statements in eastern literature. You think of the building, the sustaining, and the disappearing of a universe. Perfect, you say, is the One Existence, infinite, unchangeable; perfect in the ending is the universe, as perfect in the beginning; why then this long evolution of life with all its struggles, with all its imperfections gradually and slowly transcended. Why from the perfect should the imperfect come forth? Why should it be trained into perfection, and then return into that perfection whence it came? That question is based on a fundamental misunderstanding which it is necessary to correct; a misunderstanding which never could have risen amongst you if the Scriptures had been read in the light of the Yoga-developed consciousness, and if the broad outline which is presented had been followed out carefully in thought so that its stages might be marked. You will remember how it is written in the *Chhândhogyopanishad* that the One willed to multiply; and the moment you grasp the idea of multiplication, if you think of what it means instead of merely repeating the word, you will realise that multiplication must necessarily mean division and therefore limitation, and that limitation necessarily implies imperfection. But having gone so far, you would then have proceeded to ask: By what words is the universe described, and what idea is hidden beneath the words? And you would find that when God is spoken of as a Fire, the universe is not spoken of as a Fire, but as a spark, and the lives of men are described as millions of sparks that come from the illimitable Fire. Not only is that word "spark" used, showing you the limitation that comes with manifestation, giving you the idea that the spark, fed by suitable fuel is to be developed into the likeness of the Flame whence it came; but as the spark is of the same nature as the flame, so we are told "Thou art That," the Self in man is identical in nature with the Self that gave it birth. You will remember another word which is constantly used to describe alike the universe as a whole, and also the parts of which it is composed—the word germ or seed. Let me ask you to turn to the *Bhagavad Gîtâ* so familiar to every student amongst you, and to listen for a moment to the words chosen by Shrî Krishna when He desires to convey the idea of the nature of the universe, and its relation to the Supreme What does He say?

Mama yonir Mahad Brahma tasmin garbham dadâmyaham.

Sambhava sarva bhûtânâm tato bhavati Bhârata.

"I place the germ in the womb of Mahad Brahma." What do these words imply? for the whole turns on our understanding of that word "germ. " Mahad Brahma is the matter of the universe, vivified by Brahman in His third aspect—that which Theosophists call the Third Logos, which in the Trimûrti is spoken of as Brahmâ. Looking on Brahman as the *One*, Mahad Brahma is the third aspect of His revealing, which vivifies and makes atomic the matter of the universe, the womb of the seed of the Eternal Life. In that, brought into manifestation by Brahmâ, or the Third Logos, the Second, the generating Father, Vishnu, places that germ of life that therein it may develop; not Himself in all the might of His Deity, not Himself in the force of His unfolded powers, but the seed of His life—capable of evolution, containing everything within it potentially, but showing forth nothing in manifestation at the beginning of the universe. True, the child is the father revived; true, the child is the same as the father. None the less, the life which the father gives is the seed containing the power of development, and the universe is but the seed of Deity, with every power involved within it, and capable by its evolution of becoming the image of the Supreme: none the less is every power germinal, not developed, potential, not actual; only at the ending will that seed, grown into perfect manhood, show forth the image of its generating Sire, and give a new Íshvara to the future from whom further universes may evolve. That is the answer to the question: Why this long evolution? It is this evolution that we are to trace from the germ to the perfect, life given as germ to grow to the God.

Let us look first at the matter in which this life is to be clothed—not in detail, that is to-morrow's work—but just as to the principle involved in the evolution of the matter through which the life is to express itself. We heard the first day about tattvas. We found that they were modifications of Prakriti, the primary matter, brought out one after the other as the regions of the universe were builded. All that we need for our purpose this morning is to remember that five of these are concerned with the present evolution, that the highest of these is the A'kâsha in the highest sense of the term, then Vâyu, then Agni, then Apas, then Prithivî; all these are kosmic and they represent vast planes in the universe, but have their correspondences in the physical globe—ether, air, fire, water, earth, these being only the reflections in miniature of their great prototypes in the system at large. The only other thing we need to remember this morning with regard to matter, is that the whole of these are animated by the life of the *third* aspect of God. Here is a point where we may pause for a moment and look at other religions, and we shall find that they all tell us exactly the same. Not only do we find in Hinduism, in such a book as the *Vishnu Purâna* that the Divine creation was from Mahat—the third manifestation—that these great tattvas were evolved by modifications from the principle of individuality which is the characteristic of that aspect; but if we turn to the Hebrew teachings we shall find that it is distinctly stated that the "Spirit of God," the third aspect, or Wisdom, moved on the face of the waters. Translating the symbol of water we have matter; it is so used in every great religious scripture, and when it is said that the Spirit of God moved on the face of the waters, we have the picture of a brooding life, brooding over and permeating the ocean of primeval matter, giving to it the life that will enable it to serve as the womb for a higher life; the divine energy that thus vivifies matter comes from the third Person of the Christian Trinity. That Hebrew statement dominates the whole of Christendom, inasmuch as the Christian Churches take the older part of their scriptures from the hands of the Hebrew people; and in quoting that, I am not quoting it only as an authority from the Hebrews but as including the authority of the whole of Christendom, bound by that Hebrew teaching. I might show you, did time permit, that other great Teachers have spoken in the same sense; the outcome being that the matter in which evolution is to take place—of which our world of organisms, including our own bodies, is to be formed—that matter is permeated by the Divine life, and the aspect of Divine life that permeates it is that of the third manifestation of God. That is the fundamental reason why Brahmâ is no longer worshipped. That is why no temples are raised to Him and why worshippers do not throng to His shrines. His work was dominant in the earlier stages of the universe, but is now overshadowed by the working of another aspect of the mighty God, Vishnu as Preserver, as Sustainer, and as Organiser. He is the life which is active in all organisms; and the life which animates the atoms of matter having been given and partially evolved, the continuing aspect of that work is hidden at the present stage of the universe; the main evolution of life that is now occurring is carried on and directed by other aspects of God.

Sometimes in theosophical literature, that vivification and building up of matter is spoken of as the work of the first great life-wave in the solar system; as a wave rolling forth so does the life of God go forth for the building of the atoms whereof the system is to be composed. The critical point is this: that the life is veiled over and over again in a five-fold involution; we find it said that Prâna five-fold divides itself, for five are the types of the atoms, five are the great divisions of the materials, and in each successive type, the previous type permeates and encloses it, as we found we could read in the *Vishnu Purâna*, dealing with the building up of the tattvas. (It will be remembered that the types are really seven, but that two are concealed.) One important result comes from this which I will deal with more fully to-morrow, that the form—being built up from matter containing within it this involved and concealed life—has the power of unfolding to the highest possibility of the life thus concealed. Sheath after sheath is made in order that sheath after sheath may be brought into activity as a vehicle of the Self, and that five-fold ensheathing for the human Self is wrought in order that it may have a vehicle capable of responding to every vibration that it sets up or that it receives. As the vibrations become subtler and subtler in their character, sheath after sheath becomes active and responsive, and enables the life to function externally by means of the sheath. Let us however turn—for that will be fully worked out to-morrow—to the next great life-wave with which we are concerned; it is the life of the second aspect of Deity, spoken of in Hinduism as the life of Vishnu, spoken of in Christianity as the life of the Son of God by whom all things were made. As that life outpours into the universe prepared to receive it, as that life begins to draw together the matter which, vivified by the first out-pouring, is now ready to respond to the vibrations of the life that organises and sustains, vibrations are sent out by this Divine Life into the higher regions of the universe, beginning the task of drawing the matter together into forms. The earliest stages of these are the ante-types of what shall be in evolution—not such forms as we speak of in the lower world, concrete objects which can give rise to concrete ideas, but that which dimly we are trying to reach in the mind to-day, when we abstract from a great class of concrete objects its uniting quality, its common characteristic, and formulate this apart from the objects themselves. I have sometimes taken the triangle as the very simplest image which thought can form. You may have triangles of any size, you may have triangles of almost any shape, provided only three lines are used, and those lines are right lines, or unbent. What is the governing characteristic of the triangle? That its three angles, formed by the meeting of enclosing sides, must be equal to two right angles. Now supposing that you have the power of brain, the power of abstraction, to take ten, twenty or thirty concrete triangles and hold them in the mind as though you were looking at them in outer form, to create their mental images so that every form is present in your mind, you directing your attention to them all at the same time, then—if out of these many concrete objects that have the particular properties in common of the three right lines that enclose and the sum of the three angles equalling two right angles—if you can draw out the idea of that common property, separated from every concrete triangle, and make it an object in consciousness, then you will have risen from the concrete to the abstract, and will have some idea of what is meant by an archetype in the higher world. The earliest actions of the Deity in evolving a system are of this nature; He generates certain types or archetypes, and by the sub-division and multiplication of these the whole universe of concrete objects is formed; each one of them is capable of generating innumerable forms that reproduce its own characteristic amid endless diversities of subsidiary properties.

It is not without interest that some of our scientific men have tried to find unity amidst diversity, and to discover the types of the animal kingdom amid the innumerable diversities of the separated animal forms. One of the most famous of those men, Sir Richard Owen, tried to formulate an archetype which should represent every fundamental characteristic of the vertebrate, like no particular vertebrate but showing forth the qualities present in every vertebrate; he worked this out from a study of vertebrates, setting aside the characteristics in which they differ and synthesising into a single form the qualities possessed by all. The reverse process is what really occurred; the archetype which came forth from the Divine Mind generated in the world of matter myriad different types in each of which it is itself expressed. That gleam of genius which illuminated the mind of the modern scientist is interesting as a ray from the conception of creative action given in our sacred literature; and you will find, if you study carefully, that the earliest forms are not concrete objects but generative powers, and that these coming forth from God make models for the future types, each type being related to its ante-type, each concrete object to its abstract idea. Thus also the Greeks taught, Pythagoras and Socrates and Plato; thus also many of the Hebrews taught, the doctors of the Kabala; and both the Greek Philosopher and Hebrew Kabalist have declared that the visible world of objects could never have come into existence had not the invisible world of Ideas preceded it, so that the objects repeated in multitude what an Idea presented in unity. That Idea thus coming forth from God and drawing to itself forms in subtle matter, produces the types of forms that are gradually to be worked out in evolution; and those of you who have studied the *Secret Doctrine* of Madame Blavatsky may remember that the archetypal world is therein spoken of as the first which is created, and as that on which the whole of the evolution of denser worlds depends. It is made of the A'kâsha which contains within itself the possibility of all forms as we are told, and these Ideas are drawn forth and reproduced in greater detail by the Builder on the A'kâshic correspondences of Agni. Life is evolved by the modifications in consciousness which Íshvara brings about; the modification in the consciousness of Íshvara preceding the moulding of the matter. As that life-wave descends into denser and denser matter, it draws together more and more separate forms, that become denser in their nature, until at last, through kingdom after kingdom, it comes down to the mineral forms, where life is most restricted in its operations, where consciousness is most limited in its scope. This is the process of the involution of life in matter, the descending arc. From this lowest point the life ascends, revealing more and more of its powers, and ordinary western "evolution" begins here, the earlier process being ignored.

How did that Divine life and consciousness, in the first upward stage of evolution, evolve in the germinal life the power to respond? The life within the stone has the capacity to respond, but in a very limited fashion, partly owing to its germinal nature, partly owing to the rigidity of its surrounding vehicle; therefore the brooding life of Vishnu, nourishing this germ, at once stimulates it by impacts from without and gradually modifies the rigidity so as to make progress possible. Long, long remains the life imbedded in this rigid material, working from within outwards, as all life works, playing upon and thus softening the rigidity, and slowly giving the form more plasticity in response; we can sum up the whole of the working of the life, as the receiving of vibrations from matter without and the answering of vibrations from itself within. Notice in the earliest stages how tremendous are the impacts; if you go back to the time when the world knew not humanity, how gigantic are the operations of nature showing herself in her mineral forms; earthquakes, eruptions, crushing and grinding of materials, disintegration and reconstruction, all on the mightiest and most gigantic scale; under all that, the life, trying to make the matter more plastic and able to answer more readily; and inasmuch as there is life, there is consciousness, i. e., the power to respond, that power is developed within it, stimulated by the brooding life of Íshvara.

He dwelling within, and enveloping and permeating all objects, makes the seed of life extend and grow by his nourishing warmth, that it may become finally an independent centre. We see the life within the stone beginning to vibrate more actively as these tremendous blows come upon it from without; and mass is thrown against mass, and mountain is piled upon mountain, until at last these mineral materials gain larger power of transmitting impulses to the life within; the impulse coming through more strongly because of the lessened opposition from the form, the life responds more actively and begins to evolve, developing more definitely the power of response. As this process is repeated over and over again, the life within the minerals vibrates with ever increasing rapidity, and the matter yields to it with ever greater readiness, until a stage of plasticity is reached at which the beginnings of the vegetable world can be brought into existence. Between mineral and plant in the lowest stages no definite dividing line can be drawn by science. So general is this absence of dividing lines in nature that a separate kingdom has been recognised as including low types of both vegetable and animal, and between the vegetable and mineral kingdoms a class is recognised in which the rigid crystal which belongs to the mineral kingdom has become the plastic crystalloid that belongs to the vegetable; maintaining the outline of the mineral form, but showing the plasticity of the vegetable, and thus yielding far more readily to the moulding influences of the life within.

The life thus encased in more plastic material receives vibrations from without more easily and responds more strongly, until in the ascent that it is beginning to make, it adds the early beginnings of a power of consciousness that in the mineral was not present. We call it sensation: the power of feeling pleasure and pain, the power of responding to the outside impact by a feeling within the life. After the life in the mineral has developed the power of response, then the next stage in evolution is that the response takes on the sensations of pleasure and pain, appearing as that within the life which responds severally to harmonious or discordant impact from without. As the life develops this power of sensation, progress becomes more rapid. The animal kingdom is gradually builded and the power of sensation is the great characteristic which is developed through that kingdom, until—the animal forms having been rendered plastic through many ages by the impulse of life, and the life having formed and strengthened the power of responding by pleasure and pain to harmonious and discordant vibrations—the next stage is ready to be taken, the building of the vehicle for man.

That outer body in which man is to dwell resembles closely in its nature, in some of its fundamental characteristics, the animal bodies which the life had vivified before man was called into existence. "Out of the dust of the ground," says the Hebrew scripture, God formed the body of man, a symbolic way of saying that out of the material that had made the lowest forms of life, was also to be made the outer coating of that vessel, into which a new flood of Divine life was to be outpoured, forming the human Self, or Spirit. We learn, when we study occultism, that this third outpouring of Divine life comes neither from the Third, nor from the Second, but from the First Logos, therefore called Mahâdeva, the Great God, the Supreme. From Him comes the third impulse which is to complete evolution, the third outpouring of life, that only accomplishes its final evolution in this age by methods of Yoga; therefore is He often represented as the great Yogî, the great Guru, under whose instructions the latest stages of evolution are to be carried out. When that life-force comes down, and the human Self is sent forth to occupy its tabernacle, the ancient process is again repeated, and it is only the germ of the highest life that is given and not the completed life. Round it are vehicles that are able to respond, round it are vehicles that have the power of developing more highly, that are already capable of sending in vibrations arousing feeling in the life that they enclose, and now—enwrapped by the life of Vishnu—this germ of the Divine Self begins to stir and live as man.

At first there comes from it very little response to the life that is transmitted, very little answer to that which is outside; but what are the characteristics of this infant Self, this spark of the Eternal Fire? Triple in aspect is the life in man as it is triple in the Deity, and its characteristics are the same, Sat, Chit, Ananda. We speak thus of Brahman, and if we study the human Self we shall find these three aspects present also in that human Self; and the first to develop in man, as in the Kosmos, is Chit or knowledge. All the earliest stages of human evolution have to do with the evolution of Intelligence; it is that with which we are now concerned, as we climb this mighty ladder. We are evolving intelligence or intellect, and if we trace its stages from the earliest germs as they appear in the primeval races of the humanity of our globe, and as fostered in those races by the Great Ones who came to us as Teachers from other worlds, we shall find that the dawning intellect in man was but very slightly responsive to anything that came to it from without, and that at first every effort of the intelligence was stimulated by the promptings of the animal nature, by the sting of desire, by the passions which belong to the animal part of man. Consider a savage. When is a savage active? Only when some animal desire awakens within him. If he is hungry, yes, then he will begin to think, "where can I find food?" If he is thirsty, he will ask, "where shall I find liquid?" Any animal prompting that arises within him, his dawning mind applies itself to satisfy; and the germ of mind is stimulated by the promptings of animal desire. In that stage he knows not right from wrong; right and wrong for him have no existence; hunger and thirst, sexual desire, and the need for sleep, these are the things that make up his life and that move his dawning consciousness; these only are strong enough to stir it into activity; it cannot yet initiate activity from within. But as these play upon it, life after life, birth after birth, century after century, in successive incarnations of this germinal but growing life, as these vibrations continually arouse, awaken the life of the intelligence, which is the third aspect of the Self, these repeated vibrations, repeated over and over and over again a thousand times, by that very repetition bring about an internal tendency to repeat it again without a fresh stimulus from outside; and we find in the next stage of the evolution of intelligence, still in the savage, that the savage does not wait for hunger in order to search for food, but that the memory of hunger and the memory of food are enough to send him out, before the hunger strikes him, in search of the meal that to-morrow he will require to satisfy the needs of the body. But what a change is there if we consider it, small as it is in appearance. The man is no longer stimulated by an outer impulse coming from the animal nature; he is stimulated by a mental image, a connected picture of the painful state of the body wanting food and of the food which is able to change that state into one of pleasure; that is, he is now able to form mental images, and these stimulate him into activity. How great the change! No less than a change of the centre of consciousness from the animal to the human, one of the most significant changes in the evolving life. Now, for the first time, he does not wait to be pushed from without. He begins action from within, and the body obeys the impulse that comes from the centre, instead of the impact that strikes the centre from without. Now evolution becomes more rapid, for as this great change, one of the hardest of changes, is made, the intellect in man begins to cognise itself, and Self-consciousness begins to arise. Separation is recognised between its own centre, that thinks, and the things outside that make it think; the

"I" and the "Not-I" arise, and the centre begins to shape itself and to be capable of growth.

How shall the growth go on? By conflict. This is the characteristic of the intellect. It has to make the "I" a strong centre, a separate centre, otherwise no further evolution is possible. You may say that this looks like going downwards; nay, it is the germ of a new centre of life in which Divinity itself shall unfold when evolution is complete. There must be a clearly defined centre of consciousness, else how shall it work onward to perfection? And that centre grows by struggle. All strength comes by struggle of one kind or another. If you want your arms to become strong, it is no good to lie on a sofa and leave the muscles to grow merely by the nourishment that you give them. They want more than nourishment, they want exercise; and it is the law of all growth of form that the life must be drawn into the form, for only then can the form expand and become capable of receiving a further impulse of life; if the muscles are to grow, the cells that compose them must be stretched by exercise, and the life must flow into the expanded cell; only then does it become capable of multiplication, so that there may be many cells where before there was only one. The difference between the weak man and the strong man, the man who is feeble and the man who is athletic, is the difference brought about by exercise and struggle, by pulling against resistance, by taking up a weight and whirling it round and making the muscles strain against the weight. That is a picture of the way in which all life is working for development of form; the impulse of life leads to the exercise of the form, the exercise makes it plastic and increases the form, through which the life is thus enabled to flow more largely. That is as true in the mental world as in the physical world; for the mental world is also a world of phenomena. It is not the One; its characteristic is diversity, each being standing by himself, and regarding other things as separate. I know an object. How? By its differences from some objects and its likenesses to others; otherwise I could not know it. You cannot think of unity until you have seen variety; you cannot recognise likeness until you have seen unlikeness. The characteristic of intellectual evolution is the discrimination of differences followed by the recognition of likenesses; thus the intellect recognises object after object, each of them by its own characteristic marks. Analysis precedes synthesis. Differences are seen before an underlying unity is recognised.

As this intelligence develops, we find the recognition of the Self and the Not-Self giving rise to struggle all over the world, social struggle as well as mental struggle. In every civilisation in which the intellect is developing from its earlier stages, you must have struggle without in order to stimulate the evolution within; it is a necessary stage, although it be a passing one, and it need not distress us, who see its end, in a world guided by the Gods. All the stages through which a nation passes are necessary for its growth, and need not be condemned merely because of their being limited and imperfect. In practical politics condemnation is useful as a stimulus, as one of the agents for bringing about the evolutionary changes, but the philosopher should understand, and, understanding, he cannot condemn. The worst struggle that we may see, the most terrible poverty, the most shocking misery, the strife of man against man and nation against nation—all these are working out the Divine purpose, and are bringing us towards a richer unity than without them we could possibly attain.

Let me take one instance which seems to be the most hopeless of all— the instance of war. What can be more inhuman than war, what more brutal and more terrible, stirring the angriest passions of man and making him like a wild beast in his rage? Aye, but that is not all. Let us look at the life within a soldier which has been evolved by this terrible discipline without. What is that life learning as its vehicles are plunged into strife, into blood-shed, into mutilation, into death? It is learning lessons that without that stern experience it could not learn, without which its evolution would be checked and be unable to proceed it is learning that there is something greater than the body, something greater than the physical existence, something higher, more noble, more compelling, than the guarding of the physical vehicle from injury and even from death; and the poorest soldier who goes out on a campaign, who goes through hardship after hardship, who finds himself frozen with cold or burnt up with heat, who plunges through frozen river or toils across sandy desert, who learns to preserve discipline and submission under hardship, who learns to keep cheerful under difficulty, so that his comrades may not be depressed, who is moved, not by the thought of the body which is suffering, but by the great ideal of the military renown of his regiment, and the safety of the country which he is serving, who is learning thus to sacrifice himself for an ideal, is developing thereby qualities invaluable in lives to come. Need I say this to you, who know the place of the Kshattriya in human evolution? Did Manu when he described these different castes demarcate a caste that had not its place in the evolution of life, that had not something to teach? Was not a man kept in the Kshattriya vehicle until he had learned that life was not dependent on the body, that life was to be held at the service of the ideal, at the service of the mother-land that gave him birth, of the king who ruled him, and who to him stood, as to every Hindu the king should stand, as an Avatâra of God? He learned that when that king called him to the battle-field, he had to give his body to mutilation and to death, because the life that was in him recognised the service of the ideal as evolving the real life, and the body as a mere garment to be thrown aside when duty called? Without that training, no Brâhmana could be; no man could come into the caste of the Brâhmana, save as he had gone through that discipline in the ranks of the Kshattriya; because until he had learned that life was everything and form nothing—and that is the lesson which war teaches when it is rightly understood—until that lesson was learned, he was not prepared for the far harder evolution of the life, which is to master the lesson of unity beneath diversity, of love beneath antagonism, of being the friend of every creature and the foe of none.

When the intelligence has developed, when it has reached a fairly high standpoint, the germs of the next aspect of Deity begin to show themselves in man and that aspect is A'nanda, Joy or Bliss. But in what does A'nanda really consist? It is in the drawing together of separated objects and uniting them into one. That is the essence of Bliss, that the very core and heart of the next stage of evolution. In the old days of Hinduism, this was called the life of the Brâhmana, when the Brâhmana was really a Brâhmana and had no further birth before him on the wheel of births and deaths. In the Christian symbology it is called the Christ stage, that of Divine Sonship, and you will find in a great prayer of Jesus, called the Christ, that in praying for His disciples He asked that "they may be one in me," in union with each other and Himself. There is a grander unity yet, the unity between the Son and Father, a unity of nature not a union of the erst-separated; but before that unity can be reached, man must have realised the union with his brother men, must see humanity as united, and not as separate; that is, he must have changed his centre of consciousness—that responds to the impacts from without—from the vehicles in which the intellect and the feelings were developed to the life itself, which is one and the same in all. No longer is he to think himself as separate, inasmuch as the "I," the separated self, is now to be transcended, is to be merged in the uniting aspect of the Deity, the Vishnu or the Christ. That is to be developed as the life of man, with all its wonderful beauty and power, with its unifying force. Therefore did Shrî Krishna come as an Avatâra to this Eastern world to show forth the life of Love; for the life of A'nanda, or Bliss, is ever the life of Love, and by Love alone may we evolve it within ourselves. The aspect of God that is Bliss shows itself as Love; and in word and in action, in simile and in parable, did the Beloved and the Lover of man reveal that Divine aspect to the longing hearts of his Bhaktas. That was His special work, to show out the Love power of God; and only as that is developed within us can the life take on this lofty unfoldment that knits all selves in the One Self, that sees all lives in Him. Now, in evolution, the Self knows itself as the Life, and is no longer deluded by the ignorance that made it identify itself with the Form; it is life which realises itself as Life. When this stage is reached by the evolving life, the man who was separated becomes Humanity, and is one of the Saviours of the world. There is nothing apart from him, nothing separate to him. He stands in the very Life itself, and sheds his light in every direction into whatever Upâdhi, or vessel, may be in need of it; wherever there is want or cry for his aid, thereto flow his powers. As the sun shines forth in heaven, and may shine unto a million houses, the only condition of his rays entering being that the houses shall lay themselves open to the sunshine, so is the man who has become the second aspect of Deity, in whom that perfection of Divine Sonship is revealed. Man, as the Son of God in Heaven, is above all the distinctions that you find on Earth. He sends down his rays into the waiting hearts of men, and the only condition necessary for his entrance, the one thing that ensures his coming, is that his brother will open his heart to receive him. For he will not break his way in, he will only come where he is welcome. Thus this great life of God shows itself forth now in the man who has become the Saviour, the Son, the Initiate, as a deep compassionate love for all. Every man who reaches that stage is a new force for the uplifting of humanity. Every man who develops that aspect of life is one more wing with which to lift everything upwards. If a man be weak, his life can go to him to strengthen him; if a man be sorrowful, his life can go to him to make him glad; if a man be sinful, his life can go to him to make him pure from sin. To all men he says: "Wherever a man is there will I meet him, and there will I accept him." That is Shrî Kṛiṣhṇa in manifestation, that the love that shines forth from the bliss aspect of the Human Self.

One step remains, the last, of evolution for this rapidly perfecting life. Again I take up my Christian symbol and venture the quotation:—"As Thou, Father, art in Me and I in Thee, that they also may be one in Us. " The Son becomes in fact what he has ever been potentially, one with the Father. He enters into the mighty realm of Self-Being, where God, in the Christian phrase, is "all-in-all. " Do not let the narrower presentations of Christianity that here meet you blind you to these fundamental identities of the deeper and more spiritual Christianity with our own ancient faith. Shall these pettinesses, or even outer divergencies, separate those whom the living Spirit would unite? We learn, as we study the Hindu Scriptures, that man after having reached the second stage rises by Yoga, until he attains the last, and becomes one with the Deity Himself in full power of eternal Self-Being. It was because your own Svâmi T. Subba Rao knew this occult truth, which too many know not, that he spoke, as I before mentioned, of the innumerable Centres, or Logoi, in the One, every one of which could be the beginning of a new universe, of a new out-pouring of life. The building of those Centres is a purpose of Life-evolution. The building them up stage by stage is done as the life passes from form to form; and end or ending there is none in the infinite series of the future. What that life holds for us we cannot tell; how should we imagine that far off land, those distant reaches? But this we know: that no will of the Eternal is ever frustrate, no purpose of the Eternal lacks its fruit or misses its goal; and if our eyes fail us in the dazzle of the light wherein we see our unity with the Eternal Father—that unity that transcends our dreaming, when we shall know ourselves to be one with Him—it is enough that at last the evolution of all lives leads into that unimaginable splendour, known only to Íshvara Himself, who pours out His life that we may know it also. And Mahâdeva shall return to It with all the centres that His life has brought into existence, with all the new lives and joys that His imprisonment in His universe has made. That is enough for us to give us the hope—hope, do I say? it is too feeble a word—the joy inexpressible and the certainty which are founded on the very Life of God; for is He not the Truth, the Foundation of the Universe? And when we enter into SAT we shall know the future as we see the past, for we shall be not only immortal but Eternal.

IV. EVOLUTION OF FORM.

MY BROTHERS,—We are now to concentrate our attention on the phenomenal side of the universe, that is, on the varied appearances that surround us, whether those appearances be visible to the physical eyes or not; for we must remember that the principle of form is to be found in every stage of the manifested universe, and that when the phrase "the formless world" is used, the word "formless" is only true in relation to the worlds below the one so spoken of. All higher worlds are "formless" regarded from below, that is, regarded by the organs of perception which are fitted for exercise in the lower world; but if a person has developed the capacity to respond to the vibrations in any given world of manifestation, then that world to him is a world of form and not of formlessness. Everywhere manifestation implies form, however subtle may be the matter which composes it; and you may remember that it is said in the *Vishnu Purâna* that the one characteristic of matter which is always present is extension, that is, the capacity of taking form, of being shaped in a definite way.

Now before we take up the details of evolution, there are one or two great principles that I want to ask you to keep in mind; for we shall never be able to understand the complexity of detail, if we take it as a series of isolated details; we need to classify these under certain fundamental principles and then, those principles being clear in the mind, we can easily, as it were, pack every detail into its appropriate pigeon-hole in our thought. I shall not trouble you this morning at all with that threefold division of the evolving life with which we dealt yesterday. We can, for our work now, treat life as a unit, speaking of the Divine Life as Íshvara, and of the reflection of that life in man as the Self. We will keep these two terms to avoid confusion: Íshvara as the Divine Life which is the source of evolution; the Self as the human life which is gradually evolving. And we need these two distinguishing names, without going into any of the subdivisions that we dealt with yesterday in connection with life, in order that we may be able to see how forms are shaped, and to which principle, if I may say so, we are to refer the special modifications.

The next thing that we must realise is the respective functions of these sources of life; one working through the whole kosmos, and therefore coming to man as a part of that kosmos, the other working in man as an individual through the early stages and transcending individuality at the close. The great life of Íshvara as it rolls outwards, building the universe of forms, expresses itself, as we have seen, by a certain series of vibrations, and every modification in the form is the result of an impulse coming by way of vibrations from the ensouling life. Now the point that strikes us most in this manifestation of Íshvara, as we study it, is the unutterable patience of it. We are impatient for results, He never. We are impatient for results, because, limited by time, we crave to see the outcome of our action; He being the eternal is unspeakably patient, set upon perfection and careless of the time which that perfection may take in evolving. For the evolution of forms this patience is absolutely necessary; when we come to think, we see that any impatience in the evolution of forms would mean the over-rapid breaking up of the forms. The form is comparatively rigid as compared with the life. If the life vibrates too rapidly for the form which it is evolving, the form will shatter under the stress of those vibrations. Let me give you a very common illustration to show you what I mean; a tube of glass, or an ordinary lamp-glass if you like, has a certain note to which it vibrates; and if that note be sung near the lamp-glass, you will hear the note sound out independently from the lamp-glass, as though the lamp-glass were singing; the glass has vibrated in answer to the vibrations of the sound sung to it, it having the capacity of that vibration in it, and thus it reproduces the note. If you increase the force of that note, if you continue vibration after vibration, beyond the point at which the glass is able to respond, your glass will shiver into pieces, shivered by the force of the effort to respond to vibrations beyond its limit of rigidity. I only take that as an illustration, as a picture; it is true in every world of form; and if Íshvara were to send forth vibrations too swift, too subtle for the form which He is ensouling to respond to, that form would be shivered into pieces, and its evolution would be stopped; nature would have again to begin to build a similar form in order to again reach the point which it had already reached. This patience of Íshvara is the thing that strikes us first as we study the evolution of forms. How slow are the changes, how gradual the modifications, what thousands of successive forms are worked in, how wellnigh imperceptible are the changes in their minuteness, although so great when we look at them in the mass; that is one great principle to bear in mind.

Another great principle is the double and parallel action of Íshvara and of the evolving Self. Íshvara is present in the Self of man that is formed within Him. Every evolutionary impulse in the earliest stages comes directly from the life of Íshvara, and as He moulds the form without, He gradually strengthens the centre that He is building up within. His object is to make that centre the image of Himself, self-sustaining; but enormous reaches of time are needed for the building; as He shapes the forms, He builds the centre; and as He builds that centre, and it becomes more and more active, answering to the vibrations that He transmits to it from the outer world, it begins to take on a little action of its own and to send out vibrations, as we may say, on its own account. As this double action goes on within the form, more and more does that evolving centre begin to control the form within which it is developed. As this power of control develops and increases, He withdraws more and more of His directive energy as Íshvara; the energy drawn from Him is now beginning to work *quasi*-independently in the separated centre that He has been building, until at last that centre reflects Himself, and is able to be self-existent by the very life that it has drawn from Him. If this conception be a little abstract, let me give it again in a concrete form. There is one symbol that the sages have used over and over again, in order to express this wonder of the brooding life of Íshvara making an image of Himself and giving to that image the possibility of independent life. It is the symbol of the mother and the child within the womb. As the life of the mother passes into the child that is building within her, transmitting to that new form all the nourishment which is necessary for its growing life, the whole life of the child is dependent on the mother and the life-streams that nourish it are drawn from her own life. The building goes on, and on, and on, till the new centre of life has grown strong, but not until that centre can hold itself together amid the vibrations of the outer universe, is the new form with its ensouling life sent forth on its own independent course. So does the brooding mother-life of Íshvara envelope the children of His love, and so does He nourish them, building them within Himself as the ages pass, until they are able to hold their own centres in the illimitable life of the One, the Supreme. That is another principle which you have to remember throughout the details of the evolution of form.

One other that has two divisions and then the statement of our main principles will be sufficiently complete. There are three aspects, we recollect, which the evolving Self has to unfold. We must add to this a comprehension of the nature of these aspects, when externalised; for we did not yesterday, for lack of time, glance quite precisely at the in characteristic outer mark of each aspect of life. As these aspects modify the evolution of form, the form cannot be understood unless its relations to the aspects of life be realised. We have, as we know, to show forth Knowledge, Bliss, and Being. These will come out as powers into the world of form as evolution reaches its later stages, and the form will be able to express those powers of the evolving life. Knowledge, showing forth through form, has as its power Intelligence; Bliss, shown forth through form, has as its power Love; Being, shown forth through form, has as its power Existence; so that the fundamental aspects may be said severally to manifest as the powers of intelligence, of love, of existence. Otherwise put, the nature of intelligence is knowledge, the nature of love is bliss, the nature of existence is being. The intelligence, love and existence of our worlds are the manifested Knowledge, the manifested Bliss, and the manifested Being of the Self. That is the outward aspect of the Self as the other is the inner aspect, and these characteristic natures seek their expression in form. This expression is sought cosmically and individually, alike by the life of Íshvara and the life of the Self. Cosmically they make the planes of the manifested universe, the five planes on which we are evolving. That which manifests as existence, the power of Being, has as its form the Akâsha of the higher realm; that which manifests as love, the power of Bliss, has as its form of matter Vâyu; that which manifests as intelligence, the power of Knowledge, has as its material Agni. These are the three fundamental manifestations in form. The other two are reflections: That which is love, reflecting itself in the lower form of matter—the denser matter of Varuna—takes on the aspect of desire and passion, and becomes kâma. That which is existence, reflecting itself on the yet grosser form of Prithivî, shows forth what we call objective reality. See how the planes correspond, the one with the other. Try and make a picture of a mountain reflected in a lake; and if you have that in your mind, you will follow exactly the way the reflection takes place. There is no reflection of intelligence because it is the central quality; the intelligence is the centre of the five, two are above it and two are below it. It is the central region, the pivot on which the whole has to turn. If you look above to the higher regions, we find love and existence showing themselves forth as the powers of Bliss and Being. That is as it were, the mountain. Now look at your reflection in the lake; the middle part of the mountain is reflected half-way down in the water. The shore is the dividing line between object and image, and represents the intelligence; below that, half-way down, will come the reflection of love showing itself as emotion and desire; then we see the highest peak reflected in the deepest depth of the lake, the existence above, the power of the real Being, reflected below in the plane of physical matter as that illusory existence which man calls real. Try and keep that picture, for the principle of reflection from above to below is one of the keys to understanding both above and below. It helps you to see why emotional love passes into devotion, and how, in the passing from emotion into the higher love which is devotion, it passes from the kâmic plane to the buddhic, where bliss is the distinguishing characteristic; and you will understand why action, the most illusory of things, has to us the sense of reality. It gives that peculiarly definite sense of reality to us because it is the reflection of the real, of the existence of which it is the lower form.

Now these are the principles. Let us try to carry them out in our evolutionary study; for if you hold firm to the principles, the study of detail, of forms, will seem less confusing, less complex and less difficult; you will not lose your way among the trees, when once you have looked down on the forest as a whole; that is a simile I once heard from Professor Huxley, as illustrating principles and details, and it is a suggestive one.

We begin then the detailed evolution of form; it is like a great circle traced downwards and upwards. There is a great difference between the downward arc, the one-half of the circle, and the upward arc, the other half of the circle. In the one case, coming downwards, Íshvara imparts qualities and attributes; in the other half, going upwards, He builds the qualities and attributes into vehicles. These are the two great differences between the downward and upward arcs. In the downward, matter takes up qualities; in the upward, matter is formed into vehicles, or sheaths, or bodies, whatever may be the term we prefer. A process of specialisation goes on, up to a certain point. After a time the specialised materials are drawn together and combined into a vehicle, an organised unity, serving as a tabernacle for the Self. First comes differentiation, and the first step to that is to impart qualities to matter. Let me remind you, as the subject is so difficult a one, what is meant by tattvas, the fundamental forms of matter, and recall once more that passage in the *Vishnu Purâna* where their evolution is described, and where it is stated that the tanmâtra of sound produces A'kâsha; that is, a modification of the consciousness of Íshvara produces the form of matter that we call the atom of A'kâsha; that atom has a mere film of subtlest matter for its envelope, and the vibrating life of Íshvara for the force within. Then we are told that A'kâsha generates another tanmâtra which is touch, and that, enveloped, permeated by A'kâsha, produces the film of denser matter which is called Vâyu, the two tanmâtras and the A'kâsha being the generating force.

This goes on through the whole of the five stages, so that when we get down to the physical plane, we find an atom showing a wall of denser matter, within it the involved life and without it the magnetic field, made up of the higher tanmâtras and their atomic sheaths. The Prithivî atom hence consists of its own tanmâtra plus the matter and the life of Apas; the matter and life of Agni; the matter and life of Vâyu; the matter and life of A'kâsha: so that on the physical plane, the physical atom is a mass of five interpenetrating spheres in which is present as life the whole of the matter and the life of the worlds above it, the envelope, or wall, of the physical atom alone showing forth any characteristics of the physical world—a fact inexpressibly important for evolution. For, each of those sheaths or koshas—as the student of Vedânta calls them, and there is no better word—every one of them is latent in and around the physical atom; and in the upward evolution, every one of them becomes active and strong as evolution proceeds, sheath after sheath being vitalised. How could these koshas, or sheaths, of ours learn to respond to the vibrations of the evolving life, unless every one of them was latently present in us, waiting to be brought into activity? The root of that possibility lies in the atom itself, with all its interpenetrating spheres of life and matter, the sheaths that are within it and around it. That is not the only thing which we understand; as this conception grows clear, we understand a phrase that had often puzzled us in the old days, that "the spirit is senseless on the plane of matter. " What does that mean? The spirit, the very essence of consciousness, senseless and helpless on the plane of matter! Why? Because if you take spirit as pure spirit, the intermediate sheaths are not there by which the matter-vibrations are able to reach it, and without these sheaths it is unable to receive and respond to the vibrations of physical matter. It remains unconscious of their very existence, there being no bridge by which they can pass over and affect that life. This is really a perfectly simple statement of Madame Blavatsky's, but it is one that I have heard challenged over and over again as entirely meaningless, as conveying no idea, for how could consciousness be unconscious in any region? A little more knowledge would make us less rapid in our condemnation of our betters. That idea, then, we will take to help us in the first conception of how evolution can take place.

Now let us look how, in the downward arc that we spoke of, Íshvara is imparting qualities. According to the nature of the vibrations that He sends and of the matter that answers to them will be the quality imparted. As to the idea that difference of vibrations implies a difference of manifestation, let me buttress myself on the great reputation of Sir William Crookes. He issued, two or three years ago, I don't remember the exact date, in 1896 I think, a table of vibrations, confined of course to the physical world; a very interesting table, giving a series of classified vibrations and pointing out which were known to science, and gave rise to what we call sound, light, electricity, and so on, the difference of vibratory frequency, and the subtlety of the matter in which the vibration was set up, giving rise to a particular impression, received and answered by a sensation in us.

That is the principle which I am now applying to our system as a whole. According to the density of the matter will be the rapidity of the vibrations which that matter is capable of expressing; Íshvara sends out vibrations, and the mânasic matter, we will say, is thrown into corresponding vibrations or waves of a frequency identical with those of the life-impulse sent out from Him, so far as it is capable of responding, a limit being set by its fineness on the one side and by its density on the other. Its limit of fineness is the atom of the plane. Its limit of density is the coarsest aggregation of these atoms in the densest solid of the plane. If we take the physical plane for a moment, we have solid, liquid, gas, ether, finer ether, finest ether, and atoms. The lower five are related to the five senses in man as they are at present developed on the physical plane. These five correspond to the sense-organs and the senses that work through them, as is suggested in the names of the tanmâtras. The Solid is related to the sense of Smell; Liquid to the sense of Taste; Fire to the sense of Sight; Air to the sense of Touch; and A'kâsha to the sense of Sound. Nov these are not stated in the order given by the western scientist, but I have no time to go into the reason for the difference and to show you where his outer observation fails, because he is not able to trace beyond the limits of his senses into a finer working; in dealing with our Vâyu and A'kâsha, he classes them together, and his air is our Agni. These senses and their evolution belong to the upward arc. Coming downwards, Íshvara only gives the power to matter to respond to these particular vibrations, and these vibrations are connected on the physical plane with the sub-divisions that I have just mentioned, the different sub-divisions of matter, solid, liquid, gas, and so on, corresponding in the sense-organs to the senses.

Coming downwards, beginning on the mental plane with Intelligence— missing the two higher ones of Existence and Love—He sends out vibrations to make the matter of the mental plane answer, and the vibrations with which that matter answers, that is, a certain range of vibrations, are called mental or intelligent. You may say, Why? Just for the same reason that in Sir William Crookes' tables definite names are given to the different classes of vibrations, which produce sound, light, etc., names are given in order to express a certain limit of vibratory force; within one set of limits the vibrations affect the ether, give "light," and the eye receives them. Similarly, vibrations that fall between certain limits of vibratory frequency affect the matter of the third plane, and when they are received by an organ fitted to focus them in a centre, thus giving rise to self-consciousness, we call that organ Mind, and the action through that Mind, Intelligence. The mere name is as arbitrary as any other name, and we class these under mental, just as a certain range of etheric vibrations is classed as light, is received by an organ fitted to focus them that we call the eye, and the action through that eye is vision. If we are to talk at all, we must have names to describe different classes of phenomena, and we use the word mental or intelligent to describe the range of vibrations working in the particular kind of matter of which, in the upward evolution, an organ is builded that we call the Mind. So, again, to the vibrations that He sends out into the next coarser form of matter, called Apas, or astral, we give the name Sensory. He imparts to them the quality of responding to pleasure and pain, and as He makes this downward sweep He brings into renewed existence on each plane Devas, or beings which have as their characteristic manifestation the quality of their own plane; thus the Devas of the mental plane have the quality of intelligence as their chief peculiarity, and the Devas of the next lower plane have as their chief quality feeling, or the power of sensation, and those of the lowest plane have as their chief quality action, activity. Each Deva class shows out specially the quality of its plane, and inasmuch as these Devas draw into their own bodies the matter of the plane in which they live, they help on its evolution; for they draw it in, use it and thus develop it, and throw it out again into the general reservoir, just as man draws in physical matter, uses it in his body, and again throws it out into the physical world. As that process goes on and on and on through the ages, the whole of that kind of matter we call mental passes through the bodies of these Devas, takes on to itself the habit of responding readily to the vibrations of intelligence, and thus becomes ready for building into the mental body of man. The matter of the astral plane is builded into the bodies of the Devas of that plane until it takes up this habit of more and more definitely responding to pleasure and pain, when impacts are made on it, and thus can be used for the building up of the sensory bodies of the lower world. On each plane this downward sweep brings into activity these classes of Devas, making the intermediate links which are to work in the building of forms. The essence of the building of forms by a Deva is that he builds them of the matter of which his own body is composed. Prepared by that earlier evolution, qualities being developed in the downward sweep of the life of Íshvara, matter is, in the upward arc, gathered into definite forms, the bodies of plant, animal and man: thus definite vehicles are made, by which the highest consciousness can communicate with, and receive vibrations from, the lowest world.

Let us now, having taken this very rapid sweep downwards, begin to climb upwards. Each kind of matter is now seen to possess certain qualities. Every physical atom has a number of sheaths interpenetrating and surrounding it, the sheath of astral matter with its power of responding to sensation, the sheath of mental matter with its power of responding to intelligence, as well as the sheaths, if they may be called so, of the two higher, Love and Existence, that will not be brought into activity for a long, long time. All is there. Íshvara now begins the great stage of brooding action that I spoke of the building up of a centre, and it is His first work to build physical forms out of this prepared material, all the Devas of the physical plane being ready to act as His agents, working under His impulse and under the direction of the Lord of the Devas of the physical plane. All these innumerable intermediate agents are wanted; for innumerable are to be the forms, and every one of them has to be builded.

The building of the physical bodies begins with the formation of the minerals. As a mineral body is formed, perhaps some crystal, the crystal of an element or a salt, a definite form is built up by a Deva of the physical plane. He takes up the material of his own body and such material of the physical plane as is of similar nature to himself, and he begins shaping these crystalline forms. He builds them on the lines of the life-energy sent out by Íshvara Himself, those lines which Science calls the axes of the crystal, "imaginary" lines; "imaginary"—aye; but they are from the creative imagination of Íshvara, that is far more potent than the lower matter in which He builds. That lower matter follows the creative imagination of the Lord, and these imaginary lines govern the shaping of that crystal that is builded by the Deva. Tyndall believed not in the working of the Devas, yet when he was lecturing on crystals to a popular audience in Manchester he declared that as he pictured to himself the building of a crystal, he found himself imagining tiny architects at work, placing every atom with exact precision, with all the intelligence and skill of a human architect, employed in making a building. Tyndall was speaking better than he knew. His imagination was answering to the truth more keenly than he realised. For it is the privilege of the man of genius who loves truth as Tyndall did—who was willing to break up every fetter of dogma rather than be a traitor to his conception of truth—to unconsciously intuit the truth that he seeks, so that his words give out a higher meaning than he dreamed of. Tyndall was wise in recommending what he called the scientific flight of the imagination, for that power of imagination is a most useful thing. Never clip the wings of your imagination when you are employed in your scientific work; for it may often give you glimpses of truths that without its aid you would never find. Thus the Devas work and build crystals, and those crystals have some remarkable properties. Professor Japp tells us that some crystals turn a polarised beam of light in a particular way; and he declares that in some of these forms there is a power which is directive and somewhat akin to the intelligence of man. Truly is it akin to human intelligence, inasmuch as it is the parent of human intelligence, the latter being the child that is developing the parental powers. This building goes on through stages on which we must not tarry, through the whole of the mineral world, gradually giving to matter the power to change shape between larger and larger limits without losing cohesion. This is what is called plasticity, the power of changing shape without disintegration. Matter also gains that which science speaks of as elasticity. Now what is elasticity? Not, as people generally think the mere power of elongation, calling a thing elastic that can be pulled out like a piece of India-rubber. An elastic body in the popular sense is not an elastic body from the scientific point of view, and, strange as it may sound, glass is much more elastic than India-rubber. Yet the glass does not elongate and is brittle. The proper definition of elasticity is the power of recovering the original form after distortion, and matter gradually acquires this power. As life develops, the equilibrium of the compounds that make up the form becomes more and more unstable, while at the same time the general cohesion of the form increases; when we come to the higher forms, such as the body of man, we find a power of maintaining the central position greater than we find in any other form, together with an increased plasticity and elasticity; so that a man can adapt himself to the cold of the polar regions, and to the heat of the tropics and of the equatorial zone, without losing his body, in a way that no lower animal can match, that is, he has the power of adapting his physical body to surrounding conditions to a greater extent than is the case with any other form. Coming back to the mineral kingdom we left, let us take the next stage; Íshvara can now expand and modify His material a little more than was originally possible without breaking it up.

He begins the moulding of the vegetable kingdom, and there also he sets axes of growth, as "imaginary" and as real in their controlling force as in the crystal, though they are not always quite as easy to trace, they are nevertheless there. All the vegetable matter is built in according to these axes, and the natural classification of plants is largely determined by the numerical relations of the parts; thus the law of number shapes the form. As the matter becomes more plastic and yields more readily to the indwelling life, the higher members of that kingdom begin to show the dawning of sensation. That is due to the beginning of the vivification of the next sheath above the physical, composed of what we call astral matter, that which goes to make part of the manomaya kosha of the Vedântin. We see in that a growing susceptibility, an increasing sensory power, very slight in the vegetable world, but still present, and developed much more largely where the vegetable has a long experience of separated life. Take for instance a tree that has endured for centuries, and let me just trace the stages in which the dawning sensation is found, and even a dawn, though I hardly venture to use the word, a dawn of mental quality. That life in the tree responds to the vibrations received from outside, of cold and heat, of wind and rain, of sunshine and storm, and as the physical sheath is built up and developed by the action of the Devas working upon it, the etheric matter in it is continually thrown into vibration by the changes in temperature, light, and electrical conditions. The vibrations in the ethers that enter into the physical body are passed on to the atomic sub-plane, and as the atoms of the physical plane have their spirals made of the coarsest matter of the plane of Apas, or astral matter, a slight quivering is caused in that coarsest matter of the astral plane, and that sets up a little movement in the tree, responded to by the indwelling life by sensation, a massive and general feeling of pleasure or pain.

Have you never walked through a forest, and felt as though all nature were enjoying the sunshine? This sensation of pleasure is shown still more strikingly when the hot season comes to its ending, and the first rains fall on the thirsty ground, and the well-nigh withering vegetation sends out a conscious thrill of joy and life renewed. The very trees and bushes rejoice as the rain comes down upon them with its message of life and of hope. At such moments we recognise that the vegetable world is sensitive, although the sensation be widespread, that which is called massive in character.

Forgive me if for a moment I here digress, to say that this fact is one of the reasons why we owe a duty to the vegetable world, not needlessly to cause sensations of dawning suffering. We live too carelessly, my brothers, in this world which is all-living, where there is no atom that is dead, and especially is this sad here in India, where once there was so strong a reverence for life. That is now, alas, beginning to pass away. You are forgetting that all life is Íshvara, that according to the stage of His lower self-evolution is the power of response that is given to the form. In the old days, I remember how, when man took his food, he met the food with gracious greeting because it was sacrificing its life in order to build, through that sacrifice, his own. Though it did not possess the higher powers of sensation as we find them in the animal, but only the lesser sensation powers of the vegetable world, still, even then, he met it with reverence, as a sacrifice which was being made to him, and took it with gratitude and with love; that lower life was yielding itself up to him for his up-building. But to-day, so lost is that gentle grace in many of our Hindu people, that they not only disregard the sacrificed lives of the vegetable kingdom, but also those of the far more sentient forms which Íshvara has developed in the animal kingdom of His world. We find men who wear the outer shape of the Hindu, who have his colour, his form, his face, who boast themselves of their descent from antiquity, who hold themselves therefore in thought above the western nations, forgetting the life of the Self in this sentient creation, and nourishing their bodies with the bodies of their lower brethren, without showing any sense of the sacrifice made, or feeling even a passing gratitude for the life which is given for them.

Let us come back to the tracing of our forms. Íshvara, brooding over the evolving forms, continues His patient work—patient, that the form may never be broken by an overstrain, but may be slowly developed into a vehicle of the life that ensouls it. In every form He lives, evolving it, but He limits with illimitable patience His manifestation of life to the poor capacities of the form, that it may grow and not be destroyed. Do you remember an old story of the ancient days, in which most of you would be ashamed to acknowledge belief, for are you not graduates and men of western knowledge? Though descendants from the old time, you have naught to do with it, but I, who was trained in the West, I have no feeling of shame in acknowledging my belief in the strange things that come down to us from the times when truth was less veiled than it is now. So I dare to recall the story to you, although you may think that it is but a fable or legend. There was a boy who believed in Vishnu or Hari, in whom his father believed not, Prahlâda he was named; and that boy went through many trials, but in all his faith in the Supreme defended him; at last his father, scoffing, said, turning to a pillar in his room: "You tell me that Hari is everywhere: is He in that pillar?" "O Hari, Hari!" cried the boy, and forth from the pillar in the form of a Lion burst an avatâra of Vishnu and the pillar was shivered into pieces. Truly is He everywhere, in every particle of matter; there is no one particle from which He cannot come forth in all the might of His Godhood, in all the majesty of His Deity. But He will not, because if He did, the form could not bear that revealing, and would shiver into pieces as the God appeared. A profound truth, even if you regard the story as an allegory, a truth which teaches us what evolution means.

Thus Íshvara worked on age after age and æon after æon, with that marvellous patience of which I spoke, until matter was made sufficiently plastic to build it into the form in which His highest life was to begin its development, the form of man; building that form, He begins also to strengthen very much the centre which the form is for a while to protect. Let me say in passing one thing that I have omitted, that whenever a form has reached its highest possible point, its limit of expansion, He breaks it, in order that, in a new form better adapted, the ensouling life may continue to grow; for He knows when to break as well as when to hold; He knows when to destroy as well as when to preserve; and the moment that the limit of a form has been reached, and its matter can yield no further, He bursts the form asunder, that its materials may recombine themselves, under the impulse of life, into a more plastic organism, and that the life may thus gain further evolution, ensouling a higher form more fitted for the expression of its increasing powers. We call this breaking of the form death, and we fear and shrink from it, and if people talk to us of death, in the flush of our life, it comes as a jar and a shock. But, as I told you in the beginning, you may see very plainly that death is that beneficent aspect of Íshvara, which breaks a form that has become a prison, in order to give the life a new form in which it may continue to grow; He breaks the rigid form when it can develop no further, and gives the life the plastic form of a baby, that may be shaped more easily by the moulding forces of the life within it, yielding itself to every impulse from within. It seems then, that when we see things rightly, we should hail death as birth rather than as death. For looked at from the side of life, every death is a being born into the higher possibilities of a new shape that will adapt itself to the growing life.

When man begins his long pilgrimage, a form is ready for his ensouling, prepared to receive and to respond to the impulses which come to it from the physical, astral and—to a small extent—from the mental planes. His physical atoms are considerably evolved, the sensory sheath is working actively, and there is a very imperfect lower mental sheath; these have been built up through the evolution of the animal realm. Do not fall into the mistake of the western way of thinking, and say that man descends from the animal; that is not true. It is only a fragment of truth half seen and thereby distorted. What is true is this: that the matter of his lower vehicles has been prepared by evolving through the stages of the elemental, mineral, vegetable and animal kingdoms, in order that it may be builded into the form of man; that *in previous kalpas* forms had been evolved that might fairly be described as half-ape, half-human, that were never occupied by the triple Self, and that therefore belonged to the animal, not to the human kingdom; that in the present cycle the human form evolved, as a fœtus evolves, passing rapidly through the lower stages on the way to the human, as in pre-natal life, and it therefore has stamped upon it the stages through which it has passed. I have been going over, roughly and swiftly, those stages through which the matter of which the body is composed has gone in the past, and you will see that the true theory of evolution is different from the somewhat crude view that there is a regular succession of births from the animal into the man. The matter has been made plastic in the animal, but man in his form is the result of a higher working; the germ of his life can never develop into the animal, but only into the human, because more has been infolded into it, and that germ must unfold along a line which is that of direct human growth. Remembering that, to prevent a possible misconception, we turn to the human centre that is now definitely formed. We speak of its encircling form as the causal body, or Karana Sharîra, the form by which the Self is limited; the Karana Sharîra is not the Self, remember, but is the containing vehicle of the triple Self, and the organ of one aspect of that Self, the aspect of knowledge, shown forth as intelligence. This sheath is important, being relatively of a permanent nature, and it goes on from birth to birth; death cannot touch it, birth cannot modify it; it is the treasure-house or receptacle of all the qualities acquired by experience through human evolution, and passes through the whole cycle of re-incarnations; it is the special *human* characteristic. The form begins to adapt itself more and more to the life, and here comes in a growing difficulty. The characteristic of the life of man is the life of the intellect; this the specifically human part of evolution; but the life of sensation is far more vivid and tumultuous in the beginning, and the earlier stages of form are adapted to answer to these impulses. You may ask, why not give the man at once a mental body only, in which to work out his evolution, why must he struggle through the evolution of this body of sensation? Because, if he misses that stage, he will not be able to make up the links which are necessary for the continuity of his consciousness. At a later time the perfect man is conscious on all planes from Nirvâna downward to the physical, from the physical upwards to Nirvâna. On every plane in unbroken continuity of consciousness the Jîvanmukta lives and works. There is no link lacking. If, then, the man does not establish, in the building of his body of sensation, certain centres or, as they are called, chakras—that drawing into centres which is the work of the upward arc, as giving qualities is the work of the downward arc—if he does not draw the powers of sensation into definite centres in the sheath of his astral body, he will not have the links which he requires to receive impacts from the astral plane, and through which he can send out thrills of consciousness in order to impress it, rule it and guide it. That is why there is so much delay in the savage condition, where the life of sensation is supreme; these astral chakras are being builded up as centres of the senses, and they are built firm and strong; the outer organs, the eye, the ear, the nose, the tongue, the skin, these are merely the necessary organs in the physical body for the expression of consciousness through these chakras.

If we take, for a moment, a swift survey of the evolution of forms, we shall find that the building of organs follows the exercise of life-functions; in the earliest forms there are no organs, but the functions of life are present and active; the creature breathes and assimilates, circulation goes on; but there are no organs for digestion, no organs for breathing, no organs for circulation; the whole body does everything. But as evolution proceeds and definite organs are formed in the physical body, in the nervous system, and as later, in the astral body, chakras or astral centres of sensation are formed—as this goes on, we find a more specialised being developed with definite organs. Always the organ comes after the function, and through the organ the function expresses itself more and more perfectly. That is a fundamental principle. And do not forget that in this you are on what is thought the safer ground of western science. You do not find an organ appearing before the development of its function. You always find the life-impulse first, and then the moulding of the matter into a shape which enables that impulse to express itself more perfectly. If we trace evolution from the amœba upwards we find differentiation and specialisation becoming more marked the whole way through, yet man himself turns round, and with the very brain which has been formed under the vibrations of intelligence he reverses the whole process, and asserts that thought is produced by the brain; but every organ is formed as the organ of a function, it is produced by life, and is not its creator.

This process goes on until the necessary organs are made and the nervous system is linked to the chakras in the astral body, chiefly through what is called the sympathetic system. There are certain nervous cells of a peculiar kind in that system, of which modern science does not say much, beyond giving you the forms and contents, and these are the links between consciousness in the physical body and in the sensory body. Then come the chakras already spoken of as the centres for the working of consciousness in the astral body. A similar process goes on in the mental body under the action of thought-impulses, and there we have also an organised body able to respond to different kinds of thought, and thus to serve consciousness as its organ for expression in the mental world. As we grow mentally we build our organs for consciousness.

Coming to this building of form practically, we learn that we organise the body of sensation to higher purposes by checking the life-impulse as it runs out to the object of the senses. These objects gradually turn away from the abstemious dweller in the body, it is written, and as the lower world ceases to attract, the higher world begins to use the form for nobler ends. If we desire to increase mental power, we must practise steady thinking, and check the rovings of intelligence over the phenomenal world. As a matter of fact, many people never really think at all; what they call their thoughts are nothing more than the reflections of other people's thoughts to which their consciousness responds; their minds are looking-glasses, not productive organisms; most men's minds, I fear, are looking-glasses reflecting objects that are before them, and contemplating these reflections a man says to himself: "See! how I am thinking!" when he is only repeating the thoughts of others. Now we are not to be mere looking-glasses; when the objects of the outer world give rise to images, the mind is to work on them, analyse, re-arrange, combine; thinking is the work of the mind itself on the mental images supplied through sensation, the working on the materials which have been gradually gathered by experience. As soon might you call a loose heap of bricks that you see in the compound of a house, a building, as call the reflection of other people's thoughts, your thinking. That is only the material for thought. Thinking is the work of the architect, of the builder that builds these bricks into a definite edifice, and until we have built up thoughts in our minds, we have no right to arrogate to ourselves the name of thinkers. Practise then this independent thinking; it is hard; you will not know how hard until you try it. Never let pass a day without reading something that gives you material for thought. No matter if the book be not religious; if it be only intellectual, that will make you stronger in intellect. Even leaving spirituality aside with its nobler possibilities, take some great book worthy of being thought over, not a newspaper, not a sensational novel, not a child's book, but a BOOK— an original book, on a real topic; what Charles Lamb called a book. Read, but do not read much, perhaps not more than a dozen or twenty lines; think these lines over and over and over for at least thrice as long as you have taken to read them slowly. Do that every day regularly, and do not miss it. You find time for your dinner; why, if you can find time to feed your body and to talk, can you not find time to feed your mind? Then your mind would grow. If you do that as an experiment, say for three months only, never missing a day—for if you miss a day, you will slip back and lose the value of the automatic action of your mind—do that for three months as an experiment, as a scientific man makes an experiment, and thus train yourselves for three months in power of close attention and thought, and at the end of the three months, you will be startled to find how much these powers have grown. When you have put yourself through this experiment, then you will not want a lecturer to tell you about the value of such self-discipline, for you yourself will have proved it to be good. Take one faculty after another to train; train your reasoning faculty, your memory, your power of comparison and contrast. Take up a faculty, just as any one takes up a study that he is working at, and work at it until you are an artist in that particular faculty.

That is how form is builded, when the human Self is beginning to co-operate with the work of Íshvara, when the centre is beginning to take the control of its vehicles. It rationalises its workings, and builds and modifies them step by step. When this has been done for many lives, then comes the life for Yoga; then the man may be taught how to make more rapid progress, and how to vivify the inner and subtler sheaths of his being by certain practices, that will be taught him the moment he is ready—but that will never be taught him until he *is* ready, nay though he range the world over in search of a Guru, or live the life of an ascetic in the cave or in the jungle. That is not enough, so long as his desire is unconquered, so long as his mind is still restless. When the senses are dominated, when the mind is controlled, and not before—but then, as certainly as before there will not be the coming—a Guru will appear who will take that man by the hand and lead him along the path that is narrow as the edge of a razor, that may only be trodden by the controlled in sense and by the steady in mind, for the fall either to the one side or to the other means delay for many a birth to come. Then is developed that aspect of Bliss which shows itself outwardly as love; a faint reflection of that bliss is felt in many stages of meditation, and joy has birth within you, wells up within you, enwraps you fold by fold, until you in yogic trance reach the true A'nanda, which is the essence of beauty, and makes you quiver under its subtle vibrations of ineffable delight. And later, later still, at a stage that you may reach, when all is purified through long evolution, there comes the rising into the highest, where the subtlest matter becomes the vehicle of that developed centre, now no longer a circumference restraining and necessary, but an obedient vehicle which will serve when it is wanted and fall away when wanted it is not. As it is written that in the A'kâsha there is every possibility of form, so the life that has reached Self-existence is a being that garbs itself in any form by gathering the A'kâsha around it. Thus it may develop vehicle after vehicle until the whole of the human series is builded for use, but none of them is prison for limitation; then we say that the man is a Jîvanmukta, He is free, and all matter has become His servant, to use when He has need of it, to cast aside when He needs it not; every region of the world is His to use, no region of the world is its own to bind Him; He is liberated, and as the liberated Self He may, if He will, still work for His brother men, remaining, as Shrî Shankarâchârya taught us, until the end of His age, in order to lift humanity more rapidly on its upward climb. Thus are formed Those who are the co-workers of Îshvara in the helping of humanity, who, having gone through all suffering, throw everything they have gained at the feet of the Lord, who turn back to the world, never again to be bound by it, but still responding to the compassion which is the very life of Îshvara Himself. As long as Îshvara wills to remain in manifestation, so long does He whose will is one with that of Îshvara, will also to remain. He has nothing to gain, nothing to learn, nothing to take that any world can give Him; but He stands beside His Lord as an organ of the expression of the highest life, existing no longer for anything that He takes, but as the channel of the life of God. That is the prize of our calling, that the goal on which our hearts are fixed.

THE END.

BOOK FIVE
THE LAWS OF HIGHER LIFE

*Lectures delivered at an Annual Convention of the Indian Section of the
Theosophical Society, held at Varanasi (Benares)*

I. THE LARGER CONSCIOUSNESS

THIS year we are going to study together a subject of vital importance to the thoughtful, to the earnest, to those who desire to serve humanity, to those who wish to help the race forward in its evolution. The subject of my discourses I have called "The Laws of the Higher Life", because so many people in dealing with religion, that has to do with the Higher Life, seem inclined to remove it from the realm of law, and to bring it into some strange region of arbitrary whim, into some strange region of results without endeavour, of failure without weakness. This idea that spirituality is not subject to Law is an idea that is natural at the first sight; for we find a corresponding analogy in the way in which the laws of the physical plane have been overlooked, just in proportion as they have been unstudied and unknown.

We glance for a moment at some sudden eruption of natural forces, some tremendous explosion which throws up perhaps in a few hours a mighty mountain, or we see crags and rocky peaks where before there was verdure, and in a valley which was a plain we discern the outlines of swelling hills. In such an eruption, man once saw something arbitrary, something catastrophic, something disorderly, something unexpected, something outside the orderly growth of evolution. But we know from further study that there is nothing more disorderly in the outburst of a volcano than there is in the slow growth of the sea-bottom, until at last, after tens of thousands of years, that bottom becomes a range of mountains. The one was thought orderly, the other cataclysmic. But now we know that all natural processes, sudden or slow, unexpected or predicted, come within the realm of Law, and are utterly orderly in their happenings.

It is the same in the Spiritual World. We may sometimes see apparently sudden eruptions of the forces of the spiritual realm, a sudden change, for instance, of the whole life of a man; we may see the character wholly altered to all appearance; we may see the whole nature of the man changed even in an hour. But we have learned to understand that here also Law is supreme; that in this also there is nothing disorderly, although much that many do not yet understand. And we are beginning to realise that in the spiritual, as in the physical universe, there is the one Supreme Life, manifesting in an infinite diversity of ways, and that that Life is ever orderly in its workings, no matter how strange, no matter how wonderful, no matter how unexpected, they may seem to be to our dim and purblind eyes.

So we shall rest for a moment on the idea of Law, and see what it means. Then after explaining what I mean by "Law", I shall try to show you that, without a possibility of doubt, even apart from religion and religious thought, there is a larger consciousness than that which works in the brain and the nervous system, a larger consciousness than that which we call the waking consciousness of a man. Then tomorrow afternoon, I shall try to show you how that consciousness may begin to unfold and grow by the full recognition of the Law of Duty, by the attempt to fulfill perfectly every obligation of life. In the third and last lecture, I shall pass on to that loftier and sublimer region where the inner law takes the place of the law of outer obligation, where instead of duty, which means the payment of debt, there is sacrifice, which is the outpouring of life, where everything is done gladly, everything is done willingly, in perfect self-surrender, where the man does not need to ask: "What have I to do? What is my duty?" but where he works because the Divine outwelling finds its channel in his life, and he needs no outer compulsion because of the perfection of the inner law. Then he grows by the Law of Sacrifice, which is the Law that rules the universe as well as the hearts of men, the Sacrifice which is a faint reflection of the Divine Sacrifice by which the worlds were made, that Sacrifice which finds its small reflection, its petty, minute reproduction, wherever the heart of man throws itself at the Lotus Feet of the Lord of Sacrifice, and thus becomes a channel of the Divine outpouring, however small and insignificant at first, a channel of the life of the Logos, filled not by the little that is given, but by the great outpouring that uses man as its channel.

Now let us then try to understand what we mean by the term "Law". I have found over and over again confusion of thought on this question of what is meant by "Law", and this lands the student in many perplexities and confusions.

When we speak of the law of the land you know very well what is meant thereby. The law of the land is an ever-changing thing, changing with the change of ideas in the authority that makes the law, whether that authority comes from the mouth of an autocratic Monarch, or from the voice of a

Legislative Assembly, whether it is proclaimed in the name of the Sovereign; or of the community in which the law has to act and rule. A law is always a thing which is made, a command issued, and the authority that makes the law can change the law, the authority that creates it can annul it also. Nor is this the only thing that we may observe about the law of the land. The laws are commands: "Do this", "Do not do that"; and the commands are enforced by penalty. If you break such and such a command, such and such a punishment will follow.

Further, when we study the penalties attached to laws in different countries, the punishments for one and the same breach of the command, we find that they are as arbitrary and changing as the laws themselves. They are not the results, in any sense, of the act which has broken the law. But the penalty in every case is artificially attached to the breaking of the law, and it can be changed at any time. For instance, a man steals; one nation will punish that act with the gaol, another with the whip, another with the knife that cuts off the offending hand; another with the rope that ends the life. In every case; the penalty attached has nothing in common with the offence.

But when we speak of the Laws of Nature, we do not mean any one of the things that we have taken as characteristic of the laws of man. The Law of Nature is not a command issued by any authority. It is a statement of the conditions under which a certain thing invariably happens; not a command, but a statement of conditions. Wherever those conditions are found, there will follow a certain event; it is the declaration of a sequence, a succession, unchanging, immutable, unrepealable, because these laws are expressions of the Divine Nature, in which there is no change, nor shadow of turning, The Law of Nature is not a command: "Do this", "Do not do that". It is a statement: "If such and such conditions are present, such and such results will happen"; if the conditions change, the results will change with them.

Nor is there any arbitrary penalty attached to the Law of Nature. Nature does not punish. You have in Nature the statement of the conditions, the sequence of happening, and nothing more. Given such a condition, such and such will follow; the result is an inevitable sequence or succession, it is not an arbitrary infliction or punishment.

But the contrast of the Law of Nature and the law of man may be carried further. The law of man can be broken, but no Law of Nature can be broken. Nature knows no violation of her Laws. You may break the law of man; you cannot break the Law of Nature. The Law remains the same whatever you may do. You may break yourself to pieces against it, but the

Law will remain unchanged; you may shatter and shiver yourself against it, but the Law remains firm as a rock, against which the billows break themselves. They are unable to shake it or move it by a hair's-breadth; they can only fall into shattered foam at its base.

Such is the Law of Nature - a statement of conditions, of invariable sequences, of inviolable, unbreakable happenings; such is the Law. Thus must you think of it, when you come to deal with the higher as with the lower life.

Then there comes to you a sense of perfect security, of infinite power, of unbounded possibilities. You are not in a region of arbitrary whims, where one day this may follow, another day that. You can work with absolute certainty of results. Your own fancies will not change the Law; your ever-changing emotions will not touch the Eternal Will; you can work with a confidence of result, for you are resting on the Reality, the one Reality which is the one Law in the Universe.

But there is something wanted to work in peace and security in a realm of Law - the thing that is wanted is Knowledge.

The laws which, so long as we are ignorant of them, may toss us from place to place, may break our plans, may frustrate our endeavours, may bring our hopes to ruin, may lay us level with the dust - those same laws, which treat us thus while we are ignorant, become our servants, our helpers, and our uplifters, when knowledge has replaced ignorance. How often have I quoted in this land, as well as in others, those pregnant and significant words, spoken by an English scientist - words that ought to be engraven in letters of gold - "Nature is conquered by obedience"!

Know the Law, obey it, work with it, and it lifts you up with its infinite strength, and carries you to the goal that you desire to reach. The Law which is a danger when not known, becomes a saviour when known and understood. See how physical Nature has taught you more and more, through the years that lie behind us, this wonderful fact. You see the lightning blaze from the stormy sky, and it flashes down, strikes a turret or a tower, and behold! they fall in ruins, destroyed by the uncurbed and unbridled flash of fire. How dangerous, how terrific, how mysterious! How shall poor man face the fire of the skies? But man has now learned to harness the same fire to his service; he has yoked it by the yoke of knowledge. And behold, the same force now carries his messages over seas and lands, and joins the father to the son who has travelled thousands of miles away, in the loving bond of sympathy and communication; the lightning that destroyed becomes the electric fluid that gives hope and life to the anxious parent, and carries messages of love and goodwill over land

and sea. Nature is conquered and her forces are our servants, when we learn to work in her way.

So with all other forces, above and below; so in every field of the universe, visible and invisible. You must know the Laws of the Higher Life, if you would live it. Know them, and they will carry you onward to your goal; be ignorant of them, and your efforts will be frustrated and all your endeavours will be as though they had not been.

I now pass on to speak on what I have called the Larger Consciousness. I want to speak of it today from two standpoints: from the familiar standpoint of the East, which has learned to study consciousness from within, and which regards consciousness, working in the body, as the lowest manifestation of consciousness, a limited representation of the higher and larger consciousness. I want to speak of it, not only from that standpoint, but from the standpoint of the West as well. Chiefly for this reason; as Western thought and Western science have spread in this country, there is such an apparent certainty about them, such a glamour, that sometimes the Western thought will win a hearing when the familiar Eastern presentation of it may miss its road to the mind. I, therefore, want to show you how, among many persons trained in the habits of the materialistic thinking and materialistic science of the West; there is now a recognition that there is a consciousness larger than the brain consciousness, a recognition of a consciousness which transcends the body, and which is a matter of wonder and puzzlement, a matter of controversy and widespread dispute, on which men of science are experimenting, which they are trying to understand, which they are trying, as it were, to reduce into some familiar form within the realm of Law. The investigation is leading them by scientific experiments on the physical plane, to the same results which we find in Eastern teachings, results obtained in the East by the practice of Yoga and the consequent development of the Higher Consciousness, that looks from the higher downwards on to the physical plane. Eastern Psychology -starting from the fact of the Higher Self, and seeing that Self working in various upadhis- traces out deductively its workings on the physical plane. Western Psychology -starting on the physical plane, studying the upadhi first and then the consciousness in it- is slowly climbing up step by step, until compelled to transcend ordinary bodily conditions, until, by its own artificial methods, it is producing states of consciousness long familiar in the East, and trying, in a vague and groping fashion, to work out some theory which will make the facts intelligible and coherent. The long road is somewhat strange and unpromising, but is nevertheless coming to a similar goal to that found out long ages since by the spiritual insight of the

Seer. That is the line along which I propose to travel this afternoon. We need not delay on the subject of what is called waking consciousness - the mental faculties, emotions, etc., that you find around you in ordinary daily life. The West began to study these through the brain and nervous system. There was a time, some twenty-five years ago, when no Psychology was considered sound, which was not based on the knowledge of Physiology. The dictum was: "You must begin by studying the body, and the nervous system, and the laws of its working, and the conditions of its activities. As you know those, you will understand the workings of thought, and the activities of the mind; and thus base a sound rational Psychology on your physiological knowledge. "

I do not think that you would find that idea so completely endorsed among the most advanced students in the West today. But none the less, studying along those physiological lines, they came to very remarkable results, as men always will, when they honestly interrogate Nature.

First, they noticed that man's consciousness was not restricted to the waking state. They began to study dreams. They began to try to analyse and understand the working of consciousness when the body was asleep. They tabulated the facts after collecting a vast number of them. But they found their investigation was unsatisfactory, because it was difficult to shut out all the conditions that they did not want to study. Sometimes a dream was produced by a disorder in some organ of the body; sometimes it would be produced by over-eating or indigestion. They wanted to eliminate these conditions. Gradually they came to the idea, to try to study the workings of this dream-consciousness by inducing artificial trance, a trance which would be a dream state under certain definite conditions, which could be produced at will, and which was not the result of the disturbance of any organ of the body.

On this we have all the researches of Hypnotism, experiments repeated over and over again; that you can read in the books specially devoted to these studies.

What was the net result of these widespread, often repeated experiments? This: that under conditions in which normal thinking was impossible, because the brain was in a lethargic condition, badly supplied with bad blood, under conditions wherein coma ought to have resulted, an entirely unexpected set of results appeared. The mental qualities did not lessen in power; on the contrary, the faculties of the mind became sharper, keener, subtler, more powerful in every way, when the brain was paralysed. To their surprise they found the memory in the trance state reached back over the forgotten years of life, and gave up incidents of childhood long forgotten; not only memory, but the powers of reasoning, arguing, judging, all became stronger, more easily used, more effective in their working; under conditions wherein the senses were locked as in sleep, the functions of the senses were carried on more effectively through organs other than the ordinary ones. The eye which did not respond to the flash of the electric lamp would pierce distances that in the waking state it did not measure, read books that were kept closed, cut its way through the sheaths of flesh to the interior of the body, and describe diseases were hidden under flesh and skeleton. Similarly with the ear. The ear could hear a sound taking place far beyond the limit of the waking state of hearing, and answer questions addressed from afar, where the ordinary ear could not respond to the faint and delicate vibrations.

These results made men pause, and they began to ask questions: What is this consciousness which sees without eyes, which hears without ears, which remembers when the organ of memory is paralysed, and which reasons when the instrument of reasoning is in lethargy? What is this consciousness, and what are its instruments?

It was not only that in this trance state these strange results came about. It was found that the deeper the trance, the loftier the consciousness. That was the next step. The trance which is not very deep will only show a certain quickening of faculties. Increase the depth of the trance, and the results of consciousness shine out more brilliantly. Facts were collected which showed that man had not one consciousness, but many consciousnesses, so far as their separate working was concerned. They tried experiments with an ignorant peasant woman who in her normal state was dull, stupid, and heavy. They put her into trance, and in trance she became more intelligent; and what was stranger still, she looked down with contempt at her own consciousness in the waking state, criticised its workings, spoke disdainfully of its limitations, uttering harsh phrases, such as, "That creature", when referring to it.

Still deeper trance, still profounder slumber, and there emerged from that deeper trance a loftier consciousness, a consciousness dignified, grave, sober, looking down upon both the other manifestations, and criticising them with sternness and separation and distance, criticising their actions, blaming their faults, rising above their limitations. Thus in this peasant woman three stages of consciousness were seen, and the deeper the trance the higher the manifested consciousness.

One other strange fact appeared. In her waking state the peasant woman knew nothing of the second or the third consciousness. For her, they did not exist. The second consciousness knew the one below it, but did not know the one above it. The third looked down upon the two, but knew nothing higher than itself.

Out of this there came another idea: that not only could the consciousness show higher powers than in the waking state, but that the limited consciousness could not know the larger consciousness which was beyond its own limitations. The higher knew the lower, the lower knew not the higher. The ignorance of the lower was then no proof of the non-existence of the higher. The limitations that bound the lower consciousness could not be used as arguments against the higher condition, which it could not appreciate because of its limitations. Such are some of the results of Western science and its investigations.

Now come we to another line of study. Men, materialistic in their thought, studying carefully the mechanism of the brain, came to certain conclusions as to the kind of brain in which abnormal results of consciousness were manifested, apart from all states of artificially induced trance. That School of thinkers may be summed up in the declaration of Lombroso, a great Italian scientist. He declared that the brain of the man of genius is abnormal and diseased. "Genius is allied to madness"; wherever you find brains in which abnormal happenings are seen, you are there on the lines of disease, and the natural goal of that as insanity.

There was some such idea current even before the days of Lombroso, for we know the line of Shakespeare: "Great wits to madness near allied."

In itself this statement need not have done very much harm, had it not reached the length to which it is carried by the School of Lombroso. But as applied there, it became a weapon of terrible keenness against all religious experiences. You find men of this School basing their conclusions on physiological facts, and saying that the brain becomes abnormal when responding to certain stimuli to which the normal brain does not respond. As that idea gradually spread, they took the next step and said: "Here is the explanation of all religious experiences. We have always had visions and mystics and seers. Every religion contains testimony of abnormal happenings, declarations of visions, and of things normally invisible to the sound, to the balanced, to the rational brain. A man who sees visions is a man whose brain is diseased; he is a neuropath, he is diseased, be he a Saint or a Sage. All the experiences of the Saints and Sages, all their testimony to the phenomena of the invisible worlds - all these are dreams of disordered intellect, working in the brain which had become overstrained and diseased. "

Religious people, startled by such a statement, scarce knew how to answer it. Stunned at what seemed to them the blasphemy which regarded all religious experiences as neuropathic, the Saints as nothing but neuropaths, victims of a diseased nervous system, sufferers from obscure troubles of the nerves, they knew not what to say. The idea seemed to strike at the very root of hopes of humanity, to take away in one fell swoop the worldwide testimony to the reality of the unseen worlds.

There is one answer that might easily be given to this bold statement. I shall make the answer in the broadest possible form, before explaining the conditions under which it may be made.

Suppose it were utterly true; suppose that all humanity's greatest geniuses in religion, science, and literature were all and every one of them neuropaths, diseased as to their brains: *What then?*

When we judge the value of what a man gives to the world, we do not judge it by the state of his brain, but by its results on the hearts, the consciences; and the actions of men. If every genius were the twin brother of a lunatic, if every Saint were diseased as to his brain, if every vision of the Supreme and of the Devas and Saints came through a diseased brain in contact with *something*: WHAT THEN?

The value of what these have given us, that is the measure by which we measure them. When a man's life is utterly changed by coming into the presence of a Saint, have we explained the change by saying that the Saint's brain is diseased? If so, then the disease of the Saint is better than the health of the average plodder; the overstrained brain of the genius is a thousand times more precious to humanity than the normal brain of the man in the street. I ask what these men gave us; and I find that every highest truth that stimulates human endeavour and that has come from God to man, every truth which comforts us in our sorrows, which lifts us above the fear of death, which makes us know ourselves immortal; has come from such neuropaths. What care I for the label you fasten to their brains in your physiology? I worship those who gave to humanity these truths whereby it lives.

My second answer is: Let us consider how far there is proof for truth in this statement of the School of Lombroso. I am prepared to admit that, so far as the physiological conditions are concerned, Lombroso is to some extent right; and it is natural that it should be so. The normal brain of man, the result of man's evolution up to the present stage, is the brain which can deal best with the ordinary matters of the world, with buying and selling, cheating and swindling, getting the better of the weaker, and trampling down the feeble. The normal brain of man has to deal with the rough and tumble of life and the tug of the world; it has to do with the ordinary events of life; you cannot expect the manifestations of the Higher Consciousness through a brain nourished on unclean food, made the slave of passion, and the handmaid of selfishness and cruelty. Why expect from that brain any response to the spiritual impulses of the Higher Consciousness, or any sensitiveness to the keener vibrations of the higher worlds? It is the product of past evolution, and it represents the past.

But what of the other brain, the brain that responds to the subtler vibrations? These are the brains that have the promise of the future. They tell us of the evolution that shall be, not of the evolution that has been. Those who are in the front of evolution are likely, with their subtler, more evolved nature, to be far more easily upset by the coarser vibrations of the lower world than those adapted to it; and the very fact that their brains are responsive to the subtler; will render them less fitted to answer to the coarser vibrations of the lower world.

We have two very different conditions to consider; first, the more highly evolved brain, normally sensitive and ready to respond to subtle vibrations, in a state of very delicate equilibrium; that is the brain of the genius - spiritual, artistic, literary. Secondly, the normal brain under stress of keen emotion, rendered thereby abnormally sensitive and tense, and thrown more or less out of gear; that is the brain of the ordinary religious mystic and seer. The first will be normally healthy and sane, but not well adapted to meet the demands of the lower life, and careless of ordinary affairs; it will be easily jarred by violent vibrations, and hence often irritable and impatient; and it will be more or less easily thrown off its balance. The delicate equilibrium of its complicated nervous machinery will be far more readily disturbed than the rough self-adjusting mechanism of the less evolved brain. Later in evolution, such brains will have gained stability and elasticity; at present, they easily lose equilibrium.

The second, normally unfit to respond to subtle vibrations, can only be raised to a sufficient point of tension by a strain that injures its mechanism and shows itself as nervous disorder. Strong emotion; intense desire to reach the Higher Life, prolonged fasting and prayer, anything, in fact, that overstrains the nerves, will, for the time, render the brain sufficiently sensitive to answer vibrations from the subtler planes of being. Then visions and other abnormal happenings will occur. The super-physical consciousness finds, for a brief time, a vehicle sufficiently sensitive to receive and answer to its impulses. The neuropathic brain does not make the vision; *that* belongs to the super-physical world: but the neuropathic brain affords the conditions necessary for the vision to impress itself on the physical consciousness. Hysteria and other nervous diseases will, in thee cases, frequently accompany such phenomena.

It is true that where evolution is understood and wisely guided, it is not necessary that disease should be the condition of these higher experiences. But it is not unnatural that, in many cases, such men and women - unevolved and untrained, with no habit of introspection and self-analysis, and no knowledge of the working of the laws of consciousness, plunged in the ordinary conditions of life - should be less rational on the physical plane than their fellows, caring less for the things of this world because they care so much for the things of the Higher Life.

For a moment let us see why there should be this danger. The reason is simple. Take a string which, when loose, will not give out any musical note. Make it tense, and the note will sound out from the tightened string. It is only when stretched that it will give the musical note. But also, it is then that it is exposed to the danger of snapping. So with the brain. While it is what may be called slack, it simply responds to the slow vibrations of the physical plane; no note of heavenly music can sound out through that brain, because its nervous matter is not sufficiently tense to respond to the more rapid vibrations. It is only when the nervous matter is made tense by strong emotion, or by a great strain of some kind, that the ordinary brain can answer to them. Hence the strain which shows itself as nervous excitement, as hysteria, in daily life, does afford the condition of nervous matter capable of responding to more rapid and subtle vibrations than those of the physical plane. The tension of the nervous state is a necessary condition for the showing out of the Higher Life and Consciousness. When you understand this fact well, the great attack of the School of Lombroso on all religious experiences loses all its power and menace. The disease, the neuropathy, is natural - for you are dealing with vehicles in the ordinary stage of evolution, unfit for subtle vibrations. You have to refine them, to make them more tense, in order that they may respond to higher vibrations. In our present state of evolution, surrounded as we are by unclean circumstances, impure magnetisms, disturbing influences of every kind, it is no wonder that the unfit brain, in straining itself to answer to the higher, should be upset by the lower, and become discordant among the rough tones of earth.

Look to the East, and see how this danger has been understood and guarded against and avoided. Eastern psychology postulates a Self that gathers round him upadhi after upadhi, vehicle after vehicle, a Self which gradually shapes his own instruments. He shapes a mental body, that by that his powers of thinking may come into touch with the outer world; he shapes an astral body, that by that his powers of emotion may be expressed in the outer world; he shapes a physical body, in order that by that his aspect of activity may work in the outer world. In Eastern psychology, we are dealing with a consciousness which shapes bodies according to its needs.

Now, how shall the bodies be shaped to the needs of the Higher Consciousness? By gradually refining them and bringing them under the control of the Higher: and hence meditation is ordained as the means. But where a man wished to make very rapid progress, it was found easier to go to the jungle and temporarily isolate himself from the lower world. Thus he escaped the coarser magnetisms of the outer world, and put himself in a place in which the rougher vibrations did not reach him; hence he was less likely to be upset by these harsher and rougher vibrations. There in the jungles and forests such men began to meditate. They made the brain tense and refined by the concentration of the mind, by the gradual restraint of the lower faculties, and fixed it in rapt attention on the higher. The consciousness working from above played on the physical brain through this fixed attention, and gradually made it more tense, and tuned it to respond safely to the higher vibrations. Then it strove to draw the lower upwards, until it answered no longer to the stimuli of the outer world. The same insensitiveness to the outer vibrations that hypnotism gains by artificial means, is gained in Yoga by complete withdrawal of the consciousness from the Indriyas.

The next step, after closing the senses, was to hold quiet the powers of the mind, to make the mind steady, so that it might cease vibrating and become still, able to answer the vibrations coming from above. When the mind was made tranquil and quiet, when no desire was allowed to trouble its serenity, as a lake in perfect calm, on that mind at peace was thrown the reflection of the Self; the man saw in the tranquillity of the mind and the silence of the sense, the majesty; the glory, of the Self. That is the Eastern way.

Let us understand from this standpoint how the brain has to be changed, how it has to be refined; and how it has to be improved, how all its connecting links have to be fashioned and manufactured for the purposes of the expression of the Higher Consciousness. Following along this line of self-discipline, or Yoga, what are the conditions of brain evolution? First, purity of body; secondly, refinement of body, and increased complexity of brain. These are essential. Do not suppose that whilst your passions are still ruling you, whilst their demands can upset the mind, whilst the body is unrestrained, you are ready to receive on the mind the reflection of the Self. You must learn to rule the body, to keep it under control, by giving it proper sleep, and proper exercise, and proper food, satisfying all its needs, so as to keep it in health, not as a master, but as the obedient servant of consciousness. Hear what Shri Krishna says: "Verily Yoga is not for him who eateth too much, nor who abstaineth to excess, nor who is addicted to too much sleep, nor even to wakefulness, O Arjuna. "(*Bhagavad Gita*, vi 16.)

There is to be no extreme on either side; no torturing of the body that is to be the instrument, but also no yielding to the body that it may imagine itself the master of the Self. Where this training is followed, the brain becomes able to receive the subtler vibrations, without loss of equilibrium, and health is not sacrificed to gain delicacy and sensitiveness. The yogi is most exquisitely sensitive, but perfectly sane.

Having controlled and purified the body, we can make it sensitive to the higher vibrations, responsive to the sounding of the sublimer notes. But to do this, we must lose our interest in the lower, and become indifferent to the attractions of the outer life. Vairagya, dispassion, we must have, for that is a condition of the Higher Consciousness revealing itself in the lower world. While you love the lower things of the world, the Higher Consciousness cannot use this upadhi as its vehicle. One-pointed devotion to the Supreme, a clear, well-balanced, intelligent development of the intellect and emotions, this is the road along which we must tread, if the Higher Consciousness is to be manifested on earth. We must be pure in life, compassionate, and tender; we must learn to see the Self in every one around us, in the ugly as well as in the beautiful, in the low as well as in the high, in the plant as well as in the Deva. He who sees the Self in everything, and all things in the Self, he seeth verily, he seeth.

II. THE LAW OF DUTY

IN our talk of yesterday, we came to certain definite conclusions. We studied the nature of Law, and we found that a larger Consciousness than the waking brain consciousness of man exists in each of us. We saw that if that Consciousness was to manifest itself, then it was necessary that the senses should be utterly controlled, and the mind should be under restraint. So far we went in our study of the Higher Life yesterday.

Now we enter on another stage of our study, and we have to consider how a man should guide his conduct, in order that in him the Higher Consciousness may manifest itself in all its power. We want to see the stages of the preparation and to realise what each of us can do, now in the position that we are in, to prepare ourselves for that divine unfolding, for that blossoming of the bud of Consciousness, which is growing slowly within each of us. And in order that we may follow the subject well, let us define one or two words and expressions that we shall have to use throughout.

First, what is meant by the Higher Life? I have used it in the widest sense of the term, for all manifestations of life above the physical. It would include the manifestation of man in the various worlds invisible to the eyes of the flesh - regions of which we speak by using the word "planes" - astral plane, manasic plane, buddhic plane, atmic plane, and whatever in the vast universe may lie beyond.

What do we mean by "spiritual"? All manifestations of the Higher Life as thus defined are not necessarily spiritual. We must separate, in our thought, the form in which Consciousness is embodied and the Consciousness itself. Nothing that is of the form is spiritual in its nature. The life of form on every plane belongs to the prakritic manifestation, and not to the spiritual. The manifestation of the life in form may be on the astral plane, or on the manasic plane, but it is no more spiritual there than it is on the physical plane. Everywhere the prakritic manifestation is purely phenomenal, and nothing that is phenomenal can be said to be spiritual. That is a matter to be remembered. Otherwise we shall blunder sorely in our studies, and we shall not choose rightly the means by which the spiritual is to evolve. It matters not whether the life of form be lived on a lower or a higher plane - stone, vegetable, animal, man, or Deva. In so far as it is prakritic, phenomenal, in its nature, it has nothing to do with that which can claim the name of the Spiritual. A man may develop astral or manasic Siddhis, he may possess an eye that can see far into space, far abroad over the universe, he may hear the singing of the Devas and listen to the chanting in Svarga, but all that is phenomenal, all that is transitory. The Spiritual and the Eternal is not of the life of form.

What then is the Spiritual? It is alone the life of the Consciousness which recognises Unity, which sees one Self in everything and everything in the Self. The spiritual life is the life which, looking into the infinite number of phenomena, pierces though the veil of Maya and sees the One and the Eternal within each changing form. To know the Self, to love the Self, to realise the Self, that and that alone is Spirituality, even as to see the Self everywhere alone is Wisdom. All outside that is ignorance; all outside that is unspiritual. If once you understand this definition, you will find yourself compelled to choose not the phenomenal but the real, to choose the life of the Spirit as distinguished from the life of the form, though on the highest plane. You will be compelled to choose definite methods for evolving the life of the Spirit, and you will search for the knowledge of the law which shall enable the Consciousness to unfold, so that it may recognise its unity with all Consciousness everywhere, so that every form shall be dear not for the sake of the form but for the sake of the Self, which is the life and reality of the form. Remember how Yajnavalkya taught Maitreyi, when she desired to know this same spiritual part of the Higher Life, and he said: "Not for the sake of the husband is the husband dear, but for the sake of the Self is the husband dear; not for the sake of the wife is the wife dear, but for the sake of the Self is the wife dear"; and so on from one thing to another, to child, lover, friend, ending at last with the life that stretches beyond the physical: "Not for the sake of the Devas are the Devas dear, but for the sake of the Self the Devas are dear. "

That is the note of the Spirit. All is in the Self. The One is recognised everywhere. How shall we attain it? how shall we, blinded by matter, know it? Note that the first great step towards the attainment of this, realisation is the Law of Duty. Let us pause a moment to understand why the Law of Duty is the first truth which a man must obey, if he wishes to rise to the spiritual life. You find beings around us, belonging to the higher worlds, who are not spiritual, but who exercise enormous forces, who energise nature, bending matter to their will: mighty beings of tremendous power who range the world around us, some helping forward evolution by inspiring noble thought and high endeavour; others who are also helping forward evolution, but who do it by striving to hinder the progress of man and to bewilder him, in order that man may learn to plant his foot firmly, and by struggling against the wrong may become perfect in the right. Both these sides are of the divine manifestation; you cannot have the light without the darkness, nor progress without resistance; there is no evolution without the force that works against it. It is the force that works against evolution that gives stability to progress, and makes possible the higher growth of man. We must, however, beware that we do not fall into the common errors and confuse the functions of the two. The forces and the beings of the higher world who help evolution forward, who guide and inspire, lift and purify us, these are rightly the objects of reverence, and in their steps we may safely tread, and to them we may safely pray. The other powers are our friends, in so far as we resist them and oppose them: and they can only help us then when we strive against them. For then they strengthen the spiritual muscles and nerves. But the success that we can gain in their region in evolution lies in the power by which we combat them; and the strength that is evolved in the struggle helps forward our evolution. They are not to be followed and not to be obeyed, not to be meditated upon, nor appealed to. How then shall the wayfarer choose his path, and know the test whereby one may be distinguished from the other?

By the Law of Duty within him, by the divine Self which points out the path of progress, by obedience to Duty above all else, and by reverencing Truth as greatest, and worshipping it without a shadow of wavering or an idea of change.

Now, it is sometimes said, and it is true, that in the Sanskrit tongue there is no word for what in the West has been called Conscience. Taking the testimony of Sanskrit scholars, we learn that there is not a word which is the exact equivalent of Conscience. But we are not looking for words but for things, not searching for labels but for facts. I ask you in what Scriptures, or in what literature, you can find better expression of this idea of Conscience, than in the Eastern, where we find obedience to Conscience and reverence for Duty shining out in golden example and practice in the lives of men of ancient India, as well as in the precepts recorded in ancient Sanskrit books.

Take, for example, the conduct of Yudhishthira, the righteous King, who once in a trial at the hands of Sri Krishna Himself had fallen from truth. See him in the last scene of his life, ere he leaves this earth, when Indra the King of the Devas comes down and bids him mount his car and go to the highest heaven. Remember how, pointing to the faithful dog that had survived the terrible journey across the great desert, he says: "My heart is moved with compassion for the hound; let him come to Svarga with me". "There is no place for dogs in Svarga", replies Indra; and as Yudhishthira still refused he grew sarcastic, saying: "You let your brothers die in the great desert; you left them lying dead. You left Draupadi dying, and her corpse did not check your forward course. If brothers and wife were left behind, why cling to a dog, and why wish to take him onward?" Then replied Yudhishthira: "For the dead we can do nothing; I could not help my brothers or my wife. But this creature is alive, and is not dead. Equal to the killing of the twice-born, equal to the spoiling of the goods of the Brahmana, is the sin of deserting a helpless one, who has taken refuge with you. I will not go to heaven alone". And when he was found unshaken by divine argument, and by all appeals of Deva sophistry, then the dog vanished, and Dharma incarnate rose up before him, and bade him to mount to heaven. Stronger than command of Indra was the steadfast conscience of the king. No lure of immortality made him swerve from duty, nor could the sweet tongue of the Deva blind him as to the path of righteousness to which his conscience pointed.

Now, come further back in evolution with me, and see where Bali, King of Daityas, is offering sacrifice to the Supreme; a misshapen dwarf comes up and begs a boon: "Three steps of earth, O King as sacrificial gift". Three steps of earth, measured by those short limbs of the dwarf? - a petty gift, in truth. The boon is granted; and lo! the first step covers earth; the second spans the sky; where shall the third step be planted? The earth and sky are covered; what then remains? There is but the breast of the devotee, who throws himself down, in order that the third step may be planted upon his bosom. Then come remonstrances from every side: "It is fraud. " "It is deception. " "It is Hari Himself who is luring thee to thy destruction. Break thy word, and do not follow truth to ruin. " But although the voices strike his ear, he thinks truth and duty and conscience greater than loss of life and kingdom, and lies prone, unmoved. Presently his Guru comes, than whom none may be more revered, and the Guru bids him break his word; and when even to him Bali listens not, the Guru curses him for his disobedience - and then? Then the form of Vishnu is manifest, that mighty form which covers earth and sky, and a voice, speaking with the sweetness of the cooing of the dove, is heard in the silence that prevails: "Bali, defeated and attacked on all sides, reviled by his friends, cursed by his preceptor, this Bali will not give up truth. " Then Vishnu declares that he, in a future Kalpa, will be Indra, the monarch of the Devas, for only where truth is worshipped may power safely be entrusted.

With such cases before us, and scores of others might be cited, what matters it that no one word for "conscience" is found? The idea shines forth constantly, the idea of fidelity to duty, the recognition of the Law of Duty. And what is the one word which is the keynote of the Hindu people? It is Dharma, and this is duty, righteousness.

What is, then, the Law of Duty? It varies with every stage of evolution, though the principle is ever the same. It is progressive, as evolution is progressive. The duty of the savage is not the duty of the cultured and evolved man. The duty of the teacher is not the duty of the king. The duty of the merchant is not the duty of the warrior. So that when we are studying the Law of Duty, we must begin by studying our own place on the great ladder of evolution, by studying the circumstances around us that show our karma, by studying our own powers and capacities, and ascertaining our weaknesses. And out of this careful study we must find out the Law of Duty by which we must guide our steps.

Dharma is the same for all who are in the same stage of evolution and the same circumstances, and there is some Dharma common for all. There are duties laid down for all. The tenfold duties laid down by Manu are binding for all who would work with evolution, the general duties that man owes to man. The experience of the past has marked them out, and no doubt can arise about them.

But there are many questions of Dharma that are not so simple in their character. The real difficulty of those who are striving to advance along the path of spirituality is often to distinguish their Dharma, and to know what the Law of Duty demands.

There are many cases in our experience, day after day, in which conflict of duties appears to arise. One duty calls us one way, and another duty another way. Then we find ourselves perplexed as to Dharma, as Arjuna was perplexed on Kurukshetra.

These are some of the difficulties of the Higher Life, the tests of evolving Consciousness. It is little difficult to perform the duty that is clear and simple. Blunder is not likely to occur there. But when the path of action is tangled, when we cannot see, how then shall we tread our doubtful way through the darkness? Some dangers we know which cloud the reason and the vision, and make it hard to distinguish duty. Our personalities are our ever-present foes, that lower self which clothes itself in a hundred different forms, which sometimes puts on the very mask of Dharma, and so prevents our recognising that, in following it, we are following the path of desire rather than the path of duty. How are we then to distinguish when the personality is controlling us, and when duty directs? How shall we know when we are misled, when the very atmosphere of personality which encircles us distorts the object beyond it by desire and passion?

I know of no safer way in such trials, than to retire quietly into the chamber of the heart, to try to put personal desires aside, to strive to separate our self for a moment from the personality, and look at the question in a broader, clearer light, with prayer to our Gurudeva to guide us; then, in such light as we may win by prayer, self-analysis, and meditation, to choose the path which appears to us to be the path of duty. We may blunder; but if we blunder, having striven to see clearly, then let us remember that the mistake is necessary in order to teach us a lesson, which it is vital for our progress that we should learn; we may blunder, and choose the path of desire, misled by its influence, and when we think we are choosing Dharma, we may be moved by Ahamkara. Even if that be so, we have done rightly in struggling to see the right, and in resolving to do the right. Even if in striving to do the right, we do the wrong, we may rest assured that the God within us will correct us. Why should we despair because we make mistakes, when our heart is fixed on the Supreme, when we are striving to see the right? Nay, rather, when we have striven to do the right and have done the wrong in our blindness, we will welcome the pain that clears the mental vision, and we will cry undaunted to the Lord of the burning-ghat: "Send down yet again Thy flames to burn out everything that obstructs the vision, all dross that is mixed with the pure gold; burn Thou, O Radiant One, till we come out from the fire as pure and refined gold, whence all impurities have vanished. "

But if we, coward-like, shrinking from responsibility of coming to, a decision; and deaf to the voice of conscience, choose the easy path which another may tell us is the right one but which we feel to be wrong, and thus, against our own conscience, follow another's path, what have we done? We have dulled the divine voice within us; we have chosen the lower rather than the higher; we have chosen the easy and not the difficult; we have chosen the surrender of the will rather than its purification; and even though the path that we tread by another's choice may be the better path of the two, we have none the less injured our evolution by our failure to do that which we believed to be right. That mistake is a thousand-fold more injurious than blundering through the glamour of desire. To do what we believe to be the highest - that is the only safe path for the spiritual aspirant. If you affront your sense of right by taking that as right which in your heart you feel to be wrong, standing on another's advice and command, then you lose the very power to distinguish between right and wrong, and you put out the only light you have, however poor that light may be, and you choose to walk in darkness rather than in twilight. How will you be able to distinguish between light and dark, between the White Brothers and the Black, how will you know that this is divine and that is asuric, how will you discern the Deva from the Asura, unless you test them by the standard of duty, and by the righteousness they incarnate? Where duty is not done, where love, compassion, purity, self-sacrifice, are not seen, there, there may be power, but there, there is not the spirituality which enlightens the world, and sets an example to men.

In the path of spiritual aspiration, we must not expect to find the way easy and plain; for the spiritual life is not obtained save by repeated endeavour and constant failure, and the path of duty is not found but by undaunted perseverance. Let us but desire to know the right, and we shall surely know it, no matter by what path of anguish the right is to be found. In our daily life, let us practise to do the right, as far as we see it, and we shall surely see more clearly as we proceed.

But since many become confused as to the guides who may aid them in their upward treading, and as to how they may know such guides, let us pause and see what are the tests and proofs of spiritual life, of the spirituality which is to be copied, to be lived, which is an example, a light, in the world.

The test and proof of the advanced spiritual man, fit to be the guide, the teacher, the helper of others, is in the perfection of the qualities that the aspirant is striving to produce in himself. He performs perfectly what the aspirant performs imperfectly; he incarnates the ideal which the aspirant is striving to reproduce. What, then, are these qualities, which mark the spiritual life?

Around us on every side we see men and women seeking for light, struggling for growth, puzzled, confused, bewildered.

To all and each one that we meet we owe a duty. No one who comes within the circle of our life, but we have a duty towards that person. The world is not ruled by chance; no fortuitous happenings come into the lives of men. Duties are obligations we owe to those around us; and every one within our circle is one to whom we owe a duty. What is the duty that we owe to each? It is the definite payment of those debts with which we are familiar in our studies; the duty of reverencing and obeying those who are superior to us, who are above us; the duty of being gentle and affectionate and helpful to those around us, on our own level; the duty of protection, kindness, helpfulness, and compassion to those below us. These are universal duties, and no aspirant should fail in the attempt at least to fulfill them; without the fulfillment of these there is no spiritual life.

But even when we have discharged to the utmost the debts enjoined by the letter of the law; when we have paid and fulfilled the obligations imposed by our birth, by our family ties, by our social surroundings and national karma; there still remains one higher duty which we may place before us as the light to illumine our path.

Whenever a person comes within our circle of life, let us look to it that he leaves that circle a better man, the better for his contact with us. When an ignorant person comes and we have knowledge, let him leave us a better-informed man. When a sorrowful person comes to us, let him leave us a little less sorrowful for our having shared the sorrow with him. When a helpless person comes and we are strong, let him leave us strengthened by our strength and not humiliated by our pride. Everywhere let us be tender and patient, gentle and helpful with all. Do not let us in our daily path be harsh, so as to confuse, bewilder and perplex others. There is enough of sorrow in the world. Let the spiritual man be a source of comfort and of peace; let him be as a light in the world, so that all may walk more safely when they come within the circle of his influence. Let us judge our spirituality by our effect on the world, and let us be careful that the world may grow purer, better, happier, because we are living in it.

What are we here for, save to help each other, to love each other, to uplift each other? Is the spiritual man to hinder or to uplift his fellow-men? Is he to be a Saviour of mankind, or one who throws back the evolution of his fellows, from whom one goes away discouraged? Watch how your influence affects others: be careful how your words affect their lives. Your tongue must be gentle, your words must be loving; no slander, gossip, or harshness of speech, or suspicion of unkind motive, must pollute the lips that are striving to be the vehicle of spiritual life. The difficulty is in us and not outside of us. It is here in our own lives and our own conduct that the spiritual evolution must be made. Help your brothers, and do not be harsh with them. Lift then up when they fall, and remember, if you stand today, you too may fall tomorrow, and may need the helping hand of another, in order that you may rise.

Every scripture declares that the Heart of the Divine Life is Infinite Compassion. Compassionate, then, must be the spiritual man. Let us, in our poor measure, in our tiny cups of love, give to our fellow-man one drop of that ocean of compassion in which the universe is bathed. You never can be wrong in helping your brother, and in putting your own needs behind the supplying of his wants.

That and that alone is true spirituality, and it means coming back to the point from which we started. It means the recognition of one Self in all. The spiritual man must lead a higher life than the life of altruism. He must lead the life of self-identification with all that lives and moves. There is no "other" in this world; we all are one. Each is a separate form, but one Spirit moves and lives in all.

Listen to what spoke the Divine Lover, Shri Krishna, when, looking over the world of men, He passed His Divine verdict of the righteous and the sinful. "If the most sinful worship me", said He, "with undivided heart, he too must be accounted righteous, for he hath rightly resolved; speedily he becometh dutiful and goeth to eternal peace. O Kaunteya, know thou certainly that my devotee perisheth never" (*Bhagavad Gita*, ix 30, 31.)

Resolve rightly, then, and no fear need enter your heart. You may blunder, you may make errors, you may fall over and over again, but speedily you will become dutiful, and go to Eternal Peace.

Let us give devotion, then, to the Supreme Love. Let us recognise our oneness in Him, and therefore our oneness with each other; and because we have rightly resolved, though we have weaknesses and faults, there is the promise of Truth Itself, speedily we shall become dutiful and go to Peace.

III. THE LAW OF SACRIFICE

WE have already seen that a man can only realize himself as a Higher Consciousness in proportion as he tranquillises the senses, in proportion as he restrains the mind. We have then seen that he advances towards the realisation of the Higher Life in proportion as he obeys the Law of Duty, as he definitely and resolutely sets himself to the payment of the obligations that he has incurred.

Tonight we shall try to rise into a higher region, and see how, after he has practised the Law of Duty, the Law of Sacrifice lifts him upwards and enables him to reach union with the Divine. It is the Law of Sacrifice that we are now to study.

It has often been said, and truly said, that sacrifice is printed on the universe in which we live. And why should it not be so, since the universe in which we live itself originates in an act of sacrifice, in the limitation of the Logos in order that the world may come forth? All the religions have on this point but a single teaching, that manifestation began by an act of Divine Sacrifice. Each Scripture may in turn be quoted to prove the point, but it is so familiar to all of you that no proof is needed.

The nature of that sacrifice is seen by us as consisting in this assumption of the limitations of matter by the Immaterial, in the veiling of the Unconditioned in conditions, in the binding of the Free within bonds. The first thought that we have, as we watch the evolving of a universe, is that this manifestation of life is only possible by its limitations, that these mark out the conditions of its evolution; and that just as life becomes manifest by the taking of forms, so by the breaking of form after form and the assuming of new ones does life continually evolve. We see the life manifested in matter, drawing around itself matter which it appropriates as form. As form wastes in the exercising of life-functions, the life is ever engaged in drawing in fresh matter to replace that which has been lost. We see that the form is always decaying and always being renewed, and that the life can only find possibility of manifestation by thus taking fresh matter continually into its decaying form, and thus preserving it as the vehicle of manifestation; only by thus continually grasping after un-appropriated matter, and appropriating it for the building up and renewing of its form, can life evolve.

Thus there comes to be implanted in the very nature of the growing being, the idea that by taking, by grasping, by holding, the life is preserved, the life is increased. This seems to be what the life is learning by its contact with matter, and it does not realise, in the earlier stages, that taking, grasping, holding, keeping, is not really the condition of the life; but the condition of the maintenance of that form in which life is manifested. The form cannot continue to exist, but by virtue of the taking in of fresh matter. As the life goes on increasing, developing, this constant appropriation is the mark of the evolving Jiva. Everywhere is he learning that on the path of Pravritti, the path of forth-going, he must grasp, take, hold, and appropriate. Everywhere he is learning to try to absorb into himself other forms, and by union of other forms with his own to preserve the continuity of his existence in form.

When the great Teachers began to give lessons to the evolving Jivatma, when he had reached the necessary point of materiality, then strange teaching came to him, contrary to all his preceding experience. The Teacher began to say to him: "Life is preserved not simply by taking, but also by sacrificing that which you had already appropriated. It is a mistake to think that you can live and grow, simply by the appropriation of other forms into your own, simply by the absorption of the life around you, that your own may continue to exist. All the world is bound by a law of interdependence. All living things exist by virtue of mutual exchange, by the recognition of the fact of mutual interdependence. You cannot live alone in a world of forms; you cannot preserve your own form by the appropriating of others, without contracting a debt, which must be paid by the sacrifice of some of the appropriated object, for the maintenance of other lives. All lives are bound together by a golden chain, and that golden chain is the law of sacrifice, and not the law of grasping. "

The universe emanated by an act of supreme sacrifice, and can only be preserved by the continual renewal of sacrifice. Hear what Shri Krishna taught: "This world is not for the non-sacrificer, much less the other, O best of the Kurus. "(*Bhagavad-Gita*, iv. 31.)

Man, then, cannot even live in the world of forms, save as he performs acts of sacrifice. The revolving wheel of life cannot go on, unless each member, unless each living creature, helps to turn it by the performance of acts of sacrifice. Life is preserved by sacrifice, and in sacrifice all evolution is rooted.

In order that this new lesson might be taught in the correct way, we find the great Teachers insisting on acts of sacrifice, and showing that by virtue of these acts does that wheel of life revolve, that brings to us all good things. Thus we see established in the Hindu ritual, the well-known five sacrifices, which include in their wide circle the sacrifices which are necessary for the due maintenance of the lives of all the creatures in the world.

We are taught that our relations with the world invisible, with the Deva world, can only be preserved by the sacrifice to the Devas, in which we recognise this interdependence. We give to them, they give to us, and thus nourishing one another, we reap the highest good. (*Bhagavad-Gita*, iii. 11)

Then we learn the sacrifice, which is called the sacrifice to the Rishis, the sacrifice to the wise, the sacrifice to the Teachers. That is the sacrifice of study, by the performance of which is paid one of our debts, by the performance of which an obligation is discharged. For by study we learn in order to teach, and thus we keep up the succession of knowledge, handing it down from generation to generation.

Then we learn that we must also pay the debt to the Elders, the sacrifice to the past, the sacrifice to the Ancestors, to the Pitris; recognising in that that as we received from the past, we must pay our debt by giving to the future.

Next we learn to pay our debt to Humanity. We are taught that we must feed at least one man every day. We know that the essence of that act is not in the simply feeding one poor man. In that man who is fed, the Lord of sacrifice is also fed; and when He is fed, all Humanity is fed in Him. Just as when Durvasa came to the Pandavas in their exile, and the feast being over, demanded food where no food then existed, and the Lord of sacrifice Himself came and told the Pandavas to search for food, and one grain of rice was found, which He ate, and His hunger was satisfied, and in the satisfaction of His hunger the great host of ascetics found themselves filled; so in the sacrifice to man. In the feeding of one starving beggar, He is fed who feels Himself in all, in every human life, and thus feeding Him in the shape of one poor man, we feed humanity itself.

Lastly, we learn to sacrifice to animals. In the sacrifice to animals, in the two or three animals that daily we are bound to feed, we are feeding the Lord of animals in His animal creation, and by this sacrifice the animal world is maintained.

Such the old lessons given to young humanity, to teach it the form and essence of the sacrificial act. And we learn that the spirit of the law of the five sacrifices is far more valuable than the letter of the law; and we learn to extend to that spirit of sacrifice the recognition of the law of the obligation, of the law of duty. When the Law of Sacrifice is thus interwoven with and united to the Law of Obligation, then the next step is placed before the evolving Jiva.

You have learned to do some acts as acts of obligation. You now have to learn that the world is bound by action, save by such action as is sacrifice. (*Bhagavad-Gita*, iii. 9) You must learn that looking for the fruit of actions binds us to the world of actions, and that if we would be free from such binding we must learn to sacrifice everywhere the fruit of action: "With such object, free from attachment, O son of Kunti, perform thou action. " [*Ibid*]

That is the next step. It does not mean that some particular actions are to be separated from a man's scope of activity as sacrifices, but that all actions are to be seen in the light of sacrifice, by the renunciation of the fruit of action. When we sacrifice the fruit of action, we are beginning then to loosen the bonds of action which bind us to the world. For have we not read: "that with attachment dead, harmonious, his thoughts established in wisdom, his works sacrifices, all action melts away"? (*Bhagavad-Gita,* iv. 23)

The world is bound by karma, by action, save that action which is sacrifice. That is the lesson which begins to be breathed into our ears, as we approach the end of the Pravritti Marga, as the time comes for turning homeward, for entering the Path of Return, the Nivritti Marga. When a man begins to renounce the fruit of action, when he has learnt to perform all his actions as duty, without looking for their fruit, then comes the critical time in the history of the evolution of the human soul; then, as he is sacrificing the fruit of action, there sounds out to him a still higher note, a still higher lesson, which is to lead him over into the Nivritti Marga, the Path of Return. "Better than the sacrifice of wealth is the sacrifice of wisdom, O Parantapa," says Shri Krishna. "All actions in their entirety, O Partha, are contained in wisdom. Learn thou this by discipleship, by questionings, and by worship. The wise, the seers of the essence of things, will instruct thee in wisdom. And having known this, thou shalt not again fall into this confusion, O Pandava, for by this thou wilt see all beings without exception in the Self, and all in Me. " (*Bhagavad-Gita*, iv. 34)

There strikes out the note that we have learnt to recognise as the note of spirituality. By the "sacrifice of wisdom" we shall learn to see all beings in the Self, and thus in God. That is the note of the Path of Return, of the Nivritti Marga. That is the lesson which has now to be learnt by the evolving man.

The critical point comes now in the history of the evolving Jiva. He is trying to sacrifice the fruit of action, trying to be dead to attachments. And what is the inevitable result? The attachment to the fruit falls away, vairagya seizes him, dispassion overcomes him, he finds himself hanging, as it were, in the void. All motive for action has disappeared. He has lost the stimulus of the Pravritti Marga. He has not yet found the stimulus of the Nivritti Marga. Disgust of all objects is upon him. He seems to have wearied of the Law of Duty; he has not yet seen the heart of the Law of Sacrifice. At this moment of pause, at this moment of suspension in the void, he seems to have lost touch with the world of forms and objects, but he has not yet found touch with the world of life, with "the other side".

It is as though a man, crossing from precipice to precipice by a narrow bridge, suddenly found the bridge yield beneath his steps; he cannot return, he cannot reach out to the brink beyond. He seems to be hanging in the void, in mid-air, over the chasm; he has lost touch with all.

Fear not, O trembling soul, when that moment of utmost isolation cometh. Fear not to lose touch with the transitory, ere thou findest touch with the Eternal. Listen to those who have felt the same isolation, but have passed beyond, who have found the seeming void to be a veritable fullness: hear them proclaiming the Law of Life, upon which thou hast now to enter: "He that loveth his life shall lose it, but he that loseth his life shall find it unto Life Eternal. "

This is the test of the Inner Life. You cannot touch the higher until you have lost grasp of the lower. You cannot feel the higher, the touch of the lower is becoming that of a corpse. A child climbing up a ladder against a precipice hears the voice of his father calling him from above. He wants to reach the father, but he is clinging close to the ladder with both hands as he sees the yawning gulf below. But the voice tells him: "Loose your grasp from the ladder and stretch your hands out above your head. " But the child fears. If he looses his grasp of the ladder, will he not fall into the yawning gulf below? He cannot see above his head. The air seems empty, there is nought to grasp. Then comes the supreme act of faith. He looses grasp of his ladder. He stretches up his empty hands into the empty air above him; and lo! his father's hands clasp his own, and the strength of the father uplifts him to his own side. Such is the law of the Higher Life. In giving up the lower, the higher is secured; and by throwing up the life we know, the Life Eternal gains us as its own.

None but those who have felt it may know the horror of that great emptiness, where the world of form has vanished, but where the life of the Spirit is not yet felt. But there is no other way between the life in form and the life in Spirit. There between them stretches the gulf which must be crossed; and, strange as it may seem, it is in the moment of uttermost isolation, when the man is thrown back into himself, and there is nothing around him but the silent void, it is then that from out that nothingness of being the Eternal Being arises; and he who dared to spring from the foothold of the temporal finds himself on the sure rock of the Eternal.

Such the experience of all those who in the past have reached the spiritual life. Such the record they have left us for our encouragement and cheering when, to us too, this gulf presents itself for crossing. We read in the Shastras and in those outer actions that are full of deepest meaning, that when the disciple approaches his Teacher, he must ever come with sacrificial fuel in his hand. What is the sacrificial fuel? It represents*everything* that belongs to the life of form, everything that belongs to the personal lower self. All must be thrown into the fire of sacrifice, nought must be kept back. He must burn his lower nature, and his own hands must light the fire. He must sacrifice himself. None else may do it for him. Give, then, the life, and surrender it utterly. Keep not back alive anything, so far as you know it; cry aloud to the Lord of the burning-ghat that the sacrifice is lying on the altar, and shrink not from the consuming fire. In the blankness of isolation, trust the Law which cannot fail. If the Law of Sacrifice be strong enough to uphold the weight of the universe, will it break beneath the weight to an atom like myself? It is strong enough to be trusted; it is the strongest thing there is. The Law of Sacrifice is that the life of the Spirit consists in giving, and not in taking, in pouring itself out and not in grasping, in self-surrender and not in self-appropriation, in utterly giving all that one has, sure that the fullness of the Life Divine will enter in. And see how natural it is. The Life inexhaustible is found, that is ever bubbling up out of the illimitable fullness of the Self. Form is limited, life is unlimited. Therefore the form lives by taking, and the life grows by giving. Just in proportion as we empty ourselves of all that we have, is there room for the Divine fullness to flow in, and fill us more than we were ever filled before. Therefore the note of the Nivritti Marga is renunciation. Renunciation is the secret of Life as appropriation is the secret of Form.

This, then, is the Law of Sacrifice that we must learn. To give ungrudgingly, and ever again o give by this and this alone we live.

On first entering the Nivritti Marga, where Renunciation offers herself as our guide, her voice may seem cold and stern, her aspect may seem almost menacing. Trust her, none the less, whatever the outer appearance, and try to understand why sacrifice at first sight gives us the idea of pain.

From the standpoint of form, the aspect of sacrifice is the breaking up of forms, the throwing away of things; and the form, which feels the life withdrawing from it, cries out in its anguish, in its terror, towards the withdrawing life that maintains its very existence; and so we come to think of sacrifice as an act of pain, as an act accompanied with anguish and with terror, and this must be as long as we identify ourselves with the form.

But when we begin to live the life of Spirit, the life which recognises the One in the manifold forms, then there begins to dawn upon us the supreme spiritual truth, that sacrifice is not pain but joy, is not sorrow but delight, that that which to the flesh is painful is bliss to the Spirit, which is our true life. Then we see that the aspect of sacrifice that was sorrowful was an utter delusion, that keener than any pleasure that the world can give, more joyous than any joy that comes from wealth or position, more blissful than any bliss that the world can offer, is the bliss of the free Spirit, which, by pouring itself out, finds the union with the Self, and knows that it is living in many forms, flowing along many channels, instead of following the limitation of a single form.

Here is the joy of the Saviours of mankind, of Those who have risen to the knowledge of unity, and have become the Guides, the Helpers, the Redeemers of the race. Step by step, slowly and gradually, They have mounted upwards and upwards, They have crossed the Gulf of Nothingness that I have spoken of, and have found a footing on the other side. They have recovered the sense of the reality of life, and in the Gulf of Nothingness, in which They for a time seemed to have lost Themselves, They suddenly found Themselves above the world of forms. All forms as seen from that higher level are the vessels of one informing Life and Self. They have found with a sense of joy inexpressible, that the living Self can pour itself out into all the innumerable forms, and know no difference between form and form, but all as the channels of one Spirit.

That is why the Saviour of the world can help the race and strengthen His weaker brethren. Having risen to that great height where all selves are known as one, the different forms are all His own. He knows Himself in each. He can be joyous with the joyful, and feel sorrow with the sorrowful. He is weak with the weak and strong with the strong - all are parts of Himself. Alike to Him the righteous and the sinful. He feels no attraction to the one, nor any repulsion from the other. He can see that in every stage the One Self is living that Life which is Himself. He knows Himself in the stone, in the plant, in the brute, in the savage, as in the Saint and the Sage, and He sees one Life everywhere and knows Himself that Life. Where, then, is there room for fear; where, then, is there room for reproach? There is nothing but One Self, and nothing outside It either to fear or to challenge.

That is the true Peace, and that and that alone is Wisdom. To know the Self is alone the spiritual life, and that life is joy and peace.

Thus the Law of Sacrifice, which is the Law of Life, is also the Law of Joy, and we know that nothing has a keener pleasure than the pleasure of pouring out and not taking in, and that no limited joy can be equal to the joy of self-surrender.

Were it possible for each of us to catch for a moment a faint glimpse of the Spiritual Life, then the transitory world would assume its true proportions, and we should see the worthlessness of all that man accounts as precious. The Law of Sacrifice, which is the Law of Life and the Law of Joy and the Law of Peace, is summed up in this Mahavakya, this great Word; "I am thou; thou art I".

And now for a moment let us bring this lofty idea down to the level of our daily lives, and see how the Law of Sacrifice, in its working in ourselves, will manifest in the outer world of men.

We have learnt to realise, if but for a moment, the unity of the Self. We have learnt a word, a letter, of the Book of Wisdom. How then shall we behave ourselves to our brother men? We see a man low, degraded, ignorant, and foul. No special tie of kindred nor past karma binds us to him, nor does anything that we regard as obligation join our form to his. But, by the Law of Sacrifice, having realised the unity of the Self, when we see that outcast member of the human family, we see the Self in him, and the form vanishes, and we know that we are that man, and that man is our self. Hence compassion takes the place of what in the man of the world is repulsion. Love takes the place of hatred, and tenderness replaces indifference, and the Sacrificer is marked in his attitude to those around him by this touch of divine compassion, which cannot see the repulsiveness of the outer form, but can only realise the beauty of the Self enshrined therein.

The Sacrificer comes across a man who is ignorant, while he himself is wise. Does he feel the contempt of the man of knowledge for the man of ignorance, and hold himself above him as his superior and as separate? Nay, he does not feel his wisdom as his own, but as common property belonging to all alike, and he shares his wisdom in the separate form with the ignorance in the other separate form: and he does it without feeling the difference, because of the unity of the Self. And so with every other difference of the world of forms. The man who lives by the Law of Sacrifice realises the unity of the Self, and recognises only a difference in the containing vessel and not in the indwelling life; hence he only gathers wisdom and knowledge into his separate vessel for the sake of sharing what he gathers with others, and for others; and he loses utterly the sense of separate life, and becomes part of the Life of the World.

As he realises this, and knows that the only value of the body is to be a channel of the higher, to be an instrument of that life, he slowly and gradually rises above all thought, save the thought of unity, and feels himself a part of this great suffering world. Then he feels that the griefs of humanity are his griefs, the sins of humanity are his sins, the weaknesses of his brother are his weaknesses, and thus he realises unity, and sees through all differences the underlying One Self.

Only in this way can we live in the Eternal.

"Those who see differences pass from death to death"; thus speak the Shruti. The man who sees difference is really continually dying, for he is living in the form, which is decaying every moment and is therefore death, and not in the Spirit, which is life.

Just, then, in proportion as you and I, my brothers, do not recognise the difference between each and each, but feel the unity of life, and know that that life is common to all, and that none has a right to boast of his share of it, nor to be proud that his share is different from the share of another, only thus and in that proportion shall we live the Spiritual Life.

That is the last word, it seems, of the Wisdom that the Sages have taught us. Nothing less than this is spiritual, nothing less than this is wisdom, nothing less than this is real life.

Oh! if for one passing moment I could show to you, by any skill of tongue or passion of emotion, one gleam of the faint glimpse - that by the grace of the Masters I have caught - of the glory and the beauty of the Life that knows no difference and recognises no separation, then the charm of that glory would so win your hearts, that all earth's beauty would seem but ugliness, all earth's gold but dross, all earth's treasures but dust on the roadside, beside the inexpressible joy of the life that knows itself as One.

Hard to keep it, even when once seen, amidst the separated lives of men, amidst the glamour of the senses, and the delusions of the mind. But once to have seen it, though but for a moment, changes the whole world, and having beheld the majesty of the Self, no life save that seems worth living. How shall we make it real, how shall we make it our own, this wonderful recognition of the Life beyond all lives, of the Self beyond all selves? Only by daily acts of renunciation in the little things of life; only by learning in every thought, word, and action to live and love the Unity; and not only to speak it, but to practise it on every occasion, by putting ourselves last and others first, by always seeing the need of others and trying to supply it, by learning to be indifferent to the claim of our own lower nature and refusing to listen to it. I know of no road save this humble, patient, persevering endeavour, hour after hour, day after day, year after year until at last the mountain tops are climbed.

We talk of the Great Renunciation. We speak of These, before whose Feet we bow, as Those who have "made the Great Renunciation". Do not dream that They made Their Renunciation when, standing on the threshold of Nirvana, They heard the sobbing of the world in anguish, and turned back to help. It was not then that the real, the great, renunciation was made. They made it over and over again in the hundreds of lives that lie behind Them; They made it by the constant practice of the small renunciations of life, by continual pity, by daily sacrifices in common human life. They did not make it at the last hour, when on the threshold of Nirvana, but through the course of lives of sacrifice; until, at last, the Law of Sacrifice became so much the law of Their being, that They could not do anything at the last moment, when the choice was Theirs, save register on the record of the universe the innumerable renunciations of the past.

You and I my brothers, today, if we will, may begin to make the Great Renunciation; and if we do not begin it in the daily life, in our hourly dealings with our fellows, be assured we shall not be able to make it when we stand on the mountain crest. The habit of daily sacrifice, the habit of thinking, the habit of always giving and not taking, only thus shall we learn to make that which the outer world calls the Great Renunciation. We dream of great deeds of heroism, we dream of mighty ordeals, we think that the life of discipleship consists in tremendous trials for which the disciple prepares himself, towards which he marches with open vision, and then by one supreme effort, by one brave struggle, gains his crown of victory.

Brothers, it is not so. The life of the disciple is one long series of petty renunciations, one long series of daily sacrifices, one continual dying in time in order that the higher may eternally live. It is not a single deed that strikes the world with wonder which makes true discipleship, else were the hero or the martyr greater than the disciple. The life of the disciple is lived in the home, is lived in the town, is lived in the office, is lived in the market place, yea, amid the common lives of men. The true life of sacrifice is that which utterly forgets itself, in which renunciation becomes so common that there is no effort, that it becomes a thing of course. If we lead that life of sacrifice, if we lead that life of renunciation, if daily, perseveringly, we pour out ourselves for others, we shall find ourselves one day on the summit of the mountain, and shall discover that we have made the Great Renunciation, without ever dreaming that any other act was possible.

PEACE TO ALL BEINGS

BOOK SIX
THE SPIRITUAL LIFE

ESSAYS AND ADDRESSES

Publisher's Preface

IN addition to the large number of volumes which stand in the name of Annie Besant in the catalogue of the British Museum, there is a great quantity of literature, for which she is responsible, that has appeared in more fugitive form as articles, pamphlets and published lectures, issued not only in Great Britain but in America, India and Australia. Much of this work is of great interest, but is quite out of reach of the general reader as it is no longer in print, and inquiries for many such items have frequently to be answered in the negative. Under these circumstances the Theosophical Publishing Service decided to issue an edition of Mrs. Besant's collected writings under the title ESSAYS AND ADDRESSES. It was originally intended to arrange the matter in chronological order, commencing with the writer's first introduction to Theosophy as reviewer of Mme. Blavatsky's *Secret Doctrine*, but several considerations determined the abandonment of this plan in favour of the scheme now adopted, which is the classification of subject-matter independent of chronological order. The Publishers feel sure that this arrangement will especially commend itself to students who desire to know what the Author has written on various important aspects of Theosophy in its several ramifications, and for all purposes of study and reference the plan chosen should more effectively serve. The dates and sources of articles are given in nearly all cases, and they are printed without any revision beyond the correction of obvious typographical errors.

The importance and interest of such a collection of essays, both as supplementing treatment of many of the topics in larger works and as affording expression of the Author's views on many subjects not otherwise dealt with, will be obvious, and it only remains to express the Publisher's hope that the convenience and moderate cost of the series may insure its thorough circulation among the wide range of Mrs. Besant's readers.

Theosophical Publishing Society, London, May, 1912.

I. SPIRITUAL LIFE FOR THE MAN OF THE WORLD

A Lecture delivered in the City Temple, London, Thursday, October 10th, 1907.

THE Rev. R. J. CAMPBELL, M.A., who presided, said: In introducing the lecturer to a City Temple audience it is not my desire to indulge in personalities which might be embarrassing to her, but I feel it is due to ourselves to say that we recognise in Mrs. Besant one of the greatest moral forces of the day. She has well earned the respect now so freely accorded to her by the British public, and by many thousands of thoughtful men and women all over the world. In time past she has had to sacrifice much for her fidelity to what she believed to be the truth. It is rare in such a case that strength of conviction is untainted by any trace of bitterness or intolerance. In proportion to the price that has had to be paid for one's convictions is the intensity and, sometimes shall we say, the dogmatism, and even intolerance, with which they are held; but if there is one outstanding characteristic of Mrs. Besant's public life it is the entire absence of any trace either of bitterness or intolerance in her dealings with others. She looks for truth beneath all formal statements of belief; she excommunicates no one; and, therefore, as her acquaintance with life is so wide and deep, she has earned the position of a great spiritual teacher, and it is as such that we welcome her to the City Temple tonight.

Mrs. BESANT said: "Before beginning that which I am to say to you tonight, will you permit me one word of preface both on my presence here and on the opinions which here I shall voice? I thank your minister and I thank you for giving me the opportunity of speaking here, but I am bound to say that the opinions I give must not be taken in any way to compromise the place in which I speak, or the minister who generally occupies this pulpit. We are all grateful to the minister of the City Temple for the courage with which he has given utterance to opinions which are in the air for educated and thoughtful people, but which only the few have the courage to express. But when a truth is in the air the expression of that truth is one of the greatest services that man can render to man: For truth, you must remember, is largely dependent upon the utterance of those who see it and are brave enough to speak it, and thousands welcome a truth that they know to be true, but have not the courage to speak it out while speech is still confined to the minority. It is therefore the more important that I may not be held in anything I say to compromise in any fashion the message which here is normally delivered. For my opinions are mine, as yours are yours, and in speaking here tonight I speak the truth as I see it, not desiring that any shall accept it who as yet see it not, and least of all desiring that any word of mine shall render heavier the burden or greater the difficulty which you (turning to Mr. Campbell), sir, have to face.

Now the complaint which we hear continually from thoughtful and earnest minded people, a complaint against the circumstances of their life, is perhaps one of the most fatal. "If my circumstances were different from what they are, how much more I could do; if only I were not so surrounded by business, so tied by anxieties and cares, so occupied with the work of the world, then I would be able to live a more spiritual life." Now that is not true. No circumstances can ever make or mar the unfolding of the spiritual life in man. Spirituality does not depend upon the environment; it depends upon the attitude of the man towards life, and I want if I can tonight to point out to you the way in which the world may be turned to the service of the spirit instead of submerging it, as I admit it often does. If a man does not understand the relation of the material and the spiritual; if he separates the one from the other as incompatible and hostile; if on the one side he puts the life of the world, and on the other the life of the spirit as rivals, as antagonists, as enemies, the one of the other, then the pressing nature of worldly occupations, the powerful shocks of the material environment, the constant luring of physical temptation, and the occupying of the brain by physical cares - these things are apt to make the life of the spirit unreal. They seem the only reality, and we have to find some alchemy, some magic, by which the life of the world shall be seen to be the unreal, and the life of the spirit the only reality. If we can do that, then the reality will express itself through the life of the world, and that life will become its means of expression, and not a bandage round its eyes, a gag which stops the breath. That is what we are to seek for tonight.

Now, you know how often in the past this question, whether a man can lead a spiritual life in the world, has been answered in the negative. In every land, in every religion, in every age of the world's history, when the question has been asked, the answer has been - No, the man of the world cannot lead a spiritual life. That answer comes from the deserts of Egypt, the jungles of India, the monastery and the nunnery in Roman Catholic countries, in every land and place where man has sought to find out God by shrinking from the company of men; and if for the knowledge of God and the leading of the spiritual life it be necessary to fly from the haunts of men, then that life for the most of us is impossible, for we are bound by circumstance that we cannot break to live the life of the world and to accommodate ourselves to its conditions. I am going to submit to you that that idea is based on a fundamental error, but that it is largely fostered in our modern life, not so much so in this country by thinking of secluded life in jungle or desert, in cave or monastery, but rather by thinking that the religious and the secular must be kept apart. That is a tendency here because of the modern way of separating what is called the sacred from that which is called the profane. People here speak of Sunday as the Lord's Day, as though every day were not His equally, and He should be served on it. To call one day the Lord's Day is to deny that same lordship to every other day in the week, and so make six parts of the life outside the spiritual, while only one remains recognised as dedicated to the Spirit. And so the common talk of men - sacred history and profane history, religious education and secular education - all these phrases that are so commonly used, they hypnotise the public mind into a false view of the Spirit and the world. The right way is to say that the Spirit is the life, the world the form, and the form must be the expression of the life, otherwise you have a corpse devoid of life, and you have an unembodied life, separated from all means of effective action; and I want to put broadly and strongly the very foundation of what I believe to be all right and sane thinking in this matter. The world is the thought of God, the expression of the Divine mind. All useful activities are forms of Divine activity. The wheels of the world are turned by God, and men are only His hands which touch the rim of the wheel. All work done in the world is God's work, or none is His at all. Everything that serves man and helps on the activities of the world is rightly seen when seen as a Divine activity, and wrongly seen when called secular or profane. The merchant in his counting-house, the shopman behind his counter, the doctor in the hospital, is quite as much engaged in a Divine activity as any preacher in his church. Until that is realised the world is vulgarised, and until we can see one life everywhere, and all things rooted in that life, until then it is we who are hopelessly profane in attitude, we who are blind to the beatific vision, which is the sight of the one life in everything, and all things as expressions of that life.

Now, if that be true, if there is only one life in which you and I are partakers, one creative thought by which the worlds were formed and are maintained, then, however mighty may be the unexpressed Divine existence - though it be true as it is written in an ancient Indian scripture, "I established this universe with one fragment of Myself, and I remain" - however true it may be that Divinity transcends the manifestation thereof, none the less the manifestation is still Divine; and by understanding that we touch the feet of God. If it be true that He is everywhere and in everything, then He is as much in the marketplace as in the desert, as much in the counting-house as in the jungle, as easily found in the street of the crowded city as in the solitude of the mountain peak. I do not mean that it is not easier for you and for me to realise the Divine greatness in the splendour, say, of snow-clad mountains, the beauty of some pine forest, the depth of some marvelous secret valley where Nature speaks in a voice that may be heard; but I do mean that although we hear more clearly there it is because we are deaf, and not because the Divine voice does not speak. Ours the weakness that the rush and the bustle of life in the city makes us deaf to the voice that is ever speaking; and if we were stronger, if our ears were keener, if we were more spiritual, then we could find the Divine life as readily in the rush of Holborn Viaduct as in the fairest scene that Nature has ever painted in the solitude of the mountain or the magic of the midnight sky. That is the first thing to realise - that we do not find because our eyes are blinded.

But now let us see what are the conditions by which the man of the world may lead the spiritual life, for I admit there are conditions. Have you ever asked yourselves why around you objects that attract you are found on every side, things you want to possess? Your desires answer to the outer beauty, the attractiveness, of the endless objects that are scattered over the world. If they were not meant to attract they would not be there; if they were really hindrances, why should they have been put in our path? Just for the same reasons as when a mother wants to coax her child into the exertion that will induce it to walk she dangles before its eyes, a little out of reach, some dazzling toy, some tinsel attraction, and the child's eyes are gained by the brilliant object, and the child wants to grasp the thing just out of its reach. He tries to get on his feet, falls, and rises again, endeavours to walk, struggles to reach, and the value of the attraction is not in the tinsel that presently the child grasps, crushes, and throws away, wanting something more, but in the stimulus to the life within, which makes him endeavour to move in order to gain the glittering prize that he despises when he has won it. And the great mother-heart by which we are trained is ever dangling in front of us some attractive object, some prize for the child-spirit, turning outwards the powers that live within; and in order to induce exertion, in order to win to the effort by which alone those inward-turned powers will turn outwards into manifestation, we are bribed and coaxed and induced to make efforts by the endless toys of life scattered on every side. We struggle, we endeavour to grasp; at last we do grasp and hold; after a short time the brilliant apple turns to ashes, as in Milton's fable, and the prize that seemed so valuable loses all its attractiveness, becomes worthless, and something else is desired. In that way we grow. The result is in ourselves; some power has been brought out, some faculty has been developed, some inner strength has become a manifested power, some hidden capacity has become faculty in action. That is the object of the Divine teacher; the toy is thrown aside when the result of the exertion to gain it has been achieved. And so we pass from one point to another, so we pass from one stage of evolution to the next; and although until you believe in the great fact of continual rebirth and evercontinuing experience, you will not realise to the full the beauty and the splendour of the Divine plan, still, even in one brief life you know you gain by your struggle, and not by your accomplishment, and the reward of the struggle is in the power that you possess, or, in the great words of Edward Carpenter, narrowed down if you do not believe in reincarnation, "Every pain that I suffered in one body was a power that I wielded in the next". And even in one life you can see it, even in one brief span from the cradle to the grave you can trace the working of the law. You grow, not by what you gain of outer fruit, but by the inner unfolding necessary for your success in the struggle.

Now, if long natural experience has made wise the man, these objects lose their power to attract, and the first tendency then is to cease from effort; but that would mean stagnation. When the objects of the world are becoming a little less valuable than they were, then is the time to look for some new motive, and the motive to action for the spiritual life is, first, to perform action because it is duty, and not in order to gain the personal reward that it may bring. Let me take the case of a man of the world and a spiritual man, and see what it needs to turn one into the other. I take one in which you will not question that he is a man of the world, a man who is making some enormous fortune, who puts before himself as the one object of life money, to be rich. It is a common thing. Now, for a moment, pause on the life of the man who has determined to be rich. Everything is subordinated to that one aim. He must be master of his body, for if that body is his master he will waste with every week and month the money that he has gathered by struggle; he will waste in luxury for the pleasing of the body the money that he ought to grip, in order that he may win more. And so the first thing that a man must do is to master the body, to teach it to endure hardness, to learn to bear frugality, to learn to bear hardship even; not to think whether he wants to sleep, if by traveling all night a contract can be gained; not to stop to ask whether he shall rest if, by going to some party at midnight, he can make a friend who will enable him to gain more money by his influence. Over and over again in the struggle for gold the man must be master of this outer body that he wears, until it has no voice in determining his line of activity - it yields itself obedient servant to the dominant will, to the compelling brain. That is the first thing he learns - conquest of the body.

Then he learns concentration of mind. If he is not concentrated his rivals will beat him in the struggle of the market-place. If his mind wanders about here, there, and everywhere, undecided, one day trying one plan, and another day another plan, without perseverance, without deliberate continuing labour, that man will fail. The goal he desires teaches him to concentrate his mind; he brings it to one point; he holds it there as long as he needs it; he is steady in his persevering mental effort, and his mind grows stronger and stronger, keener and keener, more and more under his control. He has not only learned to control his body, but to control his mind. Has he gained anything more? Yes, a strong will; only the strong will can succeed in such a struggle. The soul grows mighty in the attempt to achieve. Presently that man, with his mastered body, his well controlled mind, his powerful will, gains his objects and grasps his gold. And then? Then he finds out that, after all, he cannot do so very much with it to make happiness for himself; that he has only got one body to clothe, one mouth to feed; that he cannot multiply his wants with the enormous supply that he can gain, and that, after all, his happiness-gaining power is very limited. His gold becomes a burden rather than a joy, the first delight of the achievement of his object palls, and he becomes satiated with possession, until, in many a case, he can do nothing but, by mere habit, roll and roll and roll up increasing piles of useless gold. It becomes a nightmare rather than a delight; it crushes the man who won it.

Now, what will make that man a spiritual man? A change of his object - that is all. Let that man in this or any other life awaken to the valuelessness of the gold that he has heaped together; let him see the beauty of human service; let him catch a glimpse of the splendour of the Divine order; let him realise that all that life is worth is to give it as part of the great life by which the worlds are maintained, and the power he has gained over body, over mind, over will, will make that man a giant in the spiritual world. He does not need to change those qualities, but to get rid of the selfishness, to get rid of the indifference to human pain, to get rid of the recklessness with which he crushed his brother, in order that he might climb into wealth on the starvation of myriads. He must change his ideal from selfishness to service; from strength used for crushing to strength used for uplifting; and in the giant of the money market you will have the spiritual man; his life is concentrated to humanity, and he owns only to serve and to help. Difference of object, difference of motive, not difference of the outer life, on that does it depend whether a man is of the world worldly or of the spirit spiritual.

I used just now the word duty, for that is the first step. Any one of you, whatever may be your work in the world, it matters not, if you begin to do it not because it brings you a livelihood - though there is nothing to be ashamed of in its bringing you the power to live here - if you begin to do it slowly, gradually, more and more because it ought to be done, and not because you want to gain something for yourself, then you are taking the first step towards the spiritual life, you are changing your motive; all the activities of your day will have a new object. Duty must be done; the wheels of the world must be kept turning. Men and women must be fed along the various lines of trade and commerce; the sick must be healed; the ignorant must be taught; justice must be sought as between the strong and the weak, the rich and the poor; and, looking at it thus, the tradesman, the merchant, the doctor, the lawyer, the teacher may all take a new view of life, and they may say: This activity with which I am engaged is part of the great working of the world which is Divine. I am in it to do it, and my duty lies in the perfect performance of my task. I will teach, or heal, or argue, or trade, or enter into commercial relations of all kinds, not for the mere money that it brings, or the power that it yields, but in order that the great work of the world may be worthily carried on, and that work may be done by me as servant of a will greater than my own, instead of for my own personal gain and profit.

That is the first step, and there is not one of you that cannot take it. You may do your business just the same, but you carry a new spirit with you into it; you do it because it is your work in the world, as a servant does a task for his master because he is bidden to do it, and his loyalty makes him do it well. Then every adding up of a number of figures in a ledger, every selling of an article in a shop would be done with this sublime ideal behind it: "I do it as a part of the world's work, and this is the duty that falls to my lot to do", and would be taken as coming directly from the great Will by which the worlds move, as your share of the Divine activity, your part of the universal work; and the mightiest archangel, the greatest of the shining ones, can do nothing more than his share of carrying out the Divine will. And George Herbert wrote truly that the one who sweeps a room as to the glory of God makes that and the action fine. That is spiritual life where all is done for duty, for the larger instead of for the smaller self. And, mind, it is not always easy. No shuffling, no leaving of a task undone, because the Master's eye will not be there, for our Master's eye is everywhere, and never sleeping. No scamping of work, for that is not to be one of the Divine artificers, but only an ignorant and clumsy worker. Art is only doing what you do perfectly, and God is always an artist. There is nothing, however small, no animal that only the microscope enables you to see, that is not perfect in its beauty, and the more closely you examine the more exquisite does it become. Why, those minute diatoms that you can only see by the microscope, every minute shell is sculptured with patterns geometrically perfect for whom? For the satisfaction of that sense of perfection which is one of the Divine elements in God and man alike. Not what you do, but how you do it, whether it be perfectly wrought to the utmost limit of your ability; that is the test of a man's character, and by the work you can know the character of the worker.

Now that seems a small thing when you bring it down to your own house, shop, office. Taken one by one, so small; but suppose everyone did it, how would the face of the world then appear? No scamped work, no unreliable products on the market, nothing adulterated, nothing that was not what it pretended to be, the face value and the real value always identical, every house perfectly built, every drain perfectly laid, everything done as well as the skill and strength of man can do it. Why, a world like that seems a fairy tale, an impossible Utopia, but that would be the result if every individual man did his duty as perfectly as his powers permitted. And that is the first step towards the spiritual life. It is not outside your reach; it is close to every one of you.

But that is not all; there is a higher stage of the spiritual life than that. It is much to feel yourself a co-worker with the Divine in the world, much to make your work great by knitting it to the universal work throughout this mighty system of worlds and universes; much, too, as Emerson said, to hitch your wagon on to a star, instead of some miserable post by the wayside. But even that is not the only thing within your power, even that is not the most splendid to which you can attain. For there is one thing greater even than duty, and that is when all action is done as sacrifice. Now, what does that mean? There would be no world, no you, no I, if there had not been a primary sacrifice by which a fragment of the Divine thought sheathed itself in matter, limited itself in order that you and I might become self-consciously Divine. There is a profound truth in that great Christian teaching of a Lamb slain - when? On Calvary? No, "from the foundation of the world". That is the great truth of sacrifice. No Divine sacrifice, no universe. No Divine self-limitations, none of the worlds which fill the realms of space. It is all a sacrifice, the sacrifice of love that limits itself that others may gain self-conscious being and rejoice in the perfection of their own ultimate Divinity. And inasmuch as the life of the world is based on sacrifice, all true life is also sacrificial; and when every action is done as sacrifice then the man becomes the perfect, spiritual man. Now that is hard. The first stage is not so difficult. We may give away largely; we may make our lives useful; but how difficult it is - our lives being made useful, and wrapped up in some useful work - to be able to see that work shivered into pieces, and look on its ruins with calm content.

That is one of the things that is meant by sacrifice - that you may throw the whole of your life into some good work, the whole of your energy into some great scheme, you may toil and build and plan and shape, and you may nourish your own begotten scheme as a mother may cherish the child of her womb, and presently it falls to pieces round you. It fails, it does not succeed; it breaks, it does not grow; it dies, it does not live. Can you be content with such a result? Years of labour, years of thought, years of sacrifice, and see everything crumble into dust, and nothing remain? If not, then you are working for self, and not as part of the Divine activity; and, however gilded over with love of others your scheme may have been, it was your work and not God's work, and therefore you have suffered in the breaking. For if it were really His and not yours; if it were a sacrifice and not your own possession, you would know that all that is good in it must inevitably go into the forces of good in the world, and that if He did not want the form you builded you would rather it were broken, and the life that cannot die go into other forms which fit better with the Divine plan, and work into the great scheme of evolution.

Let me put it another way, and you will see exactly what I mean, less abstractly perhaps. Take an army, an army awaiting attack from some enemy greater, stronger than itself. The commander-in-chief maps out his scheme of battle, places one regiment in one spot and one regiment in another, makes one great plan that includes the whole, and the day of battle dawns. From the side of the general goes a galloping messenger, and he sends word to some young captain in one part of the field, "Go, attack that fort that lies in front of you, capture it, and hold it until word comes to leave". And the young captain, with his little band of young men behind him, looks at the fort in front, and knows he cannot take it, sees that failure is inevitable, knows that it means mutilation and death to the men under his command - nay, he knows that if he carries out the order to the last, not one man of that little band may see tomorrow's sun, but every one will be swept away in the death-hail that will come upon them as they struggle up the hill to the impregnable fort at the top. He sees it all; does he hesitate? If he does he is traitor, dishonoured, craven. He calls his men together. "Orders have come to take the fort!" They charge up at it. They are decimated. Again they charge, and again they leave a tenth of their number on the slope. Again, and again, and again they charge, until no man is left there to stand and charge again. Meanwhile, on another side of the field progress has been made with the general's plan; meanwhile the attention of the enemy has been occupied by this handful of men who go cheerfully to death, and the plan has developed; for while the enemy were watching the forlorn hope the plan of their comrades has been carried out on the other side, and in the long run, when the sun is setting, victory belongs to the army, although those men lie spread dead and dying on the slope. Have they failed? It looks like failure to he there dying and dead; surely the men have failed. Ah! when the story of that battle is written, when a grateful nation raises a monument to the memory of the conquerors of that battle, high on that monument will be graven in imperishable gold the names of the men who died and made victory possible for their comrades by accepting defeat for themselves.

You read my parable. There is no failure where the commander-in-chief is the Divine architect of the universe, no failure, but inevitable success; and shall it not be a pride to anyone who is called to sacrifice in order that the plan may be carried out? And there is no failure, for victory is ever on the Divine side. What matters it if you and I look like failures; what matters it if our petty plans crumble to pieces in our hands; what matters it if our schemes of a moment are found to be useless and are thrown aside? The life we have thrown into them, the devotion with which we planned them, the strength with which we strove to carry them out, the sacrifice with which we offered them to the success of the mighty whole, that enrolled us as sacrificial workers with the Deity, and no glory is greater than the glory of the personal failure which ensures universal success. That is only for the strong. I grant it. That is only for the heroes. It is their work and their delight. But even to be able to see the beauty of it is to bring some of the beauty into every one of our lives. For to see a thing to be noble is to begin to incarnate that nobility in your life, and the mere recognition of the splendour of an ideal is the first step towards becoming transformed into its image.

Now suppose that you and I can shape our lives on lines such as these which inadequately I have tried to sketch, we shall become the spiritual man living in the life of the world, making the world slowly after the fashion of the Divine ideal, and making it more and more the perfectly manifested Divine thought. That is the central idea then which will transform the man of the world into the spiritual man, and in the world it can best be performed. The life of the jungle, for those who know the many lives of men, is never the last life of a saviour of his race. Sometimes such a life will be one of the many lives through which he goes to gather universal experience; sometimes a time of gathering strength together and accumulating the power that hereafter is to be used; but the life of the Christs of the race is the life in the world, and not the life in the jungle. Though we may profitably go sometimes into seclusion, the manifested God walks in the haunts of men. For only there is the great work to be done, there the trials to be faced, there the powers to be opened up. When all our powers are brought out, when we are all of us Christs, ah! then we can go out of the outer life of the world to become part of its inner life which shapes and moulds the outer activity; but those who are only growing to that stature must grow by the law of growth, and that is the law of experience. But only the perfect may pass behind the veil and thence send out the spiritual powers unfolded in the life of the world.

And so it seems to me there is not one of us who may not begin to lead the truly spiritual life, and the world will be the better for the living, while the man will unfold the more rapidly for his effort. For every one of us, if we only think of it, each one is at work to carve his own life into a perfect image, the image of the Divine manifest in man. It is not that the Divine is not within you; were it not so, how should you bring it forth? The ideal comes before the manifestation, the thought creates the form, and in every one of you there is sleeping, as it were, the Divine image, and your work is to make that image manifest, and then you are the spiritual man. Come with me to the studio of some great sculptor, not a mere marble-chipper, but one of those geniuses who show the marble living, and the ideal in spotless form. How does that man work? Do you think he is carving a statue out of the marble? He is doing nothing of the kind. He is setting free a statue within the marble, and cutting away the superincumbent, useless marble that hides from the eyes of man the beauty of the ideal that he sees. That is the sculptor of genius; in the rough block, which is all that you and I can see with our poor eyes, he sees the perfect statue imprisoned within the stone, and with every blow of mallet, and with every deft touch of chisel, he brings that prisoner nearer to freedom, his ideal nearer to manifestation. And so with you and me: we are rough blocks of marble as we live here in the studio of the world, rough, unhewn, so many of us, and the divinity within us is hidden, as the statue within the block. And you and I are sculptors, and by our life that statue is to be made manifest, that imprisoned beauty is to be set free, and with the mallet of will, the chisel of thought, we must cut away all this superincumbent, useless stone that hides the living divinity within us, hides its unmanifested glory from the sight of men. Sculptors everyone of you, shaping out what you shall inevitably be in years, in centuries, to come, and the more skillfully, with the more knowledge, with the stronger will, the more powerfully you can use your mallet and your chisel, the swifter will come the day of liberation, the nearer the manifestation of the work. And so, wherever you may be, in whatever workshop of this great world you may find yourselves at labour, keep ever in your heart the ideal that you fain would realise. Feel the presence of the imprisoned Divinity that you have the mighty privilege, and you alone, of liberating; and take in hand your tools, cut away the worthless stone, liberate the splendid statue, and then you shall know yourself self-consciously as that which you really are, men in the image of God.

Mr. Campbell, in expressing to Mrs. Besant the sense of obligation to her for her lecture, said he did not know that he had ever listened to a more magnificent oratorical effort within those walls. But that was a comparatively small matter - what of the truth itself? They had been listening to the utterances of a great preacher, and what had been said carried conviction with it. So far from the minister or the officers of the church being in any way compromised by Mrs. Besant's presence in the pulpit he hoped she would not feel compromised by her presence in the pulpit. "The fact is that we at the City Temple have learned to disregard these things; it is no use troubling about what compromises you or what does not. Speaking for myself, I can say I am only proud to have had such a great preacher enunciating great truths standing side by side with me in this historic pulpit, and I want to assure Mrs. Besant on your behalf that she will be a welcome guest at any future time when her busy life permits her to revisit the City Temple."

Mrs. Besant: Friends, when a person has something to say, or thinks that she has, for a number of people to listen to the saying is always the greatest of kindnesses, and I always think that in a question of speaker and audience the vote of thanks should be given by the speaker to the hearers, and not by the hearers to the speaker. Let me, however, in all seriousness say to you that I believe that the more a platform can be broad and all-inclusive, the more serviceable it is to human welfare. (Applause.) While I congratulate myself on the invitation that brought me here, I congratulate you on having a pastor and officers who are willing to throw this pulpit open to all who are truly in earnest, and who they believe have something to say which may be of value to all. A broad platform is a public blessing, and your City Temple is a broad platform.

II. ON SOME DIFFICULTIES OF THE INNER LIFE

("Theosophical Review", May and June, 1899.)

EVERY one who sets himself in earnest to the living of the Inner Life encounters certain obstacles at the very beginning of the pathway thereto, obstacles which repeat themselves in the experience of each, having their basis in the common nature of men. To each wayfarer they seem new and peculiar to himself, and hence give rise to a feeling of personal discouragement which undermines the strength needed for their surmounting. If it were understood that they form part of the common experience of aspirants, that they are always encountered and constantly over-climbed, it may be that some cheer would be brought to the cast-down neophyte by the knowledge. The grasp of a hand in the darkness, the sound of a voice that says: "Fellow-traveler, I have trodden where you tread and the road is practicable" - these things bring help in the nighttime, and such a help-bringer this article would fain be.

One of these difficulties was put to me some time ago by a friend and fellow-wayfarer in connection with some counsel given as to the purification of the body. He did not in any way traverse the statement made, but said with much truth and insight that for most of us the difficulty lay more with the Inner Man than with his instruments; that for the most of us the bodies we had were quite sufficiently good, or, at the worst, needed a little tuning, but that there was a desperate need for the improvement of the man himself. For the lack of sweet music, the musician was more to blame than his instrument, and if he could be reached and improved his instrument might pass muster. It was capable of yielding much better tones than those produced from it at present, but those tones depended on the fingers that pressed the keys. Said my friend pithily and somewhat pathetically: "I can make my body do what I want; the difficulty is that I do not want."

Here is a difficulty that every serious aspirant feels. The improving of the man himself is the chief thing that is needed, and the obstacle of his weakness, his lack of will and of tenacity of purpose, is a far more obstructive one than can be placed in our way by the body. There are many methods known to all of us by which we can build up bodies of a better type if we want to do so, but it is the "wanting" in which we are deficient. We have the knowledge, we recognise the expediency of putting it into practice, but the impulse to do so is lacking. Our root-difficulty lies in our inner nature; it is inert, the wish to move is absent; it is not that the external obstacles are insurmountable, but that the man himself lies supine and has no mind to climb over them. This experience is being continually repeated by us; there seems to be a want of attractiveness in our ideal; it fails to draw us; we do not wish to realise it, even though we may have intellectually decided that its realisation is desirable. It stands before us like food before a man who is not hungry; it is certainly very good food and he may be glad of it tomorrow, but just now he has no craving for it, and prefers to lie basking in the sunshine rather than to get up and take possession of it.

The problem resolves itself into two questions: Why do I not want that which I see, as a rational being, is desirable, productive of happiness? What can I do to make myself want that which I know to be best for myself and for the world? The spiritual teacher who could answer these questions effectively would do a far greater service to many than one who is only reiterating constantly the abstract desirability of ideals that we all acknowledge, and the imperative nature of obligations that we all admit - and disregard. The machine is here, not wholly ill-made; who can place his finger on the lever, *and make it go*?

The first question must be answered by such an analysis of self-consciousness as may explain this puzzling duality, the not desiring that which we yet see to be desirable. We are wont to say that self-consciousness is a unit, and yet, when we turn our attention inwards, we see a bewildering multiplicity of "I's", and are stunned by the glamour of opposing voices, all coming apparently from ourselves. Now consciousness - and self-consciousness is only consciousness drawn into a definite centre which receives and sends out - *is* a unit, and if it appears in the outer world as many, it is not because it has lost its unity, but because it presents itself there through different media. We speak glibly of the vehicles of consciousness, but perhaps do not always bear in mind what is implied in the phrase. If a current from a galvanic battery be led through a series of several different materials, its appearance in the outer world will vary with each wire. In a platinum wire it may appear as light, in an iron one as heat, round a bar of soft iron as magnetic energy, led into a solution as a power that decomposes and recombines. One single energy is present, yet many modes of it appear, for the manifestation of life is always conditioned by its forms, and as consciousness works in the causal, mental, astral or physical body, the resulting "I" presents very different characteristics. According to the vehicle which, for the time being, it is vitalising, so will be the conscious "I". If it is working in the astral body it will be the "I" of the senses; if in the mental, it will be the "I" of the intellect. By illusion, blinded by the material that enwraps it, it identifies itself with the craving of the senses, the reasoning of the intellect, and cries, "I want", "I think". The nature which is developing the germs of bliss and knowledge is the eternal Man, and is the root of sensations and thoughts; but these sensations and thoughts themselves are only the transitory activities in his outer bodies, set up by the contact of his life with the outer life, of the Self with the not-Self. He makes temporary centres for his life in one or other of these bodies, lured by the touches from without that awaken his activity, and working in these he identifies himself with them. As his evolution proceeds, as he himself develops, he gradually discovers that these physical, astral, mental centres are his instruments, not himself; he sees them as parts of the "not-Self" that he has temporarily attracted into union with himself - as he might take up a pen or a chisel; he draws himself away from them, recognising and using them as the tools they are; knows himself to be life not form, bliss - not desire, knowledge - not thought; and then first is conscious of unity, then alone finds peace. While the consciousness identifies itself with forms, it appears to be multiple; when it identifies itself as life it stands forth as one.

The next important fact for us is that, as H.P.B. pointed out, consciousness, at the present stage of evolution, has its centre normally in the astral body. Consciousness learns to know by its capacity of sensation, the sensation which belongs to the astral body. We sensate; that is, we recognise contact with something which is not ourselves, something which arouses in us pleasure or pain, or the neutral point between. This life of sensation is the greater part of the life of the majority. For those below the average, this life of sensation is the whole life. For a few advanced beings this life of sensation is transcended. The vast majority occupy the various stages which stretch between this life of sensation and that which has transcended such sensation: those of mixed sensation and emotion and thought in diverse proportions, and of emotion and thought in diverse proportions. In the life that is wholly of sensation there is no multiplicity of "I's", and therefore no conflict; in the life that has transcended sensation there is an Inner Ruler, Immortal, and there is no conflict; but in all the ranges between there are manifold "I's" and among them conflict.

Let us consider this life of sensation as found in the savage of low development. There is an "I", passionate, craving, fierce, grasping, when aroused to activity. But there is no conflict, save with the world outside his physical body. With that he may war, but inner war he knows not. He does what he wants, without questionings beforehand or remorse afterwards; the actions of the body follow the promptings of desire, and the mind does not challenge, nor criticise, nor condemn. It merely pictures and records, storing up materials for future elaboration. Its evolution is forwarded by the demands made upon it by the "I" of sensations to exert its energies for the gratification of that imperious "I". It is driven into activity by these promptings of desire, and begins to work on its store of observations and remembrances, thus evolving a little reasoning faculty and planning beforehand for the gratification of its master. In this way it develops intelligence, but the intelligence is wholly subordinated to desire, moves under its orders, is the slave of passion. It shows no separate individuality, but is merely the willing tool of the tyrannous desire -"I".

Contest only begins when, after a long series of experiences, the Eternal Man has developed sufficient mind to review and balance up, during his life in the lower mental world between death and birth, the results of his earthly activities. He then marks off certain experiences as resulting in more pain than pleasure, and comes to the conclusion that he will do well to avoid their repetition; he regards them with repulsion and engraves that repulsion on his mental tablets, while he similarly engraves attraction as regards other experiences that have resulted in more pleasure than pain. When he returns to earth, he brings this record with him, as an inner tendency of his mind, and when the desire-"I" rushes towards an attractive object, recommencing a course of experiences that have led to suffering, he interposes a feeble protest, and another I-consciousness working as mind makes itself felt and heard as regarding these experiences with repulsion, and objecting to being dragged through them. The protest is so weak and the desire so strong that we can scarcely speak of a contest; the desire-"I", long enthroned, rushes over the weakly-protesting rebel, but when the pleasure is over and the painful results follow, the ignored rebel lifts his voice again in a querulous "I told you so", and this is the first sting of remorse. As life succeeds life the mind asserts itself more and more, and the contest between the desire-"I" and the thought-"I" grows fiercer and fiercer, and the agonised cry of the Christian mystic: "I find another law in my members warring against the law of my mind", is repeated in the experience of every evolving Man. The war grows hotter and hotter as, during the devachanic life, the decisions of the Man are more and more strongly impressed on the mind, appearing as innate ideas in the subsequent birth, and lending strength to the thought -"I", which, withdrawing itself from the passions and emotions, regards them as outside itself, and repudiates their claim to control it. But the long inheritance of the past is on the side of the monarch it would discrown, and bitter and many-fortuned is the war. Consciousness, in its outgoing activities, runs easily into the worn channels of the habits of many lives; on the other hand it is diverted by the efforts of the Man to take control and to turn it into the channels hewn out by his reflections. His will determines the line of the consciousness-forces working in his higher vehicles, while habit largely determines the direction of those working in the desire body. The will, guided by the clear-eyed intelligence, points to the lofty ideal that is seen as a fit object of attainment; the desire-nature does not want to reach it, is lethargic before it, seeing no beauty that it should desire it, nay, often repelled by the austere outlines of its grave and chastened dignity. "The difficulty is that I do not *want*." We do not want to do that which, in our higher moments, we have resolved to do. The lower

"I" is moved by the attraction of the moment rather than by the recorded results of the past that sway the higher, and the real difficulty is to make ourselves feel that the lethargic, or the clamorous, "I" of the lower nature is not the true I.

How is this difficulty to be overcome? How is it possible to make that which we know to be the higher to be the habitual self-conscious "I"?

Let no one be discouraged if here it be said that this change is a matter of growth, and cannot be accomplished in a moment. The human Self cannot, by a single effort, raise to manhood from childhood, any more than a body can change from infancy to maturity in a night. If the statement of the law of growth bring a sense of chill when we regard it as an obstacle in the way of our wish for sudden perfection, let us remember that the other side of the statement is that the growth is certain, that it cannot be ultimately prevented, and that if law refuses a miracle it on the other hand gives security. Moreover, we can quicken growth, we can afford the best possible conditions for it, and then rely on the law for our result. Let us then consider the means we can employ for hastening the growth we see to be needed, for transferring the activity of consciousness from the lower to the higher.

The first thing to realise is that the desire-nature is not our Self, but an instrument fashioned by the Self for its own using; and next that it is a most valuable instrument, and is merely being badly used. Desire, emotion, is the motive power in us, and stands ever between the thought and the action. Intellect sees, but it does not move, and a man without desires and emotions would be a mere spectator of life. The Self must have evolved some of its loftiest powers ere it can forego the use of the desires and emotions; for aspirants the question is how to use them instead of being used by them, how to discipline them, not how to destroy. We would fain "want" to reach the highest, since without this wanting we shall make no progress at all. We are held back by wanting to unite ourselves with objects transitory, mean and narrow; cannot we push ourselves forward by wanting to unite ourselves with the permanent, the noble and the wide? Thus musing, we see that what we need is to cultivate the emotions, and direct them in a way that will purify and ennoble the character. The basis of all emotions on the side of progress is love, and this is the power which we must cultivate. George Eliot well said: "The first condition of human goodness is something to love; the second, something to reverence". Now reverence is only love directed to a superior, and the aspirant should seek one more advanced than himself to whom he can direct his love and reverence. Happy the man who can find such a one when he seeks, for such finding gives him the most important condition for turning emotion from a retarding force into a lifting one, and for gaining the needed power to "want" that which he knows to be the best. We cannot love without seeking to please, and we cannot reverence without taking joy in the approval of the one we revere. Hence comes a constant stimulus to improve ourselves, to build up character, to purify the nature, to conquer all in us that is base, to strive after all that is worthy. We find ourselves quite spontaneously "wanting" to reach a high ideal, and the great motive power is sent along the channels hewn out for it by the mind. There is no way of utilising the desire-nature more certain and more effective than the making of such a tie, the reflection in the lower world of that perfect bond which links the disciple to the Master.

Another useful way of stimulating the desire-nature as a lifting force is to seek the company of any who are more advanced in the spiritual life than we are ourselves. It is not necessary that they should teach us orally, or indeed talk to us at all. Their very presence is a benediction, harmonising, raising, inspiring. To breathe their atmosphere, to be encircled by their magnetism, to be played on by their thoughts - these things ennoble us, unconsciously to ourselves. We value words too highly, and depreciate unduly the subtler silent forces of the Self, which, "sweetly and mightily ordering all things", create within the turbulent chaos of our personality the sure bases of peace and truth.

Less potent, but still sure, is the help that may be gained by reading any book which strikes a noble note of life, whether by lifting up a great ideal, or presenting an inspiring character for our study. Such books as the *Bhagavad Gita, The Voice of the Silence, Light on the Path, The Imitation of Christ*, are among the most powerful of such aids to the desire-nature. We are apt to read too exclusively for knowledge, and lose the moulding force that lofty thought on great ideals may exercise over our emotions. It is a useful habit to read every morning a few sentences from some such book as those named above, and to carry these sentences with us through the day, thus creating around us an atmosphere that is protective to ourselves and beneficial to all with whom we come into contact.

Another absolutely essential thing is daily meditation - a quiet half-hour in the morning, ere the turmoil of the day begins, during which we deliberately draw ourselves away from the lower nature, recognise it as an instrument and not our Self, centre ourselves in the highest consciousness we can dream, and feel it as our real Self. "That which is Being, Bliss and Knowledge, that am I. Life, Love and Light, that am I." For our essential nature is divine, and the effort to realise it helps its growth and manifestation. Pure, passionless, peaceful, it is "the Star that shines within", and that Star is our Self. We cannot yet steadily dwell in the Star, but as we try daily to rise to it, some gleam of its radiance illumines the illusory "I" made of the shadows amid which we live. To this ennobling and peace-giving contemplation of our divine destiny we may fitly rise by worshipping with the most fervent devotion of which we are capable - if we are fortunate enough to feel such devotion - the Father of the worlds and the Divine Man whom we reverence as Master. Resting on that Divine Man as the Helper and Lover of all who seek to rise - call Him Buddha, Christ, Shri Krishna, Master, what we will - we may dare to raise our eyes to the ONE from Whom we come, to Whom we go, and in the confidence of realised sonship murmur, "I and the Father are One", "I am That".

One of the most distressing of the difficulties which the aspirant has to face arises from the ebb and flow of his feelings, the changes in the emotional atmosphere through which he sees the external world as well as his own character with its powers and its weaknesses. He finds that his life consists of a series of ever-varying states of consciousness, of alternating conditions of thought and feeling. At one time he is vividly alive, at another quiescently dead; now he is cheerful, then morbid; now overflowing, then dry; now earnest, then indifferent; now devoted, then cold; now aspiring, then lethargic. He is constant only in his changeableness, persistent only in his variety. And the worst of it is that he is unable to trace these effects to any very definite causes; they "come and go, impermanent", and are as little predicable as the summer winds. Why was meditation easy, smooth, fruitful, yesterday? why is it hard, irregular, barren, today? Why should that noble idea have fired him with enthusiasm a week ago, yet leave him chill now? Why was he full of love and devotion but a few days since, but finds himself empty now, gazing at his ideal with cold, lack-lustre eyes? The facts are obvious, but the explanation escapes him; he seems to be at the mercy of chance, to have slipped out of the realm of law.

It is this very uncertainty which gives the poignancy to his distress. The understood is always the manageable, and when we have traced an effect to its cause we have gone far on the way to its control. All our keenest sufferings have in them this constituent of uncertainty; we are helpless because we are ignorant. It is the uncertainty of our emotional moods that terrifies us, for we cannot guard against that which we are unable to foresee. How then may we reach a place where these moods shall not plague us, a rock on which we can stand while the waves surge around us?

The first step towards the place of balance is taken when we recognise the fact - though the statement of it may sound a little brutal - that our moods do not matter. There is no constant relation between our progress and our feelings; we are not necessarily advancing when the flow of emotion rejoices us, nor retrograding when its ebb distresses us. These changing moods are among the lessons that life brings to us, that we may learn to distinguish between the Self and the not-Self, and to realise ourselves as the Self. The Self changes not, and that which changes is not our Self, but is part of the transitory surroundings in which the Self is clothed and amid which it moves. This wave that sweeps over us is not the Self, but is only a passing manifestation of the not-Self. "Let it toss and swirl and foam, it is not I." Let consciousness realise this, if only for a moment, and the force of the wave is spent, and the firm rock is felt under the feet. Withdrawing from the emotion, we no longer feel it as a part of ourselves, and thus ceasing to pour our life into it as a self-expression, we break off the connection which enabled it to become a channel of pain. This withdrawal of consciousness may be much facilitated if, in our quiet times, we try to understand and to assign to their true causes these distressing emotional alternations. We shall thus at least get rid of some of the helplessness and perplexity which, as we have already seen, are due to ignorance.

These alternations of happiness and depression are primarily manifestations of that law of periodicity, or law of rhythm, which guides the universe. Night and day alternate in the physical life of man as do happiness and depression in his emotional life. As the ebb and flow in the ocean, so are the ebb and flow in human feelings. There are tides in the human heart as in the affairs of men and as in the sea. Joy follows sorrow and sorrow follows joy, as surely as death follows birth and birth death. That this is so is not only a theory of a law, but it is also a fact to which witness is borne by all who have gained experience in the spiritual life. In the famous *Imitation of Christ* it is said that comfort and sorrow thus alternate, and "this is nothing new nor strange unto them that have experience in the way of God; for the great saints and ancient prophets had oftentimes experience of such kind of vicissitudes. ...If great saints were so dealt with, we that are weak and poor ought not to despair if we be sometimes hot and sometimes cold. ... I never found any so religious and devout, that he had not sometimes a withdrawing of grace or felt not some decrease of zeal" (Bk. II. ix. 4, 5, 7.). This alternation of states being recognised as the result of a general law, a special manifestation of a universal principle, it becomes possible for us to utilise this knowledge both as a warning and an encouragement. We may be passing through a period of great spiritual illumination, when all seems to be easy of accomplishment, when the glow of devotion sheds its glory over life, and when the peace of sure insight is ours. Such a condition is often one of considerable danger, its very happiness lulling us into a careless security, and forcing into growth any remaining germs of the lower nature. At such moments the recalling of past periods of gloom is often useful, so that happiness may not become elation, nor enjoyment lead to attachment to pleasure; balancing the present joy by the memory of past trouble and the calm prevision of trouble yet to come, we reach equilibrium and find a middle point of rest; we can then gain all the advantages that accrue from seizing a favourable opportunity for progress without risking a slip backwards from premature triumph. When the night comes down and all the life has ebbed away, when we find ourselves cold and indifferent, caring for nothing that had erst attracted us, then, knowing the law, we can quietly say: "This also will pass in its turn, light and life must come back, and the old love will again glow warmly forth." We refuse to be unduly depressed in the gloom, as we refused to be unduly elated in the light; we balance one experience against the other, removing the thorn of present pain by the memory of past joy and the foretaste of joy in the future; we learn in happiness to remember sorrow and in sorrow to remember happiness, till neither the one nor the other can shake the steady foothold of the soul. Thus we begin to rise above the lower stages of consciousness in which we are flung from one extreme to the other, and to gain the equilibrium which is called yoga. Thus the existence of the law becomes to us not a theory but a conviction, and we gradually learn something of the peace of the Self.

It may be well also for us to realise that the way in which we face and live through this trial of inner darkness and deadness is one of the surest tests of spiritual evolution. "What worldly man is there that would not willingly receive spiritual joy and comfort if he could always have it? For spiritual comforts exceed all the delights of the world and the pleasures of the flesh. ... But no man can always enjoy these divine comforts according to his desire; for the time of trial is never far away. ... Are not all those to be called mercenary who are ever seeking consolations? ... Where shall one be found who is willing to serve God for nought? Rarely is anyone found so spiritual as to have suffered the loss of all things" (Bk. II. x. 1; xi. 3, 4.). The subtle germs of selfishness persist far on into the life of discipleship, though they then ape in their growth the semblance of virtues, and hide the serpent of desire under the fair blossom of beneficence or of devotion. Few indeed are they who serve for nothing, who have eradicated the root of desire, and have not merely cut off the branches that spread above ground. Many a one who has tasted the subtle joys of spiritual experience finds therein his reward for the grosser delights he has renounced, and when the keen ordeal of spiritual darkness bars his way, and he has to enter into that darkness un-befriended and apparently alone, then he learns by the bitter and humiliating lesson of disillusion that he has been serving his ideal for wages and not for love. Well for us if we can be glad in the darkness as well as in the light, by the sure faith in - though not yet by the vision of - that Flame which burns evermore within, THAT from the light of which we can never be separated, for it is in truth our very Self. Bankrupt in Time must we be ere ours is the wealth of the eternal, and only when the living have abandoned us does the Vision of Life appear.

Another difficulty that sorely bewilders and distresses the aspirant is the unbidden presence of thoughts and desires that are incongruous with his life and aims. When he would fain contemplate the Holy, the presence of the unholy thrusts itself upon him; when he would see the radiant face of the Divine Man, the mask of the satyr leers at him in its stead. Whence these thronging forms of evil that crowd round him? whence these mutterings and whisperings as of devils in his ear? They fill him with shuddering repulsion, yet they seem to be his; can he really be the father of this foul swarm?

Once again an understanding of the cause at work may rob the effect of its sharp poison-tooth, and deliver us from the impotence due to ignorance. It is a commonplace of theosophical teaching that life embodies itself in forms, and that the life-energy which comes forth from that aspect of the Self which is knowledge moulds the matter of the mental plane into thought-forms. The vibrations that affect the mental body determine the materials that are built into its composition, and these materials are slowly changed in accordance with the changes in the vibrations sent forth. If the consciousness cease to work in a particular way, the materials which answered to those previous workings gradually lose their activity, finally becoming effete matter and being shaken out of the mental body. A considerable number of stages, however, intervene between the full activity of the matter constantly answering to mental impulses and its final deadness when ready for expulsion. Until the last stage is reached it is capable of being thrown into renewed activity by mental impulses either from within or from without, and long after the man has ceased to energise it, having outgrown the stage it represents, it may be thrown into active vibration, made to start up as a living thought, by a wholly external influence. For example a man has succeeded in purifying his thoughts from sensuality, and his mind no longer generates impure ideas nor takes pleasures in contemplating impure images. The coarse matter, which in the mental and astral bodies vibrates under such impulses, is no longer being vivified by him, and the thought-forms erst created by him are dying or dead. But he meets some one in whom these things are active, and the vibrations sent out by him revivify the dying thought-forms, lending them a temporary artificial life; they start up as the aspirant's own thoughts, presenting themselves as the children of his mind, and he knows not that they are but corpses from his past, re-animated by the evil magic of impure propinquity. The very contrast they afford to his purified mind adds to the harassing torture of their presence, as though a dead body were fettered to a living man. But when he learns their true nature, they lose their power to torment. He can look at them calmly as remnants of his past, so that they cease to be poisoners of his present. He knows that the life in them is an alien one and is not drawn from him, and he can "wait with the patience of confidence for the hour when they shall affect" him "no longer".

Sometimes in the case of a person who is making rapid progress, this temporary revivification is caused deliberately by those who are seeking to retard evolution, those who set themselves against the Good Law. They may send a thought-force calculated to stir the dying ghosts into weird activity, with the set purpose of causing distress, even when the aspirant has passed beyond the reach of temptation along these lines. Once again the difficulty ceases when the thoughts are known to draw their energy from outside and not from inside, when the man can calmly say to the surging crowd of impish tormentors: "You are not mine, you are no part of me, your life is not drawn from my thought. Ere long you will be dead beyond possibility of resurrection, and meanwhile you are but phantoms, shades that were once my foes."

Another fruitful source of trouble is the great magician Time, past-master of illusion. He imposes on us a sense of hurry, of unrest, by masking the oneness of our life with the veils of births and deaths. The aspirant cries out eagerly: "How much can I do, what progress can I make, during my present life?" There is no such thing as a "present life"; there is but one life - past and future, with the everchanging moment that is their meeting-place; on one side of it we see the past, on the other side the future, and it is itself as invisible as the little piece of ground on which we stand. There is but one life, without beginning and without ending, the ageless, timeless life, and our arbitrary divisions of it by the ever-recurring incidents of births and deaths delude us and ensnare. These are some of the traps set for the Self by the lower nature, which would fain keep its hold on the winged Immortal that is straying through its miry paths. This bird of paradise is so fair a thing as its plumes begin to grow, that all the powers of nature fall to loving it, and set snares to hold it prisoner; and of all the snares the illusion of Time is the most subtle.

When a vision of truth has come late in a physical life, this discouragement as to time is apt to be most keenly felt. "I am too old to begin; if I had only known this in youth," is the cry. Yet truly the path is one, as the life is one, and all the path must be trodden in the life; what matters it then whether one stage of the path be trodden or not during a particular part of a physical life? If A and B are both going to catch their first glimpse of the Reality two years hence, what matters it that A will then be seventy years of age while B will be a lad of twenty? A will return and begin anew his work on earth when B is ageing, and each will pass many times through the childhood, youth and old age of the body, while traveling along the higher stages of the path of life. The old man who "late in life", as we say, begins to learn the truths of the Ancient Wisdom, instead of lamenting over his age and saying: "How little can I do in the short time that remains to me," should say: "How good a foundation I can lay for my next incarnation, thanks to this learning of the truth." We are not slaves of Time, save as we bow to his imperious tyranny, and let him bind over our eyes his bandages of birth and death. We are always ourselves, and can pace steadfastly onwards through the changing lights and shadows cast by his magic lantern on the life he cannot age. Why are the Gods figured as ever-young, save to remind us that the true life lives untouched by Time? We borrow some of the strength and calm of Eternity when we try to live in it, escaping from the meshes of the great Enchanter.

Many another difficulty will stretch itself across the upward path as the aspirant essays to tread it, but a resolute will and a devoted heart, lighted by knowledge, will conquer all in the end and will reach the Supreme Goal. To rest on the Law is one of the secrets of peace, to trust it utterly at all times, not least when the gloom descends. No soul that aspires can ever fail to rise; no heart that loves can ever be abandoned. Difficulties exist only that in overcoming them we may grow strong, and they only who have suffered are able to save.

III. THE PLACE OF PEACE

THE rush, the turmoil, the hurry of modern life are in everybody's mouth as a matter of complaint. "I have no time" is the commonest of excuses. Reviews serve for books leading articles for political treatises; lectures for investigation. More and more the attention of men and women is fastened on the superficial things of life; small prizes of business success, petty crowns of social supremacy, momentary notoriety in the world of politics or of letters for these things men and women toil, intrigue and strive. Their work must show immediate results, else it is regarded as failure; the winning-post must always be in sight, to be passed by a swift brief effort with the roar of the applauding crowd hailing the winner. The solid reputation built up by years of strenuous work; the patient toil that labours for a lifetime in a field wherein the harvest can only ripen long after the sower has passed out of sight; the deliberate choice of a lofty ideal, too high to attract the average man, too great to be compassed in a lifetime - all these things are passed by with a shrug of good-natured contempt or a scowl of suspicion. The spirit of the age is summed up by the words of the caustic Chinese sage of yore: "He looks at an egg, and expects to hear it crow." Nature is too slow for us, and we forget that what we gain in speed we lose in depth.

But there are some in whose eyes this whirling dance of gnats in the sunlight is not the be-all and end-all of human life. Some in whose hearts a whisper sometimes sounds softly, saying that all the seeming clash and rush is but as the struggle of shadows thrown upon a screen; that social success, business triumph, public admiration are but trivial things at best, bubbles floating down a tossing streamlet, and unworthy of the rivalries, the jealousies, the bitternesses their chase engenders. Has life no secret that does not lie on the surface? no problem that is not solved in the stating? no treasury that is not scattered on the highway?

An answer may be found without straying beyond the experience of every man and woman, and that answer hides within it a suggestion of the deeper truth that underlies it. After a week or a month of hurried town-life, of small excitements, of striving for the little triumphs of social life, of the eagerness of petty hopes, the pain of petty disappointments, of the friction arising from the jarring of our selfish selves with other selves equally selfish; after this, if we go far away from this hum and buzz of life into silent mountain solitudes where are sounding only the natural harmonies that seem to blend with rather than to break the silence - the rushing of the waterfall swollen by last night's rain, the rustle of the leaves under the timid feet of the hare, the whisper of the stream to the water-hen as she slips out of the reeds, the murmur of the eddy where it laps against the pebbles on the bank, the hum of the insects as they brush through the tangle of the grasses, the suck of the fish as they hang in the pool beneath the shade; there, where the mind sinks into a calm, soothed by the touch of Nature far from man, what aspect have the follies, the exasperations, of the social whirl of work and play, seen through that atmosphere surcharged with peace? What does it matter if in some small strife we failed or we succeeded? What does it matter that we were slighted by one, praised, by another? We regain perspective by our distance from the whirlpool, by our isolation from its tossing waters, and we see how small a part these outer things should play in the true life of man.

So distance in time as well as distance in space gives balanced judgment on the goods and ills of life. We look back, after ten years have slipped away, at the trials, the joys, the hopes, the disappointments of the time that then was, and we marvel why we spent so much of our life-energy on things so little worth. Even life's sharpest pains seems strangely unreal thus contemplated by a personality that has greatly changed. Our whole life was bound up in the life of another, and all of worth that it held for us seemed to dwell in the one beloved. We thought that our life was laid waste, our heart broken, when that one trust was betrayed. But as time went on the wound healed and new flowers sprang up along our pathway, till today we can look back without a quiver on an agony that then well-nigh shattered life. Or we broke with a friend for a bitter word; how foolish seem our anger and excitement, looking back over the ten years' gulf. Or we were madly delighted with a hardly-won success; how trivial it looks, and how exaggerated our triumph, when we see it now in due proportion in the picture of our life; then it filled our sky, now it is but a point.

But our philosophic calm, as we contemplate the victories and defeats of our past across the interval of space or time, suffers an ignominious breach when we return to our daily life and find it not. All the old trivialities, in new dresses, engross us; old joys and sorrows, with new faces, seize us. "The tumultuous senses and organs hurry away by force the heart." And so once more we begin to wear out our lives by petty cares, petty disputes, petty longings, petty disappointments.

Must this be always so? Since we must live in the world and play our part in its drama of life, must we be at the mercy of all these passing objects? Or, though we must dwell among them in place and be surrounded with them in time, can we find the Place of Peace, as though we were far away? We can, and this is the truth that underlies the superficial answer we have already found.

Man is an Immortal Being, clad in a garb of flesh, which is vivified and moved by desires and passions, and which he links to himself by a thread of his immortal nature. This thread is the mind, and this mind, unsubdued and inconstant, wanders out among the things of earth, is moved by passions and desires, hopes and fears, longs to taste all cups of sense-delights, is dazzled and deafened by the radiance and the tumult of its surroundings. And thus, as Arjuna complained, the "mind is full of agitation, turbulent, strong, and obstinate". Above this whirling mind, serene and passionless witness, dwells the True Self, the Spiritual Ego of man. Below there may be storm, but above there is calm, and there is the Place of Peace. For that Self is eternal, and what to it are the things of time, save as they bring experience, the knowledge of good and evil? So often, dwelling in its house of clay. it has known birth and death, gains and losses, joys and griefs, pleasures and pains, that it sees them all pass by as a moving phantasmagoria, and no ripple ruffles its passionless serenity. Does agony affect its outer case, it is but a notice that harmony has been broken, and the pain is welcome as pointing to the failure and as bearing the lesson of avoidance of that whence it sprang. For the True Self has to conquer the material plane, to purify and sublimate it, and only by suffering can it learn how to perform its work.

Now the secret of reaching that Place of Peace lies in our learning to identify our consciousness with the True, instead of with the apparent, Self. We identify ourselves with our minds, our brain minds, active in our bodies. We identify ourselves with our passions and desires, and say *we* hope or *we* fear. We identify ourselves with our bodies, the mere machinery wherewith we affect the material world. And so, when all these parts of our nature are moved by contact with external things and feel the whirl of the material life around them, *we* also in consciousness are affected, and "the uncontrolled heart, following the dictates of the moving passions, snatcheth away" our "spiritual knowledge, as the storm the bark upon the raging ocean". Thence excitement, loss of balance, irritability, injured feelings, resentments, follies, pain - all that is most separated from peace and calm and strength.

The way to begin to tread the Path that leads to the Place of Peace is to endeavour to identify our consciousness with the True Self, to see as it sees, to judge as it judges. We cannot do it - that goes without saying - but we can begin to try. And the means are disengagement from the objects of the senses, carelessness as to results, and meditation, ever renewed, on the True Self. Let us consider each of these means.

The first of these can be gained only by a constant and wise self-discipline. We can cultivate indifference to small discomforts, to pleasures of the table, to physical enjoyments, bearing with good-humoured tolerance outward things as they come, neither shunning nor courting small pleasures or pains. Gradually, without growing morbid or self-conscious, we shall become frankly indifferent, so that small troubles that upset people continually, in daily life will pass unnoticed. And this will leave us free to help our neighbours, whom they do disturb, by shielding them unobtrusively, and so smoothing life's pathway for feet tenderer than our own. In learning this, moderation is the keynote. "This divine discipline, Arjuna, is not to be attained by the man who eateth more than enough or too little, nor by him who hath a habit of sleeping much, nor by him who is given to over-watching. The meditation which destroyeth pain is produced in him who is moderate in eating and in recreation, of moderate exertion in his actions, and regulated in sleeping and waking." The body is not to be shattered: it is to be trained.

The second of these methods is "carelessness as to results". This does not mean that we are not to notice the result of our actions in order to learn from them how to guide our steps. We gain experience by such study of results, and so learn Wisdom. But it does mean that when an action has been done with our best judgment and strength and with pure intent, then we should let it go, metaphorically, and feel no anxiety about its results. The action done is beyond recall, and we gain nothing by worry and by anxiety. When its results appear, we note them for instruction, but we neither rejoice nor mourn over them. Remorse or jubilation takes away our attention from, and weakens us in, the performance of our *present* duty, and there is no time for either. Suppose the results are evil, the wise man says: "I made a mistake, and must avoid a similar blunder in future; but remorse will only weaken my present usefulness and will not lessen the results of my mistaken action. So instead of wasting time in remorse, I will set to work to do better." The value of thus separating oneself from results lies in the calmness of mind thus obtained and the concentration brought to bear on each action. "Whoever in acting dedicates his actions to the Supreme Spirit [the One Self] and puts aside all selfish interest in their result, is untouched by sin, even as the leaf of the lotus is unaffected by the waters. The truly devoted, for the purification of the heart, perform actions with their bodies, their minds, their understanding, and their senses; putting away all self-interest. The man who is devoted and not attached to the fruit of his actions obtains tranquility; whilst he who through desire has attachment for the fruit of action is bound down thereby."

The third method, meditation, is the most efficacious and the most difficult. It consists of a constant endeavour to realise one's identity with one's True Self, and to become self-conscious here as It. "To whatsoever object the inconstant mind goeth out he should subdue it, bring it back, and place it upon the Spirit." It is a work of a lifetime, but it will bring us to the Place of Peace. The effort needs to be continually renewed, patiently persisted in. It may be aided by fixing on definite hours, at which, for a few moments, we may withdraw ourselves like the turtle into its shell, and remember that we are not transitory but eternal, and that passing incidents can affect us not at all. With the gradual growth of this power of remaining "in the Self" comes not only Peace but Wisdom, for absence of personal desires, and recognition of our immortal nature, leave us free to judge all things without bias and without prejudice. "This tranquil state attained, therefrom shall soon result a separation from all troubles; and his mind being thus at ease, fixed upon one object, it embraceth wisdom from all sides. The man whose heart and mind are not at rest is without wisdom." Thus "being possessed of patience, he by degrees finds rest," and "supreme bliss surely cometh to the sage whose mind is thus at peace; whose passions and desires are thus subdued; who is thus in the True Self and free from sin."

This is the three-fold Path that leads to the Place of Peace, to dwell wherein ever is to have conquered Time and Death. The "path winds steeply uphill all the way," but the pinions of the Dove of Peace fan the wearied brow of the pilgrim, and at last, at last, he finds calm that naught can ruffle.

IV. DEVOTION AND THE SPIRITUAL LIFE

The soul cannot be gained by knowledge, nor by understanding, nor by manifold science nor by devotion, nor by knowledge which is unwedded to devotion. - "Mundakopanishad"; iii. II. 3, 4.

THAT, which is from the oldest Scripture of our race, is really the motto on which I am going to speak to you tonight, and I am going to try to trace for you the famous two paths of the finding of the Self - the paths which may be trodden separately, but which for the perfection of Humanity must finally blend into one. The one path is the Path of Knowledge, and it leads to Liberation; the other path is the Path of Devotion, and that, joined to right knowledge, leads to that eternity of Service which it is the greatest glory of man to attain.

But before I take up these two paths, there is just a word or two to be said on a matter which may clear the way, in order that we may definitely understand the roads along which we are to travel in thought tonight. Altogether apart, as we may say, from these Paths of Knowledge and Devotion which lead severally to Liberation and to the Great Renunciation, there are the paths which are followed by men who have not yet taken on themselves the duty of discipleship, but who are men good and earnest in their lives, and doing good work in the world - those are the paths of action, the paths where Karma is generated, and good action and good desire generate good Karma. But Karma ever brings a man back to rebirth. Myriads of years may intervene - nay, in some cases millions of years may intervene - but still the end of work is rebirth, still the end of desire is to "pass from death to death". Works which are good and useful to humanity gain their reward. Putting it in Christian phrase, we should say they gain Heaven; putting it in Hindu phrase, they gain Svarga; putting it in Theosophic parlance, they gain Devachan; and beyond the temporary Devachan, or Svarga, or Heaven, there is a possibility of work done so well with a view always to its results, that you may have that Heaven of the kosmic Devas which you read of in the Hindu writings, where one who has passed beyond ordinary humanity, and has won by effort these higher seats in Heaven, may reign throughout the course of a Manvantara, and may direct the kosmic processes of the worlds. But whatever comes of work finds its end. Neither Liberation nor the Great Renunciation can close the path of the man who works with a view to results; for nature is ever just, and what a man pays for he will obtain. If he works for the sake of reward, the reward will come to him from the unerring Justice that guides the worlds. So good deeds become exhausted; so the result of good Karma comes to an end; and, whether it be in this or in any other world, the end is sure, and back to rebirth must come the Ego who has worked for reward and whose reward at length is exhausted. But, says one of those great Scriptures, with a quotation from which began, there is a time when the study of works and of the worlds of works is exhausted. Then comes the time whereof it is written:

Let the Brahman, after he has examined all these worlds that are gained by works, acquire freedom from all desire. Nothing that is eternal can be gained by what is not eternal. ["Mundakopanishad", i. II. 12.]

When all desire is exhausted then the Path of Knowledge or of Devotion may be entered on.

Let us take the Path of Knowledge. Knowledge of what? Not the learning of the world; not those many sciences which may be gained by the intellect alone; not that long course of study laid down in the Indian books; nor even the mastery of the sixty-three sciences into which all human learning is divided. When we speak of the Path of Knowledge we mean more than intellectual learning; we mean the path which leads to spiritual knowledge, that is, to the knowledge of the ONE, of the SELF, the seeking, the finding Brahman, for by knowledge He may be found, by knowledge He may be entered into. And there are some who choose the Path of Knowledge unallied to Devotion, and who tread that Path ever, life after life, until the right to Liberation has been gained. Let us try to realise the steps of such a path. First, there must be the recognition of the ONE on whom all worlds are built, of the ONE, the SELF eternal and unchanging that throws out universes, as a spider throws out its web, and draws them in again [Ibid. i, I. 7] - the one Existence which is at the root of all, supreme, incognisable by human thought: knowledge recognises the One without a second. The next stage in that knowledge, in recognising the One, is the realisation that all things that take on separate forms must have an end, that in very truth there is no separateness in the universe, but only appearance of separation; the One without a second who alone exists, who is the One and the only Reality, THAT is realised as the Self of each, as the one Life of which all forms are only transient manifestations. Thus the recognition of the absence of separateness must be a step on this Path of Knowledge. Until absence of separateness is realised the soul passes from death to death ["Kathopanishad", Valli iv. 10] But more than this realisation of nonseparateness is needed. There is the distinct and the deliberate effort to realise that the Self of the Universe is the Self of man dwelling in the heart, that that Self, as we saw a few weeks ago, clothes itself in sheath after sheath for the purpose of gathering experience, and on the Path of Knowledge sheath after sheath is stripped from off the Self, until the very Self of all is found. For this, knowledge is necessary. First the knowledge of the existence of the sheaths, then the knowledge of the Self working within the sheaths, then the realisation that those sheaths can be laid aside one after another, that the senses can be stilled and silenced, that the Self can withdraw itself from the sheath of the senses until they no longer function save by the will, and the voice of the Self may be heard without the intrusion of the outer world.

And then the sheath of the mind - that also we considered in our study - the sheath of the mind in which the Self works in the internal world of concepts and of ideas; that also is recognised as external to the Soul, and the Soul casts that aside as it casts off the sheath of the senses. And then realising that these sheaths are not itself, realising that the Self is behind and within these, this knowledge of nonseparateness becomes a practical realisation, not only intellectually admitted, but practically realised in life. And this must inevitably lead to renunciation. But, mark you, it is the renunciation essentially of the reason, it is the renunciation which draws itself away from the objects of the senses and the objects of the mind by a deliberate retiring within the Self, and this exclusion of the outer and of the inner world is most easily followed by retiring from the haunts of men, most easily accomplished by isolation from the great Brotherhood of Humanity, most easily won if the Self, that thus seeks, separates itself from all others that are illusory, and in that quietude of an external world realises the inner isolation.

Then, supposing that that absolute exclusion be not accepted, there may still be renunciation - renunciation by knowledge, renunciation by the deliberate will that no Karma shall be generated, renunciation by the knowledge that if there be no desire then no chains of Karma are made which draw the Self back to rebirth. And, mark you - for I want you to keep this in mind, and you will see why presently - it is essentially the renunciation of the man who knows that while he desires he is bound to the wheel of births and of deaths, and that no liberation is possible for him, save as these bonds of the heart are broken. Then, realising this, if he is still compelled to act, he will act without desire; if he is compelled to live amongst men he will do his work careless of the results that flow therefrom. Renunciation which is complete, but renunciation for the sake of escape, renunciation in order that he may gain his freedom and escape from the burden of the world. And so once more it is written that:

When they have reached the Self [that is, when they have realised Brahman] the Sages become satisfied through knowledge; they are conscious of their Self, their passions have passed away and they are tranquil. The wise having reached Him who is omnipresent everywhere, and devoted to the Self, enter into Him wholly (Mundakopanishad; iii.II, 5).

That, then, is the goal of this Path of Knowledge; a lofty state, a state supremely great and mighty, where a Soul serene in its own strength, calm in its own wisdom, has stilled every impulse of the senses, is absolutely master over every movement of the mind, dwelling within the nine-gate city of its abode, neither acting nor causing to act. But a state of isolation, though a state great in its power, in its wisdom, great in its absolute detachment from all that is transitory, and ready to enter into Brahman. And into Brahman such a Soul enters and gains its liberation, to remain in that union for ages after ages - a time that no human years may reckon, that no human thought can span - having reached what the Hindu calls Moksha, in perfect unity with the One and with the All, coming out from that union only when the great Manvantara redawns, and out of that state of liberation life again passes into all manifested forms.

Turn from the Path of Knowledge to the Path of Devotion. Here right knowledge may not be ignored. Right knowledge - for that is needed, otherwise the world cannot well be served; right knowledge, because the union must be the goal, although a union differing somewhat from that which is gained by knowledge; right knowledge, because if right knowledge be absent then even love may go astray in its desire of service, and may injure where it fain would help. So that we must not have devotion unwedded to knowledge, for the knowledge is needed for the perfect service, and perfect service is the essence of the life of the devotee. But the goal of the Path of Devotion is conscious union with the supreme Self which is recognised as manifesting through all other selves, and those other selves are never left out of thought until the union of all selves is found in the ONE. For in this Path of Devotion love is the impulse, love that is ever seeking to give itself to those above it that it may gain strength for service, and to those below in order that the service may be done. So that the true devotee has his face turned upward to those that are higher than himself, that so he may gain from them spiritual force, spiritual strength, spiritual energy, but not for himself, not that he may be liberated; for he desires no liberation till all share his freedom; not in order that he may gain, for he desires no gain, save as he may give; not in order that he may keep; but in order that he may be a channel of blessing to others. So that on the Path of Devotion the Soul is ever turned to the light above, not that itself may be enlightened, not that itself may shine, but that it may serve as focus and channel for that light, to pass it on to those who are in darkness; and its only longing for the light that is above is in order that it may pass it onward to those that are below.

That then is the first, the supreme characteristic of the man who would follow the Path of Devotion. He must begin in love, as in love he has to find his end. In order that this may be, he must recognise the spiritual side of nature; he is not to be alone. It is not enough that he should recognise the Self, that he should recognise the One of whom all forms are but passing manifestations; he must recognise those passing manifestations in order that he may be equipped for service. So that he will begin by recognising that out of the One Eternal Source of Life -the SELF, that is, of all- there come out the various sparks that are spiritual Intelligences in every grade of evolution: some, mighty spiritual Intelligences that in past Manvantaras have gained Their victory, and Who come out of the Eternal Fire ready to be Lights in the world. Those he will recognise as the supreme embodiments of the Spiritual Life, Those he will recognise as the foundations of the manifested Universe, Those he will see far, far above himself; for the evolution behind Them has carried them onwards through many Nirvanas to the place at which They emerge for the manifestations of our own Universe, and he will give Them -the name matters not- but some name that will carry with it Their supreme spiritual greatness, call Them Gods, or call Them what you will, so that you realise in Them the supreme embodiments of Spiritual Life, towards Whom the Universe is tending, and in union with Whom it finds itself on the threshold of the One.

Those then first he will recognise. And then stretching downwards from Them in countless hierarchies grade after grade of Spiritual Intelligences in all the manifested forms of Life in the spiritual side of the Universe, downwards continually through the mighty Ones Whom we speak of as Builders of the worlds, Whom we speak of as Planetary Spirits, Whom we speak of as the Lords of Wisdom, downwards from them to those great Ones embodied in the highest forms of Humanity that we name the Masters, and Who reveal to us the Divine Light which is beyond themselves; and then downwards still in lower and lower grades of spiritual entities, until the whole Universe to him is full of these living forms of Light and of Life, recognised as one mighty Brotherhood of whom the embodied selves of men form part. Therefore his path is in the realisation of Brotherhood, and not in the effort for isolation. It is not liberation that he asks for himself, it is power of service that he claims from the Highest, in order that he may help those who have not yet reached the place where he stands himself. And therefore I said that the Path of Devotion begins in love and ends in love; begins in love to every sentient creature around us and ends in love to the Highest, the highest that our thought may conceive. And so recognising this Brotherhood of Helpers he would fain be a conscious helper with them all - taking his share in the burden of the Universe, bearing his part of the common burden, and ever desiring more strength in order that that strength may be used in the common helping, ever desiring more wisdom in order that that wisdom may be used in the enlightening of the ignorance around. He then will not be isolated, nor will he be content with the recognition of the Self within. On the contrary, he will ever be seeking to serve, and he will recognise the selves without as well as the Self within, and he will renounce. He too realises renunciation, as the man on the Path of Knowledge realises it; but his renunciation is of a different kind. It is not the stern renunciation of knowledge, which says: "I will not bind myself by attachment to transitory things, because they will bring me back to birth"; it is the joyous renunciation of one who sees beyond him the mighty Helpers of man, and who, desiring to serve Them, cannot care for the things that hold him back, and offers all to Them - not sternly, in order that he may be free, but full of joy, in order that he may give everything to Them; not cutting asunder desire with an axe as you might cut the chain that binds you, but burning up desire in the fire of devotion, because that fire burns up everything which is not one with its heat and with its flame. And so he is free from Karma, free because he desires nothing save to serve, save to help, save to reach onward to union with his Lord, and outward to union with men. And this service will indeed detach him from the senses, it will detach him from the mind; but the very detachment will be that he may serve better. For this is the lesson which is learnt by the devotee: that while it is his duty to act, because without action the world could not go on, while it is his duty to act in the very spot in which he finds himself, because there lies the duty for which he has come to birth, and which he therefore should perfectly discharge, he yet seeks no fruit of action. Realising that he is here for action, he will act: but it is not so much *himself*; his thought will ever be fixed on the object of service and of love, and the senses, as Shri Krishna said, the senses and the mind will move to their appropriate objects, while he himself remains unfettered within.

And then realise the gain. If we work our very best, if we work our very wisest, if for love's sake we give our best thought and our best effort to the service of man, then the very moment the act is accomplished we have no desire as to the result, save that it shall be as the Wiser Ones above us will and guide. And if thus we cut ourselves free from the action, if, having done our share in it, we leave to Them an unfettered field where all great spiritual energies may play, unbarred and untouched by our blindness and by our weakness; and if this spirit of devotion be within us, if we give of our *very* best to the service of men, then, if leaving the act to Those who guide the destinies of the world we take no further interest in the result, we leave Them to make our weakness perfect by Their strength, we leave Them to correct our blunders by Their wisdom, our errors by Their righteousness; we leave all to Them, and the very blunder that we make loses most of its power for mischief; and though we shall reap pain for the mistake that we may have made, the issue will be right, for the desire was to serve and not to blunder. And if we do not mix our own personality with it, if we leave the field clear for Them to work, then even out of our blunder will come the issue of success, and the failure that was a failure of the intellect only will give way before the mightier forces of the Spirit which is moved by love.

And then all anxiety disappears. The Life which is at peace within in this devotion has no anxiety in the outer world; it does its best, and if it blunders it knows that pain will teach it of its blunder, and it is glad to take the pain which teaches wisdom and so makes it more fit to be co-worker with the great Souls who are the workers of the world. The pain then for the blunder causes no distress; the pain for the error is taken only as lesson, and, taken thus, cannot ruffle the Soul's serenity which wills only to learn right and to do right, and cares not what price it pays if it become better servant of man and of man's great Teachers. And so doing the best and leaving the results, we find that what we call devotion is really an attitude of the Soul, it is the attitude of love, the attainment of peace, which having its face turned ever to the light of Those within it, is always ready for service, and by Their light finds fresh opportunities of service day by day.

But you may say: To whom is this devotion paid? The root of this devotion must be found by each of us in the place in which we are, to those who are living around us in the daily life we lead. No talk of devotion is worth anything if it does not show itself in the life of love, and that life of love must begin where love will be helpful to the nearest. And the true devotee is one who, just because he has no thought nor care for self, has all thought and all care for those who are around him, and he is able, out of the great peace of his own selflessness, to find room for all the troubles and strifes of his fellow-men. And so the life of devotion will begin in the home, in the perfect discharge of all home duties, in all the brightness that can be brought into the home life, in the bearing of all the home burdens that the devotee can bear, in the lightening of every burden for others and the taking on himself the burden which he takes away from them. And then from the life of the home to the life of the wider world outside, giving there his best and his choicest. Never asking, Is it troublesome? Never asking, Is it painful? Never asking, Would I not rather do something else? For his only will is to serve; and the best that he can give is that which he wills to give. And then from that outer world of service, choosing his very best capacities to lay them at the feet of mankind, out of that life of service, to the nearest first and then to those who are farther away, will come the purifying fire of devotion which will make his vision clearer for Those who lie beyond him and above. For only as man serves and loves those who are around him will the eyes of the Spirit begin to be opened, and then he will recognise that there are Helpers beyond him ready to help him as he is helping others.

For mind you, on this Path of Devotion there is no help given to the individual as individual; it is only given to him by the Great Ones beyond him if in his turn he passes it on to others. His claim to be helped is that he is always helping, and that therefore a gift to him as individual is a gift that in very truth is given to every one that needs. And then as his eyes become clearer, and he recognises these many grades of Spiritual Intelligences, he will realise that there are some of them embodied around him; and by recognising those that are embodied around him but are greater than himself, he will be able to climb upward step by step until he will see the yet greater Ones beyond these; and then having reached Them, the greater, that are still beyond. For in this path of spiritual progress by way of devotion, every step opens up new horizons, and every clearing of the spiritual vision makes it pierce more deeply into that intensity of Light in which the highest Spiritual Intelligences are shrouded from the eyes of the flesh and of the intellect. And so the Soul who is in him, the Soul of the devotee, will gladly recognise all human excellence around him, will love and admire that excellence wherever he finds it ; he will, in fact, to use a word which many scoff at - he will be a hero-worshipper, not as seeing no fault in those whom he admires, but as seeing most the good in them and loving that, and letting the recognition of the good overbear the criticism of the fault: loving and serving them for what they are to man, and throwing the mantle of charity over the faults which they may commit in their service. And as he sees and recognises this in those around him, he will come into touch with higher Disciples than those, who move most commonly in the world of men - those who have reached a little farther, those who have seen a little deeper. Spirits that are gradually burning up all ignorance and all selfishness, and who are in direct touch with Those Whom we call the Great Masters, the members of the great White Lodge; and then he will love and serve them if opportunity should offer, love and serve them to the utmost of his ability, knowing that all such service purifies himself as well as helps the world, and makes him more and more a channel for the energies which he desires to spread amongst those with less vision than himself. And then, after a while, through these into touch with the Masters Themselves, with those highest and mightiest embodiments of Humanity, high above us in Their spiritual purity, in Their spiritual wisdom, in Their perfect selflessness, high as though They were Gods in comparison with the lower Humanity, because every sheath in Them is translucent, and the Light of the Spirit shines through unchecked; not differing from men in Their essence, but differing from men in Their evolution. For the sheaths in us shroud the Light within us, while the sheaths with Them are pure, and the unsullied light shines through unchecked; and They it is who will help and guide and teach, when man has risen to Their Feet by this Path of Devotion that I have spoken of; and the touch with Them is the going forward on the Path of Spiritual Knowledge, for without this devotion the further heights may not be won.

And here I take occasion to read to you words that came only a day or two ago from an Indian Disciple, which will give you the meaning of devotion far better than any words of mine. He wrote: Devotion to the Blessed Ones is a *sine qua non* of all spiritual progress and spiritual knowledge. It gives you the proper attitude in which to work on all the planes of life. It creates the proper atmosphere for the soul to grow and flower in love and beauty, in wisdom and power. It tunes the harp of the heart, and thus makes it possible for the musician to play the correct notes. That is the function of devotion. But you must know the notes you have to play, your fingers must learn how to sweep along the strings, and you must have a musical ear, or better still, a musical heart. ... What is proper tuning to the musical instrument that devotion is to the human Monad. But other faculties are needed for the production of various sweet strains.

There you have the meaning of devotion in a few words. It is the tuning of the heart. Knowledge may be needed for the different strains that are wanted, but devotion tunes the heart and the soul, so that every strain may come out in perfect harmony. Then is the growth in love, then is the growth in knowledge, then is the growth in spiritual purity: then all the forces of the spiritual spheres are helping onwards this Soul that fain would rise for service, and all the strength of Those Who have achieved is used to help on the one who would fain achieve, in order that he may better serve.

And what does devotion mean in life? It means clearer vision so that we may see the right; it means deeper love so that we may serve the better; it means unruffled peace and calm that nothing can shake or disturb, because, fixed in devotion on the Blessed Ones, there is nothing that can touch the Soul. And ever through those Blessed Ones there shines the light which comes from yet beyond Them, and which They focus for the help of the worlds, which they make possible for our weak eyes to bear. And then there are the peace, the vision, the power of service - that is what devotion means in life; and the Self whom the spotless devotee is seeking, that Self is pure, and that Self is Light *(Mundakopanishad, iii. 1. 10)* Light which no soil may sully, Light which no selfishness may dim, until the devotee himself vanishes in the Light which is himself. For the very Self of all is Light and Love, and the time at last comes, which has come to the Masters, when that Light shines out through spotless transparent purity and gives its full effulgence for the helping of the world. That is the meaning of devotion. That, however feebly phrased - and all words are feeble - that is the inner life of those who love, who recognise that life is only meant for service, who recognise that the only thing that makes life worthy is that it shall be burnt in the fire of devotion, in order that the world may be lighted and may be warmed. That is the goal which ends, not in liberation, but in perfect service. Liberation only when all Souls are liberated, when all together enter into the bliss unspeakable, and which, when that period of bliss is over, brings them out again as conscious co-workers with unbroken memory in the higher spiritual regions; for they have won their right to be conscious workers for ever in all future Manvantaras; for the Life of Love never gives liberation from service, and as long as eternity endures the Soul that loves works for and serves the Universe.

V. THE CEASING OF SORROW

An Article in the "Theosophical Review" in October, 1897.

SAITH a great Scripture, defining pleasure as threefold, that there is a pleasure "born of the blissful knowledge of the Self", that "putteth an end to pain" (Bhagavad Gita, xviii. 36, 37). Pleasures are many, but "the delights that are contact-born, they are verily wombs of pain", whereas he only "whose self is unattached to external contacts ... enjoys happiness exempt from decay" (v. 11, 12). Looking at the faces we pass daily in city or hamlet, alike in carriage, omnibus and cart, of old, middle-aged and young, of men and women - nay, even of the little ones, too often - we see in all dissatisfaction and harassment, trouble and unrest. Rarely are our eyes gladdened by a face serene and happy, free from lines carven by worry and anxiety, a face that tells of a soul at peace with itself and with all around, of "a heart at leisure", unhurried, strong. Some cause there must be for this general characteristic, increasing with the increase of "civilisation", and yet that it is an evitable evil is evidenced by the rare sweet presences that bring with them a serener atmosphere and radiate peace as others radiate unrest. A trouble so general must have its roots deep in human nature, and some fundamental principle deep-lying as the trouble, must exist as remedy. There must be some mistake into which as a race we fall that stamps on us this mark of sorrow. But if this be so, ignorance brings about our sadness, and the knowledge of the mistake puts the remedy within our grasp.

Ages ago the knowledge was given in the Upanishads; somewhat less than five thousand years ago it was expounded in the original Bhagavad Gita; twenty-four centuries ago the Lord Buddha enforced in plainest language the immemorial teaching; nineteen hundred years ago the Christ offered the same gift to the western world. Some, learning it, have entered the supreme Peace; some earnestly striving to learn it, are feeling its distant touch as an ever-growing reality; some, seeing its far-off radiance through a momentary rift in the storm-clouds, yearningly aspire to reach it. Alas! the myriads of driven souls know not of it, dream not of it, and yet it is not far from any one of us. Perhaps a recital of the ancient teaching may help one here and there to escape from sorrow's net, to break the connection with pain.

The cause of sorrow is the thirst for separated life in which individuality begins; without that thirst the eternal seed could not develop into the likeness of its generating Sire, becoming a centre of self-consciousness able to exist amid the tremendous vibrations which disintegrate universes, able to remain without a circumference, possessing inherently the power to generate it again, and thus to act as an axis for the eternal MOTION when it is going to turn the great Wheel which is parentless, ere the Son has "awakened for the new wheel and his pilgrimage thereon". Unless the thirst for separated life were aroused, universes could never come into manifestation, and it must continue in each soul until it has accomplished its mighty task - a paradox to the intellect but a truism to the spirit - of forming a centre which is itself eternally, and at the same time is everything.

While this thirst for separated life again and again draws the soul into the ocean of births and deaths, a yet deeper constituent of its being drives it to seek ever for union. All men seek happiness, seek they never so blindly; the search needs no justification; it is a universal instinct, and even those who torture the body, and seem to be trampling happiness under foot, do but choose the valley of pain because they believe that through it lies the shortest path to a deeper and more abiding joy.

Now what is the essence of happiness, found alike in the delirious passion of the sensualist and in the rapt ecstasy of the saint? It is union with the object of desire, the becoming one with that which promises delight. The drunkard who swallows his drink, the miser who clutches his gold, the lover who embraces his mistress, the artist who saturates himself in beauty, the thinker who concentrates himself on his idea, the mystic who loses himself in the empyrean, the yogin who merges himself in Deity - all are alike in finding happiness in union with the object of desire. This one thing they have in common. But their place in evolution is shown by the object with which union is sought. Not the search for happiness, but the nature of the object which yields happiness is the distinguishing mark of the base or lofty soul.

We seem to wander from our thesis in taking our next step, but the wandering is only seeming, illusory. In any given universe one Life is evolving into many lives through an ascending series of forms. The lives manifest as energies, displayed and further developed by means of forms. In order that these lives may thus develop, the forms must be continually changing, for each form is first an instrument and later a prison. As the latent powers in a life inseparate ever from the one Life as a plant from its hidden root - are drawn out by the play of the environment upon it, the form which was its helpful vehicle becomes its encramping mould. What then can happen? Either the life must perish, stifled by the form it had shaped, or the form must break into pieces and set free the life in an embryonic form of a higher type. But the life cannot perish, being an offshoot of the Eternal; hence the form must break. The breaking of a series of forms round an ever-expanding life means - evolution.

The expansion of this life may be likened to the expansion of life in a seed - from nucleus to embryo, from embryo to seedling, from seedling to sapling, from sapling to tree, capable of yielding seeds like that from which it grew. All growth is the unfolding of hidden powers, powers that in a LOGOS have reached their highest point for that universe – His universe - and that He plants as seed of every separated life. As water ever rises to its own level so does this down-poured life strive to rise to the level of its source; as mass attracts mass so does each life separate in manifestation seek itself, the one Life. That one Life exerts ceaselessly an upward drawing, force, like the *vis a fronte* of the baffled botanist. Its embryonic Self in each answers to the Father-self and blindly reaches out, groping after the One within the many, the One that is itself. Thus external contacts arise; by the inward urging of the Self the forms meet, then cling or clash. The attractive force is the one Self in all; the variety, the pleasure or the pain, is in the forms.

Further, it is the life that seeks the life, but in the search it is the form that finds the form, thus baffling the seeker. The forms are barriers between life and life; cannot intermingle, are mutually exclusive. Life could mix with life as two rivers mix their waters, but as rivers cannot join while each is running within its own banks, so lives cannot unite while forms lock each within its own enclosure.

Let us gather up our threads and twist them together into an Ariadne-clue to guide us through the Cretan labyrinth of life that we may find and slay the Minotaur called sorrow.

There is a thirst for separated life necessary to the building of the one who endures;

There is a persistent seeking for happiness;

The essence of happiness lies in union with the object of desire;

One Life is evolving through many impermanent forms;

Each separated life seeks this Life which is itself, and thus forms come into contact;

These forms exclude each other and keep the contained lives apart.

We may now understand how sorrow ariseth. A soul seeks beauty, and finds a beautiful form; it unites itself to the form, rejoices over it; the form perishes and a void is left. A soul seeks love, and it finds a lovable form; it unites itself to the form and joys in it; the form perishes and the heart lies desolate. And this is the experience in its least sorrowful shape; far more grievous is the sad satiety of possession, the wearied relinquishment of a prize so hardly won. Disillusion treading on the heels of disillusion, and yet ever fresh illusion and ever renewed disgust.

Search the world over and we find that all the sufferings of normal evolution are due to union with the changing and dying forms, the blind and foolish seeking for a happiness that shall endure by a clinging to the form that perishes. These are "the delights that are contact-born", and because they lead to weariness or, at the best, to loss, they are truly described as "wombs of pain". As against these we are bidden to seek "the blissful knowledge of the Self". Let life seek life, and the way to happiness is found: let the self seek the Self, and the up-winding path to peace stretches before the weary heart. To seek happiness by union with forms is to dwell amid the transitory, the limited, the clashing; to seek happiness by union with Life is to rest at peace on the permanent, the infinite, the harmonious.

Does this sound as though we were stripping our lives of joy and beauty, and setting them lonely in measureless depths of space? Nay, what we love in our beloved is not the form but the life, not the body but the soul. Cleareyed love can leap across death's abyss, across birth's Lethe-stream, and find and clasp its own unerringly though new and alien form be casket for the jewel-soul it knows. When this is seen the cause of sorrow is understood, and long practice brings its certain remedy, for we, ourselves life, not form, unite our life to life, not form, in our dear ones, blend more and more as form after form is dashed in pieces by the compassionate severity of a law that is love, until we find ourselves not twain but one, one also with the Life that is in and around and through all, and, inseparate amid the separated, we have put an end to pain. This is the ceasing of sorrow, this the entering into peace.

On the way to the blissful seat, moreover, the understanding of the cause of sorrow robs sorrow itself of its sting, for we learn that it is only that stern-seeming because veiled happiness "which at first is as venom but in the end is as nectar". From this knowledge springs a strong serenity that can endure as seeing the end, can "glorify the Lord in the fires". Shall not the gold rejoice in the burning that frees it from worthless dross?

Without the experience of sorrow, strength could not be developed. Strong mental and moral muscles are not obtained without strenuous exercise, any more than physical muscles become powerful without it. Struggle is a condition of the lower evolutions in nature; it is the means by which strength is developed. Only perfect strength is calm.

Without the experience of sorrow, sympathy could not be evolved. By suffering we learn to understand at once the pain and its needs, the demand and its meeting. Having suffered under temptation, we learn how to help effectively those who are tempted; only those who have risen from falls can aid the fallen with that exquisite understanding which alone prevents help from being insult. Every bud of pain opens into a blossom of power, and who would grudge the brief travail through which an eternal Saviour is brought forth?

Without the experience of sorrow we could not gain the knowledge of good and evil; without this the conscious choice of the highest could not become certain, nor the very root of desire to unite with forms be eradicated. The perfect man is not one whose lower nature still yearns for contact-born delights, but is strongly held in check he is one who has eliminated from his lower nature all its own tendencies, and has brought it into perfect harmonious union (yoga) with himself; who passes through the lower worlds unaffected by any of their attractions or repulsions, his will unalterably pointing towards the highest, working without an effort with all the inviolability of law and all the flexibility of intelligent adaptation. For the building of such a man hundreds of incarnations are not too many, myriad years are not too long.

Never let us forget, in the wildest storm of sorrow, that these early stages of our evolution, in which pain plays so large a part, are early stages only. They bear an infinitesimal proportion to our existence; nay, the two things are incommensurables, for how can we measure time against eternity, myriad years against an unending life? If we spake of the cycle of reincarnation as the infant stage of humanity, full of infantile ailments, we should utterly exaggerate its relative importance. Verily "our light affliction, which is but for a moment, worketh for us a far more exceeding and eternal weight of glory". Therefore when the storm-clouds gather, look beyond them to the changeless sky; when the billows buffet, lift the eyes to the eternal shore. Let earth and hell pour forth their angriest forces to overwhelm, they shall only lift us upwards, bear us onwards. For we are unborn, undying, constant, changeless and eternal, and we are here only to forge the instruments for an immortal service, the service which is perfect freedom.

VI. THE VALUE OF DEVOTION

An Article in the "Theosophical Review" in May, 1900.

AMONG the many forces which inspire men to activity, none, perhaps, plays a greater part than the feeling we call devotion, - together with some feelings that often mask themselves under its name though fundamentally differing from it in essence. The most heroic self-sacrifices have been inspired by it, while the most terrible sacrifices of others have been brought about by its pseudo-sister fanaticism. It is as powerful a lever for raising a man as is the other for his degradation. The two sway mankind with over-mastering power, and in some of their manifestations show an illusory resemblance; but the one has its roots in knowledge, the other in ignorance; the one bears the fruits of love, the other the poison-apples of hate.

A clear understanding of the nature of devotion is necessary, ere we are in a position to weigh its, value and to distinguish it from the false Duessa. We must trace it to its origin in human nature, and see in what part of that nature it takes its rise. We must know in order that we may practise; for as knowledge without practice is barren, so practice without knowledge is wasted. Emotion unregulated by knowledge, like a river overflowing its banks, spreads in every direction as a devastating flood, while emotion guided by knowledge is like the same river running in appointed channels and fertilising the land through which it flows.

If we study the inner nature of man, we find that it readily reveals three marked aspects that are distinguished from each other as the spiritual, the intellectual and the emotional. On studying these further, we learn that the spiritual nature is that in which all the separate individualities inhere, that it is the common root, the unifying influence, that principle which, when developed, enables a man to realise in consciousness the oneness of all that lives. The intellectual nature may be said to its antithesis; it is the individualising force in man, that which makes the many from the One. Its self-realisation is "I", and from this it sharply divides the "not-I". It knows itself apart, separate, and works best in isolation, drawn inwards, self-concentrated, indifferent to all without. Not herein can be found the root of devotion, of a feeling which rushes outward; intellect can grasp, it cannot move. Remains the emotional nature, the energising force that causes action, that which feels. This it is that attracts us to an object, or repels us from it, and herein we shall find that devotion has its source. For as we study the emotional nature we see that it has two emotions - attraction and repulsion. It is ever moving us towards or away from objects surrounding us, according as those objects afford us pleasure or pain. All the feelings which draw us towards another fall under the head of attraction and are forms of Love. All those which repel us from another fall under the head of repulsion and are forms of Hate.

Now Love takes different forms, and is called by different names, according as its object is above it, equal with it, or below it. Directed to those below it we name it pity, compassion, benevolence; directed to those equal with it, we call it friendship, passion, affection; directed to those above it, we style it reverence, adoration, devotion. Thus we trace devotion to its origin in the love-side of the emotional nature, and we define it as love directed to an object superior to the lover. When love is directed to the Guru, to God, we rightly term it devotion, for then it is poured out before the superior, and shows in perfection the characteristic of all love given to those who are greater than ourselves, the characteristic of self-surrender.

Here we have the touchstone by which we can separate it from the fanaticism which has inspired religious wars, religious persecutions, religious animosities. These have their roots in hatred, not in love; they repel us from others instead of drawing us towards them. In the name of love to God men injure their fellows; but when we analyse the motive power of their actions we do not find it in the love, but in their sense that they are right and others wrong, in the separateness they feel from others, in the feeling of repulsion from them because of their supposed wrongness, i.e., in hate. Out of this come the bitter waters that sterilise the heart over which they flow. By this we can judge what we regard as devotion in ourselves; if it makes us humble, gentle, tolerant, friendly to all, then it is true devotion; if it makes us proud, harsh, separate, suspicious of all, then, however fair its seeming, it is dross, not gold.

Now devotion being a form of love, it can only flow out when an object presents itself which is attractive in its own nature, i.e., happiness-giving. All men seek happiness, and that attracts them, draws them towards itself, which seems to them to make for happiness. Happiness is the feeling which accompanies the increase of life, and true and permanent bliss lies in union with the Self, the All-life, in conscious Self-identification with and expansion into the All; all efforts after happiness are efforts to unite with objects in order to absorb their life, thereby expanding the life that absorbs them. Happiness results from this union, because thereby the feeling of life is increased. Fundamentally the impulse to seek union comes from the Self, seeking to overpass the barriers which separate its selves on the lower planes, and the attraction between selves is the seeking by the Self in each of the Self in the other. "Lo, not for the sake of the husband is the husband dear, but for the sake of the Self the husband is dear. Lo! not for the sake of the wife is the wife dear, but for the sake of the Self the wife is dear." And so also with sons, wealth, Brâhmanas, Kshattriyas, the worlds, the gods, the Vedas, the elements, until: "Lo! not for the sake of the All is the All dear, but for the sake of the Self the All is dear (*Brihadâranyakopanishad; VI. v. 6)* The Self seeks the Self, and this is the universal search for happiness, ever frustrated by the clash of form with form, the obstruction of the vehicles in which the separated selves abide.

In order to draw out devotion, then, an object which is attractive must be presented to man, and we find such objects presented most completely in the revelations of the Supreme Self made through human form in the "God-Men" who appear from time to time - the Avatâras, or Divine Incarnations. Such beings are rendered supremely attractive by the beauty of character they manifest, by the rays of the Self which shine through the human veil, imperfectly concealing their divine loveliness. When He who is Beauty and Love and Bliss shows a little portion of Himself on earth, encased in human form, the weary eyes of men light up, the tired hearts of men expand, with a new hope, a new vigour. They are irresistibly attracted to Him, devotion spontaneously springs up. Among Christians the intensity of religious devotion flows out to Christ, the Divine Man, regarded as an incarnation of Deity, far more than to "God" in the abstract. It is His human side, His life and death, His sympathy and compassion, His gentle wisdom and patient sufferings, which stir men's hearts to a passion of devotion; as the "Man of Sorrows", the innocent and willing Sufferer, He wins perennially the love of men; it is the memory of Him as Man that holds men captive; as phrased by one of His devotees: -

The cross of Christ

Is more to us than all His miracles.

And so in the God-Men of other faiths; it is Shri Râma the Divine King, Shri Krishna the Friend and Lover, who win the undying, passionate devotion of millions of human hearts. They render Deity attractive by softening its dazzling radiance into a light that human eyes can bear as it shines through the veil of humanity; They limit the divine attributes till they become small enough for the human intelligence to grasp. These stand as Objects of devotion, attracting love by Their perfect lovableness; They need only to be seen to be loved; where They are not loved it is merely because they are not seen. Devotion to Divine Men is not a matter for discussion or for argument; the moment one of Them is seen by the inner vision the heart rushes out to Him and falls unbidden at His feet. Devotion may be cultivated by the reason, may be approved of and nurtured by the intelligence; but its primary impulse comes from the heart, not from the head, and flows out spontaneously to the Object that attracts it, to the shining of the Self through a translucent veil; to the Heart's Desire in manifested form.

Next, as objects of devotion, come the Teachers who, having Themselves obtained liberation, remain voluntarily within touch of humanity, retaining human bodies while the Jivâtmâ enjoys nirvanic consciousness. They stand, as it were, between the Avatâras and the earthly Gurus who are Their disciples and who have not yet reached liberation, but to the eyes of men on earth They are scarce distinguishable from the Avatâras Themselves, and they draw men with the same overmastering attraction. The Avatâra truly is greater, but that greatness lies on the side turned away from earth, and we can imagine no completer perfection than that of the Masters of Wisdom.

Then come, in more constant physical communication with men, the Gurus who are the immediate spiritual teachers of those whose faces are turned to the steep path that leads to the heights, to the snowy mountains of human perfection. Still marred by weaknesses though they be, these have advanced sufficiently beyond their fellowmen to serve as their guides and helpers; and for the most part the earlier stages of progress are trodden by devotion to them. Further, as they are near the threshold of liberation, they will shortly pass into the class beyond them, and, as spiritual links are imperishable, will then be able, with added force, to draw their devotees after them. Love given to them strengthens and expands the nature of their lovers, and there is no surer path to devotion, in its highest meaning, than the love and trust given to the earthly Guru. Nowhere has this been realised so strongly as in the East, where the love and service of the Guru have ever been held as necessary to spiritual progress. Much of the decay of modern India is due to the ignorance, the pride, the un-spirituality of those who still wear the ancient name while devoid of all the qualities once implied by it; for as the best wine makes the sharpest vinegar, so is the degradation of the highest the lowest depth.

How shall devotion, then, be evoked and nourished? Only by meeting in the outer or inner world a fit object of devotion, and by yielding fully and unreservedly to the attraction it exercises. The glad and cordial recognition of excellence wherever found, the checking of the critical and carping spirit that fixes on defects and ignores virtues, these things prepare the soul to recognise his Guru when he appears. Many a one misses his teacher by the mental habit of fixing the attention on blemishes rather than on beauties, by seeing only the sun-spots and not the Sun. Further the recognition of excellence shows the capacity to reproduce it; sympathetic vibrations are given out only by a string tuned to produce by itself a similar note; the soul knows his kin, even though they be elder than himself, and only those akin to greatness are awakened by the great to response.

When the Guru is found and the tie with him is made, the first great step is taken. Then follows the steady culture of devotion to him, and through him to Those beyond and to the Supreme Self, manifested in form. This must never be forgotten, for the Guru is a means not an end, a transmitter not an originator of the divine light, a moon not a sun. He helps, strengthens, guides, evolves his pupil; but the end is the shining out of the Self in the disciple, the Self who is one, and is in Guru and chelâ alike.

Devotion to the embodiment of the Self spoken of as the Avatâra may be nourished and increased by reading and meditating on His sayings and the incidents of His life on earth. It is a good plan to read over an incident and then vividly picture it in the mind, using the imagination to produce a full and detailed picture, and feeling oneself as present in it, a spectator or an actor therein. This "scientific use of the imagination" is a great provocative of devotion, and it actually brings the devotee into touch with the scene depicted, so that he may one day find himself scanning the akashic record of the event, a very part of that living picture, learning undreamed of lessons from his presence there.

Another way of cultivating devotion is to be much in company with those in whom devotion burns more brightly than in ourselves. As burning wood thrown into a smouldering fire will cause a flame to burst out brightly again, so the nearness of the warm fire of devotion in another rekindles the flagging energy of a weaker soul. Here again the disciple may gain much by frequenting the company of his Guru, whose steadier force will energise his own. Narâda, in his admirable Sûtras, thus instructs us on the culture of devotion, and who should teach better than that ideal devotee?

Almost needless to add that the direct contemplation of, meditation on, adoration of the object of devotion quicken and intensify the love. In the hurry of modern life we are apt to forget the power of quiet thought and to grudge the time necessary for its exercises. Thought of the one we love increases love, and the would-be devotee must give time to the object of his devotion, and it is not his thought alone that is at work. As little can a plant grow without sunlight as devotion without the warming and energising rays that stream from its object; the older soul pours out far more love than he receives, and his light and heat permeate and strengthen the younger soul. The Guru loves his chelâ, God loves his devotee, far more than the chelâ loves his Guru, or the devotee his God. The love of the devotee for his Lord is but a faint reflection of the love of Him who is Love itself. It is said that if a child throws a pebble to the ground, the whole great earth moves towards the pebble as well as draws the pebble to itself; attraction cannot be one-sided. In the spiritual world when man makes one step towards God, God makes a hundred steps towards man, for greatness there means greatness in giving, and the ocean pours forth its measureless depths towards any drop that seeks its bosom.

Having seen what devotion is, what its objects, how it can be increased, we may fitly measure its value so as to find motive for attaining it.

Devotion changes the devotee into the likeness of the one he loves. Solomon, the wise Hebrew, declares that as a man thinks so he is. The Chhândogyopanishad teaches that man is created by thought; what he thinks on that he becomes. But the intellect alone cannot easily be shaped into the likeness of the Supreme. As cold iron is hard, and incapable of being worked, but heated in the furnace becomes fluid and flows readily into any desired mould, so it is with the intellect. It must be melted in the fire of devotion, and then it will quickly be shaped into the likeness of the Beloved. Even love between equals, where it is strong and faithful and long continued, moulds them into each other's likeness; husband and wife become like each other, close friends grow similar each to each. And love directed to one above us exercises its transforming power still more forcibly, and easily shapes the nature it renders plastic into the likeness which is enshrined in the heart.

Devotion prevents the making of new karma, and when the old is exhausted the devotee is free. The great Christian teacher, St. Paul, writing of himself, declared that he no longer lived but Christ lived in him, and this saying becomes true of each devotee as his devotion leads him to surrender himself utterly to the one he loves. He thinks of his body not as his, but as an instrument used by his Lord for the world's helping; all his actions are done because they are the duty given him by his Beloved; does he eat, it is not to gratify the palate, but to keep in working order his Lord's instrument; does he think, it is not for the pleasure of thinking, but in order that his Lord's work may be the better done; he merges his life in the life he loves, thinks, works, acts, in union with that higher life, merging his smaller rill of being in the larger stream, and finding a deep joy in feeling himself part of the fuller life. So it is written: "Whatsoever thou doest, whatsoever thou eatest, whatsoever thou offerest, whatsoever thou givest, whatsoever thou doest of austerity, O son of Kunti, do thou that as an offering unto Me. Thus shalt thou be liberated from the bonds of action (yielding) good and evil fruits" (Bhagavad-Gitâ, ix. 27, 28.). Where fruits of action are not desired, where actions are done only as sacrifice, no karma is made by the actor, and he is not bound by them to the wheel of births and deaths.

Devotion cleanses the heart. Once again Shri Krishna teaches us, and the words at first seem strange. "Even if the most sinful worship me with undivided heart, he too must be accounted righteous." Why? we naturally ask; and the answer comes: "Because he hath rightly resolved; speedily he becometh dutiful, and goeth to peace eternal" (Bhagavad-Gitâ, 30, 31.) In the higher world men are judged by motives not by actions, by inner attitude not by external signs. When a man feels devotion to the Supreme, he has turned his back on evil and has turned his face to the goal; he may stumble, stray, even fall, but his face is turned in the right direction, he is going homewards; he must needs become dutiful by the force of his devotion, for seeking union with his Beloved he will swiftly cast away everything that prevents the union; to Him who sees the end from the beginning he is righteous when his face is turned to righteousness, and his love will burn up in him the evil that veils from him the Being he adores and produce in him the likeness that he worships. So sure is this action, so inviolable the law, that he is "accounted righteous". To the two great classes of the self-seekers and the seekers of the Self, he has changed from the first into the second.

Devotion puts an end to pain. That which we do for the object of our love is done with joy, and pain is merged in gladness when it is endured for the sake of one we love. The mere earthly lover will gladly undergo hardships, perils, sufferings, to win approval from, or to gain something desirable for, his beloved. How should not the one who has caught a glimpse of the beauty of the Self do joyfully all that brings him nearer to union, sacrifice ungrudgingly, nay, with delight, all that withholds him from the bridal of the inner life? For the sake of being with one we love, we readily endure inconvenience, sacrifice comfort, the joy of the presence of the loved one lends charm to the surmounting of all obstacles that separate. Thus devotion makes hard things easy, and painful things pleasant. For love is the World-alchemist and transmutes all to gold.

Devotion gives peace. The heart at peace in the Self is at peace with all. The devotee sees the Self in all; all forms around him bear the impress of the Beloved. How then can he hate or despise or repel any, when the face he loves smiles at him behind every mask? "Sages look with equal eye on a Brâhmana adorned with learning and humility, on a cow, an elephant, and even a dog and a dog-eater" (Bhagavad-Gîtâ, v. 18.) No one, nothing; can be outside the heart of the devotee, since nothing is outside the embrace of his Lord. If we love the very objects touched by the one we love, how shall we not love all forms in which the Beloved is enshrined? A child in his play may draw over his laughing face a hideous mask, but the mother knows her darling is underneath; and when in the world-lîlâ the Lord is hidden under form repulsive, His lovers are not repelled, but see only Him. There is no creature, moving or unmoving, that exists bereft of Him, and in the heart-chamber of the vilest sinner the Holiest abides.

Thus we return to our starting-point and learn to recognise the devotee by his aspect to his fellow-creatures. His abounding love, his tenderness, his compassion, his pity, his sympathy with all faiths and all ideals, these mark him out as a lover of the Lord of love. It is told of Shri Râmânûjâchârya that a mantra was once given him by his Guru, and he asked what would happen if he told it to another: "Thou wilt die", was the answer. "And what will happen to the one who hears it?" "He will be liberated." Then out ran the devotee of Shri Krishna, and flying to the top of a tower, he shouted out the mantra to the crowded streets below, careless what happened to himself so that others should be set free from sin and sorrow. There is the typical devotee, there the lover transformed into the likeness of the Beloved.

VII. SPIRITUAL DARKNESS

An Article in the "Theosophical Review" in February, 1900.

FEW of the perils which beset the path of the serious aspirant are more depressing in their nature, more fatal in their effects, than what is called spiritual darkness - the gloom which descends on the heart and brain, wrapping the whole nature in its sombre folds, blotting out all memories of past peace, all hopes of future progress. As a dense fog pervades a great city, stealing into every nook and corner, effacing every familiar landmark, shutting off every vista, blurring into dimness even the brilliant lights, until, to the bewildered wayfarer, nothing seems left save himself and the stifling mephitic vapour that enfolds him, so is it when the fog of spiritual darkness comes down on the aspirant or the disciple. All his landmarks disappear, and the way vanishes in the gloom; his wonted lights are shorn of their lustre, and human beings are mere shadows that now and again push up against him out of the night and into the night again disappear. He is alone and lost; a sense of terrible isolation shuts him in, and no one shares his solitude. The human faces that smiled on him have vanished; the human voices that cheered him are silent: the human love that caressed him has grown chill. His "lovers and friends are put away from" him; and no words of comfort reach him across the deadly stillness. To move forward, when the ground on which the foot must be planted is invisible, feels as if he were stepping over a precipice, and a dull surging of waves at a far depth seems to threaten destruction, while their very distance below intensifies the nearer silence. Heaven is shut out as well as earth; sun, moon and stars have vanished, and no glimmer of their radiance pierces the gloom from above. He feels as though suspended in an abyss of nothingness, and as though he would shortly pass into that nothingness himself; his flame of life seems to flicker in the darkness, as though, in sympathy with the universal gloom, it would itself cease to shine. The "horror of great darkness" is upon him, paralysing every energy, crushing every hope. God and man have deserted him - he is alone, alone.

The testimony of every great mystic proves that this picture is not overdrawn; there are no cries of human anguish more bitter than those which wail out from the pages on which noble and saintly souls have recorded their experiences on the Path. They had looked for peace, and combat surrounds them; for joy, and sorrow is their portion; for the Beatific Vision, and the darkness of the pit hems them in. That lesser souls have not faced the ordeal, and look unbelievingly on its possibility, putting their theories of what should be against the iron facts of what is - this proves nothing save that their hour is not yet come. The child cannot measure the man's struggle, nor the babe feel the anguish that pierces the breast which feeds it. To every age its proper fruitage, and while we can understand the experiences that lie behind us, none may grasp the nature of those that lie ahead. Let the undeveloped soul, if he will, scoff at the agony he cannot appreciate, depreciate the suffering he cannot yet feel, even deride as weakness the signs of an anguish whose lightest touch would shrivel up his own vaunted strength. Those growing into divine manhood know the reality of the darkness, and only those who know can judge.

At a very early stage of real apprenticeship to the higher life, darkness - less absolute than that above described, but sufficiently trying to the as yet undeveloped soul - will strain and test his powers. The earnest aspirant soon finds that fits of gloom, the cause of which he cannot discover, descend upon him and subject him to much distress. He is apt, in the over-sensitiveness which accompanies this stage of growth, to blame himself for these accesses of sadness, and to take himself sharply to task for the loss of the serenity which he has put before himself as his ideal. When the gloom is upon him, every surrounding object takes an unwonted and exaggerated shape. Small annoyances loom large, distorted by the mists that surround him, petty troubles grow into great shadows that over-cloud the sun, and friction that in happier seasons would pass unnoticed now rasps every nerve and tortures every sensibility. He feels that he has fallen from the place to which he had climbed by prolonged efforts, and that all his past struggles are wasted and their fruits rent away from his grasp. As has been well said: "It is wonderful how the Powers of the Dark seem to sweep away as it were in one gust all one's spiritual treasures, garnered with such pain and care after years of incessant study and experience." What wonder that the trembling and bewildered soul of the neophyte feels a touch almost of despair as the spoils of victory on many a hard-fought field crumble into ashes in his hands.

Let us examine into the cause of the darkness, for though, while it is upon us, all merely theoretical knowledge breaks down under our feet, yet that knowledge may help to clear it away more rapidly, when once it begins to lighten. Nothing but repeated practical experience can keep us as steady and as serene in the darkness as in the light, but theoretical knowledge has its place in the evolution of the mind.

We will take separately the cases of the aspirant and of the accepted disciple, for though the causes of the darkness which affects the former may also play their part in bringing down the night on the latter, there are additional causes at work where the accepted disciple is concerned.

First comes the well-known fact of the quickening of karma, once a man has set his face resolutely towards the portal of the Path. We need not dwell on this, for it has been often explained, and it plays a comparatively small part in the bringing down of the darkness. One element, however, perhaps less often alluded to, may be mentioned here. Pleasure and pain, connected with the emotions and passions, belong to the astral world and are experienced through the astral body; consequently a very large amount of karma belongs, by its very nature, to the astral plane, and is there exhausted. Bad karma can, therefore, be largely worked out by suffering, apart from events; the suffering which normally accompanies misfortunes, disasters of every description on the physical plane, has its habitat on the astral, and we suffer on the astral while we are passing through our troubles on the physical. Now this astral suffering can be disjoined from the physical events with which it is normally associated, and can be passed through apart from those events. In the quickening of karma this result is largely brought about, and some of the darkness experienced by the aspirant is due to this cause; he is working out his bad karma by enduring the suffering that belongs to events not yet ripe for manifestation on the physical plane; and if he observes his own life, he will find that, later on, he passes through events that would ordinarily be regarded as of the most distressing character with a calmness and indifference that surprise himself. The fact is that he has already borne the suffering normally attached to them, and he meets on the physical plane the mere shells and semblances, the empty forms, which are all that remain when the astral consciousness that normally vivifies these forms has been withdrawn. (Students may be reminded - though the subject is too large a one to be entered on here - that man's consciousness is astral, at the present stage of evolution.) The aspirant may therefore comfort himself when an apparently causeless gloom descends upon him with the knowledge that he is exhausting some of his karmic liabilities, and that the payment of karmic debts is never demanded twice.

Secondly, the aspirant is seeking to purify and ultimately to destroy the personality. Pleasures increase and intensify the life of the personality, while pains diminish it. His own deliberate will has offered the personality as a sacrifice to the Lord of the Burning-ground, and if the sacrifice be accepted, the flame falls and devours it. What cause for sorrow is here? But the fire, as it burns up the dross of personality, setting free the pure gold of the life, must needs bring keen suffering to the life which is thus rapidly purged from elements that have for millenniums formed part of its being, mingling with all its activities. And here comes in the peril which makes spiritual darkness so fatal. Can the aspirant hold out while the dark fire burns up that which seems to be his very life? Can he bear the strain, live through the darkness, and be found, when it lifts, still at his post, weary and wornout, perchance, but *there*? If he can, then a great peace will succeed the darkness, and in the peace he shall hear the song of life. New strength will flow in upon him, and he will be conscious of a deeper vision, of a firmer grasp on truth; the darkness will prove but the mother of light, and he will have learned in it priceless lessons that will stand him in good stead in future trials. Alas! but too often courage breaks and endurance fails, and the darkness proves to be the darkness of a temporary tomb, and perhaps for the remainder of the incarnation, brings "ruin to many a noble soul that has not yet acquired strength enough to endure".

Thirdly, the darkness is often a glamour thrown over the aspirant by the destructive forces that play in the world. To the process of evolution destruction is as necessary as construction, disintegration as integration. That which apparently delays really strengthens, as death is but an aspect of birth. The occultist knows that every force in nature represents the working of an invisible Intelligence, and that this is as true of the destructive as of the constructive forces. And he knows that the destructive Intelligences - the Dark Powers, as they are often called - set themselves to beguile, entrap, and bewilder the aspirant the moment he has made sufficient progress beyond ordinary humanity to draw their attention, and render himself worthy of attack. Endeavouring to delay the higher evolution and to prolong the sovereignty of matter, they regard as their natural enemy anyone who steps out of the normal path and seeks to lead the spiritual life. These are the "powers of nature", so often mentioned in mystic books, who strive to hold back the aspiring soul. Their most favourite device of all, perhaps, is to cause discouragement and, if possible, to drive to despair, by enveloping the soul in darkness, and by making him feel forsaken and alone. Theirs the touch which gives the peculiar poignancy to the isolation; the thoughts that whisper of despair are but the echoes of their mockery. As progress is made on the Path, all the powers of nature must gradually be faced and conquered, and the facing and the conquering must be done alone. Alone? ah! not alone in reality; what shall separate us from the One Life which is our very Self, or from the love of the Masters who watch every step of the combatant? but alone so far as the intellect is concerned, which feels the "I" as standing unaided and forlorn.

When we study the life of the accepted disciple, we find at work in it the causes which we have seen in the life of the aspirant, but a new cause also arises, which, as he advances, ever plays a more and more prominent part in his experience. As the shackles of his own karma fall off him, he becomes free to bear part of "the heavy karma of the world", and he also begins to face the greater destructive forces for the world's sake, standing between them and humanity and drawing on to himself as much as is practicable of their energies. The sin and the sorrow of the world, its pathetic ignorance, press upon him, and until he reaches the strong peace which has its sure root in perfect knowledge, he cannot escape, from time to time, the gloom which comes down upon him, as though the whole world's sorrow crushed his heart, and made it bleed at every pore with "helpless pity" for the blindness that breeds misery and the ignorance which is sin. Nor dare he strive to shake of this feeling of sorrow, since, by virtue of the more and more realised unity of his life with that of all men, his sorrow is theirs, and he shares by it in their karma and quickens their evolution. But he gradually learns to bear it with a peaceful satisfaction, deepening into a sense of profound inner joy, until the crushing power of it diminishes and finally disappears, and only an all-abounding compassion remains, so that the very sorrow becomes dearer than all that the world calls joy, and the gloom is but a tender twilight, fairer and sweeter than the brilliance of the noonday sun.

Sharper and keener is the suffering that he faces when he "turns his back on the light and goes down alone into the darkness to meet and overcome the Powers of Evil". This is the work of the world's Saviours, and the hour comes for the disciple when this solemn and glorious duty devolves on him. He is trained for its more arduous struggles by gradually learning to draw into himself inharmonious and disruptive forces, so that they exhaust themselves in him, often tearing and rending him in the process, and are then sent forth, harmonised and rhythmical, forces for building up instead of forces that destroy. Disciples are the crucibles of nature, wherein compounds that are mischievous are dissociated, and are recombined into compounds that promote the general good. As the seething compounds break up with explosive violence, the sensitive human crucible quivers under the terrible strain, and little wonder that, at times, it breaks, unable to endure. By such discipline, long-continued, the disciple strengthens his power, and becomes fit to bear heavier burdens, fit to bear the gloom of the awful darkness in which he feels himself forsaken of God and man, in which he seems flung to the Dark Powers that they may work their will upon him, in which life is only torture, and the anodyne of loss of consciousness is craved. Then comes the subtle alluring temptation "come down from the cross"; and he knows that nothing holds him stretched thereon save the nails of his own fixed purpose and indomitable will; at any moment he can bid the torment cease, if he be willing to escape at the cost of the world he has sacrificed himself to help. If he escape, the world must suffer; if he can bear the agony, the burden of humanity is a little lifted. "He saved others; himself he cannot save." The gibe of the unbeliever is the life-law of the Christ.

But at last, even this hope that was sustaining his fortitude is rent away from him, and the darkness of despair enfolds him, whispering that all the anguish is in vain, that he is beaten, overpowered, and all his hoped-for service to the world is but the "baseless vision of a dream". Never again shall he serve his Master in joyful obedience; never again shall weary souls be gladdened by the light he bears; he has taught others to tread the Path, but has himself fallen from it; he has preached on everlasting love, and behold! love itself has abandoned him and leaves him to sink into the abyss. Can he hold out through this? can he still bless the good, while evil triumphs over him? can he be content to perish, if that be his karma? can he still rejoice that the world shall be saved though he bear no part in the saving, and joy that love shall triumph though he be outcast from its embrace? If he cannot, then the darkness has stifled him, and the world has for a while lost a helper. If he can - then, with that uttermost surrender of the separated self, the darkness lifts; the eternal Self wells up within him; the Face of his Master shines out and he knows that He has been there all the time; in a moment of clear spiritual vision, he sees through the rent veil the Holy of Holies, where abides "The Heart of Silence, the Hidden God", and the pinions of the white peace enfold him. Then brief rest in the calm stillness of the silent sealed cave; the coming forth into a new and larger life, with deeper wisdom, firmer faith, stronger love; the greater power to serve humanity, the strength to endure still heavier strain. Above all he has learned something of the power of illusion, has caught a glimpse of the nature of Mâyâ, and has that to help him in all future darkness, the realised knowledge that it cannot wreck unless he himself yields to its delusive force. Such is the priceless fruit of spiritual darkness, and by such strain and such struggle the man evolves the God.

VIII. THE MEANING AND THE METHOD OF THE SPIRITUAL LIFE

An Article in the "Theosophical Review", in January, 1906.

IN considering the meaning and the method of the spiritual life, it is well to begin by defining the meaning of the term "spiritual", for on that there exists a good deal of uncertainty among religious people. We constantly hear people speaking of "spirit" and "soul" as though they were interchangeable terms. Man has "a body and soul", or "a body and spirit", they say, as though the two words "spirit" and "soul" had no definite and distinct meaning; and naturally if the words "spirit" and "soul" are not clearly understood, the term "spiritual life" must necessarily remain confused. But the Theosophist, in dealing with man, divides him in a definite and scientific way both as regards his consciousness and as regards the vehicles through which that consciousness manifests, and he restricts the use of the word "spirit" to that Divine in man that manifests on the highest planes of the universe, and that is distinguished by its consciousness of unity. Unity is the keynote of spirit, for below the spiritual realm all is division. When we pass from the spiritual into the intellectual we at once find ourselves in the midst of separation.

Dealing with our own intellectual nature, to which the word "soul" ought to be restricted, we at once notice that it is, as is often said, the very principle of separateness. In the growth of our intellectual nature we become more and more conscious of the separateness of the "I". It is this which is sometimes called the "I-ness" in man. It is this which gives rise to all our ideas as to separate existence, separate property, separate gains and losses; it is just as much a part of the man as spirit, only a different part, and it is the very antithesis of the spiritual nature. For where the intellect sees "I" and "mine" the spirit sees unity, non-separateness; where the intellect strives to develop itself and assert itself as separate, the spirit sees itself in all things and regards all forms as equally its own.

It is on the spiritual nature that turn all the great mysteries of the religions of the world, for it is a mystery to the ordinary man, this depth of unity in the very centre of his being, which regards all around it as part of itself, and thinks of nothing as separately its own.[Page 134 That which is called in the Christian religion the "Atonement" belongs entirely to the spiritual nature, and can never be intelligible so long as the man thinks of himself as a separate intellect, intelligence apart from others. For the very essence of the Atonement lies in the fact that the spiritual nature, being everywhere one, can pour itself out into one form or another; it is because this fact of the spiritual nature has not been understood, and only the separation of the intellect has been seen, that men, in dealing with that great spiritual doctrine, changed it into a legal substitution of one individual for other individuals, instead of recognising that the Atonement is wrought by the all-pervading spirit, which, by identity of nature, can pour itself into any form at will.

Hence we are to think of the spirit as that part of man's nature in which the sense of unity resides, the part in which primarily he is one with God, and secondarily one with all that lives throughout the universe. A very old Upanishat begins with the statement that all this world is God-inveiled, and going on then to speak of the man who knows that vast, pervading, all-embracing unity, it bursts into a cry of exultation: "What then becomes of sorrow, what then becomes of delusion, for him who has known the unity?" That sense of a oneness at the heart of things is the testimony of the spiritual consciousness, and only as that is realised is it possible that the spiritual life shall manifest. The technical names - by which we, as Theosophists, mark out the spirit - matter not at all. They are drawn from the Samskrit, which for millennia has been in the habit of having definite names for every stage of human and other consciousness; but, this one mark of unity is the one on which we may rest as the sign of the spiritual nature. And so again it is written in an old Eastern book, that "the man who sees the One Self in everything, and all things in the Self, he seeth, verily, he seeth". And all else is blindness. The sense of separation, while necessary for evolution is fundamentally a mistake. The separateness is only like the branch that grows out of a trunk, and the unity of the life of the tree passes into every branch and makes them all a oneness; and it is the consciousness of that one-ness which is the consciousness of the spirit.

Now in Christendom the sense of one-ness has been personified in the Christ; the first stage - where there is still the Christ and the Father - is where the wills are blended, "not my will but thine be done"; the second stage is where the sense of unity is felt: "I and my Father are one". In that manifestation of the spiritual life we have the ideal which underlies the deepest inspiration of the Christian sacred writings, and it is only as "the Christ is born in man", to use the Christian symbol, that the truly spiritual life begins. This is very strongly pointed out in some of the Epistles. S. Paul, writing to Christians and not to the profane or heathen - to those who have been baptised, who are recognised members of the Church, in a day when membership was more difficult to gain than it is in these later times - says to them: "Ye are not spiritual: ye are carnal. And the reason he gives for regarding them as carnal and not spiritual is: "I hear that there be divisions among you"; for where the spiritual life is dominant, harmony, and not division is to be found. And the second great stage of the spiritual life is also marked out in the Christian scriptures, as in all the other great world-scriptures, when it is said that, when the end cometh, all that has been gathered up in the Christ, the Son, is gathered up yet further into the Father, and "God shall be all in all". Even that partial separation of Son and Father vanishes, and the unity is supreme. So that whether we read the *Upanishats*, the *Bhagavad Gîtâ*, or the Christian *New Testament*, we find ourselves in exactly the same atmosphere as regards the meaning, the nature of the spiritual life; it is that which knows the one-ness, that in which unity is complete.

Now this is possible for men, despite all the separation of the intellect and of the various bodies which bar us out the one from the other, because in the heart of our nature we are Divine. That is the great reality on which all the beauty and power of human life depend. And it is no small thing whether, in the ordinary thought of a people, they rest upon the idea that they are Divine, or have been deluded into the idea that they are by nature sinful, miserable and degraded. Nothing is so fatal to progress, nothing so discouraging to the growth of the inner nature, as the continual repetition of that which is not true: that man fundamentally and essentially is wicked, instead of being Divine. It is a poison at the very heart of his life; it stamps him with a brand which it is hard indeed for him to throw off; and if we want to win even the lowest and most degraded to a sense of inner dignity, which will enable them to climb out of the mud in which they are plunged up to the dignity of a Divine human nature, we must never hesitate to preach to them their essential Divinity, and that in the heart of them they are righteous and not foul. For it is just in proportion as we do that, that there will be within them the faint stirrings of the spirit, so overlaid that they are not conscious of it in their ordinary life; and if there is one duty of the preacher of religion more vital than another, it is that all who hear him shall feel within themselves the stirring of the Divine.

Looking thus at every man as Divine at heart, we begin to ask: If that be the meaning of spirit and spiritual life, what is the method for its unfolding? The first step is that which has just been mentioned, to get people to believe in it, to throw aside all that has been said about the heart of man being "desperately wicked"; to throw aside all that is said about original sin. "There is no original sin save ignorance, and into that we are all born, and we have slowly to grow out of it by experience, which gives us wisdom. That is the starting point, as the conscious sense of unity is the crown. And the method of spiritual life is that which enables the life to show itself forth in reality as it ever is in essence. The inner Divinity of man, that is the inspiring thought which we want to spread through all the Churches of the West, which too long have been clouded by a doctrine exactly the reverse. When man once believes himself Divine, he will seek to justify his inner nature.

Now the method of the spiritual life in the fullest sense cannot, I frankly admit, be applied to the least developed amongst us; for them the very first lesson is that ancient lesson: "Cease to do evil". In one of my favourite Upanishats, when it speaks of the steps whereby a man may search after and find the Self, the God within him, the first step, it is said, is to "cease to do evil". That is the first step towards the spiritual life, the foundation which a man must lay. The second step is active: to do the right. These are two commonplaces which we hear on every side, but they are no less true because commonplace, and they are necessary everywhere and must be repeated until the evil is forsaken and the good embraced. Without the accomplishment of these, the spiritual life cannot be begun. And then, as to the later steps, it is written that no man who is slothful, no man who is unintelligent, no man who is lacking in devotion, can find the Self. And again it is said that: "The Self is not found by knowledge nor by devotion, but by knowledge wedded to devotion." These are the two wings that lift the man up into the spiritual world.

To fill up these broad outlines which are set to guide us to the narrow ancient Path, we may find a mass of details in the various scriptures of the world, but what is specially needed just now, is the way in which people living in the world, bound by domestic ties, and ties of occupation of every sort, how these people may have a method by which the spiritual life may be gained, by which progress in real spirituality may be secured. It is true that in all the different religions of the world there has been a certain inclination to draw a line of division between the life of the world and the life of the spirit; that line of division, which is real, is, however, very often misunderstood and misrepresented, and is thought to consist in circumstance, whereas it consists in attitude - a profound difference, and one of the most vital import to us. Owing to the mistake that it is a difference of circumstances which makes the life of the world and the life of the spirit, men and women in all ages have left the world in order to find the Divine. They have gone out into desert and jungle and cave, into mountain and solitary plain, imagining that by giving up what they called "the world", the life of the spirit might be secured. And yet if God be all-pervading and everywhere, He must be in the marketplace as much as in the desert, in the house of commerce as much as in the jungle, in the law-court as much as in the solitary mountain, in the haunts of men as well as in the lonely places. And although it be true that the weaker souls can more easily sense the all-pervading life where the jangle of humanity is not around them, that is a sign of weakness and not a sign of spirituality. It is not the strong, the heroic, the warrior, who asks for solitude in his seeking for the spiritual life.

Yet in the many lives that men lead in their slow climbing to perfection the life of the solitary has its place, and often a man or woman for a life will go aside into some lonely place and dwell there solitary. But that is never the last and crowning life, it is never the life in which the Christ walks the earth. Such a life is sometimes led for preparation, for the breaking off of ties which the man is not strong enough otherwise to break. He runs away because he cannot battle, he evades because he cannot face. And in the days of the weakness of the man, of his childhood, that is often a wise policy; and for any one over whom temptations have still strong power it is good advice to avoid them. But the true hero of the spiritual life avoids no place and shuns no person; he is not afraid of polluting his garments, for he has woven them of stuff that cannot be soiled. In the earlier days sometimes flight is wise, but it should be recognised as what it is - weakness, and not strength. And those who live the solitary life are men who will return again to lead the life of the world, and having learned detachment in the solitary places will keep that power of detachment when they return to the ordinary life of men. Liberation, the freeing of the spirit, that conscious life of union with God which is the mark of the man become Divine, that last conquest is won in the world, it is not won in the jungle and the desert.

In this world the spiritual life is gradually to be won, and by means of this world the lessons of the spirit are to be learned - but on one condition. This condition embraces two stages first, the man does all that ought to be done because it is duty. He recognises, as the spiritual life is dawning in him, that all his actions are to be performed, not because he wants them to bring him some particular result, but because it is his duty to perform them easily said, but how hard to accomplish! The man need change nothing in his life to become a spiritual man, but he must change his attitude to life; he must cease to ask anything from it; he must give to it everything he does, because it is his duty. Now that conception of life is the first great step towards the recognition of the unity. If there be only one great life, if each of us is only an expression of that life, then all our activity is simply the working of that Life within us, and the results of that working are reaped by the common Life and not by the separated self. This is what is meant by the ancient phrase: "give up working for fruit" - the fruit is the ordinary result of action.

This advice is only for those who will to lead the spiritual life, for it is not well for people to give up working for the fruit of action until the more potent motive has arisen within them, that spurs them into activity without the prize coming to the personal self. Activity we must have at all hazards; it is the way of evolution. Without activity the man does not evolve; without effort and struggle he floats in one of the backwaters of life, and makes no progress along the river. Activity is the law of progress; as a man exercises himself, new life flows into him, and for that reason it is written that the slothful man may never find the Self. The slothful, the inactive man has not even begun to turn his face to the spiritual life. The motive for action for the ordinary man is quite properly the enjoyment of the fruit. This is God's way of leading the world along the path of evolution. He puts prizes before men. They strive after the prizes, and as they strive they develop their powers. And when they seize the prize, it crumbles to pieces in their hands - always. If we look at human life, we see how continually this is repeated. A man desires money; he gains it, millions are his; and in the midst of his millions a deadly discontent invades him, and a weariness of the wealth that he is not able to use. A man strives for fame and wins it; and then he calls it: "A voice going by, to be lost on an endless sea." He strives for power, and when he has striven for it all his life and holds it, power palls upon him, and the wearied statesman throws down office, weary and disappointed. The same sequence is ever repeated. These are the toys by holding out which the Father of all induces His children to exert themselves, and He Himself hides within the toy in order to win them; for there is no beauty and no attraction anywhere save the life of

God. But when the toy is grasped the life leaves it, and it crumbles to pieces in the hand, and the man is disappointed. For the value lay in the struggle and not in the possession, in the putting forth of powers to obtain, and not in the idleness that waits on victory. And so man evolves, and until these delights have lost their power to attract, it is well that they shall continue to nerve men to effort and struggle. But when the spirit begins to stir and to seek its own manifestation, then the prizes lose their attractive power, and the man sees duty as motive instead of fruit. And then he works for duty's sake, as part of the One Great Life, and he works with all the energy of the man who works for fruit, perhaps even with more. The man who can work un-wearying at some great scheme for human good and then, after years of labour, see the whole of it crumbling to pieces before him, and remain content, that man has gone far along the road of the spiritual life. Does it seem impossible? No. Not when we understand the Life, and have felt the Unity; for in that consciousness no effort for human good is wasted, no work for human good fails of its perfect end. The form matters nothing; a form in which the work is embodied may crumble, but the life remains.

And in order to make it very clear that such a motive may animate men even outside the spiritual life, we may consider how sometimes in some great campaign of battle it is realised that success and failure are words that change their meaning, when a vast host struggles for a single end. Sometimes a small band of soldiers will be sent to achieve a hopeless, an impossible task. Sometimes to a commanding officer may come an order which he knows it impossible to obey: "Carry such-and-such a place" - perhaps a hillside, bristling with cannon, and he knows that before he can gain the top of that hill his regiment will be decimated, and, if he presses on, annihilated. Does it make any difference to the loyal soldier who trusts his general and leads his men? No. The man does not hesitate when the impossible task is put before him; he regards it only as a proof of the confidence of his commander, that he knows him strong enough to fight and inevitably fail. And after the last man dies, and only the corpses remain, have they failed? It looks so to those who have only seen that little part of the struggle; but while they held the attention of the enemy, other movements had been made unnoticed which rendered victory secure, and when a grateful nation raises the monument of thanks to those who have conquered, the names of those who have failed in order to make the victory of their comrades possible will hold a place of honour in the roll of glory, and of the nation's gratitude. And so with the spiritual man. He knows the plan cannot fail. He knows the combat must in the end be crowned with victory, and what matters it to him, who has known the Oneness, that his little part is stamped by the world as failure, when it has made possible the victory of the great plan for human redemption, which is the real end for which he worked? He was not working to make success here, to found some great institution there, he was working for the redemption of humanity. And his part of the work may have its form shattered; it matters not, the life advances and succeeds.

That is what is meant by working for duty. It makes all life comparatively easy. It makes it calm, strong, impartial, and undaunted; for the man does not cling to anything he does. When he has done it, he has no more concern with it. Let it go for success or failure as the world counts them, for he knows the Life within is ever going onwards to its goal. And it is the secret of peace in work, because those who work for success are always troubled, always anxious, always counting their forces, reckoning their chances and possibilities; but the man who cares nothing for success but only for duty, he works with the strength of divinity, and his aim is always sure.

That is the first great step, and in order to be able to take it there is one secret that we must remember: we must do everything as though the Great Power were doing it through us. That is the secret of what is called "inaction in the midst of action". If a man of the world would become truly spiritual, that is the thought that he must put behind all his work. The counsel, the judge, the solicitor, what must be the motive in each man's heart if in these ordinary affairs of life he would learn the secret of the spirit? He must regard himself simply as an incarnation of Divine Justice. "What," a man says, "in the midst of law as we know it? "Yes, even there, imperfect as it is, full of wrongs as it may be, it is the Justice of God striving to make itself supreme on earth; and the man who would be a spiritual man in the profession of the law must think of himself as an incarnation of the Divine Justice, and always have at the heart of his thought: "I am the Divine hand of Justice in the world, and as that I follow law." And so in all else. Take Commerce. Commerce is one of the ways by which the world lives - a part of the Divine activity. The man in Commerce must think of himself as part of that circulating stream of life by which nations are drawn together. He is the Divine Merchant in the world, and in him Divine activity must find hands and feet. And all who take part in the ruling and guidance of the nation, they also are representatives of the Divine Lawgiver, and only do their work aright as they realise that they incarnate His life in that aspect towards His world. I know how strange this sounds when we think of the strife of parties, and of the pettiness of politicians; but the degradation of man does not touch the reality of the Divine Presence, and in every ruler, or fragment of a ruler, the Divine Lawgiver is seeking to incarnate Himself in order that the nation may have a national life, noble, happy, and pure. And if only a few men in every walk of life strove thus to lead the spiritual life; if, casting aside all fruits of individual action, they thought of themselves as only incarnations of the many aspects of the Divine activity in the world, how then would the life of the world be made beautiful and sublime!

And so in the life of the home. The head of the household, the husband, incarnates God in his relation of supporter and helper of the life of His universe. So much has this been seen in older days, that the LOGOS of the universe, God manifest, is said in one old Hindu book to be the Great Householder. And so should every husband think of himself as incarnating the Divine Householder, whose wife and children exist not for his comfort or delight, but in order that he may show out the Divine as perfect man, as husband and father. And so also the wife and mother should think of herself as the incarnation of the other side of Nature, the side of matter, the nourisher, and show out the ceaseless providing of Nature for all her children's needs. As the great Father and Mother of all protect and nourish their world, so are the parents to the children in the home where the spiritual life is beginning to grow. Thus might all life be made fair; and every man and woman who begins to show the spiritual life becomes a benediction in the home and in the world.

The second great step that men may take, when duty is done for duty's sake, is that which adds joy to duty - the fulfilment of the Law of Sacrifice; that noblest, highest, view of life, which sees one's self not as the Divine Life merely in activity in the world, but as the Divine Life that sacrifices Itself that all may live. For it is written that the dawn of the universe is an act of sacrifice, and the support of the universe is the continual sacrifice of the all-pervading Spirit that animates the whole. And when that mighty sacrifice is realised as the life of the universe, what joy more full and passionate than to throw oneself into the sacrifice and have a share in it, however small, to be part of the sacrificial life by which the worlds evolve. Well might it be said by those who see life, and realise what it means: "Where, then, is sorrow, where, then, delusion, when once the Oneness has been seen?" That is the secret of the joy of the spiritual man. Losing everything outside, he wins everything within.

I have often said, and it remains true ever, that while the life of the form consists in taking, the life of the spirit consists in giving, and it is that which made the Christ, as the type of the Spiritual Giver, declare: "It is more blessed to give than to receive"" For, truly, those who know the joy of giving have no hankerings after the joy of receiving; they know the upwelling spring of joy unfailing that arises within the heart as the Life pours out. For if the Divine Life could flow into us and we keep it within ourselves, it would become even as the mountain-stream becomes if it be caught in some place whence it may not issue, and gradually grows stagnant, sluggish, dead; but the life through which the Divine Life pours unceasing knows no stagnation and no weariness, and the more it outpours the more it receives. Let us not, then, be afraid to give. The more we give the fuller shall be our life. Let us not be deluded by the world of separateness, where everything grows less as we give it. If I had gold my store would lessen with every coin that I gave away; but that is not so with the things of the spirit; the more we give, the more we have; each act of gift makes us a larger reservoir. Thus we need have no fear of becoming empty, dry, exhausted; for all life is behind us, and its springs are one with us; once we know the life is not ours, once we realise that we are part of a mighty unity, then comes the real joy of living, then the true blessedness of the life that knows its own eternity. All the small pleasures of the world which once were so attractive fade away in the glory of the true living, and we know that those great words are true: "He who loseth his life shall find it unto life eternal."

IX. THEOSOPHY AND ETHICS.

An Address given *at the Parliament of Religions, Chicago, 1893.*

IN the part of the Syllabus that we are considering this afternoon, we have to conclude the discussion opened by our Indian brother, tracing on from step to step the meaning of Altruism, the growth of morality, the sanction, the motive of ethics, and the identity of moral teaching in every great religion in the world. That we have chosen as a final presentment in this Congress of our philosophy, for all philosophy has its right ending in ethics and in conduct, which is of the most vital importance to men and women in their daily life.

First of all, then, we have the word Altruism, "incumbent", it is said, "because of man's common origin, common training, common destiny", and so on. And it is true that in the earliest stages of moral life, altruism must be the goal that we set before ourselves. The service of others is what we should strive to perfect. But sometimes it has also seemed to me that altruism is itself but a stage of progress rather than the goal. That as long as service is consciously service of others, that is, of others separated from our own self, that there is still incompleteness in the ethics, there is still lack of spirituality in the soul.

Some of you may remember that exquisite Persian poem in which the lover, seeking his beloved, finds closed against him the door of her chamber, and knocks, pleading for admission. From within the closed room sounds a voice asking "Who asks for admission?" And believing that his love was the best claim that could be given for his entry, he answered, "It is thy beloved that knocks." But there was silence within the room and the door remained closed against the suppliant. Out into the world he went and learned deeper lessons of life and of love; and coming back once more to the closed door, he struck thereon and asked for entry. Again the voice came, "Who is it that knocks?" But the answer this time was other than at first. No longer "Thy beloved" came the words, but, "It is thyself that knocks," and then the door unclosed, he passed the threshold. For all true love has its root in unity, and there again it is not twain but one. So it would seem that in the highest ethic this is the true note that we should strike, inasmuch as for our best beloved there is no such thing as service regarded as altruistic, because the deepest joy and the highest pleasure come in serving that which is in very truth the better self of each; so as we grow in spiritual life and understand the true oneness of humanity, we shall find in that humanity the best beloved. We shall serve our higher self in serving it, and thus once more we come back to that from which we started, the Invisible, the One and the All.

And Altruism, glorious as it is in the lower stages of morality - Altruism itself - is lost in the Supreme Oneness of the human soul, in the absolute indivisibility of the Spirit in Man. While, however, we are still consciously separate. Altruism may rightly be regarded as the Law of Life, based on a common origin in the Divine, based in the common training, the pilgrimage which every soul of man must tread, based also in common experience, in that life after life where we have to learn every lesson, acquire all knowledge, share the various possibilities of human lot, and build out of common material a sublime character. In that life our destiny is one, the perfection of a divine humanity; one in origin, one in training, one in destiny, what shall avail to separate Man from Man and to build up walls of division between brothers?

Thus this Unity is the foundation of our brotherhood, as Brotherhood is the word that includes all our ethics. For it is in the law of Love that all true conduct has its root. As long as external law is needed, that law is the measure of our imperfection; it is only when no law is wanted, when the nature expressing itself spontaneously is one with the divine law, it is only then that humanity is perfected and liberty and law become one for evermore.

Here again is the sanction of right ethics, found in this fact of brotherhood everywhere discoverable in nature. All our European World discussing ethical systems today, is asking for some categorical imperative which shall announce duty and right to man. Take what systems you will in our German Schools of Philosophy, the system of Kant in Germany or any of the many schools of ethics being gradually built by our English-speaking people - everywhere you will find the question propounded, What is the Imperative? What is the Ought? What is the Thou Shalt, which is to be the training in human life?

"It is not possible," say some schools, and you may find this expressed very clearly and well in one of the well-known books of Professor Sedgwick in dealing with the question of Ought - we are face to face with a difficulty as to why we ought. Can we get any further than a conditional imperative? Can we go beyond the statement to Men, If you want to reach such a goal, such-and-such is the path you should pursue?

To take his own illustration, you may say to a pupil, "If you want to paint and be a great artist, you must hold your brush in such fashion; you must train your eye by such-and-such rules; you must gradually gain the knowledge which underlies form, and by these many steps you shall at last reach your goal."

Is morality the same in this sense as Art or Science? Is it always to depend upon an If, so that if Man refuses the goal he shall reject right conduct and stand lawless in a universe of law? If that be so, it seems to me that progress will be very slow amongst men, for you would have them first to evolve the conscience, and it is the very training of the conscience for which right ethics is needed. You would be walking constantly in a vicious circle having no point of starting. You would be endeavouring to use a lever with an absent fulcrum, and so find no vantage point to which your force could be applied. It is the categorical imperative we need, not the conditional. Not "If Thou wilt be perfect, do this or that," but, "Thou shalt be perfect, and the Law of Life is Thus."

And is it not true that Nature speaks in such fashion? Is it not true that from the lips of Nature, physical, we will say, there sounds ever the categorical imperative? Man, ignorant and foolish, unknowing the laws that surround him, desires to follow the promptings of his own untrained will, driven perhaps by the desires of the lower nature and hearing in them the voice that allures and compels. From the lips of Nature drop sternly the words, "Thou shalt". Answers the will of Man able to choose, "I will not". And then there falls upon the silence but the two words, "Then suffer".

Such is the way in which physical nature teaches the inviolability of law. Man, following his own untrained will, strives to follow it, be a fence of physical law around him or not. He dashes himself against the iron wall he cannot break, and the pain of the bruising, the anguish of the mutilation, teaches him that law is inviolable and unchangeable, that it must be obeyed or the disobedient will perish in the struggle.

Is Nature different on her different planes? Does she speak clearly, as well in the moral and in the spiritual world as in the physical? Yea, for all nature is one. The expression of the one divine will is nature, and until you can change the divine will no law that is the expression of that will can be altered; and, therefore, in morals as much as in physics, this imperative, this categorical imperative, is hers. But unhappily, it has not been undisputed; unhappily, men have thought they could play with morals where they would never dream of playing with physical necessity. They have thought that they could sow one seed and reap another, when they were sowing virtue and vice instead of the mere corn or oats. And they have wondered and they have not understood when each seed is ripened after its own nature, and the moral seed has ripened according to law, and given a corrupt society and degraded humanity and a soul stupefied and drugged by sense.

Does such teaching seem stern and cold? Does it seem as though Man in a remorseless universe, found in the wheels of destiny rolling round him no place of refuge, no harbour in which he might escape? Does he feel that these wheels moving round him crush him, that law is iron, and destiny cannot be escaped? My brothers, ill do you read the Universe if to you law seems cruel, if to you death may seem soulless. Law is but the will of the divine, and the divine who desires your happiness. Law is but the expression of the perfect, and only in perfection can joy and peace be found. Lose sight of this will for a moment, of those wheels that seem to crush you, for though the wheels roll on unchanging, the very heart of the universe is love. Therefore it is that some of us who have caught glimpses of this unity, who have seen that love and justice are one, and that injustice and cruelty would be identical, therefore it is sometimes that, looking at the universe, we feel that while the law is changeless it lifts us instead of crushing us. And has not your own Emerson taught you the same lesson? Can you remember in one of those marvelous essays of his he taught the great truth that Nature only looks cruel while we oppose her; she is our strongest helper when we join ourselves to her. For every law that crushes you while you oppose it lifts you when you are united to it. Every force that is against you while you are lawless, is on your side when you make yourself one with law. He tells you to hitch your wagon on to a star, for then the wagon shall move with all the force of the planet above you; and is it not a greater destiny even to suffer until we learn the law, than to escape it and remain in ignorance when the law is that which brings us ultimately to triumph? Nature is conquered by obedience, and the divine is found in a unity of justice and of love.

Brotherhood, then, in its full meaning, is a law in nature. Stress has more than once been laid on this in our meetings, but not too much stress has thereon been laid. For it is the very object, the desire, of our work that brotherhood shall become practical in society, and it will never become practical until men understand that it is a law, and not only an aspiration. It is a common experience that when, men have discovered a law of nature, they no longer fight against it. They at once accommodate themselves to the new knowledge. They at once adapt themselves to the newly-understood conditions, and in that very way have preached brotherhood. And yet brotherhood is but so little known in our Western World! Is it not possible that men have disobeyed, not because they do not recognise the beauty of the ideal, but because they have not understood its absolute necessity, and the failure of every effort that goes against the universal law in life.

Brothers in our bodies by that interaction of physical molecules of which our Brother W.Q.Judge has already spoken; brothers in our minds by that interaction of mental images and mental pictures whereby every one of us is constantly affecting his brothers. In our spirits, above all, and on every plane of life, brotherhood exists as fact.

And it must be remembered, in dealing with this brotherhood, that the word is meant to imply everything that it means in what we call the closest relationships of daily life. We are apt to make a distinction between brethren in churches and those outside. We should follow in that which we preach of, if it is that real brotherhood of love that we desire amongst men. Sometimes it is said that by ceasing to love the nearest we shall grow to love impersonal humanity. It is not so. The life of love is a growth upward, an expansion ever widening, growing out from the family to the city, from the city to the state; from the nation to humanity. It does not begin by dwarfing the love of the home. It starts there and it carries on all the passions - the passion and the pity that the mother feels for the child of her own body, and extends that love to embrace every child and son of man - not by cooling down love, but by strengthening and widening it out.

Thus is brotherhood to grow and the race to become practically, as it is essentially, one. For it is these relationships that teach the wider possibility, and so, in the Book of the Golden Precepts, one of the most exquisite gifts that we have received from the East through H. P. Blavatsky, we are told, "Follow the wheel of life; follow the wheel of duty to race and kin"; as those duties are properly discharged we become worthy of the wider work. The heart widens out because it is never closed against any. And at the very beginning of the path, the first step the disciple is bidden to take is to make his heart respond to every cry of nature, so that, as the heart-sling quivers under the touch, he, as string, shall quiver to every cry of need that comes from his brother's lips. But if we confine our love to those with whom nature has put us, it is lower love. The lower love is selfish, exclusive, taking from the outside to give to the personally beloved, and careless for the wants of others provided one's own is satisfied. I mean one's own in the family, not one's own personally. That is not true love. It is a form only of selfishness, and when you find in our teaching that such love is to be destroyed, it means that love must be purified of every taint of personality, and so we must grow ever upward, widening as we grow, because the love that we are to give to our brother man is to be measured by his want of it, and not by any of the lesser ties of personality that may bind us to him or may be absent between him and us. The measure of want - that is the measure of giving. The agony that cries for help - that is the claim that we have to answer. And so our teachers train us to discharge the nearest duty so that we may carry on the strength of that to the wider duty, and thus make our love to man as the love of husband to wife, as the love of brother to sister, finding in the pain but joy in the sacrifice, because the happiness of the beloved is deeper than the momentary pain of that which is given to us.

Thus, then we learn, as it were, the sanction, the motive, that which nature tells us as regards this human brotherhood, and from that we step onward to deal with those who are not yet quite touched with that light of reality which makes the appeal to the divine in man the mightiest of impulses.

For as man develops he answers to nobler and nobler impulses, and at first, very often, the method of the teacher must be the method of Nature, which allows men to learn by pain the reality that I was speaking of with regard to the law. And so by Karma we scent another sanction for right ethics; so we teach men that selfishness can but breed sorrow and evil, can have no other offspring than misery. If they will not learn by love they must learn by pain. If they will not learn by longing for God, they must learn by experience of the evil; and if that real tree of life which is in every human heart does not sufficiently attract them to the eating of its fruit, the tree of Life Eternal whose fruits are but of love and duty, then they must eat of the tree of knowledge of evil as well as of good, so that if, to quote one of the sweetest of our English poets - "if Goodness lead him not, then Weariness may toss him to my breast". For that is the voice of the Spirit crying in the world, crying to all that has gone out from it to come back. If its voice does not attract, then suffering must be used for a time to drive. Back the wanderer must come; the exile cannot remain abroad; his seat is empty in the home, it waits for his return, and if he will not come by love, then by starving on the husks that are fit food for swine he must learn the lesson. And the unrest of the transitory, the dissatisfaction of the temporal - that shall turn his steps once more homeward till he come near enough to be drawn by love and no longer by pain.

Thus, then, we have the foundation which deals with facts as sanction for righteousness, and thus Reincarnation once more comes in order to show us that only by right living can progress be made, that if selfishness is to be eradicated unselfish acts must be performed, selfish thoughts must be destroyed, for in reincarnation it is thought which moulds the character, and none can mould the character towards evil and thus discover tendencies to good. Thus we remove arbitrariness from the moral world by knowledge of self. Knowledge has removed it from the physical. Thus we take away all the doubt and the hope that springs from the doubt, that we may escape the results of our own actions and creep into unearned bliss by some side door of vicarious atonement where we have not laboured and where we have not wrought. We learn that each must walk on his own feet that each man must grow by his own effort. Though brother souls must help him, he must also help himself. For Truth does not need invertebrate people saved by the goodness of another. Truth needs men and women strong to stand in the strength they have acquired for themselves, strong that by their example the still weaker may be inspired, and gradually each one may show himself divine.

But all this is not new. There is nothing new save the words that clothe it, nothing new save the garment that is woven round it. We have had all this as our priceless heritage for millions of years, and yet we have not recognised our treasure. Every great teacher of Religion has taught what here I feebly repeat today. Every great one who has come into the world in order to strike the keynote of morality has spoken the same language, has uttered the same thought.

Turn to the scriptures of the world and see how one moral nutriment is found in all. Will you go to China, Lao-tze will teach you the law of love, and teach you the very doctrine familiar in your own creed; for Lao-tze, speaking six hundred years before Christ was born, laid down that law of curing evil by good. Yes, we have not yet learned the only law of Peace.

"The untruthful," he said, "I will meet with truth, as I meet the truthful also. I will meet the liberal with liberality, I will meet the illiberal with liberality also. The faithful I will meet with faith, the unfaithful I will meet with faith also. I will cure the miser by generosity, I will cure the liar by truth."

So, as from the lips of a Chinese teacher, there drops from those of a great Hindu sage exactly the same thought, when in the tenfold system of duties Mano put forgiveness of injuries as the vital law of the progress of the soul. So, six centuries before Christ, the Buddha repeated the lesson - "To him that causelessly injures me I will return the protection of my ungrudging love. The more evil comes from him the better shall flow from me." Exactly the same lesson flows from the lips of the great Jewish teacher when in the Sermon on the Mount he bids his disciples: "Love your enemies, bless them that curse you, do good to them that hate you, that you may be the children of your Father in Heaven, who sendeth his sunlight on the evil and on the good, and sendeth rain alike on the just and on the unjust."

The Voice is one, whether from Jew or Buddhist, whether from Hindu or Chinese, the words are well-nigh one, the spirit is identical. What want we, then, of new morality, while the old remains unfulfilled? Why ask for new teaching when the old is so high above our accomplishment today? It may be that amongst far-off generations, when the growth of Man has been perfected, it may be that in some future cycle of evolution, some morality undreamed of today, some ethic more noble, more sublime, more pure, may come from the lips of some God to man. We are not ready for such teaching, we are not yet prepared for such instruction. Enough for us the ancient law of love, for until we have fulfilled that no other horizon can open before our eyes.

And so, at this last of our sessional meetings, we close with that with which we started, the law of a divine life that brings all things with it, the law of a divine love that is the guiding light of man.

Born of the spirit, we go towards the Spirit. Born of the divine love, we live until that love is perfected in us, and when that love is made perfect, what lips of Man may syllable, what brain of Man may conceive, what further heights of beauty, what further depths of joy, what further possibilities of illimitable expansion, lie before those souls whose life is one with the divine. Bound to the feet of divinity, they last as long as it. Boundless as deity itself, no limitations can check the spirit that lives in man.

X. THE SUPREME DUTY

An Address given at the Parliament of Religions, Chicago, 1893.

I SPEAK tonight on the supreme duty. I proclaim tonight the universal law of life; for only by service is fulness of life made possible, to the service of man the whole of the universe today is yoked. For under the name of man, man past, present, and future, man evolving up to the divine man, eternal, immortal, indestructible, that is the service to which every individual should be pledged, that the object of life, that the fashion of evolution; and I shall try to put for you tonight in few words something of the elements of this service, something of its meaning in daily life, as well as something of the heights whereto the daily practice may at length conduct the human soul, for poor indeed is that religion which cannot teach the men and women of the world the duty of daily life, and yield to them inspiration which shall aid them in their upward climbing to the light.

Great is philosophy which moulds the minds of men, great is science which gives light of knowledge to the world; but greater than all is religion which teaches man his duty, which inspires man with strength to accomplish it; greatest of all is that knowledge of the human soul which makes daily service the path of progress and finds in the lowest work the steps that lead to the highest achievement.

According to the philosophy which we stand here to represent, we have in the universe and in man various planes of being, sevenfold in their full enumeration. A briefer classification will serve me for the hints which alone I can throw out tonight. Let us take the plane of the physical man and see what on that plane the service of man may connote. First of all, the service of man implies what was called by the Buddha right livelihood, that is, right fashion of gaining ordinary life, honest way of gaining the means of ordinary existence. Not a livelihood based on the compelled service of others, not a livelihood which takes everything and gives nothing back, not a livelihood which stretches out its hands to grasp and closes its fists when gift is asked instead of gain. Right livelihood implies honesty of living, and honesty implies that you give as much as you take, that you render back more than you receive, that you measure your work by your power of service, not by your power of compulsion. That the stronger your brain the greater your duty to help, that the higher your position the more imperative the cry to bend that position to the service of human need. Right livelihood is based on justice. Right livelihood is made beautiful by love, and if there is to be a reckoning between the giving and the taking, then let the scale of giving weigh the heavier, and give to man far more than you take from him.

But on the material plane more is asked of you than the discharge of this part of duty, right livelihood, that inures none and serves all. You have also a duty of right living that touches on the plane of the body, by which I include tonight the whole of the transitory part of man, and right living means the recognition of the influence that you bring to bear upon the world by the whole of your lower nature as well as by the higher. It implies the understanding of the duty that the body of each bears to the bodies of all, for you cannot separate your bodies from the bodies amidst which you live, since constant interchange is going on between them. Tiny lives that build up you today help to build up another tomorrow, and so the constant interaction and interweaving of these physical molecules proceed. What use do you make of your body? Do you say: "It is mine. I can do with it as I will. Shall not a man do as he will with his own?" Even so. But there is nothing a man has that is his own, for all belongs to that greater man, the aggregate humanity, and the fragments have no rights that go against the claim of service to the whole. So that you are responsible for the use that you make of your bodies. If when these tiny lives come into your charge you poison them with alcohol, you render them coarse and gross with over-luxurious living and send them out into the community of which you form a part, and send them out to other men and women and children, they sow there the seeds of the vices they have learned from you, of the gluttony, of the intemperance, the impurity of living that you have stamped on them while they remained as part of your own body. You have no right to do it. No excuse can bear you guiltless of the crime. There are drunkards amongst us. Granted they are responsible for their crime, but also every human being is responsible for them who helps to spread the poison in a community which is focalized in those miserable creatures. And so every atom that you send out alcohol-poisoned from yourself helps to make drunkenness more permanent, helps to make its grip tighter upon the victims already in its grasp, and you are guilty of your brother's degradation if you do not supply pure atoms of physical life to build up others who in very truth are one with yourself.

And so you have something of what service of man means on this lower plane, and another service that you, above all, richer people in this land and in others, could set an example of, so that others from your voluntary action may learn to follow in the same path, you should simplify the physical life, you should lessen the physical wants, you should think less of luxury and more of the higher life, less labour wasted to minister to the artificial wants of the body, and more time for the souls of men to grow less encumbered with the anxieties of life. If you take such teaching to the poor, true as the teaching is, one hardly dares to put it to them on whom the iron yoke of poverty presses, and who find in so much of physical suffering one of the miseries of their life. You should set the example, because with you it is voluntary action. You should set the ideal of plain living and high thinking instead of the ideal of senseless luxury, of gross materialistic living on every side. Can you blame the poor that they think so much of earthly pleasure, that they desire so passionately material ease? Can you blame them if in every civilised country discontent is growing, threats are filling the air, when you set the ideal which they copy in their desire, and when you, by the material pleasure of your lives, tell them that man's aim and object is but the joy of the sense, is but the pleasure of the moment? This also is your duty in the service of man on a material plane, so that, lessening the wants of the body, he may learn to feed the soul, and making the outer life more nobly simple may give his energies rather to that which is permanent and which endures.

But not only on the physical, the lowest plane, is the service of man to be sought. We rise to the mental plane, and there too must man be served far more efficaciously than he can be served on the physical plane. Do you say that at least I cannot do service on the mental plane? That the mental plane is all very well for the great thinker that publishes some work that revolutionizes thought? That it is all very well for the speaker who reaches thousands where I can reach but units? It is not so. The great thinker, be he writer or be he speaker, has not such enormous over-plus of impulse as you, judging by the outer appearance, may imagine. True, his work is great, but has it never struck you in what lies the power of the speaker, whence comes the strength with which he moves a crowd? It does not lie in himself; it lies not in his own power, but in the power he is able to evoke from the men and women he addresses, from the human hearts he wakes. It is their energy and not his in the tide of his speech. The orator is but the tongue that syllables out the thoughts in the hearts of the people; they are not able to speak them, they are not able to articulate them. The thoughts are there, and when some tongue puts them into speech, when the other inarticulate sense takes the force of the spoken word, then they think it is oratory. It is their own hearts that move them, and it is this voice, inarticulate in the people, which from the lips of the speaker makes the power that rings from land to land.

But that is not all. Every one of you in your daily thinking, every one of you has thoughts that you pour out to the world. You are making the possibilities of the morrow, you are making or marring the potencies of today. Even as you think, the thought burning in your brain becomes a living force for good or for evil in the mental atmosphere just as far as the vitality and the strength that are in it may be able to carry it on in its work of this world of mind. There is no woman, however weak, there is no man however obscure, who has not in the soul within him one of the creative forces of the world. As he thinks, thoughts from him go out to mould the thoughts and lives of other men. As he thinks thoughts of love and gentleness, the whole reservoir of love in the world is filled to overflowing; and as he contributes to them, so every day is formed that public opinion which is the moulder of men's ideas more than sometimes we are apt to dream. So that in this everyone has share, so that in this all men and women have their part. Your thought-power makes you creative Gods in the world, and it is thus that the future is built, it is thus that the race climbs upward to the divine.

Not alone in the physical nor alone in the mental sphere is this constant service of man to be sought; but of the service of the spiritual sphere, no words of platform oratory can fitly describe its nature or its sacredness. That is the work that is done in silence, without sound of spoken word, of clatter of human endeavour. That work lies above us and around us, and we must have learned the perfection of the service in the lower ere we dare aspire to climb where the spiritual work is done. What, then, is the outcome of such suggestion, what the effect in life of such philosophy applied to the life of each as it is made or met in the world today? Surely it is that we should think nobly. Surely it is that our ideals should be lofty. Surely it is that in our daily life we should ever strike the highest keynote, and then strive to attune the living to the keynote that at our noblest we have struck. According to the ideal the will is lifted. In the old phrase, the man becomes that which he worships. Let us see, then, that our ideals be lofty. Let us see that what we worship shall have in it the power that shall transform us into the image of the perfect man; that shall transmute us into the perfect gold of which humanity shall finally consist. If you would help in that evolution, if you would bear your share in that great labour, then let your ideal be truth; truth in every thought and act of life. Think true, otherwise you will act falsely. Let nothing of duplicity, nothing of insincerity, nothing of falsehood soil the inner sanctuary of your life, for if that be pure your actions will be spotless, and the radiance of the eternal truth shall make your lives strong and noble. Not only be true, but also be pure, for out of purity comes the vision of the divine, and only the pure in heart, as said the Christ, shall see God. That is true. In whatever phase you put it, that is true, whatever words describe it. Only the pure in heart shall have the beatific vision, for that which is itself absolute purity must be shared in by the worshipper ere it can be seen.

And then add to these ideals of truth and of purity one that is lacking in our modern life, the ideal of reverence for what is noble, of adoration for that which is higher than one's self. Modern life is becoming petty because we are not strong enough to reverence. Modern life is becoming base, sordid, and vulgar because men fear that they will sink if they bow their heads to that which is greater than they are themselves. I tell you that worship of that which is higher than yourself raises you, it does not degrade you. That the feeling of reverence is a feeling that lifts you up, it does not take you down. We have talked so much about rights that we have forgotten that which is greater than a man's right with himself. It is the power of seeing what is nobler than he has dreamed of, and bowing in the very dust before it till it permeates his life and makes him like itself. Only those who are weak are afraid to obey; only those who are feeble are afraid of humility. Democrats we are in our modern phrase, and with the world of today as we have it democracy in the external world is the best fashion of carrying on the outer life. But if it were possible that as in the days of old in Egypt and India the very gods themselves wandered the earth as men, and taught the people the higher truth, trained the people in the higher life, conveyed to the people the higher knowledge, would we claim that we were their equals, and that we should be degraded by sitting at their feet to learn? And if you could weave into your modern life that feeling of reverence for that which is purest, noblest, grandest; for wisdom, for strength, for purity, till the passion of your reverence should bring the qualities into your own life - Oh, then your future as a nation would be secure. Then your future as a people would be glorious, and you men and women of America, creators of the future, will you not rise to the divine possibilities which every one of you has hidden in his own heart? Why go only to the lower when the stars are above you? Why go only to the dust when the sun sends down his beams that on those beams you may rise to his very heart? Yours is the future, for you are making it today, and as you build the temple of your nation, as you hope that in the days to come it shall rise nobly amongst the peoples of the earth and stand as pioneer of true life, of true greatness, lay you the foundations strong today. No building can stand whose foundations are rotten, no nation can endure whose foundations are not divine. You have the power. Yours is the choice, and as you exercise it the America of centuries to come will bless you for your living or will condemn you for your failure; for you are the creators of the world, and as you will so it shall be.

XI. THE USE OF EVIL

Delivered in India in 1894.

MY BROTHERS, - I am to speak to you this evening on a problem which has tasked the intellect of man for thousands and thousands of years, and which is still discussed today, as though it had never been considered before, with as much energy and eagerness and with as much interest. That it remains unsolved still is shown by the continuance of the discussion and by this unwearied turning to it of the mind of man. Man seems instinctively to imagine that this problem is one which would teach lessons of value and importance, if it could be understood, and that behind the "Mystery of Evil" there is hidden some priceless truth.

I do not pretend that I am going to solve this immemorial problem, but I hope to lay before you certain considerations which may throw light upon it, if you apply yourselves to thinking over them. And in order that you may carry them more easily in your minds I divide the subject under four heads:

1- The Origin of Evil

2-The Relativity of Evil.

3-The Use of Evil.

4- Then ending of Evil

Under these four heads I hope to show you that evil is a necessary part of manifestation, a necessary condition of manifestation, and originates with manifestation. That also it does not exist absolutely, in and by itself, but is relative, relative in that it exists in relations between things and not in the things themselves, and also because it varies with time, with succession of events, and with the progress of the universe. Then I hope to show you the purposes it subserves, the uses it fulfils, and, lastly, how we may escape from it, how we may, by the use of evil, break the bonds that tie us to the wheel of birth and death; how although living in the world, we may live in it without generating Karma, and so, to use a well-known phrase, may burn up Karma in the fire of Knowledge. Following these divisions under which I shall arrange the details, I may be able to give to your minds, the minds of the rising and educated youth of India, ideas that may be worthy of your consideration, in order that you may not simply listen for an hour, but, taking them at leisure, may have materials to work upon after you have left this hall.

Now let us consider the origin of evil. Realise, to begin with, that no universe can come into manifestation at all, that no manifestation can occur, that no multiplicity can become, that no diversity can appear, unless there be limitation. That is the first point that I wish to make clear to your minds. The one existence, spoken of sometimes as *Brahman,* that existence is absolute and undivided; no attributes are there, no qualities are there. There is unity, no diversity; there is unity, no multiplicity. It is "the One without a second". So that, when for a moment you try even to think this Existence, in the very thinking by which you must separate yourself from It, by which you as a mind endeavour to consider some thing which is thought of and is not the thinker, by that very effort of thought you introduce duality into that which you are trying to realise as unity; and when there is separation between the thinker and thought, which is implied in the effort, there is diversity, - not Brahman as One in whom there is no duality, in whom there is no separated Being, in whom there is neither thinker nor thought. Thought implies perception and an object of perception; but Brahman is absolute unity, absolute identity. We speak of thought where thought cannot exist. It is unconditioned, therefore unintelligible; unconditioned, therefore without limitation. And, therefore, truly is it written, *That* is neither conscious nor unconscious - albeit there is some deeper essence which when conditioned becomes consciousness, because consciousness implies duality, consciousness implies something which is conscious, and something of which it is conscious. That is, at least duality is implied the very moment the word consciousness is used, so that in that absolute unity, where there is identity and not diversity, where there is but the secondless *One,* there is no possibility of thinking, because there is absence of conditions, there is absence of limitation. But the very moment the universe has, as it were, to come into being, then there must be conditions, there must be limitation. Limitation is a condition of manifestation, for the very moment you arrive at the point of manifestation, a circumference must be drawn from the central point, the circle of a universe; without that thought is lost in the absolute one-ness, the identity. Within that circle thought may be exercised, and the very word "manifestation" implies at once this limitation. Manifestation, by a law of mind, at once implies its antithesis, the absence of manifestation. To anything which you may think comes the opposite, for the opposite is implied in the very act of defining. "A" implies "not-A". Therefore we are compelled to formulate "absence of manifestation", and yet cannot truly be said to think it. But, as I have just said, manifestation must imply limitation. There is limitation in the very existence of a universe; it is conditioned, and as soon as you think of the matter you at once begin to understand that a universe implies limitation, and that only by a process of limitation can a universe come into being;

conditions self-imposed within the Infinite One-ness that can be recognised as the boundary that limits thought. Well, when that is thought and understood, the next step is very simple. Having diversity, having limitation, there is at once imperfection implied. The perfect is unlimited; the limited, imperfect. So imperfection must be the result of limitation. In the totality you may find perfection; in the whole, but not in the parts. The very moment you have parts, multiplicity, various bodies; each body separately considered is imperfect, because it is less than the whole. The very fact that it is a part proves that it is imperfect; a fragment cannot be perfect; only the whole can have perfection predicated of it. So that we have here a second step. The first is the fact of manifestation implying limitation, and thus limitation making a diversity of objects; the second is that separate bodies must be imperfect, in that each is less than the whole of which only perfection can be declared.

Notice now the links of the argument. Notice that the very fact of a universe implies this imperfection; that if you object to imperfection you must object to manifestation. If you object to limitation, you must object to there being anything which can be thought of, of which consciousness can be predicated, anything save that absolute unity, utterly incomprehensible to thought. So that we have this solid ground to start from, that the existence itself of the universe by the very fact of limitation, implies imperfection in the limited, and that every object being necessarily limited, is also necessarily imperfect, being less than the whole. Now when that is realised, you have your origin of imperfection, of what is called evil. Thus imperfection is co-eternal with the universe. Limited, imperfection is a necessary condition, so that whenever there comes a universe into existence, imperfection must come into existence at the same time. The fact of manifestation is the origin of imperfection.

But when we go on to deal with what is called evil, we find something more in our thoughts than this necessary imperfection of separated bodies; although the essence of imperfection is in the very existence of the universe, that which we call evil lies in the degree of imperfection, and in its relation to the rest. But in the very words "good and evil" relativity is fundamentally implied, the "pairs of opposites" necessary to thought; the word "good" is not fairly to be predicated. of any thing until the idea of evil is recognised - the "not-good"; for good and evil are correlative terms, and the one can only be distinguished as being the opposite of the other which is implicitly present in the mind at the same time. It is a fundamental law of mind that thought must work by difference, discriminating the difference, technically, between "A" and "not-A"; "A" representing the individual thing which is thought of, and "not-A" everything else which is excluded from that individual thing, so that if you say "good" you separate the good from that from which it is distinguished, - the "not-good": and without this separation no idea of good can be present in the mind, for we realise "good" only by contrast with that which is "not-good" and which is distinguished from it. In the absence of that distinguishment there would be nothing which we could call "good". "Good" and "not-good", then, are a pair of opposites, and one is only possible by the existence of the other. Similarly you may take another pair of opposites. Compare light with darkness. Light would have no meaning to you in thought if it were not for darkness or no-light. Light is only cognisable by thought because of no-light. Light-giving bodies can be recognised in thought, because all bodies do not give light; and this is so much the case that the presence of non-light-giving bodies is necessary for realisation of light. Astronomers tell us, startling as seems the statement, that the depths of space are dark, not light, although they are full of the vibrations of the ether which on the earth we recognise as light. Why? Because there are vast spaces of the mighty universe where there are no light-reflecting bodies, themselves non-luminous; and in the absence of these dark ones light cannot be thrown back, reflected; hence space which is full of the vibrations of ether is absolutely dark, because of the absence of those bodies which are the reflectors of light, themselves being dark.

Take still further an extension of the same thought. Evil does not exist in and by itself, as we may judge from the phenomena around us; evil, like good, lies in the relationship between one thing and another; it is relative, not absolute. What we speak of as evil in one place may be not evil in another; for evolution implies this changing character, and what is good at one stage may be evil at another. Presently I will take certain things which we say are evil, and show you that the evil does not reside in the things but in the relationships between them and certain other things, and that it is in the relationship alone that what we call evil resides. Let me take an illustration to show you what I mean. You may have a violently vibrating body, vibrating without touching any other body; vibrating inwards and outwards, which would do no harm, which would cause no pain, and the result of that active motion of the body would not be anything which you would recognise as evil. But place in contact with that violently vibrating body another body, and it will produce what we call a pleasure or a pain - that is if the second body has got the power of response, the power of answering to that which is outside, and of feeling the vibration to which it answers. By coming into contact with the body which is violently vibrating, and by receiving the blow, what we call the sensation of pain might arise. Now pain is regarded as part of the evil of the universe; pain is regarded as one of those things which are the results of what is called evil. But as a matter of fact, pain is the result of contact between two things which separately are innocuous, and arises from the inter-relation of those things which in their separate aspects are not individually pain-producing, but only imperfect, each by itself. When coming into relation with each other, they, as it were, work against each other, then there comes out what we regard as evil, and the nature of the result will depend upon the relation between the two, not even upon the inherent imperfections of each that I spoke of, but on their relations to each other.

Now that leads me to point out to you that as evolution proceeds, that which we call evil must necessarily be developed more and more. As evolution proceeds, the result of the evolution is to bring into conscious existence higher and higher types of organisations, higher and higher types of living things, which enter into more and more complicated relationships with others which surround them, and in these organisations there is developed more and more of this power of response. There is developed also the memory of response; there is developed not only memory but the power of placing things side by side, that is of comparison, and then of considering the results of the comparison and drawing therefrom volitions. And then there is the experience gradually gathered which illumines the developing consciousness, enables it to recognise certain things as things found to be against progress, to be against the higher evolution, certain things which retard evolution, certain things which check it, which tend to bring about disintegration instead of higher integration. Now what means evolution? It is merely the building together of higher and more complicated organizations that express with ever greater and greater perfection the Life that is Divine, the Life that in the universe is seeking manifestation. When we speak of manifestations as higher or lower, we really mean they express more or less of the Divine. We call them higher and lower merely as they manifest qualities, which tend towards the lessening of separateness and the developing of unity, that is which lead away from the pole of matter and lead towards the pole of Spirit. The grosser side of manifestations of the One Life is that which we describe as matter. Now there are two poles in manifestation the form side or that of matter on the one hand, and the life side or that of Spirit on the other. They are the two opposite aspects of the one Eternal Life, and the process of evolution consists in that life in its dual aspects going outwards to cause diversity, and when the limit of diversity is reached, drawing inwards to reintegrate the diverse separated units into a mighty and enriched unity. The outward-going life seeks diversity and may be said therefore to tend to the pole of matter; the inward-going life seeks unity, and may be said therefore to tend to the pole of Spirit. Here is a truth that the thoughtful should ponder over. If we take good to mean all that is working in harmony with the Great Law, and evil to mean all that is working against it, then qualities now regarded, and rightly regarded, as evil - selfishness, desire for material gain, etc. - would have been good during the "descent into matter", as only by these could diversity be obtained, whereas now they are evil as retarding the process of integration, as checking the inward-flowing tide of life towards the pole of Spirit. Thus again we realise the relativity of evil, and understand that a quality which at one time was good, as subserving the progress of the universe, becomes evil when it should have been left behind in the sweep of evolution, and when persisting into a stage higher than that to which it belonged, it retards the progress which once it had accelerated.

Evolution, on its returning path, is unfolding the life-side of nature, and is making, as it were, matter more and more plastic, more and more delicate, more and more complicated in its organisation, until by its very complexity its equilibrium is so unstable that it takes very easily shapes of various kinds under impulses from within and becomes a mere graceful garment in which life is expressed, until, finally, matter is nothing more than the subtle form which expresses life by limiting it, and it changes form with every impulse from the life, and takes on new shapes with the different impulses of the out-going and in-coming life; and this is evolution. When man begins to understand what evolution means, he then regards everything which helps towards evolution as being on the lines of harmony with the purposes of the universe, and therefore with being now on the side of greater and greater integration, of the building together of a complicated unity. Then he names "good" all that works in that direction, and calls "evil" all the tendencies which persist from the stage of evolution in which greater diversity was sought. Realising that evolution is now the process of building together the separated objects into a perfect unity, he calls "good" everything which tends directly to harmony, which tends towards aggregation, which tends towards the unfolding of the higher unity, which tends towards the expression of the Divine life, with ever increasing and increasing perfection; and he calls "evil" every thing which checks that aggregation and which introduces the earlier forms into the present and retards the passing on to what is relatively perfect and relatively higher.

Now suppose we carried that thought out, what would we find? We should find that that which in the past caused evolution and was not evil, becomes evil when it persists in the evolution of the higher organisation and so retards its growth. For instance, in the mineral kingdom you have minerals and stones hurled about by some volcanic eruption; you see that eruption, with its shivering of certain bodies, with its tremendous evolution of gases, accompanied by explosions, and then with the rebound of the separate materials making a desert where before was a fertile plain, and you say: "See this is evil." Yet wise minds, on the contrary, regard it as part of the regenerative processes of nature by which, by disintegration and collision, new combinations are rendered possible, the face of the earth is changed, mountain ranges are thrown up, rivers and channels are created, and by means of this violent destructive agency new continents are built, homes for higher forms of life are rendered possible in the course of the evolution. Let us pause for a moment and contemplate the way in which a continent is built. Let us watch the tremendous action of those volcanic forces, and at one place see a mountain range flung up; then let us watch the formation of mighty glaciers, great masses of ice, and see them presently begin to grind their way down the mountain-side into the plain which lies below; see their resistless course, ploughing out their way, and listen as they go on, smashing, grinding, shivering, tossing up masses which fall again rebounding; watch the processes of that world of struggle, of strife, of noise, of disturbance, of difficulty, and see the marshalling of those energies which seem to be working for ruin and for nothing else. But as centuries go on, and still you are watching, you find that where there was a grinding glacier there is now a new channel, a channel which has been dug out of the mountain side and through the plains by its giant action, and as you watch you find water collecting in this channel and gradually more and more flowing into it, until where there was the destructive action of the ice there is a great river full of life-giving water; and as the water flows down through the plain vegetation springs up on the banks, and great cities are building, food can be grown for keeping up the life of man, trees are growing luxuriantly, and human homes are seen, and happiness on every side. But what would have been man's lot without that previous evolution? We can see that unless the disturbing agency had had full sway in these earlier growths of life you would never have had the later; so you cannot call that evil. There is nothing evil in itself, for these are simple destructive and attractive forces at work, and the Being who is the source of all life, the great One, The Lord, is known sometimes as the Destroyer and sometimes as the Regenerator, for, until the lower is destroyed the higher cannot be born, and every death is but the lower aspect of a higher birth.

But if we turn to man, to those who been gradually evolved, those human beings who have begun to reason, who have begun to remember, to compare, and therefore to judge and to understand - when amongst them there appears a disturbing agency, which lies at the root of all the angry passions of man, then man having evolved to a stage at which the infliction of pain on others is against his evolution towards the Divine Love, we call that infliction of pain a "Crime". Why for instance do we call a murder an evil act? We call it an evil because the murderer is there reverting to a previous stage in evolution that he ought to have outgrown; as a man he should have evolved towards a higher life of harmony, but he is giving way to an inclination which will bring about the retardation of growth, and which at the stage which he has reached is harmful. At the point of evolution he should have reached, he ought to be one of the forces evolving towards the Divine Harmony and not one of the forces which are retarding that evolution, and rendering it slower of accomplishment.

I am going to deal with the use of this retarding agency. Let us now take a man who begins to understand that in the sphere of thought and action he can place himself either upon the side of progress or upon the side of retardation; who realises his place in the universe, who realises the true working of nature, and who may deliberately set himself either on the side of the evolving life, or upon the side of the forces which are retarding evolution, which are holding it back, which are against progress, which are not in harmony with it. Such a man has to choose with which side he shall identify himself. He may choose to identify himself with the side which is progressing on to the gods or he may choose to identify himself with the side which is retarding that evolution. His choice is in his own hands. He must realise that if he chooses the side which retards evolution he has chosen destruction, by identifying himself with the disintegrating agency; whereas if he chooses harmony with evolving life, he has chosen continuation, because he has identified himself with that which is the law of progress, and the fact of his identification with that law will give to him the permanence which results from harmony. You may say, why should identification with the retarding forces lead to destruction? The answer is this: because the Divine Life going on and causing evolution returns to unity, and everything which harmonises with its mighty course is carried onwards without waste of energy; whereas everything which sets itself against it, and causes friction and retardation, wears itself out by the very friction which it causes. It is one of the laws of motion that a moving body continues to move if not opposed, but if friction is generated by its coming into contact with another body it will gradually come to a standstill; wherever there is friction there is this expenditure of energy, and this friction transmutes moving energy into another form, such as heat, and the energy is dissipated; continued friction causes the dissipation of the form which is subject to it. It is not that the energy is annihilated; it is not that the energy is destroyed; that cannot be. It is that the form is destroyed which comes into contact with that in which the opposite force is manifested. The form perishes because the opposition breaks it - into pieces, or rather it breaks itself into pieces against the opposing force, but the energy persists because it is part of one eternal life. But you may say, why this retarding force? Why should there be in evolution this action of retardation? Why should there be in evolution something which opposes? How can it come? If everything is from the One, how can it develop?

First, because the condition of any diversity is the manifestation of the opposing poles of Spirit and matter, of light and darkness, that I spoke of in the beginning; and, secondly, because for the development of all positive qualities, it is necessary that they should be exercised against opposition. Without opposition no development is possible; without opposition no growth is possible. All growth and development result from the exercise of energy against some thing which opposes. Think for a moment and; you will see how true this statement is. You have muscles in your arms; if you want to develop the strength of the muscles, how are you to do it? By exercising them, by stimulating them, not by keeping them still. You know there are some people who practise a particular form of asceticism, who extend the arm and keep it rigid, so that muscular contraction cannot take place. What is the result? After a time the arm becomes fixed in that position, it becomes rigid, the muscles lose the power of contraction; they are no longer the channels of living energy; in fact, there is stagnation, absence of effort, absence of muscular contraction, of pulling against resistant forces; the result is to throw the arm backwards, as it were, into a lower form of living thing, to which motion as a whole does not belong, and the arm becomes as rigid as a stone or a piece of wood; it has lost the muscular power for want of exercise, because it has remained quiet and stagnant, and therefore the power of motion has disappeared. But if a man wants to develop his muscles what does he do? He takes a club which has weight, he takes a dumb-bell which has weight, he takes any object which has weight, and then sets muscle against weight and pulls against it, whirls it round, but always puts the muscle against the opposing force in the weight. He lifts it from the ground; and the weight tries to drag him down and he tries to drag it up. The effect of this conflict is the development of muscular energy, the development of force in the muscle. Muscularity is drawn out and developed by working against the opposing weight; it becomes stronger and becomes able to overcome opposing forces, and so the muscle grows and develops the more the more it is exercised, and becomes more powerful than before. This development arises entirely because it has been used in opposing weight, and by exercise has overcome the opposition; from this it has gathered life and strength, for as the muscle increases its capacity for holding life, life flows into it, and ever the strength we can draw from, the surrounding Divine life is limited only by our capacity to receive and hold.

There is the use of evil. The life that is in you cannot manifest its higher capacities unless you are placed under conditions in which you can develop yourselves by struggling against opposition. Evil is, as it were, the weight opposing the muscle, and as you develop the body by struggling against the opposing external weight; so do you develop the moral character by struggling against evil which is the opposite of every virtue. Every virtue has its opposite evil. Truth and falsehood, courage and cowardice, compassion and hatred, humility and pride. All these things are, pairs of opposites. How can you develop truth save by struggling against the false, save by realising that in the world around you there is falsehood on every side of you? What can you do when you realise the force of this, save contradict it and place yourself in opposition to it, and yourself be true? Never let a false word escape your lips; never let a false thought find habitation in your brain, never let a false action disfigure your conduct, and the result of the recognition of falsehood will be to develop in you the necessary power for truth. As you struggle against the tendency to falseness, there is developed in you the increasing power to be true. Now what is Truth? Truth is Brahman: Truth is life: Truth is the essence of what we call the Divine Life; and we reach it by struggling against falsehood, developing, as it were, the virtue which is the receptacle of the Divine Life, and as you enlarge it and increase it by your struggling against falsehood - as the muscle grows larger by practice against the weight you are making your character a receptacle for the Divine Life, that Divine Life which shall flow in ever-increasing volume and give you greater power. Thus you are developing those qualities of Truth which without opposition you could never have evolved, and which, in proportion to the energies evolved by your efforts against falsehood, will purify your nature from falsity, and render true the life which you are developing. So also with every other virtue. Courage is developed in the presence, not in the absence, of an object which you fear. If there were no objects which gave rise to the sensation of fear, then courage could never be evolved. But the presence of these objects that give the sensation of fear increases the experience of that Soul and gradually evolves courage. Have you ever noticed in an infant, that that which at first was terrifying to it, that which was an object of terror to it when first seen, gradually loses its terrifying quality as it becomes more and more familiar? See how timid a little child is; see how he sees even in a strange face an object which terrifies him. How shall that child lose that timidity and become brave in the face of men? Not by shutting him up in a room where he will never see anybody. If you keep him in a room where there is no strange face the child has no fear. Fear is generated by letting him face unknown objects, and presently he begins to understand them, until out of constant experiences fear is eliminated, and strength and courage take its place.

And so I might take virtue after virtue to show that they grow only in the face of opposition, and that in the result of these opposing forces lies the value of this retarding energy *there* is the value of the evolution of evil which acts as - a weight against the effort towards perfection and thereby develops the strength which checks the desire for these forms which are doomed to destruction; for the men who choose to ally themselves with that which is doomed to destruction, must share the fate of those forms they have selected for their own. But the energy which is necessary for evolution towards the condition of perfection would be absent without evil, and the presence of evil in the universe makes it possible for good to grow and for perfection to triumph.

Nor must we forget as a fundamental use of evil the evolution of the power to discriminate between good and evil, and thus of volition, of choice. How should we distinguish Truth save by discerning it as different from that which is not true? How should we learn its value if we did not find from experience the destructive effects of falsehood, in man and in society. "A" is only brought into consciousness by the presence of "not-A" and the latter is necessary to the definition of the former in the mind. So our mind would remain a blank as regards Truth, we could not realise it, cognise it, define it, save as distinguishing it by its differences from not-Truth. And so with each virtue, with good in its totality. Only by recognition of evil can we know good. And to recognition of evil, experience of evil is necessary.

Useful also is evil as a scourge that drives us to good. For as evil is discordance with the evolving forces of the Divine Life in manifestation, it must result in pain. Pain verily *is* discordant vibration. Therefore evil inevitably brings suffering as a result, not by an arbitrary penalty but by an inherent necessity. And suffering gives rise to a feeling of repulsion towards the cause of suffering, and so drives man away from the side of nature which in-harmoniously and tumultuously is plunging into disintegration, and carrying with it the personalities who elect to identify themselves therewith. In the mighty stream of Divine Life that circles as a universe all men are carried along; but one current whirls downwards all monstrous and disorderly growths, that they may be disintegrated into the rough materials for a new building, while the other current carries onwards all that are moulding themselves into orderly expressions, and that by making themselves vehicles of the Law share its permanence as an essential manifestation of the One Reality. I said, when dealing with pain, that I would show you how it was possible that this evil which we see around us and recognise as evil might gradually lose over us its retarding power as the God in us evolves outwardly and fills us with strength. Remember that the line along which I have been leading you will enable you to look with understanding and, therefore, with absolute charity on all the forms of evil which surround you; you will see in them inevitable imperfections; if you see the human Soul struggling in corruption and in evil, you will not feel anger nor intolerance, nor hatred, but you will know that this Soul, just because of the evil with which it is struggling, will gradually gain strength and become triumphant over it. So that at last you will understand how the Divine is in everything, in good as in evil, that Shri Krishna is the vice of the gambler as well as the purity of the righteous, and our universe will become full of hope; for you will recognise that the whole is working towards perfection, and that good and evil are the two forces which cooperate to liberate the Soul, the one by drawing it upwards, the other by shattering everything to which it clings and which is not God.

But the point to which I wish to lead you is that as you gradually recognise these facts you will see that the aim of the individual self is to become perfectly at one with the inward-going stream of Divine Life; this is the beginning of understanding, the beginning of the realisation of the meaning of the universe, and you will begin to utilise what seems to be evil in order that you may get rid of everything which binds you down to the transitory side of nature, and so take pain as a real helper. Pain is said to be an evil. Pain is not pleasant, but it is not an evil; it is desirable and not undesirable, for it is a condition of gaining perfection, and without it perfection cannot be. And why? For this reason: that development must become conscious, that is, there must be a gradual development of thought within us. But by what process can this be secured? When we go outward towards an object which attracts us we at first seek only satisfaction. But in the external there is no permanent satisfaction; in the external which attracts the deluded Soul of man there is nothing that can give permanent satisfaction to the Soul. The Soul has been compared to a charioteer, standing in the chariot of the body, and using the mind as the reins to curb the horses of the senses; when the galloping horses of the senses carry the Soul away to the objects of desire, how shall the Soul learn that these objects are not truly desirable? How shall it lose the desire which goes out to these things which can never satisfy? And how shall it learn to turn inward to the centre, and seek for Brahman alone? It can only be led to turn towards its desires when it finds that everything which is not Brahman passes away, and in the passing away gives pain. You desire the gratification of the senses. How shall that desire be eliminated? Only by discovering that the pleasure they yield is very transitory, that if it is followed too far it brings about disgust and suffering and pain, and that therefore the freedom and the wisdom of man lie in getting rid of the desire for sense-pleasures, if having been attracted by the sensation of taste because it is pleasant, we find that to gratify it to the utmost brings disgust, then we begin to see that it will be wiser to choose an object which has more permanence than the gratification of taste. Then the root of desire is pulled up and can send out these lower shoots no more. But you can never convince men that this is so unless they have tried the following of the objects of the lower desires and have found the results which flow from them. Argument would not do it, reasoning would not do it; but when men have had the experience, when men have gratified their taste to the full, when they have become gluttonous, presently they will find that they have made their bodies miserable, their lives one long suffering, that diseases result from the gratification they have experienced, that the gratification brings *pain* as a result; then they will no longer desire to gratify themselves in that way, and the root of desire will be cut away; or rather the process of cutting it away will have begun, for the process is a long one. And that is the only way desire can be finally extirpated. You can only get rid of it by gradually realising through experience the knowledge that the gratification of all desire which is not going upwards is a womb of pain, and brings forth woe as a child. Nothing but this experience can get rid of desire; not by outward compulsion but inward will must the destruction of desire take place, and this is wrought by pain. Hence is pain, miscalled an evil, one of the greatest blessings bestowed upon man, in order to turn him from the transitory and fix him upon the eternal; for only by pain can he possibly learn, only out of disgust with the world will arise those inward aspirations which shall at last be gratified in the vision of *Truth Divine*.

Do not misunderstand me, for misunderstanding on this matter is very easy but very dangerous. The stage of the full gratification of desire that I have been speaking of is the stage of the Soul's childhood, ere yet the memory of the Soul recalling past suffering following on gratification, translates itself as the voice of conscience, and warns the lower nature of the peril of yielding to desire. When once experience has been sufficient to bring about such warning from the Soul, then it is madness to disregard it and gratify desire in its despite. Full gratification of desire belongs to the stage where the outer attraction is yielded to without a pause, without a doubt, without a question, and is followed by no regret, by no shame, by no remorse. The rising of any question in the mind as to the propriety or the wisdom of gratifying the desire, shows that the memory of the Soul contains a record of suffering following on similar gratification in the past; otherwise no question could arise. If the man yields, against the warning, the pain of remorse will be added to the pain of satiety, and thus only progressive lessons are learned; until at last he realises that his wisdom lies in refusing to purchase future pain by temporary pleasure. And then he begins to starve out the desires by refusal to feed them, while by dwelling on the pains that gratification brings he cuts at their root with the axe of knowledge, wrought out of experience. All average men, all but the lowest and most brutish, have reached the stage when the voice of conscience is heard, and should therefore begin to consciously cooperate with the upward tendency out of the mire of materiality into the spiritual life.

How then can we break our bonds? The real answer is suggested in that law which I have been showing to you. The bonds are broken by these inevitable experiences which life after life teach the Soul the nature of the universe into which it has come. But desire is a binding force, and as long as there is desire so long must men come back to birth. The desire for good will draw it back as well as the desire for evil, the desire for religious happiness will draw it back, as well as the desire for earthly joys; the desire for the praise of men, for love, for knowledge even. A Soul may desire results of a high and noble character; still there is a desire for results, and this must bind it to places where the results are to be found. Therefore in order to get rid of *Karma* we must get rid of *desire*. Not cease from action - that is unnecessary, but act without desire - making every effort which is necessary, yet indifferent to the result. This is the familiar lesson given by Shri Krishna, this the essence of all truth. It is renunciation of desire, not of action, which makes the real Sannyasi, which makes the renunciator, which makes the Yogi, a *real* Yogi - not one only in the wearing of yellow garments and ashes - but a Yogi who has broken all the bonds of desire, and not simply one who is an outward renunciator. For the man of action who performs every action because it is his duty, and remains indifferent to the fruits thereof, that man in the world is the servant of God; he is one who performs every action, - not for what it brings him but because it fills up something lacking which ought to be done in the world in which he lives as an agent of God. A man who realises that the wheel of life must turn, and who takes part in the turning of the wheel, not for what the turning of the wheel may bring to him, but in order that the Divine life may circle in its course, - he plays his part in working without attachment, without desire, and turns the wheel whether it brings him pleasure or pain, whether it brings him praise or blame, fame or ignominy, Divine knowledge or ignorance - anything the wheel may bring him. He only perceives that it is his duty to cooperate with God while manifestation persists and he therefore identifies himself with the God from Whom the turning of the wheel proceeds. He is then *one* with Shri Krishna who declared that He had nothing to obtain in Heavens or on earth, but that if He stopped acting all would stop. And therefore the devotee who acts, not in order that he may get anything but in order that the Divine purpose may be fulfilled, he works by way of sacrifice; he offers all his actions as sacrifices to God and remains indifferent to the fruits of the sacrifice, for they lie at the feet of God and not in the heart of the devotee. Such a man makes no *Karma*, for such a man has no *desire*; such a man creates no links which bind him to earth, such a man is spiritually free, although around him actions may spring up on every side. Thus is it when a man is born into the sphere of knowledge; thus is it when a man is born into the sphere of devotion; and the life of such a man is as an altar, and burning upon that altar is the flame of devotion and of knowledge. Every action is cast into the fire and is consumed therein, rising up as the smoke of a sacrifice and leaving behind on the altar nothing save the fuel of knowledge and the fire of love.

Such then imperfectly sketched - for the subject is too vast - are the lines along which you may study the ancient problem, and which may make more clear to you the reason why pain and imperfection exist; we have seen that evil originates in limitation, we have seen that evil is a but relative thing, and how what we call evil is often only a veil of evil and beneath it a future good. We have seen how actions of men, when they are developed become evil, which in a lower organisation would not at all be evil; how as man proceeds onward and onward, he can use evil for his own perfecting; how man tries to escape from pain and to pursue pleasure; how desire remains in his heart, and brings him back to earth, and he goes forward and forward, purifying desire, identifying himself with the Divine Actor in the universe; then how no further actions have binding force upon him; how such a man is free from evil, and free from all those bonds which tie the Souls of men; and finally how he becomes an altar from which the smoke of sacrifice goes up continually to the Eternal. This indeed the life which alone is worth the living, this indeed the road along which lies peace and calm. This is realised by the true Yogi alone. Compare this with the life of the man who clings to the world full of dissatisfaction, full of discontent. Look at the men and women around you; look at their faces; see how they are full of anxiety and of desire, of trouble and injustice; and see how men's hearts are pierced by pain and laid desolate by catastrophes, by miseries, by hopes and by fears; how they are tossed about and flung from side to side, and too often brought to ruin!

And then realise that Brahman is bliss. Bliss, but how? Bliss, because there is unity; bliss, because there is an absence of desire; bliss, because there is knowledge of permanence, which nothing that is transient can disturb. So shall the despairing human Soul find hope, if it is fixed on *Brahman*; so shall the disturbed human soul find peace. Who can deny *that* to the Soul that knows its source, that has found the Self? Thou art *Brahman*. There is nothing which can shake that; there is nothing which can undo that; there is nothing which can change that. It is fixed indissolubly upon the changeless, upon the Eternal Truth. It has nothing in it of earth, that it should ever pass away. The body is not the Soul; disease may mar it, accident may injure it, death may strike it away, but the Soul remains unchanged. The lower mind you may destroy, but there is no real loss; changed may be the individual circumstances, but the "I" is changeless. Separation between bodies may come, but the inner unity remains unbroken, and so any outer change must fail to drive to misery or to despair. Such a Soul stands as a rock in the midst of warring, surging billows. The waves of misfortune boil up around it, they may dash up against it, but only to be shattered into foam against its sides, and fall in snowy wreaths to decorate its base, and thus render it more beautiful than it was before. So is it with the Soul which identifies itself with the One; so is it with the Soul which by knowledge and devotion has removed everything which is fleeting, and has founded itself on that which is Divine. That is the goal; the goal which may be reached by you all, and the reaching of that goal is the USE OF EVIL IN THE UNIVERSE.

XII. MAN'S QUEST FOR GOD

An Article in the "Theosophical Review" in December, 1897.

MAN has for ages fashioned theories about God, theories ranging from the fetish of the savage to the loftiest dream of the mystic, the profoundest conception of the philosopher. Omitting fetishism, we may class the theories of living interest under Monotheism and Pantheism, including under the first the "Theism" of modern thought, and under the latter the scientific Polytheism of the great Eastern religions.

In the West, of late years, many of the more thoughtful and highly-educated people repelled by the crude Theism of the masses and by the unintelligent theories of the divine Existence presented by popular Christianity have taken refuge in agnosticism, a confession of intellectual despair. Feeling that knowledge about God was unattainable, that "no thoroughfare" was written above every path along which humanity was groping after God, these people, truthful and sincere, thoughtful and candid, have preferred the modesty of silence to the insolence of disbelief. They elected to starve the heart rather than to stifle the intellect, and consoled themselves with the undeniable facts of this world for what they considered as the unverifiable fancies about another. But the ineradicable longings of the human heart for the knowledge of God will sooner or later overthrow any edifice of agnosticism that the intellect can rear, and agnosticism can never be more than the temporary refuge of the wearied intellect, where it may gather strength and courage to start on another stage of the eternal quest.

The popular Christian conceptions of God are dominated by the ideas inherited from exoteric Hebraism, by the crude anthropomorphism of its published scriptures. The Jehovah, or Jahveh, of the Hebrews, imaged as a "man of war", with human passions and superhuman powers, walking in the garden, coming down from heaven to look at a tower, descending to a mountain to proclaim his law, demanding the slaughter of countless animals in sacrifice, declaring himself to be jealous, angry, revengeful, remembering offences generation after generation - this deity of an undeveloped race has been largely instrumental in forming the God-idea of the uneducated in Christendom.

The contact of the Hebrews with Chaldean thought added dignity and grandeur to their idea of God, and their post-Babylonian writings show a nobler view of the divine Being. The God of the prophets, as of the later Isaiah and of Micah, is a grandiose and inspiring conception, a Power that makes for righteousness. This remodeled thought about God was softened into the ideal of a perfect man of superhuman greatness, the Father and Lover of men, in the later rabbinical teachings and in the Jewish-Christian scriptures. The limitations were removed while the ideal humanity was left, power remained without cruelty and justice without severity. But in Christian theology such as we find in Tertullian, and less nakedly in other Fathers of the Church, the savagery of the earlier Hebrews reappears, and the gracious lineaments of "the Father" vanish under the fierce mask of Jahveh, again the vengeful God whelming his foes under fire-floods. None the less the nobler conception remained as an encouragement and inspiration, gradually becoming focused in the person of the Son, the Divine Man, supreme in tenderness and compassion. From the troublous times of the fourth, fifth, and sixth centuries, enough emerged to satisfy the heart but not enough to content the intellect; the conception of God was left vague, hazy, and somewhat terrifying, while the object presented for adoration, on which all love was lavished, was the Son, self-sacrificed, redeeming, surrendering power to pity - a figure that drew all hearts, that satisfied all aspirations, the Man divine enough for worship, the God human enough for love.

Among ourselves, uprising from the Unitarian school of Christians, there is a somewhat curious but most instructive sect, that of modern Theism, represented by Theodore Parker, Francis Newman, Frances Power Cobbe, and Charles Voysey. These assert and worship "the Father", purging away from that conception all that is harsh, unlovely, stern, in the view of popular Christianity, adorning it with all the heart-compelling attributes of the perfect man, turning, in fact, the second Person of the orthodox Trinity into the first, and investing this now wholly divine Figure with all the far-reaching qualities of deity. The Trinity disappears, the Unmanifested is ignored, and a vast superhuman personal God is regarded as at once the Father of spirits and the all-sustaining, self-existent Life, beyond whom, embracing and pervading all, naught else exists: He is at once the "One without a second", and the personal Lover and Friend of man. If all the harsher traits were expunged from the God of Mohammed, and the fierce wrath were replaced with an immeasurable compassion, then, for the unity and personality of the Supreme, Theism and Islam might link hands.

Says Theodore Parker: "The mode of man's finite being is of necessity a receiving: of God's infinite being, of necessity a giving. You cannot conceive of any finite thing existing without God, the infinite ground and basis thereof; nor of God existing without something. God is the necessary logical condition of a world, its necessitating cause; a world, the necessary logical condition of God, his necessitated consequence. ... It is the idea of God as infinite - perfectly powerful, wise, just, loving, holy - absolute being, with no limitation. ... His Here conterminous with the all of space, His Now coeval with the all of time." (*Ten Sermons on Religion*, pp. 338. 339, 341.)

"The Soul contemplates God as a being who unites all these various modes of action, as manifested in truth, in right, and in love. It apprehends him, not merely as absolute truth, absolute right, and absolute love alone, but as all these unified into one complete and perfect being, the Infinite God. He is the absolute object of the soul, and corresponds thereto, as truth to the mind, as justice to the conscience, as love to the heart" (p.9.)

As intellect developed and knowledge increased, science began to undermine the popular theory about God, and to see inconsistencies in the loftier thought. The widening out of the universe, the opening of immeasurable depths of space, the glimpses of far suns which dwarfed our own to rush-light, the whirling infinities of innumerable systems, the gold-dust sprinkled afar that was found to be galaxies of stars - each star a sun, each sun the centre of its circling worlds - the faint mist-wreaths that turned out to be uncounted hordes of luminaries on the edges of new fields of being, the unplumbed profundities of living things in ever-diminishing minuteness presented by our own globe, the infinities of life on the one hand too small for scanning, the infinities of life on the other hand too vast for measuring - from all this the brain staggered back, dizzied and confounded, overturning, as it reeled against it, the idol of an extra-cosmic God. Jean Paul Richter's dream became a reality, and void pealed back to void, orb tossed back to orb, the mournful cry, "Children, you have no Father". But when the intellect was crushed beneath immensities, the soul uprose in indomitable and admirable audacity, flinging out into the seeming void its ineradicable belief in the Life whence it sprang, to find the void a plenum, Deity immanent throughout "empty" space.

Then Pantheism unveiled its all-alluring beauties, and the inter-cosmic God shone forth dispelling all the clouds of doubt and fear, and turning into gardens of delight the erstwhile desert sands. Had it come in its native garb, it would have won all to itself, but to intellectual Europe the most generally recognised exponent of this theory was Spinoza, and while his strong thought fascinated and compelled the intelligence, presented - as it often was by opponents - without the ethic based on it, it left the spirit starving and the heart a-cold. The idea got abroad that "Pantheism" was a chill and stern philosophy, that its God was unconscious, inaccessible - the "Father" had disappeared. "God is a being absolutely infinite; a substance consisting of infinite attributes, each of which expresses His eternal and infinite essence" (*Ethics*, Book 1, Definition 6.). Of these attributes man knows but two, extension and mind or will. Mr. Froude in his *Short Studies* (*p. 360*) -from which the quotation from Spinoza is borrowed- says, summarising Spinoza's views, that God "is not a personal being, existing apart from the universe; but Himself in His own reality, He is expressed in the universe, which is His living garment". All things exist as He willed them to be, evil is not positive, there is "an infinite gradation in created things", "all in their way obedient". Two things in Spinoza have repelled the emotional - his steady logical destructive analysis and calm acceptance of its results, and his theory of necessitarianism. The latter has been held fatal to morals, the former to devotion. Yet Spinoza was so far from being incapable of strenuous devotion that he was described by his enemies as "a God-intoxicated man", and his lofty, serene virtue and calm acquiescence in the law of life as he saw it were in themselves evidences of the fine fibre of his soul.

Western thought is swinging between Pantheism and a more or less coherent Theism; at one time the thinker is driven to accept the one infinite, self-existent Substance, impersonal, all-pervasive, and his emotions are chilled and paralysed; at another he expands in love and devotion to a consciously touched Father, and is checked by the logical contradictions in which he finds himself entangled. The compulsion of the intellect, the longings of the heart come out strongly in the poet who voiced so often the restless mentality of his age:

> The sun, the moon, the stars, the seas, the hills, and the plains
>
> Are not these, O Soul, the Vision of Him who reigns? ...
>
> Earth, these solid stars, this weight of body and limb,
>
> Are they not sign and symbol of thy division from Him?
>
> Dark is the world to thee: thyself art the reason why;
>
> For is He not all but thou, that hast power to feel "I am I"? ...
>
> Speak to Him, thou, for He hears, and Spirit with Spirit can meet
>
> Closer is He than breathing, and nearer than hands and feet.
>
> (Tennyson's "Works"; Page 277.)

In all Western forms of Pantheism there is a common lack - the lack of the great ladder of beings stretching from the grain of dust to the loftiest spirit. All apparently end with man, and see in him the highest expression of God, while man, feeling his own littleness in the immensity of the God-pervaded universe, stretches out groping hands to find his elder brothers, the outcome of evolution in past eternities, in other realms of space. If none such exist, if an immeasurable past has brought as fruit no mighty beings, far above his pigmy growth as he above the mote in the sunray, must not all universes be but an ebb and flow of the ocean, in which he is but a bubble in the foam of a breaking wave? He sees himself within measurable distance of his end, for why should his world bear a harvest for eternity when other like worlds have gone down into the past and no fruit of them remains? The failure of the dead universes to produce continuing lives, exhibiting loftier powers, appears to prophesy for him an evolution equally limited, and to presage his approaching doom. Chilled by the dank vapours of annihilation he flies back into the warmer regions of faith, and submits to any outrage on reason rather than stifle the ever-recurring conviction, "Not all of me shall die".

Here steps forward to his rescue Eastern Pantheism, satisfying alike to head and heart, impregnable intellectually as that of Spinoza, but solving the problems of life as no philosopher can do who reduces intelligent beings to the narrow compass of man and the lower kingdoms of nature. Other worlds in disappearing have left the lives evolved by their aid, and beings greater than man, intelligences deeper, wider, loftier, crowd the realms of space, soaring to unimaginable grandeur, angels of worlds, Gods of countless systems, rising ever higher, with consciousness expanded to embrace vaster areas, offering countless objects for worship, extending loving hands to help, the Fathers and Mothers of the systems that roll in space - all that heart can long for, all that aspiration can soar to, all that reason can demand. Through each pours out the One Life, in each is expressed some marvel of the else unintelligible Glory; They reveal part of THAT which eludes all grasping in totality; some so mighty and so vast that They sustain a universe, some so individually tender that a child, unafraid, might nestle on Their breast.

In Eastern Pantheism the One and the Many are distinguished in thought, while the fundamental unity - the Many being but rays of the One, manifested centres of consciousness, channels of the One, each in His measure - is never left out of sight. "He verily is all the Gods". "They call Him Indra, Mittra, Varuna, and Agni". "He who is Brâhma, who is Indra and Prajâpati, is all these Gods" (*Brihadâranyakopanishad*, quotations from the Shruti, in Commentary on the Fourth Brâhmana, chapter 1). The Gods truly live as separate intelligences, but they no more mar the divine unity than does the existence of men as separate intelligences. Polytheism adds to the philosophy of Pantheism the religious element needed for spiritual evolution, but Gods and men, as well as all other parts of the universe, live and move and have their being in the One. THAT is the One without a second, incognisable, infinite, the causeless Cause of Being. "It is beyond the range and reach of thought - in the words of the *Mândûkya*, 'unthinkable and unspeakable'" (*The Secret Doctrine*, Volume 1, page 42). As salt in water, as butter in milk, the One Life is in all, invisible to eye, but immanent in all. The symbol of THAT to our conditioned intelligence is the supernal Trinity, Brahman in His threefold aspect, God in manifestation, the highest point to which our thought can soar.

He is the One Self, and veils himself in innumerable forms, amid which the "Seven Spirits" take the loftiest place, and below Them many divine Beings, grouped in threes and sevens, according to their functions in any given department of the kosmos, and in many other groupings, familiar in world-scriptures, and reducible to the same fundamental complex units[*Thus in a seven the one is placed in the centre and six are round it; this doubled, the centres coinciding, gives twelve round the one; hence all multiples of twelve. Again, the three taken as a centre with the seven round it yield the ten, the decade (our system perfected at its close), and out of this arise multiples of ten. Or, this central three being regarded as a unit, eight represents the one and seven, and multiples of eight result. Further groupings appear when each of these threes or sixes, or sevens, is taken as double, positive-negative, male-female, etc. But this number system in all its ramifications is too big to deal with here]*

A three and a seven form the Rulers, it would seem, in many systems of our kosmos. Below These are vast hierarchies of graduated intelligences, guiding the kosmic order, superintending its various departments, Gods of the seven great Elements, the permutations and combinations of which make up the material side of nature - the three gunas (qualities) and the seven tattvas (elements) composing this material side as the three Logoi and the seven Spirits compose the life or energy side.

When we think of the Logos as the Self of all, we think of Him as One, as the Lord of the world and of men. The highest LOGOS, we have heard, is One who has climbed the ladder of Being until He can hold His centre of consciousness, Himself un-paralysed, fully conscious, amid the mighty vibrations of the Great Life. Coming into manifestation He limits Himself to be the channel of that One Life to a universe; He has been man in an incalculable past, and has risen through every phase of superhuman being to the highest level of conditioned existence. Hence He can condition Himself at any point of such existence. When for some gracious purpose He thus takes on the human condition and is born into one of His worlds, we call him an Avatâra, a God-man. He lives again on some globe as man, but the glory of Deity lightens through Him, and He is Emmanuel, God-with-us. To such a one, or to any spiritual intelligence, men of all grades of head and heart can turn in worship, in love, in trust; from all such beings, men can ask for aid, counsel or guidance. For a very lowly-developed type of man an intelligence of a comparatively low grade may be the most effective "God"; the untrained brain cannot grasp the vast idea of an intra-cosmic God, all-pervasive, all-sustaining; the concept bewilders the intellect and chills the heart. Yet without love and trust and worship the spiritual nature cannot awake, cannot develop; it is not the object of worship but the attitude of the worshipper that rouses the emotions which stimulate spiritual growth. God is the life of every object, and it is He that is worshipped in each, not the outer form that is His veil. He is the all-attractive charm, the all-alluring power, and as the mind and heart of the worshipper expand and rise, form after form breaks away from Him, each successive form showing more of His radiant loveliness, until He stands as manifest Lord of all, and the devotee made one with Him becomes one with the Supreme.

Limited as we are at present, every conception of God we form is limited, inadequate, even grotesque in its imperfection. Well may we try in gentlest reverence to improve and purify conceptions lower and cruder than our own, recognising that our own must be equally low and crude in the sight of those beyond us, however inspiring they may be to us at our less developed stage. Let us worship the highest we can dream in our purest moments, and strive to live the beauty we adore. Worship and life reveal God above us, because they waken the powers of God within us. Man becomes that which he worships and loves, and when the twain become one in Nirvâna the Quest is over, the spark has become the Flame.

XIII. DISCIPLESHIP

An Article in the "Theosophical Review" for July, 1906.

MUCH has been said and written on the Qualifications for Discipleship, as they are set down in Eastern Scriptures; they are laid down therein as the ideal according to which the aspirant should try to shape his life, and are intended to help a candidate for discipleship by pointing to the direction in which he should turn his efforts. Among the Eastern peoples, Hindus and Buddhists, to whom they were given, they have always been so regarded, and men have taken them as guides in self-culture, as pupils may strive to copy, to the best of their ability, the perfect statue set up in the midst of the class for study. As these qualifications have become known in the Western world through theosophical literature, they have been used in a somewhat different spirit, as a basis for the criticism of others rather than as rules for self-education. Frederic Denison Maurice spoke once of people who "used the bread of life as stones to cast at their enemies"; and the spirit which thus uses information is not uncommon among us. It may be open to question whether Those who have spread through the world much information that once was kept secret, may not occasionally have felt a twinge of doubt as to the wisdom of pouring forth teaching liable to so much misuse.

Our great Teacher, H. P. Blavatsky, has suffered much at the hands of those who use the qualifications for discipleship as missiles for attack, instead of as buoys to mark out the channel. It has been asked - as in the Vâhan last year - why a person who smoked, who lost her temper, who was lacking in self-control, should have been a disciple, while - this was not said but implied - many eminently respectable people, with all the family virtues, who never outrage conventionalities, and are models of deportment, are not considered worthy of that title. It may not be useless to try to solve the puzzle.

Those who have read carefully the unpublished letters from Those whom we call the Masters must have been sometimes struck with surprise over the opinions therein expressed, so different is Their envisagement of people and things from the current appreciations in the world. They look at many things that to us seem important with utter indifference, and lay stress on matters that we overlook. So surprising are sometimes the judgments passed that they teach the readers a great lesson of caution in the formation of opinions about others, and make one realise the wisdom of the Teacher who said: "Judge not, that ye be not judged." A judgment which has not before it all the facts, which knows nothing of the causes from which actions spring, which regards superficial appearances and not underlying motives, is a judgment which is worthless, and, in the eyes of Those who judge with knowledge, condemns the judge rather than the victim. Eminently is this true as regards the judgments passed on H. P. Blavatsky, and it may be worth while to consider what is connoted by the words "disciple" and "initiate", and why she should have held the position of a disciple and an initiate, despite the criticisms showered upon her.

Let us define our terms. A "disciple" is the name given, in the occult schools, to those who, being on the probationary path, are recognised by some Master as attached to Himself. The term asserts a fact, not a particular moral stage, and does not carry with it a necessary implication of the highest moral elevation. This comes out strongly in the traditional story of Jesus and His disciples; they quarreled with each other about precedence, they ran away when their Master was attacked, one of them denied Him with oaths, and later on showed much duplicity. The truth is that discipleship implies a past tie between Master and disciple, and a Master may recognise that tie, growing out of past relationship, with one who has still much to achieve; the disciple may have many and serious faults of character, may by no means - though his face be turned to the Light - have exhausted all the heavy karma of the past, may be facing many a difficulty, fighting on many a battlefield with the legions of the past against him. The word "disciple" does not necessarily imply initiation, nor saintship; it only asserts a position and a tie - that the person is on the probationary path, and is recognised by a Master as His.

Among the people who occupy that position in the world today are many types. For those who are perplexed regarding them it is well that the law should be recalled, that a man is what he desires and thinks, not what he does. What he desires and thinks shapes his future; what he does is the outcome of his past. Actions are the least important part of a man's life, from the occult standpoint - a hard doctrine to many, but true. Certainly there is a karma connected with action; the past evil desire and thought, which are made manifest in an evil act in the present, have had their evil fruit in the shaping of tendencies and character, and the act itself is expiated in the suffering and disrepute it entails; the remaining karma of the action grows out of its effect on others, and this reacts later in unfavourable circumstance. Action, in the wide sense of the term, is composed of desire, thought and activity; the desire generates thought; the thought generates activity; the activity does not generate directly but only indirectly. Hence the man's desires and thoughts are the most vital elements in the formation of the judgment passed on the man. What he desires, what he thinks, that he is; what he does, that he WAS. It follows that a man with past heavy karma may, if he become a disciple, expedite the manifestation of that karma, and its fruitage in the outer world may be of actions that do not bring him credit in the eyes of his world. From the occult standpoint such a man is to be helped to the utmost, so that he may be able to pass through the awful strain, the bearing of which successfully means triumph, the succumbing to which means failure.

Moreover, in passing right judgments on actions, not only must we know the actor's past, in which the roots of the actions are struck, but we must know the immediate past, that which immediately preceded the action. Sometimes a wrong action is done, but it has been preceded by a desperate struggle, in which every ounce of strength has been put forth in resistance, and only after complete exhaustion has the action supervened. From outside we see only the failure, not the struggle. But the struggler has profited by the efforts that preceded the failure; he is the stronger, the nobler, the better, and has developed the forces which will enable him to overcome the difficulty when it next presents itself, perchance even without a struggle. In the eyes of Those who see the whole, and not only a fragment, that man condemned by his fellows as fallen has really risen, for he has won as the fruit of his combat the strength which assures him of victory.

This disciple stands on the probationary path; he is a candidate for initiation. He comes under conditions different from those that surround men in the outer world; he is recognised as pledged to the service of Light, and hence is also recognised as an opponent of the power of Darkness. His joys will be keener, his sufferings sharper, than those experienced without. He has called down the fire from heaven; well for him if he shrinks not from its scorching. And well too for him, if, like the Red Indian at the torture-stake, he can face an unsympathetic world with a serene face, however sharply the fire may burn.

What of the famous qualifications for initiation which he must now seek to make his own? They are not asked for in perfection, but some possession of them there must be ere the portal may swing open to admit him. In the judgment passed on him, which opens or bars the gateway, the whole man is taken into account. With some, so greatly are other qualities developed, that but a small modicum of those specially demanded weighs down the scale. With others, more average in general type, high development of these is demanded. It is, so to speak, a general stature that is expected, and the stature is made up in many ways. A candidate may be of great intelligence, of splendid courage, of rare self-sacrifice, of spotless purity, and bringing such dower with him may lack somewhat in the special qualifications. Something of them, indeed, he must have. If he have no sense of the difference between the real and unreal; if he be passionately addicted to the joys of the world; if he have no control over tongue or thought, no endurance, no faith, no liberality, no wish for freedom, he could not enter. The completion of the qualities may be left for the other side, if the beginnings are seen; but the initiate must fill up the full tale, and the more there is lacking the more will there be to be done.

It is not well to minimise the urgency of the demand, for these qualities must be reached some time, and far better now than later. Every weakness that remains in the initiated disciple, who has entered the path, affords a point of vantage to the Dark Powers, who are ever seeking for crevices in the armour of the champions of the Light. No earnestness is too great in urging the uninitiated disciple to acquire these qualities; no effort is too great on his part to compass their achieving. For there is something of pathos in the case of a hero-soul who has "taken the kingdom of heaven by violence" and has to pause to give a life-time to the building up of the lesser perfections which in the past he neglected to acquire.

Though the mills of God grind slowly

Yet they grind exceeding small;

Though He stands and waits with patience

With exactness grinds He all.

The lofty initiate who has left some minor parts of human perfection unbuilt must be born into the world of men to lead a life in which these also shall be perfected. And if any chance to meet such a one in the flesh he would do wisely to learn from his best rather than to use his worst as his excuse for his own shortcomings, making it a justification for his own faults that he shares them with an initiate.

Pre-eminently is this true of the criticisms leveled against H. P. Blavatsky. "She smoked." But smoking is not the sin against the Holy Ghost. The use of it to depreciate a great teacher is a far worse crime than smoking, which, at the worst, is only a habit disagreeable to a small minority.

"She had a bad temper." So have a good many of her critics, without a thousandth part of the excuse she well might have pleaded. Few could bear for a week the strain under which she lived year after year, with the dark forces storming round her, striving to break her down, because the breaking down meant a check to the great spiritual movement which she led. In the position she was bidden to hold the nervous strain and tension were so great, the cruel shafts of criticism and unkindness were rendered so stinging by the subtle craft of the Brothers of the Shadow, that she judged it better at times to relieve the body by an explosion, and to let the jangled nerves express themselves in irritability, than to hold the body in strict subjection and let it break under the strain. At all hazards she had to live, with strained nerves and failing brain, till the hour struck for her release. It is ill done to criticise such a one, who suffered that we might profit.

"She lacked self-control." Outside sometimes, for the reasons above given, but never inside. Never was she shaken within, however stormy without. It may be said that such statement will be used as an excuse for ill-temper in ordinary people. Let them stand where she stood, i.e., become extraordinary people, and then they may fairly claim the same excuse.

H. P. Blavatsky was one of those who are so great, so priceless, that their qualities outweigh a thousand-fold the temporary imperfections of their nature. Her dauntless courage, her heroic fortitude, her endurance in bearing physical and mental pain, her measureless devotion to the Master whom she served these splendid qualities, united to great psychic capacities, and the strong body with nerves of steel that she laid on the altar of sacrifice, made all else as dust in the balance. Well might her Master joy in such a warrior, even if not free from every imperfection. But where a person has no heroism, little devotion, and but small tendency to self-sacrifice, a strong manifestation of the special qualifications may well be demanded to counterbalance the deficiencies. Man worships the sun as a luminary and not for his spots. In the sunlight of H. P. Blavatsky's heroic figure, the spots are not the things that catch the eye of wisdom. But these spots do not raise to her level those who are nearly all spots, with little gleams of light. It is ill done in these days of small virtues and small vices to criticise harshly the few great ones who may come into our world.

Often, with S. Catherine of Siena, have I felt that intense love for some one even but a little higher than ourselves is one of the best methods for training ourselves into that lofty love of the Supreme Self which burns up all imperfections as with fire. Hero-worship may have its dangers, but they are less perilous, less obstructive of the spiritual life, than the cold criticism of the self-righteous, directed constantly to depreciation of others. And still I hold with Bruno, the hero-worshipper, that it is better to try greatly and fail, than not to try at all.

XIV. THE PERFECT MAN

An Article in the "Theosophical Review" in April, 1905 •

THERE is a stage in human evolution which immediately precedes the goal of human effort, and when this stage is passed through man, as man, has nothing more to accomplish. He has become perfect; his human career is over. The great religions bestow on this Perfect Man different names, but, whatever the name, the same idea is beneath it; He is Mithra, Osiris, Krishna, Buddha, Christ - but He ever symbolises the Man made perfect. He does not belong to a single religion, a single nation, a single human family; He is not stifled in the wrappings of a single creed; everywhere He is the most noble, the most perfect ideal. Every religion proclaims Him; all creeds have in Him their justification; He is the ideal towards which every belief strives, and each religion fulfils effectively its mission according to the clearness with which it illumines, and the precision with which it teaches the road whereby He may be reached. The name of Christ, used for the Perfect Man, throughout Christendom is the name of a *state*, more than the name of *man*; "Christ in you, the hope of glory", is the Christian teacher's thought. Men, in the long course of evolution, reach the Christ state, for all accomplish in time the centuried pilgrimage, and He with whom the name is specially connected in western lands is one of the "Sons of God" who have reached the final goal of humanity. The word has ever carried the connotation of a state; it is "the anointed". Each must reach the state: "Look within thee; thou art Buddha". "Till the Christ be formed in you."

As he who would become a musical artist should listen to the masterpieces of music, as he should steep himself in the melodies of the master-artists, so should we, the children born of humanity, lift up our eyes and our hearts, in ever-renewed contemplation, to the mountains, on which dwell the Perfect Men of our race. What we are, They were; what They are, we shall be. All the sons of men can do what a Son of Man has accomplished, and we see in Them the pledge of our own triumph; the development of like divinity in us is but a question of evolution.

I have sometimes divided interior evolution into sub-moral, moral, and super-moral; submoral, wherein the distinctions between right and wrong are not seen, and man follows his desires, without question, without scruple; moral, wherein right and wrong are seen, become ever more defined and inclusive, and obedience to law is striven after; super-moral, wherein external law is transcended, because the divine nature rules its vehicles. In the moral condition, law is recognised as a legitimate barrier, a salutary restraint; "Do this"; "Avoid that"; the man struggles to obey, and there is a constant combat between the higher and the lower natures. In the super-moral state the divine life in man finds its natural expression without external direction; he loves, not because he ought to love, but because he is love. He acts, to quote the noble words of a Christian Initiate, "not after the law of a carnal commandment, but by the power of an endless life". Morality is transcended when all the powers of the man turn to the Good as the magnetised needle turns to the north; when divinity in man seeks ever the best for all. There is no more combat, for the victory is won; the Christ has reached His perfect stature only when He has become the Christ triumphant, Master of life and death.

This stage of the Christ-life, the Buddha-life, is entered by the first of the great Initiations, in which the Initiate is "the little child", sometimes the "babe", sometimes the "little child, three years old". The man must "regain the child-state he hath lost"; he must "become a little child" in order to "enter the kingdom". Passing through that portal, he is born into the Christ-life, and, treading the "way of the Cross", he passes onwards through the successive gateways on the Path; at the end, he is definitely liberated from the life of limitations, of bondage, he dies to time to live in eternity, and he becomes conscious of himself as life rather than as form.

There is no doubt that in early Christianity this stage of evolution was definitely recognised as before every individual Christian. The anxiety expressed by S. Paul that Christ might be born in his converts bears sufficient testimony to this fact, leaving aside other passages that might be quoted; even if this verse stood alone it would suffice to show that in the Christian ideal the Christ-stage was regarded as an inner condition, the final period of evolution for every believer. And it is well that Christians should recognise this, and not regard the life of the disciple, ending in the Perfect Man, as an exotic, planted in western soil, but native only in far eastern lands. This ideal is part of all true and spiritual Christianity, and the birth of the Christ in each Christian soul is the object of Christian teaching. The very object of religion is to bring about this birth, and if it could be that this mystic teaching could slip out of Christianity that faith could no longer raise to divinity those who practise it.

The first of the great Initiations is the birth of the Christ, of the Buddha, in the human consciousness, the transcending of the I-consciousness, the falling away of limitations. As is well known to all students, there are four degrees of development covered by the Christ-stage, between the thoroughly good man and the triumphant Master. Each of these degrees is entered by an Initiation, and during these degrees of evolution consciousness is to expand, to grow, to reach the limits possible within the restrictions imposed by the human body. In the first of these, the change experienced is the awakening of consciousness in the spiritual world, in the world where consciousness identifies itself with the life, and ceases to identify itself with the forms in which the life may at the moment be imprisoned. The characteristic of this awakening is a feeling of sudden expansion, and of widening out beyond the habitual limits of the life, the recognition of a Self, divine and, puissant, which is life, not form; joy, not sorrow; the feeling of a marvelous peace, passing all of which the world can dream. With the falling away of limitations comes an increased intensity of life, as though life flowed in from every side rejoicing over the barriers removed, so vivid a feeling of reality that all life in a form seems as death, and earthly light as darkness. It is an expansion so marvelous in its nature; that consciousness feels as though it had never known itself before, for all it had regarded as consciousness is as unconsciousness in the presence of this upwelling life. Self-consciousness, which commenced to germinate in child-humanity, which has developed, grown, expanded ever within the limitations of form, thinking itself separate, feeling ever "I", speaking ever of "me" and "mine" - this Self-consciousness suddenly feels all selves as Self, all forms as common property. He sees that limitations were necessary for the building of a centre of Selfhood in which Self-identity might persist, and at the same time he feels that the form is only an instrument he uses while he himself, the living consciousness, is one in all that lives. He knows the full meaning of the oft-spoken phrase the "unity of humanity", and feels what it is to live in all that lives and moves, and this consciousness is accompanied with an immense joy, that joy of life which even in its faint reflections upon earth is one of the keenest ecstasies known to man. The unity is not only seen by the intellect, but it is felt as satisfying the yearning for union which all know who have loved; it is a unity felt from within, not seen from without; it is not a conception but a life.

In many pages of old, but ever on the same lines, has the birth of the Christ in man been figured. And yet how all words shaped for the world of forms fail to image forth the world of life.

But the child must grow into the perfect man, and there is much to do, much weariness to face, many sufferings to endure, many combats to wage, many obstacles to overcome, ere the Christ born in the feebleness of infancy may reach the stature of the Perfect Man. There is the life of labour among his brothermen; there is the facing of ridicule and suspicion; there is the delivery of a despised message; there is the agony of desertion, and the passion of the cross, and the darkness of the tomb. All these lie before him in the path on which he has entered.

By continual practice, the disciple must learn to assimilate the consciousness of others, and to centre his own consciousness in life, not in form, so that he may pass beyond the "heresy of separateness", which makes him regard others as different from himself. He has to expand his consciousness by daily practice, until its normal state is that which he temporarily experienced at his first Initiation. To this end he will endeavour in his everyday life to identify a his consciousness with the consciousness of those with whom he comes into contact day by day; he will strive to feel as they feel, to think as they think, to rejoice as they rejoice, to suffer as they suffer. Gradually he must develop a perfect sympathy, a sympathy which can vibrate in harmony with every string of the human lyre. Gradually he must learn to answer, as if it were his own, to every sensation of another, however high he may be or however low. Gradually by constant practice he must identify himself with others in all the varied circumstances of their different lives. He must learn the lesson of joy and the lesson of tears, and this is only possible when he has transcended the separated self, when he no longer asks aught for himself but understands that he must henceforth live life alone.

His first sharp struggle is to put aside all that up to this point has been for him life, consciousness, reality, and walk forth alone, naked, no longer identifying himself with any form. He has to learn the law of life, by which alone the inner divinity can manifest, the law which is the antithesis of his past. The law of form is taking; the law of life is giving. Life grows by pouring itself out through form, fed by the inexhaustible source of life at the heart of the universe; the more the life pours itself out the greater the inflow from within. It seems at first to the young Christ as though all his life were leaving him, as though his hands were left empty after outpouring their gifts on a thankless world; only when the lower nature has been definitely sacrificed is the eternal life experienced, and that which seemed the death of being is found to be a birth into a fuller life.

Thus consciousness develops, until the first stage of the path is trodden, and the disciple sees before him the second Portal of Initiation, symbolised in the Christian Scriptures as the Baptism of the Christ. At this, as he descends into the waters of the world's sorrows, the river that every Saviour of men must be baptised in, a new flood of divine life is poured out upon him; his consciousness realises itself as the Son, in whom the life of the Father finds fit expression. He feels the life of the Monad, his Father in Heaven, flowing into his consciousness, and realises that he is one, not with men only, but also with his heavenly Father, and that he lives on earth only to be the expression of the Father's will, His manifested organism. Henceforth is his ministry to men the most patent fact in his life. He is the Son, to whom men should listen, because from him the hidden life flows forth, and he has become a channel through which that hidden life can reach the outer world. He is the priest of the Mystery God, who has entered within the veil, and comes forth with the glory shining from his face, which is the reflection of the light in the sanctuary.

It is there that he begins that work of love symbolised in the outer ministry by his willingness to heal and to relieve; round him press the souls seeking light and life, attracted by his inner force and by the divine life manifested in the accredited Son of the Father. Hungry souls come to him, and he gives them bread; souls suffering from the disease of sin come, and he heals them by his living word; souls blinded by ignorance come, and he illuminates them by wisdom. It is one of the signs of a Christ in his ministry, that the abandoned and the poor, the desperate and the degraded, come to him without the sense of separation. They feel a welcoming sympathy and not a repelling; for kindness radiates from his person, and the love that understands flows out around him. Truly the ignorant know not that he is an evolving Christ, but they feel a power that raises, a life which vitalises, and in his atmosphere they inbreathe new strength, new hope.

The third Portal is before him, which admits him to another stage of his progress, and he has a brief moment of peace, of glory, of illumination, symbolised in Christian writings by the Transfiguration. It is a pause in his life, a brief cessation of his active service, a journey to the Mountain whereon broods the peace of heaven, and there - side by side with some who have recognised his evolving divinity - that divinity shines forth for a moment in its transcendent beauty. During this lull in the combat he sees his future; a series of pictures unrolls before his eyes; he beholds the sufferings which lie before him, the solitude of Gethsemane, the agony of Calvary. Thenceforth his face is set steadfastly towards Jerusalem, towards the darkness he is to enter for the love of mankind. He understands that ere he can reach the perfect realisation of unity he must experience the quintessence of solitude. Hitherto, while conscious of the growing life, it has seemed to him to come to him from without; now he is to realise that its centre is within him; in solitude of heart he must experience the true unity of the Father and the Son, an interior and not an outer unity, and then the loss even of the Father's Face; and for this all external contact with men, and even with God, must be cut off, that within his own Spirit he may find the One.

As the dark hour approaches he is more and more appalled by the failure of the human sympathies on which he has been wont to rely during the past years of life and service, and when, in the critical moment of his need, he looks around for comfort and sees his friends wrapt in indifferent slumber, it seems to him that all human ties are broken, that all human love is a mockery, all human faith a betrayal; he is flung back upon himself to learn that only the tie with his Father in heaven remains, that all embodied aid is useless. It has been said that in this hour of solitude the soul is filled with bitterness, and that rarely a soul passes over this gulf of voidness without a cry of anguish; it is then that bursts forth the agonised reproach: "Couldst thou not watch with me one hour?" - but no human hand may clasp another in that Gethsemane of desolation.

When this darkness of human desertion is overpast, then, despite the shrinking of the human nature from the cup, comes the deeper darkness of the hour when a gulf seems to open between the Father and the Son, between the life embodied and the life infinite. The Father, who was yet realised in Gethsemane when all human friends were slumbering, is veiled in the passion of the Cross. It is the bitterest of all the ordeals of the Initiate, when even the consciousness of the life of sonship is lost, and the hour of the hoped-for triumph becomes that of the deepest ignominy. He sees his enemies exultant around him; he sees himself abandoned by his friends and his lovers; he feels the divine support crumble away beneath his feet; and he drinks to the last drop the cup of solitude, of isolation, no contact with man or God bridging the void in which hangs his helpless soul. Then from the heart that feels itself deserted even by the Father rings out the cry: "My God! my God! why hast Thou forsaken me?"

Why this last proof, this last ordeal, this most cruel of all illusions? Illusion, for the dying Christ is nearest of all to the divine Heart.

Because the Son must know himself to be one with the Father he seeks, must find God not only within him but as his innermost self; only when he knows that the eternal is himself and he the eternal, is he beyond the possibility of the sense of separation. Then, and then only, can he perfectly help his race, and become a conscious part of the uplifting energy.

The Christ triumphant, the Christ of the Resurrection and Ascension, has felt the bitterness of death, has known all human suffering, and has risen above it by the power of his own divinity. What now can trouble his peace, or check his outstretched hand of help? During his evolution he learned to receive into himself the currents of human troubles and to send them forth again as currents of peace and joy. Within the circle of his then activity, this was his work, to transmute forces of discord into forces of harmony. Now he must do it for the world, for the humanity out of which he has flowered. The Christs and their disciples, each in the measure of his evolution, thus protect and help the world, and far bitterer would be the struggles, far more desperate the combats of humanity, were it not for the presence of these in its midst, whose hands bear up "the heavy karma of the world".

Even those who are at the earliest stage of the Path become lifting forces in evolution, as in truth are all who unselfishly work for others, though these more deliberately and continuously. But the Christ triumphant does completely what others do at varying stages of imperfection, and therefore is he called a "Saviour", and this characteristic in him is perfect. He saves, not by substituting himself for us, but by sharing with us his life. He is wise, and all men are the wiser for his wisdom, for his life flows into all men's veins and pulses in all men's hearts. He is not tied to a form, nor separate from any. He is the Ideal Man, the Perfect Man; each human being is a cell in his body, and each cell is nourished by his life.

Surely it had not been worth while to suffer the Cross and to tread the Path that leads thereto, simply to win a little earlier his own liberation, to be at rest a little sooner. The cost would have been too heavy for such a gain, the strife too bitter for such a prize. Nay, but in his triumph humanity is exalted, and the path trodden by all feet is rendered a little shorter. The evolution of the whole race is accelerated; the pilgrimage of each is made less long. This was the thought that inspired him in the violence of the combat, that sustained his strength, that softened the pangs of loss. Not one being, however feeble, however degraded, however ignorant, however sinful, who is not a little nearer to the light when a Son of the Highest has finished his course. How the speed of evolution will be quickened as more and more of these Sons rise triumphant, and enter into conscious life eternal! How swiftly will turn the wheel which lifts man into divinity as more and more men become consciously divine!

Herein lies the stimulus for each of us who, in our noblest moments, have felt the attraction of the life poured out for love of men. Let us think of the sufferings of the world that knows not why it suffers; of the misery, the despair of men who know not why they live, and why they die; who, day after day, year after year, see sufferings fall upon themselves and others and understand not their reason; who fight with desperate courage, or who furiously revolt, against conditions they cannot comprehend or justify. Let us think of the agony born of blindness, of the darkness in which they grope, without hope, without aspiration, without knowledge of the true life, and of the beauty beyond the veil. Let us think of the millions of our brothers in the darkness, and then of the uplifting energies born of our sufferings, our struggles and our sacrifices. We can raise them a step towards the light, alleviate their pains, diminish their ignorance, abridge their journey towards the knowledge which is light and life. Who of us that knows even a little that will not give himself for these who know naught?

We know by the Law immutable, by Truth unswerving, by the endless Life of God, that all divinity is within us, and that though it be now but little evolved, all is there of infinite capacity, available for the uplifting of the world. Surely, then there is not one, able to feel the pulsing of the divine Life, that is not attracted by the hope to help and bless. And if this Life be felt, however feebly, for however brief a time, it is because in the heart there is the first thrill of that which will unfold as the Christ-life, because the time approaches for the birth of the Christ-babe, because in such a one humanity is seeking to flower.

XV. THE FUTURE THAT AWAITS US

An Address given before the London Lodge of the Theosophical Society on November 25th, 1895.

TONIGHT I propose to speak to you on human evolution, leading you onwards to the future that lies before the race, and endeavouring to guide you step by step - though the steps will be somewhat long ones - up the staircase which, through the ages, the race will climb. In order to do this intelligibly I must carry your thoughts backwards for a few moments over ground that will be familiar to you as students of our sublime philosophy, and I may run over it hastily because it *is* familiar, though the glance over it is necessary as a preliminary reminder even for those who already know the facts, in order that we may have the whole great scheme before us from the beginning to the end of the Manvantara.

Think then for a moment, so far as thought be possible of that high region, of the beginning of a universe, when from the great Logos from Whom the universe proceeded there issued that Breath which comes forth but once in a Manvantara and once returns - the mighty LifeBreath in which all systems, all worlds, all individuals, live, breathe, and exists. Let there be in your minds for a moment a picture of that vast cycle of evolution - evolution as yet unaccomplished, evolution existing in the thought of the LOGOS but not in the facts of the manifestation. Then, running swiftly onwards from that beginning, place before your minds another picture, that of the making of the planes of a universe, region after region: how the energy of the LOGOS flashing forth pours Itself out as Atma, the one Self, into a universe yet to be, to make plane after plane in sevenfold order; Itself the energy, the first spirit; and the first matter but Its own outer aspect, the ring within which It limits Itself for the purpose of manifestation; then this energy passing outwards enfolded in that first matter as in a garment, and its outer aspect again forming a new phase of matter, that of the second plane, so that the energy of the second plane is the first energy *plus* first-plane matter, and round this the fresh differentiation of the matter of the second plane is wrapped; and so the energy of the third plane is the first energy *plus* first and second-plane matter, and the outer limit becomes third-plane matter; and so on, making region after region until the seven (the root-number of this universe) are complete, all differentiations of the One - all Atmâ, but Atmâ modifying itself in manifestation; then, touching the limiting surface of the sphere - the self-ordained "ring Pass-not" - the great Life-wave rushes back upon itself, drawing in from circumference to centre, and having touched the outermost limit, the lowest world of matter, it begins to unfold what erstwhile it infolded. Having thus brought into objective existence the spirit-matter of each plane, it begins to use this as material, and to build that spirit-matter into various organisations and forms of living things who are to be vehicles of consciousness in this universe, to be ultimately fit to form the living temples of the undifferentiated Atmâ as it streams forth as the energy of the LOGOS; the unfolding energy climbs from mineral to vegetable, from vegetable to animal, and so upwards to animal man. Still in mind imaging this vast aeonian succession, see how in these bodies over which the undifferentiated Atmâ itself is brooding there are unfolding one by one the successive types of spirit-matter which had been infolded during the descent, and how, going upwards to the animal and yet further to animal man (with whom we are concerned), there unfold gradually within the coarser matter of his physical body these subtler, less dense types of spirit-matter which belong to the different planes formed by the infolding of the Life. At last the moment comes when man is to begin to be - not merely animal man, but man himself; when this upward-climbing, unfolding energy reaches the point at which it is possible for it to stretch upwards to the ever-living Fire that flashes downwards from above, the life below reaching up to the life above, till they meet and man is born. Let me aid our halting thoughts with a simile drawn from everyday experience: you know the way in which the electric arc is formed, the blazing light of the electric lamp; two carbon poles one positive, the other negative come ever nearer and nearer to each other; all still is darkness, but in the darkness they are coming closer and closer, till at last they are so near each other that the resistance of the air is overcome, the current springs from pole to pole, the electric arc is formed, and light blazes out. That electric arc may not inaptly serve us as a symbol of the sudden formation of the individual, the real man, born when what we may call the negative current of Atmâ reaching upwards and the positive current of Atmâ reaching downwards rush together and meet, and man comes into existence, to live through the measureless ages of eternity. All this will be just enough to remind you of what lies behind us in the past, of facts already familiar, but which must be clearly in your minds if you are to see the future that awaits us, the future which I am to try to sketch.

This great Life-Breath then is sweeping on and man is beginning to be, and that wave is the wave of evolution, the law by which all must live, the progress by which all is carried onwards - man as well as the planet on which he lives, the universe and all worlds that are therein; all that goes with its current is carried onward and upward, all that sets itself against it is cast downward as wreckage, to be worked up again in some far-off future in which all missed possibilities shall be realised. We may think of man now as the individual beginning his upward climbing, and coming up to the place at which we stand today. In order to make a difficult subject a little clearer, let me ask you to image in your minds the three great kinds of activities in which mankind progresses. I could fancy them as a mighty three-sided pyramid, with upward - pointing apex piercing heaven, each side of the pyramid typifying one of the three great activities of the universe; one side would be power, another wisdom, another love, and within these all minor activities would group themselves, all possibilities would be included. On the sides you may see figured many lines that seem parallel but are really convergent, the varied lines of progress, mental, moral, spiritual, along which the race is to evolve. And if you think of this pyramid as made of great blocks, each block a great stage of progress symbolising one of the regions of the universe, then at the base we should have the physical world, and working there all the powers and energies of man that are manifested as physical consciousness in the physical body, and are there gradually evolving the three sides of his nature - power, wisdom, and love. Next above it, the second great block symbolizing the astral plane, another great region to be occupied by human consciousness; above that the plane of Manas - the devachanic plane, the region of the mind itself; above that a region nobler yet and loftier, that of Buddhi or spiritual intuition, the plane of Samadhi, sometimes called Sushupti; above that again the, plane of Atmâ, Nirvanâ, the crown, enfolding all, within all. To think of this picture may help us as we pass from step to step - from block to block - for we have to trace mankind rising from stage to stage, and to understand in what the evolution of man consists.

It consists in expanding consciousness, consciousness beginning at the very base of our pyramid as a mere thread of living light; it expands as it mounts from region to region, widening out and taking in more and more; at last the thread has become a cone of fire, and it rises to the very apex and joins the ocean of Living Fire in which all light and all life reside.

Expansion of consciousness is the note of human evolution, and as it expands, taking more and more within its limits, mankind thus rising will increase in power, wisdom, and love. Not that the three can really be disjoined, save for clearness of explanation, for love is but the outward expression of wisdom, and power its effectual agent; still, the separate consideration of each may help to systematise our thinking, and that is not without advantage in a subject so complex and so difficult.

Taking the race as a whole, we may say that its self-conscious life is in the body on the physical plane; man himself as before defined may indeed be said to have come down from higher regions into his physical encasement, but those regions are not yet subdued by his consciousness, and in them mankind at large cannot at present be said to live in self-conscious activity. Man inhabits them, but his consciousness in them is the consciousness of a babe, not yet awake. Still, that mistake may not arise, let me say that though it is true that mankind as a whole has not risen above the consciousness on the physical plane, there are even now some who have risen above it, and are able to work on other planes; and these are an everincreasing number. In all that I may say of the future, I shall speak of nothing that is not known at least to one or two among us, who have gained a partial realisation of the future of the race, who know at least something of these different planes which in the future all mankind shall know perfectly and possess fully.

In glancing over the physical region, how do its activities group themselves on the three sides of our pyramid? Upon the side of love we have the service of those above us and the help and compassion we extend to those around us and below; upon the side of wisdom we have all that which is not yet wisdom but is only knowledge, yet knowledge that will become wisdom when it is transmuted; all scientific thought, all philosophical thought, all artistic thought - these are the great lines along which thought is ascending on the side of wisdom. On the side of power we have government, rule, the organisation of society, and that creative power that even now resides in man, though as yet he knows it not.

As the world is just now it strikes us as strange, almost as startling, that on each of these sides man seems to be reaching the limits of the physical, continually coming to walls he is unable to overleap; with a successful past behind him, no doubt, yet seeming as though his progress in the physical were over, and something else must be found if success is to continue. If we look at the region of love which has religion for one of its lines of growth - the service of those above us - we see that during the last fifty years the great religions of the world have been pushed backward by the advancing tide of skeptical intelligence, so that they are now in a position of extreme difficulty, even those who love them most feeling a doubt at the back of their minds as to whether they are on the right road. It is recognised that in the great domain of religion faith has too much taken the place of knowledge, hope too much the place of certainty, and authority too much the place of vision. The result of this is that, go to what country you may, take what religion you please, you find the great mass of the people sunk in superstition, a prey to terrors of every kind, terror of the unknown future in front of them, a future terror-filled because unknown. Where among the masses there is not superstition there is atheism, eating away ideals. And in addition to this religious degradation of the crowd there is a class of more highly educated people, skeptical at heart and in life if not always in phrase, but often skeptical in phrase as well; challenging all religion because they know that its mere exotic presentation cannot be intelligently held as true in fact - challenging all and not yet finding hope beneath the challenge, hope of a truth that may be realised though they feel the ground giving way beneath their feet. If we turn to the other line on the side of love -its aspect to those around us and below us, its helpful activity and compassion- we see a few brave hearts well-nigh overwhelmed, despairing before the mass of human misery which they are incompetent to meet or heal; poverty heart-breaking as to the body, ignorance more heart-breaking as to the mind, so that those who are lovers of mankind scarce know from what direction effective aid may come.

On the side of wisdom, also, dead walls meet our gaze on each ascending line. Science, which has done so much and accomplished so many triumphs, is apparently reaching its limit in the exquisite delicacy and accuracy of its physical apparatus, and yet there come pouring into the laboratories energies too subtle for its measures to gauge, substances too rare for its balances to weigh. Science on every side is groping after new methods. In medicine it finds itself blind, the doctor unable to diagnose disease for lack of clearness of vision, unable to trace definitely the action of his drugs, merely experimenting, and ever hoping that out of experiments some certain knowledge may emerge. In physical science materialism is breaking down, with its theories of the universe proved to be inadequate, while idealism is not ready to take its place, to speak clearly and to explain intelligibly. In the greatest of idealistic systems, the Vedânta of India, as it is now taught, we find intellect devoted to useless hairsplitting instead of profound thinking, a subtle deterioration of character, and modes and habits of thought which undermine morals; men becoming careless of conduct in life and of difference between right and wrong, self-hypnotised by an unintelligent repetition of the profound truth "Thou art THAT". In East and West alike blindness and gropings, a vague craving that knows only that it has lost its ideals and that where ideals are not there no truth can be.

And power; what shall we say of the human activities that play on the side of power? Society at war within itself, class against class, sex against sex; kings with no authority to control, who no longer reign, who have no responsibility, to whom has been left the social power to do evil while the governing power to do good has been wrested from them; the power torn from them placed in the hands of a many-millioned ignorance, in some vague hope that this will be pulling in so many directions that no very harmful movement will occur; and as a result moral and physical deterioration visible everywhere, poverty and misery well-nigh invincible, with no wisdom that is able to guide, no power that ventures to control. Men look dimly backward and fearfully forward, wondering when a social cataclysm will occur, and some dream sadly of the days when there were kings who were Initiates and who gathered the nations under the safe shelter of their thrones, where knowledge and power grew into mighty life and realised a true society. And what of the power of creation? but, as I said, that is now unknown, and it is useless to speak of it.

Well, let us glance forwards, and see how mankind shall advance to greater peace, security and happiness on this physical plane. All the changes that will come into the physical plane in the future will come from the working downwards of the higher powers that will then be generally evolved in man. We can now picture to ourselves the nearest step, that into the second region - the mounting of mankind to the second great stage of our pyramid; mankind will become self-conscious on the astral plane, conquering the astral realm, and will thus find itself in a new world. Here man will take to himself new powers, adopt new methods, with new vistas opening before him, new potentialities blossoming forth on every side. It is the race that is rising, not merely stray individuals that are outstripping their fellows. Let us try to realise this next stage in human progress, when the majority of mankind will have expanded from self-consciousness in the physical to self-consciousness in the astral world; let us see how along the lines that we have considered in the physical world mankind will evolve and grow. For what is this astral world, and what do we mean by the expanding of consciousness to embrace this second region in the universe?

First, there is expansion of sense-power. The astral senses, while still distinguishable from each other - for we are not beyond these walls of separation in the astral world - are not so limited as the physical; astral vision sees behind, before and around, it sees every side of an object and pierces through it; the senses acquire fresh subtlety and acuteness and refinement, and from every direction wider knowledge pours in through these wider windows of the soul; the keener, stronger senses pierce through and make of none effect the obstacles that hindered man when his consciousness could only work through the physical body.

Taking up the activities on the side of love, and first the service of those above us, we find that when man passes into the astral world he will see there as phenomena which he can investigate much that he only dreamed of, or took on faith, when restricted to the physical world. And there are great truths, great realities, mighty intelligences with whom he will first come into touch in this astral world - only touching the fringe and not yet understanding the nature - only a far-off touch, but still it will make them real to him, and no longer only matters of faith. As this unknown world opens up before the awakened vision of man, as it is now open only to the few, he will find that he is not only able to see with far-reaching vision, not only able to use astral senses in the physical body, but that he can leave the physical body whenever it is an inconvenience or a hindrance, and can use his astral body to travel through the astral world. Then there will come within the compass of his possibilities communication with the great intelligences who may there be reached when the limits of the physical are overstepped. And we shall find that religion will take to itself new life, for the very basis of scepticism will be struck away when mankind can see and investigate phenomena now wrongly deemed supernatural, and when men come again into direct touch with beings whose very existence is now denied. So also must superstition disappear when men can range at will the world beyond the grave; that which is no longer the unknown will no longer be a land of terrors, and men's fears will no more be played upon by those who seek to subjugate them through dread of the unseen world. All men will know that world, all will understand its phenomena, marvelous now, but then to be familiar, then to enter into daily life. What we call death will be practically shorn of its sorrows, for man will be able to live in the astral world, to mingle with those who have altogether shaken off for a time the limitations of the physical body; the astral world will have come within the compass of the ordinary life, and the division caused by death will be swept away. The contact with the greater Ones, the teaching that then will be thrown open to the world, the possibilities of reaching them - space having no longer power to divide in view of the swiftness of passage that belongs to that subtler region - these will place within the reach of all opportunities of knowledge that today come only to the very few, knowledge that will change the whole aspect of life, and open up before the mind of man his still diviner possibilities. There too men will meet the great teachers of the past, and will know that they are not dreams but living men - that all that has been taught of them as noblest is verily true, while all that the ignorance of men has done to obscure them will fade away in that brighter light, in the clearer vision of that purer day. And when from the line of religion we turn to that of help to those around us and compassion to those below, what will not mankind be able to accomplish when a majority can do what only a minute minority can do now - grasp the astral forces and use them constantly both in the physical and the astral worlds? In the physical world a man will be able to aid others, to protect others by consciously sending forces from the astral to effect his purpose, thinking a useful thought and clothing it in elemental essence, thus creating an artificial elemental which he can direct to the helping of the weaker, the safeguarding of the unprotected, the warding-off of danger, forming a continual shield for anyone to whom it is sent. All this will be within the easy reach of those who are the vanguard of human evolution, and the most backward will be aided by those who have advanced further, all these powers coming within the reach of the majority of men. Help to all who need it in the astral world will also be given, help to all the souls of the backward ones who, on casting off the physical body, enter for the first time a world that is new to them; for all mankind will not be equal then any more than they are equal now. The great majority will be working self-consciously on the astral plane, but there will still be vast numbers whose consciousness will not have risen to it; the majority will be available from which to draw helpers to guide, comfort and direct all the more ignorant souls who have cast off the garment of the physical body, to do the work that only the few do now. There are great opportunities upon that plane today, for even now comfort may be brought to the souls that go thither helpless, hurried into that region full of fear; their terrors may be soothed, their minds enlightened, and in the future this blessed work will lie open to mankind for all who reach these higher possibilities of man along the line of compassion.

Another blessing that will come to the world, working down from the astral to the physical plane, will be along the line of the education of the children. How will education be changed when the astral senses are awakened, when the minds of children lie open before their parents and teachers, when their characters are plainly limned in colour and form as they are to astral vision, when all their evil tendencies are recognised in the germ in childhood and are starved, while all the good are helped and strengthened, encouraged to the blossoming! The education of children in the future - which, after all, is not so far away - will be one that will make their progress a thousand-fold swifter than it is today. What might not be done for the children of the present, if they were trained by those who possess astral vision - if all seeds of vice were starved, if all seeds of good were encouraged into blossoming? Instead of seeing them grow up mere copies of the elder people around them, we should see them growing up as a verily new generation, unfolding the possibilities that even now are within. Alas for the ignorance that encourages the evil and discourages the good, for the blindness that is as a bandage on the eyes of our people, so that they are unable to see and therefore to guide the young!

When we turn from the side of love to that of wisdom, we find that with the expansion of consciousness on the astral plane a complete change must occur. The methods of science will be altered, the old methods that already are beginning to be outworn will be cast aside in favour of keener and subtler tools, all scientific men using these better instruments of the astral senses in order to study and understand the phenomena of the physical as well as those of the astral world. I have only time to indicate a few of the new methods that will then come into common use, but a brief indication will show you how wide is their scope; and I trust that your President, who is so well able to do it, will ere long deal with this subject in detail in a way that I cannot do, touching it but in passing. Take medical science, and imagine the difference in certainty and precision when the doctor diagnoses by vision and traces the action of his drugs by astral sight; neither the physician nor the surgeon will be shut out by the surface of things as they are today, but every doctor will see exactly what is at fault and will apply his remedies accordingly.

Or take the methods of chemistry. The chemist will no longer theorise, but will see; his "atoms" will no longer be possible abstractions but things that can be easily examined and traced [See the article on "Occult Chemistry" in "Lucifer", November, 1895, reprinted as a pamphlet] all combinations will be studied with astral vision, stage after stage watched and followed; he will test, dissociate, combine, rearrange, all with the certainty that comes from vision, and he will manipulate his materials by the new forces at his command. In psychology how changed will be the methods when the mind lies before the psychologist as an open book; instead of speculating on mind in animals, drawing inferences from their actions, guessing at their motives, he will see the way in which the animal is thinking, the strange world that dawns on the animal intelligence - a world so different from our own because the standpoint from which it is seen is so different. Then indeed will man be able to deal effectively with the animal mind, training the dawning intelligence, guiding its advance with clear and competent knowledge. Thought will be studied as it is sent from mind to mind, and psychology will no longer be a jumble of words, a grouping of unenlightened ideas; the whole will fall into order, will be gradually understood and mastered, for the psychologist will then know in what the mind of man consists, and will begin to understand the method of its working and the possibilities of its unfolding powers.

Think too of philosophy. There will no longer be any possibility even of discussion as to its basis in view of the wider knowledge, of powers before unaccredited, of matter with potentialities unimagined, matter found to be so much subtler than had been thought possible, but still ever acting as a garment for the life. Then will be supplied what is now lacking in idealism - the understanding of the relationship between force and matter as the two aspects of the One, between life and the garment in which life is clothed. Man will comprehend further how matter is subject to the life, how it assumes the form that thought commands, how the creative power is able to function, though this will be grasped far more fully in the regions beyond.

Consider also writing of history. How different that will be in a world where all the astral records lie open to be read, when history can no longer be written from one side or the other, to support a theory or to bolster up some view of the writer, but when those who are historians will throw themselves back into the past, will live and move among the scenes which they depict! When history is told it will be told from the astral records, the living scenes, and they who tell it will live as it were in the period, and trace events step by step with the men and women of the time. And all this with the certainty of observation - reverified at will by different students - neither guess nor inference necessary, but patient looking and faithful recording; just as we live and move among our fellows today will the historian live and move in the world we call the past, a world living and present to those who know how to tread their way therein.

Again, how different will art be in those days that are coming - different even from the merely mechanical standpoint. So many more colours will then delight the eye, brilliant and vivid of hue, translucent, exquisite and soft; such varieties of changing forms in the astral world, so much more to delineate, to reproduce for even down in the physical world the canvas of the painter will glow with the beauties of the astral. And when the musician writes some great symphony or marvelous sonata, he will not only breathe forth sounds to charm the ears of men, but colours will flash out as the notes fall sweetly, and every symphony will be a dazzling series of colours as well as of sounds, with a beauty that is now undreamed of, with a perfection and a delicacy which as yet man cannot know.

From the side of wisdom let us pass to the side of power. Society will then be replaced on its ancient basis, with better materials for its builders' hands. All the different functions of a perfectly ordered State will be discharged by those who are fitted for each by their natural evolution. Then all men's auras will be visible to those who guide the State, and according to the knowledge and the power and the benevolence visible to the astral sight will be the duty each is called on to discharge. Each man has around him in his aura the delineation of his character and of his powers, marking the functions which he is best suited to perform, so that each man will then be sent to his rightful place; a feeling that justice is done will make men harmonious, each knowing that he is doing that for which he is fitted, that power which sees gives him his rank and marks out the region of his activity. Most, indeed, seeing for themselves, will endorse the justice of the ruling authority, and those who cannot see will be kept in check by the overwhelming public opinion. Then knowledge will rule ignorance, and power will shield and guide impotence, and men will laugh at the insane idea that the multiplication of ignorance is wisdom. In those days as youths are growing into manhood their paths in life will be selected, marked out clearly by the colour, fineness and size of their auras, which will show - as they show now to those whose eyes are opened - the range their faculties can cover and the powers they have within them for development. Then work will be joy, as all work is joy when it is fitted to the powers of the worker; the labour, the pain, of work come when it frustrates powers which we possess, when the work is not fitted to the capacity; when man shall be ever doing that for which his faculties are best suited, then will there be harmony and content in society instead of discontent and threats of revolution.

In those days how different also will be the law, especially as to criminal jurisprudence; as soon as astral sight becomes a power common to even a strong minority, there must be an entire change in the national dealing with evil and evildoers. If men now possessed astral sight it would not be possible for them to do many of the things that are done by nations and by society at the present time. It would not be possible that nation should fling itself against nation in war, for then they would perceive the misery and disturbance brought into the astral world by the souls hurled there into in terror and in wrath. And there could be no such thing as capital punishment among men who could trace the after-life of man and who knew that every murderer set free by execution can injure society more effectually than when he is bound within the body. Then, too, man will take up his duty towards the animal kingdom around him as well as towards his own brethren of the human race. Men with astral vision could not act towards animals as blind men now act, and in a civilised world there will be no slaughter-houses, no butchers' shops, with their terrible surroundings of loathsome elemental creatures, and of astral forms of animals driven out from their physical bodies in fear and horror, to send back upon the world a wave of terror that separates animals from men. For as man slays these helpless creatures they send back into the world which they left vibrations of distrust and hatred of men, affecting the animals living upon the earth and bringing about the "instinctive" repulsion which so largely marks the attitude of the animal-world towards man. In those days the crime called "sport" will no longer disgrace mankind, staining with innocent blood the hands that should be pure. Men will cease to be the chief agents who bring misery into the world, and when once they see what they are doing these evils will be swept away for evermore.

Thus as man rises in self-consciousness to the astral world, there will come about wonderful changes that will alter the whole face of society, and will make the earth far fairer, love, wisdom and power having been developed along the lines which we have considered, and along many another that time permits us not to follow.

Another stage arises now before our eyes the devachanic world, the region of the mind itself; and the time will come when mankind shall rise into that loftier consciousness, shall be able to function in the devachanic body and use the devachanic senses. How shall I tell of the possibilities of that wondrous world, of all its marvels and its glories, its flashing colours and its melodious sounds, its intense life and radiant light? Save in its own language how shall any idea of it be given? for there they speak in colour and in music, in living forms of light resplendent. Here we speak and hear but clumsy phrases, word-symbols expressing only a fragment of such thought as we can formulate through the brain. But there no halting, articulated speech is needed, for there mind speaks direct to mind, and matter is so subtle that every thought at once takes form. If we pass into the devachanic world and think, the images of the thought spring up all around us, flashing, glorious in colours vivid and exquisite beyond all telling, delicate hues shading into one another in swift changeful succession, inexpressibly, fascinatingly fair. The more beautifully the thinker is thinking, the fairer are the forms that surround him, the greater and the purer his ideas the more exquisite are the shapes that body themselves forth as the radiant offspring of his mind. All that he thinks is there before him; he thinks of a friend and the image of his friend smiles upon him - of a place and it lies stretched at his feet; space cannot divide, for mind is not limited by space; time is beginning to yield, and past, present and future begin to melt into the now; not wholly so yet in the lower devachanic regions, though we feel there the beginning of the blending which is perfected in loftier spheres. When friend speaks to friend they speak in form and colour and music, and the world around them is the richer for their outpouring as its wondrous matter follows the thrilling vibrations of their thought. Thus all the region of Devachan is ever radiant with changing colours of which earth knows nothing, musical with tones that physical ears cannot hear; mere living is bliss ineffable where nothing evil or inharmonious can disturb. No note of discord can pass into that world, for thought which cannot frame itself in harmony and beauty can there find no expression; each changing form seems fairer than the last, each tone fuller, sweeter, richer than the one before it. If all here had the devachanic senses awakened and functioning, then ere words could fall from my slow lips the whole room would seem full of music and colour and form, the exquisite vesture of thought, and every sense at once would be stimulated and delighted, for all senses are there but one.

If we ask more closely as to the activities that belong to Devachan, and how man will function in that lofty region when he becomes self-conscious there, again we must look to experience for the answer - the experience of those who have outrun their fellows and are already familiar with many of its powers and its possibilities. Service there takes on a new aspect, for as mind touches mind the lesser comes into direct contact with the Great Ones - so far as the lesser can touch the greater - and the knowledge they impart is so full, so rich, that as it is studied new possibilities seem always to be welling up within it, and what is told is not a hundredth part of that which is placed within reach; it seems to encircle and penetrate the mind till the man is plunged into a sea of wisdom and knowledge which permeates him through and through. There again compassion expands, rejoicing in the new channels which it finds for its outward flowing. The man on the devachanic plane reaches downwards to all planes, sending down the forces that belong to those higher regions to strengthen and illuminate the minds of men, affecting them by masses instead of one by one, affecting numbers by farreaching thoughts, helping them to see truth as true, and impressing on the inner mind that which the outer brain is unable to comprehend. Thus part of the help given to those who are aided consists in the working on the inner or higher mind, suggesting a new idea, a scientific "discovery", a missing link of knowledge, and this higher mind grasping the presented truth works it down into its own lower nature, so that this innermost conviction overpowers all logic and all the slow processes of reasoning, illuminating the lower mind, making comprehensible the thought, dominating the will, until all the lower nature is enlightened by the ray from its higher Self. That is part of the help rendered to men by those who have reached the devachanic region, and it will be rendered more and more fully to the backward of the race as larger numbers learn to function on the devachanic plane. Here are possibilities that as yet are hardly dreamed of, the training of thought to reach heights unimagined, the making of mighty elementals and the sending them forth to aid into the world of men, the guiding of minds groping after truth, the breathing of loftiest inspirations into those who have fitted themselves to receive them. As thought takes form and the forces of devachanic life are thrown into it, such a form becomes a most potent agent, and thus one worker can aid myriads of his fellow-men.

Wisdom is so different on that level that it is scarcely possible to give even a glimpse of its methods and its workings. It is not the observation of bodies but the understanding of essences, not the observation of effects but the understanding of causes, so that wisdom there sees and hears and knows, and deals with the causes of things instead of with results, with the things themselves instead of with their appearances. Mankind will have vision reaching forward into the future, creating causes which will be worked out in following centuries. Help in evolution will then pour in from every side, for the majority instead of hindering will forward, instead of making obstacles, will lift the backward over them, for they will understand the Divine Law and become co-workers with it in the progress of the world.

See how the sides of the pyramid seem to be approaching each other as we climb upwards, and love and wisdom are blending their activities. So also with power. From what has been said is seen the kind of power that then will be in the world, and how it will quicken evolution. For to have power on the devachanic plane is to be a fuller expression of the Good Law, a deeper channel for its mighty current; perfect execution is guided by perfectly rationalised obedience, while each is the Law in action and is therefore overwhelming in strength. We go so slowly now from century to century, from millennium to millennium, that if we look back millions of years we see the human race still climbing on its way. But then the progress will be enormously swifter, obstacles will be a memory of the past, and all forces will be working consciously towards a fulfilment that is divine.

Even still higher mankind must rise. Beyond the glorious devachanic world opens yet another more glorious, the region of Samadhi, where a few of our race can function, though it is utterly unknown to the vast majority. It is a region there thought entirely changes its character and exists no longer as what is called thought on the lower planes; where consciousness has lost many of its limitations and acquires a new and strange expansion; where consciousness knows itself to be still itself, and yet has widened out to know other selves as one with it, so that it also includes the consciousness of others; it lives, breathes, feels, with others, identifying itself with others, yet knowing its own centre; embracing others and being one with them, and yet at the same time being itself. No words can express it; to be known it must be experienced. This great expansion gives a hitherto unknown unity; the divisions of earth are lost, for we are nearing the centre and looking outwards, thus feeling the oneness, instead of dwelling on the circumference and seeing the multiplicity. Then all that has been felt of service to those above us and compassion to those below us takes a new aspect, foreshadowing a yet more perfect unity - the unity of those who are higher and, just because they are higher, who realise their oneness with all below, seeing mankind in the unity of its spiritual nature instead of in the diversity of its material manifestations. Then outflows that compassion that sees itself and knows itself in every human soul, that understands all and therefore is able to help all, that feels with all and therefore is able to raise all, that in the worst and most degraded still realises the possibilities that to it are actualities, seeing in every man what he is in reality, not what he is in appearance, seeing him as he will be (as we should say) in the future, as he eternally *is* in the eyes of those who know. There incomprehensible problems find simple solution, and things that seem unknowable come within the limits of the knowable; man, rising higher and higher, finds wisdom more far-reaching, power mightier, love more all-embracing, till even to the freed spirit it seems as though there could be no higher climbing, no greater possibilities to be realised. Then before it unfolds a yet mightier world which dwarfs all that went before. One other range is still within the limit of human vision - within the reach, I dare not say of human thought, but to some extent of human apprehension, where Nirvana binds up all these glories of humanity, and where its possibilities are seen and realised and are no longer mere lovely dreams. Life beyond all fancy of living, activity in wisdom and power and love beyond men's wildest imaginations, mighty hierarchies of spiritual intelligences, each seeming vaster and more wonderful than the one before. What here seems life is but as death compared with that life, our sight is but blindness and our wisdom but folly. Humanity! what has it to do in such a region, what place has man in such a world as that? And then sweeping as it were from the very heart of it all - from the LOGOS who is its Life and Light - comes the knowledge that this is the goal of man's pilgrimage, that this is man's true home, that this is the world to which he really belongs, whence have come all the gleams of light that have shown upon him in his weary journey. Then it comes into the dazzled consciousness that man has been living, and experiencing, and climbing from the physical to the astral, from the astral to the devachanic, from the devachanic to the samâdhic, from the samâdhic to the nirvanic for this end: that he might at last find himself in the Logos whence he came, that he might know his consciousness as the reflection of That, a ray from That. The end of this mighty evolution - the end of this stage of it, for final end there is none - the end of this stage is that each should be in his turn the new LOGOS of a new universe, the perfect reduplication of the Light whence he came, to carry that Light to other worlds, to build from it another universe. That which awaits man is that mighty growth into the God, when he shall be the source of new life to others, and bring to other universes the light which he himself contains.

But what words can tell of that vision, what thought even flashing from mind to mind may hope to give the faintest image of that which shall be? Faint and imperfect the sketch must be - how faint and how imperfect only those can know before whose eyes have been unrolled the vast reaches of the untrodden vistas of those unborn years. Faint and imperfect, truly; yet still a sketch, however dim, of the future which awaits us - still a ray, however shadowy, of the glory that shall be revealed.

THE END.

BOOK SEVEN
SOME PROBLEMS OF LIFE

FOREWORD

AN attempt is made in the following pages to discuss some of the Problems of Life and Mind that exercise the brains and wring the hearts of thoughtful people. These problems will be studied with the aid of the light thrown upon them by Theosophy, that Divine Wisdom which enlightens us just so far as we are able to receive it. There is no idea in my mind so ambitious as that of solving these problems: I only seek to offer to my fellow students some thoughts that have been helpful to myself and may also be serviceable to others.

Theosophy, from its very nature, cannot form a new religion, a new church, or even a sect separate and apart. It is a unifier, not a divider; an explainer, not an antagonist. Whenever a Theosophist is aggressive, combative, denunciatory, he is failing in his high mission, for the "wisdom that cometh from above is first pure then peaceable." He is bound to be tolerant even with the intolerant, knowing that no evil can be destroyed save by its opposite good. Hence in seeking solutions for life's problems he does not vehemently assail the solutions already suggested, but seeks to distil from each any trace of truth it may contain. In all the schools of thought around us, ethical, sociological, scientific, and religious, some aspect of the truth is being set forth, and the fact that its exponents regard it as the whole truth does not lessen the intrinsic value of the particular fragment they present. Any view which has been held by large numbers of people, for long periods, over wide areas, recurring time after time, showing a perennial life, has in it some truth which preserves it; it is the duty of the Theosophist to seek for this truth and to bring it to light, freeing it from the errors which have enveloped it. Whenever human hearts and lives attach themselves to any view, they are not attracted by the errors which compose its form but to the truth which is its life. The failure to appreciate this distinction between the life and the form which temporarily envelops it has given rise to the bitterness of controversy, to the extremes of intolerance that we find in the history of thought. The Divine Wisdom which includes all truth cannot be hostile to any fragment of itself, whatever may be the transitory form in which it is set. The student of the Divine Wisdom, then, must recognise and revere it under every veiling form, as Isis recognised and reverently gathered up the torn fragments of the body of Osiris the beloved. Thus may the errors which belong to Time fall away, while the Eternal Truth endures, manifesting itself with ever-increasing fullness.

In our study, then, of the problems which surround us, we must search diligently in each school of thought for the truths which it is seeking to express, for the facts in nature which underlie its teachings. If this search be conducted successfully, the various schools will to a great extent be unified, Theosophy synthesising their different fragments. Quarrels arise because each school regards its partial truth as the whole, denying the truths of its neighbours while affirming its own. Peace will brood over the world when all schools concern themselves with the duty of outlining as perfectly as possible the aspects of truth which they perceive, and refrain from censuring as falsehoods those aspects which are invisible from the standpoints they severally occupy. "Men are usually right in that which they affirm, wrong in that which they deny," once quoth a philosopher, and his remark might be printed in golden letters over the desk of every student.

ANNIE BESANT.

LONDON, *July,* 1899.

I. PROBLEMS OF ETHICS.

THE problems of Ethics are concerned with the relations which exist between man and man, between nation and nation, and between man and the non-human world. Ethics has been called the Science of Conduct, therefore the Science of Relations, and its aim is to regularise and render harmonious the relations between an individual and his fellows, human and non-human. A man is not an isolated unit, but a part of an organic whole; Ethics considers him as such a part, and lays down the laws by which that whole may accomplish its orderly evolution.

Every system of Ethics, if incomplete, may be brought in a final analysis under one or other of three heads - authority, intuition, utility. Anyone of these three offers itself as a separate foundation on which a system of Ethics may be erected, and only a complete system recognises the value of each of the three, and sets each in its place as a corner-stone in the pyramid of conduct.

Those who base Ethics on authority appeal to some revelation given by a divine Being, or to some teachings of highly developed men, sages of the past, whose knowledge was greater than that of their contemporaries or of subsequent generations, and who spoke with the authority derived from that knowledge. These teachers - Prophets, Rishis, Magi, call them by what name we may - were men who knew the worlds beyond the physical, and laid down definite precepts out of their wide experience; these precepts were submissively accepted by the nations among whom they lived, they themselves being regarded either as directly inspired by God, or as sharing the divine nature. All the Scriptures of the world, the Bibles of our race, serve, each to the believers in it, as the foundation of morality, each laying down a certain code of ethics; this code is regarded as of direct and binding authority, not depending on reason but on the possession by the teacher of higher knowledge, whether that knowledge were due to his inspiration by some divine Being or to his own evolution into Deity.

The second great ethical school declines to submit itself to any external authority, and founds itself on the existence in man of an interior faculty akin to Deity - intuition. Intuition is variously defined; some identify it with conscience, and declare that conscience is the voice of God speaking in the human soul; others, shrinking from so extreme a position, and admitting that conscience is liable to error, and varies with the evolution of the individual, regard intuition as a faculty belonging to the spiritual nature, thus as being inherently superior to the physical, emotional, and intellectual natures, and therefore the proper guide of conduct.

The third school of Ethics bases morality on utility, appealing to reason as the authority which judges the facts and tendencies of life, traces the results of actions, and deduces from them a moral code, seeking to found its precepts on the generalised experience of the race. This school has many divisions, but they all found themselves ultimately on experience, and regard conscience as the product of evolution, as the moral instinct.[6]

However various may be the ethical opinions found among men, they may all, in the final analysis, be reduced to these three: the authority appealed to is (*a*) divine, of the nature of a revelation; (*b*) spiritual-human, depending on intuition; (*c*) rational-human, based on the recording of experience and the logical deduction of rules of conduct therefrom.

In studying these three great ethical systems it is necessary to consider the attacks made on each of them by their opponents, as well as the principles relied on by those who accept them. We shall seek in each for an aspect of Truth, which will contribute to the elucidation of ethical problems, seeing in each a value which may not rightly be overlooked or discredited. Each affords a partial guide for conduct and treating them theosophically we can unify them, antagonistic as they have been held to be, and as their supporters believe them to be.

(*a*) What is revelation? It is a teaching generally given in the early days of a race, in order to mark out a path for humanity not yet sufficiently evolved and trained to rely safely for guidance on either its intuition or its reason. The object of this authoritative declaration is the rendering of progress more rapid than it would be were the race left to make experiments unaided in matters of right and wrong. Many blunders would be made, many blind alleys entered, in the vague gropings of primitive man, driven by the imperious instincts of his animal nature, without experience to guide or reason to restrain. We may put aside all the aspects of revelation which deal with the inner constitution of man, with the relation of Deity to the universe, and with other weighty matters - aspects found in the great Scriptures of the world; we will confine ourselves to those parts of revelation which deal with morals, for it is against these that attacks are levelled by those who assail revelation as a foundation for an ethical system, and who refuse to the world's Scriptures any place in building up a sane morality. Every student is struck, when he considers any of the earlier codes of morality - nay, it is not necessary to be a student to be startled by it - by the presence of precepts which to him are immoral,

---

[6] Instinct has been defined as accumulated racial experience, and this is a true definition, whether we consider it, with the materialists, as transmitted by the modification of the organism, or with the Theosophists, as stored in the group-soul, the over-soul of a group.

not moral. Yet, if he accept occult teaching, he believes that the Scriptures containing these precepts were given by men who possessed very lofty and wide knowledge, men of the noblest morality, of very high spiritual development. Further, he comes across such precepts in books that contain hints as to God and man fragrant with pure and sublime spirituality, so that they give a painful jar to the mind intent on higher things. True, some of them might, nay would, be ejected by the analytic hand of critical scholarship, and would stand confessed as interpolations of later date. But however far historical criticism may go, that criticism, guided by occult knowledge and not merely by scholarship, must confess the salient fact that these ancient Scriptures contain teachings from men who were giants, spiritually and morally, above the men of the present as they were far above the men of the past. Fragments at least of their teachings have come down to us in these Scriptures, no matter how much of alien matter may have crept into them in the efflux of time and by the ignorance of successive generations. And among these teachings are some of the precepts which jar on us as unsuitable to their noble surroundings and as unworthy of the great instructors from whose lips they fell.

To solve this problem aright we must grasp the necessary corollaries of evolution, and place clearly before the mind some of the conditions inevitably bound up with the growth of a race from moral nescience to moral perfection. In far-off antiquity we see an infant humanity strong in its passions, but weak in its reasoning powers, plunging wildly at the entrance to the path of morality. It begins in blind ignorance of all distinctions between right and wrong. The first training could be but in broad principles, and withal these very principles must not press too harshly on the hitherto uncurbed animal nature. Many an action that would be a step backwards for us now was a step forwards for it then. On the infinite ladder of progress each rung is trodden in its turn, and we call the rungs below us "evil" and the rungs above us "good." Evil and good are relative: they appertain to progress, to growth. Our good of yesterday is our evil of to-day, and our good of to-day will be our evil of to-morrow. In the world there is a steady purpose that may be seen in the light of the history of human evolution. Souls in their infancy, ignorant of right and wrong as we now recognise them, gradually learn by experience, and looking backwards over the growth of humanity, we see that saints and sages have trodden the path up which these souls in their turn are climbing. We perceive that men are living in the world and are treading this long ascent in order that the soul may evolve. This soul is to be a self-conscious and self-moving intelligence; it is to develop a will that is free, which shall learn to choose the highest. This will is never to be coerced into choosing the best, but is to be left free to take what it will, under the sole condition that having taken it shall keep, having chosen it shall abide by its choice. As we watch the evolution of this growing intelligence we find that it is learning to choose between that which makes for progress, and that which makes for retardation. We perceive that the very things which at one stage helped it on its way upwards at a later stage pull it backwards, and, persisted in, would hold it in a lower state of being. When a soul is at a very low stage of evolution there is many an action that is right for it, because it carries it a step onwards, that becomes wrong for it after that step has been taken. Lifting forces are right, down-dragging forces are wrong. This study leads us to the conclusion that what is "right" at any period of the world's history is that which aids in lifting the soul into a higher condition than that in which it is at the time, and thus works in harmony with the divine will for the growth of the soul, helping it to become nobler, purer, wiser, more rational. That which is "wrong," on the other hand, is anything which goes against the current of evolution, anything which keeps the soul stationary or drives it backward against the upward tendency of the whole. "Evil" is the setting of the will of a part against the will of the whole, the separating oneself from the purpose of the world and going against it instead of helping it on. The kosmos is evolving from the inorganic to the organic, from nescience to omniscience, and any part of it which dislocates itself from its connections, which puts itself into antagonism to that movement, which for its separate purposes strives to delay the coming of that

Far off divine event

To which the whole creation moves,

commits sin, embraces evil, weds itself to death.

Let us take a few cases in which commands were given which jar on modern thought. We may imagine a race given to cannibalism, commanded to take the flesh of animals as food; assuredly a step forward would be taken by the substitution of animal for human flesh. As soon as the nation had entirely outgrown the eating of men and slaughtered animals only for food, the teacher would try to gradually lead it away from that barbarous custom by allowing the use of flesh only in connection with religious services, permitting to be used as food only the flesh of animals offered as sacrifices, and encompassing these sacrifices with burdensome conditions so as to restrict their number. To put together the slaughter of animals in sacrifice respectively to certain deities and to man's palate may strike many as a strange and incongruous juxtaposition. Yet some, not all, of the commands with respect to animal sacrifices were given for this very purpose. Among people who slaughtered all kinds of living things for food, it was an advance to restrain their killing to certain times and seasons, to surround it with rigidly enforced ceremonies. If, as in some cases, a man was not allowed to kill an animal without a year of preparation during which no flesh might be taken, if he might only eat flesh which had been offered in sacrifice, it is easy to see that such a man was being weaned from flesh-eating, and was learning to break off an evil habit. During his year of preparation the habit of living on flesh would be conquered, and the very restrictions surrounding the final ceremony would tend to make him reverence sentient life and regard its sacrifice as a solemn act, not lightly to be performed. Although to the modern mind the sacrifice of animals as a religious act appears to be brutal and degrading, one cannot but ask oneself whether it marks a lower stage of national immorality to slay animals only for sacrifice than to slay them wholesale for the gratification of the palate; whether the rare holocausts in Solomon's temple, for instance, were more degrading to the public conscience than the daily slaughterings in Chicago. The restrictions which in some civilisations of the past surrounded the slaying of the brute would press heavily on our modern western civilisations, and those ancient nations were at least learning that recklessness of animal life was a sin. People who disfigure their streets with the bleeding carcass of animals hung up to attract buyers should not look down too contemptuously on the ancient temple.

So with other points of conduct, which, rightly condemned to-day, were yet in the past sanctioned, even commanded by ethical teachers. Polygamy, for instance, introduced relations between the sexes far better than the promiscuity which preceded it. Among people at the lowest stage of sexual relations polygamy was a step upwards and therefore was right, not wrong. When the soul evolves, polygamy gives place to monogamy. As a rising from promiscuity polygamy was an advance; as a sinking from monogamy polygamy would be a degradation.

Such cases show us in what sense morality is, and must be, relative for evolving souls, and we see that any teacher who understands human nature, and who is more anxious to help his younger brothers than to express his own full thought, may rightly, in training a people, give ethical precepts that would now be degrading in practice. Looking at ancient ethical codes in this way, we can solve many of the difficulties that press on believers in their own Scriptures; the recognition of the principle of relativity in morals makes the way clear, and we understand that ethics is an advancing science, evolving with the evolution of the soul. We see that we must not swathe the limbs of the present with many of the bands useful in the past; that while the sublime spiritual truths contained in them give the world's Scriptures an eternal value, many of their precepts belong to a stage now outgrown. We must not dwarf the conscience and drug the moral sense by defending as perfect, because within the limits of a "revelation," precepts which were good for their own age but would be mischievous in ours. We make the Bibles of our race clogs instead of wings if we treat past commands as now binding, or if we explain them in a non-natural sense because they shock the more highly developed moral instinct which is the very result of that moral training through which our souls have passed. Enough if such precepts were ahead of the moral practice of their time, if they struck notes higher than the people could themselves utter, if they put before them an ideal not so lofty as to be impossible to strive after, though sufficiently lofty to exercise over them an elevating power. Unless we can thus throw ourselves backward in thought into those times of ignorance, we shall fail to grasp the meaning and the wisdom of the teachers, and may cast aside other teachings of inestimable value because they are mingled with instructions suitable for their own age, though not for ours. For let it never be forgotten that the very books which contain passages that now jar on us contain also ethical precepts of a character so sublime that while we are now able to recognise their exalted beauty we stumble feebly along the lower stages of the road of which they are the goal. The use of a revelation is to set before a race knowledge it is as yet unable to compass for itself, knowledge of dangers from which it warns, of possibilities which it holds out as encouragement. A revelation is the knowledge of the elder brothers placed at the service of the younger, one of the most effective means of lifting the world, of hastening the evolution of the soul.

(*b*) Repelled by these moral difficulties which surround revelation and may even be said to be inseparable from all revelations given to a primitive people, many of the most thoughtful and cultured people of our day reject it altogether as of authority, and regard conscience as the direct arbiter in morals; some go so far as to declare that it is the voice of God in man, and ought to be obeyed as a divine authority. This ethical school has been effectively attacked by the blunt pointing out of the fact that conscience is a very variable quantity - varying with civilisation, with intellectual development, with public opinion, with the general tradition and training of a nation. Further, that conscience in one man contradicts conscience in another, so that a person acting conscientiously may do things which another person as conscientiously condemns. Thus conscience speaks with many voices, yet always preserves the note of authority, of imperious command, and tortures with remorse the man who disobeys. When a man listens to conscience he feels himself to be listening to something that comes from outside or beyond himself, something that does not argue but asserts, that does not plead but commands. This voice, with its imperious "Do this," "Avoid that," seems by this very imperiousness to claim unquestioning obedience, and this has led to the ascription to it of divine authority. Yet if - as is clear from a study of the facts of human history - it sometimes commands crimes, we cannot rightly describe it as the voice of God. The inquisitor was sometimes conscientious when he racked and burned his brother man for the glory of God and the salvation of the souls of others who might be inclined to follow that heretical brother; he acted with a clear conscience, honestly believing himself to be doing service both to God and to man. Yet we can scarcely admit that in his case conscience was an infallible guide, or regard it as the voice of God speaking in the human soul.

The question, then, arises: What is this conscience which arrogates to itself such supreme authority, speaking as though it ought to be obeyed without challenge? Here Theosophy steps in and explains the genesis of conscience, and hence the limitations that surround it in the evolving - the not yet evolved - man. According to theosophical teaching the human soul, or intelligence, is a growing and developing quality, evolving by the experience gathered in life after life. Born into the world utterly ignorant and therefore without knowledge of good or evil, the soul at first could not recognise any difference between right and wrong. At that early period every experience was useful simply as experience, and everything encountered in life had some new lesson to impart to the infant soul. Whether an action were right or wrong, in our sense of the terms, it was equally useful to the soul, for only by the results which followed could knowledge of law be obtained. It was found that happiness followed some actions - those that were in harmony with the laws of nature - and that misery followed others - those that were in contravention with these laws; by these results the soul slowly learned to distinguish between the actions that made for progress and those which made for retardation. As the soul passed through incarnation after incarnation, it gathered a large store of these experiences of actions and their results: these experiences were increased by those reaped in the intermediate world, wherein the soul sojourned for awhile after leaving the earth, and found that suffering followed on the heels of the physical yielding to the impulses of the animal nature. Continuing its pilgrimage and arriving in the heavenly world, the soul rested and looked back over these varied experiences, and cast up the ledger of the concluded life-cycle. Certain classes of actions had led to happiness and growth, other classes to unhappiness and delay. The first classes, it decided, were those which it was desirable to repeat, while the latter should be entirely avoided. When the time had arrived for the return to earth, and the soul was employed in making for itself a new mind, it wove into this new mind the conclusions on desirable and undesirable actions to which it had come when reviewing its previous earth-life. Some of these were clear and definite: "That course of action led to sorrow, this course to joy; performing that deed I reaped misery, performing this I found content and peace. In the future I will avoid that, and I will do this." These decisions it implants in the mind it is forming, to be utilised in the coming life, and when it comes into the world in a new body these conclusions appear as innate ideas. The events from which the conclusions were drawn remain in the memory of the soul but are not imprinted on the mind; for the latter the conclusions themselves are enough, and they form a summary sufficient for guidance, unencumbered with a mass of unnecessary and burdensome detail. These conclusions form what we call conscience, or moral instinct, which responds at once to external impacts; when the parents or the teacher tells the child, "This is right, that is wrong," the mind of the child promptly acquiesces in the statement, if it fall within the limit of the registered results of its own experience; if it do not, the mind of the child remains bewildered and unconvinced, and withholds the inner assent although it may yield an outer obedience. Here comes in the value of education; the innate ideas may lie latent, if not aroused and brought out by external stimulus, however promptly they may respond to that stimulus when it is applied. Further, the weaker among them are strengthened when a statement of results is made externally beforehand, and the results follow the course of action described.

Regarding the nature of conscience in this way, we arrive at an understanding of its limitations. When anything comes before the soul similar to its past experiences, the registered decision asserts itself and the "voice of conscience" is heard; but when new circumstances arise, and no registered decision is available, conscience is dumb, and the man is compelled to rely wholly on the judgment then formed by the reason. Such a judgment will be largely influenced by the atmosphere in which he lives, by the customs and traditions of his time, by the prepossessions arising from racial and religious prejudices and from his own personal idiosyncrasies.

As the soul develops and gains fuller and fuller control over its vehicles, it is able to utilise more fully the experiences of the past, and to draw upon its memory for help beyond the well-digested conclusions registered in the mind as innate ideas of right and wrong. When it seeks to influence the lower vehicles, its communications must always have in them the note of authority, for the mind-consciousness can only know that some thought or impulse comes to it from a hidden and unexplained source, and there is nothing to approve to the reason that which is yet felt to possess compelling power.

When we study the subject from this standpoint it is easy to see why conscience, lacking experience, should make wrong decisions and give wrong commands, and we can accept the fact with equanimity, since the very experience of the sorrowful results that accrue from the mistake will give the soul wider knowledge, and thus ensure a wiser decision under similar circumstances in the future. Further, we see that the saying that a man should follow conscience is true, for even supposing the dictate of conscience be mistaken in any given case, it is none the less the best available judgment possessed by the individual, and its faultiness being due to insufficiency of experience it will be partly corrected by the results of the obedience rendered. The soul grows in the dark hours when a problem of action is presented to it that it is unable to solve. For the fairly moral person no difficulty arises in making the choice between the clearly wrong and the clearly right; to see is to decide. The problems which rack our brains and wring our hearts are those which arise when, standing before two courses of action, both seem right or both seem wrong, so that duty appears to be divided. The theosophist, finding himself in such straits, understands why he is thus groping in the darkness, and sets to work to do his best with a calm and steady mind-the result of knowledge. He puts before himself as fully and clearly as possible the two courses of action and their probable results, and brings to bear upon them his best powers of reason and judgment; he tries to eliminate as far as possible "the personal equation," to ignore the bearing of the alternative courses on his own wishes or fears, likes or dislikes, and to free himself from bias and prejudice; he then, with the whole force of his heart, wills to do the better of the two, seeking the illumination of spiritual intelligence; having thus done his best, he chooses, and fearlessly advances along the selected path. He may have chosen amiss, but even then, his intention being pure, that good intent will prevent the arising of any very serious harm; he will suffer for his mistake, and will thus increase his knowledge and be able to choose more wisely in the future, but the powers which "make for righteousness" will use his pure will to neutralise the results of his intellectual blunder. Results are guided more by motives than by actions, for the force liberated by a high motive is more potent than that generated by action, and will produce more good than the mistaken method will produce harm. Further, the motive works upon character, while the action only brings results on the physical plane. Thus, trusting to the Law, relying on the Law, we may act fearlessly even when darkness enshrouds us, for we know that the Law to which we commit ourselves will break in pieces our mistakes, while conscience will grow wiser through the exercise of our highest faculties, and will become stronger by the very conflicts through which it passes.

Conscience then - or moral intuition, as it is sometimes called - is not an infallible guide, but it has a place in directing our conduct; it does not decide between right and wrong without experience, but yields at any time the decisions arrived at by the study of experience by the soul. Thus understanding it we can use it, without being greatly troubled when it fails us at the hour of our sorest need, and in these cases of failure we must fall back on our best judgment to form a decision, abiding contentedly by the results.

(c) Let us consider utility as affording the basis for ethics, and see how far this ground commends itself to our reason. The formula often given, "the greatest happiness of the greatest number," needs, as every thoughtful utilitarian declares, some explanation for its due application. The nature of the happiness meant must be defined, both as to quality and quantity of duration; the higher must not be sacrificed to the lower; nor the lasting to the transient. Utilitarianism stated partially and without due discrimination lays itself open to effective attack as selfish and calculating, but put as the theosophist might put it, in the deep and wide sense, it is sound and philosophical. It should mean that if we act in accordance with law we must be acting for ultimate happiness; that ultimate happiness and ultimate right are inseparable, since we live in a world of law; that in this world, where every law is an expression of the divine nature, obedience to law in bringing about harmony must necessarily bring about happiness, and must at the same time be identical with the highest good. When we see that the law of the world is a law of progress, that we are evolving towards a more perfect condition, that the divine will is bringing about the perfection of all, that in perfection there can be no disharmony and therefore no suffering; when this is seen, we see also the underlying truth of utilitarianism beneath the partial expression, and that in the ultimate analysis there is no distinction between virtue and happiness. We are often blinded to this important truth by the fact that in the process of evolution the following of virtue repeatedly brings pain; and this must be until the lower nature is wholly transcended, until we have wholly outgrown the brute in us, and let "the ape and tiger die." We gradually learn that nature incessantly demands pleasure - i.e., harmonious and adapted co-operation - but that when the pleasure is attached to the possession of a form that breaks into pieces, such pleasure is followed by pain; we learn that in following the lower pleasures we are grasping at things which pierce us in the grasping, that such pleasures are delusive, and that all that is against the law - and therefore "wrong" - must inevitably lead to pain. We learn that we are the higher, not the lower, nature, and must transfer our centre of consciousness from the animal self to the divine Self; that we are not the body, as many think, nor the mind, as more highly developed people imagine, but the Self which is unity, in which all live and move. Evolution emphasises, strengthens, makes strong and defined the individual in order that he may become a centre of consciousness able to endure as a centre amid the keenest and strongest vibrations after the protective scaffolding of the individuality has been removed. The progress of man is from consciousness to self-consciousness through all the stages of selfishness and self-assertion, until self-consciousness can persist without losing memory and identity and all that is valuable as giving stability, while casting aside the limits that prevent interpenetration of numberless self-consciousnesses; nay, it is to expand to all-consciousness without losing its centre, expanding and contracting at will. In the course of this progress each man learns by sad and bitter experience the intangible unity of all beings, finding that nothing that injures one can be good for any, that that which brings happiness to all can alone bring happiness to each. Not the happiness of the greater number but the happiness of all is necessary for the happiness of one.

Oneship is not in the lower but in the higher, not in the body or the mind but in the spirit, the divine, the eternal life. Virtue and happiness are ultimately the same, because virtue is that which serves the life of all, not the separated life, and it is virtue merely because it aids evolution and is lifting the many towards the One. If in utilitarianism anything less than unity be postulated, if any point be set up short of that eternal oneness which is hidden in us and is being brought into manifestation, then the system is incomplete. No system can be really rational unless it be spiritual in its foundation and recognise the one Spirit as the life in all.

These three systems then, of authority, of intuition, of utility, contain truth and should be mutually helpful; they are complementary, not antagonistic, and each brings its useful lesson for the teaching of man. No system of ethics can be sound if it do not recognise the *evolving* life of the soul as its foundation and inviolable law as the condition of evolution. These two fundamental principles, so familiar to us as reincarnation and karma, are the basis of ethics, and without these no ethical problem can be solved.

One divine Life, given as a seed for the life of man; that seed growing by reincarnation, the infolded powers of the Spirit becoming the unfolded powers of the man made God - such is the secret of evolution. Those who in the early days of humanity gave to it revelation dealt with the early stages of the human soul, stimulating its growth; those who appealed to intuition recognised the growing soul which possessed a harvest of experience; those who spoke of happiness and virtue as one - if they knew the inner truth of their teaching - were grasping after the oneness of all things and the perfect happiness that lies only in the development of all. Thus the human soul develops out of ignorance into partial knowledge, out of partial knowledge into divine life, where the highest good is the highest bliss. On one or other stage of that ladder everyone of us, readers mine, is standing; the problems we meet in daily life belong to our stage of growth, and we solve them by knowing and by living. Sometimes a wiser and an older soul brings its experience to the helping of the younger, and by speaking out its knowledge for the guidance of the less advanced makes their evolution more rapid; the very proclamation of a law makes the recognition of that law the easier. Such souls are the Revealers, and all such teachings are of the nature of revelation. For such helping divine Teachers, liberated souls, remain among us, bearing the burden of the flesh; by their spoken words they quicken our nascent intuition, and by this revelation of truth aid us to climb more swiftly towards the light. From that Brotherhood has ever come revelation, the revelation of fragments of the Divine Wisdom. They send out their disciples as messengers, who repeat the truths they in humbleness have learned, in order that the world may evolve more rapidly. But never let it be forgotten that we progress more by living than by studying. As we destroy separateness and live compassion our eyes will be opened to the visions of ideal beauty. Now, as ever, is it true that only those who do the will shall know of the doctrine, and in no age of the world more than in the present has it been possible for man to be truly "taught of God."

II. PROBLEMS OF SOCIOLOGY.

Few questions, perhaps only those that are connected with religion, rouse as much hot feeling as those of sociology. Enthusiasts of any school can see no good, can scarcely admit common honesty, in enthusiasts of another. Folly or knavery, deliberate or invincible ignorance, is held to be the only conceivable explanation of views in antagonism to those cherished by the speaker. "Of course, no decent person can be a socialist," says one. "Of course, no humane person can be anything but a socialist," says another. And so on, with all the pairs of opposites into which sociology is divided.

Needless to say that here, as everywhere, the extremist is in the wrong, and truth lies in the golden mean. The great schools of sociological thought are none of them based on a fundamental error, but each on a partial truth; each manifests an aspect of the truth, necessary for social well-being, and denies other aspects of the truth because of the limitations of its exponents. The heat shown by the combatants may very well be excused in view of the importance of the issues at stake; for sociology is concerned with the external happiness of people everywhere, with their condition, their welfare, their comfort, their daily lives. Some, moved strongly by sympathy with the suffering before their eyes, will plunge headlong along any road that promises immediate relief; others, further-sighted and recognising hidden dangers, oppose vehemently all reform, lest while bringing a transient good it should result in deeper ill. These two tendencies lie deep in human nature, and by their interplay work for gradual evolution. Separated, as they generally are in action, they are wont to precipitate social catastrophes. Looking at human history, we often find it difficult to say which of these two classes-those who would have change at all hazards, or those who would stand on the old paths at all hazards - have most contributed to revolutions; whether these have been brought about mostly by the violent advocacy of those desiring change, or by the stubborn obstinacy of those who refused in any fashion to alter with the changing circumstances of man. If the two forces could be united in harmonious co-operation, progress would be at once rapid and safe, but while our limitations remain as narrow as they are at present, the hasty action followed by reaction, the forward rush and hasty retreat, are likely still to alternate in social affairs.

No person in whom heart and brain are developed can look at modern social conditions without recognising the intellectual ineptitude and the moral obliquity that have brought modern nations to their present pass. Not order but disorder, not government but anarchy, face us on every side, and we find everywhere unrest and discontent, the eloquent witnesses to the failure of modern civilisation. The air is full of confused murmurs, of inarticulate complainings, and despite the efforts of the unselfish and the growing sensitiveness of the social conscience, the hatred bred of a dull sense of injustice faces the repression bred of suspicion. The brotherhood which is a fact in nature is daily contradicted and defied in social life, and the friction generated by disregard of natural law threatens to burst into flames which will consume society, and leave the ground clear for another attempt to build a civilisation, or possibly, if men be sufficiently evolved, for the construction of a system ordered in accordance with facts.

All are agreed that the present state of things is unsatisfactory, and the century has been rife with proposals for change. These may be classified under three heads: political, dealing with the external organisation of society; economic, dealing with the production and distribution of wealth, and hence with ownership of the means of production; and at the close of the century, Theosophical, dealing with the broad principles under-lying all human relations. The politicians deal with the fabric of society, and political remedies can but concern themselves with externals that can be dealt with by legislation; none the less there must arise under this head a question of vast importance - the root of the authority swaying national affairs. A very large and increasing party, comprising many of the broadest-minded among the young thinkers of our time, entirely turns its back on politics, declaring that political arrangements are not at the root of the troubles of the day. These thinkers say that we shall never get rid of our troubles - poverty, ignorance, class antagonisms, recurrent strife between capital and labour - by working from the political standpoint; that below the political basis is the economic, and that politics can only deal with the surface of things. Let political arrangements be as good as the wit of man can devise, nevertheless with an unsound economic system misery must continue. A third party, small in numbers at present, says that even when we have reached the economic basis we have not yet touched the social bed-rock. They admit that economics go deeper than the questions which agitate the political world, but they allege that there is something that underlies both politics and economics, and that is human nature. They say that until human nature is understood, with its fundamental, ineradicable tendencies; until a study is made of man as man, both as an individual and in his social relations with his fellows, man in the past, the present, and the future, with his weaknesses and his powers; until this be done, we shall never be able to build a society which will endure. The people who talk in this strain are usually called Theosophists. All Theosophists certainly would agree in this, however much they may differ as regards present-day politics and economics. Whether or not they take part in political or social questions, they always hold these to be subsidiary to that which they regard as basic - a wide view of humanity as composed of souls evolving through vast ages of time under a definite law of growth. Hence they recognise the necessity for understanding the constitution of human nature and the conditions necessary for its evolution.

Yet theosophical teachings lend themselves with peculiar force to the elucidation of the very problems that politics and economics propound. The theosophical view of life must profoundly modify the atmosphere through which these problems are seen, since it presents men as evolving souls - under whatever political and economic condition they may at anyone time be born coming back to this world over and over again, inheriting their past and building their future while living in their present. Looking further backwards and further forwards than any political or economic system, theosophical teachings deal with man as an evolving entity, creating his future environment by his present activities, and modifying his present surroundings according to his place in the scheme of evolution. Theosophy applies the principle of evolution to society in a more radical fashion than does any school of thinkers, seeing in society not only an evolving organism - as do many others - but an evolving organism made up of souls, each one of which is also evolving. Those who see each man evolving during millions of years must necessarily look on all political and economic schemes as partial and temporary - as local and parochial, if the phrase may be permitted. Any political and economic system can but represent a passing phase in the vast evolution of humanity. Hence the Theosophist tends to a peaceful attitude of mind towards the different conflicting parties in the State; he is not inclined to rush wildly with one or the other, but sees that each embodies a principle necessary for the well-being of the whole, serving as a temporary vehicle for a fundamental tendency in human nature. He sees that the solution of problems will lie in the wise blending of principles and methods that are now in antagonism to each other, so that the total experience of humanity may be utilised in the social structure.

It may be well to remark, in order to avoid mistake, that theosophical teachings with reference to sociology have not yet been clearly formulated, and that any attempt to state them will certainly be coloured by the idiosyncrasies of the particular thinker concerned. The most that can just now be done is to indicate certain salient points and to make a tentative effort to apply these broad principles to present-day problems; with the help afforded by the history of the past, as we learn it from theosophical teachings, and the revelation of the occult side of nature in those same teachings, it should be possible to shed some light on the conditions necessary for a satisfactory solution, and to see the place and working of the tendencies now in collision that should be brought into harmony. The conservative and the liberal in politics, the socialist and the individualist in economics, severally represent necessary factors in social evolution, and the man who could utilise them all, putting each into his own place and holding all in balanced stability, would be a veritable saviour of society. This was done of old, we have learned, by the King-Initiates, who in far-off ages gave to humanity its earliest lessons in social construction, and it may be - nay, the time shall surely come - that in another Golden Age it will again be done, in a fashion suited to more highly evolved souls and to a humanity grown out of infancy into manhood. Society must again be based on a recognition of the fundamental laws of brotherhood, reincarnation, and karma, for these alone can unite progress with order, assign social functions with justice, and ensure abundance of material goods with propriety of distribution. Ignorance of these facts has brought about anarchy; knowledge will give right government, and the content that springs from justice.

Let us consider, first, the political problem: What should be the government of a nation, what its external organisation? A large body of thoughtful people, though far less in number now than in the early days of the century, concern themselves mainly with politics, regarding political order as the chief factor in national happiness. In considering the political aspect we will exclude the economic from view for a time, for the sake of clearness, and confine ourselves to the fashion of the instrument with which the law works in the nation. We are not here concerned with details, such as the political parties of any given time, or the way in which two or more sets of people may struggle for the direction of the government of a country; our study lies with the fundamental question of national organisation: "Where is the root of government, the source of authority?" This question must be answered in principle in one of two ways; however much the answer may be hedged about with qualifications, it can be ultimately reduced to a basic idea - that of monarchy or of democracy. At present among ourselves authority is supposed to grow from two roots, a limited monarchy and a limited democracy - a manifest compromise, a transitional state. Under monarchy comes all the varieties of personal rule, wherein the ruler is ruler by virtue of some quality pertaining to himself, some inherent natural qualification acknowledged by the ruled as giving him sovereignty over them. Under democracy come all the varieties of national organisation based on some system of the election of the government by the governed, those in which the root of power lies in the ruled, not in the ruler. The executive may be called a monarch, a president, a dictator, a council, or anything else, but he or it wields merely a delegated authority derived from the subjects, and resumable in the last resort by those who gave it.

Most people would probably say, at this point, that no discussion can arise in the present day between the principles of monarchy and democracy thus defined, and certainly very few persons would now accept the basic idea of monarchy, and frankly say that they believed in the "Divine Right of Kings." Yet, considering the part played by this idea in the history of the world, its endorsement by religion, and its acceptance by the wisest and best of our race in the past, its origin cannot be without interest. It comes down to us from the days of Lemuria and Atlantis, when perfected men belonging to an earlier humanity dwelt among our infant races and guided their earliest steps. They ruled the nations without question, in virtue of their manifest and unchallenged superiority, as a father rules his children; by their wisdom, compassion, and justice they enthroned the idea of monarchy in the hearts of men, and knit together in their minds religion and royalty, being in very truth to their peoples the representatives of God upon earth, embodying in their rule so much of the divine order as was suitable to the place and the time. There was no doubt in the minds of any as to the innate difference between the primitive kings and the nations that they ruled; they gave to the people their arts, their sciences, and their polity; they were at once their teachers and their guides; they built the outer fabric of the nation, and nursed its dawning life. From those heroic figures of antiquity, encircled still with the magic of their deeds, enshrined in myth and poem, there has come down an ideal of kingship in which the king was greater, wiser, nobler, diviner, than the people over whom he ruled, when his valour was their buckler and his wisdom their enlightener, where selfishness played no part, self-seeking held no place, when he gave himself and his life to the people, toiled that they might rest, waked that they might sleep, fasted that they might eat, when kingship meant supreme self-surrender in order that the nation might be guarded, taught, and raised.

When our own Aryan race was segregated, its Manu was naturally its king, and in his direct line were incarnated the mighty souls who carried on his work under his immediate supervision. The purest physical heredity, maintained by these great souls, afforded suitable encasement of flesh for these early monarchs, and the physical heredity remained when, in process of time, Initiates of lower rank incarnated in his family to continue the royal duties. Thus the divine right of kings became wedded to the idea of hereditary birthright, and for tens of thousands of years the connection of the two was maintained - a view quite intelligible as a tradition from these earlier times. The King-Initiate did not become possessed of "divine right" because he was born in a given family; but having in himself the necessary qualities, he took birth in that given family as the recognised and convenient method of obtaining the fealty of the nation, and the conditions suitable for training the new body and mind in which he was to function during that incarnation. An experienced and highly developed soul was chosen as a ruler of a nation by the great spiritual hierarchy that guides the evolution of humanity; *there* lay the recognised root of supreme authority, that hierarchy being the vehicle of the LOGOS in the department of His realm we call our world. Hence such a soul came as ruler, dowered with the right divine to rule, delegated by the hierarchy that was the expression of the ruling life of the LOGOS, chosen for his fitness, his capacity, developed through hundreds of incarnations in all the ascending grades of a past humanity. The taking birth in a particular family was merely a convenient way of publicly designating the chosen ruler, so that the kingship might pass from one personality to another without confusion, jar, or strife. To the people for many ages that birth gave the right to rule them, they knowing not the facts behind the veil; only a tradition was handed down of a golden age when kings were gods, and the hereditary kings of later millenniums traced their ancestry back to some divine King; Son of the Sun, Son of Heaven - some such name was the proudest of their royal titles, until in the efflux of time the title was regarded as a superstition, the fact on which it was based being lost in the night of the past. As the soul that incarnated in the Aryan race to finish their human evolution passed on into loftier regions, less developed souls stood at the head of humanity, and gradually, as the karma of the race accumulated, there was less and less direct interference by the Great Ones. The nursling had become the child on his own feet.

Less removed from their subjects in development, and not having yet outgrown the human weaknesses of selfishness, ambition, and pride, the kings began to use their unrestricted powers for their own advantage instead of for their people's good. Losing touch with their superiors in the invisible world, they lost the sense of responsibility to them, and gradually came to regard themselves as independent, and as arbitrary "lords over God's heritage." Then the people, misruled, began first to rebel against and later to limit the authority of their kings - feeling, truly enough, that monarchs who used their unbounded power to ensure enjoyment for themselves instead of welfare for their people, were no longer true incarnations of divine right. In Europe, the disappearance of the idea of reincarnation and karma intellectually involved the disappearance of the idea of hereditary divine right, while its practical destruction was brought about by the wickedness or mediocrity of the kings themselves. And yet if the idea of monarchy be admitted at all, we are brought logically to the view that the king must derive his authority from some invisible spiritual superior, who delegates to him the administration of a department in the divine world-government, and to that end invests him with the authority necessary for the effective carrying on of the administration. There is an impassable gulf between the hereditary being ruling a nation for life and the minister elected by the nation to a certain post, with power revocable at will. A monarch who is not a monarch; a ruler who does not rule; a supreme head (in name) of a nation who at every point of activity is precluded from action; such a personage may be a most useful and admirable functionary, worthy of all respect, but his office is in a transitional condition and cannot permanently exist. He is too great not to be greater; too small not to be smaller. If he be "king by the grace of God" he should have the power and the responsibility of kingship as well as its name; if he be "king by the will of the people," holding his office by virtue of an election by the nation - an election declared and revocable by some assembly representing the nation - and deprived of all reality of power, the title of king is somewhat too splendid for the limited reality.

If we look back some thirty years, we shall find in England a fairly strong party representing the republican ideal. Anyone who took a share in the political movements of that time will remember that a definite feeling in favour of republicanism was very widely spread, more especially among the manual workers, who displayed distinctly anti-monarchical sentiments. That feeling - as popular waves of feeling often are - was due to causes that had not in them the elements of permanency, and that have for the most part disappeared during the last twenty years. Philosophic republicans there have always been, and they will continue to be, but we are concerned here with practical problems rather than with academical debates. The popular feeling which showed itself against the heir to the crown was chiefly due to what we are bound to admit was the lamentable example of reckless extravagance and carelessness of life shown by the then young man who stood highest on the steps of the throne. This feeling has subsided as years have brought dignity and sobriety in public life. Another thing that has contributed to make republicanism in England a practically dead issue is the obvious failure of that system alike in France and in the United States. In the latter country the failure is the most marked. The interference with private life, greater there than here; the increasing wars between capital and labour, waged with a terrible bitterness unknown in older lands, and with a violence on both sides that shocks humanity; the poverty which holds in its grip a huge population surrounded by natural advantages; the corruption and police oppression that are rotting municipal government; the withdrawal from public life of the most thoughtful and refined people, in consequence of the intolerable conditions connected with it, conditions such that the very name of "politician" has become a reproach; all these and other causes have brought about a complete disillusion as to republicanism in action, whatever arguments may be adduced for it theoretically by those who believe in human equality. Men who twenty years ago were concerned in questions of government have now for the most part passed on into questions of economics, and declare that whatever may be the form of government, it is a sound economic system which is needed to make a nation prosperous, contented, and happy.

We may then put aside the issue as between monarchy and republicanism, as not coming within practical purview. And as though to mark its unreality there stands the wonderful celebration of the year 1897, acclaiming the conclusion of the sixty years of rule by our present monarch. Everyone admits - no matter what may be his personal opinions or prejudices - that we witnessed an unexampled uprising of sentiment in every part of the English-speaking world, an uprising that submerged for the time every other feeling. England and all her colonies were swept by one wave of enthusiastic devotion to the sovereign who sits on the throne of this vast empire, and all observers were struck by the strength and the passion of the sentiment, the hold it had on the popular heart, the transfiguring effect on the object of that devotion. The truth is that, deep in the heart of nations, despite all the crimes that evil kings have wrought, there lives a passionate desire to look up and see as the Head of the nation one human being who incarnates all it has of greatness, of glory, and of power, who stands as its symbol to the world. This tendency in human nature seems to be ineradicable, and its strength is witnessed by its survival through all strain of royal crimes. History testifies to the fact that extremity of misery and despair has ever been needed to goad a nation into revolt.

Rebellion is not the natural tendency of the human brain and heart. Man desires with a passionate longing to be taught, to be guided, to be ruled, as is shown by the pathetic inextinguishable loyalty of the masses to one man after another who rises into power on their shoulders. But man also demands that the one who claims to teach shall be able to teach; that the one who stands as guide shall be able to guide; that the one who is crowned as ruler should be able to rule. In this country, amid our political parties, there is no one man who stands out as leader, whom all would unitedly acclaim as great, who incarnates the ideal of a nation's Head. Were it possible that in a royal House a man should be born with the genius of a Ruler, with the power to awaken popular enthusiasm, with the brain to guide the nation, and the heart to love the people with a wise and all-embracing tenderness, seeing their sufferings, understanding the causes, and applying with a firm unflinching hand the sufficient remedies, then should we see what loyalty means in the heart of a nation, and the power that such a one would wield, amid glad assent, to eradicate wrongs and establish better conditions, with all the concentrated force and directness of an individual will, guided by a keen intellect and a noble heart.

Government would no longer be a series of compromises arrived at by decisions depending on the varying strength of parties, but a clear rational application of definite principles to definite ends.

In our own days the study of economics is leading many into various forms of Socialism. These forms are all democratic, and are based, explicitly or implicitly, on the assumption of the basic rights of man, and the counting of heads. The majority of heads is to fix the form of government, no matter what the contents of the heads may be. Empty ones, if the hands connected with them can scratch a cross on a ballot-paper, are to count as much as full ones, the drunken profligate is to balance the noblest sage. Truly it is said that under a proper system there would be no empty heads and no drunken profligates; but the proper system is yet to be established, and social derelicts are meantime to have an equal hand in making it, and to form part of the materials out of which it is to be constructed. "The sovereign people" cannot logically exclude any. This is the rock on which democratic socialism must split. It is the condition of success in all compulsory or voluntary groupings of men for the attainment of an object, that the head of the association shall be superior in faculty knowledge, and grip of the whole situation to those who compose the active constituents of the working body; if he cannot rule and they cannot obey, disaster is certain. Hence the manifold failures in co-operative production. The head of a business, the captain of a ship, the general of an army, the principal of a college, the father of a family - each of these must be superior to his subordinates in the matter in hand else chaos results. Only in a democratic State are the ruled supposed to elect the ruler, an equal to govern equals.

It is argued that a man might be elected to a position of authority and be vested with full power during the period of his official status; it is, however, very difficult for the official superior to impose a strict discipline on and to control effectually those to whom he is ultimately responsible, and by whom he may be ejected; the prompt obedience necessary to success is also not easily yielded by those in whose hands is the power of throwing off their chief. Even were these difficulties overcome, greater ones remain behind; in voluntary associations trust must be given to the elected officer, while he must be ruled by a sense of keenest honour to do his duty to the full; these qualities are lacking both in men and their chosen leaders for the most part, as is evidenced by the bitter suspicions of his fellows, that have broken many a labour leader's heart after fettering his energies for years, and by the failures in integrity among officials that have so hampered trade organisations. Trust and high honour are among the noblest and rarest of human qualities at the present stage of evolution, yet without the general diffusion of these democratic Socialism must fail.

If we look at governing bodies belonging to the State - such as socialistic communities would organise - we see staring us in the face the hideous difficulty of corruption. Men elected to office are continually found using their office for personal gain. In democratic America municipal and other public bodies are sinks of corruption, and there is scarcely any attempt to hide the fact that officials must be bribed when any undertaking is in question with which they are able to interfere. Where are we to find the men who may be trusted with office and will not turn it to their own ends? Such men are found where office is accepted for love of country and from traditional sense of obligation to the public service, but - until human nature be changed - such qualities are not to be found often in those who seek elective office as a means of livelihood.

That a noble form of Society is possible in which all the forces of the State shall be organised to subserve the general good, and in which all the plenty and happiness for which Socialists are rightly yearning shall be realised, is indeed a truth, as we shall presently see. But it will not be what we now call democratic, for democracy runs counter to the all-compelling laws of nature.

The fundamental error on which this system is based is the idea that "men are born equal," the keynote of the "declaration of the rights of man," which was the legacy of the last century to the present. Truly if men were born into this world but once, this fundamental error ought in justice to be a natural truth, and each man should be as good as anyone else, and have equal rights in the community. If the soul be newly created when it comes into the world in a new body, or if, as some think, man is only a body; if everyone now living in England was born for the first time during the present century and will pass away from earth for ever when the grave closes over his head or the fire consumes his body; if our only experience of earthly life lies in this brief space which stretches from the cradle behind us to the grave in front of us; then we might expect that one man should not be innately wiser or better than another, one fitted to rule, another only fitted to obey.

As we know by observation, men are not born equal but very unequal; some with tendencies to virtue, others to vice; some with genius, others with narrowest intellect. Never can a stable society be built if we start by disregarding nature, and treat as having right to equal power the ignorant and the wise, the intellectual and the stupid, the criminal and the saintly; on that uneven ground no edifice that will endure can ever be based. Yet if man be born but once, it would be unjust to build on any other foundation; for it would be a shocking injustice to subordinate one man to another, save by his own free choice, if both come freshly to the world, neither having learned anything, nor struggled, nor experienced, in former lives. In such case it would seem as though everyone had an equal right to everything, and should have his equal turn at governing among the rest; ignorance should have as great a voice in the guiding of a nation as wisdom, and a free fight and free scramble should give each man his chance in so irrational a world.

Nor are matters mended if "equal" be translated to mean "should have equal opportunities," for to give equal opportunities to the unequally equipped is to condemn the weaker to perish in the struggle for existence. We have, in our selfishness, left the weaker as a prey to the stronger, instead of training the stronger to regard his strength as imposing on him heavier responsibilities - among which are the helping and protecting of the weaker. Our economic system is one of free combat, with the inevitable "Woe to the vanquished." In former days it was a battle of bodies, now it is chiefly a battle of minds, but a battle none the less. We have learned that a man must not use his muscles to plunder his neighbour; we have yet to learn that he must not use his brains to the same end. It is no more right to trample on others because we are cleverer, smarter, shrewder than they, than in the days that are called barbarous it was right for a man to use his strength to rob, to crush, to enslave. The free combat that we call "civilisation" is not a state that can endure. I am not denying the necessity of passing through this stage in evolution, in order that the individual may be developed, but am looking to the next stage, for which we may rightly begin to work.

No one with a human heart in him can go through one of our great cities, seeing the condition of thousands of our people, realising the hopelessness of them for those who are born into them, without feeling a bitter pain, even if he think the state of things to be without remedy. To see into what surroundings children are born, how they grow up, how their parents live and die - these things are enough to break the heart if it be not wise enough to understand, and strong enough to labour. And I, for one, cannot have harsh condemnation for words, however wild, and schemes, however ill-considered, that spring from suffering, misery, and starvation, embittered by ignorance alike of causes and of ends. I have seen too much of the life of the poor, of the wearing anxiety and blinding pain, of the brutalisation and crushing out of hope and energy, to feel aught but tenderest compassion for their woes and sympathy with the motive that underlies all honest efforts for their relief. The wildest words are often but cries of pain, half-inarticulate, born of the blind feeling that something is wrong and of ignorance how to change, of the despair that grows out of patience long outworn and breaking hearts that find no help in man or God.

The worst of all is that this is of modern development and belongs especially to western lands; it is not of more than a century and a quarter's growth, and dates from the substitution in general use of machinery for handicrafts. The huge aggregations of population brought about by the methods of production are the superficial cause of much of the degradation; another of these causes is the crushing out of individual faculty. In the older days those who were employed in supplying objects needed by the community were men who, to a great extent, had joy in their work, the joy of the creator in his finished product. The craftsman of days not long gone by was an artist in a humble way, and his faculties were drawn out by the effort to invent, to improve, to adorn his work. Looking back even a couple of hundred years to the things in common use amongst us, we find everywhere traces of the individual hand and fancy. Farmhouses are still found where treasures of oaken tables, dressers, chests, &c., have come down in the family for generations, and these things in common use are eagerly bought up by connoisseurs, though but the work of ordinary craftsmen, often of "farm-hands," who in the long winter's evenings - as still in Norway and Sweden - would carve rough copies of flowers and twisted stems, adding a leaf or a bud or a tendril as the whim suggested itself, or some onlooker put in his word.

It is not, of course, possible to turn back the wheels of time and bring back the era of handicraft, even though it was more conducive to widespread comfort and development than the era of machinery in which we live. Machinery is here, and is here to stay, and we must adapt our society to the new conditions. As yet we have taken no steps to meet the difficulties caused by it, nor to make up for the deprivations imposed by it on manual workers employed on it. More and more in our modern life the man who tends a machine is becoming a machine himself, a flesh and blood lever of the things of steel and iron. He is deprived of the joy of the artist and becomes an automaton, turning out millions of fragments, say the heads of pins, but never an entire thing in which he can take delight or pride, into which he can put himself, which makes him feel himself to be a living man and not a mere hand to produce. The brains of a large number of those from whom the bulk of the nation is born are thus being partially atrophied and the physical development of the workers is injured.

Not without incurring a national Nemesis may a nation allow millions of its workers to be thus arrested in their growth. Into the lower physical types born of parents thus stunted can only come souls of low development, for nations, like individuals, reap that which they sow. If men's faculties are no longer, under modern conditions, cultivated in their labour as they used to be, then the enormous increase of the powers of production due to machinery must be utilised to give more leisure to the machine-workers, so that their faculties may be cultivated outside their labour. The English workman of the past was more of a man than is his compeer of to-day, and if we would not see the nation composed of souls of lower types it is necessary to redress the balance. The stunting of the mind in mechanical work is the justification of the cry for shorter hours of labour, and should be met by the co-operation of all classes of the commonwealth in bringing them about. It is not labour that takes the heart out of a man, but the dwarfing, stunting, deadening labour to which so many myriads are now condemned. Where such labour is necessary it should be brief, and should be balanced by the cultivation of faculties at other times. Otherwise our system tends to the dissolution instead of to the evolution of society.

The Theosophist, believing in reincarnation and karma, is able to see the roots of our social troubles and their remedy, and to work patiently in sure dependence on the law. He sees that the ideals of society must be changed, and that the Socialists are aiming at a right end - the general happiness - by mistaken methods. And he finds in the history of the past social conditions brought about, and for a time superintended, by Adepts, that they realised the most beautiful dreams of the idealist Socialist, while the basis and the methods were entirely different from those of the modern schools. Ere considering these, let us see the ideals which are created by a belief in reincarnation and karma.

Reincarnation implies the evolution of the soul, and when evolution is recognised equality is seen to be a delusion. Evolution is as a ladder up the steps of which humanity is climbing, and all men do not stand on the same rung. As evolution is a matter in which time plays the greatest part - at any rate until a late stage of growth - difference of stage in evolution implies difference of time during which the evolving entity has been climbing up the ladder. In other words souls, while eternal in their essence, are of different ages in their individuality, and herein lies the fundamental natural truth on which a stable human society must be based. For the ideal then of organisation based on the mutual contracts of individuals of equal age, each born with equal rights, we must substitute the ideal of a family, the members of which are of different ages, each born into duties dependent on the faculties they bring with them. The family, not the chartered company, is to be the ideal of the State; the discharge of duties, not the enforcing of rights, is to be the keynote of the individual life.

As evolution of the soul comes to be recognised as a factor which must enter into the organisation of society, the corollary that evolution is by law will also be accepted - karma will accompany reincarnation. Then the faculties with which a man is born will mark his stage in evolution, and will therefore determine his position in the State. And as the law guides the soul into the environment it has rendered necessary by its past actions, so in a State that was a living natural organism instead of a legal machine, souls would be as normally guided to the social grade fitted for the working out of the results of their past and their own further evolution, as in the building of the human frame the necessary materials are guided to where nerve or bone is required. Abnormal cases would appear, owing to the complexity of the causes generated by the past, but could be met, as we shall see, by special methods.

From this way of regarding the State, as an organisation based on natural laws and intended to aid and further the progress in evolution of every soul entering into it, certain principles of conduct will flow. In the family the heaviest burdens are borne by the elders and not by the children; the youngest are carefully trained, tenderly guarded, shielded from trouble, anxiety, and undue strain. If food run short, it is not the children who are first stinted; if anything be lacking, the elders bear the suffering and strive to let the children feel no want. Their greater strength is regarded as imposing on them responsibilities and duties, not as giving the right to plunder and oppress. These principles are to be worked out in the solution of social problems, and we may now turn to the question of their practical application in sociology.

In the early systems of sociology, imposed by authority on infant races by their initiate Rulers, all that modern Socialism aims at for the benefit of the masses - and far more - was definitely secured. Provision was made for the abundant production of all the necessaries of life, for the training of varied types of mind to the best advantage, for the full evolution of all the faculties brought by each with him into the world, and for the direction of the energies of each into the channel best fitted for their utilisation and development. The conception of the social scheme was due to the divinely illuminated wisdom of perfected men, and its administration was confided to the most advanced souls of our own humanity, working in graduated order under the immediate direction of the King-Initiate. The basic principles of this scheme may be thus stated: government is a task demanding the highest human qualities, spiritual and intellectual, and to be rightly carried on must be undertaken in the spirit of entire self-abnegation and of devotion to the common weal, the highest being most completely the servant of all; the more highly developed the man the more highly placed should he be in the social order, and the heavier therefore his responsibilities; further, the smaller will be his personal demand on material resources, his nature expanding itself chiefly in the mental and spiritual worlds, and being related to the material for service rather than for enjoyment; the governing class should therefore consist of the wisest, the purest, the most self-denying of the nation, those who can see the farthest and who ask for themselves the least, who have their hearts set on the common good, who count no labour heavy that promotes the general growth and happiness, who seek nothing but give everything, who are wise by ages of experience, and who having learned the lessons of the world are able to apply them to the circumstances of the day. The first duty of the government is to maintain in comfort, prosperity, and suitable conditions for progress, the less developed types, needing for their happiness abundance of material goods; these things are requisite alike for their evolution and their contentment, and the smaller their resources within themselves the larger are necessarily their demands on the outer world. Abundance can only be provided by labour, and to avoid waste of energy the labour must be carefully organised, directed into the most fruitful channels, and guided to the most efficient co-operation. This can only be done by those who have the whole field under their eyes, and can thus dispose of the available energies to the best advantage. The undeveloped must yield labour and obedience in exchange for comfort and absence of material care; by this labour and obedience their mental and moral qualities are evolved and trained, fitting them in later birth to take a higher position in the State.

Avoiding details, which varied at different times and places, the general scheme placed the responsibility for the organisation and direction of labour within a given area on the officials administering the area; each governmental unit formed part of a larger unit, and training in the smaller units prepared for the administration of the larger; famine or any scarcity of the comforts of life, discontent, uneasiness, crime, ignorance - these things being regarded as due to the fault of the administrators, each ruler was called to account by his immediate superior for the prevalence in his district of any of these evils, rightly regarded as evitable. The ruler was there to direct labour, to ensure education, to equalise distribution, to repress violence, to decide disputes, to keep order, to promote happiness; if he could not do these things he was unfit to rule and must give place to a better man. He might be the ruler of a village, of a town, of villages and towns aggregated into a province, of provinces grouped into a viceroyalty, but whatever the size of his district, he was responsible for its good government; and all were thus held responsible, from the pettiest village official up to the highest governors holding directly from the monarch, the monarch answering to the occult hierarchy only. He appointed some as his viceroys over grouped provinces, these in turn appointed the rulers of provinces, and these again the subordinate officials, and so on to the end of the ladder; thus was ensured a graduated and orderly administration, which served at once as a government machinery and a training ground for the evolving souls who constituted it, its highest and most responsible members being Initiates. It will be observed that this whole system made the lower and less evolved subordinate to the higher and more evolved throughout; each rendered obedient to his superiors and received it from his inferiors, and the responsibility of each was to those above him, never to those below. Hence "rights" had no place, "duties" only were recognised, but these duties imposed on the more evolved the obligation to provide for the less evolved everything that could conduce to their growth, their happiness, and their improvement. All was given, nothing was snatched, and consequently there was order and contentment instead of struggle. The land belonged to the monarch, but was divided as to control into definite portions, assigned to the different classes. One half was set aside for the producers engaged in active work and for their families; the second half was again divided, one portion of it going to the monarch, and supporting the whole governing class, and such imperial charges as the defence of the nation, the keeping up of internal communications, and similar necessaries for the people as a whole; the administration of justice, like the rest of the work of this governing class, entailed no direct charges, all the officials being supported from this land. The second portion of the half of the land went to the priesthood, who formed a class apart, side by side with the governing class, and were charged with the public education; the whole of this education, again, for children and youths, entailed no direct charges, the priests being the teaching class of the nation; this land further supported all sick and incapable persons, and all - outside the governing class - who had passed middle age, generally fixed at about forty-five. The period of labour extended over only about twenty-five years; before it, the youth was educated, and after it his time was given to the leisurely development of whatever faculties he had evolved. The admirable organisation of labour rendered it so productive that this ample leisure could be secured to all the producing class, thus ensuring their definite evolution in each life-period. The half of the land used for the governing and priestly classes was cultivated by the manual workers, this labour being their contribution to the State. Among the institutions maintained by the land of the priesthood in each province were central agricultural colleges and experimental farms, where professors and students were constantly engaged in the scientific study of agriculture; it was their duty to improve the methods of cultivation, to make experiments in cross-breeding plants and animals, to search for new ways of utilising natural forces, of enriching the soil, &c. Any discovery was tested on these government farms, and all the information gathered was circulated among the cultivators by popular teachers; improved breeds of cattle, grains and seeds were distributed through the province, and all that science and trained intelligence could devise was placed at the general service, being freely imparted to the workers. Agricultural work was further assisted by the publication throughout the year of the best times for the various field and garden operations, astronomy and astrology being utilised for the prediction of the changes of the weather, early and late seasons, favourable and unfavourable magnetic conditions, &c. All this work was demanded from the official class as their contribution to the State, even more rigidly than labour was exacted from the manual workers, for the pressure of opinion and the accepted code of honour prevented dereliction of public duty. One principle of administration was significant of the spirit in which the business of the nation was carried on: in times of scarcity of grain, the land of the priests was first sown, then that of the people; lastly that of the king and officials; if irrigation failed, the water was supplied in the same order. The children, sick, aged, and superannuated, considered as the weakest members of the national household, were those whose needs were the first to be supplied; burdens must fall on the elder and the stronger, not on the feeblest.

The products of a district were gathered into central granaries and storehouses for distribution as needed, the methods of distribution varying much with time and place. In good seasons the surplus products were stored for use in times of scarcity - a custom we find surviving in Egypt in historical times. This centralising of the products of a district and their careful distribution enabled the results of improved cultivation and of mineral discoveries to be shared among all, the whole family, as it were, profiting by any advance. Further, a competence was assured to each and harassing anxiety as to the means of subsistence was unknown - that anxiety which breeds desperation in the undeveloped soul, and renders impossible the evolution of higher qualities.

Education was universal, but was adapted to the life that was to be led; reading and writing were not, as now, considered indispensable, but all who showed capacity for study were instructed in these instruments of learning and were then sent on from the primary to the secondary schools; thus children born into any class could rise out of it if they brought with them into the world capacities fitting them to rise, *but not otherwise*. The bulk of the population were trained in technical schools for agriculture or handicrafts, according to their tendencies, the capacities of the child deciding his walk in life, but a sound knowledge of his work was always imparted to him, so that he might perform his duties intelligently and with pleasure. The children of the governing and priestly classes, together with the pick of the working population, boys and girls, received a careful educational training, specialised to meet individual tendencies after the broad and deep foundation had been laid. Religious, moral, and physical education was universal, varying in character according to the capacities and future work of the pupil, and no pains were spared to develop to the utmost the intellectual, moral, and spiritual faculties of those destined to guide and rule the community; above all were they trained to regard duty as all-compelling, and self-abnegation and hard work as the inevitable accompaniments of high station; this austere training and this rigorous exaction of duty from the young who were to be highly placed may be found recounted both in fourth and fifth race literature, and those who fancy that ancient rulers were mere luxurious idlers might well correct their ideas from the extant accounts. The hours of work for the labourer were short, his life was free from anxiety, and he was discharged from hard work ere old age overtook him; but the ruler must work as long as any needed him, all the responsibility of the welfare of the community weighed on him, and death alone lifted from his shoulders the burden of duty to his people.

Looking back to that ancient time and comparing it with the present, we naturally ask why so noble a system faded away, and why man passed into a state of struggle. As souls less highly evolved succeeded to the post originally held by the Divine Kings and the Initiates of various grades, the powers wielded by the rulers were prostituted to selfish purposes instead of being devoted to the common good. Rulers failing in their duties, discontent took birth among the peoples, tyranny bred hatred, and oppression begot rebellion. Was this a necessary stage in human evolution? It would seem so. Man in his early days was child, not man; he was in the nursery and the school, and the troubles of his manhood lay in the future. Between the stage when humanity was an infant, guided, taught, and trained by divine Teachers and their immediate pupils, and the stage of divine Manhood when each shall have the law within him instead of without him, there stretches a long and weary struggle, a time of hopes disappointed, of efforts continually frustrated, of attempts breaking down, of experiments and failures. This is a time of transition, like that of early manhood, and humanity is like the young man or woman who thinks that he can set everything right in a moment, that the wisdom of the ages is as nothing beside his keen insight, that only the sloth and stupidity of his elders stand in the way of the abolition of every abuse and the righting of every wrong. Everybody else has failed, but he will succeed; he will solve in a moment the problems of ages, and in a few years the world will be happy. So the surging democracies of modern days are very young; one moment all will be right if we get rid of a king; next moment all is saved if an Established Church be crushed; yet again, happiness is secured if capitalists be destroyed. All superficial enough truly, as we see as experience ripens and we recognise that our difficulties are rooted in the lack of development in our own natures. Yet may it not be that through these very struggles, these shiftings of power, these experiments in government, these failures of the ignorant, the experience may be gained which shall again place the hand of the wisest on the helm of the state, and make virtue, self-sacrifice, and high intelligence indispensable conditions for rule? Passengers do not take turns on the bridge of the ship to navigate the ocean; the skilled workman does not entrust his delicate machine to the loafer; the crossing-sweeper is not called in to perform a delicate surgical operation. And it may be that by failure and by social revolutions, if by no other way, we may learn that the guiding of a nation, politically and economically, is not best done by the ignorant or even by amateurs, but demands the highest qualities of head and heart.

In economics also it is probable that this stage of competition and misery was necessary for the evolution of individuality, and that man needed to grow first by combat of bodies and then by combat of brains, by the constant claim of the individual to plunder according to his powers and his opportunities. None the less it is true that this stage shall be outgrown, and we shall learn to substitute co-operation for competition, brotherhood for strife. But we can only outgrow it by cultivating unselfishness, trust, high character, and sense of duty, for we must improve ourselves ere the body politic of which we are constituent parts can be healthy.

But how to find a motor power to bring about such changes? While steadily disciplining and training ourselves, we can place before our fellows ideals which shall be so wise, so well considered, that they shall win the allegiance of the intellect as well as satisfy the cravings of the heart. We must change our estimate of the relative value of things, and substitute intellectual and spiritual wealth for material riches as a standard of social consideration. May it not be possible to influence public opinion to value men and women for greatness in intellect and virtue, in self-surrender and devotion, and not for wealth or luxury? - making the multiplicity of material wants the recognised mark of inferior development, and simple and pure living hand in hand with richness of the higher nature the title to honour. May not the wealthy learn that it is an essentially infantile view of man to value him by his show instead of by his worth, by the number of his material wants rather than by the grandeur of his spiritual aspirations? Wherever the ideal is the possession of material goods combat must be the social condition, since material goods perish in the using, and possession by one excludes possession by another. Intellectual, artistic, spiritual wealth increase in the sharing, each who shares adding to the store. This is the fundamental reason why progress towards peace and contentment must be towards intellectuality, artistic development, and spiritual life, and not towards material splendour and the vulgarity of outer ostentation. These are for the undeveloped, the others for the developed. And inasmuch as the ignorant will copy the more advanced and the lowly the highly placed, the example must be set by those who lead the social and intellectual world. Moreover they would themselves gain by the change in so far as they lead luxurious lives, for the pampering of the body is even more fatal to the growth of the higher nature than is the stern discipline of poverty. Man need demand from the outer world no more than absence of harassing anxiety; sufficiency, not luxury; beauty and harmony, not ostentation; leisure, not exhausting toil; time and opportunity to develop the God in him, not the overfeeding of the animal.

Further, we must have faith in humanity and appeal to what is best in man, not to what is worst. It is not true that it is necessary to build society on selfishness and to rely on selfish instincts. That which is deepest in man is not the animal, and to mould society for the brute that man is outgrowing is to build on a sinking foundation. It is a curious illustration of this that even with men of poor moral development honour is more compelling than law, and social opinion than legislation. A man will ruin himself to pay a "debt of honour" while he seeks to evade a debt enforceable by law - a perverted sense of duty, truly, but still eloquent of the important truth that more can be done by appealing to a sense of obligation imposed by the social opinion surrounding a man than by compulsion of an impersonal law. If the sense of honour, of duty to a class, can be expanded to include the nation, we shall have at work in our midst the most binding form of obligation. Duty will become the keynote of life, each asking "What do I owe?" instead of "What can I successfully demand?"

It seems possible that in the future we may arrive, even by the slow method of failure, at some scheme of government in which the wisest shall hold the reins of power, and obedience shall be gladly rendered to recognised superiors; and at some economic system in which wealth shall be distributed according to needs. Then the maxim will be acted upon - noblest of all maxims when given by love, not grasped by hate - "From every man according to his capacities; to every man according to his needs." That which has been the battle-cry of men maddened by suffering shall become the axiom of distribution in the rational human family.

Most certainly the putting forward of such ideas as are here suggested will not change social conditions in a moment, but no permanent improvement can be wrought in sudden fashion. Yet are they on the line of progress, of the upward evolution of man. The majority of men on the earth to-day are men of the fourth race, but the fifth race - the keynote of which is individualism - is leading human development. The dawn of the sixth race is yet afar in the future, and of that the keynote will be unity not individualism, brotherhood not combat, service not oppression, spirit not intellect. And the birthmark of the spirit is the longing to pour itself out in sacrifice, never asking what it can take but only what it can give. The fundamental unity of mankind is the central truth of the coming race, and the nation which first grasps and practises that great conception will lead the future, humanity falling into line behind it. Those who see it, who teach it, may fail for the moment, but in their failure is the seed of inevitable success.

It is for us who are Theosophists, who hold as truth the spiritual unity of mankind, to put our belief into practice by teaching peace, brotherhood, the drawing together of classes, the removing of antipathies, the recognition of mutual duty; let the strongest do the best service, the wisest the loftiest teaching; let us all be willing to learn and ready to share; so shall we hasten the dawn of a better day, and prepare the earth to receive the coming race.

III. PROBLEMS OF RELIGION.

To the true Theosophist every man's religion is a sacred thing, and he would not consciously jar on the feelings of any; for whether a statement of religious truth be adequate or inadequate, crude or well-considered, it is sacred for the one who accepts it as embodying his special ideal. We may rightly use our keenest intelligence and our most patient thought in searching for the wisest and most adequate presentations of things spiritual; but on the other hand we do well to remember that spiritual truths are so many-sided that the utmost the intellect can do at one time, is to present a single aspect of such a truth. Even when that aspect is given in a crude form, it but shares the crudity of all intellectual statements of spiritual truths, the difference between the crude and the polished being but a difference of degree, not of kind. We might put side by side, for instance, the crudest idea of God that might be obtained from the most ignorant costermonger and the subtlest conception formed by the loftiest philosopher, and might be struck by the wide discrepancy; yet if that same subtle conception could be compared with the adoring thought of a lofty spiritual Intelligence, able to live consciously in the splendour of the LOGOS, we might realise that any thoughts of God that can express themselves through the physical brain can only represent degrees of inaccuracy, grotesque in their inadequacy. Even the greatest of spiritual Seers must fail when he seeks to lisp in mortal numbers the glory of the Vision that blinds his raptured gaze; much more then, when we are dealing with the ideas of Deity formulated by half-developed men and women like ourselves, may we learn humility and charity in criticising - if we must criticise our brother's faith. It is wiser to seek, even in the strangest view, for a faint suggestion of an aspect that we may have missed, than to use our critical fangs to rend in pieces an ideal which is helping some human soul to rise, and is evolving in some undeveloped intelligence the germs of aspiration and worship.

Therefore in dealing with some of the Problems of Religion, I shall seek at least to deal with them reverently, careful to avoid jarring on human feelings, and mindful of the maxim, "Nothing that is human is alien to me." In indicating the lines along which, in the light of Theosophy, solutions seem possible, I would not force on any reader ideas which are unacceptable to his own reason and intuition, for the thought on religion which a man originates is far more helpful to him than the parrot-repetition of words that do not represent his individual conception of truth.

There are five problems of religion which stand out as of perennial and universal interest, and while each might well demand a volume for itself for adequate treatment, it may not prove useless to present them with brevity, showing how the theosophic method is at once suggestive and illuminative; for very often in religion, as in ethics and sociology, it reconciles the adherents of opposing schools by harmonising concepts that are superficially discordant, proving them to be facets of the same truth when their mutual relations are seen. These five are as follows: the nature of God in manifestation; the existence and growth of the human soul;

freewill and necessity; the place of prayer in the religious life; the atonement.

First let us take up the problem of problems, that of the existence of God and the conceptions of Divinity formulated by man. There is one fundamental principle that must be recognised in approaching this problem - the unity of existence. If God and man be regarded as basically different, a mighty unspanned gulf stretching between them, then the problem of the divine existence and of man's relation thereto seems to frown upon us as defying solution. But if God and man be seen as of one essence, humanity as an offshoot of the one Tree of Life, and as one of myriad offshoots, sub-human and super-human - one radiant arch of beings, each instinct with divine life - then the question as it affects man appears as by no means a hopeless one. The West, tending to the former conception - that of a fundamental difference of nature between "the Creator and the created" - has swung between the unacceptable extremes of crude, anthropomorphic Monotheism and philosophic Agnosticism; the East, founding its religions on the second conception - that of unity - has contentedly accepted a religious Pantheism as intellectually necessary and as emotionally satisfying. Pantheism in the West has hitherto been an exotic, and has appealed strongly only to the highly intellectual; its God has remained a cold abstraction, intellectually sublime but emotionally chill. In the East, Pantheism, while asserting as clearly as possible the One Existence, meeting all intellectual difficulties by the affirmation of the universality of that Existence - God is everything and everything is God - yet passed naturally into the recognition of endless gradations of Beings expressing very various measures of the divine Life, some so lofty in their nature, so vast in their power, so far-reaching in the range of their consciousness, that they include every element that Christian Monotheism has found necessary for the satisfaction alike of the intellect and of the heart.

It is apparent in reviewing Christian Monotheism that anyone who approaches the study of the divine Existence from the standpoint of the intelligence is sure ultimately to land himself in Pantheism; if he does not openly reach it, it is because he shrinks from formulating the logical conclusion from his premises. No better example of the inevitableness of this conclusion can be found than the Bampton Lectures of the late Dean Mansel; following purely metaphysical lines, he saw himself led more than once into the "dreary desolation of a pantheistic wilderness," and so passionately did his heart revolt against a view that robbed him - as he misconceived Pantheism - of his Father in heaven, that he flung aside the irresistible conclusions of his logic and took refuge in the dicta of revelation, as a shelter from the arid glare of an empty sky and a barren land. The Eastern Pantheism - which, as already said, posits a universal existence in which all beings are rooted, and accepts to the fullest the belief that in God "we live and move and have our being" - recognises also that the divine Life manifests itself in modes of existence which bridge over the gulf between man and God manifesting as God. It acknowledges mighty Intelligences who rule the invisible and visible worlds, the presiding Gods who guide the order of nature and watch over the destinies of men, the agents of the supreme Will in every department of life, the fitting objects of reverence and of worship. Just in proportion as the existence of these great Beings is recognised and enters practically into human life - whatever may be the name given to them - is religion strong against the attacks of Agnosticism and unbelief. For these ranks of spiritual Beings, rising in ascending hierarchies till they culminate in the supreme God of the system to which they belong, give to men intelligible ideals of divinity, which rise as they rise, expand with the expansion of their consciousness, and meet at every stage of evolution the craving of the human heart for some superior Being far above itself, whom it can love, trust, reverence, worship, appeal to for aid when human help is far. It makes possible and real the "Father in heaven" for the child and the peasant as well as for the philosopher, presenting for adoration the concrete Being with enlarged faculties and powers that the heart is ever seeking. The just arguments of the metaphysician and the logician, against the existence of a God at once infinite and personal, have shattered themselves time after time against the immovable conviction of the spirit in man that it is akin to, is the offspring of, some mighty divine Being, and man has doggedly refused to surrender his conception of such a Being - however illogical it might be - until a higher conception was offered including everything he was seeking in the lower.

This view of the life-side of the cosmos is one that in no way outrages reason or transcends possibility; on this the statement of an avowed Agnostic may help us; "Looking at the matter from the most rigidly scientific point of view, the assumption that, amidst the myriads of worlds scattered through endless space, there can be no intelligence, as much greater than man's as his is greater than a black beetle's; no being endowed with powers of influencing the course of nature as much greater than his, as his is greater than a snail's, seems to me not merely baseless, but impertinent. Without stepping beyond the analogy of that which is known, it is easy to people the cosmos with entities, in ascending scale, until we reach something practically indistinguishable from omnipotence, omnipresence, and omniscience. If our intelligence can, in some matters, surely reproduce the past of thousands of years ago, and anticipate the future, thousands of years hence, it is clearly within the limits of possibility that some greater intellect, even of the same order, may be able to mirror the whole past and the whole future; if the universe is penetrated by a medium of such a nature that a magnetic needle on the earth answers to a commotion in the sun, an omnipresent agent is also conceivable; if our insignificant knowledge gives us some influence over events, practical omniscience may confer indefinably greater power."[7] This possibility of the learned Agnostic is known as truth by the Seer, and moreover it represents the life-side as corresponding with the form-side delineated by science. For the worlds around us are at various stages of evolution and are grouped in an ascending order. Our own planet is part of a group of planets, having their common centre in the sun; our solar system is part of a group of systems, having their common centre in a distant star; probably that group of systems, again, has a common centre with other similar groups of systems, and so on and on. Thus the universe is seen as made up of departments, each successive unit forming a section in a wider department - graded hierarchies of forms. The analogy of nature thus leads us to look for similarly graded hierarchies of living Intelligences, guiding the forms, and we are thus brought face to face with the Gods.

Occultism teaches us that over each department in nature there presides a spiritual Intelligence; to put the matter in a more concrete form, over our solar system presides a mighty Being, the LOGOS, the manifested God of that system. He would be called the Father by the Christian, Ishvara by the Hindu, Allah by the Mohammedan. His consciousness is active at every point in His cosmos; His life sustains it, His power guides it, everywhere within it He is present, strong to help, mighty to save. Dimly we know that beyond Him there are yet greater Ones, but for us it is easier to conceive of the Power that maintains our system, to whom we are definitely related, than of the vaster Consciousness which includes myriad systems within His realm. Each LOGOS is to His own universe the central object of adoration, and His radiant ministers are rightly worshipped by those who cannot rise to the conception of this central Deity. As the intelligent beings within His kingdom rise higher on the ladder of evolution, their ideal of God enlarges, deepens, and expands; at each point of their growth their ideal shines alluringly above them - narrow enough at the lowest point to meet the needs of the most limited intelligence, vast enough at a higher to task the intellect of the profoundest thinker. Thus a

---

[7] 'Essays upon some Controverted Questions', by T. H. Huxley, p. 36, ed. 1892. It is not pretended that Dr. Huxley believed that things are so; wise men, he thought, would say "not proven," and be agnostics."

448

conception of Deity may be found which is intelligible to the child, to the ignorant, to the undeveloped, and which is to them inspiring, consoling, and sublime. If a lofty conception were offered to them, they would merely be dazzled by it, and they would be left without anything to which their hearts could cling. The idea that satisfies the philosopher would convey nothing to the ignorant, the words that express it would to him be meaningless; he is told of a Being in terms that convey to him the chill void of an immeasurable space, and he is practically forced into Atheism; he is given nothing under pretence of giving him everything, for a thought that he cannot grasp is to him no thought at all.

What is needful to man in his conception of God? A Being that satisfies his heart and compels the homage of his intelligence, that gives him an ideal that he can love and worship, and towards which he may aspire. It is more important that a man should realise some One before whom his heart can expand in loving adoration than that his concept should be philosophically satisfactory and metaphysically correct. The spiritual nature is to be stimulated into activity; the soul is to be helped in its growth; the spark, which is the essence of the divine Fire on the altar of the heart, must bum up into the Flame whence it came forth and towards which it endlessly aspires. The attitude of love, of worship, of aspiration, is necessary for the growth of the soul, and if the lips falter, if the words be halting, if the infant soul can only utter the broken lispings of its infancy, does the Supreme Love despise its offspring because the expression of the filial love is clumsy and the thought inarticulate? "As one whom his mother comforteth" does the young soul feel the clasping of the everlasting Arms, and while the form in which Deity is clothed may be that of a subordinate God, the life that thrills through is a manifestation of the one Life, the one Love.

The Roman Catholic Church has met the varieties of human need by presenting for the worship of her children not only the "Blessed and glorious Trinity," but the mighty Archangels and Angels - the "Gods" of the Ancient Wisdom and of Eastern Faiths - and the sweet human familiar image of Mother Mary and her infant Son. Hence the vast power wielded by the Church over the ignorant, who are comforted in their daily struggles and homely lives by the vision of these celestial visitants; the humble country-woman can whisper her troubles into the ear of the gentle nursing Mother, and feel assured of womanly sympathy; the child can smile up into the face of his Guardian Angel and sink peacefully to sleep beneath his veiling wings. It is noteworthy that the Roman Catholic Church holds the learned while attracting the ignorant, satisfies the philosopher while consoling the peasant. And this is because she adapts her teaching to her pupil, and does not offer the stone of an abstract idea to those who crave the bread of a concrete presence. Moreover, by thus giving intelligible objects for the worship of the unevolved she guards from degradation the sublime concepts of Deity that the advancing soul demands. The all-pervading mighty presence of God omnipotent, omnipresent, omniscient, and the gracious divine Motherhood of the Virgin immaculate, remain as deep spiritual verities in nature, unvulgarised by the cramping materialising of the undeveloped mind. The Holy of Holies is kept unpolluted, while the thronging multitudes find all they need in the outer courts. Only those who have been anointed with the chrism of spirituality may pass within the veil, and see the dazzling glory of the Shekinah lightening the most holy Place.

IV. THE EXISTENCE OF THE SOUL.

LET us next consider the problem concerning the existence of the soul, entering a region where the pinions of thought flag less than in that where they essayed to soar into the existence of God. Men ask, "Is there a soul?" "I am a soul," answers the spiritually enlightened philosopher. But how can we make this answer effective for the thousands of educated men and women who to-day doubt the very existence of the soul?

Let it be clearly understood from the outset that their doubt is not the outcome of a wish to doubt, still less of a desire to live licentiously - as some bigoted folks imagine; it arises from the play of the mind on facts around them, and from the exigencies of an intellect that they cannot honestly escape; they cannot accept ideas about the soul that appear to them to be illogical and imbecile, and prefer to grope in the twilight of Agnosticism rather than be false to their conception of truth. And verily such scepticism is nearer the kingdom of God than the easy-going repetition of a formula that is not the expression of the speaker's thought. It is the fashion among many religious people to speak harshly of unbelief; they have never faced the problems which the unbeliever has faced and has tried to solve. They have never endured the bitterness of despair that overwhelms the mind and heart ere the man who has once believed can say that he believes no longer, and that in the deeper loyalty to truth he must surrender loyalty to creed. No one who has passed through that storm, who has entered into that darkness, can ever again feel aught but keenest sympathy with those who are enveloped in it and who prefer the nakedness of unbelief to the soiled garments of dishonesty. To every such soul, loyal to truth in this life or in any other, the sun shall arise in the darkness; to every soul that refuses a light it knows to be false, and would rather live in the darkness than accept it, shall come the light of knowledge and faith conjoined; it matters little whether in this brief span of life it come or not, provided that under all stress of unbelief the soul remains loyal to truth and to righteousness and keeps unstained its faith in virtue and its love to man.

In seeking to help such as these to solve the problem of the existence of the soul, it is useless to adduce metaphysical arguments, for these have been tried and rejected; it is useless to appeal to an intuition which for the time is clouded, and the voice of which has been disregarded as likely to be mistaken. We must meet the sceptic on the only ground that for the time being he recognises as secure, and submit certain elementary arguments based on experiment; these while they will not prove the existence of the soul - that will come at a later stage - will carry the student into the position of acknowledging a super-physical consciousness, a consciousness not dependent for its activity on the normal physical conditions, but in direct conflict with them. The first difficulty that we have to surmount is the idea that the consciousness normally working in the brain is dependent upon that brain for its existence, that thought is the result of nervous activity and cannot work apart from it. To overcome this difficulty we need not prove the existence of the soul, with all the wide connotations of that word; by leaving the student to prove for himself that consciousness can function despite the paralysis of its physical organ and outside physical limitations of time and space, we enable him to reach a position where other lines of proof will lie open before him, and he can take these up one after the other till he finds himself face to face with the knowledge of the soul.

The first step is to see that the consciousness of a man includes much that is not normally present in his waking hours, and that there are many "layers of consciousness" that emerge from obscurity when the avenues of the senses are closed and the outer world is excluded. Further, that the more complete the exclusion, the larger appears to be the content of consciousness. The action of consciousness when the body is sleeping may form the first object of study. A first idea of the range of this study may be gathered from such works as Du Prel's 'Philosophy of Mysticism', and Sully's 'Illusions, Delusions, and Hallucinations'. Dreams should be classified (see Leadbeater's 'Dreams'), and special note should be taken of cases where author's obtain suggestions and plots in dream, as R. L. Stevenson with 'The Strange Case of Dr. Jekyll and Mr. Hyde', his own account of his "Brownies" may be read with advantage. Many people can solve problems asleep that baffle them awake, and the student might on this head experiment on himself. The extreme rapidity of dream-consciousness should be studied, the succession of states of consciousness enormously exceeding in speed any rate of vibration of which physical nervous matter is capable. The curious results of suggestion during sleep may be tried, resulting in the proof that conduct may be controlled by a part of the consciousness which does not show itself during waking hours.

From sleep the student may pass to the consideration of abnormal conditions resembling it in the exclusion of the outer world, such as trance, delirium, and the excitation of consciousness sometimes preceding death. Mozart and Tennyson bear witness to a state familiar to each of them, transcending the normal and setting at naught its limits of time; from this state Mozart brought back some of his noblest inspirations. Drowning men, brought back to waking consciousness, have testified to having seen, as in a picture, the whole of their past lives. Dying men have been recorded as speaking languages forgotten since childhood, and babbling of minute incidents of the past long sponged from the slate of waking memory. As we come face to face with these facts consciousness insensibly changes its aspect, and we see a vast ocean surrounding us, only a little of which trickles through our brains. Nothing seems to be lost; it is pushed out of the brain by a stream of fresh impressions, but is not allowed to drift out of reach. It is somewhere in that ocean of consciousness that is ours, and yet not ours, that we must explore.

The trance condition may be most closely studied through mesmerism and hypnotism, and it is not necessary to enter here into a detailed examination of the experiments which may be studied in standard works and reverified by personal observation. Richet's 'Etudes sur la Grande Hysterie', Binet and Fere's 'Animal Magnetism', and Sinnett's 'Rationale of Mesmerism', may serve as a commencement, the last-named book giving plentiful references to other works. It will suffice here to summarise the facts: suggestion can cause and prevent physical lesions, as burns and blisters; it can make the senses respond to objects that exist only in thought, and dead to objects that normally stimulate them - as seeing and feeling an object where none is physically present, and seeing only empty space where a physical body is standing; it can transfer a disease from one side of the body to the other, and from one person to another, and can heal it altogether; it can impose at will the feeling of pleasure, pain, horror, wrath, love, hatred; it can make an honest person steal, a kind person cruel; it can wipe out memory, and do a myriad other things beside. That is, an outside consciousness can take possession of a brain and work it for its own ends, the real owner being meanwhile ejected. Further, in trance the real owner may show himself far more fully than he does when normally working through the brain; memory is intensified both as to past events and present adhesive capacity; reason becomes keener and subtler; imagination takes flights it cannot reach when clogged in nervous matter; power of expression appears and the halting tongue is eloquent; latent faculty awakens and a factory girl rivals Jenny Lind. Nay, physical boundaries are transcended, and the entranced person diagnoses internal disease, the diagnosis being later confirmed by *post-mortem* investigation; or he sees what is occurring hundreds of miles away, he reports a conversation held at a far distance. Space fails me even to summarise the facts, but this matters not, for the student must read, must investigate for himself, in order that the force of the ever-accumulating evidence may play on his own mind, forcing him to the conclusion that but a small part of consciousness expresses itself through the brain.

Very important - but also very scanty - are the results obtained by hypnotising lunatics. Cases are on record in which, in the trance condition, the lunatic became sane, returning to his normal lunacy when he emerged from trance - or, as I should say, when he again began to try to function through the imperfect instrument of his brain. It is difficult to imagine more definite evidence that the brain is but the instrument of the waking consciousness than that obtained along this line, and it is much to be desired that doctors in charge of lunatics should collect facts in relation to them under the influence of mesmerism or hypnotism.

The student should next study the evidence for the appearance of "the double" apart from the physical body, the "phantasms of the living" as they have been called. Messrs. Gurney and Myers' work on this subject will serve as starting-point, and each may collect evidence on this head for himself from his own circle of acquaintances. A few will find that they can themselves reach distant friends in this way by an effort of the will, but the experience will be rare. But if human evidence is to be held as worth anything, the fact that phantasms of the living do appear can be put beyond doubt, and this means that consciousness can function far away from the physical body which it normally uses as its instrument.

The next stage is to show that the individual consciousness, thus found able to work outside the body during "life" survives "death." Here the phenomena classed as "spiritualistic" have their place as evidence, and no better work can be first studied than that in which Sir William Crookes records his own investigations. Any sincere and patient investigator may convince himself by personal experiment of the fact of individual survival, and apart from all *seances* and formal seekings there is evidence and to spare of volunteered communications, visible and audible, from those who had passed "beyond the veil" but for some reason strove to reach again their friends in the flesh.

When in this way a strong *prima facie* case, to say the least, has been established for the separability of consciousness from its physical organ and for its survival after the death of that organ, the student may be willing to submit himself to the training and the discipline necessary to obtain a true knowledge of the soul's existence. The way of meditation, reaching the higher consciousness, is the path he must now tread, and he cannot be expected to enter on it until he thinks that there is a possibility of gaining the knowledge he seeks. The process is toilsome and laborious, and demands long perseverance ere much apparent progress is made; but scores upon scores, nay, hundreds upon hundreds, of men and women have pursued it both in the past and in the present, and they bear witness to the results obtained by it. If complete control be gained over the mind, so that it can be directed unswervingly on a single point, and then, dropping that point, can remain poised and steady, the brain still, the senses asleep, then there arises above the horizon of the mind another kind of consciousness, recognised by the thinker as himself, but as himself in a higher condition of being. As he rises into this condition his powers suddenly enlarge, limitations vanish, a new and keener, subtler life pulses through him, he seems thought rather than thinker. Problems that puzzled him offer their solutions; questions that were unanswerable are answered simply and clearly; difficulties have vanished; all is luminous.

Does anyone say that this state is a mere day-dream, in which the dreamer is at the mercy of his imagination? Surely the evidence of those who have experienced it is more valuable than the assertions of those who have never reached it, and their testimony is unvarying and covers thousands of years. This is one of the methods that has been pursued in the East for uncounted generations, and this practice has developed not mere dreamers, not mere poets - if poets are to be despised by scientists - but some of the keenest metaphysicians, the profoundest philosophers, that humanity has yet produced. The mighty literature of India - to say nothing of the sacred books of other lands - bears witness to its efficacy, for the writers of the noblest Indian works were men of meditation. It is not the view of the enthusiast only, but the view of many of the keenest minds in Europe, that Indian thinkers offer solutions of psychological problems and theories of man and thought that deserve the most respectful consideration and the most careful study. Meditation, as the way to transcending mere brain consciousness, is recommended not only by the mystic but by the metaphysician, by intellects that plunge into the Ocean of Existence and swim where the majority drown. By it may be obtained the knowledge that man is a consciousness transcending physical conditions, and only when that consciousness is reached can the existence of the soul be proved by way of the intellect.

There is another way, the way of devotion, that reaches the goal attained by way of the intellect, and for many of us that way is more attractive, that road is more readily trodden. In that our meditation is directed to an Object adored and loved, and the passion of the soul for that high spiritual Being burns away every sheath that separates it from the object of its worship, until in union with Him it finds the certainty of its own immortality, knowing itself as self-existent since one with the One who is life. Then knowledge replaces faith, and the devotee, like the philosopher, knows himself eternal.

V. FREEWILL AND NECESSITY.

WHEN a problem has been under discussion for hundreds of years, and when it has been debated by the keenest intellects with varied results, it seems arrogant to say that it may be solved by grasping three main factors in human evolution. Nevertheless, the Theosophist cannot well avoid this statement when he envisages the problem of freewill and necessity, for in the light of the identity of the divine and human natures, reincarnation, and karma, the difficulties will away and the solution presents itself as obvious. Without these three truths the problem can never be solved. There is a necessity which compels and guides us; there is a freewill which decides and selects. Thus stated, a paradox appears. How can a soul at once be free and yet compelled by an inexorable destiny?

"Man is made in the image of God." In one form or another this allegation appears in every world-religion. It has been believed everywhere, at all times, and by all. It bears the hall mark of catholicity. In this truth lies hidden the reconciliation of necessity and freewill.

When we seek to study some of the attributes of the manifested God, we recognise among them that of Will. In fact, Will seems as though it were the supreme attribute of the LOGOS, and it represents to us the ultimate of force, all-pervading, all-directing, irresistible. Majestically free, Self-determined, it appears to us, moving all things to harmony and order but moved by none. We rest upon it in perfect confidence as on a rock that cannot be shaken, and the exquisite order and invariableness of nature are for us rooted in that steadfast all-compelling Will.

When we think of a man as containing within himself the germs of all divine potencies, as the acorn contains within itself the potentiality of becoming the perfect oak-tree, we naturally seek in him the germ of this imperial will, since he must be in the divine image in the power of will as much as in anything else. We find in him the attribute of will, and see him exercising a power of choice; but when we analyse this attribute and go below the surface of the apparently free choice, we find that the will is continually limited and hampered, and that the choice: is pressed from every side by pre-determining forces which push it in one direction. The freedom is seen to be but apparent, the choice is perceived to be determined. And yet there remains an obstinate conviction that no argument, however logical and irresistible, is wholly able to dispel, that the activity of the will contains a factor not accounted for in the rigorous analysis of determinism, a subtle element that has escaped recognition by the keen scrutiny of the metaphysical chemist.

This conviction is strengthened by the observation that what we call will in man is a power in process of evolution, and is indeed still rudimentary in the majority.

We cannot trace such a power at all in the mineral kingdom; there the affinities and repulsions are fixed and stable, the preferences can be measured and their recurrence can be depended upon. In even the highest members of the vegetable kingdom selective action is exceedingly feeble, and can scarcely be said to show any spontaneity. Given similar conditions, similar plants act in a similar way. So again in the animal kingdom there is a marked absence of spontaneity; for the most part the actions of an animal can be calculated beforehand by anyone who has made a study of the species to which it belongs, and experienced hunters utilise this regularity of action in pursuing and trapping their prey. Nevertheless we do observe occasional aberrations, especially in the higher animals, and in those, most of all, who have been much under the stimulating influence of man. When we come to study the less evolved members of the human family, we find that in them also there is comparatively little deviation from lines that can be laid down beforehand. They are played upon by forces the existence of which they do not recognise, and to which they unconsciously yield. They are moved to activity chiefly by the attractions and repulsions exercised over their desires by external objects; hopes and fears pull and drive them, and since they are mainly moved by these pullings and pushings from outside, their lines of action can be predicted with a fair amount of certainty. None the less we observe that as we ascend in the scale of humanity, spontaneity of action becomes a less and less negligible factor, and that while with a very highly developed man we can prophesy with certainty as to a number of things that he will *not* do, it is practically impossible to predict what his action will be. And this becomes more and more apparent the more highly the man is evolved. The will of the saint, of the hero, shows something of the imperial character of self-motion that we think of as characteristically divine.

For by "will" we mean the determination of force from the inmost centre of life, while by desire - which stands as the illusive reflection of will in the majority - we mean the determination of force from that which is outside that inmost centre, outside the inner immortal Man. In the lower types of mankind the motor energy is in the desires of the animal nature, imperiously demanding satisfaction and urging the man along the road leading to the objects which gratify those desires. For this reason the actions of the majority can be predicted with certainty, the objects which yield gratification being known and the desires which seek gratification being similar. The result of our study of evolution in general, then, leads us to the conclusion that this part of the divine image in us is one of the later outcomes of our growth, and that the characteristic of spontaneity is found to be marked in proportion to the degree of development.

If we turn our attention especially to the order of evolution of mental qualities, we shall arrive at a similar conclusion. Will does not manifest itself until after memory, comparison, reason, judgment, imagination, have reached a considerable amount of development. For a long period these growing mental faculties are yoked to the service of the desire-nature. They are the handmaids of kāma, and fly to obey the commands of desire. But at length a new figure rises slowly in the dim background of the mind, and after the mental faculties have completed their work on a given subject an authoritative voice comes forth from the mists which form the boundaries of the waking consciousness, and commands that a particular line of action should be followed. The council of mental faculties finds its premier, and authority silences dispute. Reason may sometimes challenge the orders of the will, but it finds itself compelled to yield, and there is in the will some strange energy welling out from the very fount of being which enthrones it as monarch over the realm of mind. Latest born, it yet asserts its pre-eminence, and all else bows down under its sceptre. But being yet in its childhood, it shows but little of its true majesty; only we can recognise in it the spontaneity of the Parent Will, the Will that rules the worlds.

If we betake ourselves to introspection, the will is the faculty which most resists our analysis. We cannot reach its root, which seems to pierce deeply into our life's centre. It appears to arise in a region veiled from our waking consciousness; to call all else to account, but to render account to none. We see that it is moving in chains, yet sense beneath those chains a living energy; the chains are not the generation of that living force, the determining causes are not the generator of the will.

So far, then, we see in will the directive energy which arises above or beyond the mind rather than in it, appearing at a late stage of human evolution, and being in its essence identical with that majestic divine and self-moved Will which guides the universe.

So far we find ourselves coming to the conclusion that the will, in its essential nature, is free, being an offshoot in each man of the universal Will. How then has it come to be bound, and how are its chains forged? To these questions reincarnation and karma supply the answer.

It is not necessary here to deal with reincarnation in its details. It will suffice us to regard man as an evolving individual, in whose life-career births and deaths are recurring incidents. Birth is not the beginning of a life nor is death its ending; birth and death begin and end only a single chapter in the life-story; the story runs through many chapters and the plot is continuous throughout. As a man lives through a day, falls asleep for a night, and wakes again the next morning for a new day, so does the evolving individual experience again and again the morning of birth and the night-time of death, remaining the same continuing life, passing in unbroken continuity through births and deaths.

If to-day I incur a debt, and sleep unconscious of it, my debt faces me in the morning on my awakening. It is not cancelled by the passing of the night. Many days may pass, and the remembrance of the debt may fade away from my mind, but the day of reckoning arrives, and the creditor presents himself for payment, his claim being rendered none the less valid for my lapse of memory. Such debts are contracted by each evolving individual, and they are rigidly collected when the payment falls due. Inexorable Destiny is at our door, and we cannot evade his claims. When we come to consider these debts of the past we find that we come into the world with the greater part of our destiny already fixed. We are born with a mentality and a desire-nature that have been built by us in the past, formed by the activities of the same individual who must inhabit his own past building in the present. Our character, our powers and our limitations, our faculties and our deficiencies, our virtues and our vices, these are the most potent factors in our destiny and they condition the whole of our present life. The same kind of life cannot be led by a man of narrow intelligence and vicious propensities, born in a miserable environment, and by a man of broad intelligence and virtuous inclinations, born amid the happiest surroundings. Each is compelled by necessity; the same output cannot fairly be demanded from each, nor can the one be blamed for being utterly inferior to the other. Necessity imposes lines of thinking, lines of acting, and the developing will is hampered by these at every turn. We are compelled by our past, by our thinkings and longings and desires in the lives that lie behind us, and only a very small part of our present is fashioned by our present will. Just as we may make a habit and that habit becomes a compelling force, so that we follow it unconsciously and have to exert much energy to change it; so are we pushed into thoughts and actions by the habits we have formed in the past and brought with us into our present life. We call this heritage of the past our karma, and it is the determining force in our lives. I think in certain ways because I have made a habit of thus thinking; I act in certain ways because my thoughts have dug the channel along which my energies run. On every side necessity compels me, my will moves in self-forged chains.

Where then is freedom? Within the limits of these self-drawn obligations the captive will moves wearily; but still it is the living force, with its power of spontaneity, of initiative. He who made the present in his past is still here in the midst of his makings, no puppet but a living soul; he can change and modify that which of yore he formed, he can file the chains which he riveted on himself long ago. The products of his past thoughts are there, but *he* is still the Thinker, and even within the narrowest of limits he can still work, and widen, and modify, and break. The evolving God is there, albeit encased in the web woven by ignorance; he is still in the centre and there is free, while constrained without by the results of past follies and mistakes. Just in proportion as he grows, and by effort breaks his chains, will his freedom extend, until at last his past is outworn and he reaches divine liberty.

In ourselves, as in external nature, knowledge of law means power to achieve. The ignorant man is driven hither and thither by the laws of nature, a helpless piece of drift-wood on the stream of life. But the learned man, subject to the same laws, exercises his selective power, balances one against another, and obtains his chosen object; he works by fixed laws, but he throws his life-force with the law-forces that help his purpose, and neutralises those that antagonise him by the activity of other energies. In every part of nature we live and move amid fixed laws, fettered by our past and blinded by our ignorance; in proportion as we outwear our past and change ignorance into knowledge, we become free. Power grows as vision clears, as we climb higher liberty increases, until finally we shall reach the centre where self-motion abides. We are constrained by necessity, but we are outgrowing it; we are not yet free, but we are evolving towards freedom. The more nearly we approach the realisation of our divinity the freer we become, and when our separated wills, evolved and self-moved, merge harmoniously in the Parent Will, we shall experience that reality of freedom the dim presage of which made us cling to the belief in freewill. Here again the teachings of Theosophy prove to be our light-bearer, our Lucifer, star of the morning.

VI. PRAYER.

THE question is continually asked: "Do you Theosophists believe in prayer?" and it may be helpful to some to study the subject of prayer in the light of occult knowledge, prefacing the study with the remark that the belief of Theosophists will vary according to their knowledge, and that no Theosophist save the writer is committed to the statements that follow. The public does not yet realise that a Theosophist is not fitted with a ready-made suit of beliefs when he enters the Society, but is only supplied with materials from among which he may choose those which suit him, and must then proceed to fashion his garments for himself. The views that are here submitted are given simply as the views of a particular student, as materials for study.

The first thing necessary in considering the utility of prayer is to analyse prayer itself, for the word is used to cover various activities of consciousness, and they cannot be dealt with as though they formed a simple whole. We find prayers that are petitions for definite worldly advantages, for the supply of physical needs - prayers for food, clothing, money, employment, success in business, recovery from illness, &c. These we will group together as Class A. Then we have prayers for help in moral and intellectual difficulties and for spiritual growth - for the overcoming of temptations, for strength, for insight, for enlightenment. These can be grouped as Class B. Lastly there are the prayers that ask for nothing, that consist in contemplation and adoration of the Divine Perfection, in intense aspiration for union with God - the ecstasy of the mystic, the meditation of the sage, the soaring rapture of the saint. These we will call Class C.

The next thing that we must realise is the great ladder of living beings from the sub-human elemental to the LOGOS Himself, a ladder in which no rung is wanting. This occult side of nature is a fact, not a dream. The world is filled with living things, invisible to fleshly eyes. The astral world interpenetrates the physical, and crowds of intelligent conscious creatures throng round us at every step. Some are below man in intelligence and some soar high above him. Some are easily influenced by his will, others are accessible to his requests. In addition to these independent entities, the elemental essence of the three kingdoms is responsive to his emotions and his thoughts, and is swiftly shaped into forms whose very life is to carry out the feeling or the thought that ensouls them; thus he can create at will an army of obedient servants who will range the astral world to do his pleasure. Yet again there are available human though invisible helpers, whose attentive ear may catch a cry for aid, and who gladly serve as veritable "ministering angels" to the soul in need. And to crown all there is the ever-present, ever-conscious life of the LOGOS Himself, potent and responsive at every point in His realm, of Him without whose knowledge not a sparrow falleth to the ground, not a dumb creature thrills in joy or pain, not a child laughs or sobs - that all-pervading, all-embracing, all-sustaining Life and Love, in which all live and move. As nought that can give pleasure or pain can touch the human body without the sensory nerves carrying the message of its impact to the brain-centres, and as there thrills down from those centres through the motor nerves the answer that welcomes or withdraws, so does every vibration in the universe, which is His body, reach His consciousness and draw thence responsive action. Nerve-cells, nerve-threads, and muscular fibres may be the agents of feeling and motion, but it is the *man* that feels and acts; so may myriads of intelligences be the agents, but it is the LOGOS that knows and answers. Nothing can be so small as not to affect that delicate omnipresent consciousness, nothing so vast as to transcend it. We are so limited that the very idea of such an all-embracing consciousness staggers and confounds us; yet perhaps the gnat might be as hard bestead if he tried to measure the consciousness of Pythagoras.

It is impossible to deny the fact that prayers *are* answered, and that many can give out of their own experience clear and decisive cases of "answers to prayer." Moreover, many of these do not refer to what are termed subjective experiences, but to hard facts of the so-called objective world. A man has prayed for money, and the post has brought him the needed amount; a woman has prayed for food, and food has arrived at her door. In connection with charitable undertakings, there is plenty of evidence of help prayed for in direct need, and of speedy and liberal response. On the other hand, there is also plenty of evidence of prayers left unanswered, of the hungry starving to death, of the child snatched from its mother's arms by death, despite the most passionate appeals to God. Any reasonable view of prayer must take into consideration these conflicting facts, must neither refuse to admit the answers nor evade the recognition of the failures to obtain any. All facts must fall into their place in any true theory of prayer.

We will take separately our three classes of prayers, and we shall find that the occult lives in nature are the agents which bring about answers to prayer, the particular agents at work being those suitable to the kind of prayer put forth.

When a man utters a prayer of Class A, he may obtain an answer through one of several agencies. His concentrated thought and earnest will affect the elemental essence of the astral plane, and he creates a powerful artificial elemental, whose one idea is to bring about what its creator desires. This elemental, where the prayer is for money, food, clothing, employment, for anything that can be given by one man to another, will seek out a person able to give, and will impress on that person's brain the image of its creator and of his special need, this impression giving rise to the thought of sending the man help. "I thought of George Muller and his orphanages this morning," a rich man will say, "I may as well send him a cheque." George Muller's prayer is here the motor power, the artificial elemental is the agent concerned in bringing about the desired result, and the cheque, unasked for of man on the physical plane, comes as the "answer to prayer." The result could have been obtained as readily by a deliberate effort of the will, without any prayer, by a person who understood the mechanism concerned and the way to put it into motion. But in the case of most people, ignorant of the forces of the invisible world and unaccustomed to exercise their wills, the concentration of the mind and the earnest desire necessary for success are far more easily reached by prayer than by a deliberate mental effort to put forth their own strength. They would doubt their own power, even if they understood the theory, and doubt is fatal in all exercise of the will. That the person who prays does not understand the machinery he sets going in no wise affects the result; a child who stretches out his hand and grasps an object need not understand anything of the working of the extensor muscles, nor of the chemical and electrical changes set up by his movement in muscles and nerves, nor need he elaborately calculate the distance of the object by measuring the angle made by the optic axes; he wills to take hold of the thing he wants, and the various parts of his body obey his will although he does not even know of their existence. So also is it with the man who prays, unknowing of the creative force of his thought or of the proceedings of the creature he has sent forth to do his bidding; he acts as unconsciously as the child, and like the child grasps what he wants.

A prayer of Class A may also be answered in other ways than by the action of an artificial elemental. A passing disciple, or other helper at work on the astral plane, may hear his prayer and bring about the desired result. Especially is this likely to be the case when the utterer of the prayer is a philanthropist in need of aid for the carrying on of some beneficent work. The helper will throw the thought of sending him the assistance he needs into the fertile soil of a charitable brain, and the result will follow as before. Sometimes, but I think more rarely, the will of the praying person affects a nature spirit, or elemental proper, and he actively exerts himself to bring about the wished for effect; some people exercise a peculiar power over nature spirits of various kinds, and the "little people" will take much trouble in order to supply the needs of their favourites.

The failure of earnest and strongly-willed prayers to bring about the object aimed at seems to be due to the fact that they dash themselves against some karmic cause too strong for them to turn aside or to modify to any appreciable extent. A man condemned by his own action in the past to die of starvation may hurl his prayers against that destiny in vain. The artificial elemental he has created by such prayers will find all its efforts futile; no helper will come in his way to cause the desired relief to be sent to him; no nature spirit will pay any attention to his cry. Where the relations that had existed in the past between the souls of parents and of a dying child necessitate in the present life the breaking of the tie at a particular period, the current of force set free by prayer will not avail to prolong the thread of the young life. Here, as everywhere, we are living in a realm of law, and forces may be modified or entirely frustrated by the play of other forces with which they come in contact. Two exactly similar forces might be applied to set in motion two exactly similar balls; but in one case no other force might be applied to the ball and it might fly to the mark aimed at, in the other a second force might strike the ball and send it entirely out of its course. And so with two similar prayers; one may be karmically unopposed, or even aided on its way by a karmic force, while the second may be flung aside by a karmic force far more energetic than the original impulse. One prayer is answered, the other falls to the ground apparently unheeded; in both cases the result follows the law.

Let us consider Class B. Prayers for help in moral and intellectual difficulties are efficacious both in action and reaction. They draw the attention of those servants of humanity who are ever-seeking to help the bewildered soul, and counsel, encouragement, illumination, are thrown into the brain consciousness, thus giving the answer to prayer in the most direct way. Ideas are often suggested which clear away an intellectual difficulty, or throw light on an obscure problem, and the sweetest comfort is poured into the distressed heart, soothing its perturbations and calming its anxieties. This may be called the objective answer to such prayers, where the help of stronger and more advanced souls - of a disciple, an angel, a Master - is readily given in response to the cry for aid. But there is also a subjective answer, not so readily recognised, as a rule, by those who pray, that may be regarded as the reaction of the prayer itself on the one who offers it. His prayer truly places his heart and mind in the receptive attitude, which makes it easy to render him objective aid but it also opens the channel of communication between his higher and lower natures, and thus allows the strength and illuminative power of the higher to pour downwards into the brain-consciousness. The currents of energy which normally flow downwards, or outwards, from the Inner Man are as a rule directed to the external world, and are utilised in the ordinary affairs of life by the brain-consciousness for the carrying on of its daily activities. But when this brain-consciousness turns away from the outer world, and, shutting its outward-going doors, directs its gaze inwards; when it deliberately opens itself to the inner and closes itself to the outer; then it becomes a vessel able to receive and to hold instead of a mere conduit-pipe between the interior and exterior worlds. In the silence obtained by the cessation of the noises of external activities, the quiet voice of the soul can make itself heard, and the concentrated attention of the expectant mind enables it to catch the soft whisper from the Inner Self.

Even more markedly is this the case when the prayer is for spiritual enlightenment, for spiritual growth. Not only do all helpers most eagerly seek to forward spiritual progress, seizing on every opportunity offered by the upward aspiring heart, but the longing for such growth liberates energy of a higher kind, the spiritual longing calling forth an answer from the spiritual realm. Once more the law of sympathetic vibrations asserts itself, and the note of lofty aspiration is answered by a note of its own order, by a liberation of energy of its own kind, by a vibration synchronous with itself. The divine life is ever pressing against the limits which bind it, and when the upward-rising force strikes against those limits, the separating wall is broken through, and the life floods the soul.

When a man, becoming strong in spiritual aspiration, no longer seeks for gain nor looks to God for gift; when his sole longing is to resemble That which he adores, and his prayer becomes an act of contemplation and worship; then the result of the prayer is to draw an answer from the high spiritual region to which the thought of the suppliant aspires. The subtle vibrations of the spiritual realm play on the up-reaching soul, awakening the corresponding divine elements that lie latent within it, and these, thrilling into answer, flood the man with a new sense of power and make him realise something of the nature of divinity. Inasmuch as the Divine is everywhere, as in Him we live and move, that appeal to the Divine without us causes an activity which reacts on us, awakening the Divine within us, and this "God-with-us" imparts to the mind and heart the energy of the spiritual nature, making us conscious of our own divine power.

Thus we pass from the spiritual aspirations almost imperceptibly into the prayer which is pure worship, pure adoration, from which all petition is absent, and which seeks only to pour itself forth in sheer love of the Perfect, dimly sensed. Such prayers, grouped as Class C, are the means of union between man and God, drawing the worshipper into the Being he adores. In these, the consciousness limited by the brain contemplates in mute ecstasy the Image it creates of Him whom it knows to be in truth beyond all imagining, and oft, rapt by the intensity of its love beyond those concrete limits imposed by the intellect, it soars upwards into the realm where limits are not, and feels and knows far more than on its return it can tell in words or clothe in intellectual form. Then in prayer the mystic gazes on the Beatific Vision, then the sage rests in the infinite calm of the wisdom that is beyond knowledge, then the saint is penetrated with the radiant purity in which God is seen. Such prayer irradiates the worshipper, and from the mount of such high communion descending to the plains of earth, the very face of flesh shines with supernal glory, translucent to the flame which burns within. Happy they who know the reality which no words may convey to those who know it not; those whose eyes have seen the King in His beauty will remember, and they will understand.

VII. THE ATONEMENT.

There is a profound spiritual truth underlying the various doctrines of atonement that have been put forth from time to time by Christian churches. In all of them Jesus the Christ has been the central figure, and the atonement has been wrought by him.

In the early days of the Christian Church the death of Jesus was regarded as a payment made to Satan for the ransoming of mankind from his power. Mankind was in thrall to the devil in consequence of the Fall, and man was the "bondsman of the devil." To redeem that unhappy bondsman God gave His own Son, the ransom paid being his agonising death. The debt of man being thus discharged, he was liberated from the kingdom of darkness, and became the free-man of him who had paid his debt.

In later phases of Christian thought on this subject, a far darker doctrine arose. The sacrifice of suffering and death offered up by God the Son, incarnated as man, was declared to be offered to God the Father to appease his wrath and to expiate vicariously the sins of men. Human ingenuity devised the idea of a contract entered into in heavenly places between two Persons in the Godhead for the redemption of fallen men, and then followed all the painful presentations of divine wrath on one side and divine agony on the other, against which the conscience of more spiritually minded Christians has revolted in our own day. Many of the noblest Christian clergy have headed an ever-increasing school of thinkers which indignantly repudiates this harsh form of medieval doctrine as at once blasphemous towards God, dishonouring to justice, and profoundly erroneous as to the relation between God and man. Men such as Mr. McLeod Campbell of the Scottish Church, as F. D. Maurice and F. Robertson of the English, are exponents of a purer and truer teaching; they see that the office of a Divine Man is not to create a new relationship between God and man, but to make manifest and vindicate a relationship already existing. Many devout persons have been so disgusted with these legal quibblings, in which one divine Person is angry and another propitiatory, one demanding and another paying - have felt it all to be so unreal, so unspiritual, that they have flung aside the whole doctrine of atonement with impatience, forgetting that even under the veil of repellent errors a truth may lie hidden that we cannot afford to lose. Such a truth there is in this doctrine of atonement, and it is this truth which has given the doctrine its hold over the hearts of men. Is it not strange, when we come to think of it, that a doctrine so narrow, unfair, and mistaken, has yet afforded an impulse to noble living to some of the purest and most self-denying among the children of men? In this very doctrine, that seems to us so repellent, many loving and gentle Christian souls have found their strongest stimulus to self-sacrifice, their surest foundation for saintly lives of wide-spreading beneficence. Where we find such incongruity between the verbal statement and the effect produced by it on high types of soul, we may be sure that such souls, by spiritual insight, have caught a glimpse of a truth which is veiled by the crude and erroneous presentation. What is this Truth?

As the human soul evolves, it continually enlarges its limits, the limits of the individualised consciousness, embracing more and more within its bounds. The narrow and unevolved soul shows a lack of embracing sympathy, and this lack proves that the spiritual evolution has not yet begun. As we study human evolution we see the consciousness expanding and taking more within its scope; first limited to the physical, it expands to include the astral; expanding further, it includes the mental. In process of time the man passes through the first great initiation, and in Christian phrase "the Christ is born in him;" in theosophical terminology, the consciousness begins to function on the buddhic plane, the plane of love, and bliss, and unity, the lower spiritual plane. Slowly "the Christ" grows, the consciousness works more and more in the spiritual world, and a new attitude becomes habitual. The man feels himself to be one with all around him, one with all that lives. He no longer feels himself to be separate, but to be one with all the lives amid which he moves. He does not lose hold of his own centre of consciousness, but in some strange, subtle way he interpenetrates all other consciousnesses and feels them as his own. He expands to contain all others, and makes no difference between "himself" and "them." In that spiritual realm he feels as others feel, thinks as they think, suffers as they suffer, joys as they joy; verily, there are no "others," but all is himself. Every child of man is part of the life of this man; they do not stand outside him to be sympathised with; they are forms of him; he is living, sinning, fearing, hoping, struggling, in everyone of them. When that consciousness is definitely established, the Christ has grown to manhood, and the consecration of the true baptism marks him as a manifested Son of God. Then he comes to the knowledge of his place in the world, his function in nature - to be a Saviour and to make atonement for the sins of the people. He stands in the inner heart of the world, the sanctuary of Buddhi, as a High Priest of humanity. He is one with all his brethren, not by a vicarious substitution, but by the unity of a common life. Are any sinful? he is sinful in them that his purity may purge them. Are any sorrowful? in them he is the man of sorrows; every broken heart is broken in his, every pierced heart in his heart is pierced. Are any glad? in them he is joyous and pours out his bliss. Are any craving? in them he is feeling want that he may fill them with his utter satisfaction. He has everything, and because it is his it is theirs. He is perfect; then they are perfect with him. He is strong; who then can be weak, since he is in them? He climbed to his high place that he might pour out to all below him, and he lives in order that all may share his life. He lifts the whole world with him as he rises; the path is easier for all men because he has trodden it.

Every Son of man may become such a manifested Son of God, such a Saviour of the world. In each such Son is "God manifest in the flesh," the atonement which aids all mankind, the living power that makes all things new. Only one thing is needed to bring that power into manifest activity in any individual soul; the soul must open the door and let him in. Even he, all-permeating, cannot force his way against his brother's will; the human will can hold its own alike against God and man, and by the law of evolution it must voluntarily associate itself with divine action and not be broken into sullen submission. Let the will throw open the door, and the life will flood the soul, While the door is closed it will only gently breathe through it its unutterable fragrance, that the sweetness of that fragrance may win where the barrier may not be forced by strength.

This it is, in part, to be a Christ; but how can mortal pen depict the immortal, or mortal words tell of that which is beyond the power of speech? Tongue may not utter, the unillumined mind may not grasp, that mystery of the Son who has become one with the Father carrying in His bosom the sons of men.

That is part of the glorious truth that is travestied in the doctrine of the atonement as it has been taught for many a century; that the secret of the influence that, even in its erroneous forms, has proved so great an inspiration to many noble hearts. Even when error blinds the intellect, the vivifying power of that supernal love is felt, and souls, sensitive to spiritual influences, answer to its sweet compulsion, and, in their small measure, also, they begin to share the joy of giving, of living the life that is love. A spiritual religion has no separated reward to offer, has no separated penalty to threaten. It can but say: "In so far as you love and serve, the Divine Life is finding a channel for expression in you, and when you reach the higher world, expand to the wider consciousness, then also you will know what every saint has yearned for, what every Master has accomplished; you will feel in you the Divine Life as your life; you will thus enter into the joy of your Lord."

THE END.

Made in United States
Troutdale, OR
01/08/2025

27625764R00263